WHERE TO ~~GO~~
GREAT B
& IRELAND

WHERE TO GO WHEN
GREAT BRITAIN
& IRELAND

DK | Penguin Random House

LIST MANAGER Christine Stroyan
EDITOR Vicki Allen
ASSISTANT EDITOR Claire Bush
DESIGN MANAGER Mabel Chan
DESIGNER Shahid Mahmood
DTP DESIGNER Jason Little
PICTURE RESEARCHERS Ellen Root, Marta Bescos
SENIOR CARTOGRAPHIC EDITOR Casper Morris
CARTOGRAPHERS Suresh Kumar, Mohammad Hassan
PRODUCTION CONTROLLER Kerry Howie

PUBLISHER Vivien Antwi

First edition produced for Dorling Kindersley by

cobaltid

The Stables, Wood Farm, Deopham Road,
Attleborough, Norfolk NR17 1AJ
www.cobaltid.co.uk

EDITORS Kati Dye, Louise Abbott,
Robin Sampson, Sarah Tomley, Maddy King,
Neil Mason, Marek Walisiewicz
DESIGNERS Lloyd Tilbury, Paul Reid,
Annika Skoog, Claire Dale, Darren Bland

First Published in Great Britain in 2010
by Dorling Kindersley Limited
80 Strand, London WC2R 0RL

Reprinted with revisions 2012, 2016

Printed and bound in China

Every effort has been made to ensure that this book is as up-to-date as
possible at the time of going to press. Some details, however, such as
telephone numbers, opening hours, prices, and travel information are liable
to change. The publishers cannot accept responsibility for any consequences
arising from the use of this book, nor for any material on third-party websites,
and cannot guarantee that any website address in this book will be a suitable
source of travel information. We value the views and suggestions of our
readers very highly. Please write to: Publisher, DK Travel Guides,
Dorling Kindersley, 80 Strand, London, WC2R 0RL, Great Britain.

www.traveldk.com

MAIN COVER IMAGE: Twr Mawr lighthouse, Llanddwyn Island
HALF TITLE PAGE IMAGE: Sphinx rock on Great Gable, Lake District
TITLE PAGE IMAGE: Sunset over Esthwaite Water, Lake District
CONTENTS: View of River Wye from Symonds Yat, Herefordshire;
Temple Bar district by the Liffey River, Dublin

CONTENTS

SPRING

A bluebell wood in Hertfordshire, England

SPRING IN GREAT BRITAIN AND IRELAND

IN THE GARDEN COUNTIES OF SOUTHERN ENGLAND and along the mellow Atlantic shores of the south of Ireland, spring flowers begin to bloom and winter's weakening grip on the land is signalled by the appearance of the first migrant swifts and swallows in the skies. In the countryside, you might hear the distinctive call of a cuckoo. With luck, Easter will be warm and sunny enough for barbecues in back gardens and picnics in the country. But spring, more than any other season, highlights the amazingly varied microclimates of Britain and Ireland. In Cornwall or Cork, it may be warm enough for a day at the beach, but in the high wilderness of the Cairngorms, winter sports enthusiasts will be revelling in fresh-fallen snow and the best ski conditions of the year. Further north, the Orkney and Shetland Isles may still be swathed in freezing fog. A spring journey in Britain and Ireland calls for careful planning.

> Winter's weakening grip on the land is signalled by the appearance of the first migrant swifts.

Even along the south coast of England, winter sometimes clings to the countryside until March. It is not unheard of for Kent – nicknamed the "garden of England" – to be blanketed in snow just a few weeks before Easter. So the sudden appearance of green buds and of cherry, hawthorn and apple blossom is sometimes as surprising as it is welcome. The first spring sunshine normally bathes the south coast of England, warming resorts such as Margate in Kent, Brighton in Sussex and Torquay in Devon – where carefully tended palm trees bear witness to one of England's balmiest climates – and the rugged shores of Cornwall that stretch down to the southernmost point of mainland Britain.

In and around London some of the world's most famous gardens and green spaces are already in bloom. The Royal Botanic Gardens at Kew are carpeted with more than a million crocuses in early spring, and blossoming camellias soon give way to sweet-scented lilacs. The Privy and Pond Gardens at Henry VIII's Hampton Court Palace are at their best in April, when the long lines of pretty spring flowers bring the formal shapes of this historic garden to life.

On the North Sea coast, from Yorkshire to Scotland, spring brings migrant birds in ones and twos, or in vast, spectacular flocks. At Bempton Cliffs in East Yorkshire, more than 200,000 birds gather to breed, including puffins, guillemots, fulmars and razorbills, building nests on every ledge and in every nook of these high, vertiginous cliffs. Further north, on the Bass Rock in the Firth of Forth, so many gannets gather to nest

Below (left to right): Apple blossom in an orchard in Kent; gannets nesting on a cliff at Bass Rock, on the Firth of Forth

that they whiten the rocks; these large birds have a 2-m (6-ft) wing span, and the sight of their flocks at sea is one of Britain's greatest wildlife spectacles.

The woods and waters of the Lake District are famously linked with spring. The first daffodils emerge in March, and within a few weeks there are broad swathes of vivid yellow in gardens, by roadsides, and all along the shores of Ullswater and Grasmere, where the daffodils nod and dance in vivid contrast to the dark woodlands behind them, which are only just beginning to come into leaf.

> St Patrick's Day turns all of Ireland – but especially Dublin – into a great place for the *craic*.

Yellow is the signature colour of spring in Scotland, too: the blossoming broom and gorse runs in bright swathes across the wild hills and curlew-haunted moors, dotted with the purple of heather. A sunny mid-April day may tempt you to walk up Arthur's Seat – the main peak of the high hills in the heart of Edinburgh – wearing just shorts and a T-shirt. But there's likely to be a cutting wind at the summit, and the gleam of snow-capped peaks on the northern horizon, so don't be deceived by the April sunshine, even in southern Scotland. Fresh snow can fall on the slopes of the Cairngorms and the northwest Highlands as late as May, and walkers may find unmelted pockets even in June. But there are areas of unexpected warmth even in Scotland's far northwest; at the National Trust for Scotland's gardens at Inverewe, sub-tropical exotics, such as Tasmanian gum trees and Chinese rhododendrons, flourish within sight of snow-tipped summits.

Spring is not just a season of natural splendour. Easter is one of the most important festivals of the Christian year, when Easter services, choral performances and midnight Masses take place at great English cathedrals such as St Paul's, Canterbury, Winchester and York Minster in late March or early April. In Wales, St David's Day (1 March) is celebrated throughout the country, from the small festivities in towns and villages to the awesome sound of a 1,000-strong, male-voice choir in full song in St David's Hall in Cardiff. St Patrick's day turns all of Ireland, but especially Dublin, into a great place for the *craic* on 17 March, with music, dancing and a drop of two of Irish whiskey. And in England, St George's Day, on 23 April, is another excuse for public celebration, with concerts and colourful processions in London and other cities.

Below (left to right): Reflections of flowering gorse in Loch Duich, in the Scottish Highlands; tortoiseshell butterfly; Hampton Court Palace Pond Garden

Britain in Bloom

Above: 1893 advert with slogan "Carters' Bouquet of Pretty Cut Flowers, Easily Grown from Seed"

From colourful cottage flowerbeds and lovingly tended inner-city allotments to the serenely landscaped estates of grand English houses and botanical gardens that continue centuries-old traditions of research into the healing powers of plants, Britain's gardens are legendary.

Great Britain and Ireland start to come into bloom as early as February, when the first, aptly named, snowdrops appear in woods and gardens, to be followed soon after by bluebells, daffodils and early crocuses. Around the same time, the first sunny days bring out bumblebees and tortoiseshell butterflies that have overwintered under cottage eaves and in attics and greenhouses. Myriad microclimates make it possible for imaginative gardeners to cultivate an array of exotic imports. Some of our grandest and most fascinating gardens date from Britain's colonial heyday, when botanists searched the Himalayan foothills, Alpine meadows and the jungles of Brazil and Borneo for ever-more-exotic decorative, commercially useful or simply unusual plant species. The grand country estates of Scotland and Ireland are splashed with the pink, white and purple blooms of azaleas and rhododendrons, originally imported from sub-tropical Asia, and it's hard to imagine south-coast resorts, such as Torquay in Devon, without their decorative palms.

HARLOW CARR

LOST GARDENS OF HELIGAN

THE EDEN PROJECT

SISSINGHURST CASTLE GARDENS

Royal Botanic Garden Edinburgh, Southern Scotland Britain's tallest palm house, giant sequoias, a Highland heath garden and a world-famous Alpine rock garden can be found here. *www.rbge.org.uk*

Mount Stewart House and Gardens, Northern Ireland Thanks to the mild microclimate of the Ards Peninsula, spring comes early to these glorious gardens. *www.nationaltrust.org.uk*

Blarney Castle and Gardens, Southern Ireland Spring bluebells burst into flower in the beautiful gardens on the estate of this famous castle, where cattle graze in lush lakeside pastures. *www.blarneycastle.ie*

Bodnant Garden, North Wales Azaleas, rhododendrons, magnolias and camellias put on a stunning show in spring in this garden, which has superb views of Mount Snowdon. *www.bodnantgarden.co.uk*

Wordsworth Daffodil Garden, Northwest England In spring, this space between Grasmere's church and the River Rothay is smothered in the daffodils that inspired William Wordsworth (*see pp50–1*).

Harlow Carr, Northeast England Bluebells and mixed primulas flourish in sun-dappled clearings in the woods of this Yorkshire garden, with its streams and rocky outcrops. *www.rhs.org.uk*

Biddulph Grange Garden, West Midlands A Chinese garden, Egyptian courtyard, stumpery and "upside-down tree" make this one of Britain's quirkiest gardens. *www.nationaltrust.org.uk*

Hidcote Manor Garden, West Midlands Gardens designed as "outdoor rooms" and enclosed by immaculately trimmed hedges are the keynote of this masterpiece of Arts and Crafts design. *www.nationaltrust.org.uk*

Anglesey Abbey and Gardens, Eastern England Outstanding garden created in the 1930s by Lord Fairhaven as an ambitious, Classical landscape of trees, sculptures and pretty borders. *www.nationaltrust.org.uk*

Royal Botanic Gardens, Kew, London One of the world's most important centres for plant science and conservation, with palm houses, hothouses, landscaped lawns and shrubberies. *www.kew.org*

Chelsea Physic Garden, London A sanctuary in the heart of London with beds of ferns, herbs and aromatics. Founded in 1673, it continues research into medicinal plants. *www.chelseaphysicgarden.co.uk*

Wisley, Southeast England The flagship garden of the Royal Horticultural Society is more than a century old and boasts lavishly planted borders, velvety lawns, lush rose gardens and glasshouses. *www.rhs.org.uk*

Sissinghurst Castle Gardens, Southeast England A charming complex of gardens and courtyards created by the writer Vita Sackville-West and her husband, Harold Nicholson. *www.nationaltrust.org.uk*

The Eden Project, Southwest England In March, the beds are awash with daffodils in every shade of yellow. In April, it's the turn of English wild flowers, such as campions and violets. *www.edenproject.com*

Lost Gardens of Heligan, Southwest England Neglected for almost a century, the gardens of this Cornish estate have been lovingly restored; fruit, bamboo and banana plants flourish here. *www.heligan.com*

Rosemoor Garden, Southwest England A magnificent 260 hectares (65 acres) of gardens, including bluebell woods, two rose gardens, a formal garden, a French-style potager and stream. *www.rhs.org.uk*

ROYAL BOTANIC GARDENS, KEW

BODNANT GARDEN

A LITERARY PILGRIMAGE

ORTIFIED AGAINST WELSH REBELS in medieval times by English lords, the border town of Hay-on-Wye now welcomes a very different type of invasion. Every spring, the Hay Festival (late May/early June) brings some 85,000 literary pilgrims to 10 days of readings, masterclasses, debates and entertainment centred on a tented village. There are dense daily programmes of ticketed events, which often book up well in advance, but it's free to go in and simply soak up the vibrant atmosphere while you read or people-watch from one of the many deck chairs scattered around the site. Later in the day, festival-goers and star guests spread out informally between the live bands, comedy performances and town pubs to continue the fun. Hip young families and cultured book-lovers might rub shoulders with authors, poets and performers, as well as a horde of TV commentators and journalists. Famous names that have made an appearance include Alan Bennett, Carol Ann Duffy, Stephen Fry and Archbishop Desmond Tutu. Hay Fever, the parallel children's festival, offers younger visitors a hands-on chance to make their own puppets and pottery.

This cosmopolitan festival was started in 1988 by local actor Peter Florence, who still runs the event and is now exporting the concept to new venues such as Segovia, Nairobi and, famously, Cartagena in Colombia. There's a strong US connection. In the festival's second year, playwright Arthur Miller agreed to be the star guest – after reportedly asking if Hay-on-Wye was some kind of sandwich; in 2001 former President Bill Clinton described it as "the Woodstock of the mind".

For some, the greatest surprise of the festival is its setting. The site is normally pasture: this is hill-farming country, where for most of the year there are more sheep than people. Hay's stone buildings huddle together in typical Welsh small-town fashion, around a market place and a clock tower, with a semi-ruined castle on the skyline and the slopes of the Black Mountains in the distance. The town's famous bookshops and traditional stores have been joined by specialist and fashion shops, putting Hay firmly on the cultural map of Britain.

THE ESSENTIALS

GETTING THERE AND AROUND
Hay-on-Wye is on the Welsh side of the border with England. Cardiff and Birmingham airports are 115 km (71 miles) and 137 km (85 miles) away respectively. Trains run from London to Hereford, from where there are both festival and regular bus services to Hay-on-Wye.

WEATHER
This area is dryer than west Wales, but it can be cold and windy on the hilltops, with an average daytime temperature of 8–12°C in late spring.

ACCOMMODATION
Splashing Out The Swan at Hay, in Hay-on-Wye, is a Georgian coaching inn with fine dining and beautiful gardens. *www.swanathay.co.uk*

On a Budget Outdoors at Hay, in Hay-on-Wye, is a camp site that also offers adventure activities. Open from March to November, it is just 5 minutes' walk from the festival site. *www.training-activities.co.uk*

EATING OUT
Splashing Out The Swan at Hay's elegant restaurant overlooks the hotel's gardens and boasts French-trained chefs who use local produce. *www.swanathay.co.uk*

On a Budget The Blue Boar, in Hay-on-Wye, is a friendly pub with an evocative medieval bar, a bright, cheery atmosphere and hearty traditional food. *Tel: 01497 820884*

PRICE FOR TWO PEOPLE
Around £210 a day for food, accommodation and entrance fees.

WEBSITE
www.hay-on-wye.co.uk

Main: Book-lovers of all ages delight in the literary atmosphere
Below: Festival visitors browse outdoor bookshelves in Hay-on-Wye

FURTHER DETAILS

HAY FESTIVAL

Hay-on-Wye. The festival takes place over 10 days
annually, around the late-May Bank Holiday weekend
(dates vary); tickets for festival events can be purchased
in advance using the online booking service, or through
the festival box office (tel: 01497 822 629).
www.hayfestival.com

WHAT ELSE TO SEE AND DO

Brecon Beacons
You can drive from Hay-on-Wye up the winding Forest
Road towards Hay Bluff, park at the viewpoint and walk
uphill on the Offa's Dyke Path to the windswept ridge.
Here you can see far across the Welsh border country
and the Brecon Beacons National Park (see pp202–3).
www.breconbeacons.org/walking

River Trips
It's possible to hire a canoe or a kayak, take a picnic and
canoe downstream on the tranquil River Wye. Paddles
and Pedals, based in Hay-on-Wye, offer a pick-up
service that returns you to your starting point.
www.paddlesandpedals.co.uk

Riding
The Black Mountains and Brecon Beacons, with their
springy grass trails, make superb riding country. You can
hire a pony for as little as an hour or take a longer trip
involving an overnight stay. Tregoyd Mountain Riders in
Tregoyd, Powys, offers a range of options for all ages
and levels of experience. FreeRein in Clyro, Radnorshire,
offers tours with accommodation at farms and country
inns, including unescorted trips for experienced riders.
Tregoyd Mountain Riders: www.tregoydriding.co.uk
FreeRein Riding Holidays: www.free-rein.co.uk

Below (top to bottom): Richard Booth, founder of
the festival, and the self-appointed "King of Hay";
Brecon Beacons National Park

THE KEY TO ENGLAND

STEEPED IN HISTORY, and besieged today by little more than fantastic views and wheeling seagulls, the magnificent cliff-top medieval bastion of Dover Castle dominates the famous White Cliffs. Strategically located, the battlements that once roared with cannon fire and the shouts of soldiers today welcome far more serene invasions of holidaying families, weekending couples and camera-toting tourists, but the castle remains a commanding and imposing edifice. April and May – as the days lengthen and fine weather returns – are particularly pleasant months for exploration and photography, with blossoming trees and all the colour of spring in this coastal corner of Kent.

Long regarded as the "key to England" – guarding the shortest distance to once-hostile French shores – the castle's lofty keep (the Great Tower) and curtain walls constitute one of southeast England's hallmark fortresses. There was once an Iron Age fort here, and the first castle was erected by William the Conqueror in 1066. The one we see today dates from the reign of Henry II, around 100 years later. Unlike many other castles, Dover has survived largely intact, and the

The battlements that once roared with cannon fire and the shouts of soldiers today welcome far more serene invasions of holidaying families and weekending couples.

rooms of the Great Tower have been restored to re-create the atmosphere of Henry II's fortress. Climb to the top for far-reaching views over the Strait of Dover all the way to the shores of France – historically England's greatest enemy.

Parts of the site date from the times of those other famous foreign invaders, the Romans – the 24-m (80-ft) high, well-preserved *pharos* (lighthouse) is England's tallest surviving Roman relic. Adjacent to the lighthouse stands the ancient Saxon church of St Mary-in-Castro ("St Mary-in-the-Castle"), which dates from the 7th century.

There's a lot to do at Dover Castle, so prepare for extensive reconnaisance: after exploring the castle and its grounds, sit down with a picnic and recharge for the next assault – on its secret tunnels. Once you've finally exhausted the castle's possibilities, head down to the town of Dover, home to a museum that chronicles this important settlement's eventful history. Round off your day with a boat tour of the famous White Cliffs themselves.

FURTHER DETAILS

DOVER CASTLE
Dover, Kent; open Apr–Jul: 10am–6pm daily; Aug: 9:30am–6pm daily; Sep: 10am–6pm daily; Oct: 10am–5pm daily; Nov–Mar: 10am–4pm Sat–Sun.
www.english-heritage.org.uk

Dover
The town of Dover is much more than just a ferry port. There's a Roman fort and Napoleonic fortifications to explore, and walks along the seafront and the Prince of Wales Pier. The Dover Museum provides a good account of this strategic town's history over the centuries. **Dover Museum:** www.dovermuseum.co.uk

White Cliffs Walk
Dover's signature image, the imposing chalk cliffs are ideal for walks and views out over the Strait of Dover. A hike up to the coastal fortifications of the Western Heights offers views of the continent on a clear day.

White Cliff Boat Tours
These boats bounce over the waves, giving the best perspective on the white cliffs (and Dover Castle). Vessels leave regularly for the 40-minute cruise. www.doverwhitecliffttours.com

WHAT ELSE TO SEE AND DO

Deal Castle & Walmer Castle
The two Tudor castles of Deal and Walmer, at picturesque seaside Deal northeast along the coast, provide an opportunity to compare and contrast with Dover Castle. Regular buses from Dover take 30 minutes.
www.aboutdeal.co.uk

Canterbury
The historic cathedral city of Canterbury, 29 km (18 miles) northwest of Dover, is easily reached by train or coach from Dover. It has a host of things to see, including the famous Cathedral – site of the murder of St Thomas Becket, and pilgrimage destination of Chaucer's *Canterbury Tales*. The town is also home to the Canterbury Heritage Museum, a Roman Museum and the Canterbury Tales attractions – a re-creation of 14th-century Canterbury.
www.canterbury.co.uk

Hop Over to France
There are regular crossings to France on the ferry from Dover. It's quite feasible to visit Calais or Boulogne for the day. Don't forget your passport.
www.poferries.com

Main: Aerial view of Dover Castle, overlooking the Strait of Dover
Far left (top to bottom): Historical re-enactment at the castle; interior view of the castle's Grand Shaft Staircase
Above: Main entrance gate to Dover Castle **Below:** Iconic White Cliffs of Dover

THE ESSENTIALS

GETTING THERE AND AROUND
The Suffolk Heritage Coast is in the east of England, running from south of Lowestoft to Felixstowe. The nearest international airport is London Stansted, which is 72 km (45 miles) west of Felixstowe. The best way to explore the area's country roads is by bicycle or car.

WEATHER
March to May are the driest months on the Suffolk coast. The weather is mild, with average spring daytime temperatures of 7–13ºC, but there can be brisk sea breezes, so bring warm clothing.

ACCOMMODATION
Splashing Out The Swan, on Market Square in Southwold, superbly blends old coaching-inn traditions with luxurious modern comforts.
www.adnams.co.uk

On a Budget Field End, in Leiston, offers good-quality 4-star guesthouse accommodation in an Edwardian house just north of Aldeburgh.
www.fieldendguesthouse.co.uk

EATING OUT
Splashing Out The Butley Orford Oysterage, in Orford, is a characterful café-style restaurant that has cultivated its own oysters since the 1950s.
www.pinneysoforford.co.uk/the-restaurant

On a Budget The Randolph Inn, in Reydon near Southwold, is gastronomic heaven with a menu of innovative but affordable dishes.
www.therandolph.co.uk

PRICE FOR TWO PEOPLE
Around £210 a day for accommodation, food and entry to the reserves.

WEBSITES
www.visiteastofengland.com
www.visitsuffolk.com

A BOOMING BUSINESS

The STRANGE AND UNEARTHLY BOOMING CALL of a bittern is something that, once heard, is never forgotten. It was a sound that was on the wane in Britain until the early 2000s, when conservation programmes enabled the bittern population to grow again. The Suffolk Heritage Coast is a favourite haunt of these enigmatic birds; wait patiently at one of the region's wonderful nature reserves, and you might be lucky enough to hear that haunting noise.

Spring also brings migrant birds to these shores in their thousands. They nest all along the coast, but especially in the three RSPB reserves at Minsmere, North Warren and Havergate Island. The unspoilt landscape, the peace and quiet and the abundant local seafood are a draw not only for birds but also for visitors to this tranquil corner of England.

The Suffolk Heritage Coast, running between Lowestoft and Felixstowe, is not a dramatic coastline of high cliffs and rugged bays. It is an area of understated beauty, of quiet beaches interspersed with marshes and reed beds that sprawl underneath vast expanses of sky. It is also dotted with sophisticated seaside towns, such as Southwold and Aldeburgh. Creative types may know Aldeburgh for its music and opera festival in the summer, but naturalists visit in spring for the flocks of avocets that arrive at this time of year. The RSPB reserve on Havergate Island, in the River Ore near Aldeburgh, is one of the delights of this quiet coast. You can only reach it by boat, which adds to its otherworldly charm, and in spring you are sure to see the rare and beautiful avocets, sifting through the sands for food with their unusual upturned bills.

Also near Aldeburgh is the North Warren reserve, a place where bitterns gather and where the equally rare and beautiful sound of the nightingale can still be heard. The biggest reserve on the coast, RSPB Minsmere, south of Dunwich, is home to a huge number of birds, including avocets and nightingales. In spring, marsh harriers – birds of prey that have inhabited England since the Iron Age – perform acrobatic displays to impress their mates, wheeling and diving above the marshland where the shy, booming bitterns lurk, hidden among the reeds.

Main: Elusive bittern in its reed bed habitat
Below: Avocets wading in the mud

FURTHER DETAILS

RESERVES OF THE SUFFOLK HERITAGE COAST

RSPB Havergate Island Nature Reserve
Havergate Island is only accessible by boat from Orford Quay; open for pre-booked trips Aug–Apr on first Saturday of the month (boat leaves at 10am); also open for special weekend events. See website for details.
www.rspb.org.uk

RSPB Minsmere Nature Reserve
Minsmere is just off the A12 between Yoxford and Blythburgh, signposted with brown tourist signs; open daily during daylight hours.
www.rspb.org.uk

RSPB North Warren Nature Reserve
North Warren is to the north of Aldeburgh, on the Thorpe Road which leads to Thorpeness; open 24 hours a day.
www.rspb.org.uk

WHAT ELSE TO SEE AND DO

The Suffolk Coast and Heaths Path
This long-distance footpath follows the Suffolk Heritage Coast for 80 km (50 miles) between Lowestoft and Felixstowe, passing close to all three of the RSPB reserves.
www.suffolkcoastandheaths.org

Dunwich
Sandwiched between Southwold and Aldeburgh, Dunwich was once a substantial medieval town and the capital of East Anglia. Since the 14th century, major coastal erosion has reduced it to the size of a village, but it is still an important site of historical interest.
www.visit-dunwich.co.uk

Adnams Brewery
One of the most highly regarded breweries in the country, Adnams, in Southwold, offers guided tours, demonstrations of the beer-making process and beer-tastings.
www.adnams.co.uk

Below (top to bottom): Minsmere RSPB reserve; coastal town of Southwold

THE ESSENTIALS

GETTING THERE AND AROUND
Liverpool is on the northwest coast of England. It has its own international airport, Liverpool John Lennon Airport, which is about 12 km (7½ miles) southeast of the city centre and is easily reached by rail (2½ hours from London). Many of the city-centre sights are easily reached on foot or by the Merseyrail rail network, which also has a station close to Aintree Racecourse.

WEATHER
Liverpool has a rather wet climate in the spring, with rainfall above the national average. Spring daytime temperatures range from 6 to 12ºC.

ACCOMMODATION
Splashing Out The Hard Day's Night Hotel is a 4-star Beatles-themed hotel in a Grade-II-listed building in the city centre.
www.harddaysnighthotel.com

On a Budget The Cocoon is a "pod" hotel on South Hunter Street providing small but comfortable rooms a short walk from the city centre.
www.cocoonliverpool.co.uk

EATING OUT
Splashing Out Panoramic34, on Brook Street, does indeed offer a panoramic view over the city, and serves equally impressive contemporary food.
www.panoramic34.com

On a Budget Ma Boyle's Alehouse and Eatery, off Water Street in Tower Gardens, dates back to 1870 and serves classic northern pub fare.
www.maboyles.com

PRICE FOR TWO PEOPLE
Around £230 a day for food, accommodation, local transport and entrance fees.

WEBSITE
www.visitliverpool.com

Above (top to bottom): Photomontage at the Beatles Story Museum; Walker Art Gallery; Grand National at Aintree Racecourse **Main:** Albert Dock and the Port of Liverpool Building

THE MERSEY BEAT

Some people might have been surprised when Liverpool was named European Capital of Culture for 2008. After all, this historic port on the River Mersey is better known for its distinguished football clubs; for the famous Grand National steeplechase that takes place at Aintree Racecourse in April; and as the home of The Beatles. But there's more to Liverpool than meets the eye, and spring is an ideal time to explore this lively city's thriving cultural scene.

During its maritime heyday in the 18th and 19th centuries, Liverpool was the second city of the British Empire and handled 40 per cent of the world's trade, but its extensive docks and quays gradually fell into dereliction in the 1970s and 1980s. Now, however, after major regeneration of the area, the rough-and-tumble waterfront has become a UNESCO World Heritage Site and its renovated warehouses hold world-class museums and art galleries.

At Albert Dock on the waterfront, you can find out more about Liverpool's seafaring past. The Merseyside Maritime Museum has displays on the rise and decline of the city's docks and the smuggling of goods, and poignant mementos of the ill-fated *Titanic* and *Lusitania* ocean liners. The heart-wrenching International Slavery Museum, in the same building, reveals a darker side to Liverpool's past – at one time the city was the world's biggest slave port.

FURTHER DETAILS

LIVERPOOL

The Grand National
Aintree Racecourse, Ormskirk Road, Aintree, Liverpool.
The race is run in the first or second week of April.
www.aintree.co.uk

Merseyside Maritime Museum
Albert Dock; open 10am–5pm daily.
www.liverpoolmuseums.org.uk

The Beatles Story
Britannia Vaults, Albert Dock; open 10am–6pm daily.
www.beatlesstory.com

Tate Liverpool
Albert Dock; open 10am–5pm daily.
www.tate.org.uk

Walker Art Gallery
William Brown Street. The Gallery showcases diverse
works of art, from the 13th century to the modern day;
open 10am–5pm daily.
www.liverpoolmuseums.org.uk

World Museum
William Brown Street. The Museum houses historic
treasures from across the globe; open 10am–5pm
daily. www.liverpoolmuseums.org.uk

Museum of Liverpool
Pier Head; open 10am–5pm daily.
www.liverpoolmuseums.org.uk

Anglican Cathedral Church of Christ
St James's Mount; open 8am–6pm daily.
www.liverpoolcathedral.org.uk

Catholic Metropolitan Cathedral of Christ the King
Mount Pleasant; open 7am–6pm daily.
www.liverpoolmetrocathedral.org.uk

Mersey Ferry
Pier Head, Georges Parade. River Explorer ferries
run to Woodside Ferry Terminal in Birkenhead
10am–4pm daily.
www.merseyferries.co.uk

Mendips and 20 Forthlin Road
Allerton and Woolton, Liverpool. The childhood homes
of two members of the Beatles; open late Feb–Nov:
Wed–Sun; admission by National Trust guided tour only
www.nationaltrust.org.uk

Liverpool Beatles Tours
Personalized tours to suit visitors' time and level of
interest, from 2 hours to 3 days long, by booking only.
www.beatlestours.co.uk

Liverpool has something to satisfy every cultural taste. If you are
interested in pop culture, the Beatles Story museum at Albert Dock traces
the rise of the Fab Four, with memorabilia including a real-life yellow
submarine, and you can also sign up for an organized Beatles-themed tour
of the city. For art lovers, Tate Liverpool is the northern home of the
National Collection of Modern Art and hosts major international exhibitions.
The city centre also boasts the Walker Art Gallery, the World Museum and
the Museum of Liverpool, which charts the unique geography, history and
culture of this iconic city.

The city's architecture is particularly impressive. Maritime wealth left a
legacy of monumental buildings, and lining the waterfront at Pier Head are
the "Three Graces" – the imposing Port of Liverpool Building, the Cunard
Building and the Royal Liver Building, whose "Liver Birds" sculptures on its
clock tower are the city's symbol. The Anglican Cathedral, which took 74 years
to construct, is the fifth-largest in the world and is rivalled in the city only by
its Catholic counterpart – the Metropolitan Cathedral – with its striking
modernist design.

In the 1960s, pop star Gerry Marsden eulogized Liverpool in his hugely
popular song *Ferry 'Cross the Mersey*. You can still catch the Mersey ferry from
Pier Head to Birkenhead – a perfect way to step back and admire this vibrant
city's magnificent and historic waterfront.

Below: Liverpool Metropolitan Cathedral

THE ESSENTIALS

GETTING THERE AND AROUND
Speyside is in the northeast of Scotland.
The nearest airport and mainline rail
services are at Inverness, 61 km (38
miles) from Elgin, with flights from
several UK airports and trains from
Glasgow, Edinburgh and London.
ScotRail (*www.scotrail.com*) operates
trains to Knockando and Rothes.

WEATHER
Be prepared for any kind of weather
on Speyside in spring, with daytime
temperatures of 0–10°C. Warm,
waterproof clothing and footwear
are essential.

ACCOMMODATION
Splashing Out Glenmorangie House
at Cadboll is an informal, luxurious
country-house hotel.
www.theglenmorangiehouse.com

On a Budget Tannochbrae, in Dufftown,
is a quaint little guesthouse with cosy
rooms and a decent bar.
www.tannochbrae.co.uk

EATING OUT
Splashing Out The Muckrach Country
House Hotel, beside the village of
Dulnain Bridge, serves fine-dining with an
emphasis on local and seasonal produce.
www.muckrach.com

On a Budget Ord Bàn Restaurant Café,
in Aviemore, offers delicious, simple,
locally sourced food and home-baking.
Tel: 01479 810005

PRICE FOR TWO PEOPLE
£160–230 a day for food,
accommodation and entrance fees.

WEBSITE
www.greaterspeyside.com

ONE SIP AT A TIME

In the words of Scotland's bard, Robert Burns, "freedom and whisky gang the gither" (go together), and there's no denying that whisky is the very essence of Scotland. For many connoisseurs, Speyside is the heartland of Scotland's malt industry, the home of Glenlivet and Glenfiddich, and the birthplace of many other world-renowned whiskies.

The Spirit of Speyside Whisky Festival is a wonderful opportunity for aficionados to sample some of the world's best whiskies, while also enjoying a broader range of Scottish delights. The festival takes place each year from late April to early May, when Speyside opens its doors for ten days of whisky sampling, gourmet food and outdoor activities from hill walking to golf, plus whisky auctions and live music on the banks of the River Spey.

Speyside is at its loveliest in late spring, with the fresh greenery of silver birch and rowan trees on the riverbanks, blazing swathes of yellow broom on the slopes above, nodding fields of barley in the fertile farmlands, and streams gushing from heathery hillsides to join the lovely River Spey. The pure water of the Spey's many tributaries has always been an essential ingredient of the region's fine whiskies, along with a ready supply of barley from the farmlands of Moray and Aberdeenshire.

Combine the Whisky Festival with the world's only Malt Whisky Trail for a trip that will satisfy the most demanding connoisseur, linking eight world-famous distilleries, each offering tours, tastings and insight into *uisghe beatha*: a Gaelic term meaning "water of life". The Trail meanders through lush countryside, wending its way to the waters of the Moray Firth.

Just as each malt whisky has a unique flavour, each distillery is a unique slice of living history, from the old-fashioned distillery at Dallas Dhu to little Benromach, which re-opened in 1998, and Glenlivet, one of Scotland's largest distilleries, producing a world-renowned malt. Speyside's whisky-makers have a passion for their art, and Speyside's distillers continue to create new and inspiring malt whiskies. Just take them one sip at a time.

Main: Drams of finest Speyside malt whisky
Below: Glenlivet Whisky Distillery

FURTHER DETAILS

SPEYSIDE WHISKY
Speyside Whisky Festival
www.spiritofspeyside.com

Malt Whisky Trail
www.maltwhiskytrail.com

The Glenlivet Distillery
Balindalloch; open mid-Mar to mid-Nov: 9:30am–4pm Mon–Sat, 12pm–5pm Sun.
www.theglenlivet.com

Glenfiddich Distillery
Dufftown; open Apr–Oct: 9:30am–4pm daily; Nov–Mar: 11am–3pm Sun.
www.glenfiddich.com

Dallas Dhu Distillery
Mannachie Road, Forres; open Apr–Sep: 9:30am–5:30pm daily; Oct: 9:30am–4:30pm daily; Nov–Mar: 9:30am–4:30pm Mon–Wed, Sat and Sun.
Tel: 01309 676548

Benromach Distillery
Invererne Road, Forres; open May–Sep: 9:30am–5pm Mon–Sat; Oct–Apr: 10am–4pm Sun.
www.benromach.com

Cardhu Distillery
Knockando, Aberlour; open Apr: 10am–5pm Mon–Fri; May–Jun: 10am–5pm Mon–Sat (to 7pm Fri in Jun); Jul–Sep: 10am–5pm Mon–Sat (to 7pm Fri), 11am–4pm Sun; Oct–Dec: 10am–3pm Mon–Fri.
Tel: 01479 874635

Glen Grant Distillery
Rothes, Aberlour; open mid-Jan–mid Dec: 9:30am–5pm daily.
www.glengrant.com

Glen Moray Distillery
Bruceland Road, Elgin; open Oct–April: 9am–5pm Mon–Fri; May–Sep: 9am–5pm Mon–Fri, 10am–4:30pm Sat.
www.glenmoray.com

Strathisla Distillery
Seafield Avenue, Keith; open Apr–Oct: 9:30am–5pm Mon–Sat, noon–5pm Sun.
Tel: 01542 783044

WHAT ELSE TO SEE AND DO
Speyside Cooperage
You can see skilled coopers make wooden casks here.
www.speysidecooperage.co.uk

Below: Stacked whisky casks, Speyside Cooperage

GEORGIAN CHARM

T HE QUAINT HAMPSHIRE TOWN OF NEW ALRESFORD (pronounced "Allsford") bustles with life. Its pretty streets are energized by busy residents dipping in and out of its many charming independent shops, and by visitors who pour into the area daily to appreciate the town's historic houses and picturesque surroundings. Its bright, colour-washed Georgian street frontages offer both a friendly face to the world and an architectural continuity that puts many other towns in Britain to shame. All this is set against glorious rolling fields hiding a necklace of idyllic chalk streams that feed the thriving local watercress industry. This small town is many people's idea of perfection.

The 13th-century Bishops of Winchester were Alresford's original architects, but it is thanks to a devastating fire in 1689 and the quick thinking of an American World War II pilot that New Alresford is the Georgian wonder you see today. After the fire, vulnerable timber was replaced by resilient red brick, and in 1942, Captain Robert Cogswell averted another major disaster by steering his failing bomber plane away

THE ESSENTIALS

GETTING THERE AND AROUND
Alresford is in Hampshire in the south of England, 13 km (8 miles) from Winchester and 18 km (11 miles) from Alton; both have mainline rail connections to London. The nearest international airports are at Heathrow and Gatwick, 82 km (51 miles) and 106 km (66 miles) from Alresford respectively. You can arrive by steam train on the Mid Hants Railway and explore the compact town centre on foot, but to visit outlying villages or nearby Winchester, a car is essential as buses are infrequent.

WEATHER
Alresford experiences typically mild but changeable English spring weather; be prepared for both sunshine and rain. Daytime temperatures average 7–12ºC.

ACCOMMODATION
Splashing Out Lainston House, in nearby Sparsholt, is an award-winning hotel set in its own 26-hectares (63-acres) of beautiful parkland.
www.lainstonhouse.com

On a Budget The Bell, in Alresford, is a centrally located former coaching inn with a great restaurant and en suite rooms.
www.bellalresford.com

EATING OUT
Splashing Out The Hotel du Vin bistro, in Winchester, offers classic European cuisine with a contemporary twist.
www.hotelduvin.com/hotels/winchester/bistro.aspx

On a Budget The Bush Inn in nearby Ovington boasts good pub food and lovely gardens beside the River Itchen.
www.thebushinn.co.uk

PRICE FOR A FAMILY OF FOUR
£315 a day for food, accommodation, entrance fees and tickets for the Watercress Line.

WEBSITES
www.alresford.org
www.visitwinchester.co.uk

Set against glorious rolling fields hiding a necklace of idyllic chalk streams… this small town is many people's idea of perfection.

from the town, bailing out just before it crashed near old Alresford Pond. Today, a plaque can be seen near the water's edge honouring his bravery.

This thriving town is also a historical time capsule. Antiquated buildings house jolly cafés and heritage trains regularly steam into the town's "olde worlde" station. On the banks of the River Arle, the impossibly pretty Fulling Mill charms passers-by and the Eel House parades its unique past. Children will enjoy learning about the ingenious methods the river-keepers used to catch young eels before they left the Arle for their spawning grounds in the Atlantic Ocean. They will also love the many river walks, which offer the chance of spotting swans and otters.

There can be no better reason to visit Alresford in springtime than to catch May's Watercress Festival, when the town centre becomes a stage for an entertaining celebration of Alresford's star export. Food, music, dancing and comedy announce the season's first watercress harvest. Hop on board an old-fashioned steam train for a nostalgia-filled journey along the Watercress Line, and arrive at this fun-packed festival in style.

FURTHER DETAILS

ALRESFORD

Eel House
The centre of the town's eel-catching industry, the Eel House is open on festival days and on selected dates each year.
www.towntrust.org.uk/eel_house.htm

Millennium and Arle River Trails and Old Alresford Pond
These trails use a series of existing paths around the town to provide pleasant and informative walks.
www.alresford.org/millen.php

Watercress Festival
The festival is held on the third Sunday in May, from 10am to 4pm.
www.watercressfestival.org

Mid Hants Railway Watercress Line
The 16-km- (10-mile-) long family-oriented line operates between Alresford and Alton.
www.watercressline.co.uk

WHAT ELSE TO SEE AND DO

Winchester Science Centre and Planetarium
Set in an award-winning 3,500 sq m (38,000 sq ft) building near Winchester, this hands-on science centre and planetarium has more than 100 fun, interactive exhibits that demonstrate fundamental science principles and ways in which we use them.
www.winchestersciencecentre.org

Jane Austen's House
This 17th-century country house at nearby Chawton is where the novelist spent the last eight years of her life, and wrote most of her comedies of middle-class manners in Georgian England, including *Pride and Prejudice*.
www.jane-austens-house-museum.org.uk

Gilbert White's House and Oates Museum
Home to the renowned naturalist, this fascinating museum commemorates important pioneers in the exploration of the natural world. The house is set in the historic village of Selborne and is surrounded by exquisite countryside.
www.gilbertwhiteshouse.org.uk

Marwell Wildlife
You can see over 250 species of exotic and endangered animals at this wildlife park near Eastleigh, including Humboldt penguins, bat-eared foxes, Siamang gibbons and snow leopards. The park covers 56 hectares (140 acres) of beautiful landscaped grounds.
www.marwell.org.uk

Main: Fulling Mill on the River Arle
Above: Horse and carriage at the Watercress Festival, on its way to the watercress farms
Left panel (top to bottom): Watercress harvest; steam train on the Watercress Line
Below: Colour-washed Georgian buildings in Alresford

THE ESSENTIALS

GETTING THERE AND AROUND
Pendle Hill is in Lancashire in the northwest of England, 1.6 km (1 mile) from the village of Barley. The nearest major airport is Manchester International Airport, 77 km (48 miles) south of Barley. There are bus services connecting the villages around Pendle Hill, but a car is best for exploration if you are comfortable with the area's narrow country roads.

WEATHER
The climate around Pendle Hill varies enormously; expect anything from torrential rain to hot sunshine – sometimes on the same day. Average spring daytime temperatures range from 5 to 10°C.

ACCOMMODATION
Splashing Out Northcote, in Langho, offers a Michelin-starred restaurant in a 19th-century manor house, with luxury bedrooms and landscaped gardens.
www.northcote.com

On a Budget Dam Head Barn, in the "witches' village" of Roughlee, is a converted barn with spacious en suite rooms.
www.damheadbarn.com

EATING OUT
Splashing Out Piccolino Clitheroe's open kitchen serves up modern and classic Italian dishes and freshly made pasta.
www.individualrestaurants.com/piccolino/clitheroe/

On a Budget The Well Springs, in Sabden, on the opposite side of Pendle Hill from Barley, is a popular Spanish/Mexican restaurant.
www.thewellsprings.co.uk

PRICE FOR TWO PEOPLE
Around £150 a day for food and accommodation.

WEBSITE
www.visitlancashire.com

Main: Rays of sunlight illuminating Pendle Hill
Right (top to bottom): "Witch graves" in St Leonard's graveyard; public footpath sign for Pendle Hill circular walks

BEWITCHING VIEWS

THE BROODING FORM OF PENDLE HILL became infamous in the 17th century as the focal point for the most celebrated witch trial in English history. If you approach the isolated 557-m- (1827-ft-) high Lancashire hill on a misty day, it's not difficult to imagine the uneasy atmosphere here in the early 1600s. At the time, religious fervour and superstition ran riot throughout the country, even amongst royalty. When King James I came to the throne, he enacted a death penalty for anyone suspected of causing harm through magic. Pendle Hill, long regarded as a wild and lawless part of England, experienced this legislation first-hand when ten women and two men from villages around the hill were accused of witchcraft.

In 1612 a pedlar named John Law suffered a stroke after an altercation with a village woman, Alizon Device. He accused her of witchcraft, and the allegations snowballed with the ensuing investigations. Elderly women who acted as village healers, attempting medical cures using herbs and potions, were also accused. Healing was a common way to make a

Pendle Hill

FURTHER DETAILS

PENDLE HILL

Walking Routes
There are several paths up to the top of Pendle Hill. The route from the village of Sabden, on the southwest side of the hill, is a 3–4-hour round trip. There is a good car park at Barley – which also has restaurants and hotels – on the southeastern side of the hill, and the round trip from here is about 6 km (just under 4 miles); it should take anyone of average fitness just under 3 hours. It is a very popular walk and likely to be busy on a fine spring day. Check the weather forecast, as conditions are often changeable and mist or rain can descend quickly.

WHAT ELSE TO SEE AND DO

Roughlee
This village is a 5-minute drive east of Barley. It features the pretty stream known as Pendle Water and the picturesque Roughlee Hall, once thought to be the home of the most famous Pendle witch, Alice Nutter.

Blacko
A few minutes' drive east of Roughlee is the village of Blacko. Here the "witch" with the splendid name of Old Mother Demdike – although her real name was the rather more prosaic Elizabeth Southern – lived at Malkin Tower Farm, now converted into holiday cottages.
Malkin Tower Farm: www.malkintowerfarm.co.uk

Newchurch
About 1 km (½ mile) south of Barley, Newchurch village is named after St Mary's Church, which has the "Eye of God" painted on its tower to ward off evil. Alice Nutter is supposed to lie buried in the churchyard, but no grave has yet been found.

Downham
This quaint village is popular with film-makers – it lies in an estate whose owners forbid the erection of overhead cables and satellite dishes. One of the period dramas filmed here over the years was the 1960s classic, *Whistle Down the Wind*.

Below (top to bottom): Village of Downham; hiking up Pendle Hill

living in the early 17th century, and it's thought that some Pendle healers made false charges to discredit their rivals. The witch hunt turned deadly, however, and of the 12 accused, only one was acquitted – the rest were hanged and buried in the graveyard of St Leonard's church in Downham.

Today the locals are happy to exploit their notorious past. Signposts for walking routes show silhouettes of witches on broomsticks, and the villages surrounding the hill – Barley, Downham, Roughlee and Sabden – do a roaring trade in occult souvenirs. That isn't the only reason to pay a visit, however. The quaint stone houses and narrow streets have changed little over the years, and when the sun shines over these quiet backwaters, they easily rival the more famous Cotswold villages for beauty and charm, giving you the perfect start to a day of hiking. If you climb up the not-too-strenuous slopes of Pendle Hill on one of the well-marked paths, you will be rewarded with bewitching views that stretch as far as the Lancashire coast, 50 km (31 miles) away. You may not encounter a witch, but the scenery is definitely magical.

THE ESSENTIALS

GETTING THERE AND AROUND
Derry is in the northwest of Northern Ireland, close to the border with the Republic of Ireland. It has its own small airport, the City of Derry Airport, 11 km (7 miles) southwest of the city. Belfast International Airport is 96 km (60 miles) southeast of Derry, with airport coach connections between the two. Derry's city centre is easily explored on foot.

WEATHER
Ireland gets a lot of rain, but Derry is at its driest in spring. The average daytime temperature is cool, at 8–10°C.

ACCOMMODATION
Splashing Out The 4-star City Hotel Derry, on Queens Quay, offers luxury rooms right on the banks of the River Foyle, within walking distance of the centre.
www.cityhotelderry.com

On a Budget The Derry City Independent Hostel, on Great James Street, has private rooms as well as dormitories, and offers comfort and good value.
www.derryhostel.com

EATING OUT
Splashing Out Mange2, on Strand Road, serves Irish produce cooked in delicious French-bistro style.
www.mange2derry.com

On a Budget Fitzroy's Bistro, on Bridge Street, is a relaxed restaurant in the city centre serving international cuisine.
www.fitzroysrestaurant.com

PRICE FOR TWO PEOPLE
Around £150 a day for accommodation, food and entrance fees.

WEBSITE
www.derryvisitor.com

Previous page: The Royal Pavilion in Brighton, East Sussex

THE WALLED CITY

DERRY MAY BE NORTHERN IRELAND'S SECOND CITY, but first-rate music echoes from within its historic walls each spring, when it hosts the City of Derry Jazz and Big Band Festival. The region's biggest and most-renowned jazz event, it attracts national and international performers over four days in late April and early May. The range of music is impressive, blending traditional and contemporary jazz and big-band sounds with hip-hop, salsa, reggae, blues and swing. You can hear free concerts at pubs and hotels around the city, or take in headline acts at the Millennium Forum, a modern landmark inside its venerable walls.

Once you've satisfied your musical cravings, take a tour of the city's old town. Its impressive 6-m- (20-ft-) high defensive walls were built between 1613 and 1618 by Protestant settlers from London. Despite three Catholic sieges – including the 105-day Siege of Derry in 1688–89, the longest siege in British history – these well-preserved walls were never breached. You can walk along the top of them, following their 1.5-km (1-mile) circuit round the city, and drop down to visit any of the fascinating historical sites you see en route. If you start your day with a visit to the spectacular Neo-Gothic Guildhall, or the Tower Museum, with its high-tech displays that tell the city's story, you'll find yourself very near Shipquay Gate, where there are steps leading to the top of the walls. The ramparts here are dotted with original cannons. Follow the walls anti-clockwise, and you'll soon be tempted down by the fascinating Siege museum, the small but beautiful St Augustine's Church and St Columb's Cathedral – the first Protestant cathedral in the British Isles, built after the Reformation and dedicated to the Ulster monk who founded the first settlement here. It too contains relics of the great Siege.

From the height of Derry's walls there are thought-provoking views of this once-divided city. To the west lies the Catholic Bogside district, its large, distinctive political murals a reminder of Northern Ireland's troubled history, while to the east, across the River Foyle, Maurice Harron's profound *Hands Across the Divide* sculpture symbolizes reconciliation.

Main: Cannon on the walls of Derry **Below:** Jazz band playing at the City of Derry Jazz and Big Band Festival

FURTHER DETAILS

DERRY
The City of Derry Jazz and Big Band Festival
The festival is held over four days in late April/early May.
www.cityofderryjazzfestival.com

Millennium Forum
Newmarket Street. This theatre and conference centre lies in the heart of the city.
www.milleniumforum.co.uk

The Guildhall
Guildhall Square; open 10am–5:30pm daily.
www.derrystrabane.com

The Tower Museum
Union Hall Place; open 10am–5:30pm daily.
www.derrystrabane.com

Siege Museum
Society Street; 10am–5pm Mon–Sat.
www.thesiegemuseum.org

St Augustine's Church
Palace Street; open daily.
www.derryandraphoe.org/st-augustine-s

St Columb's Cathedral
London Street; open 9am–5pm Mon–Sat.
www.stcolumbscathedral.org

WHAT ELSE TO SEE AND DO
Derry City Tours
An informative hour-long walking tour of Derry, covering history such as the Bloody Sunday story, and sights such as the historic Derry Walls.
www.derrycitytours.com

Below (top to bottom): St Columb's Cathedral; the *Hands Across the Divide* sculpture

THE ESSENTIALS

GETTING THERE AND AROUND
Bempton Cliffs Reserve is in the northeast of England, 108 km (67 miles) east of Leeds. The reserve is 2.5 km (1½ miles) from Bempton village and railway station. Several of the cliffside viewpoints within the reserve are wheelchair-accessible.

WEATHER
Be prepared for cold winds and rain off the North Sea, with spring daytime temperatures of around 8–12ºC.

ACCOMMODATION
Splashing Out The Crown Spa Hotel, in Scarborough, has the distinction of being the only 4-star hotel on the Yorkshire coast.
www.crownspahotel.com

On a Budget An Oasis Guest House, in Bridlington, is a cosy B&B that offers comfortable beds and hearty breakfasts.
www.anoasisbrid.co.uk

EATING OUT
Bempton is a small and relatively remote village, with limited dining options that all offer a mid-priced menu.

Rags Hotel & Restaurant, in Bridlington, is a classy restaurant that specializes in fresh seafood and other local delicacies.
www.ragshotel.co.uk

The White Horse, on Bempton High Street, is a family-friendly pub serving real ales and pub grub, within walking distance of Bempton Cliffs.
Tel: 01262 850266

PRICE FOR TWO PEOPLE
From around £150 a day for accommodation, food and entrance fees for the nature reserve and other attractions.

WEBSITE
www.yorkshire.com

Main: Puffin in flight from the cliffs at Bempton
Right (top to bottom): Two black-legged kittiwakes sparring with their beaks; colony of guillemots

BIRD-WATCHERS' PARADISE

COMICAL, CUTE AND CLUMSY-LOOKING, puffins are the most enchanting of British sea birds. To see them is to love them, and at Bempton Cliffs on the Yorkshire coast you can see them by the hundred in spring and early summer, along with vast flocks of other sea birds.

Bempton's white chalk cliffs rise dramatically out of the waves, offering the perfect nesting place for puffins, which wheel and soar from the shore far out above the grey waters of the North Sea. It's a wildlife spectacle unequalled in Britain, and it has to be seen – and heard – to be believed. From viewing points on the cliffs, you can watch these fat little creatures setting off on fishing expeditions from which they return with flimsy-looking wings beating gallantly and their colourful beaks stuffed with silvery sand eels – dinner for the chick that huddles in their cliffside burrow. Out at sea, the adult birds can be seen afloat in large flocks that suddenly vanish beneath the waves when they detect a shoal of fish below.

FURTHER DETAILS

RSPB BEMPTON CLIFFS NATURE RESERVE
Near Bempton, East Yorkshire; reserve is open at all
times; visitor centre open Mar–Oct: 9:30am–5pm daily;
Nov–Feb: 9:30am–4pm daily.
www.rspb.org.uk

WHAT ELSE TO SEE AND DO
RSPB Blacktoft Sands Nature Reserve
These vast reedbeds are home to bearded tits, bitterns
and marsh harriers; open 9am–9pm daily.
www.rspb.org.uk

RSPB Dearne Valley Old Moor Nature Reserve
This moorland reserve is home to kingfishers and
huge flocks of lapwings; visitor centre open Feb–Mar:
9:30–5pm daily; Apr–Oct: 9:30am–8pm daily; Nov–
Jan: 9:30–4pm daily.
www.rspb.org.uk

RSPB Fairburn Ings Nature Reserve
Kingfishers, little ringed plovers and garganey ducks are
among the species here in spring and early summer;
visitor centre open 9am–4pm daily.
www.rspb.org.uk

Flamborough Head, Flamborough
This looming headland, with its historic lighthouse,
affords breathtaking views out to the North Sea.
www.flamboroughhead.co.uk

The Deep, Hull
This spectacular aquarium offers a puffin's-eye view of
the undersea world. You can view sharks and 3,500
other fish of various species from an underwater tunnel.
www.thedeep.co.uk

Scarborough Castle, Scarborough
There are superb views of the North Sea coast from the
imposing ramparts of this ruined castle, built during
the reign of King Stephen in the 1130s.
www.english-heritage.org.uk/yorkshire

Below: Grass-topped chalk cliffs at Bempton

The puffins arrive at their breeding colonies in the spring and, after breeding,
they leave en masse in mid-July. Towards the end of the breeding season,
Bempton Cliffs throngs with adults feeding greedy chicks. A few days later, it is
bereft of puffins, with adult birds heading back into the wide spaces of the
North Sea and their newly fledged offspring struggling to keep up as they set
out on their first maritime pilgrimage. These youngsters will spend five or six
years at sea, before returning to lay their own eggs on Bempton's chalk ledges.

Puffins are the starring players at Bempton, but there is always a strong
supporting cast. Gannets – among the most impressive of British sea birds
– patrol the waters close inshore and can be seen plummeting after fish from
altitude. Dainty little kittiwakes fill the air with their distinctive calls and huddle
together on their precarious nesting ledges; razorbills and guillemots crowd
rocky ledges and, like the puffins, arrow out to sea in squadrons in search of a
fish supper. If you are a nature-lover at heart, you could spend a day's blissful
bird-watching on this beautiful coastline; with over 20 species of bird to watch
out for, you will be spoilt for choice.

THE BARD'S BIRTHDAY

THE MODEST SOUTH WARWICKSHIRE TOWN of Stratford-upon-Avon would be no more than an inconsequential blip on the tourist radar but for the dazzling brilliance of its most famous luminary, William Shakespeare. Literary pilgrims the world over dream of coming to England specifically to visit Stratford-upon-Avon; to such aficionados, exploring the rest of the United Kingdom can be a mere afterthought. With legions of British schoolchildren also visiting Stratford-upon-Avon to learn about the author of *King Lear* and *Hamlet*, the town is guaranteed to offer an uninterrupted tourist bonanza.

Stratford-upon-Avon offers an overflowing cornucopia of sights associated with the playwright and all things Shakespearean. The museum – the half-timbered house where the Bard was born in 1564 – is the first stop on the trail, and almost certainly the most visited house in Britain. Nash's House, on Chapel Street, is an attractive period building that houses an exhibition centre for New Place, which is next door and is where Shakespeare lived when not in London, and where he died in 1616. Two other houses are well worth a visit: Hall's Croft,

Stratford-upon-Avon offers an overflowing cornucopia of sights associated with the playwright and all things Shakespearean.

a snapshot of Elizabethan England, was the home of Shakespeare's eldest daughter, while the half-timbered and thatched Anne Hathaway's Cottage and Gardens was the home of Shakespeare's wife. The playwright's resting place, Holy Trinity Church, draws a natural conclusion to literary explorations. A late-afternoon trip down the River Avon provides perfect calm in which to muse over his life, and see the town from a different perspective.

Shakespeare's birthday on 23 April has been commemorated in the town for over 200 years. Today it is celebrated with a number of days of cultural events, from street theatre to poetry readings, musical performances, folk dancing, processions and marching bands. The Shakespeare Birthday Parade is held on the Saturday closest to 23 April, when a procession forms a pilgrimage from Shakespeare's birthplace to his grave. The Bard's plays are staged everywhere – from the Royal Shakespeare Theatre to the streets and even boats. It's impossible not to become swept up in this celebration of Britain's most famous writer.

FURTHER DETAILS

SHAKESPEARE SITES
Details of places and events can be found at:
www.shakespeare-country.co.uk
www.shakespeare.org.uk

Shakespeare's Birthplace
Henley Street; open summer: 9am–5pm daily; winter: 10am–4pm daily.

Nash's House & New Place
Chapel Street; closed for renovations until July 2016. See website for opening times after reopening.
www.shakespeare.org.uk

Hall's Croft
Old Town; open mid-Mar–Aug: 10am–5pm daily; Nov–mid-Mar: 11am–4pm.

Anne Hathaway's Cottage and Gardens
Shottery; open spring and summer: 9am–5pm daily, winter: 10am–4pm daily.

Holy Trinity Church
Shakespeare's burial place, in Trinity Street; open Apr–Sep: 8:30am–6pm Mon–Sat, 12:30–5pm Sun; Mar and Oct: 9am–5pm Mon–Sat, 12:30–5pm Sun; Nov–Feb: 9am–4pm Mon–Sat, 12:30–5pm Sun.

Avon Boating
Rowing-boat and motor-boat rental, plus guided river cruises on quiet, electric-powered boats.
www.avon-boating.co.uk

Royal Shakespeare Company
Britain's most famous repertory theatre company produces plays by Shakespeare and his contemporaries as well as living playwrights at their two Stratford homes: the Royal Shakespeare Theatre and the Swan Theatre.
www.rsc.org.uk

WHAT ELSE TO SEE AND DO
Charlecote Park
Shakespeare was apocryphally caught poaching deer on the estate of this beautiful Tudor house, 8 km (5 miles) from Stratford-upon-Avon. The magnificent gardens by the River Avon were designed by "Capability" Brown.
www.nationaltrust.org.uk

Mary Arden's Farm
The childhood home of Shakespeare's mother lies just outside Stratford at Wilmcote.
www.shakespeare.org.uk

Main: Rowing boats on the River Avon
Far left (top to bottom): Performance of Love's Labour's Lost in Stratford; Shakespeare's birthplace
Above: Shakespeare Birthday Parade in Stratford
Below: Holy Trinity Church in Stratford, Shakespeare's resting place

Below: Anne Hathaway's thatched cottage at Shottery

THE ESSENTIALS

GETTING THERE AND AROUND
Hadrian's Wall Path National Trail crosses northern England, from Wallsend near Newcastle-upon-Tyne in the east to Bowness-on-Solway in the west. The closest international airport is at Newcastle. The A69 and B6318 lead to major sections of the wall. The AD122 bus operates Easter–Sep, running from Newcastle Central Station to Carlisle with stops at all the wall's main visitor centres.

WEATHER
Spring weather is variable, and you could see anything from snow to warm sunshine. Daytime temperatures average 3–11°C.

ACCOMMODATION
Splashing Out Jesmond Dene House, in Newcastle, is in a 19th-century Grade II listed building and offers luxurious rooms and fine dining.
www.jesmonddenehouse.co.uk

On a Budget The Centre of Britain Hotel and Restaurant, in Haltwhistle, is set in a 15th-century building.
www.centreofbritain.org.uk

EATING OUT
Splashing Out The Bouchon Bistrot, in Hexham, close to the Corbridge site, serves up classy French-style dishes.
www.bouchonbistrot.co.uk

On a Budget The Rat Inn, at Anick, between Corbridge and Hexham, is an 18th-century inn serving superior pub food as well as sandwiches and bar snacks.
www.theratinn.com

PRICE FOR TWO PEOPLE
£190–200 a day for food, local transport, accommodation and entrance fees.

WEBSITE
www.hadrians-wall.org

Main: Hadrian's Wall, looking east from Holbank Crags
Right (top to bottom): Housesteads Fort on Hadrian's Wall; hiking beside the wall

BORDER PATROL

IT WAS BUILT BY AN INVADING FORCE as a symbol of control and military might. Yet there's something romantic about Hadrian's Wall, which curves so majestically through the rolling hills of northern England. The Romans erected the wall early in the 2nd century, and for nearly 300 years it marked the northern frontier of their empire. Some sections are no longer visible, as much of the stone was recycled in churches and other local buildings over the centuries. Enough remains, however, for its designation as a UNESCO World Heritage Site.

The 135-km (84-mile) Hadrian's Wall Path National Trail follows the historic line of the wall. Starting in the east at Segedunum Roman Fort in Wallsend, it follows the river in Tyneside, runs through pretty Tynedale farmland and snakes up and down the stark, windswept fells of Northumberland. The wall reaches its highest point of 345 m (1130 ft) at Whinshields Crags, before descending gently through the fertile pastures of Cumbria on its

FURTHER DETAILS

ROMAN SITES ALONG HADRIAN'S WALL

Segedunum Roman Fort
Buddle Street, Wallsend. Interactive computer
displays, excavated finds, a reconstructed bathhouse
and more paint a picture of Roman life as it played
out here at the wall's eastern end. There are splendid
views over the ruins from the watchtower; open
10am–2:30pm Mon–Fri.
www.segedunumromanfort.org.uk

Chesters Roman Fort
Chollerford, Humshaugh, Hexham. This cavalry fort, in
a lovely riverside setting, was one of the first along the
wall. It has well-preserved gateways and foundations,
and a military bathhouse. Its museum displays
important archaeological discoveries; open Apr–Sep:
10am–6pm daily; Oct–Mar: 10am–4pm daily.
www.english-heritage.org.uk

Vindolanda
Bardon Mill, Hexham. Some of the finest and most
unusual Roman artifacts were found at this settlement
and are on display in the excellent museum here.
They include jewellery, shoes and even letters written
on wooden tablets. A temple and other buildings
are reconstructed in the garden, and you can watch
ongoing excavations; open Feb–Mar: 10am–4pm daily;
Apr–Sep: 10am–6pm daily; Oct–Dec: 10am–5pm
daily (closed Jan).
www.vindolanda.com

Housesteads Roman Fort and Museum
Bardon Mill, Hexham. Many features have been
excavated at Britain's best-preserved Roman fort,
including double portal gateways, turrets, a hospital
and even latrines. The museum contains a model
of how the site looked in its entirety; open Apr–Oct:
10am–6pm daily; Nov–Mar: 10am–4pm daily.
www.english-heritage.org.uk

Corbridge Roman Town
Corchester Lane, Corbridge. The remains of this bustling
garrison town include barracks, temples, granaries and
a fountain house with an aqueduct. The museum
displays the broad range of Roman artifacts found
here; open Apr–Oct: 10am–6pm daily; Nov–Mar:
10am–4pm Sat and Sun.
www.english-heritage.org.uk

way to the saltmarsh estuary of the Solway Firth. The central sections of the wall
within Northumberland National Park are some of the best-preserved, and they
cut through dramatic scenery little changed since Roman times. It takes between
four and seven days to walk the entire length of this ancient fortification, but
there are more than 80 shorter paths and circular routes to either side. There's
also a cycle trail that runs the length of the wall.

Whichever route you choose, picture the wall as it was in Roman times: 5 m
(16 ft) high, with a deep ditch bordering the south side, and whitewashed to
make it stand out against the landscape and intimidate the Scottish tribes. Some
15,000 soldiers were stationed along its length. There was a watchtower every
500m (about 550 yards), a "milecastle" and gate every 1.5 km (the Roman mile
of 1,000 paces – just over 1,600 yards), and a fort every 11 km (7 miles) or so.
Archaeological sites, such as Chesters Roman Fort, Vindolanda, Housesteads
Fort and the Corbridge Roman Site still remain, giving you a glimpse of life in this
distant and most heavily fortified frontier of the Empire.

Below: Bathhouse complex at Chesters Roman Fort

THE ESSENTIALS

GETTING THERE AND AROUND
Brighton is on England's southeastern coast, 85 km (53 miles) from London. The nearest airport is London Gatwick, 48 km (30 miles) north of Brighton. Fast trains run regularly to Brighton from central London and from Gatwick, with a journey time of less than an hour. Brighton town centre is easily navigable by foot.

WEATHER
Brighton enjoys a mild maritime climate, with average daytime temperatures of 7–14°C in spring.

ACCOMMODATION
Splashing Out Drakes, on Marine Parade, is a comfortable, 4-star boutique town house on the seafront that describes its ambience as "laid-back glamour".
www.drakesofbrighton.com

On a Budget Gulliver's, on New Steine, is a centrally located B&B in an elegant and charming Georgian townhouse close to the beach.
www.gullivershotel.com

EATING OUT
Splashing Out Bistrot du Vin, on Ship Street, offers classy gastropub lunches and suppers, all sourced from local ingredients, in a former arts centre.
www.hotelduvin.com/locations/brighton

On a Budget Bardsleys, on Baker Street near the railway station, serves up perhaps the best fish and chips in town in a restaurant that has been owned by the same family for four generations.
www.bardsleys-fishandchips.co.uk

PRICE FOR TWO PEOPLE
From £160 a day for food, accommodation and entertainment.

WEBSITES
www.visitbrighton.com
www.realbrighton.com

BRIGHTON ROCKS!

Cherry-picking many of the best features of the English capital and relocating them to the beach, the city of Brighton has earned itself the nickname "London-by-Sea". Attracting the most fashionable of visitors and residents, Brighton combines urban chic with flip-flops and salty air and, like London, is composed of many individual districts, each with its own unique vibe. Exploring the city, you could be in Amsterdam one minute, Greenwich Village the next; yet it's important to draw no such comparisons, for Brighton's personality is all its own.

Once a fishing port and small market town, Brighton's fortunes were transformed in the late 18th century, when the fashion for curative bathing in sea water took hold among the gentry. The patronage of the Prince Regent, who first visited Brighton in 1783, sealed the town's aristocratic credentials. Brighton's regal side can be seen today in its early 19th-century Regency architecture, and in the Royal Pavilion, an extravagant Asian-style royal palace.

BRIGHTON'S SIGHTS

The Royal Pavilion
This former palace, remodelled by John Nash from 1815 to 1823, contains Queen Victoria's apartments and lavish music and banqueting rooms. The gardens have been restored and replanted according to Nash's original vision; open Oct–Mar: 10am–5:15pm; Apr–Sep: 9:30am–5:45pm.
www.royalpavilion.org.uk

Brighton Festival
www.brightonfestival.org

The Lanes and North Laine
www.visitbrighton.com/shopping/the-lanes
www.northlaine.co.uk

Brighton Pier
Madeira Drive, Brighton. Iconic Victorian pleasure pier now packed with funfair-style attractions; open daily (except 25 Dec); opening and closing times vary and are weather dependent – check the website.
www.brightonpier.co.uk

WHAT ELSE TO SEE AND DO

Brighton Marina Village
The slick Marina Village development on the eastern edge of the town provides mooring for more than 1,500 boats and yachts as well as plenty of entertainment. Street performers, a boardwalk, shops, cafés and restaurants, a cinema, casino and bowling complex draw plenty of visitors, many of whom make the short trip from Brighton on Volk's Electric Railway, the world's oldest operating electric railway.
Marina Village: www.brightonmarina.co.uk
Volk's Electric Railway: www.volkselectricrailway.co.uk

The South Downs
A designated National Park and an Area of Outstanding Natural Beauty, the South Downs' chalk hills and clifftop paths stretch through Sussex into Hampshire. It's a short car journey to these superb walks and beautiful views; alternatively you can take special "Breeze up to the Downs" buses from Brighton's centre.
www.southdowns.gov.uk

Charleston Farmhouse
Approximately 30 minutes' drive east of Brighton, beyond Lewes, this country residence was the meeting place of famed literary set the Bloomsbury Group in the early 20th century. There are tours of the house and grounds, and a busy events and workshop calendar.
www.charleston.org.uk

Main: Brighton's renowned Pier at sunset

Left (left to right): Regency terraced housing in Brighton; the town's shingle beach

Right: Shopping in the Lanes

The town has evolved from a royal summer resort to the year-round home of famous artists, musicians and bright young creative things escaping the oppression of London without leaving it far behind; high-speed trains connect the two in under an hour. The town's cultural scene punches well above its weight for its size, most notably during the annual Brighton Arts Festival, a glossy celebration of traditional and fringe music, theatre, literature and art. Brighton is also home to a thriving gay scene and is famous for its relaxed atmosphere.

There is much to be had by way of retail entertainment too, much of it in the quirky independent specialist boutiques of The Lanes. Lose yourself in this maze of small shops and find retro gems and one-off jewellery, or browse the antiques and flea market in the bohemian district of North Laine. To relax, take a stroll through arty Kemp Town "village", with its lively squares and cafés, and indulge in some people-watching. For traditionalists, the quintessential British seaside must-haves are certainly all in place: arcades and fairground rides on the Palace Pier, a huge shingle beach, and, most famously, sticks of delicious Brighton Rock.

Below: The Royal Pavilion, inspired in part by the Taj Mahal

THE ESSENTIALS

GETTING THERE AND AROUND

The Welsh Narrow-gauge Railways are concentrated in northwest Wales. The area is approximately 4 hours' drive from London. There are three main starting points for the narrow-gauge trains: Porthmadog, Caenarfon and Llanberis. Mainline rail services along the north Wales coast call at Porthmadog. The Sherpa bus service connects Porthmadog to Caenarfon and Llanberis, and runs buses to all the most popular tourist points in Snowdonia.

WEATHER

Spring is generally mild but windy, with rain showers. Daytime temperatures vary from 7 to 15ºC in the valleys and from 0 to 11ºC on the summit of Snowdon.

ACCOMMODATION

Splashing Out Tan-yr-Allt, just outside Porthmadog, is an early-19th-century country house that was once the home of the Romantic poet Shelley. *www.tanyrallt.co.uk*

On a Budget Lake View, in Llanberis, within the Snowdonia National Park, is a friendly family-owned hotel with lake views and good locally sourced food. *Tel: 01286 870422*

EATING OUT

Splashing Out The Peak, in Llanberis, offers an interesting melange of excellent Welsh and international cuisine, such as roast Welsh lamb, rib-eye steaks, lentil dahl and bouillabaisse. *www.peakrestaurant.co.uk*

On a Budget Russell Tea Room, in Porthmadog Station, is a classic old station café with mugs of tea and filling meals.

PRICE FOR A FAMILY OF FOUR

From £275 for accommodation, food and train tickets.

WEBSITE

www.visitwales.com

FULL STEAM AHEAD

WALES HAS MORE THAN ITS FAIR SHARE of narrow-gauge steam railways, especially in the northern region, around Snowdonia. These steam engines were used to transport slate from the area's world-famous slate quarries to the coast, for shipping around the British Empire during the 19th and early 20th centuries. No longer used for their original purpose, many have been renovated by enthusiasts and now offer short but evocative journeys through glorious countryside. All the trains travel at a delightfully modest speed, so you can gently soak up the wonderful views. In fact, by using Snowdonia's "Sherpa" bus services to plug the gaps, it's possible to travel from the sea to the summit of Mount Snowdon by steam train.

From Caernarfon on the Welsh coast you can take a Welsh Highland Railway train through stunning scenery to Pitt's Head, a starting point for a trek to the top of Snowdon, or travel on to Beddgelert before looping around, via a dramatic plunge through a hillside tunnel, for the return journey. Or disembark at Beddgelert and take the bus to nearby Llanberis, the starting point for two magical steam-train rides: one around tranquil twin lakes and through the Padarn Country Park, with great views of the peaks; the other chugging its way up the slopes of Snowdon itself to Hafod Eryri – the summit's visitor centre (*see also pp66–7*).

Buses connect Caernarfon with Porthmadog, further up the coast, where there are another two trips to savour. From Porthmadog's Harbour Station the Ffestiniog Railway heads east, climbing straight into the heart of Snowdonia. It runs through glorious oak woods and past magnificent lakes and waterfalls, clinging to the sides of the mountains or even tunnelling through them, and up to Blaenau Ffestiniog station, at the head of the valley. The Welsh Highland Heritage Railway is a loop of line only 1.6-km (1-mile) long, starting and finishing at Porthmadog, but the stop at its engine sheds en route is a must for enthusiasts young and old. The line offers visitors over 18 the opportunity to drive a steam engine called "Gelert" – an experience likened to "driving a car using bath taps". While younger visitors may be disappointed at missing out, they can still clamber into the locomotive cabs in the engine sheds and learn how it all works. Each train has a wheelchair-accessible, pushchair-friendly coach and the railway will even take well-behaved dogs – so this really can be a day out for all the family.

Main: Welsh Highland Railway train
Below: Snowdon Mountain Railway train climbing the last section of rail before the summit

FURTHER DETAILS

WELSH NARROW-GAUGE RAILWAYS
Great Little Trains of Wales
Ten of Wales's best steam railways are grouped together under the Great Little Trains of Wales banner, with a website detailing all the routes. Each train line has its own schedules and prices, but you can buy a Great Little Trains Discount Card, which is valid for one year and gives you a 20-per-cent discount on all the trains. Many of the trains connect with mainline stations and bus services. Note that the steam-train services are less frequent in winter and may run at weekends only.
www.greatlittletrainsofwales.co.uk

Sherpa Buses
The Sherpa bus network covers the Snowdonia National Park, connecting Porthmadog, Caernarfon, Llanberis and Betws-y-Coed. Winter services are reduced, but at Easter the summer timetable, with more frequent services, comes into operation.
www.visitsnowdonia.info

National Slate Museum
Llanberis; open Easter–Oct: 10am–5pm daily; Nov–Easter: 10am–4pm Sun–Fri.
www.museumwales.ac.uk/slate

WHAT ELSE TO SEE AND DO
Caernarfon Castle
North Wales is home to some of the finest medieval castles in the world, and this is possibly the most impressive fortress in the British Isles.
www.caernarfon.com

Below (top to bottom): Snowdon Mountain Railway train pushing its carriage up Snowdon; Ffestiniog Railway steam train

GREEN PARTY

S
T PATRICK'S DAY IS CELEBRATED AROUND THE WORLD, by Irish communities as far away as Australia, the USA and Tokyo. 17 March is an excuse for anyone with a drop of Irish blood – real or honorary – to don a shamrock, let down their dyed-green hair and parade through the streets in the colours of the Emerald Isle. Nowhere is it celebrated more enthusiastically than in Ireland itself, where the liveliest celebration of its national holiday takes place in the capital, Dublin.

A week-long festival of culture and the *craic* – the Irish term for fun and entertainment – makes this party-loving city the place to be in springtime. It culminates with a grand parade on St Patrick's Day that begins at noon in Parnell Square and wends its merry way through the city centre to St Patrick's Cathedral. More than half a million people line the streets to watch the spectacle. Extravagant floats and pageants illustrate the theme of each year's parade, accompanied by marching bands. Colourfully costumed characters create a carnival atmosphere with dancing, singing and acrobatic routines. Actors also portray St Patrick himself, complete with flowing beard, staff and shamrock.

The parade passes by some of Dublin's most famous landmarks. It heads down O'Connell Street past the General Post Office, where the Republic of Ireland was proclaimed in 1916, and the Spire of Dublin, the city's millennium monument. After crossing the O'Connell Bridge, the procession turns west at the gates of Trinity College and heads along Dame Street, passing the stately Dublin Castle. At Christ Church Cathedral, Dublin's oldest building, it turns south towards St Patrick's Cathedral – Ireland's largest church.

In the days leading up to the parade, the St Patrick's Festival stages a range of events that celebrate Irish culture. There are music concerts and art exhibitions; numerous theatre, film, comedy and modern-dance performances; *céilí* – traditional Irish dancing; and family activities from funfairs to treasure hunts. Street performers from around the country fill Dublin's Georgian-era squares with free music and entertainment.

When the festival comes to a close in a blaze of fireworks, you can't help thinking that old St Patrick himself would approve.

THE ESSENTIALS

GETTING THERE AND AROUND
Dublin is located halfway down the east coast of Ireland, and has its own international airport, 11 km (7 miles) north of the city centre. Driving in the city can be slow-going, and most of the main sights can be easily reached on foot or by bus, or by using the excellent DART (Dublin Area Rapid Transit) train service.

WEATHER
Ireland is known for experiencing four seasons in one day, and that undoubtedly applies as much to Dublin as anywhere else. Average spring daytime temperatures range from 6 to 10°C.

ACCOMMODATION
Splashing Out Dylan, in Eastmoreland Place, is a 5-star boutique hotel that offers the the ultimate in comfortable accommodation.
www.dylan.ie

On a Budget The Charles Stewart, in Parnell Square, is a modest but cosy, centrally located B&B.
www.charlesstewart.ie

EATING OUT
Splashing Out Patrick Guilbaud, on Upper Merrion Street, has 2 Michelin stars and serves extravagant modern cuisine prepared from Irish produce.
www.restaurantpatrickguilbaud.ie

On a Budget The Gotham Café, on St Anne Street, is one of the city centre's most popular and atmospheric eating places, with great *craic* and great food.
www.gothamcafe.ie

PRICE FOR TWO PEOPLE
From €235 a day for accommodation, food, entrance fees and the odd pint of Guinness

WEBSITE
www.visitdublin.com

Main: St Patrick's Day Parade, O'Connell Street
Below: Revellers crowding the streets of Dublin during the parade

FURTHER DETAILS

DUBLIN

St Patrick's Day Festival
www.stpatricksfestival.ie

St Patrick's Cathedral
Patrick's Close. St Patrick was said to have baptized early Christians at this spot in the 5th century. The present cathedral was built on the site in 1191 and is the largest in the country; open Mar–Oct: 9:30am–5pm Mon–Fri, 9am–6pm Sat, 9am–10:30am, 12:30–2:30pm & 4:30–6pm Sun; Nov–Feb: 9:30am–5pm Mon–Fri, 9am–5pm Sat, 9am–10:30am & 12:30–2:30pm Sun.
www.stpatrickscathedral.ie

Trinity College Library
College Street. Set within the lovely Trinity College campus, the college's old library is home to the Book of Kells, a beautiful medieval manuscript illustrated by 9th-century monks on the Scottish island of Iona; open 9:30am–5pm Mon–Sat, noon–4.30pm Sun (Jun–Sep: 9am–6pm Mon–Sat, 9:30am–6pm Sun)
www.tcd.ie/library

Dublin Castle
Dame Street. Located at a strategic site in use since Viking times, the 13th-century castle was built by the invading Normans and remained the seat of English rule until 1922. Tours take in the ornate State Apartments, the Chapel Royal and the Undercroft; open 10am–4:45pm Mon–Sat, noon–4:45pm Sun.
www.dublincastle.ie

Christ Church Cathedral
Christchurch Place. The cathedral was founded by the Vikings in 1038, and rebuilt in stone by the Anglo–Norman warrior Richard de Clare – known as "Strongbow" – in 1169; open Mar & Oct: 9am–6pm Mon–Sat, 12:30–2:30pm & 4:30–6pm Sun; Apr–Sep: 9am–7pm Mon–Sat, 12:30–2:30pm & 4:30–7pm Sun; Nov–Feb: 9am–5pm Mon–Sat, 12:30–2:30pm Sun.
www.christchurchcathedral.ie

Below: Marching band in parade; fireworks over Dublin's waterfront

THE ESSENTIALS

GETTING THERE AND AROUND
The West Highland Way is in the west of
Scotland. It runs for 154 km (96 miles),
from Milngavie in the south to Fort
William in the north. Trains and buses
travel between Glasgow and Milngavie
(train journey time around 30 minutes).
Fort William can be reached by coach
from the north, east and south, and by
train from Glasgow (journey time around
3 hours).

WEATHER
Spring weather along the trail is
extremely changeable. Be prepared for
anything from bright sun to gusty winds
and driving rain. Average spring daytime
temperatures range from 0 to 15°C.
Warm, waterproof clothing is essential.

ACCOMMODATION
Splashing Out Inverlochy Castle, near
Fort William, is an opulent country-house
hotel in the heart of the Highlands.
www.inverlochycastlehotel.com

On a Budget Crianlarich Youth Hostel,
in Crianlarich, is midway along the
route, and has modern facilities and
family rooms.
www.syha.org.uk

EATING OUT
Splashing Out Crannog, on Waterfront
Town Pier in Fort William, offers superb
seafood dishes including locally caught
lobster, crab and scallops.
www.crannog.net

On a Budget Ben Nevis Inn, in Achintee,
just outside Fort William, is a cosy
walkers' inn serving hearty pub meals.
www.ben-nevis-inn.co.uk

PRICE FOR TWO PEOPLE
Around £130 a day for accommodation,
picnic lunch and evening meal.

WEBSITES
www.visitscotland.com
www.west-highland-way.co.uk

Previous page: Ha'penny Bridge over
the River Liffey in Dublin, Ireland

Main: Dramatic Rannoch Moor on the West Highland Way

HIGHLAND HIKING

O NE OF THE GREAT JOYS OF SCOTLAND is the ease with which you can leave behind city life
and plunge into wild open country. The West Highland Way is the perfect way to do this.
Its southern end wends its way through the genteel suburbs of Glasgow and the rolling hills
near Loch Lomond before travelling on over wild heather moors and through bleak but
beautiful glens to the foot of Ben Nevis at Fort William. It's a challenging – but not too
challenging – venture. Determined long-distance hikers can aim to complete its 152-km
(95-mile) length in one assault of around a week, but the route can also be broken down into
a series of sections that any reasonably fit walker can complete in a day's energetic stroll. It is
well worth the effort; no other long-distance walk in Britain offers such stunning contrasts
and beautiful scenery.

Most walkers set off from the quiet commuter village of Milngavie, where a granite obelisk
on Douglas Street marks the southern end of the Way. There is a good reason for this: the
gentle first section of the walk, skirting Loch Lomond's tranquil shores, lets you stretch your

FURTHER DETAILS

WEST HIGHLAND WAY

The following website covers the route of the West Highland Way and provides comprehensive visitor information.
www.west-highland-way.co.uk

Mountain Biking

It is possible to cycle along the Way, although you have to carry a bicycle over fences and any rough terrain. Certain sections are signposted as prohibited to bicycles, but these pre-date a change to the Scottish Outdoor Access Code in 2005, which allows cycling.

Rob Roy's Cave

About 1.5 km (1 mile) northwest of Inversnaid, on the eastern shore of Loch Lomond, on the Inversnaid to Inverarnan section of the Way.
www.explorelochlomond.co.uk

St Fillan's Chapel

About 1.5 km (1 mile) from Tyndrum, on the Crianlarich to Tyndrum section of the Way.
www.west-highland-way.co.uk

WHAT ELSE TO SEE AND DO

Glengoyne Distillery

To reward yourself for a day's hard walking, pick up a bottle of fine malt whisky at this pretty distillery near Strathblane, close to the start of the Way.
www.glengoyne.com

Ben Nevis

Britain's highest peak is close to the northern end of the Way. The ascent of the mountain begins around 3 km (2 miles) east of Fort William. Abacus Mountain Guides offers guided trips to the summit.
Abacus Mountain Guides: www.abacusmountain guides.com

Below (top to bottom): Cyclists on the Devil's Staircase; Inverlochy Castle viewed from the West Highland Way

legs and warm up your walking muscles for the more demanding northern sections of the Way. The route is studded with landmarks from history and legend. Before leaving the shores of Loch Lomond, it passes "Rob Roy's Cave" – a crevice in the rock that was one of the legendary outlaw's many hideouts. Between Crianlarich and Tyndrum, the ruined shell of St Fillan's Chapel is all that remains of a church endowed by Robert the Bruce in the 14th century.

But it is natural splendour, not man-made history, that makes the West Highland Way special. On the long day's walk across the wild peatlands of Rannoch Moor you may, with a little luck, see red deer grazing and golden eagles soaring, making it one of the few great adventures left in Britain. Seemingly deceptively easy; the last third of the journey, covering a vast expanse of heather moor and peat bog, is more challenging. It calls for excellent trail skills if the weather closes in, as it can do at any time. The climax of the Way, stretching over the route's highest point – the 550-m- (1850-ft-) high, aptly named "Devil's Staircase" – through the Lairigmor pass and on to Fort William by the sea, is breathtaking in every sense of the word.

THE ESSENTIALS

GETTING THERE AND AROUND

The British capital is served by five major airports; the largest two being Heathrow and Gatwick, 30 minutes by train to the west and south respectively. Northwards, Stansted and Luton airports are further out, although still well served by public transport into the centre. London City Airport, in east London, serves the city's financial district. Once in London, the best way around is via the extensive Underground network or iconic red buses, although a London black cab should be experienced at least once.

WEATHER

Pack layers; shorts and T-shirts could be useful, but so could waterproofs, woollens and umbrellas. Average spring daytime temperatures range from 6 to 14°C.

ACCOMMODATION

Splashing Out Hotel 41, on Buckingham Palace Road, is a meticulously managed and excellently located boutique hotel. www.41hotel.com

On a Budget EasyHotels have five no-frills properties (in Earls Court, Victoria, Paddington, Old Street/ Barbican and South Kensington) in the centre of London. www.easyhotel.com

EATING OUT

Splashing Out Pétrus in Knightsbridge offers fine gourmet dining. www.gordonramsayrestaurants.com/ petrus

On a Budget Princi, in Wardour Street, Soho, offers delicious Italian food in a friendly atmosphere. www.princi.co.com

PRICE FOR TWO PEOPLE

£210–330 a day including food, accommodation, transport and entry fees.

WEBSITE

www.visitlondon.com

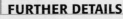

LONDON CALLING

LONDON – WHATEVER THE SEASON – IS A PHENOMENON. This vibrant, invigorating and ardently cosmopolitan metropolis is among the world's truly great cities. Its historic architecture and vast, treasure-filled museums jostle for space with stylish Michelin-starred restaurants, world-class cultural events, effortlessly cool nightlife and outstanding shopping. And when you need to slow down, its fresh, green patchwork of public parkland brings the countryside to the heart of the capital. There are over 400 green spaces offering sanctuary in the city, from the spacious Royal Parks, such as Hyde Park and Green Park – havens from the bustling streets and the perfect spots for a picnic – to botanical wonders such as Kew Gardens.

The capital celebrates spring with its biggest gardening festival – the Chelsea Flower Show– which bursts into bloom over five days in late May, astonishing visitors with its beautifully assembled show gardens. The London Marathon is another seasonal high point, when more than 35,000 runners – from professional athletes to fundraising amateurs and celebrities – are cheered on by thousands of spectators lining the route from Blackheath to The Mall. As the evenings draw out, even the arts events spill outside – Regent's Park's programme of alfresco plays provide an unforgettable alternative to West End shows or Shakespeare at The Globe.

One way to appreciate just how much there is to see is to take a spin on the South Bank's London Eye and tick off iconic views, from the Houses of Parliament, Big Ben and the dome of St Paul's Cathedral to Canary Wharf's skyscrapers and the soaring Shard. You'll quickly realize that you need to plan a strategy to get the most out of London, a city that truly has something for everyone. Whether you're interested in art, science, music, finance, technology or fashion, you can explore them here from their beginning to their projected future. From the Natural History and Victoria and Albert Museums to Tate Modern, a classy cocktail bar to a cosy Soho pub, and from Harrods department store to Topshop, London embraces life in all its forms and glory, and invites you to join in.

Main: Houses of Parliament and the London Eye **Below (left to right):** Theatres on Shaftesbury Avenue in London's West End; Natural History Museum in South Kensington

FURTHER DETAILS

LONDON

The Royal Parks
www.royalparks.org.uk

Royal Botanic Gardens, Kew
Nearest tube station: Kew Gardens;
open 10am daily; closing times vary.
www.kew.org

The RHS Chelsea Flower Show
Nearest tube station: Sloane Square; May.
www.rhs.org.uk/shows-events/rhs-chelsea-flower-show

The London Marathon
Route runs from Blackheath to the Mall; April.
www.virginmoneylondonmarathon.com

Regent's Park Open Air Theatre
Nearest tube station: Baker Street.
www.openairtheatre.com

The Globe Theatre
Nearest tube stations: Mansion House, London Bridge.
www.shakespeares-globe.org

London Eye
Nearest tube stations: Waterloo, Embankment,
Charing Cross, Westminster; open Sep–Apr: 10am–
8:30pm daily; May–Aug: 10am–9:30pm daily.
www.londoneye.com

St Paul's Cathedral
Nearest tube stations: St Pauls, Mansion House,
Cannon Street; open 8:30am–4pm Mon–Sat.
www.stpauls.co.uk

Natural History Museum
Nearest tube station: South Kensington;
open 10am–5:50pm daily.
www.nhm.ac.uk

Victoria & Albert Museum
Nearest tube station: South Kensington; open
10am–5:45pm Sat–Thu; 10am–10pm Fri.
www.vam.ac.uk

Tate Modern
Nearest tube stations: Southwark, Mansion House,
St Paul's; open 10am–6pm Sun–Thu; 10am–10pm
Fri–Sat.
www.tate.org.uk/modern

Harrods
87–135 Brompton Road, Knightsbridge; open
10am–9pm Mon–Sat, 11:30am–6pm Sun.
www.harrods.com

Below: Spring daffodils in Green Park

THE ESSENTIALS

GETTING THERE AND AROUND
The Lake District is in the northwest of England, to the south of the Scottish border. Manchester Airport and Newcastle International Airport are 156 km (97 miles) and 154 km (96 miles) respectively from Grasmere. The best way to explore the Lake District is by car, but there are good bus services between the major towns.

WEATHER
The Lake District is the wettest part of England, so be prepared for rain and hill fog at any time of the year. Average spring daytime temperatures are 6–10°C.

ACCOMMODATION
Splashing Out The Miller Howe Hotel, 13 km (8 miles) southeast of Grasmere by Windermere, is one of England's best country-house hotels.
www.millerhowe.com

On a Budget The How Foot Lodge Country Guest House, built in 1843, is a few seconds' stroll from Dove Cottage.
www.howfootlodge.co.uk

EATING OUT
Splashing Out The restaurant at the Holbeck Ghyll Country House Hotel, a few minutes' drive from Grasmere, has a Michelin star and is not to be missed.
www.holbeckghyll.com

On a Budget The Jumble Room, in Grasmere, is an informal restaurant that serves top-quality food, and is rated by several food guides.
www.thejumbleroom.co.uk

PRICE FOR A FAMILY OF FOUR
Around £210 a day for accommodation, food and entrance fees.

WEBSITE
www.golakes.co.uk

Main: Daffodils covering the shore of Ullswater
Right (top to bottom): Dove Cottage, home of William Wordsworth; Grasmere; red squirrel

GOLDEN DAFFODILS

IN THE SPRING OF 1802, WILLIAM WORDSWORTH and his sister Dorothy went for a walk at Gowbarrow Park, by the shore of Ullswater in the Lake District. They saw whole hillsides covered in bright-yellow daffodils, and two years later Wordsworth published "I Wandered Lonely as a Cloud" – regularly voted one of Britain's best-loved poems – immortalizing those "… golden daffodils; beside the lake, beneath the trees…". More than 200 years later, those hillsides are just as thickly swathed in daffodils in spring. It may be the vast, still beauty of the lakes and the dramatic grandeur of the mountains that attracts most people to the Lake District, but Wordsworth and other Lakeland writers also saw joy in nature's finer details.

When Wordsworth wrote his famous poem, he and Dorothy were living at Dove Cottage in the picturesque village of Grasmere – described by the poet as "the loveliest spot that man hath ever found". The cottage is open to visitors today, and remains much as it was when they called it home, from 1799 to 1808. To follow in Wordsworth's footsteps and discover

FURTHER DETAILS

EXPLORING WORDSWORTH'S LAKELAND
Much of the land around Ullswater and Grasmere is owned by the National Trust, and so can be enjoyed by everyone. The National Trust and local Tourist Information Centres sell leaflets and books that include information on Wordsworth and literary Lakeland walks. www.nationaltrust.org.uk

Dove Cottage
Grasmere; open Mar–Oct: 9:30am–5:30pm daily; Nov–Feb: 10am–4pm daily. www.wordsworth.org.uk

Wordsworth Point
This can be reached from the Glencoyne Bay National Trust car park on the A592 between Glenridding and Watermillock, 1.6 km (1 mile) north of Glenridding. www.nationaltrust.org.uk

Aira Force Waterfall
There is a 1.6-km (1-mile) circular walk to the waterfall from the National Trust car park on the A592 between Glenridding and Watermillock, 100 m (330 ft) after the junction with the A5091 to Matterdale End and Troutbeck. www.nationaltrust.co.uk

Hill Top
Near Sawrey, Hawkshead, Ambleside; House open Feb–Mar: 10am–3:30pm (closed Fri); Apr–May: 10am–4:30pm (closed Fri); Jun–Aug: 10am–5:30pm Mon–Thu, to 4:30pm Fri–Sun; Sep–Oct: 10am–4:30pm Sat–Thu. www.nationaltrust.org.uk

Beatrix Potter Gallery
Main Street, Hawkshead; open Feb–Mar: 10am–3:30pm Sat–Thu; Apr–mid-May: 10am–5pm Sat–Thu; mid-May–Aug: 10am–5pm daily; Sep–Oct: 10am–4pm Sat–Thu. www.nationaltrust.org.uk

WHAT ELSE TO SEE AND DO
Ullswater Lake Cruises
Ullswater Steamers run lake cruises year-round between the shoreside villages of Glenridding, Howtown and Pooley Bridge, giving stunning views of the lake and surrounding mountains from the water. www.ullswater-steamers.co.uk

Cumberland Pencil Museum
This unusual museum in Keswick showcases the history of pencil-making in the Lake District; it has an 8-m (26-ft) pencil that was, until 2005, the world's longest. www.pencilmuseum.co.uk

Below: Hill Top, the home of Beatrix Potter

Lakeland's daffodils, walk along the western side of Ullswater around Wordsworth Point. If you're lucky, you might also see a red squirrel scampering about in the trees; this charming and now-rare animal still thrives in these woodlands. While exploring the southern end of the lake, don't miss the spectacular waterfall Aira Force, which crashes through steeply sloping woodland.

No family outing in the Lake District is complete without a visit to Hill Top near Windermere – the former home of another of its famous residents, Beatrix Potter, whose love of this landscape inspired her to write *The Tale of Peter Rabbit* and other cherished children's stories. The farmhouse is now a museum exhibiting her personal belongings. You can see many of her original drawings at the Beatrix Potter Gallery in nearby Hawkshead.

It may be harder these days to wander lonely in the ever-popular Lake District, but if you choose a quiet day of the week and a secluded spot, it is still possible to find, as Wordsworth did, a "bliss of solitude" among these soaring mountains and cool, glassy lakes.

THE ESSENTIALS

GETTING THERE AND AROUND
Cork is on the south coast of Ireland, and is the second biggest city in the Republic of Ireland after Dublin. It has its own busy international airport, only 6 km (4 miles) south of the city centre. There are scheduled and chartered flights to Cork from cities throughout Europe. Driving can be difficult in the city centre so taxis, buses and walking are the best options.

WEATHER
For the festival the weather should be crisp and brisk, with perhaps a hint of summer in the air. Average daytime temperatures range from 4 to 14ºC.

ACCOMMODATION
Splashing Out The Clarion, on Lapps Quay, is a modern 4-star luxury hotel that overlooks the river.
www.clarionhotelcorkcity.com

On a Budget The Blarney Stone Guesthouse, on Western Road, is a welcoming Victorian B&B near the university with en suite accommodation.
www.blarneystoneguesthouse.ie

EATING OUT
Splashing Out Jacobs On The Mall, on South Mall, is one of the city's best fine-dining choices, in the setting of a former Turkish bath.
www.jacobsonthemall.com

On a Budget The Quay Co-op is an organic, vegetarian and vegan self-service restaurant on Sullivan's Quay, serving salads, lasagne, pizza and veggie burgers and has a list of organic wines.
www.quaycoop.com

PRICE FOR TWO PEOPLE
Around €240 a day for food, accommodation and entrance fees.

WEBSITE
www.visitcorkcounty.com

THE SOUND OF MUSIC

MOST EVENINGS, THE EVOCATIVE STRAINS of fiddle and bodhrán (an Irish drum) drift from pubs around the ancient city of Cork. Ireland's second city grew initially from a 7th-century monastery on the south bank of the River Lee, and the city today stands on an island created by two channels of the river. Cork's rich Gaelic heritage makes it a lively centre for all types of Irish music, and in spring it celebrates the Cork International Choral Festival.

Founded in 1954, this five-day festival in April/May is one of the leading events of its kind in Europe, attracting many of the world's finest amateur choirs. But there's more to their spirited singing than sheer love of music – this is a competitive event, with the winners taking home the coveted Fleischmann International Trophy. In addition to the international choirs, up to 100 Irish adult and youth choirs attend the concurrent national competitions. With around 5,000 participants overall, music fills the air in a great heralding of spring. The competitions and the Opening Gala Concerts, which feature professional musicians, are ticketed events. But outside the contests, you can see the choirs in a variety of free public performances and fringe concerts, and experience a sweeping range of vocal styles. You might head to the Church of St Anne Shandon, home of the famed Shandon Bells, at sunrise, to hear the glorious sound of the dawn chorus sung from its tower in an ancient May Day rite. Later on, in the atrium of the Clarion Hotel, you might choose to relax and enjoy an informal taster of international choirs, after browsing (and eating) at the delicious Food Fair outside.

The big public events take place in City Hall, Cork's finest public building and one of the best acoustic venues in the country. The international competitors are especially innovative, as each choir must present an *a capella* (unaccompanied) programme that includes work from past and present composers. The national competition for church music is held in the spectacular Gothic landmark of St Fin Barre's Cathedral, dedicated to Cork's patron saint. The many and varied highlights of the festival provide a great way to appreciate this most musical of cities.

Main: Shandon Tower, Church of St Anne Shandon
Below: Cork City Hall, site of many of the performances during the Cork International Choral Festival

FURTHER DETAILS

CORK INTERNATIONAL CHORAL FESTIVAL
The festival is held over the five days leading up to the May Day Bank Holiday each year.
www.corkchoral.ie

Church of St Anne Shandon
Church St, Cork; open Nov–Feb: 11am–3pm daily (from 11:30am Sun); Mar–May & Oct: 10am–4pm Mon–Sat, 11:30am–3:30pm Sun; Jun–Sep: 10am–5pm Mon–Sat, 11:30am–4:30pm Sun.

The Clarion Hotel
The hotel is right beside the River Lee on Lapps Quay.
www.clarionhotelcorkcity.com

City Hall
Anglesea St, Cork. Home to the city's administration, the concert hall here is also Cork's main venue for concerts and festivals; open 9am–5pm Mon–Fri.
www.corkcity.ie

St Fin Barre's Cathedral
Bishop St, Cork; open 9:30am–5:30pm Mon–Sat; 12:30–5pm Sun Apr–Nov.
http://cathedral.cork.anglican.org

The English Market
Access via Princes St, Oliver Plunkett St or Grand Parade, Cork; open 8am–6pm Mon–Sat.
www.englishmarket.ie

WHAT ELSE TO SEE AND DO

Blarney Castle
Whether you see kissing the Blarney Stone as a silly custom or a must-do, it's worth the short drive out of town to visit its fascinating home, Blarney Castle.
www.blarneycastle.ie

Cork City Gaol
This castle-like gaol on Sunday's Well Road recreates its grim 19th-century conditions with wax figures.
www.corkcitygaol.com

Below: Aerial view of Blarney Castle

SUNNY ISLES

L YING WAY OUT IN THE ATLANTIC off the western tip of Cornwall, the gloriously sub-tropical, unpolluted and unspoilt Isles of Scilly don't really feel like a part of England at all. There are virtually no cars on the smaller off-islands and no-one locks their front doors; there are endless empty and secluded beaches and wonderful walks, often close by unique and largely undisturbed prehistoric sites, such as Bant's Carn, a neolithic dolmen (burial chamber). Late spring is one of the best times to visit, just before the main season gets underway, when the famous winter daffodils are still in bud, the rock pools are warm enough for children to explore, and the islanders still have the time, and the inclination, to chat.

Scilly comes awake after the long winter at Easter; at dawn on Easter Day crowds gather at the Buzza windmill above the harbour on the main island of St Mary's to see the sun rise. The biggest event in the islands' calendar, the World Pilot Gig Championships, takes place in early May, when you can join dozens of tripper boats filled with spectators for a long weekend of

THE ESSENTIALS

GETTING THERE AND AROUND
The Isles of Scilly are 48 km (30 miles) off the coast of Cornwall. You can fly here all year round by light aircraft from Land's End, Newquay, Exeter, Bristol and Southampton, or by helicopter from Penzance. The *Scillonian* ferry runs daily from Penzance (Apr–Oct only). There are no hire cars on the islands, and virtually no buses, but plenty of taxis on St Mary's – otherwise it's all by boat or foot.

WEATHER
The islands are generally sunnier and milder than the mainland. Average daytime temperatures in spring are 10–15°C, but are often above 20°C.

ACCOMMODATION
Splashing Out Karma St Martin's, in St Martins, is a luxurious hotel masquerading as a cluster of granite cottages, set right on the beach.
www.karmagroup.com

On a Budget Isles of Scilly Country Guest House, on St Mary's, is 25 minutes' walk from Hugh Town. It is a family-friendly B&B with a relaxed atmosphere.
www.scillyguesthouse.co.uk

EATING OUT
Splashing Out Spero's, in Porthmellon, St Mary's, is a classy restaurant converted from a gig shed right on the beach.
www.speros.co.uk

On a Budget Dibble and Grub, on Porthcressa Beach, St Mary's, is a cheap and cheerful seaside café.
Tel: 01720 423 719
www.dibbleandgrub.com

PRICE FOR A FAMILY OF FOUR
Around £265–295 a day for accommodation and food.

WEBSITE
www.simplyscilly.co.uk

The real charm of Scilly lies in its simplicity – boating, walking, splashing about in sheltered coves, or just admiring the extraordinary seascape.

wonderful traditional rowing races, followed by a huge bonfire on the beach. The main pastime for holidaymakers is island-hopping. Each morning tripper boats leave St Mary's quay for expeditions to the smaller off-islands: Tresco, with its exotic Abbey Gardens; St Martin's and its beachside Caribbean-style hotel, where cocktails can be sipped beneath stunning sunsets while the children paddle in the azure water; and St Agnes, the most southwesterly place in England, with its spectacular views over the Bishop's Rock Lighthouse.

There are specialist boat trips for diving and snorkelling, and to observe hundreds of grey seals basking in the sunshine on the Eastern Isles, or the puffins that come to Scilly at this time of year to breed on the granite outcrops of the northern coast. The real charm of Scilly lies in its simplicity – boating, walking, splashing about in sheltered coves, or just admiring the extraordinary seascape and rare wildlife. There are no hills or tall buildings here, so it's one of the few places in Britain where you can see the sun rise and set from the same spot.

FURTHER DETAILS

THE ISLES OF SCILLY

Bant's Carn and Halangy Down
Bant's Carn dolmen and the ancient village of Halangy Down are on the northwest coast of St Mary's, 2 km (1 mile) north of Hugh Town.
www.english-heritage.org.uk

Buzza
This former windmill can be found by footpath from the eastern end of Porthcressa beach, St Mary's.

The World Pilot Gig Championships
The Championships are held every year over the first Bank Holiday weekend in May.
www.worldgigs.co.uk

Island-hopping
Boats leave St Mary's quay for the other islands Apr–Oct, 10:15am daily (30 minutes' journey time); limited service Nov–Mar.
www.scillyboating.co.uk

Tresco Abbey Gardens
These gardens feature more than 20,000 exotic plants; open 10am–4pm daily.
www.tresco.co.uk

Sealife and Shipwreck Tours
Island Sea Safaris offer 1- and 2-hour boat trips to view sealife and wrecks off the coast of St Mary's, as well as 45-minute excursions to view gig races.
www.islandseasafaris.co.uk

WHAT ELSE TO SEE AND DO

Minack Theatre
This wonderful open-air theatre in Porthcurno, just outside Penzance in Cornwall, was built into the cliffs overlooking the sea, adding extra drama to its performances of Shakespeare and other classics.
www.minack.com

Porthcurno Telegraph Museum
This fascinating museum in Porthcurno gives the history of what was once the world's most important cable station, connected to more than 160,000 km (100,000 miles) of cable radiating out under the oceans in a global network.
www.porthcurno.org.uk

St Michael's Mount
The dramatic hilltop home of the St Aubyn family in Marazion, Cornwall, is modelled on the monastery of Mont-Saint-Michel in Normandy on the coast of northern France. It is run by the National Trust and is accessible on foot at low tide.
www.stmichaelsmount.co.uk

Main: Aerial view of St Martin's, Isles of Scilly
Left (top to bottom): World Pilot Gig Championships at Hugh Town in St Mary's; Bishop's Rock Lighthouse
Above: Grey seal bull
Below: Tresco Abbey Gardens

Below: Holiday-makers on the beach at Tresco

THE ESSENTIALS

GETTING THERE AND AROUND
Oxford is in the area known as "the Heart of England", 88 km (55 miles) northwest of London (1–2 hours by car). The nearest airport is London Heathrow (72 km/45 miles away). Trains run regularly from London Paddington and London Marylebone (journey time 1 hour). Once there, you can explore the city centre by bike or on foot, although a car is useful for visiting the surrounding countryside.

WEATHER
Oxford's weather in spring is variable; with luck you'll have bright skies and warm days, but be prepared for four seasons in one day. Average daytime temperatures range between 6 and 12°C.

ACCOMMODATION
Splashing Out Malmaison, in Oxford Castle, is based in a converted prison, and now caters for a more discerning clientele.
www.malmaison.com

On a Budget Keble, Lady Margaret Hall, Queen's, University, Exeter and Trinity Colleges offer fully refurbished student rooms during the university vacations.
www.universityrooms.com

EATING OUT
Splashing Out The Cherwell Boathouse, on Bardwell Road, offers atmospheric riverside dining.
www.cherwellboathouse.co.uk

On a Budget Pizza Mamma Mia, on South Parade, offers relaxed Italian food at great prices.
www.mammamiapizzeria.co.uk

PRICE FOR TWO PEOPLE
From £210 a day for food, accommodation and entrance fees.

WEBSITE
www.oxfordcityguide.com

A CLASS OF ITS OWN

ONE OF THE TWO TOWERING PILLARS OF ENGLISH EDUCATION, Oxford, like Cambridge, is home to punting, pedalling pedagogues and earnest students in striped scarves. The home of the oldest university in the English-speaking world, Oxford is a city steeped in tradition, history and – for the less highbrow – student revelry. All three are combined in the annual May Morning festivities, when the choir of Magdalen College heralds the dawn with the *hymnus eucharistus*, sung from the top of the college's tower to the onlookers below.

Matthew Arnold's "sweet city with her dreaming spires" may nowadays have her fair share of distinctly non-classical high-street shops, traffic jams and café chains, but hidden behind the High Street or the Cornmarket – a stone's throw from a cappuccino machine or a sale rail – is another world: old Oxford is a Lewis Carroll-esque wonderland of ancient doorways and cobbled passageways, tranquil quads and bicycles leaning against golden limestone walls. Don't be daunted; despite the city's intellectual heritage, Oxford's attractions don't all require a

FURTHER DETAILS

OXFORD

Oxford Colleges
Colleges can usually be visited 2–5pm daily all year, but check noticeboards outside each college for individual opening times. Entrance fees apply.
www.ox.ac.uk

Ashmolean Museum
Beaumont Street, Oxford. The University's museum of art and archaeology displays everything from Chinese prints to coin collections, with a good café in the basement; open 10am–5pm Tue–Sun (open bank holiday Mondays.)
www.ashmolean.org

Pitt Rivers Museum
South Parks Road, Oxford. This anthropological gem is packed with over 500,000 artifacts from around the world. Entry is free; open 10am–4.30pm Tue–Sun, noon–4:30pm Mon.
www.prm.ox.ac.uk

Turf Tavern Public House
Hidden down an alley off New College Lane, Oxford, the foundations of this pub were laid in the 14th century.
www.turftavern-oxford.co.uk

Eagle and Child Public House
St Giles, Oxford. Locally known as the Bird and Brat, this has been a pub since the 1600s, when it lodged the Chancellor of the Exchequer during the English Civil War.
Tel: 01865 302925.

The Trout Inn
Lower Wolvercote, Oxford. A favoured watering-hole of Colin Dexter's fictional detective Inspector Morse.
www.thetroutoxford.co.uk

Botanic Garden
Rose Lane, Oxford. Britain's oldest botanic garden, lying alongside the river opposite Magdalen College, in the heart of the city; open daily Mar–Apr and Sep–Oct: 9am–5pm; May–Aug: 9am–6pm; Nov–Feb: 9am–4pm.
www.botanic-garden.ox.ac.uk

Radcliffe Camera
The reading room of the University's Bodleian Library in Radcliffe Square is inaccessible to visitors, but its beautiful domed exterior is a must-see tourist attraction.

WHAT ELSE TO SEE AND DO

The Cotswolds
A short journey from Oxford brings you to the impossibly pretty rolling meadows and picture-perfect towns and villages of the Cotswolds.
www.the-cotswolds.org

Main: Aerial view of Oxford University buildings, including the Radcliffe Camera (centre)

Left (left to right): Choristers singing at the top of Magdalen Tower on May Morning; students gathered to listen on Magdalen Bridge

Right: The Trout Inn on the banks of the Thames River

brain the size of a planet. To take away a true feel of the place, a tour of the archaeological displays of the university-owned Ashmolean Museum or the tribal treasures of the Pitt Rivers Museum should be swiftly followed by a pint of real ale in the tumbledown Turf Tavern – a hidden favourite of both "town" and "gown" (academia). Once on the pub trail, make a stop, too, at the Eagle and Child, the watering hole of choice for the Inklings – a regular group of drinkers and thinkers that included C S Lewis and J R R Tolkien amongst their number.

On a fine spring day, look upwards as you walk around the town, so you don't miss the more unusual architectural details such as the gargoyles on historic Queen's Lane. Take a boat trip on the Cherwell or the Thames rivers, stopping at riverside pubs such as the Trout Inn for a glass of ale, or take a picnic to Christ Church Meadow. Climb Carfax Tower for its sweeping views, browse the Covered Market, and amble through the spring flowers of the Botanic Garden. It's no surprise that large parts of the Harry Potter films were shot in this magical city.

Below: Punts gathered by Magdalen College Bridge

More Great Ideas for **Spring**

Atmospheric ruins of Laugharne Castle

River Rhaeadr plunging down lush slopes in Powys

Cottages lining steep, cobbled Gold Hill in Shaftesbury

LAUGHARNE CENTRAL WALES
Laugharne is the "lulled and dumbfound town" that Dylan Thomas wrote about in his 1954 play *Under Milk Wood*. He lived here for most of his adult life and it is where his body is buried. The little coastal town boasts a 12th-century castle, the boathouse where Thomas lived – now a museum, a fine Norman church and walks around the estuary. There is also an annual award-winning spring festival celebrating Thomas and Celtic culture.
www.visitwales.com

BEVERLEY MINSTER NORTHEAST ENGLAND
One of the finest Gothic churches in England, the minster took two centuries to build, has a twin-towered west front, and has been described as "a symphony in stone".
www.beverleyminster.org.uk

CULLODEN BATTLEFIELD HIGHLANDS AND ISLANDS
As the Battle of Culloden raged, the skies were leaden and gales drove sleet into the faces of the troops, so to evoke the awfulness of that tragic day on 16 April 1746, go in appalling weather. Visitors can roam the battlefield, visit the clan graves and learn interactively about the routing of Bonnie Prince Charlie's exhausted Jacobite force by 9,000 government troops – a conflict that took less than an hour but changed the course of Scottish history.
www.nts.org.uk/culloden

DUN AENGUS WESTERN IRELAND
This mysterious Iron Age fort on Inishmore, the largest of the Aran Islands, has stunning views from its clifftop position above the Atlantic Ocean.
www.aranisland.ie

TREVITHICK DAY SOUTHWEST ENGLAND
Robert Trevithick's contribution to the industrial revolution is honoured on the last Saturday in April, when the town band, dancers and steam engines parade down the streets.
www.trevithick-day.org.uk

PISTYLL RHAEADR WATERFALL NORTH WALES
The 19th-century author George Burrow likened Pistyll Rhaeadr to a great length of silk that is agitated by violent gusts of wind. At 74 m (240 ft), this magical waterfall is the highest in Wales. Its peaceful setting in the Berwyn Mountains in Powys is great walking country, and offers respite from a busy world. Look out for the abundant bird life and the "fairy bridge", a natural stone arch over the River Rhaeadr, between two stages of the waterfall.
www.pistyllrhaeadr.co.uk

BLUE POOL SOUTHWEST ENGLAND
Tiny particles of clay suspended in the waters of this former clay pit, just north of the Purbeck Hills, account for its shimmering and seductive blue-green colour. Rare fungi and mosses, and animals such as green sand lizards, sika deer and even Dartford warblers can been seen on its banks in spring. You can walk through the expanse of heathland around the pool, descend to the water's edge and enjoy a delicious cream tea at the 1930s tea house next to the pool.
www.bluepooltearooms.co.uk

BALRANALD NATURE RESERVE HIGHLANDS AND ISLANDS
Rare birds and unusual flowers thrive in this jewel in Scotland's natural crown in spring. Flocks of turnstones, purple sandpipers, sanderlings, dunlins, and the occasional endangered corncrake can be spotted. From the Greenland barnacle geese on the coast to the lapwings on the marshy grasslands, the air is filled with birdsong, and the ground is carpeted with sea rocket, sea sandwort and silverweed.
www.rspb.org.uk

COTON MANOR GARDENS WEST MIDLANDS
This 17th-century manor house is renowned for its landscaped gardens, but in spring it offers the added attraction of long walks in a large bluebell wood.
www.cotonmanor.co.uk

CANTERBURY SOUTHEAST ENGLAND
You need to step inside Canterbury's 800-year-old cathedral to absorb its sheer splendour. At Easter, there are services throughout Holy Week, concerts and exhibitions.
www.canterbury-cathedral.org

SHAFTESBURY SOUTHWEST ENGLAND
Quintessentially English, beautiful Gold Hill is a highlight of Shaftesbury, one of the country's oldest and highest towns. Ancient cottages tumble down its cobbles towards Blackmore Vale, recalling a famous bread advertisement in which Gold Hill starred. The town is also proud of its links with the novelist Thomas Hardy, and two interesting museums chronicle the town's past. A few miles away is Old Wardour Castle, with an unusual 14th-century hexagonal tower house.
www.shaftesburydorset.com

BALLYCASTLE NORTHERN IRELAND
Perfectly placed for touring the Causeway coast and the Glens of Antrim, this seaside town also offers temperate diving waters in late spring.
www.ballycastle.info

BACUP NORTHWEST ENGLAND
One of Britain's best-preserved historic mill towns, Bacup is also famous for its "Britannia Coco-Nut Dancers", who dress up and dance along the town boundaries on Easter Saturday.
www.coconutters.co.uk

STIRLING CENTRAL SCOTLAND
An historic and elegant town, Stirling stands at a strategic point of the River Forth – a location that has helped mould its past. It lies in Braveheart country, where the battles of the Scottish War of Independence were fought 700 years ago. Stirling also has a fabulous castle, perched high on a volcanic plug, which is a treasure house of history, having witnessed Scottish and Stuart kings, Mary Queen of Scots, wars, intrigue and murders in its 600-year history.
www.destinationstirling.com

See also pp16–17, 26–7, 34–5.   *See also pp18–19, 32–33.*   *See also pp20–21, 30–1, 38–9, 48–9, 56–7.*

Tourists setting off for Ramsey Island

Discovering a letterbox in the wilderness of Dartmoor

Costumed revellers taking part in Helston's Furry Dance

ST DAVIDS AND RAMSEY ISLAND CENTRAL WALES

St Davids is the smallest city in Britain – in reality, a small village with a beautiful cathedral – but it is surrounded by vast and idyllic walking country, its sweeping coastlands dotted with prehistoric sites and tiny chapels. Offshore, its nutrient-rich sea waters ensure abundant sea life; porpoises, seals, whales and dolphins can be seen on boat tours. The nearby RSPB reserve of Ramsey Island is home to falcons and sea birds in spring, which build their nests among the flower-covered cliffs.
www.ramseyisland.co.uk

TARKA TRAIL SOUTHWEST ENGLAND

The Tarka Trail is a 48-km- (30-mile-) long disused railway line in rural Devon, which has been given a new lease of life as a cycling and walking trail. From Braunton in the north to Meeth in mid-Devon, users pass coastal cliffs, sandy bays and the river estuaries where Henry Williamson's literary creation Tarka the Otter lived. As the trail wends south, it crosses wooded river valleys and rugged moorland. The route can be cycled in 4 hours or walked in 10.
www.devon.gov.uk/tarkatrail

KEYHAVEN'S SOLENT SHORE SOUTHEAST ENGLAND

A delightful 15-minute ferry trip from Keyhaven to Hurst Castle takes you past a saltmarsh nature reserve rich in sea birds, unusual plant life and brackish water creatures. Crouching low and menacing at the end of Hurst Spit, in a perfect position to defend the western approach to the Solent, is Hurst Castle – part-Tudor fortress, part-Victorian battery – and a fascinating historical interlude for visitors.
www.new-forest-national-park.com

ARDNAMURCHAN PENINSULA
HIGHLANDS AND ISLANDS

The most westerly point of mainland Scotland has it all: wildlife, including red deer and eagles, hiking, cycling, fishing, boating and beaches.
www.ardnamurchan.com

LETTERBOXING SOUTHWEST ENGLAND

Letterboxing began in 1854 when a Dartmoor guide left a bottle at Cranmere Pool and challenged hikers to make the long walk there and leave a calling card to mark their achievement. Today, clues are placed to help hikers locate letterboxes; on finding one, a rubber stamp in the box is used to record the find in a visitors' book and in the hunter's own book. There are many letterboxes hidden around Dartmoor, providing hours of orienteering fun.
www.dartmoorletterboxing.org

WOOLSACK RACES
SOUTHWEST ENGLAND

Thousands flock to the races and street fair in Tetbury every May to watch competitors carry heavy woolsacks on their backs for 220 m (240 yards) up the steep Gumstool Hill.
www.tetburywoolsack.co.uk

BEATRIX POTTER EASTER EGG HUNT
NORTHWEST ENGLAND

The World of Beatrix Potter attraction hides 100 eggs in Cumbria – finders are rewarded with great prizes, including Lake District holidays.
www.hop.skip.jump.com

CASTLE WARD NORTHERN IRELAND

Overlooking Strangford Lough, this quirky 18th-century house oozes personality. One half is built in the Classical style, while the side facing the lough is Gothic. The extensive grounds are crammed with interest, from a sunken garden and the Temple Water canal – built to reflect the ruins of Audley Castle – to woodlands, scenic views, an adventure play area, animals and a wildlife centre. Children can also dress up in Victorian clothes and play with Victorian toys.
www.nationaltrust.org.uk/castle-ward

SOUTH HARRIS BEACHES HIGHLANDS AND ISLANDS

Some argue that the beaches of South Harris beaches are the best in the world. While the climate may not measure up to Hawaii, the stunning white sandy stretches, crystal-clear Atlantic waters and shell-sand pasture called machair, spectacularly strewn with wild flowers, are without doubt some of nature's greatest triumphs. All this is set against a fabulous backdrop of dramatic mountains, notably Traigh Scarasta and Luskentyre.
www.visitscotland.com

COAL-CARRYING CHAMPIONSHIP
NORTHEAST ENGLAND

Participants carry coal sacks through Gawthorpe every Easter Monday in this race begun in the 1960s by two competitive friends.
www.gawthorpemaypole.org.uk

FURRY DANCE SOUTHWEST ENGLAND

Helston's Floral Dance – or The Furry Dance, as the locals call it – takes place on 1 May and features a dignified procession with men in morning suits and top hats, and women in long dresses. It's a colourful occasion to welcome in the spring and the promise of summer, and sees the town decorated with greenery, bluebells and gorse. Thousands descend on Helston for the revelry, with dancing from 7am to 5pm and partying that continues well into the night.
www.cornwall.co.uk/Helston

OLIMPICK GAMES SOUTHWEST ENGLAND

Introduced in the early 17th century by Robert Dover, an extrovert lawyer, the Olimpick Games take place on Dover's Hill, above Chipping Campden, in late May. The games involve traditional and less-common sports, such as falconry, hot-air ballooning, motorbike scrambling and a shin-kicking contest. Fireworks and dancing end the day, and the next morning the Scuttlebrook Queen is crowned, and there's a colourful display of fancy dress, maypole dancing and a fair.
www.olimpickgames.com

PAN CELTIC FESTIVAL SOUTHERN IRELAND

This lively festival promotes all things Celtic from six Celtic "nations" – Ireland, Scotland, Wales, Cornwall, Brittany and the Isle of Man. Started in 1971, and held annually in the week following Easter, the event is hosted by different Irish towns and cities. Language, food, music, singing and the craic – light-hearted mischief – are all embraced as the host town's streets come alive with pipe bands, ceilidhs, street entertainers and competitions.
www.panceltic.ie

SUMMER

Burton Bradstock,
part of Dorset's
Jurassic Coast,
England

SUMMER IN GREAT BRITAIN AND IRELAND

A T ITS BEST, SUMMER IN THE BRITISH COUNTRYSIDE can be as close to perfection as it's possible to get. Wild flowers bloom along hedgerows, wheat turns golden in vast fields and flocks of swallows flit gracefully across azure skies. Sunlight dapples the rich green woodlands of the New Forest and the rolling moors of Yorkshire, and sparkles on the still waters of the Lake District. But this lush perfection comes at a price: the British summer is notoriously unpredictable, and our fickle, ever-changing climate often leaves even professional meteorologists looking foolish. A dank and misty morning can easily turn into a gloriously sunny afternoon, which is why the weather is, famously and inescapably, one of the most popular topics of conversation all over England, Scotland, Wales and Ireland. But it is this constant mix of sunshine and showers that creates our "green and pleasant land", from the Highland forests to the humble village greens – the quintessentially British venue for local cricket matches, fêtes and morris dancers. Ireland would not be known as the "Emerald Isle" were it not for its forty shades of green, encouraged by the ever-changing weather. It's hard to imagine William Turner painting his breathtaking seascapes without the inspiration of England's shifting skies, and you need only visit the villages of the Stour Valley in summer to see how the fluctuating qualities of English summer light influenced Constable, whose work was inspired by the countryside around villages such as Clare and Dedham. British and Irish writers and poets, from Shakespeare to Shelley, Yeats to Keats and Burns to Betjeman, have all sung the praises of this most capricious of seasons.

> Summer in the British countryside can be as close to perfection as it's possible to get.

Summer is, of course, the ideal time to venture outside, whether to take part in energetic sports or merely laze around on a picnic rug, reading a book or newspaper. On thousands of village greens, the whack of leather on willow signals the beginning of the cricket season, when local sides compete for honour, batting as fiercely as their county and national counterparts do at legendary cricket grounds such as Lords and the Oval. In late June and early July, the eyes of the tennis world are on the Wimbledon Championships, while around the same time, the waters off the Isle of Wight are coloured with the sails of more than 1,000 racing yachts and dinghies taking part in Cowes Week – the largest sailing regatta of its kind in the world. Many of the same boats will be seen in Irish waters during Cork Week, Ireland's biggest sailing event. Away from the action, or, often, alongside it, people quietly enjoy another British summer tradition: the picnic. Ideally held under whispering oaks in grassy meadows,

Below (left to right): Hiker admiring the view in the Lake District; yacht racing during Cowes Week

these casual feasts involve hampers packed to bursting with cucumber sandwiches, strawberries and cream, scones and a bottle or two of chilled Pimm's. At the seaside, the grand traditions of paper-wrapped fish and chips and a gentle stroll along the esplanade still thrive.

The summer sun might lull the south of England, but for those adventurous souls who prefer wide open spaces to neatly trimmed hedgerows and gardens, the lakes, moors and dales of northern England, the vast, empty Atlantic beaches of western Ireland and the wild sea lochs of northwest Scotland call out for exploration. The longest days of the year bring almost 18 hours of daylight to northern Scotland. Head out to sea in the choppy waters around the Isle of Mull, and there's an excellent chance of seeing dolphins, seals, basking sharks and even huge minke whales. Take a rod and line, and with any luck you can come back from a day's sea fishing with enough mackerel, gurnard or sea bass to make the perfect summer barbecue. Further south, off Cornwall, Wales or the west coast of Ireland, a sea fishing trip may even yield a shark or other exotic fish. Inland, a summer day spent cycling in the Yorkshire Dales, sailing on the sublime Norfolk Broads, or scaling the breathtaking peaks of Snowdonia can be an idyllic experience. Even if the weather isn't always beautiful, it is never less than bracing, and striding out in the wide, windy open spaces of the Exmoor countryside or exploring a dramatic stretch of seashore, such as Dorset's Jurassic Coast, can be exhilarating.

Summer's zenith is Midsummer's Eve, celebrated with music, bonfires and dancing by modern pagans beside the ancient megaliths of Stonehenge, where thousands greet the dawn of Midsummer's Day, the longest day of the year. Watching the sun come up over equally ancient but less-frequented stone circles in Scotland and Ireland can be an even more moving and spiritual experience. The season's grand finale is perhaps the legendary Last Night of the Proms, which traditionally brings a summer programme of orchestral music at London's Royal Albert Hall to an exuberant crescendo. Linked to open air concerts in Scotland, Wales and Northern Ireland, these celebrations mark the end of the great British summer for another year.

> The longest days of the year bring almost 18 hours of daylight to northern Scotland.

Below (left to right): Wild flowers bloom in a Gloucestershire meadow; bottlenose dolphins off the coast of Scotland; village cricket match on Sarisbury Green in Hampshire

Beside the Sea

Above:
Postcard of children
enjoying donkey rides on the beach,
posted at Blackpool in 1919

When the summer sun puts his hat on, few places are more fun than the British seaside. After all, it was the British who invented the seaside resort, complete with donkey rides, amusement piers, ice cream and "bathing machines" – moveable changing rooms that could be wheeled into the water, concealing the lissom limbs of Victorian ladies from the public gaze. The expansion of the railways in the mid- to late 19th century brought the masses to seaside towns, and by the 1930s, bank-holiday trains would be heaving with city-dwellers flocking to the beach.

In the 21st century, the British are rediscovering the charms of their coast. Some resorts have reinvented themselves: Brighton has embraced the arts, while Newquay has become Britain's pre-eminent surf resort. Others, such as Blackpool, remain fabulously brash. Piers, donkey rides and fish and chips are still seaside staples, and few sights are more quintessentially British than a row of colourful beach huts. Childhood memories of rock pools and sandcastles bring parents in search of these simple pleasures for their own children. It is nostalgia, as well as the beauty of much of the British coastline, that is drawing people back to the sea.

KINSALE

BRIGHTON

NEWQUAY

BRIDLINGTON

Arran, Southern Scotland Pebbly coves and sandy beaches ring the rugged shores of Scotland's most accessible island. Brodick, Arran's biggest village, has great pubs and fish-and-chip shops. *www.visitarran.com*

Largs, Southern Scotland For years, this great sweep of beach has been Glasgow's summer getaway. Much more sophisticated now than in its heyday, it boasts a shiny, modern marina. *www.largsonline.co.uk*

Kinsale, Southern Ireland Set on a superb natural harbour not far from Cork, Kinsale boasts great restaurants, charming hotels and old-fashioned pubs, as well as pretty beaches nearby. *www.kinsale.ie*

Llandudno, North Wales This legendary Welsh resort's North Shore beach has a Victorian pier *(see p212)*, while the sandy West Shore has fabulous sea views and sunsets. *www.visitllandudno.org.uk*

Blackpool, Northwest England With its trams, sing-along pubs and roller coasters, Blackpool is the epitome of the seaside resort. Despite attempts to go upscale, it's still gloriously tacky *(see pp132–3)*.

Morecambe Bay, Northwest England This resort is renowned for its abundant birdlife, fabulous sunsets and fast-moving tides, which can rush in at the speed of a good horse. *www.morecambebay.org.uk*

Scarborough, Northeast England Sweeping North Sea views, sandy bays, dramatic cliffs and delicious fresh seafood are among the charms of this Yorkshire resort. *www.visitscarborough.com*

Bridlington, Northeast England This town is home to a seaside museum and the John Bull World of Rock, celebrating the confectionery that is synonymous with seaside fun. *www.bridlington.net*

Filey, Northeast England Known since Victorian times for its bracing sea air, Filey is a fishing harbour with beaches overlooked by the chalk cliffs of Bempton *(see pp32–33)* and Flamborough Head. *www.filey.co.uk*

Southwold, Eastern England A swathe of sea-smoothed pebbles, a long line of brightly painted beach huts, a brewery and great fresh crab make this quirky Suffolk seaside village irresistible. *www.visitsouthwold.co.uk*

Brighton, Southeast England The Prince Regent (later King George IV) made this city fashionable in the early 19th century. A hub of the arts, it's still where London goes for a weekend by the sea *(see pp38–9)*.

Margate, Southeast England A favourite with Londoners for years, this bucket-and-spade resort also has the Turner Contemporary – a gallery named after the famous English artist. *www.visitthanet.co.uk*

Weston Super Mare, Southwest England This resort has been famous for its donkey rides and arcades for almost a century. An observation wheel adds to its appeal. *www.visit-westonsupermare.com*

Newquay, Southwest England England's answer to Bondi Beach has become the southwest's party town *par excellence*, loved by surfers, yachties and gap-year party animals *(see pp162–3)*.

St Ives, Southwest England Gorgeous beaches and a heritage bequeathed by some of the 20th century's best British artists are the hallmarks of this Cornish fishing village. *www.stives-cornwall.co.uk*

Torquay, Southwest England Palm trees line the esplanade and sub-tropical blooms adorn the gardens of stylish Art Deco hotels in genteel Torquay. Don't miss the town's superb Devon cream teas. *www.torquay.com*

TORQUAY

ST IVES

THE ESSENTIALS

GETTING THERE AND AROUND
Snowdonia National Park covers an area of 2,170 sq km (838 sq miles) in North Wales and is around 4 hours' drive from London. The main railway station is Llandudno Junction, from where regular services run to Betws-y-Coed in the heart of the park. The Sherpa bus service covers the park; day passes are available.

WEATHER
Summer in Snowdonia is generally mild and wet, though sunny spells are not uncommon. Daytime temperatures average 9–11°C on Snowdon's summit, although it can get considerably colder.

ACCOMMODATION
Splashing Out Y Meirionydd Townhouse, situated in the small Snowdonia town of Dolgellau and close to the coastal resort of Barmouth, has been providing comfortable rooms and good food for over 150 years.
www.themeirionnydd.com

On a Budget Pen-y-Gwryd Hotel, in the foothills of Snowdon, hosted the successful 1953 Everest team while they trained in the area – their signatures can be seen scrawled on the ceiling.
www.pyg.co.uk

EATING OUT
Splashing Out Ty Gwyn, in Betws-y-Coed, is an award-winning restaurant in the heart of the mountains.
www.tygwynhotel.co.uk

On a Budget Pete's Eats, in Llanberis, is the classic mountaineer's café where you can stuff yourself to bursting after a hard day on the hill.
www.petes-eats.co.uk

PRICE FOR TWO PEOPLE
£190–210 a day for food and accommodation.

WEBSITE
www.visitsnowdonia.info

Main: Above the clouds at the summit of Mount Snowdon **Right (top to bottom):** Scrambling across Crib Goch Ridge; waterfall beside the Miners' Track route up the flanks of Snowdon

WHERE EAGLES DARE

ERYRI, THE WELSH NAME FOR SNOWDONIA, has its Celtic roots in the word for "eagle's nest". It is a fitting appellation for the most spectacular highland region and most celebrated national park in Wales. Breathtaking walks above the clouds, exhilarating scrambles to boulder-strewn summits and enthralling views down to icy lakes and razor-edged ridges are the highlights of a visit to the north of the region, where the rocky shoulders of Mount Snowdon dominate the landscape. Rising to 1,085 m (3,560 ft), Mount Snowdon is the highest point in Britain south of Scotland, but it is not reserved for eagles and dedicated mountaineers: many thousands of people make the 6-hour ascent every year.

Several routes of varying difficulty lead to the summit; if you're feeling intrepid, take the ridge walk along the "Snowdon Horseshoe", negotiating the jagged edge of Crib Goch Ridge, where the ground falls away dizzyingly to either side. At 11 km (7 miles) long and with 975 m (3,200 ft) of ascent, this route demands a head for heights, good fitness and thorough preparation, even in the summer months. For less of a white-knuckle experience, try the popular "Miners' Track" from Pen-y-Pass, which extends for 6.5 km (4 miles) and ascends 730 m (2,400 ft), passing gushing waterfalls and the derelict buildings once used by the mountain's copper miners. This undemanding, well-made trail ends at Llyn Glaslyn – a lake

FURTHER DETAILS

SNOWDONIA NATIONAL PARK
The national park's many information centres can advise on events, activities, transport and accommodation.
www.eryri-npa.co.uk

Snowdon Mountain Railway
Trains run regularly from Llanberis in late-Mar–Nov; at the very beginning and end of the season, they may stop short of the summit, at Clogwyn, if the weather is bad.
www.snowdonrailway.co.uk

WHAT ELSE TO SEE AND DO
Mountain biking
There are excellent mountain-biking trails within the national park; find mountain-bike hire and information centres at Betws-y-Coed and Coed-y-Brenin.
www.mbwales.com

Rock-climbing
Some of the finest rock-climbing in southern Britain is to be had here. Renowned crags include Idwal Slabs on Glyder Fawr, and Dinas Mot, Dinas Wastad and Dinas Cromlech at Llanberis Pass.
British Mountaineering Council: *www.thebmc.co.uk*

Watersports
The River Tryweryn is the best rafting and kayaking river in Wales. Visit the National Whitewater Centre near Bala to check out the action. You can also sail and windsurf on Lake Bala, Wales's biggest freshwater lake.
National Whitewater Centre: *www.ukrafting.co.uk*
Lake Bala: *www.visitbala.org.uk*

Below (top to bottom): Mountain-biking in Snowdonia; rock-climbing on the Snowdon Horseshoe at Capel Curig

coloured blue by copper salts, set like a jewel 600 m (1,970 ft) up on the eastern flank – only very experienced walkers should attempt the challenging ascent to the summit from here.

By far the easiest way to conquer Snowdon is to hop aboard Britain's only rack-and-pinion railway, the Snowdon Mountain Railway, which takes you on an enthralling ride through woodland, across an impressive viaduct and along high ridges to the summit, where a striking and modern visitor centre offers welcome refreshments. On a clear day, views from the train and especially from the cairn right at the top of the mountain are astonishing: you can look across Snowdonia's many peaks to see the Isle of Man, the east coast of Ireland, the Lake District, the Yorkshire Dales and even parts of southern Scotland.

But there's more to Snowdonia than this jewel in its crown. There is fine mountain walking across the park, especially further south among the purple-tinged peaks of the Moelwyn range, and countless activities to suit the adventurous, such as hiking, rafting, canyoning and canoeing, as well as woodland and coastal walks for more gentle exercise and contemplation.

ALL ABOARD

A	S THE WORLD'S PREMIER SAILING REGATTA, Cowes Week in August is a red-letter day for the small but perfectly formed Isle of Wight. With a huge programme of daily races, the regatta attracts more than 1,000 boats, as seasoned professionals rub shoulders with amateur skippers, weekend sailors, Olympic veterans, celebrities, novices and some 100,000 enthusiastic spectators. Cowes Week may be the world's oldest regatta – dating back to 1826 – but it's totally up-to-date and alive with the latest nautical buzz.

Although it's ultimately a celebration of sailing, Cowes Week is also a crucial slot on the island's social calendar – a huge, week-long party. For extraordinary views, hop aboard one of the spectator boats and get closer to the action. The traditional fireworks celebrations on Friday evening are a pyrotechnic curtain-call on eight days of competition and festivities. If you get the sailing bug, book onto a sailing course with UKSA, where you can learn how to tack and get the chance to race, or call in at the Cowes Maritime Museum to get some fascinating insights into the island's sailing history and shipbuilding industry.

THE ESSENTIALS

GETTING THERE AND AROUND
The Isle of Wight is located in the English Channel, off the south coast of England. As many as 350 ferry sailings a day link the island to the mainland, including from Southampton to East Cowes (taking around 55 minutes). Ferries also sail from Portsmouth Harbour and Lymington to other points on the island. High-speed passenger catamarans run between Southampton and West Cowes (around 25 minutes). The island has a comprehensive bus network.

WEATHER
The Isle of Wight enjoys a mild climate with daytime temperatures of 16–19°C. Always prepare for changeable weather.

ACCOMMODATION
Splashing Out The Albert Cottage Hotel, in Cowes, is an imposing former royal residence that offers 10 luxurious rooms, or Queen Victoria's Indian Summer House in the garden, which you can rent exclusively for perfect seclusion. *www.albertcottagehotel.com*

On a Budget The Dorset Hotel, in Ryde, 10 km (6 miles) from Cowes, offers great value B&B. *www.thedorsethotel.co.uk*

EATING OUT
Splashing Out The Hambrough, in Ventnor, is a Michelin-starred restaurant with glorious sea views. *www.thehambrough.com*

On a Budget The Pierview Public House, in Cowes, is popular with thirsty sailors and spectators during Cowes Week. *www.pierview.co.uk*

PRICE FOR TWO PEOPLE
From £150 a day for accommodation, food, local transport and entrance fees.

WEBSITE
www.visitisleofwight.co.uk

Ultimately a celebration of sailing, Cowes Week is also a crucial slot on the island's social calendar – a huge, week-long party.

Ever since the Victorians first started holidaying on the Isle of Wight, it has become a popular destination for mainlanders, and beyond the yachts there's no shortage of attractions. Osborne House, outside East Cowes, was Queen Victoria's main residence in her later years, and you can visit both its sumptuous state rooms and private apartments. The island has several other historic treasures, such as the Brading Roman Villa, home to magnificently-preserved mosaics and an extensive collection of Roman archaeology. Carisbrooke Castle, in the island's capital, Newport, has some intriguing exhibits detailing its history – including items belonging to King Charles I, who was incarcerated here before his execution in 1649. A visit to Yarmouth Castle, an artillery fort built during the reign of King Henry VIII, provides solid evidence of the island's strategic importance over the centuries. Finally, if you visit in early summer, don't overlook the Isle of Wight Festival in June – this popular annual music festival has always attracted top international stars, from The Killers to Jay-Z.

FURTHER DETAILS

ISLE OF WIGHT

Cowes Week
The regatta takes place in the first week of August. Races begin at 10am and run through the afternoons. Places on spectator boats can be booked online from June or on site (subject to availability).
www.cowesweek.co.uk

UKSA
A youth charity based in Cowes. Offers a huge range of sea-based courses including dingy sailing, yachting and navigation.
www.uksa.org

Cowes Maritime Museum
Cowes Library, Beckford Road; open 10am–12:30pm and 1:30–5pm Mon, Tues, Fri, 10am–4:30pm Sat.
www.iwight.com/museums

Osborne House
East Cowes; open Apr–Sept: 10am–6pm daily; Oct–Nov: 10am–4pm daily; Nov–Mar: 10am–4pm Wed–Sun (pre-booked guided tours only)
www.english-heritage.org.uk

Brading Roman Villa
Brading; open 10am–5pm daily.
www.bradingromanvilla.org.uk

Carisbrooke Castle Museum
Newport; open Apr–Oct: 10am–4:45pm daily; Nov–Mar: 10am–3:45pm on weekends only.
www.carisbrookecastlemuseum.org.uk

Yarmouth Castle
Yarmouth; open Apr–Sep, 11am–4pm Sun–Thu.
www.english-heritage.org.uk

Isle of Wight Festival
Seaclose Park, Newport. The festival is held over the second weekend of June.
www.isleofwightfestival.com

The Needles
Alum Bay. Boat trips depart from Alum Bay; open 10am–4pm daily.
www.theneedles.co.uk

WHAT ELSE TO SEE AND DO

Isle of Wight Steam Railway
Take a trip back in time aboard the dark-green carriages of a steam train on this quaint old railway. It runs along an 8-km (5-mile) route from Smallbrook Junction in the east of the island to Wootton in the north.
www.iwsteamrailway.co.uk

Blackgang Chine
This eccentric amusement park, near Blackgang, is a collection of pirate-, cowboy- and fairytale-themed rides, set within rambling Victorian gardens, and provides a great day out for families with younger children.
www.blackgangchine.com

Below: The Needles, stretching into the English Channel

Main: "Class 1" yachts taking part in a Cowes Week race **Far left (top to bottom):** Dinghy race during Cowes Week; Osborne House, the family home of Queen Victoria and Prince Albert **Above:** Isle of Wight Festival in full flow

A GRAND GARDEN

Human endeavour rarely matches the pure natural beauty of the Emerald Isle, but Powerscourt Estate is a happy exception. Set a few miles outside Dublin in County Wicklow, a region famed as the "garden of Ireland", the estate's breathtaking landscaped gardens are made all the more remarkable by the tragic story of the great house behind them.

In 1731 the renowned German architect Richard Cassels began converting a 13th-century Anglo-Norman castle into a Palladian mansion for the third Viscount Powerscourt, Richard Wingfield. A decade later this exquisite hilltop manor boasted the finest ballroom in the land, attracting nobles and royalty for the next two centuries. But in 1974, a terrible fire gutted the building, leaving a burned-out shell. Only the façade and the ballroom, which now houses a historical exhibition, have been restored to their former glory.

Thankfully, the magnificent gardens were spared, and this is what people come to see. There can be few finer views in the British Isles than that from Powerscourt's cobblestone balcony, sweeping down the terraced hillside and across the lake and woodlands to the distant peak of Great Sugar Loaf Mountain. Much of this harmonious vista was created in the middle of the

Main: Magnificent lake that lies in front of Powerscourt House **Below (top to bottom):** Powerscourt House, damaged by fire but retaining its splendour; dramatic Powerscourt Waterfall, the highest in Ireland

THE ESSENTIALS

GETTING THERE AND AROUND
Powerscourt Estate lies near the town of Enniskerry, County Wicklow, about 35 km (22 miles) south of Dublin Airport and 22 km (14 miles) south of Dublin city centre. You can reach it by taking a combination of the DART train from Dublin and public buses, but a car is the best way to get there.

WEATHER
The summer weather can be beautiful, but you are close to the Wicklow Mountains so it can also be changeable, with average daytime temperatures of 11–19°C.

ACCOMMODATION
Splashing Out The Powerscourt Hotel, a Palladian-style house on the stunning Powerscourt estate, is one of the finest hotels in Ireland, complete with a luxury spa, Irish pub and signature restaurant. www.powerscourthotel.com

On a Budget Ferndale House, in Enniskerry, is a good-value, welcoming B&B in a listed Victorian building. www.ferndalehouse.com

EATING OUT
Splashing Out The Sika restaurant at the Powerscourt Hotel has to be the first choice for gourmets, with dining at the Chef's Table in the kitchen the ultimate indulgence.

On a Budget Emilia's Ristorante, in Enniskerry, is a cheerful trattoria-style eatery serving good thin-crust pizzas baked in a wood-burning oven. www.emilias.ie

PRICE FOR TWO PEOPLE
From €190 a day for entrance fees, food and accommodation.

WEBSITE
www.visitwicklow.ie

19th century to the designs of landscape architect Daniel Robertson. Suffering from gout, he allegedly directed workers from a wheelbarrow while sipping sherry to dull his pain.

The formal terraces, decorative ironwork and statuary reflect Robertson's love of Italianate garden design. Other generations added specimen trees, woodland paths, grottoes, Japanese gardens and a pepper-pot tower. Earliest are the fragrant walled gardens, laid out at the same time as the original house. There's even a pet cemetery with engraved headstones.

The gardens are in their full glory in summer. There's much to explore, but, if you do nothing else, walk down the monumental staircase to the lake, framed by two winged horses. In the centre the Triton Fountain spurts a jet of water high in the air. Stroll around the lake and look back on the handsome mansion, with its impressive twin-domed round towers. You can almost imagine ballroom music drifting from the windows. For the more sedentary visitor, the Terrace Café offers its own astounding views.

FURTHER DETAILS

POWERSCOURT HOUSE AND GARDENS
Powerscourt Estate, Enniskerry, County Wicklow;
open 9:30am–5:30pm daily.
www.powerscourt.com

WHAT ELSE TO SEE AND DO
Bray
One of Ireland's oldest seaside resorts, Bray sits just to the east of Enniskerry, at the end of Killiney Bay between Bray Head and a sweeping shingle beach. Stroll along the ocean on the promenade, or take the 5-km (3-mile) scenic cliff walk to the fishing village of Greystones. Children can also enjoy the National Sea Life Centre, one of the country's largest marine zoos. Bray Sea Life Centre *www.sealife.ie*

Killruddery House and Gardens
Killruddery has been the home of the Earls of Meath since 1618. The present house, built in the 1820s, contains many treasures and the magnificent formal gardens are among the earliest in Ireland, with many original 17th-century features.
www.killruddery.com

Mount Usher Gardens
These wild, romantic gardens, just outside the town of Wicklow, are spread along the banks of the River Vartry. Laid out in naturalistic style in the 19th century, the gardens contain many exotic species.
www.mountushergardens.ie

Russborough House
West of Enniskerry and over the Wicklow mountains near Blessington, Russborough is another Palladian mansion designed by Richard Cassels, considered by many to be Ireland's loveliest stately home.
www.russboroughhouse.ie

Below (top to bottom): Triton Fountain, framed by two statues of winged horses; vista of Powerscourt Estate with Great Sugar Loaf Mountain in the background.

THE ESSENTIALS

GETTING THERE AND AROUND
The Norfolk Broads are in Norfolk and Suffolk in eastern England, 145 km (90 miles) northeast of London. Norwich, Norfolk's biggest city, is just 16 km (10 miles) from the heart of the Broads and has a small airport, as well as regular rail services from other parts of Norfolk and from London. The Broads are accessible by a network of small roads but are, of course, best explored by boat.

WEATHER
The Broads are at their absolute best in summer, when there should be plenty of warm, sunny days and the least chance of rain. Average daytime temperatures range from 16 to 21°C.

ACCOMMODATION
Splashing Out The Fritton Arms is an upscale pub in a manor house just moments away from the beautiful Fritton Lake.
www.frittonhouse.co.uk

On a Budget Blackhorse Cottage at Brancaster Staithe is a delightful thatched cottage overlooking the harbour. Sleeps up to 6 people.
www.blackhorsecottagenorfolk.co.uk

EATING OUT
Splashing Out The Lavender House, in Brundall, is a superb restaurant with a stunning menu and a great atmosphere.
www.thelavenderhouse.co.uk

On a Budget The Earsham Street Café, in Bungay in Suffolk, serves Brancaster mussels and other tasty local fare.
www.earshamstreetcafe.co.uk

PRICE FOR TWO PEOPLE
Around £170 a day for food, accommodation and entrance fees.

WEBSITE
www.visitnorfolk.co.uk

Above (left to right) Horning village; canoeing on the Broads
Main: Hickling Broad from the air

BROAD HORIZONS

Pure silence is so rare, that when we experience it we are compelled to stop and listen to the quiet. One place where it is possible to capture this elusive stillness is in a canoe on the Norfolk Broads. Although this watery region attracts millions of visitors every year, its 200 km (120 miles) of navigable lakes and rivers provide ample space to lose oneself and find those peaceful moments.

The Broads stretch from the historic city of Norwich to the eastern coastlines of Norfolk and Suffolk. Despite their stunning natural beauty, they are, in fact, a joint effort of man and nature – the result of the digging of peat for fuel and building materials over hundreds of years. The excavated areas slowly flooded as sea levels rose in the 13th century, creating the network of rivers and lakes that now form Britain's third-largest inland waterway.

The Broads is the nation's largest protected wetland, sheltering some of the UK's rarest birds, including bitterns and marsh harriers, as well as more common species such as swans and grebes. The birdwatcher's motto has always been "let the birds come to you", and if you take a moment to pause in your canoe, wildlife usually emerges from the reedbeds. To see a great crested grebe, with its tufted head and russet ruff, is always special, and if you're lucky you might spot a graceful heron in flight or a cormorant diving for fish. Kestrels and sparrowhawks circle the skies here too, and you will share the water with geese, ducks, moorhens and coots.

If you prefer to stay on dry land, there are many other ways to enjoy summer in the Broads. There are over 322 km (200 miles) of paths and boardwalks along which to hike or cycle, or you can explore the region by car and find spots to relax by the water's edge. There are dozens of pretty villages, among them Horning, featured in the novels of Arthur Ransome, and Hickling, with its 14th-century flint-and-stone church. But it's in a canoe that you can truly immerse yourself in this region's haunting landscape. The peace comes when you stop paddling, and let the immensity of the Broads and their strange beauty embrace you.

Below (left to right): Windmill at How Hill; greylag goose flying over reedbeds; sunset over the Broads

FURTHER DETAILS

THE NORFOLK BROADS
Broads Authority: www.broads-authority.gov.uk
Broads Tourism: www.norfolkbroads.com

Canoe Hire
Canoes can be hired by the day or the half-day, and some companies run canoe safaris with guides to help you navigate. Canoes and other boats can be hired at several centres including Norwich, Beccles, Wroxham, Stalham, Wayford Bridge and the Sutton Staithe Boatyard.
www.thecanoeman.com

WHAT ELSE TO SEE AND DO
The Museum of the Broads
This award-winning museum in Stalham has enjoyable displays on life in the Broads, the people, the boats, the wildlife and how the Broadland was created.
www.museumofthebroads.org.uk

Bure Valley Railway
This beautiful old steam-engine line follows a 29-km (18-mile) circular route between the market towns of Aylsham and Wroxham, at the heart of the Broads. The trains travel through the picturesque Bure Valley countryside, following the River Bure through meadowland and ancient pasture.
www.bvrw.co.uk

Somerleyton Hall and Gardens
Just outside Lowestoft on the Suffolk coast, the grand Somerleyton Hall and its beautiful gardens are open to the public and are well worth a look.
www.somerleyton.co.uk

> The peace comes when you stop paddling, and let the immensity of the Broads and their strange beauty embrace you.

DICKENS' RETREAT

Tucked between the resorts of Ramsgate and Margate on the Isle of Thanet – a peninsula of north Kent flatland that juts into the Strait of Dover – the pint-sized Victorian settlement of Broadstairs is hands-down the most delightful of the towns that fringe this sandy coastline. This tranquil, easy-going and totally unfussy coastal town makes for a breezy escape from the Big Smoke and urban England. Its chalky cliff-top perch overlooks Viking Bay, historically used by smugglers who also infested coves up and down the coast.

The town's evocative name is said to derive from the wide steps that gave access to the sands below, which were cut from the rock in the 15th century. More importantly, Broadstairs finds itself indelibly marked on the literary atlas for its associations with the towering genius of Charles Dickens, who found the town inspirational and penned *David Copperfield* here. A regular visitor between 1837 and 1859, the brilliant novelist is celebrated in the Dickens House Museum, and the house overlooking Viking Bay where Dickens lodged was perhaps unsurprisingly rechristened Bleak House.

Summer is naturally the best season to dip your toes in the Broadstairs brine, especially as June sees enthusiasts trooping to the annual Dickens Festival, which first took place in 1937. During the festival there's a theatrical buzz in town, with Dickens enthusiasts dressing up in Victorian attire and sauntering along Viking Bay beach. Events include country fairs, historical walks, parades, dramatizations of the novelist's works and musical concerts. A grand gala ball brings the curtain down on the event. Later in summer there's the excitement of Broadstairs Folk Week, an enthusiastic celebration of folk music and dance. The festival attracts folk musicians from all over Britain, and hums with events and activities for adults and children. Handy workshops in a variety of musical instruments offer a chance for both novices and experts to play together.

The town's small size means Broadstairs is easily navigable on foot, leaving time for exploring other sights in the locality. After wandering the sands on Viking Beach, consider exploring Louisa Bay and Dumpton Gap to the south and the coastline towards Margate, where a string of quiet, secluded coves and bays extends north: Stone Bay, Joss Bay, Kingsgate Bay – overlooked by Kingsgate Castle, now housing flats – and Botany Bay.

THE ESSENTIALS

GETTING THERE AND AROUND
Broadstairs is on the Kent coast, in the southeast of England. Trains run to and from London Victoria to Broadstairs every half-hour (every hour on Sundays). The regular Thanet Loop bus service runs through Margate, Broadstairs and Ramsgate.

WEATHER
In summer, Broadstairs is generally sunny and pleasant, with average daytime temperatures of 16–22°C. However, be prepared for rain.

ACCOMMODATION
Splashing Out Charles Dickens was a regular visitor at the Royal Albion, on Albion Street, a classic Regency seafront hotel; the spacious superior rooms at the front look over Viking Bay.
www.albionbroadstairs.co.uk

On a Budget Number 68 B&B, on West Cliff Road, is a stylish but cosy little place near the seafront with themed rooms.
www.number68.co.uk

EATING OUT
Splashing Out Osteria Posillipo Pizzeria, on Albion Street, was voted 4th best Italian restaurant in the UK by Antonio Carluccio, who called it "a little bit of Naples in Kent".
www.posillipo.co.uk

On a Budget Morelli's Cappuccino, on Victoria Parade, is a lovely family-run café and ice cream parlour on the seafront; great for snacking, coffees, sandwiches, hot dishes and smashing sundaes.
Tel: 01843 862500.

PRICE FOR TWO PEOPLE
£80–110 a day for accommodation, food and entrance fees.

WEBSITE
www.visitthanet.co.uk

Main: Viking Bay in Broadstairs, overlooked by Bleak House (top right) **Below (left to right):** Cliffs at Kingsgate Bay; bust of the town's most famous tourist, Charles Dickens

FURTHER DETAILS

BROADSTAIRS

Broadstairs Dickens Festival
Various venues; late Jun.
www.broadstairsdickensfestival.co.uk

Broadstairs Folk Week
Various venues; mid-Aug.
www.broadstairsfolkweek.org.uk

Dickens House Museum
2 Victoria Parade; open Jul–Sep: 10am–5pm daily;
Easter–Jun and Oct: 2pm–5pm daily.
www.visitbroadstairs.co.uk

WHAT ELSE TO SEE AND DO

St Peter's Village
A short walk inland from Broadstairs, the pretty village
of St Peter's is an attractive diversion. The graveyard
of the church of St Peter in Thanet is among the
largest to be found in England.
www.villagetour.co.uk

Margate
The Thanet resort town of Margate, to the north of
Broadstairs, is far better known than its sibling to the
south, but is consequently busier and less genteel.
Margate was one of the very first resorts to lure British
holiday-makers to paddle in the sea as a leisure activity.
A big reason to earmark Margate for exploration is the
presence of the new Turner Contemporary Art Gallery.

Ramsgate
Either hop on a bus or walk to Ramsgate, 3 km
(2 miles) south of Broadstairs. It's an attractive and
much larger resort situated on the top of a cliff, with
an excellent crop of Regency architecture.
www.portoframsgate.co.uk

Sandwich
The attractive town of Sandwich lies 12 km
(9 miles) south of Broadstairs. It once enjoyed fame
as a great medieval port.
www.discoversandwich.co.uk

Deal
This coastal town, 15 miles (24 km) southeast of
Broadstairs, has two Tudor castles: Deal and Walmer.
William Pitt the Younger (British Prime Minister,
1783–1801 and 1804–6) lived here with his niece,
Lady Hester Stanhope. An inspiration to Picasso and
friend of James Joyce, Lady Hester later became the
most famous woman traveller of her time.
www.aboutdeal.co.uk

Below: Beach and harbour at Broadstairs

THE ESSENTIALS

GETTING THERE AND AROUND
The Peak District is in central England, largely in the county of Derbyshire. The nearest international airport is Manchester Airport, 16 km (10 miles) northwest of the Peak District National Park boundary. Trains run regularly from London to main Peak District stations, such as Chesterfield, Derby and Sheffield, with journey times of around 2 hours 30 minutes. The region is well served by buses.

WEATHER
Much of the Peak District experiences higher than average rainfall in summer, when daytime temperatures are at their highest, ranging from 14 to 16°C.

ACCOMMODATION
Splashing Out Fischer's Baslow Hall, near Baslow, is a beautiful country-house hotel on the Chatsworth Estate that boasts a Michelin-starred restaurant. *www.fischers-baslowhall.co.uk*

On a Budget Crown Cottage, on the Main Road in Eyam, is a 4-star B&B located in a 200-year-old building that was once an inn. *www.crown-cottage.co.uk*

EATING OUT
Splashing Out Rowley's, in Baslow, on the edge of the Chatsworth Estate, specializes in locally sourced food. *www.rowleysrestaurant.co.uk*

On a Budget The Chequers Inn, in Froggatt, dates from the 16th century and is a great example of the Peak District's many gastropubs. *www.chequers-froggatt.com*

PRICE FOR TWO PEOPLE
From £160 a day for food, accommodation and entry fees.

WEBSITE
www.visitpeakdistrict.com

WELL-DRESSED WELLS

THE DERBYSHIRE PEAK DISTRICT has an air of mystery about it, and the origins of the region's time-hallowed and fascinating tradition of well dressing are suitably obscure. From the end of April to mid-September, throughout Derbyshire – and to a lesser extent in neighbouring Staffordshire – the inhabitants of over 60 towns and villages decorate the local village wells that have all but disappeared in other parts of rural England.

In pre-Christian Britain, all villages would have had access to a well or natural spring, and offerings – usually in the form of flowers and other plants – were placed beside them to thank the gods for the supply of fresh water. When Christianity arrived in Britain in the 4th century AD, this custom was condemned as a form of water worship. However, the tradition lingered on in this part of the Peak District, perhaps due to the region's isolation and lack of major roads.

In 1665, the bubonic plague that was sweeping the country arrived in the village of Eyam, in a bundle of cloth that had been sent from a tailor in London. In a noble act, the inhabitants of Eyam voluntarily quarantined themselves for 16 months to prevent the plague spreading further. They were naturally thankful for the fresh water provided by the village well and the well dressing ceremony, as it is known today, was born. Eyam's well dressing lasts for a week in August, giving you enough time to explore Derbyshire's Peak District; you can tour its many pretty villages, and go hiking on nearby Eyam Moor and the green hills of the Derwent Valley.

Visitors to Eyam and other places known for well dressing – such as Tissington, Bakewell, Hope and Hathersage – have the chance to see for themselves how the dressings are created, and can admire the finished results. Boards are soaked in the local pond or river and then covered in clay, onto which a design is sketched. Then flowers, seeds, berries and other natural materials are skilfully used to create an incredibly colourful collage that will be placed beside the well. These works of art last for up to a week – enough time to thank the ancient gods for their munificence in ensuring that this endearing tradition survives in our hectic modern world.

Main: Village of Hathersage, nestling in the Derwent Valley
Below: Chatsworth House, overlooking the River Derwent

FURTHER DETAILS

**DERBYSHIRE PEAK DISTRICT
WELL DRESSING**
Well dressing ceremonies take place in many villages around the Derbyshire Peak District between late April and mid-September.
www.welldressing.com

WHAT ELSE TO SEE AND DO
The Hope Valley Line
This is one of the most scenic rail routes in the UK, travelling through the Peak District National Park to connect Sheffield and Manchester via a scattering of pretty villages in the beautiful Derwent, Hope and Edale valleys. Many of them are "folk trains", featuring onboard musicians who will invite you to alight at one of the village stations and continue the festivities at a local pub.
www.hvlptp.org.uk

Peveril Castle
One of England's earliest Norman castles, Peveril Castle, in Castleton, was founded in 1066. Its high grounds provide some of the best views of Derbyshire's Peak District.
www.english-heritage.org.uk/peveril

Chatsworth House
Residence of the Duke and Duchess of Devonshire, Chatsworth House, near Bakewell, is one of Britain's most impressive country houses, containing an art collection that ranges from Roman sculptures to paintings by Rembrandt and Lucian Freud.
www.chatsworth.org

Haddon Hall
Overlooking the River Wye at Bakewell, Haddon Hall is a vast, fortified 12th-century manor house. The house was modified by each generation of its inhabitants until the 17th century, when it was abandoned and left to decay gracefully. Both the house and its Elizabethan gardens were lavishly restored in the 1920s.
www.haddonhall.co.uk

Below: Beautiful example of well dressing at Coffin Well

THE ESSENTIALS

GETTING THERE AND AROUND
The Scottish Borders are in the southeast of Scotland, along the national border with England. They begin about 24 km (15 miles) south of Edinburgh, where the nearest international airport is situated. There are bus and train connections from Edinburgh, but with the Borders' beautiful scenery and widely spaced towns, it is best to travel the region by car.

WEATHER
While summer in the southeast of Scotland is generally warmer and dryer than in the Highlands, be prepared for rain at any time. Average daytime temperatures range from 18 to 22°C.

ACCOMMODATION
Splashing Out The Roxburghe Hotel & Golf Course, near Kelso, is a relaxed country-house hotel on the wooded Roxburghe estate.
www.roxburghe.net

On a Budget The Tontine Hotel, in Peebles, is a historic hotel with an excellent restaurant, a stone's throw from lovely walks along the River Tweed.
www.tontinehotel.com

EATING OUT
Splashing Out Bardoulet's Restaurant at The Horseshoe Inn, in Eddleston, has won awards for its innovative food featuring local produce and many Scottish specialities.
www.horseshoeinn.co.uk/restaurant

On a Budget The Waggon Inn Bar and Restaurant, in Kelso, offers something for everyone, from home-made pub classics to steaks and seasonal specials.
www.thewaggoninn.com

PRICE FOR TWO PEOPLE
£200 a day for accommodation and food.

WEBSITE
www.visitscottishborders.com

Main: Standard Bearer at the Selkirk Common Riding **Right (top to bottom):** Traditional Scottish dancing; festivities during the Langholm Common Ridings; mounted participants heading to the Ride Out in Langholm

RIDING OUT

A S DAWN APPROACHES, THE PIPER PLAYS, summoning the townsfolk to an ancient duty. A crowd gathers in anticipation, until at last the clatter of horses' hooves is heard, growing louder as their flag-bearing riders approach the town square. The Common Ridings have begun. Each summer this scene is played out in towns throughout the Scottish Borders. The ritual of the Common Ridings dates back to the 14th century, when the region suffered constant turmoil in the border wars with England. While kings and noblemen fought over territory, ordinary families had to defend their livestock against *reiving* – cattle thieving – a common practice in those lawless times. So the townspeople decided to gather together and patrol the boundaries (or "marches") of their lands themselves, in a practice known as the "Ridings of the Marches".

The Common Ridings are a re-enactment of these patrols and they have become a yearly tradition, commemorating the Borders' turbulent past. They take place in the Border towns every summer and have grown to become great festive affairs, with parades, pageants and

FURTHER DETAILS

THE COMMON RIDINGS

Ridings take place annually in many of the border towns, and in Edinburgh, between June and August. Towns with the most extensive festivites are listed below.
www.returntotheridings.co.uk

Hawick
Here the Ridings honour a group of young local men who routed an English raiding party near Hawick after the Battle of Flodden in 1514, capturing their flag.

Langholm
"Langholm's Great Day", as the Ridings are known, takes place on the last Friday in July. Three unusual emblems are carried aloft: the thistle, spade, and crown and barley banna (barley bread nailed to a platter with a salted herring).

Selkirk
In the largest of the Common Ridings, up to 400 riders set off on a 19-km (12 mile) ride, galloping back to the Market Place for the Casting of the Colours ceremony.

Galashiels
The "Braw Lad" leads riders to the Raid Stane – where the townsfolk massacred English plunderers in 1337 – before returning to the Old Town Cross for colourful ceremonies.

Melrose
Activities at this event include parades, ride outs, the ceremonial crowning of the Festival Queen and the swearing-in of the "Melrosian", the town's representative.

Jedburgh
The Callants Festival lasts two weeks, celebrating the bravery of the Jedburgh ("Jethart") Callants during the Redeswire Raid – the last of the border skirmishes.

Peebles
The Riding of the Marches takes place during Beltane Week, in mid-June, which celebrates an even older pagan festival marking the return of summer.

Lauder
One of the original Common Ridings, this culminates with the Cornet leading the riders to the only surviving boundary stone in the Borders.

Below: Jedburgh Abbey in the Scottish Borders

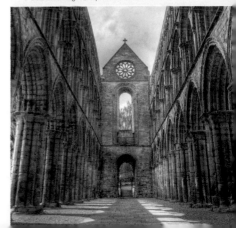

carnivals. Each town has its own unique agenda and ceremonial customs, but in each of the towns, one man is chosen to lead the procession and is bestowed with an honorary title, such as Cornet (in Hawick and Langholm), Standard Bearer (in Selkirk) or Braw (fine) Lad (in Galashiels). A principal Lass ties a ribbon to the man's Burgh Flag, or Standard, just as a knight's lady would have attached her "favour" (such as a ribbon or veil) to his lance before battle. There are moving speeches, rousing songs and marching pipe bands.

But the essence of every gathering is the "Ride Out". These great displays of horsemanship often see hundreds of horses and riders thundering across the beautiful Borders landscape, in some of the largest mounted gatherings in Europe. Horses are ridden proudly and passionately, whether owned or hired by their riders for this great day. There's a warm feeling of community pride as each crowd follows its riders to the edge of town. And as the townsfolk ride the marches, age-old boundaries are redrawn, and ties to a common history and culture once again renewed.

THE ESSENTIALS

GETTING THERE AND AROUND
The Stour Valley is in the east of England, on the coastal border of Essex and Suffolk. The nearest major airport is London Stansted, 65 km (40 miles) west of Dedham. The closest rail station is at Manningtree, 8 km (5 miles) from Dedham. The area is best explored on foot or by bicycle, although a car is useful for longer journeys.

WEATHER
The summer climate in the Stour Valley is generally mild, but be prepared for rain. Average summer daytime temperatures range from 15 to 18°C.

ACCOMMODATION
Splashing Out Maison Talbooth, in Dedham, is a Victorian country-house hotel by the River Stour with 12 luxury suites, massage treatment rooms and a restaurant.
www.milsomhotels.com

On a Budget May's Barn Farm, in Dedham, is a quiet B&B in a secluded location with views over Dedham Vale.

EATING OUT
Splashing Out Le Talbooth, in Dedham, is part of the Maison Talbooth complex, and serves some of the best-quality food for miles around.
www.milsomhotels.com

On a Budget The Essex Rose Tea House, part of the Tiptree brand, is a traditional tearoom with table service. It offers a wide range of sandwiches, cooked lunches and classic cream teas.
www.trooms.com

PRICE FOR TWO PEOPLE
From around £150 a day for accommodation, food and entrance fees.

WEBSITE
www.visiteastofengland.com

CONSTABLE COUNTRY

IT MAY SURPRISE YOU TO FIND THAT there is an area of England that has hardly changed in two centuries – yet is scarcely an hour's drive from London's suburbs. The Stour Valley lies along the River Stour, forming the border between the counties of Essex and Suffolk. It was the setting of many paintings by the renowned artist John Constable (1776–1837). One of Britain's best-loved artists, Constable was more popular in France than in Britain during his lifetime, and was forced to take up portrait painting to subsidize his real love: landscape painting. He painted the Stour Valley region extensively in the early 1800s, capturing the majestic water meadows, the willowy bank-side trees and scenes of rural life along the lowland river valley in Dedham Vale. These quintessentially English countryside tableaus – a gentle landscape of lazy little rivers, quaint English churches, country pubs and cricket on the village green – are today preserved in an Area of Outstanding Natural Beauty. In the patchwork of fields, June's spectacular harvest of bright-yellow oilseed rape later gives way to crops of wheat, barley and onions. Oxeye daisies, bee orchids and clover flower in the ancient hedgerows bordering the quiet rural lanes and attract a flurry of butterflies in August.

In this warm summer glow, Constable painted some of his best-loved works. Born in East Bergholt in Suffolk, the son of a wealthy corn merchant, he was most inspired by the landscape in and around nearby Dedham. In 1802 he painted one of his most famous scenes, *Dedham Vale*, which captures the river winding towards the distant tower of Dedham Church. It was a view he returned to and painted again and again.

Not far from here is Flatford Mill, where Constable composed perhaps the best known of his great works, *The Hay Wain*. The mill itself is not open to the public, but you can book Constable-related art courses at the Field Centre here and are allowed to walk past in order to view Willy Lott's Cottage, the building at the left-hand side of *The Hay Wain*. The cottage was built sometime in the 16th century and was around 300 years old when Constable finished his painting in 1821. To see it still standing today, almost two centuries later, is just one of the spirit-lifting moments that you will experience in the quite literally picturesque landscapes of Constable Country.

Main: Willy Lott's Cottage near Flatford Mill
Below (left to right): Flatford Mill; fields of oil-seed rape in bloom near Dedham

FURTHER DETAILS

STOUR VALLEY CONSTABLE COUNTRY
The Flatford Mill Field Centre
Flatford Mill. Field Centre, East Bergholt, Suffolk. The Field Studies Council, based at the Flatford Mill Centre, runs over 170 arts, crafts and natural history short courses lasting from two days to a week – naturally including artistic explorations of Constable Country.
www.field-studies-council.org/flatfordmill

WHAT ELSE TO SEE AND DO
Flatford Bridge Cottage
Adjoining Flatford Mill is the lovely old thatched Bridge Cottage, which also features in many of Constable's paintings of the area. It has been restored and now houses an exhibition on the artist and a tea room. In summer guided walks can be booked here.
www.nationaltrust.org.uk

The Beth Chatto Gardens
The renowned gardening expert and author Beth Chatto has opened her gardens – in Elmstead Market, just over 8 km (5 miles) south of Dedham – for public viewing. Established in 1960, the gardens are most famous for the non-irrigated, gravel-planted section, where only truly drought-hardy plants survive. The "island planting" of the main gardens is inspirational, and most of the garden's unusual plants are available to buy in the nursery.
www.bethchatto.co.uk

Sir Alfred Munnings Museum
Castle House, in Dedham, was the home of the artist Sir Alfred Munnings – a former president of the Royal Academy of Arts. The house is now an art museum that displays over 200 of his works, and his studio has been preserved just as it was in his lifetime.
www.siralfredmunnings.co.uk

Below: Cows drinking from the River Stour

A SUMMER PLAYGROUND

W ITHIN MINUTES OF ESCAPING the thundering traffic of the A38 Devon Expressway, the air changes, life slows and all becomes right with the world. Unspoilt villages welcome you along the network of narrow, high-banked lanes, many of which are drawn south towards a magnetic coastline of such beauty that you may never want to leave. At the heart of this ravishing haven, anchored between Torbay and Plymouth on the edge of a deeply wooded estuary, lies Salcombe, a glorious summer playground of flaxen sands and leisurely waves.

The small town's self-consciously smart Fore Street and Island Street – with its boatbuilders' workshops – are the focus of activity on shore, and there are dozens of pubs, restaurants, cafés and clothing shops. Away from retail heaven, difficult choices await the summer visitor – should it be the bare-faced indulgence of Salcombe Dairy ice cream, the excitement of crabbing on the embankment or the fascination of ancient tales of shipwrecks and smugglers at the Museum of Maritime and Local History? Of course, salty sea dogs can't wait want to be on the water exploring the cobalt-blue estuary and its backwater creeks, where ferries, tourist

▌ THE ESSENTIALS

GETTING THERE AND AROUND
Salcombe is on the Devon coast in southwest England. The nearest airport is Exeter, 80km (50 miles) to the northeast. Totnes has a railway station and there are trunk roads to within half an hour of Salcombe. Once there, ditch the car and explore using the town's buses and ferries, or on foot. Salcombe also operates a park-and-ride service.

WEATHER
Salcombe has a mild climate and in summer is routinely warmer than other parts of the UK, with average daytime temperatures of 15–18°C.

ACCOMMODATION
Splashing Out The Sea Balcony, an uber-modern apartment overlooking the Salcombe Estuary, has luxurious rooms and unrivalled views.
www.salcombefinest.com

On a Budget Waverley, on Devon Road, is a comfortable, unspoilt B&B.
www.waverleybandb.co.uk

EATING OUT
Splashing Out The Winking Prawn, on North Sands, serves the freshest seafood in a beautiful beachfront location.
www.winkingprawn.co.uk

On a Budget Captain Flint's, on Fore Street, is a massively popular pizza and pasta restaurant that's great for children.
Tel: 01548 842357

PRICE FOR A FAMILY OF FOUR
Around £300 a day for food, accommodation and boat hire.

WEBSITES
www.salcombeinformation.co.uk
www.southhams.gov.uk

Previous page: Sandown Pier on the Isle of Wight, Hampshire

At the heart of this ravishing haven… lies Salcombe – a glorious summer playground of flaxen sands and leisurely waves.

cruisers and fishing boats ply their routes between yacht races, dinghy lessons and visiting sailing boats. In August, the week-long Salcombe Regatta takes over land and water, with lots of sailing and rowing races, but also mud races, torch-lit processions and even daring aerial displays by planes and helicopters. There are also activities to keep children amused, including crab-catching contests, treasure hunts, sand-castle competitions.

For landlubbers, there are half-a-dozen clean and safe beaches for relaxing and sandy fun – they also provide perfect vantage points for estuary-watching. One of the prettiest and most sheltered is Mill Bay, just a short ferry-ride from Salcombe. As families wend their way home at the end of each day, the chances are they are already planning the next   perhaps a visit to the sub-tropical gardens created by the Edwardian eccentric Otto Overbeck, a ramble along the South West Coast Path's heart-leaping stretches with their sensational views or – and why not? – another day on the beach. Worried about summer boredom? In Salcombe, it's impossible.

Main: Stunning Mill Bay, backed by rolling hills
Far left (top to bottom): Pastel-coloured houses on Salcombe's Fore Street
Above: Crabbing, a popular pastime for children
Below: Salcombe viewed across the water

FURTHER DETAILS

SALCOMBE

On the Water
Salcombe offers lots of ways to have fun on the water: you can learn to sail, kayak or paddle-surf; charter your own boat; or go on a relaxing Rivermaid ferry cruise, with guides to help you spot seals and myriad sea birds.
Island Cruising Club: www.icc-salcombe.co.uk
South Sands Sailing: www.southsandssailing.co.uk
Salcombe Rib Charter: www.salcomberibcharter.com
Ferry Cruises: www.kingsbridgesalcombeferry.co.uk

Salcombe Maritime Museum
Market Street, Salcombe; open Easter–Oct: 10:30am–12:30pm & 2:30–4:30pm daily.
www.salcombemuseum.org.uk

Salcombe Regatta
Salcombe's colourful August water festival.
www.salcombeyc.org.uk

Overbeck's Museum and Garden
Sharpitor, Salcombe; opening times vary throughout the year; see website for details.
www.nationaltrust.org.uk

South West Coast Path
www.southwestcoastpath.com

WHAT ELSE TO SEE AND DO

Dartmoor
Wild, mysterious and only 40 minutes' drive from Salcombe (see pp192–3).
www.visitdartmoor.co.uk

Bantham
Stunning sands not far from Bigbury and Burgh Island, where a sea-tractor crosses the causeway at high tide.
www.visitsouthdevon.co.uk

Slapton Ley National Nature Reserve
Slapton Ley is a beautiful freshwater lagoon, home to hundreds of species of flora and fauna. Nearby is Slapton Sands where, in 1944, hundreds of US troops died after German U-boats torpedoed a D-Day exercise.
www.slnnr.org.uk

Woodlands Leisure Park
Located just outside of Dartmouth, this theme park is perfect for boisterous youngsters.
www.woodlandspark.com

THE ESSENTIALS

GETTING THERE AND AROUND
The Dingle Peninsula, County Kerry, is on the southwest coast of Ireland, stretching west from Tralee. The nearest major airports are at Cork, about 130 km (80 miles) to the southeast, and Shannon, 126 km (78 miles) to the northeast. There are buses serving the area, but the best way to get around is by car or bicycle.

WEATHER
The Gulf Stream brings a mild climate, but there's a good chance of wind and rain even in summer, so come prepared. Daytime temperatures average 12–20ºC.

ACCOMMODATION
Splashing Out The Dingle Skellig Hotel and Peninsula Spa, on the harbour just outside Dingle Town, is a 4-star modern hotel with fantastic views over Dingle Bay.
www.dingleskellig.com

On a Budget James G Ashes is a bright and clean B&B with downstairs bar and restaurant in the centre of Dingle Town.
www.ashesbar.ie

EATING OUT
Splashing Out The Chart House, in Dingle Town, is an award-winning restaurant serving modern cuisine in an atmospheric old cottage. Dinner only.
www.thecharthousedingle.com

On a Budget Grey's Lane Bistro, in the heart of Dingle Town, serves delicious dishes using locally sourced ingredients (including plenty of fresh fish).
www.greyslanebistro.com

PRICE FOR TWO PEOPLE
From €190–210 a day for food, accommodation and entrance fees.

WEBSITE
www.dodingle.com
www.dingle-peninsula.ie

THE END OF THE ROAD

THERE ARE FEW PLACES MORE ENCHANTING than Ireland's Dingle Peninsula. Its very name has a magical ring, and its chain of Kerry-green hills, studded with ancient stone cottages and strange little beehive huts, just might make you believe in leprechauns. Though this slim finger of the western coast stretches just 56 km (35 miles) into the Atlantic, it encompasses idyllic beaches, high rugged mountains, stunning seascapes and fascinating historical sites.

Magical too are the songs that you'll hear in the pubs of Dingle Town. It's renowned as a centre for traditional Irish music and lively "sessions" – both organized and impromptu – take place almost every night. In summer, the narrow streets of colourful shops and houses winding up from the harbour are packed with visitors who've come to enjoy the legendary *craic* (fun).

One of the best ways to see Dingle's wild and remote landscape is on a drive around the region. Head east out of town along Dingle Bay to one of Ireland's most heavenly beaches, Inch Strand, its 6 km (4 miles) of soft sand overlooked by the Slieve Mish mountains. To the west lies adventure, starting with the road signs: Dingle Peninsula is an Irish-speaking region, and there are few English translations. Follow Slea Head Drive for dramatic coastal views. The eerie ruins of Dunbeg Fort, a dramatic Iron Age promontory fort, cling to surf-pounded cliffs. Nearby, explore the curious stone *clochans* (beehive huts) at Fahan – dwellings built by prehistoric farmers. Around the peninsula's tip there are breathtaking views across the sound to the Blasket Islands. Now uninhabited, they were once known as "the last parish before America". Reaching toward them is Garraun Point, the most westerly spot on the mainland – perfect for sunset-watching.

A short detour inland brings you to the phenomenal Gallarus Oratory. Like the *clochans*, this early Christian church was built of stone without mortar, yet has remained watertight for centuries. To the north, Mount Brandon is Dingle's highest peak, rising 953 m (3,127 ft) high. From Brandon Bay below, the 6th-century navigator St Brendan allegedly set sail for the New World. Modern-day explorers are more likely to end their journeys on the fine sandy beaches that stretch along Tralee Bay on Dingle's northern shore.

Main: The Blasket Islands from Clogher Head on the Dingle Peninsula
Below (left to right): Ancient remains of Dunberg Fort; Mount Brandon; dramatic drive around Slea Head

FURTHER DETAILS

THE DINGLE PENINSULA
Dunbeg Fort
Slea Head Drive, Fahan; open access.
www.dunbegfort.com

Fahan Beehive Huts
On private land; farmers often charge a small fee for up-close access.

Gallarus Oratory
Near Ballyferriter; tel: 066 915 5333; open daily Easter–Oct.

WHAT ELSE TO SEE AND DO
The Blasket Islands
These beautiful, windswept islands, 9.5 km (6 miles) off the tip of the Dingle Peninsula, were settled as far back as the Iron Age. Though they are now home only to a great variety of seabirds, the fascinating story of life as it was in this remote community is told in the Blasket Centre in Dunquin, a village on the mainland. Weather permitting, you can take a boat trip from Dunquin Pier to visit the picturesque Great Blasket Island.
Blasket Centre: tel: 066 915 6444
Blasket Islands Eco Marine Tours: www.marinetours.ie

Tralee
Kerry's county town puts on the Rose of Tralee International Festival each August, with a famous beauty pageant and a week of parades, funfairs and other activities. The National Folk Theatre of Ireland is also based here and stages performances of traditional music and dance throughout the summer.
Rose of Tralee: www.roseoftralee.ie
National Folk Theatre: www.siamsatire.com

The eerie ruins of Dunbeg Fort, a dramatic Iron Age promontory fort, cling to surf-pounded cliffs.

THE ESSENTIALS

GETTING THERE AND AROUND
Bristol is in the southwest of England.
The nearest airport is Bristol International
Airport, around 13 km (8 miles) from
the centre. Regular trains run to Bristol
Temple Meads from London Paddington,
and take just under 2 hours. Most of
the central sights in the city can be
seen on foot, with recourse to buses for
outlying destinations.

WEATHER
Bristol has a mild climate with generally
dry summers. Average summer daytime
temperatures range from 13 to 22°C.

ACCOMMODATION
Splashing Out Hotel du Vin & Bistro,
in Narrow Lewins Mead, is situated
in restored warehouse buildings, and
offers style, comfort and great food in
a city-centre location.
www.hotelduvin.com

On a Budget The Greenhouse B&B, on
Greenbank Road, is a pretty Victorian
cottage with modern interior styling.
www.thegreenhousebristol.co.uk

EATING OUT
Splashing Out Riverstation, on The
Grove, is a converted former police
station that serves tasty modern
European cuisine.
www.riverstation.co.uk

On a Budget El Puerto, on Prince
Street, serves tasty tapas in a lively
and fun atmosphere with flamenco
dancing on Sundays and paella-cooking
demonstrations.
www.el-puerto.co.uk

PRICE FOR TWO PEOPLE
From around £170 a day for
accommodation, food and entrance fees.

WEBSITE
www.visitbristol.co.uk

Main: Hot-air balloons over Clifton Suspension Bridge **Right (top to bottom):** Bristol Harbourside Marina at night;
interior of Bristol City Museum and Art Gallery; aerial view of Bristol Floating Harbour with Queen Square at the centre

ON THE WATERFRONT

Straddling the river Avon, the vital and dynamic inland port and university city of Bristol is the cultural nucleus of England's rural southwest. The city's longstanding relationship with sea trade – the shipping of tobacco, wine and slaves in the main – survives in its pronounced historic port character. The Floating Harbour, so called because lock gates insulate it from the tides, celebrated its 200th anniversary in 2009. It is the city's focal point, an attraction for residents and visitors alike. In late July or early August, the area also hosts the exuberant Bristol Harbour Festival, when the water swarms with boats and the waterside comes alive with festivities, from music to dance, circus acts and a cavalcade of fireworks that concludes the celebrations at the end of the long weekend.

Other summer events include August's Bristol International Balloon Fiesta, when dozens of hot-air balloons fill the skies above the city, and the "birthday party" of the *SS Great Britain*, held annually on 19 July. Designed by the daring Victorian engineer Isambard Kingdom Brunel, and launched in Bristol in 1843, she was the first iron-hulled ocean-going vessel to be powered by propeller, transforming world travel. After a million miles at sea, she

FURTHER DETAILS

BRISTOL

Bristol Harbour Festival
Held over a weekend in late Jul or early Aug.
www.bristolharbourfestival.co.uk

Bristol International Balloon Fiesta
Held over four days in mid–Aug.
www.bristolfiesta.co.uk

SS Great Britain Birthday Party
Held on 19 Jul annually, 6:30–10pm.

SS Great Britain
Bristol Dock. Tickets also include entry to the dry dock,
the replica of *The Matthew* and the Maritime Heritage
Centre. Open Apr–Sep: 10am–5:30pm daily; Oct, Feb–
Mar: 10am–4.30pm daily; Nov–Jan: 10am–4pm daily.
www.ssgreatbritain.org

Bristol Cathedral
College Green; open 8am–5pm Mon–Fri;
8am–3pm Sat–Sun.
www.bristol-cathedral.co.uk

Explore-at-Bristol
Anchor Road, Harbourside; open 10am–5pm
Mon–Fri: 10am–6pm Sat–Sun.
http://explore-at-bristol.org.uk

Theatre Royal
Bristol Old Vic, King Street.
www.bristololdvic.org.uk

City Museum and Art Gallery
Queens Road, West End; open 10am–5pm daily.
www.bristolmuseums.org.uk

St Mary Redcliffe
Colstone Parade; open 8:30am–5pm Mon–Fri;
8am–8pm Sun.
www.stmaryredcliffe.co.uk

Arnolfini Arts Centre
Narrow Quay; open 11am–6pm Tue–Sun and Bank
Holiday Mon.
www.arnolfini.org.uk

Clifton Suspension Bridge
www.clifton-suspension-bridge.org.uk

WHAT ELSE TO SEE AND DO

Cheddar Caves and Gorge
Take in the amazing geological formations in the
Mendip Hills and explore the cavernous secrets of
Cheddar Gorge.
www.cheddarcaves.co.uk

Glastonbury Abbey
Set in idyllic parkland, this sublime ruined abbey – once
the largest in England – is a highlight of the area.
www.glastonburyabbey.com

returned to Bristol in 1970 for restoration. Today she lies adjacent to a replica of another iconic vessel, *The Matthew*.

Away from the waterfront, Bristol still has plenty to offer. The city's 12th-century cathedral is an outstanding example of a hall church, where the nave, choir and aisles all reach a uniform height. The streets off Park Street north of the cathedral boast some fabulous examples of Georgian architecture, while Explore-at-Bristol is an entertaining combination of hands-on science centre and planetarium, perfect for children. Across Pero's Bridge, Queen Square is an elegant Georgian Square, north of which lies the cobbled 17th-century King Street, home of the Theatre Royal. If rain strikes, the City Museum and Art Gallery, alongside the Neo-Gothic Wills Memorial Tower, provides not just shelter but a first-rate collection of artifacts ranging from ancient Egyptian relics, dinosaurs and fossils to art works by Old Masters and contemporary names. If it's sunstroke you're escaping, seek refuge in the cool interior of St Mary Redcliffe or chill out at the excellent waterfront Arnolfini Arts Centre. Finally, in Clifton, to the west of the city centre, you can admire the iconic Clifton Suspension Bridge – also designed by Brunel – that dramatically spans the River Avon.

Below: Bristol Harbour Festival

THE ESSENTIALS

GETTING THERE AND AROUND
Bath is in Somerset, in the southwest of England. The nearest airport is Bristol International, about 30 km (19 miles) away. There is a regular train service between Bath and London (journey time 90 minutes), and a fast and frequent rail service connecting Bath with Bristol. Buses connect Bath with the nearby city of Wells. Open-air bus tours of Bath are plentiful, and in summer months river trips run along the River Avon.

WEATHER
Bath enjoys a mild summer climate, with average daytime temperatures ranging from 15 to 17ºC.

ACCOMMODATION
Splashing Out The Bath Priory, on Weston Road, is a fabulous historic house with delightful gardens and a Michelin-starred restaurant.
www.thebathpriory.co.uk

On a Budget Apsley House Hotel, on Newbridge Hill, is an elegant Georgian country house with outstanding service and divine gardens.
www.apsley-house.co.uk

EATING OUT
Splashing Out The Olive Tree at the Queensberry Hotel, on Russell Street, majors in modern British cooking using local, seasonal ingredients.
www.olivetreebath.co.uk

On a Budget The Circus Café and Restaurant, on Brock Street, changes its menu every month.
www.thecircuscafeandrestaurant.co.uk

PRICE FOR TWO PEOPLE
From £135 a day for food, accommodation and entrance fees.

WEBSITE
www.visitbath.co.uk

MAKING A SPLASH

Named after its celebrated hot springs, which the Romans developed into a temple and bathing complex, Bath – a UNESCO World Heritage Site – is one of England's most elegant cities. The city's long history, its Palladian-style crescent architecture and ample parkland breed a languorous refinement that few newer towns can muster.

Summer sees the arrival of the Bath Music Festival in late May or early June, when a galaxy of musicians comes to town. The festival – two weeks of classical, world music, folk, jazz and contemporary music events – is celebrated at venues across town. Artists from across the musical spectrum come to perform: past guests include Brian Eno, Branford Marsalis, the Charles Mingus Big Band, bluegrass star Ralph Stanley and noted soprano Emma Kirkby. But it's not just about music: there's also dance, film, workshops, multimedia performances, lectures, free events and a host of exhibitions, all bringing a cultural buzz to Bath.

Situated just southwest of the city's imposing abbey, the Roman Baths – work on which commenced around AD 60 – constitute some of England's most important Roman architectural relics. A visit to the baths is a direct link to the Roman occupation of England: take your time exploring the Sacred Spring and the Great Bath or pop into the adjacent Pump Room and its excellent restaurant. For a more hands-on appreciation of Bath's thermal waters, immerse yourself in the luxurious Thermae Bath Spa – the rooftop pool, with its spectacular views, is the best possible conclusion to a day's exploring. Overlooking the Roman Baths is the 16th-century Bath Abbey, parts of which date back to Norman times.

In the 18th century, Bath became fashionable as a spa resort and the city's grand Georgian buildings, built in distinctive Bath stone, date from this era. Designed by John Wood the Younger in 1767 and completed in 1775, the elegant bow of Royal Crescent is Bath's best-looking slice of Georgian grandeur; you can visit No. 1 Royal Crescent's sumptuous interior. Further examples of the city's Georgian heritage can be seen in the shop-lined elegance of Pulteney Bridge, designed by Scottish architect Robert Adam, and in The Circus and Queen Square, designed by John Wood the Elder.

Main: Magnificent Royal Crescent in Bath
Below (left to right): Roman baths with Bath Abbey in the background; Thermae Bath Spa

FURTHER DETAILS

BATH

Bath Music Festival
Various venues, Bath; late May/early Jun.
www.bathfestivals.org.uk/music

Roman Baths
Stall Street, Bath; open Sep–Jun: 9am–6pm daily;
Jul–Aug: 9am–10pm daily.
www.romanbaths.co.uk

Thermae Bath Spa
New Royal Bath open 9am–9:30pm daily; Cross Bath
open 10am–8pm daily.
www.thermaebathspa.com

Bath Abbey
Open Apr–Oct: 9:30am–5:30pm Mon, 9am–5:30pm
Tue–Fri, 9am–6pm Sat, 1–2:30pm and 4:30–5:30pm
Sun; Nov–Mar: 9am–4:30pm Mon–Sat, 1–2:30pm and
4:30–5:30pm Sun.
www.bathabbey.org

No. 1 Royal Crescent
Open Feb–Dec: noon–5:30pm Mon, 10:30am–
5:30pm Tue–Sun.
www.no1royalcrescent.org.uk

Walking Tours
Free 2-hour walking tours leave from Abbey Church
Yard at 10:30am daily and 2pm Sun–Fri.
www.visitbath.co.uk

WHAT ELSE TO SEE AND DO

Bristol
The maritime city of Bristol (see pp88–9), a 15-minute
train journey from Bath, has dozens of sights, including
the 12th-century Bristol Cathedral, the Clifton
Suspension Bridge and the steamship SS Great Britain
www.visitbristol.co.uk

Wells
The compact city of Wells is most famous for its
splendid cathedral, encasing a stunning English Gothic
interior. Wells can also be used as a jumping-off point
to Cheddar Gorge, Wookey Hole and Glastonbury.
Wells Cathedral www.wellscathedral.org.uk

Below (top to bottom): Operatic production in the
historic Roman Baths; Pulteney Bridge

THE ESSENTIALS

GETTING THERE AND AROUND
The Orkney Islands are 16 km
(10 miles) off the northern coast of
Scotland. Mainland Orkney has its
own airport at Kirkwall, with flights from
several Scottish city airports. Other
islands have smaller airports and there
are also connecting ferries for cars and
for foot passengers.

WEATHER
The summer climate in the Orkneys is
surprisingly mild, with very long daylight
hours and average summer daytime
temperatures of 12–16°C.

ACCOMMODATION
Splashing Out The Orkney Hotel, in
Kirkwall on Mainland, is a restored
17th-century inn.
www.orkneyhotel.co.uk

On a Budget Berstane House, in
St Ola on Mainland, offers superior
B&B accommodation set in woodland,
with breathtaking views over the sea.
www.berstane.co.uk

EATING OUT
Eating options in this remote place are
limited, with little price variation.

The Foveran Hotel's restaurant, near
Kirkwall on Mainland, overlooks Scapa
Flow and serves superb local dishes.
www.foveranhotel.co.uk

The Ferry Inn, in Stromness on Mainland,
offers tasty home-cooking with daily
specials and many vegetarian dishes.
www.ferryinn.com

PRICE FOR TWO PEOPLE
Around £210 a day for food,
accommodation and entrance fees.

WEBSITE
www.visitorkney.com

STONE-AGE SETTLEMENT

Britain has a wealth of prehistoric sites, but some of the oldest and most
fascinating are scattered across the far-flung Orkney Islands. This archipelago of around
70 islands lies off the northern tip of Scotland, where the Atlantic Ocean merges into the
North Sea. It's a meeting point of cultures too, with a strong Scandinavian heritage that
reflects its early Viking rulers as well as its Scottish ancestry.

But Orkney's human history goes back much further. Its largest island, simply called
Mainland, is home to the most complete Neolithic village in Northern Europe, Skara Brae.
Inhabited between 3200 and 2500 BC, it lay buried in the dunes on the west coast of
Mainland until a storm uncovered it in 1850. The 10 partly subterranean houses were built
of dry-stone slabs, surrounded by midden (refuse) mounds and linked by covered
passageways. With their turf and animal-skin roofs long gone, you can look down into these
dwellings and marvel at their sophisticated comforts. Each had a hearth, stone beds, wall

Main and left images

Main: Ring of Brodgar on Mainland

Left (left to right): Walker surveying the islands of the Orkney archipelago; interior of a prehistoric house at Skara Brae

Right: Viking runes engraved on a stone in the chambered cairn at Maeshowe

FURTHER DETAILS

UNESCO ORKNEY WORLD HERITAGE SITE

Skara Brae
31 km (19 miles) northwest of Kirkwall on the B9056 on Mainland; open Apr–Sep: 9:30am–5:30pm daily; Oct–Mar: 10am–4pm daily.
www.historic-scotland.gov.uk

Maeshowe Chambered Cairn
Admissions to the cairn are via Tormiston Mill Visitor Centre, 14 km (9 miles) west of Kirkwall on the A965 on Mainland; open Apr–Sep: 9:30am–5pm daily; Oct–Mar: 10am–4pm daily; twilight tours Jun–Aug at 6pm and 7pm; advance booking is required.
www.historic-scotland.gov.uk

Ring of Brodgar
8 km (5 miles) northeast of Stromness on Mainland; open access.
www.historic-scotland.gov.uk

Stones of Stenness
Just over 1 km (¾ mile) southeast of the Ring of Brodgar; open access.
www.historic-scotland.gov.uk

WHAT ELSE TO SEE AND DO

St Magnus Cathedral
Orkney's capital, Kirkwall, is home to Britain's most northerly cathedral, St Magnus, named after the islands' martyred patron saint. The handsome red sandstone building dates back to 1137. The ornate interior features enormous Romanesque pillars and decorated stonework.
www.stmagnus.org

Italian Chapel
During World War II, Italian prisoners of war on Orkney converted two Nissen huts into this delightful memorial chapel on the tiny island of Lamb Holm. The interior is a work of creativity and imagination, decorated with frescoes and trompe l'oeil artwork.
www.undiscoveredscotland.co.uk/eastmainland/italianchapel

Walking Trips
Wilderness Scotland offers guided walking trips around the islands' coastal paths and famous geographical formations, such as the Old Man of Hoy and Cuilags on the island of Hoy. Tours of the Neolithic sites are also included.
www.wildernessscotland.com

cupboards and a stone dresser. The inhabitants' jewellery, pottery and tools are now displayed in the site's visitor centre.

Skara Brae is part of UNESCO's Heart of Neolithic Orkney World Heritage Site, together with three other sites on Mainland. The grassy mound at Maeshowe hides a monumental chambered cairn dating to around 2800 BC. Bend low to walk through the narrow passage leading to the mysterious inner chamber, where you'll find runic graffiti carved by Viking tomb raiders. The Ring of Brodgar is a huge stone circle some 104 m (340 ft) in diameter, surrounded by a deep ditch. Though only 36 of its original 60 stones remain, with just 27 still standing, it is strikingly set on an isthmus (land bridge) between two lochs. The nearby Stones of Stenness, one of the earliest recorded stone circles, date from around 3100 BC. Four of the original 12 stones remain, the tallest standing 6 m (20 ft) high. These great megaliths are all the more dramatic in summer, looming up in stark contrast to Orkney's windswept, almost treeless terrain, their striking shadows creeping far across the ground in the long hours of daylight.

Below: Stones of Stenness in late-afternoon sunlight

THE ESSENTIALS

GETTING THERE AND AROUND
The Yorkshire Dales National Park covers 1,769 sq km (680 sq miles) of northern England. The nearest international airports are Leeds Bradford Airport and Manchester Airport, 22 km (14 miles) and 80 km (50 miles) respectively from the park's southern boundary. There are good bus services in the Yorkshire Dales, but a car is convenient for more remote areas.

WEATHER
The weather in the Dales varies greatly. Summers can be glorious, but be prepared for showers. Average summer daytime temperatures range from 16 to 19ºC.

ACCOMMODATION
Splashing Out Swinton Park, near Masham, is a luxurious 31-room castle hotel set in 80 hectares (200 acres) of its own grounds in Wensleydale.
www.swintonpark.com

On a Budget Beck Hall, in Malham, is a friendly guesthouse with log fires, four-poster beds and brilliant breakfasts.
www.beckhallmalham.com

EATING OUT
Splashing Out The Burlington Restaurant, at the Devonshire Arms Hotel on the Bolton Abbey Estate, has four AA Rosettes for its fantastic modern cuisine.
www.thedevonshirearms.co.uk

On a Budget The George and Dragon, in Aysgarth, serves excellent food at reasonable prices in a great location near Aysgarth Falls in Wensleydale.
www.georgeanddragonaysgarth.co.uk

PRICE FOR TWO PEOPLE
Around £180 a day for food and accommodation.

WEBSITE
www.yorkshire.com

LIMESTONE LANDSCAPE

ONE OF BRITAIN'S BEST-LOVED LANDSCAPES, the Yorkshire Dales stretch across northwest Yorkshire and into Cumbria. Collectively, these dales – from the Norse for valleys – make up the vast and glorious Yorkshire Dales National Park. There are around 40 dales to explore via footpaths, cycle ways and the tiny roads that wind their way through this pastoral upland region of limestone hills and glacier-carved river valleys. Most of the valleys here take their names from the rivers that run through them, such as Wharfedale, which is named after the River Wharfe.

Summer sees the national park at its most beautiful, when the sloping fields are at their brightest green and the rustic, grey, dry-stone walls march over the steep hills. Under the sun's golden glow, sheep and cattle graze contentedly in pastures that are dotted with charming old stone barns. Elsewhere the upland hay meadows are cleared of livestock, allowing them to burst spectacularly into flower from June through to July. The wild flowers provide a colourful habitat for a wide variety of animals, insects and nesting birds, and include dozens of traditional British plant species, such as pignut, lady's mantle, meadow buttercup, wood cranesbill and globeflower.

The Yorkshire Dales also contain vast stretches of moorland, at its best in August when the heather covering it is in full bloom, creating a sea of colour. This is prime bird-watching country; the merlin – Britain's smallest bird of prey – can be seen here, as can other raptors, such as peregrines, kestrels and buzzards. Look out for golden plovers, lapwings and yellow wagtails too.

The national park's most celebrated features are its dramatic limestone landscapes. Aysgarth Falls in Wensleydale is a series of broad limestone steps in the river that create a stunning scenic waterfall. At Malham Cove, a massive, sheer white cliff towers over the head of the valley. It is topped by limestone pavement, a natural feature in which rainwater etches deep fissures, called grykes. Nearby Gordale Scar is a rugged ravine that boasts two cascading waterfalls. There's a weird and wonderful landscape below the Dales too; don't miss an opportunity for an unforgettable underground adventure.

Main: Network of dry stone walls running over the Dales
Below (left to right): Hikers following a footpath alongside a dry-stone wall, caver abseiling down a gorge at Alum Pot cave system; hawthorn tree on the Dales' limestone pavement

THE ESSENTIALS

GETTING THERE AND AROUND
Arundel is in West Sussex, in the southeast of England. The nearest airport is London Gatwick, 45 km (28 miles) away. Regular trains take 90 minutes to travel from London Victoria to Arundel, and buses run between Arundel and Brighton. The castle is a 10-minute walk from the train station.

WEATHER
In summer the weather in Arundel is generally pleasant, with long days and average daytime temperatures of 14–21°C. However, always prepare for rain and changeable weather.

ACCOMMODATION
Splashing Out Live like a lord at the sumptuous, 900-year-old Amberley Castle, just north of Arundel, and watch the portcullis being lowered at midnight.
www.amberleycastle.co.uk

On a Budget Bonnie's Boutique in Binsted, 5 km (3 miles) outside Arundel has three B&B suites with a spacious garden, heated swimming pool and snooker room.
www.bonniesboutique.net

EATING OUT
Splashing Out The Town House, in Arundel High Street, has spectacular views of the castle and boasts a top-tier menu.
www.thetownhouse.co.uk

On a Budget The Bay Tree, in Tarrant Street, is an excellent family-owned restaurant with a winning British and European menu.
www.thebaytreearundel.co.uk

PRICE FOR TWO PEOPLE
£160–210 a day for accommodation, food and entrance fees.

WEBSITES
www.arundel.org.uk
www.arundelmuseum.org

Main: Arundel Castle overlooking the River Arun
Right (top to bottom): Town buildings overlooking the Arun; aerial view of the castle and grounds

JEWEL OF THE SOUTH

THE CRENELLATED MEDIEVAL FORM OF ARUNDEL CASTLE, historic seat of the dukes of Norfolk, sits picturesquely on a hilltop in the South Downs. It towers above the charming West Sussex market town of Arundel and the winding River Arun. The river historically served as a vital link to the sea, and for centuries the town was a flourishing port. Wandering through Arundel's attractively cobbled streets and antique shops is a day out in itself, but it is the dominating presence of the castle that draws visitors to this historic town. Although its foundations originally date to Norman times, the castle has evolved dramatically during its 950-year existence. A combination of disrepair, fire and wartime damage, compensated for with extravagant restoration and lavish embellishments over the centuries, has resulted in the majestic building that we see today.

Climb the castle's keep for simply stunning views of the South Downs, and look out for marks on the walls caused by cannonballs fired during the English Civil War. Admire the magnificent collections of armour, paintings (including works by Van Dyck), china, tapestries and furniture on display, and allow time to wander around the fine gardens. Overflowing with heritage and history, the castle also has a gaggle of ghosts, obligatory perhaps for a bastion with this pedigree. Past dukes of Norfolk lie interred in the Fitzalan Chapel, located within the

FURTHER DETAILS

ARUNDEL

Arundel Castle
High Street, Arundel, West Sussex; open Apr–Oct only, Tue–Sun: castle rooms noon–5pm; castle keep 11am–4:30pm; Fitzalan Chapel, gardens and grounds 10am–5pm. Guided tours (75 minutes) run prior to the opening of the castle to the public, from 10:30am to 11:45am; advance booking is essential.
www.arundelcastle.org

Arundel Cathedral
London Road; open 9am–6pm daily.
www.arundelcathedral.net

Carpet of Flowers Festival
Arundel Cathedral celebrates the Catholic feast of Corpus Christi with a carpet of flowers and a procession from the cathedral to the castle. Corpus Christi falls on a Thursday between late May and the middle of June (depending on the date of Easter).
www.arundelcathedral.net

Arundel Festival
Runs for around 10 days in late August.
www.arundelfestival.co.uk

WHAT ELSE TO SEE AND DO

Petworth House and Park
Petworth House is a magnificent 17th-century mansion famed for its lavish collection of art, including works by Turner, Bosch and Titian. The house sits in 280 hectares (700 acres) of parkland landscaped by "Capability" Brown – England's most famous landscape gardener.
www.nationaltrust.org.uk

Bignor Roman Villa
Arundel has a few relics from the Roman era, but nothing compared to the excellently preserved Roman mosaics from the 3rd century AD at this celebrated heritage site in Bignor, 10 km (6 miles) north of Arundel. No buses run here, so you will need either your own car or a taxi.
www.bignorromanvilla.co.uk

Below: "Carpet of Flowers" in Arundel Cathedral

castle grounds. This Catholic chapel is attached to, but not part of, the Anglican Church of St Nicholas; an unusual arrangement that allowed, albeit somewhat dangerously, the Catholic dukes to observe their faith in Protestant England during the Reformation.

Summer is without doubt the perfect season to visit: the beaches at Littlehampton and Worthing, or Brighton and Hove further east, are not far away, and the town of Arundel celebrates two of its most popular and spectacular events. The renowned "Carpet of Flowers" festival takes place at Arundel Cathedral in late May or early June. The cathedral itself is a huge, awe-inspiring edifice in the Neo-French Gothic style, dating back to 1873. Its distinctive annual festival celebrates the Catholic festival of Corpus Christi, when a floral "carpet" – comprising more than 15,000 blooms – is laid out in a pattern, stretching 27 m (90 ft) along the main aisle of the cathedral, to be trampled underfoot during mass. The Arundel Festival takes place later in the summer, towards the end of August, when the castle and town play hosts to top performers from the worlds of theatre, dance and music.

FESTIVAL OF SONG

THE SMALL WELSH TOWN OF LLANGOLLEN becomes a whirl of colour for one week every July. Take a stroll up the main street and you may encounter African dance troupes in bright, flowing kaftans; women's choral groups from Eastern Europe, resplendent in their richly embroidered tunics; and, from closer to home, members of traditional Welsh male-voice choirs walking proudly in their immaculate, navy-blue blazers. All are in town for the International Eisteddfod, one of Europe's largest multicultural musical events. Every year, children and adults from more than 50 countries descend on Llangollen's festival field to compete in a range of choral and musical disciplines. Many of the competitors, from solo instrumentalists to folk-dance groups and barbershop quartets, remain in their national dress throughout the festival, which begins with the colourful opening pageant. Witnessing this uplifting and joyful celebration of choral music in this small Welsh town feels like stumbling upon hidden treasure.

The first Eisteddfod was held in Cardigan Castle in 1176, when Lord Rhys invited poets and musicians from all around Wales to perform there. The National Eisteddfod continues this tradition, but Llangollen takes a more global approach. Since 1947 it has been hosting the International Eisteddfod, bringing together national folk traditions from all around the world. It was the brainchild of Harold Tudor, a journalist from nearby Wrexham who wanted to promote

THE ESSENTIALS

GETTING THERE AND AROUND
Llangollen is in northeast Wales, about 20 km (13 miles) southwest of Wrexham. The nearest airports are at Liverpool and Manchester, 82 km (51 miles) and 91 km (57 miles) away respectively. The nearest rail station is Ruabon, 8 km (5 miles) from Llangollen, with direct services to Birmingham and Cardiff; buses run from the station to Llangollen. The festival site is within easy walking distance of the town centre.

WEATHER
Llangollen enjoys a mild summer climate, but be prepared for rain and mountain breezes. Average daytime temperatures range from 14 to 17°C.

ACCOMMODATION
Splashing Out The Wild Pheasant, in Llangollen, is housed in a quaint 19th-century building but boasts a modern luxury wing and spa.
www.wildpheasanthotel.co.uk

On a Budget Plas Hafod, in Llangollen, is a friendly B&B in a Victorian house with great views over the vale of Llangollen.
www.plas-hafod.co.uk

EATING OUT
Splashing Out The Corn Mill, in Llangollen, is an acclaimed gastropub in an old watermill on the River Dee.
www.brunningandprice.co.uk/cornmill

On a Budget Gales, also in Llangollen, is an established favourite, serving delicious, simple home-cooked food in a wood-panelled wine bar.
www.galesofllangollen.co.uk

PRICE FOR TWO PEOPLE
Around £150 a day for accommodation, food and entrance fees.

WEBSITES
www.llangollen.com

Previous page: Dovedale, in Derbyshire's Peak District National Park

Main: The International Eisteddfod's lively opening pageant **Below (top to bottom):** Llangollen railway station; male-voice choir performing at the International Eisteddfod; horse-drawn barge on the Llangollen Canal

reconciliation and mutual cultural understanding within postwar Europe. The inaugural event featured only a handful of choirs, with one group, from Hungary, hitchhiking across Europe to attend. Today, some 4,000 competitors and 50,000 spectators converge on Llangollen every summer.

The focus of the Eisteddfod rests on the Royal International Pavilion. A series of concerts takes place there during the evenings, but it is the pavilion's daytime competitions that really create excitement. The standard of performers is high and an eclectic mix of world-class acts are attracted here, such as Bryn Terfel, Joan Baez, José Carreras and Katherine Jenkins. You may be lucky enough to discover choral music's next big thing – in 1955, the then-unknown opera supremo Luciano Pavarotti experienced his first musical success here, as part of a male-voice choir. His concert in 1995 is still fondly remembered. But remember that potential stars are just as likely to appear on the festival field as in the pavilion, so take time to simply wander and enjoy the multicultural delights.

The contests culminate in the Choir of the World, a sing-off between all the winning choirs on the Saturday night, and the winners receive the Pavarotti Trophy, named after the Eisteddfod's most eminent supporter.

FURTHER DETAILS

EISTEDDFOD FESTIVALS
International Eisteddfod
Royal International Pavilion, Abbey Road, Llangollen; Tue–Sun in the second week of July.
www.international-eisteddfod.co.uk

National Eisteddfod
The Eisteddfod takes place in the first week of August; the venue changes each year *(see website for details)*.
www.eisteddfod.org.uk

WHAT ELSE TO SEE AND DO
Plas Newydd
The "Ladies of Llangollen" were a pair of eccentric spinsters who turned their backs on their Anglo–Irish aristocratic background and took up residence together at Plas Newydd, near Llangollen. In the early 1800s the couple – Lady Eleanor Butler and Miss Sarah Ponsonby – were the toast of society. Their elegant Gothic house, with its formal gardens and woodland walk, now houses a small museum about the ladies and Regency society.
www.nationaltrust.org.uk

Horse-drawn Canal Trips
Llangollen Wharf is the departure point for horse-drawn boat trips along the beautiful Llangollen Canal. The quiet waterway – now a UNESCO World Heritage Site – offers the most relaxing way of travelling through the stunning Welsh mountains. The 45-minute cruises depart every half-hour during school holidays; every hour at other times. Two-hour cruises are also on offer.
www.horsedrawnboats.co.uk

Llangollen Railway
One of Britain's most scenic heritage lines, the Llangollen Railway runs steam and preserved-diesel trains through the beautiful Dee Valley, from Llangollen to Corwen. The timetable changes throughout the year, and the railway offers special events such as family days and murder-mystery tours.
www.llangollen-railway.co.uk

Angling on the River Dee
Llangollen Maelor Angling controls a 16-km (10-mile) stretch of the River Dee in and around Llangollen. The Dee is particularly renowned for salmon, brown trout and grayling.
www.llangollen-maelor-angling.com

Below: Plas Newydd, home of the "Ladies of Llangollen"

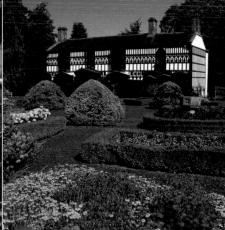

THE ESSENTIALS

GETTING THERE AND AROUND
The Lulworth Ranges are in Dorset, in the southwest of England. The nearest airport is at Bournemouth, 40 km (25 miles) away. The nearest train station is at Wool (on the Dorchester/ Poole line), 8 km (5 miles) away; buses run from Wool to Lulworth Cove. Please note that roads in the ranges are restricted during live firing exercises – telephone 01929 404819 for the latest information.

WEATHER
The summer climate in Dorset is pleasant and mild, with average daytime temperatures ranging from 14 to 17°C.

ACCOMMODATION
Splashing Out Mortons House Hotel, in Corfe Castle, 8 km (5 miles) from Kimmeridge Bay, is a very pretty 16th-century manor house converted into an award-winning luxury hotel.
www.mortonshouse.co.uk

On a Budget Cove House B&B, in West Lulworth, is a converted Victorian house with spacious rooms and amiable owners.
www.covehouse.net

EATING OUT
Splashing Out The restaurant at Mortons House Hotel, in Corfe Castle, spices up classic British ingredients with modern fusion flavours – but also serves up a traditional Sunday lunch.
www.mortonshouse.co.uk

On a Budget Lulworth Cove Inn, in West Lulworth, offers dependably flavoursome seafood and shellfish dishes.
www.lulworth-cove.co.uk

PRICE FOR TWO PEOPLE
From around £105 a day for accommodation, food and entrance fees.

WEBSITE
www.lulworthonline.co.uk

THE JURASSIC COAST

ONE OF ENGLAND'S FINEST SECTIONS OF COASTLINE, Dorset's Lulworth Ranges run from Kimmeridge Bay in the east to Lulworth Cove in the west. They offer spectacular hikes but are also home to firing ranges for the British army, so plan a visit when the paths are open and artillery practice has been put on hold. It's worth the wait – the stunning views from this heathland path include sweeping bays and rugged, folding white cliffs. The absorbing cliff-side limestone geology and beauty of the Jurassic Coast has resulted in the Ranges being designated a UNESCO World Heritage Site and Area of Outstanding Natural Beauty (AONB). It's no walk in the park, however, and the cresting and falling path can be demanding in sections.

Before setting off, visit the Lulworth Heritage Centre, which has lots of useful information on the area and its geology. Then make your way to Lulworth Cove, a scenic, horseshoe-shaped bay formed over the millennia by persistent waves. The nearby Stair Hole is a cove-in-the-making where you can see "Lulworth Crumple" – the distinctive folded rock found in this area. A further geological marvel is the Fossil Forest, east of Lulworth Cove: weird, ring-shaped formations in the rock that are the 145-million-year-old petrified remains of Jurassic treetrunks.

A string of bays unfurls along the coast east of Lulworth Cove, including Mupe Bay and Arish Mell. Mupe Bay is overlooked by Bindon Hill (said to be haunted by a spectral Roman army), while Arish Mell, further east, is a pretty, sheltered cove. Beyond this lies the ancient Iron Age hill fort and earthen burial mound of Flower's Barrow. To the east of Tyneham Village, the dark Jurassic shale layers of Kimmeridge Bay are worth exploring – there are thousands of amazing fossils embedded in the local rock. There is also an excellent marine wildlife reserve in the bay. The three-storey Clavell Tower, just to the east above the bay, was built in 1830 as a folly; in 2006, the tower was moved 25 m (82 ft) back from the crumbling cliff to stop it from pitching into the sea. The exhilarating views, archaeological treasures and potential fossil finds make the Lulworth Ranges one of the most exciting places to walk in summer.

Main: "Lulworth Crumple" rock strata at Stair Hole
Below: Clavell Tower on the clifftops overlooking Kimmeridge Bay

FURTHER DETAILS

LULWORTH RANGES
The Lulworth Ranges are live-ammunition training grounds used by the army, so it is essential to coincide with opening times to the public: late-Jul–Aug daily, plus most weekends, school holidays and Bank Holidays. Red flags indicate that the firing range is in use. Do not stray away from the path.
www.gov.uk

Lulworth Visitor Centre
Lulworth Cove; open from 10am daily.
www.lulworth.com

Purbeck Marine Wildlife Reserve
Kimmeridge Bay; open Apr–Sep: 10:30am–5pm Tue–Sun; Oct–Mar: 12–4pm weekends and school holidays.
www.dorsetwildlifetrust.org.uk

WHAT ELSE TO SEE AND DO
Durdle Door
A few miles west along the coast from West Lulworth, this well-known and iconic limestone arch is a geological highlight of the Jurassic Coast.

Corfe Castle
Magical castle ruins to explore, not far from Kimmeridge, with engaging exhibitions, activities and family trails based on the castle's turbulent past.
www.nationaltrust.org.uk

Below (top to bottom): Tranquil Lulworth Cove; Durdle Door arched rock formation in Durdle Bay

THE ESSENTIALS

GETTING THERE AND AROUND
The Irish National Heritage Park is 5 km (3 miles) west of Wexford on the N11, and is best reached by car. The nearest airport to Wexford is Waterford, 50 km (30 miles) to the west, with flights from the UK. The nearest international airport is at Dublin, 140 km (85 miles) north.

WEATHER
Summer is the best time to visit County Wexford, with average daytime temperatures of 13–18°C, though as always in Ireland, be prepared for rain.

ACCOMMODATION
Splashing Out The Ferrycarrig Hotel is a 4-star choice with stunning views across the River Slaney, and is very close to the Heritage Park.
www.ferrycarrighotel.ie

On a Budget Maple Lodge is a simple but excellent family-run B&B in a period home 5 km (3 miles) from Wexford.
www.mapleludgewexford.com

EATING OUT
Splashing Out La Cote is one of Wexford's top dining establishments, with daily fish specials and seasonal menus.
www.lacote.ie

On a Budget Simon Lambert & Sons, in Wexford, is a good-value gastropub; with an excellent breakfast and lunch menu and home-brewed beer on tap.
www.simonlambertandsons.ie

PRICE FOR A FAMILY OF FOUR
From €190 a day for entrance fees, food and accommodation.

WEBSITE
www.visitwexford.ie

Main: Reconstruction of a *crannog*, or island settlement, built in the middle of a lake at the Irish National Heritage Park
Right (top to bottom): Replica of a dolmen, or portal tomb; Celtic cross painted with Biblical images

A JOURNEY TO THE PAST

IRELAND IS AN ANCIENT LAND, and traces of its early inhabitants are scattered across the green hills like snapshots of history. Here, a massive dolmen (stone tomb) stands guard in a lonely field; there, a grassy mound marks a prehistoric burial site. It can sometimes be hard to understand the character of the people who built them, and how they must have lived.

The Irish National Heritage Park is like a time-trail into this past. Spread out through reclaimed marsh and woodlands, 9,000 years of history are displayed in a series of reconstructed dwellings. First you come across a Stone Age hut, its sapling frame covered in earth and animal skins. Next is an early Irish farmstead with conical, thatched houses and animal shelters. As you enter the dark, smoky interiors you start to imagine what life was like in these ancient abodes. Costumed guides are on hand to demonstrate how people cooked and what they ate.

The park is an educational experience for young children and history buffs alike. You can explore a Neolithic dolmen, see inside a Bronze Age *cist* (a stone-built, box-shaped grave) and stand within one of the mysterious stone circles that seem to watch over these ancient tombs.

FURTHER DETAILS

IRISH NATIONAL HERITAGE PARK
Ferrycarrig, County Wexford; open May–Aug: 9:30am–
6:30pm daily; Sep–Apr: 9:30am–5:30pm daily.
www.inhp.com

WHAT ELSE TO SEE AND DO

Wexford
Take a stroll through this attractive harbour town
founded by the Vikings. Explore its medieval lanes,
ruined Selskar Abbey, 18th-century Commarket and the
West Gate Tower from the old city walls.
www.visitwexford.ie

Kilmore Quay
This picturesque little village with its thatched cottages
is one of the main fishing ports in southeast Ireland.
June and July are good months to take a boat trip
to the Saltee Islands – one of Ireland's largest bird
sanctuaries, home to thousands of cormorants, puffins,
gannets and other birds, as well as seals. A boat trip
from Kilmore Quay Marina with Kilmore Quay Angling
Charter identifies local wildlife.
Kilmore Quay Angling Charter tel: 087 983 2996
www.visitkilmorequay.com

Wexford Wildfowl Reserve
In summer, wading birds and birds of prey can be
seen at this reserve, located on the mudflats, or
"slobs", 5 km (3 miles) northeast of Wexford town.
www.wexfordwildfowlreserve.ie

Curracloe Beach
The closest place to spread your beach towel on a
sunny day is beyond the mudflats, 10 km (6 miles)
northeast of Wexford town. The opening scenes of
Steven Spielberg's war film *Saving Private Ryan*
were filmed here.

Below (top to bottom): Gannet colony at Great Saltee
Island; Kilmore Quay harbour, the starting point for
many boat trips to the Saltee Islands

Each turn in the woods brings you into another era. Children love the Celtic ring
fort with its timber stockade and secret underground passage. The brightly
coloured Celtic cross at the monastic settlement may come as a surprise, but this is
how the weathered high crosses originally looked. Nearby is the drying kiln and
water mill that the monks used to grind grain.

Perhaps the most striking homestead is the *crannog*, a medieval settlement
located on a man-made island in a reedy lake. You can also explore a Viking ship
and walled household, and an early Norman feudal castle, the whitewashed façade
of which makes a gleaming contrast to the rare stone ruins that are left in Ireland
today. Each dwelling is recreated in fantastic detail.

The Irish National Heritage Park really comes to life on summer weekends when
living history events are enacted throughout the grounds. A deeper understanding
of so many of Ireland's ancient heritage sites awaits you amid this lush and
pleasant Wexford countryside.

EXPLORING EXMOOR

S TRADDLING THE NORTH COAST OF SOMERSET AND DEVON, Exmoor National Park can present very different faces. The high moors evoke a bleak and haunting beauty when the mists roll in from the sea, while sunshine exposes a timeless rural idyll of green hillside pastures, divided by dry-stone walls and solitary farms that date back as far as the 11th century. In summer, you can cross fallow fields knee-deep in sun-burnished grass and wild flowers, and hike through the forested valleys of the rivers Exe and Barle, before cooling your feet in clear rushing water beside the stone arches of a packhorse bridge.

Though it covers just 692 sq km (267 sq miles), Exmoor is criss-crossed by more than 1,000 km (621 miles) of footpaths and bridleways. The park is also popular with cyclists, who can often be seen pedalling en masse up to Dunkery Beacon – Exmoor's highest point at 520 m (1,705 ft) – where there are sweeping views over the heather-covered moors to the sea. Here, and on the moor near Simonsbath to the west, you are likely to see wild Exmoor ponies, a rare and ancient breed that roams free in the park. England's only wild herd of red deer lives

THE ESSENTIALS

GETTING THERE AND AROUND
Exmoor National Park is in southwest England on the north coast of Somerset and Devon, around 48 km (30 miles) north of Exeter. The closest major airport is Bristol, 50 km (31 miles) northeast of the Exmoor boundary. The best way to explore the region is on foot or by bicycle, but a car is also recommended for more remote areas. There are buses between the main Exmoor villages.

WEATHER
Exmoor has a temperate climate and is warmest during the summer months, with average daytime temperatures ranging from 15 to 17°C.

ACCOMMODATION
Splashing Out The Luttrell Arms, in Dunster, is a small and atmospheric hotel in a 15th-century building with an excellent bar and restaurant.
www.luttrellarms.co.uk

On a Budget Town Mills, in the beautiful Exmoor town of Dulverton, is a charming converted millhouse.
www.townmillsdulverton.co.uk

EATING OUT
Splashing Out The Royal Oak Inn, in Luxborough, has several dining rooms that all share the same tasty menu, which includes unusual and innovative dishes.
www.theroyaloakinnluxborough.co.uk

On a Budget Cobblestones, in Dunster, is an old-fashioned restaurant with friendly staff. It boasts a fantastic menu and reasonable prices.
www.cobblestonesofdunster.co.uk

PRICE FOR TWO PEOPLE
Around £170 a day for food and accommodation.

WEBSITE
www.visit-exmoor.co.uk

In summer, you can cross fallow fields knee-deep in sun-burnished grass and wild flowers, and hike through the forested valleys.

here too, numbering several thousand. Keep an eye out for their fawns, which are born in early summer.

Charming villages and hamlets with quaint churches and cosy pubs are scattered throughout the park. Favourite beauty spots include Selworthy, with its thatched cottages and whitewashed church, and Allerford with its double-arched packhorse bridge. Exford, in the heart of the park, is a stag-hunting centre; packs of dogs and horses are a common sight in this pretty village around the River Exe. Nearby Winsford is a collection of thatched cottages, pubs and picturesque bridges.

A handful of larger villages form the main tourist hubs. Dulverton is the starting point for fine walks along the River Barle. Overlooked by its turreted castle, Dunster is a lovely medieval wool-exporting village with an octagonal Yarn Market in the high street. There are more thatched cottages and an ancient parish church at Porlock, perhaps the most attractive village on the north coast. Lastly, perched on a high cliff, the Victorian resort of Lynton affords fine views over the beach at Lynmouth below, and across the Bristol Channel to Wales.

FURTHER DETAILS

EXMOOR NATIONAL PARK
The three main national park centres at Dulverton, Dunster and Lynmouth offer maps, trail guides, details of local events and information about the park.
www.exmoor-nationalpark.gov.uk

Dulverton National Park Centre
Fore Street; open 10am–2pm Mon–Wed, Fri & Sat.

Dunster National Park Centre
Dunster Steep; open 10am–2pm Sat & Sun.

Lynmouth National Park Centre
The Esplanade; open 10am–5pm daily.

WHAT ELSE TO SEE AND DO
Dunster Castle
A 13th-century gateway leads to this romantic fortress in Dunster, set on a hill with terraced gardens and splendid views over Exmoor and the Bristol Channel. It was the seat of the aristocratic Luttrell family for nearly 600 years.
www.nationaltrust.org.uk

Coleridge Cottage
Samuel Taylor Coleridge wrote *The Rime of the Ancient Mariner* and other works while living here in 1797–9. His cottage is on the Coleridge Way, a 58-km (36-mile) footpath named in his honour, and visitors can view the parlour, reading room and a collection of personal mementoes.
www.nationaltrust.org.uk

The Cliff Railway
Take a delightful ride on the Cliff Railway, a remarkable Victorian hydraulic cable car that is powered by counter-balanced water tanks. It has been transporting passengers between the clifftop resort of Lynton and the beach at Lynmouth since 1890.
www.cliffrailwaylynton.co.uk

Outdoor Activities
Exmoor has an abundance of varied terrain that is suitable for all manner of outdoor pursuits, including hiking, fishing and mountain biking. You can also learn to canoe and windsurf on the reservoir at Wimbleball Lake.
www.visit-exmoor.co.uk

Main: Typical Exmoor cottage by the double-arched packhorse bridge in Allerford
Left (top to bottom): Yarn Market in Dunster; mountain bikers cycling past gorse bushes
Above: Wild ponies grazing on Exmoor

Below: Rolling Exmoor countryside

THE ESSENTIALS

GETTING THERE AND AROUND
Mull is an island in the Inner Hebrides, off the coast of northwest Scotland. The main ferry route (with a journey time of 45 minutes) operates from Oban on the mainland to Craignure on Mull. There are also ferries from Lochaline to Fishnish (taking 15 minutes) and Kilchoan to Tobermory (taking 35 minutes). There are buses, taxis and car hire available on Mull.

WEATHER
Summer weather on Mull is mild, with daytime temperatures of 15–23°C, but strong winds and choppy seas are normal. Weatherproof clothing is essential.

ACCOMMODATION
Splashing Out Glengorm Castle, near Tobermory, offers luxury B&B rooms in a stunning family-owned mansion.
www.glengormcastle.co.uk

On a Budget Tobermory Youth Hostel, in Tobermory, has cheap dormitory accommodation and also offers private and family rooms.
www.syha.org.uk

EATING OUT
Splashing Out Highland Cottage, in Tobermory, offers exceptional gourmet food in an elegant setting. Book in advance.
www.highlandcottage.co.uk

On a Budget Fisherman's Pier Chip Van, in Tobermory, is legendary for its fantastic fresh-fried fish and chips to take away.
www.tobermoryfishandchipvan.co.uk

PRICE FOR TWO PEOPLE
£190 a day for accommodation, food, trips and entrance fees.

WEBSITES
www.visitscotland.com
www.tobermory.co.uk

Main: Minke whale, a regular visitor to the waters around Mull
Right (top to bottom): Colourful façades on the harbour-front in Tobermory, Mull; puffin colony

A WHALE OF A TIME

I T'S IMPOSSIBLE TO DECIDE which of Scotland's many islands is the most enchanting. Mull, with its miles of heather moorland, azure seas and picture-postcard villages, is definitely a strong contender. But Mull is more than just a pretty face. Its hinterland and its waters are home to a vast array of wildlife, making it a nature-lover's paradise in the summer months.

Sea eagles soar above a rugged coastline where crags and rocky headlands are interspersed with coves of pristine white sand. Otters, recovering their numbers after decades of decline, patrol its silver streams and rock pools. Inquisitive seals pop their heads up as if to greet passing boats, or loll on seaweed-covered rocks at low tide. The waters around Mull and its smaller sister islands are also the home of permanent populations of bottlenose dolphins and harbour porpoises, and blooms of plankton attract huge, ponderous basking sharks – a little scary at first sight, but completely harmless. With a bit of luck and determination, you may be able to view many of these species on even a short visit to Mull. Stay for a week in summer, and it's almost guaranteed that you'll encounter one or more of these amazing creatures. However, it's another summer visitor that can make a trip to this island very special. Huge minke whales – which can reach up to 11 m (36 ft) in length – are drawn to the west coast of

FURTHER DETAILS

MULL WILDLIFE

Wildlife Cruises
Sea Life Surveys offer 6-hour day cruises that visit the
best areas to see whales, dolphins, porpoises, sharks,
seals and a variety of sea birds. Day cruises depart from
Tobermory Apr–Oct, 9:30am daily; shorter boat trips are
also available year-round.
www.sealifesurveys.com

Overland Expeditions
Wild About Mull, in Pennyghael, offers minibus tours of
the island, led by naturalists who know the best wildlife
sites. www.wildaboutmull.co.uk

WHAT ELSE TO SEE AND DO

Torosay Castle
This Victorian mansion is closed to visitors but the
beautiful gardens are occasionally open to the public.
The Japanese garden, with its spectacular sea views, is
particularly impressive.

Duart Castle
The ancestral seat of the Maclean clan – one of the
most powerful families on Mull – was built near
Lochdon, on Mull, in the 13th century. You can explore
both the evocative castle and its grounds.
www.duartcastle.com

Below (top to bottom): European otters play on seaweed
along Mull's beaches; white shell-sand of west-coast beaches

Scotland by the nutrient-rich waters that well up from the Atlantic depths. In the
summer months, it's possible to sight minke whales up to half-a-dozen times a
day. Despite suffering centuries of whaling, the whales can be surprisingly
fearless, swimming right up to small boats before rolling over to pass beneath.
More commonly, they can be spotted as they breach, or surface, blasting out a
spume of spray as they exhale before sliding back below the waves.

Minke are not the only whales seen in these waters. orcas (killer whales) are
also spotted occasionally in summer. Humpback whales have also been recorded,
and there has been at least one sighting of a fin whale – second only in size to
the blue whale – in recent years. Look out, too, for sea birds such as puffins,
razorbills, shearwaters and kittiwakes. They prey on the same shoals of fish that
feed the minke, so large flocks may indicate the presence of whales.

Mull has a thriving wildlife industry, with many companies offering day trips
– and sometimes longer cruises – from various points on the island. There are
also overland tours that allow you the chance to see such rare sights as golden
eagles, red deer and adders. A day out in Mull offers plenty of potential thrills:
you just have to keep your eyes wide open.

CASTLES AND COASTLINE

With its lush green valleys and windswept mountains, South Wales is rich in natural beauty. There are few sights that beat the sunset at Rhossili, on the Gower Peninsula, or the rugged coastline of Cardigan Bay. But this ancient land has man-made wonders too: a string of grey-stone castles that stud the countryside like uncut gems. Some are crumbling ruins, providing a picturesque backdrop for family picnics and endless opportunities for games of hide and seek. Others look much as they did when they were first built – historic treasure troves ringed with battlements and containing grand halls and mighty towers. All have their own unique and compelling story to tell.

Chepstow Castle is particularly dramatic. Stunningly situated above the River Wye, on the border with England, it is a brooding reminder of a turbulent past. Built by the Normans in 1067 just after the Conquest, it was the first stone castle in Britain – a strategic base for aggressive raids into Wales. Then there's Caerphilly, a little town dominated by an imposing castle. Built in the 13th century, the castle was a medieval masterpiece of military engineering, with impenetrable walls and formidable water defences. Cardiff Castle, by contrast, is noted for its flamboyant 19th-century interiors, created for the eccentric Marquis of Bute by William Burgess. Its rooms are a Neo-Gothic fantasy of gilded ceilings, mirrors and elaborate carvings.

Travellers with an artistic streak will love the romantic ruins of Laugharne Castle, a favourite of the poet Dylan Thomas, while families with budding young historians might prefer Pembroke Castle. Founded by one of William the Conqueror's most trusted lords, and the birthplace of Henry VII, it is often used for energetic re-enactments of historic events.

Perhaps the most striking sight of all is Carreg Cennen Castle, in rural Carmarthenshire. The castle is perched precariously on a crag above the River Cennen, and legend has it that one of King Arthur's knights lies asleep deep beneath it, ready to awaken when Wales is in peril.

THE ESSENTIALS

GETTING THERE AND AROUND
South Wales lies on the western coast of Britain and shares a border with England. Cardiff International Airport is 23 km (14 miles) from Cardiff; there are direct train connections from Cardiff to London, Birmingham and Manchester. South Wales's castles are best reached by car; most are located within a couple of hours' drive of Cardiff.

WEATHER
In summer the weather in South Wales is generally pleasant, with daytime temperatures averaging 17–22°C. You should be prepared for rain too.

ACCOMMODATION
Splashing Out St David's Hotel and Spa, in Cardiff, is a luxury option and a favourite with visiting celebrities. *www.thestdavidshotel.com*

On a Budget The Glynhir Estate, in Carmarthenshire, offers B&B and self-catering options and is ideally situated for visiting the coastal castles of Dinefwr and Carreg Cennen. *www.theglynhirestate.com*

EATING OUT
Splashing Out
Le Monde, in Cardiff, is as dark as a dive bar but has the best fish in the city. The sea bass in rock salt is a house speciality. *www.le-monde.co.uk*

On a Budget The Greendown Inn, in St-Georges-Sur-Ely near Cardiff, is a friendly inn that serves simple local fare, including home-made beef pie. *www.greendownhotel.com*

PRICE FOR A FAMILY OF FOUR
£295–315 a day for accommodation, food, transport and entrance fees.

WEBSITE
www.visitwales.com

Main: Visitors in the grounds of the impressive Laugharne Castle in Carmarthenshire
Below: Cardigan Island, lying in Cardigan Bay

FURTHER DETAILS

CASTLES OF SOUTH WALES

Chepstow Castle
Bridge Street, Chepstow, Monmouthshire;
open Mar–Jun & Sep–Oct: 9:30am–5pm daily;
Jul–Aug: 9:30am–6pm daily; Nov–Feb: 10am–4pm
Mon–Sat, 11am–4pm Sun. *www.cadw.gov.wales*

Caerphilly Castle
Caerphilly; open Mar–Jun & Sep–Oct: 9:30am–5pm
daily; Jul–Aug: 9:30am–6pm daily; Nov–Feb:
10am–4pm Mon–Sat, 11am–4pm Sun.
www.cadw.gov.wales

Cardiff Castle
Castle Street, Cardiff; open Mar–Oct: 9am 6pm daily;
Nov–Feb: 9am–5pm daily. *www.cardiffcastle.com*

Laugharne Castle
King Street, Laugharne, Carmarthenshire;
open Apr–Oct: 10am–5pm daily. *www.cadw.gov.wales*

Carreg Cennen Castle
Llandeilo, Carmarthenshire; open Mar–Oct: 9:30am–
5:30pm daily; Nov–Feb: 9:30am–4pm daily.
www.carregcennencastle.com

WHAT ELSE TO SEE AND DO

Cardiff
In Cardiff, the lively Welsh capital, you can take a tour
of the Millennium Stadium, visit the Welsh Millennium
Centre – a stunningly modern centre for the arts – or
head to St Fagans National History Museum. The huge
variety of theatres, galleries and nightspots provides a
welcome contrast to the region's historical architecture.
www.visitcardiff.com

Swansea and the Gower Peninsula
Try the famous cockles with vinegar and pepper
at Swansea Market, or savour an ice cream in the
Mumbles – a large village just outside of Swansea,
where you can also view the ruins of yet another castle,
Oystermouth. The nearby Gower Peninsula offers
beautiful scenery and spectacular sunsets over Rhossili
Bay from its headland, which is known as Worm's Head.
www.swansea.gov.uk

Llanelli Wetland Centre
Stretching over 180 hectares (450 acres) on the
Burry Inlet, this magnificent mosaic of lakes, pools
and lagoons is home to countless wild species, from
dragonflies to egrets.
www.wwt.org.uk

Below: Great Hall of Caerphilly Castle

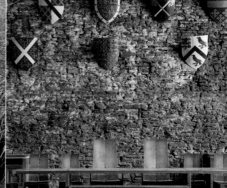

THE ESSENTIALS

GETTING THERE AND AROUND
The Cheshire Ring is located in northwest England, near Manchester, Stoke-on-Trent and Northwich. Manchester Airport is within half an hour's drive of the canals. Railway stations close to boatyards include Manchester Piccadilly, Macclesfield, Sandbach and Northwich.

WEATHER
At the height of summer, Cheshire can be pleasantly warm and dry (13–17°C), but be prepared for rain.

ACCOMMODATION
Splashing Out The Place Hotel, in Manchester, provides comfortable and contemporary one and two-bedroom family apartments with kitchen and living room.
www.theplaceaparthotel.com

On a Budget Premier Inn Macclesfield South West is useful for a stopover at the beginning or end of your trip, with Macclesfield and boatyards nearby.
www.premierinn.com

EATING OUT
Splashing Out Sutton Hall Hotel, near the Macclesfield Canal, is a splendidly converted 16th-century manor house now run as a dining pub, with an interesting changing menu.
www.brunningandprice.co.uk

On a Budget Dukes 92, in Castlefield, provides real ales, pizzas and good bar food. Children are welcome until 8:30pm.
www.dukes92.com

PRICE FOR A FAMILY OF FOUR
Around £190–265 a day including boat hire and food.

WEBSITE
www.waterscape.com

Main: Narrowboat navigating the Bridgewater Canal at Walton
Right (top to bottom): Mills alongside the canal at Macclesfield; Anderton Boat Lift at Barnton, near Northwich

CANAL CRUISING

Taking to the water on Britain's historic canal network gloriously uncomplicates your lifestyle for a week or so, and in the heat of summer it can provide the perfect relaxation fix. One of the most diverse circular routes takes in six canals to form the 156-km (97-mile) Cheshire Ring, which is possible to navigate in about a week.

For families, this trip can be an unbeatable way of sharing the sheer pleasure of travel: the boat is your home, your kitchen, and your entire life, while the rest of the world glides effortlessly by. Added to that, it's a brilliant history lesson. Your children may be learning about the Industrial Revolution at school – here, they'll find out how travel was in the brief heyday of the canal, before the coming of the railways. They'll be helping to open and close the 92 locks, and older children can take a turn at steering the craft. You'll head through tunnels and under packhorse bridges, and there's always the towpath on hand to let off steam, on foot or by bicycle. If you start your journey on the lock-free Bridgewater Canal, you

FURTHER DETAILS

CHESHIRE RING
You do not need a licence to pilot a canal boat, and piloting is quickly learned. A full fuel tank is supplied at the start of the week and will easily last for the whole trip. It is often possible to take bicycles and pets on boats.
Blakes: *www.blakes.co.uk*
Claymoore Canal Holidays: *www.claymoore.co.uk*

Little Moreton Hall
Congleton. Cheshire's most iconic country house is considered to be one of the finest examples of English Tudor architecture. Built without foundations in 1450, and extensively added to over the following 120 years, it is spectacularly crooked, with barely a straight vertical line; open mid-Feb–Oct: 11am–5pm Wed–Sun; Nov–mid-Dec: 11am–4pm, Sat–Sun.

Museum of Science and Industry (MOSI)
Liverpool Road, Castlefield. The MOSI tells the fascinating story of Manchester's scientific and industrial past, present and future; open 10am–5pm daily.
www.msimanchester.org.uk

Manchester United Museum and Stadium Tour
Old Trafford, Sir Matt Busby Way. Manchester United's stadium, Old Trafford, famously called the "Theatre of Dreams", offers a perfect day out for supporters, and enough to see even for those who aren't football fans; open 9:30am–5pm Mon–Sat, 10am–4pm Sun.
www.manutd.com

Anderton Boat Lift
Lift Lane, Anderton, near Northwich; trips on the lift run daily in the summer months. Check the website for days of operation outside the summer season.
www.canalrivertrust.org.uk

WHAT ELSE TO SEE AND DO
New Mills
A popular short add-on to a Cheshire Ring cruise is to take the Upper Peak Forest Canal to New Mills, where the town perches over the dramatic Torrs gorge, which is great fun to explore.
www.newmillstowncouncil.com

can travel right into central Manchester, where you can moor at Castlefield and explore the city centre. Some of the best diversions are the Museum of Science and Industry and the tour of Manchester United Football Club's huge stadium. You can then continue along the Rochdale Canal, winding between atmospheric backdrops of Victorian warehouses before rising steadily through the outskirts.

At Marple there are two spectacular canal features: the imposing Marple Aqueduct and an impressive flight of 16 locks. From there you skirt brooding Peak District hills as the Macclesfield Canal passes by old silk mills, before the 12 Bosley locks lower you on to the Cheshire Plain, where you can visit the eye-catching riot of half-timbering that is Little Moreton Hall. Turn right at Stoke to cruise up the Trent and Mersey Canal and, just before you rejoin the Bridgewater Canal, you'll pass an unmissable sight: the Anderton Boat Lift, which once carried working barges up to the River Weaver. You can park up your canal boat and join the Lift's own pleasure craft to "have a go" on this engineering marvel, a theme park ride from Britain's industrial past.

Below: Little Moreton Hall, a fine example of half-timbered architecture

THE ESSENTIALS

GETTING THERE AND AROUND
Edinburgh is located in the southeast of Scotland. The nearest airport is Edinburgh International, 16 km (10 miles) west of the city. Hourly trains (fastest 4 hours 20 minutes) run from London King's Cross to Waverley Station in Edinburgh. Trains also run to Edinburgh from other cities across the UK. Most of the city centre can be easily explored on foot.

WEATHER
Edinburgh enjoys a temperate climate with summer daytime temperatures averaging 14–22°C. However, Scotland's weather is fickle, so be prepared for rain at any time.

ACCOMMODATION
It is essential to book accommodation for the festival up to 6 months in advance. Expect premium prices at this time of year.

Splashing Out The Balmoral Hotel, on Princes Street, has a fantastic location and offers excellent comfort and service. *www.roccofortehotels.com*

On a Budget Glendale House, in Craigmillar Park, 3 km (2 miles) from the city centre, is a clean, well-equipped B&B. *www.glendaleguesthouse.co.uk*

EATING OUT
Splashing Out The Kitchin, in Commercial Quay, is an award-winning restaurant by the waterfront in Leith, with an inventive menu and great ambience. *www.thekitchin.com*

On a Budget Petit Paris, on Grassmarket, offers an authentic French menu. *www.petitparis-restaurant.co.uk*

PRICE FOR TWO PEOPLE
Around £265 a day for accommodation, food and festival tickets.

WEBSITE
www.edinburgh.org

FUN AT THE FRINGE

WITH ITS GRAND ARCHITECTURE AND COSMOPOLITAN VIBE, Edinburgh has long been a centre for enlightened thinking, earning it the title "the Athens of the North". Today, Scotland's capital city conserves this noble tradition by playing host to the world's biggest arts festival. The world-famous Edinburgh Festival is not one event, but rather a constellation of individual arts and culture festivities that bring a creative frisson to the city. The original event, the Edinburgh International Festival, boasts an inspiring programme of classical music and theatre productions, but it's the world-famous Edinburgh Fringe that steals much of the limelight, attracting performers from over 60 countries every year. Ranging across the full dramatic spectrum, from theatre, mime, comedy, dance and musicals to performances aimed exclusively at little ones, the Fringe sees almost 20,000 participants displaying their creative talents across the city – every available public space simply overflows with performers.

With so many concurrent events in town, something is bound to catch your interest: there's the Edinburgh International Film Festival, the Edinburgh Jazz and Blues Festival, the Edinburgh Art Festival, the Edinburgh International Book Festival and the Edinburgh Annuale. The festival period is wildly popular, bringing in more visitors than the city's entire resident population, so you'll have to battle for every square foot of space. But summer is usually kind weather-wise, and the long days encourage extensive exploration.

When you have time to put aside your festival schedule, explore the city's melange of medieval, Gothic and Georgian architecture. Both the medieval Old Town and the adjoining Georgian New Town are UNESCO World Heritage Sites. A trip to Edinburgh Castle, on its perch of Castle Rock, offers panoramic views over the city; during festival time, the spectacular Edinburgh Military Tattoo is performed here nightly. Admire the architecture of the Royal Mile and explore the exhaustive collection of Scottish heritage at the National Museum of Scotland. The Scottish National Gallery and the Scottish National Gallery of Modern Art will surely satisfy art-lovers. The royal Abbey and Palace of Holyroodhouse, St Giles' Cathedral, the Scottish Parliament and the Royal Yacht Britannia are all other excellent sights. If you get hooked in summer, you can always come back to the city for the New Year's Eve Hogmanay.

Main: Festival fireworks over Edinburgh's skyline
Below (left to right): Crowds gathering on the Royal Mile during the festival; *Swan Lake* performed at the Edinburgh International Festival; Edinburgh Tattoo

FURTHER DETAILS

EDINBURGH FESTIVAL
Edinburgh International Festival: www.eif.co.uk
Edinburgh Fringe Festival: www.edfringe.com
Edinburgh International Film Festival:
    www.edfilmfest.org.uk
Edinburgh Jazz and Blues Festival:
    www.edinburghjazzfestival.com
Edinburgh Art Festival: www.edinburghartfestival.com
Edinburgh Book Festival: www.edbookfest.co.uk
Edinburgh Annuale: www.annuale.org

EDINBURGH
Edinburgh Castle
Castle Hill; open Apr–Sep: 9:30am–6pm daily;
Oct–Mar: 9:30am–5pm daily.
www.edinburghcastle.gov.uk

Edinburgh Military Tattoo
Performances in August: 9pm Mon–Fri, 7:30pm and
10:30pm Sat; fireworks display on Sat nights.
www.edintattoo.co.uk

National Museum of Scotland
Chambers Street; open 10am–5pm daily.
www.nms.ac.uk

Scottish National Gallery
The Mound; open 10am–5pm Fri–Wed,
10am–7pm Thu.
www.nationalgalleries.org

Scottish National Gallery of Modern Art
Belford Road; open 10am–5pm daily.
www.nationalgalleries.org

Abbey and Palace of Holyroodhouse
Royal Mile; open Nov–Mar: 9:30am–4:30pm daily;
Apr–Oct: 9:30am–6pm daily.
www.royalcollection.org.uk

Royal Yacht Britannia
Leith; open Jan–Mar and Nov–Dec: 10am–3:30pm
daily; Apr–Sep: 9:30am–4:30pm daily; Oct: 9:30am–
4pm daily.
www.royalyachtbritannia.co.uk

Camera Obscura and World of Illusions
Castlehill; open Jul–Aug: 9:30am–9pm
daily; Sep–Oct: 9:30am–7pm daily; Nov–Mar:
10am–6pm daily; Apr–Jun: 9:30am–7pm daily.
www.camera-obscura.co.uk

WHAT ELSE TO SEE AND DO
Aberdour
This charming village on the Firth of Forth has several
sights, including Aberdour Castle, an extended 12th-
century residence; the 12th-century St Fillan's Church;
two beaches and a summer festival.
www.historic-scotland.gov.uk

More Great Ideas for **Summer**

HISTORY AND HERITAGE

Evocative remains of Rievaulx Abbey in Helmsley

WILDLIFE AND LANDSCAPE

Red squirrel on Brownsea Island

CITIES, TOWNS AND VILLAGES

Picturesque Welsh town of Barmouth

CHILTERN OPEN AIR MUSEUM
SOUTHEAST ENGLAND
Rescued and re-erected local buildings, from an Iron Age house to a Victorian farm, bring history alive for visitors to Chalfont St Giles.
www.coam.org.uk

RIEVAULX ABBEY NORTHEAST ENGLAND
A majestic and amazingly intact 900-year-old Cistercian abbey, Rievaulx is set in the stunning River Rye valley with sublime views of the dale. This atmospheric building once housed 650 monks and became one of the wealthiest abbeys in England. It was dissolved by Henry VIII in 1538, but much of the church and parts of the chapter house and refectory remain standing. The site houses an interesting interactive museum and there are wonderful walks nearby.
www.english-heritage.org.uk

TOLPUDDLE MARTYRS PROCESSION AND FESTIVAL SOUTHWEST ENGLAND
Every July, a three-day festival of music, performance and debate, combined with a Trades Union Congress parade, celebrates the birthplace of trade unionism in the village of Tolpuddle. In the 1830s six impoverished agricultural labourers started the Friendly Society of Agricultural Labourers to demand a minimum wage. They were deported to Australia, then returned following a public outcry.
www.tolpuddlemartyrs.org.uk

BARDSEY ISLAND
NORTH WALES
Bardsey, off the Llŷn Peninsula, was a place of pilgrimage for the early Celtic Christian church. The abbey's 13th-century tower houses a 1,200-year-old stone carving.
www.enlli.org

FLOORS CASTLE
SOUTHERN SCOTLAND
Overlooking the River Tweed and the Cheviots, this fairy-tale castle is dotted with turrets and surrounded by beautiful grounds, where massed piped bands play in late August.
www.roxburghe.net

BROWNSEA ISLAND SOUTHWEST ENGLAND
Brownsea Island, at the entrance to Poole Harbour, teems with flora and fauna in its mixed woodland, wetland and heath nature reserve. There are rare plants, insects and birds, such as the bar-tailed godwit, as well as red squirrels, sika deer and shy water voles. Trail and tracker packs are available for lovely walks with beautiful views, and the island has an open air theatre. The Baden Powell Outdoor Centre allows you to camp on the site of the world's first scouting camp, held in 1907.
www.nationaltrust.org.uk

SLIEVENACLOY
NORTHERN IRELAND
Northern Ireland's newest nature reserve is home to many rare flora and fauna, including species of orchids and fungi, as well as Irish hares, curlews and kestrels.
www.ulsterwildlife.org

DOZMARY POOL
SOUTHWEST ENGLAND
Wild and desolate, Dozmary Pool is said to be the resting place of King Arthur's sword, Excalibur, thrown into the water by a loyal knight to be caught by the Lady of the Lake.

FETLAR
HIGHLANDS AND ISLANDS
"The Garden of Shetland", is a fertile haven for exquisite flowers and ground-nesting birds, including 90 per cent of the British population of red-necked phalaropes.
www.fetlar.org

BOARSTALL DUCK DECOY SOUTHEAST ENGLAND
A duck decoy is an inventive device that was employed in the 17th–19th centuries to trap ducks. The Boarstall Duck Decoy is one of only four surviving in England and is still in working order. Regular demonstrations show how the ducks were coaxed by a fake duck, the "decoy", into a small patch of water and then corralled by man and dog into a wickerwork tunnel. Originally trapped for food, birds that are "caught" today are ringed and released into the wild.
www.nationaltrust.org.uk

BARMOUTH NORTH WALES
An attractive stone town set between an enormous sandy beach and the dramatic Mawddach Estuary, Barmouth backs onto a craggy hillside, on top of which is Dinas Oleu ("Fortress of Light"), the first piece of land acquired by the National Trust and a great viewing point. Once a major ship-building centre, Barmouth is now a seaside resort hosting entertaining summer events, such as kite-flying festivals, and is the starting point of the Three Peaks Yacht Race.
www.barmouth-wales.co.uk

PEEBLES
SOUTHERN SCOTLAND
On the River Tweed, Peebles is famous as a centre of arts and for the Beltane Festival, a week-long celebration of legend and history that takes place every June.
www.peebles-theroyalburgh.info

WHITSTABLE SOUTHEAST ENGLAND
A historic harbour and noisy fish markets draw the crowds to this small Kent coastal town. Pebbled beaches and colourful beach huts provide a flavour of traditional "Englishness", while restaurants offer delicious fresh seafood. The lively Oyster Festival in late July celebrates Whitstable's history and heritage through music, art and street theatre. Delicious food and drink stalls abound, and the festival week kicks off with a ceremonial "landing of the oysters" on the beach.
www.seewhitstable.com

RYE SOUTHEAST ENGLAND
Once a coastal town, Rye now lies 3 km (2 miles) from the sea, leaving sheep to graze where boats once moored. The town became a cinque port in the 12th century, gaining trading and tax concessions for supporting the Plantagenet kings with ships, men and safe harbour. Today, it has a thriving artistic community and its ancient buildings, cobbled streets, pubs and shops are a tourist magnet. Look out for the entertaining summer Raft Race.
www.visitrye.co.uk

See also pp70–71, 76–7, 92–3.

See also pp80–81, 86–7, 94–5, 108–9.

See also pp74–5, 88–9, 96–7, 106–7.

Traditional narrowboat crossing the Pontcysyllte Aqueduct

Giant chess set at Groombridge Gardens

Horse racing on Laytown Beach

PONTCYSYLLTE AQUEDUCT NORTH WALES
For a memorably scary experience, take a narrowboat ride along the Llangollen canal from Llangollen Wharf to the Pontcysyllte Aqueduct. Built over the River Dee by Thomas Telford and William Jessop in 1805, the cast-iron, 38-m- (126-ft-) high structure has been given World Heritage status. With very little protection on one side except for a low iron "wall", crossing the 307-m- (1,007-ft-) long aqueduct in a boat gives the feeling of being suspended in mid-air.
www.pontcysyllte-aqueduct.co.uk

GROOMBRIDGE GARDENS SOUTHEAST ENGLAND
For horticulturalists with kids, Groombridge has it all – award-winning gardens for adults and an enchanted forest for children. The formal gardens are organized into "rooms", including the "drunken" garden, the oriental garden and glorious herbaceous borders. In the forest, youngsters will be amazed by unusual animals, such as the "zedonk" – a rare zebra and donkey cross-breed. There is also a playground, as well as birds of prey and landscape art to admire.
www.groombridgeplace.com

LAYTOWN BEACH RACES EASTERN IRELAND
Turf meets surf at Laytown for the only officially approved beach strand race in Europe. These popular races have been taking place in late summer on the beautiful Laytown Beach since 1868, and thousands turn up every year to watch the spectacular sight of horses thundering across the sandy shore. A field above the beach is transformed into a racing enclosure with a ring, weighing area, bookies, grandstand, restaurants and bars.
www.laytownstrandraces.ie

INNER HEBRIDES
HIGHLANDS AND ISLANDS
Summer ferries run trips to the smaller islands including the pretty Iona, and Staffa, home of the dramatic Fingal's Cave. The Treshnish Isles shelter thousands of sea birds.
www.staffatours.com

RUTLAND WATER
EAST MIDLANDS
This small county contains a reservoir the size of Lake Windermere. Perfect for fishing and sailing, the lake also hides the half-submerged Normanton Church Museum.
www.discover-rutland.co.uk

THE HOPPINGS
NORTHEAST ENGLAND
Europe's largest travelling fair comes to Newcastle in June. There is a huge variety of white-knuckle rides to enjoy, as well as old favourites such as carousels and dodgems.
hoppingsfunfairs.com

SPEYSIDE WAY
HIGHLANDS AND ISLANDS
The Way runs from the Moray Firth to the Cairngorms, but shorter treks between villages offer a folk museum, a castle or two and the Glenfiddich whisky distillery.
www.speysideway.org

SIDMOUTH FOLK WEEK
SOUTHWEST ENGLAND
One week of music, singing, dancing, ceilidhs, workshops and performances in a lovely Devonshire Regency seaside town in August.
www.sidmouthfolkweek.co.uk

CALSHOT
SOUTHEAST ENGLAND
Calshot Activities Centre, on the Solent Coast, is one of the most popular water sports locations in Britain. It offers sailing, windsurfing, canoeing and powerboating.
www.calshot.com

TATTON PARK NORTHWEST ENGLAND
There is something for everyone at this imaginatively presented visitor attraction. The magnificent house is full of historic treasures, including a Tudor great hall, complete with costumed guides. The estate also boasts a 400-hectare (1,000-acre) deer park, landscaped gardens and a farm that still uses traditional methods. The park hosts over 100 events every year, including the Royal Horticultural Society's five-day Flower Show in July.
www.tattonpark.org.uk

FLYING LEGENDS AIR SHOW EASTERN ENGLAND
An international line-up of historic fighter aircraft awaits the thousands of spectators who attend this nostalgic two-day annual event, organized by the Imperial War Museum and the Fighter Collection. Every July, classic aircraft are displayed and flown at Duxford in Cambridgeshire. Aeroplanes from Britain, the USA, Germany, Italy and Russia, including famous models such as Spitfires, Hawkers, Mustangs and Focke-Wulfs, take part in a mass take-off and flypast.
www.iwm.org.uk

SCAFELL PIKE NORTHWEST ENGLAND
Soaring to 980 m (3,200 ft), Scafell Pike is the highest mountain in England. Its rough and rugged terrain is surrounded by a spectacular range of fells – Sca Fell, Kirk Fell, Pillar and Great Gable – giving you a fantastic panorama of views as you tackle the long walk to the summit. Start your trip with a visit to the historic Wasdale Head Inn, Wasdale, a traditional starting point at the foot of Scafell Pike that has been offering sustenance and advice to climbers since the 19th century.
www.scafellpike.org.uk

MARBLE ARCH CAVES GLOBAL GEOPARK
NORTHERN IRELAND
This geopark offers boat trips on an underground river and tours of the awe-inspiring caverns.
www.marblearch cavesgeopark.com

LAKE DISTRICT SHEEPDOG TRIALS
NORTHWEST ENGLAND
The one-day trials at Hill Farm, Ings, in August demonstrate the traditional skills of dog and shepherd moving sheep through a series of obstacles.
www.isds.org.uk

CORACLE RACES
CENTRAL WALES
Water-based frolics in the traditional Welsh boats take place on the River Teifi for one day in August, including a race for novices, a non-swimmers' race, a water-polo match and net-fishing displays.

See also pp66–7, 72–3, 102–3.

See also pp84–5, 104–5, 110–11, 112–13.

See also pp68–9, 78–9, 90–91, 100–101, 114–15.

AUTUMN

Kilchurn Castle
on Loch Awe in
Argyll, Scotland

AUTUMN IN GREAT BRITAIN AND IRELAND

AUTUMN, IN BRITAIN AND IRELAND is a long, mellow time between the two more extreme seasons of summer and winter. John Keats, in his ode "To Autumn", called it the "season of mists and mellow fruitfulness". He was inspired by the River Itchen near Winchester, where autumnal mists rise from the river early in the morning and late in the afternoon, and the boughs of nearby orchards hang heavy with fruit. All around Britain, fruit trees are laden with plums, pears and apples, and hedges are rich with wild blackberries. Occasionally, September brings an "Indian summer", when days are unusually warm, and in Scotland and northern England early autumn can often be a gentler season than wet, windy and unpredictable spring. On the coast of North Cornwall, the beginning of autumn marks the start of the prime surfing season, when the big waves begin to roll onto the sandy shores just as the last summer visitors head for home.

> The honking of geese winging in from Scandinavia haunts the skies above wetlands.

A few late-blooming plants, such as the mauve and yellow Michaelmas daisy (so called because it flowers around St Michael's feast day, on 29 September) bring pretty dabs of colour to cottage gardens. In fields and woodlands, connoisseurs of wild fungi have fun hunting for delicious edible versions, such as chanterelles and ceps. The leaves change colour across the gardens of stately homes, city parks and rural woodlands, as far apart as Loch Lomond in Scotland and the spectacular Wye Valley on the Welsh border, creating great swathes of red and gold, punctuated by the scarlet splashes of rowan berries, haws and rosehips. Soon, these and other berries, nuts and seeds will begin to attract Arctic migrant birds, such as vividly coloured waxwings, rare, tiny redwings and sociable fieldfares, which all spend winter in Britain. The honking of skeins of geese winging in from Scandinavia haunts the skies above wetlands, such as the Firth of Tay on the east coast of Scotland, in one of the characteristic sounds of autumn.

Only a few miles inland, keen anglers bid for access to the choicest stretches of the River Tay, where the last few weeks of autumn offer some of the best angling of the season. Autumn is the time, too, to seek out some of Britain's most spectacular wildlife, such as red deer stags, as they clash antlers during the rutting season on the heathlands of the New Forest, Hampshire or Richmond Park in London, or on the moors of Islay in the Inner Hebrides.

Below (left to right): Red deer stag roaring during rutting season, in Richmond Park, London; surfer in Newquay, Cornwall; Parade of Fire on Lewes Bonfire Night

Autumn is harvest time, and food festivals all over Britain celebrate the successful growing season. In Scotland, Braemar is the home of the Royal Highland Games, where kilted muscle-men toss cabers and fight to win the "tug-o-war", Highland dancers perform the Highland Fling, and the music of pipe bands and lone pibroch players fills the air. The event is always attended by the British Royal Family, who stay at their home in nearby Balmoral. For those with an interest in Britain's royal heritage, this is a wonderful time to visit Windsor Castle, a royal residence just outside London. Visitors gain access to five additional, magnificent chambers – the Semi-State Rooms – in autumn and winter, complementing the State Apartments that are always open. Fallow deer stags roam free in Windsor Great Park, the vast, Saxon hunting forest that encircles the castle and is open to all-comers, for walking, cycling and horse-riding.

Smuggler-costumed revellers tour the streets in noisy torchlit processions.

As autumn moves inexorably towards winter, the days begin to dawn under a covering of frost, and all but the most stubborn of leaves falls from the trees. Hearts are gladdened, though, by a festival that occurs all over the world, and is celebrated here in a peculiarly British way. Halloween, or – to give its original Celtic name – Samhain, was a pre-Christian festival that marked the coming of winter, on a night when spirits of the dead were thought to mingle with the living, held at bay only by masks and bonfires. It was incorporated into the Christian calendar more than 1,000 years ago as All Saints' Day, or All Hallows' Eve, and today it is celebrated on 31 October. In England it sometimes merges with Guy Fawkes Night – a festivity of firework displays and bonfires, celebrating the failure of a Catholic plot to blow up King James I and the Houses of Parliament in 1605. Some of the most spectacular celebrations, held on the anniversary of the Gunpowder Plot each 5 November, take place in Lewes in Sussex, where smuggler-costumed revellers tour the streets in noisy torchlit processions, before ritually burning effigies upon bonfires. Public bonfires and fireworks displays take place all over England, and in recent years many of them have become more multicultural because the date sometimes overlaps with Diwali (Festival of Lights), a Hindu festival that is also celebrated with fireworks. All of these celebrations provide an exciting (if noisy) seasonal signpost, marking the end of autumn and the coming of winter.

Below (left to right): Still, deep waters of Loch Lomond in western Scotland; trees lining the Long Walk at Windsor Great Park

Food, Glorious Food

Above: Wartime poster

With crops ripening in the fields – from the hops and barley that make English ale and Scotch whisky, to the golden wheat that goes into our bread – autumn has long been a time to celebrate nature's bounty. Though pagan in origin, the Harvest Festival is traditionally one of Britain's best-loved church festivals, when parishioners and schoolchildren give thanks for the harvest by bringing baskets of food to decorate their local churches and singing hymns. The event usually takes place in late September or early October, on the Sunday closest to the "harvest moon" – the full moon nearest to the autumn equinox.

Today, the fine quality of the food itself is likely to be celebrated as much as the provision of it. Those planning a trip to sample the best of Britain and Ireland's produce will find September and October packed with food festivals and events. Whether it's apples from the orchards of Herefordshire, venison from the Scottish Highlands or oysters from the coast of Ireland, this time of year is an opportunity to celebrate the very best of seasonal and local fare. Unsurprisingly, many of the most attractive and exciting festivals take place in the heart of rural Britain, where farming is still a traditional way of life, but there are festivals and seasonal events in towns and cities too, often celebrating world influences and cosmopolitan cooking, as well as local produce.

THE GREAT CORNISH FOOD FESTIVAL, TRURO

HARVESTING A CORN FIELD

CARDIFF COUNTRY FAIR

ABERGAVENNY FOOD FESTIVAL

Shetland Food Fair, Highlands and Islands Britain's northernmost isles unveil an array of local delicacies at this event in late October, from seawater oatcakes to fudge. *www.shetland.org*

Venison Season, Highlands and Islands The deer-stalking season in Scotland peaks in October; red deer, roe stags and hinds roam wild in the Highlands, so the quality of the meat is fantastic.

Dartmouth Food Festival, Southwest England This "feast for the senses," in late October, showcases the best food and drink the region has to offer, with tastings and workshops. *www.dartmouthfoodfestival.com*

Forest Showcase Food and Drink Festival, Southwest England Artisan food producers from the Forest of Dean gather in early October, in the idyllic grounds of a 17th century hunting lodge. *www.forestshowcase.org*

Clarenbridge Oyster Festival, Western Ireland The first shellfish of the season, fresh from the Irish Sea, are served up by the bucket in September in this welcoming fishing harbour. *www.clarenbridge.com*

Conwy Honey Fair, North Wales Celebrate Conwy's long-standing history with beekeeping, in September, when beekeepers line the streets to sell their honey. *www.conwybeekeepers.org.uk*

Abergavenny Food Festival, South Wales Celebrity chefs, food writers, farmers and brewers descend on Abergavenny every September for this popular foodie event. *www.abergavennyfoodfestival.com*

Cardiff Country Fair, South Wales Cardiff Castle plays host to this September event, where you can sample 400 cheeses made from cow, sheep, goat and buffalo milk. *www.cardiffcastle.com*

Isle of Man Food Festival, Northwest England Sample everything from moorland lamb and local cheese to organic ice cream at this irresistible event, held in Douglas in September. *www.visitisleofman.com*

York Festival of Food and Drink, Northeast England Yorkshire is renowned for its ale, cheese, beef, lamb and seafood. Try them all in September in historic York. *www.yorkfoodfestival.com*

The Big Apple, West Midlands Every October, Herefordshire villages celebrate their apple- and pear growing heritage with tastings of local cider and perry (pear cider). *www.bigapple.org.uk*

Norwich Beer Festival, Eastern England Run by the Campaign for Real Ale, which champions traditional British beers, this October event celebrates more than 200 ales. *www.norwichcamra.org.uk*

Faversham Hop Festival, Southeast England This medieval town comes alive with music, dancing and street entertainment at the annual hop-harvest festivities in September. *www.favershamhopfestival.org*

Northamptonshire Food Festival, East Midlands In the grounds of Grade I listed Holdenby House, this festival celebrates the dynamic food and drink scene of Northamptonshire. *www.glynde.co.uk*

Sturminster Newton Cheese Festival, Southwest England Cheese, chutney and more than 30 kinds of beer, cider and perry make this Dorset event, held in September, go with a bang. *www.cheesefestival.co.uk*

The Great Cornish Food Festival, Southwest England The best of Cornish food and drink is served up in September on Truro's Lemon Quay. *www.greatcornishfood.co.uk*

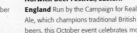

DEER-STALKING SEASON IN SCOTLAND

FAVERSHAM HOP FESTIVAL

THE ESSENTIALS

GETTING THERE AND AROUND
The Lower Wye Valley gorge marks the southern end of the border between England and Wales. Cardiff and London Heathrow airports are 95 km (60 miles) and 230 km (143 miles) from the valley respectively. There are trains to Hereford and Chepstow, and local buses run approximately hourly between the two, along the Wye Valley, via Monmouth.

WEATHER
The Wye Valley often enjoys fine weather in autumn, but be prepared for cool evenings and rain. Average daytime temperatures are around 6 to 12°C.

ACCOMMODATION
Splashing Out The Old Court Hotel, in Symonds Yat West, is a characterful 16th-century house near the River Wye.
www.oldcourthotel.co.uk

On a Budget The Nurtons, in Tintern, has spectacular views of the valley and offers organic breakfasts and evening meals.
www.thenurtons.co.uk

EATING OUT
Splashing Out The Crown at Whitebrook is an acclaimed Michelin-starred restaurant with rooms, in a remote setting just off the Wye Valley.
www.thewhitebrook.co.uk

On a Budget The Saracen's Head, in Symonds Yat East, is a riverside inn serving above-average pub grub made with local, seasonal produce. It also has a children's menu.'
www.saracensheadinn.co.uk

PRICE FOR TWO PEOPLE
From around £180 a day for food, accommodation and activities.

WEBSITES
www.wyedeantourism.co.uk
www.wyevalleyaonb.org.uk

SPECTACULAR COLOUR

IF BRITAIN HAD A "FALL FOLIAGE" REGION to rival New England's, it would be the Lower Wye Valley gorge. The mixed native forest of ash, beech and oak produces one of the country's best displays of autumn colour. The winding river and high slopes of the gorge make this an enticing landscape to explore, and the soaring roofless remains of Tintern Abbey rank among the most evocative of ruins. From the late 18th century, the Wye Valley became a place of pilgrimage for those in search of the "picturesque". The first of Britain's landscapes to be "discovered", the gorge had everything the romantically minded traveller desired: brooding forests and cliffs punctuated by medieval ruins, all easily observed from the water.

Leaving England, you're likely to approach the Lower Wye Valley by the M48 motorway, crossing the iconic 1966 suspension bridge over the River Severn – very much the gateway to Wales. Heading north from Chepstow, there's a real feeling of a change of pace and time as you are enfolded by the wooded landscape, with every turn in the winding road promising a new autumnal viewpoint.

Tintern village sits on a looping curve in the river, with Tintern Abbey occupying much of the flat land by the banks. Henry VIII dissolved the 14th-century Cistercian monastery here in 1536, and the buildings were let out to locals: the great church was used for playing quoits. The area soon became part of the Industrial Revolution, when Tintern began to produce brass and wire. The ruins lay more or less forgotten until the poets and artists of the Romantic movement sought it out – they inspired one of William Wordsworth's most celebrated works, "Lines Composed a Few Miles Above Tintern Abbey", and J M W Turner painted the scene several times.

North of Monmouth, the main road swings away from the river, and it's worth exploring the lanes and paths around the spectacular Symonds Yat Rock, a towering viewpoint set high on a narrow neck of land. The village of Symonds Yat straddles the Wye; a hand-pulled rope ferry opposite the Saracen's Head Inn takes you across the river, and an easy 5-km (3-mile) round walk returns over a wire suspension bridge. There's also level cycling between here and Monmouth on the Peregrine Path, which runs for 10 km (6 miles) along the line of a former railway, and canoeing from the Wyedean Canoe and Adventure Centre.

Main: River Wye from Symonds Yat Rock **Below (left to right):** Autumn colour in the Lower Wye Valley; canoeing and kayaking on the River Wye

FURTHER DETAILS

WYE VALLEY GORGE

Tintern Abbey
Tintern, Chepstow, Monmouthshire; open Mar–Jun:
9:30am–5pm daily; Jul–Aug: 9:30am–6pm daily;
Nov–Feb: 10am–4pm Mon–Sat, 11am–4pm Sun.
www.cadw.wales.gov.uk

Wyedean Canoe and Adventure Centre
Symonds Yat East, Ross-on-Wye. Canoes are available
to hire by the day, the half-day or the hour.
www.wyedean.co.uk

WHAT ELSE TO SEE AND DO

Chepstow Museum
This local history museum, in an elegant 18th-century
house, has exhibits detailing the development of
Chepstow – a historic walled town and former port.
www.chepstow.co.uk

Chepstow Castle
This well-preserved medieval castle has a dramatic
setting on slopes above the River Wye.
www.cadw.wales.gov.uk

Goodrich Castle
There are substantial remains of this 11th-century
hilltop castle, which guarded the entrance to the north
end of the Wye Valley gorge near Symonds Yat.
www.english-heritage.org.uk

River Cruises
The *Kingfisher* offers short cruises on the river, with
commentary, from Symonds Yat East.
www.wyenot.com

The Kymin
Set high above Monmouth, this wooded hill has
pleasure grounds to explore and a circular Georgian
banqueting hall and Naval Temple memorial to visit.
www.nationaltrust.org.uk

Monmouth
This unspoilt old border town offers many sights:
a remarkable gated medieval bridge, handsome
Georgian buildings and the Nelson Museum and Local
History Centre, which has a tremendous collection of
Admiral Nelson memorabilia.
www.monmouth.org.uk

Wye Valley Walk
This marked walking route runs from Chepstow to
Monmouth and beyond; the full route runs 218 km
(136 miles) to the remote mountain source of the Wye.
www.wyevalleywalk.org

Below: Imposing ruins of Chepstow Castle

THE ESSENTIALS

GETTING THERE AND AROUND
Braemar is 90 km (56 miles) west
of Aberdeen, the site of the nearest
international airport. Trains connect
Aberdeen with London – with a journey
time of over 7 hours – and with most
Scottish and English cities. Buses run
daily between Aberdeen and Braemar,
with a journey time of around 2 hours.
A car is useful for travelling in the remote
countryside around Braemar.

WEATHER
Braemar's weather is usually mild in early
September, but rain is always possible in
the Scottish Highlands. Average daytime
temperatures range from 15 to 17°C.

ACCOMMODATION
Splashing Out Darroch Learg, in Ballater
(24 km/15 miles from Braemar), is a
mansion-house hotel with high-quality
rooms, set in a beautiful location.
www.darrochlearg.co.uk

On a Budget Braemar Youth Hostel,
in Braemar, offers comfortable
accommodation located in a former
shooting lodge.
www.syha.org.uk

EATING OUT
Splashing Out The Spirit Restaurant,
in Ballater, is an excellent establishment
with a menu that features local produce
such as lamb, venison and rabbit.
Bookings only.
www.theauldkirk.com

On a Budget Gordon's Tearoom, in
Braemar, is a traditional restaurant and
tearoom serving breakfast, full meals
and snacks.
www.gordonstearoom.com

PRICE FOR TWO PEOPLE
Around £190–250 a day for tickets to
the games, food and accommodation.

WEBSITE
www.visitscotland.com

Main: Highland dancing in full flow   **Right (top to bottom):** Tossing the caber at Braemar; tug-of-war;
contestant in the stone-putting competition

FUN AND GAMES

Pipers, highland dancers and kilted muscle-men make the Royal Braemar Gathering
the most dramatic and exciting of all Scotland's many Highland games events. This is
Highland pageantry at its most spectacular. Only a spoilsport would point out that most of
the ancient traditions celebrated here go back no further than the early 19th century, when
the romantic novels of Sir Walter Scott prompted a surge of interest in Highland life – a
fascination that was shared by Queen Victoria, who first visited the Gathering in 1848, and
later bestowed the title "Royal" onto the Highland Society and its games. Today, members of
Britain's Royal Family are always in attendance at the Braemar games, usually dressed in their
finest Highland attire. Their Scottish residence, Balmoral Castle, lies only a few miles away.

For many onlookers, the highlight of the Gathering is the fiercely contested Highland
dancing competition. Various Scottish dances – reels, jigs and strathspeys – are performed
by teams of nimble dancers, accompanied by traditional music. The haunting strains of

FURTHER DETAILS

BRAEMAR

Braemar Gathering
The Princess Royal and Duke of Fife Memorial
Park, Braemar. Held on the first Sat in Sep; advance
booking from 1 Feb.
www.braemargathering.org

Balmoral Castle
Crathie, near Ballater. The Royal Family's Highland
retreat since the reign of Queen Victoria is closed during
the Gathering, but you can admire it from a distance.
www.balmoralcastle.com

WHAT ELSE TO SEE AND DO

Braemar Castle
This sturdy little stronghold in Braemar is steeped
in history – it was garrisoned by British troops until
1831 – and has been restored to its full glory by
community volunteers
www.braemarcastle.co.uk

Old Royal Station
This station in Ballater, with its luxurious waiting room,
was built especially for Queen Victoria in the 19th
century. A life-size replica of the royal railway carriage
used by Victoria and her many offspring stands outside.
www.royal-deeside.org.uk

Royal Lochnagar Distillery
This historic distillery, near Balmoral Castle in Crathie,
offers tours and tutored whisky tastings.
www.discovering-distilleries.com

Lochnagar
One of Scotland's most spectacular summits, Lochnagar
is 1,154 m (3,787 ft) high. It can only be reached by
walking, taking a path that starts at the Spittal of Glen
Muick. There are superb views all along the ascent, and
it takes around 7–8 hours to reach the summit. Proper
walking footwear and waterproof clothing are essential.
www.cairngorms.co.uk

Golf Clubs
The Deeside region has a number of excellent golf
clubs, including Braemar Golf Club – home of the
highest 18-hole golf course in Britain. The upmarket
Inchmarlo Golf Club, 62 km (39 miles) east of Braemar,
boasts an excellent location and luxurious facilities.
Braemar Golf Club: www.braemargolfclub.co.uk
Inchmarlo Golf Club: www.inchmarlo-golf.com

bagpipes are, of course, omnipresent, but to those who are only familiar with
military bands, the eerie *pibroch* – a lament played by a lone piper – will be a
revelation. The "heavy events" at the games, in which strongmen from all over
the world clash in a display of straining sinews, clenched teeth and sweating
muscle that is unique to Highland gatherings, are an unmissable spectacle. The
events – from tossing the caber (a telegraph pole-sized length of wood), putting
the stone and throwing the hammer, to the strength-sapping hill race – all have
their origins in the trials of prowess and martial skills practised by the clan
warriors of Scotland's past.

But it's not all deadly serious. Despite the extreme exertion required by each
competitor, the tug-of-war is a good-humoured event, and the children's sack race
gives younger visitors a chance to shine. Whether you put your own skills to the
test – anyone can enter – or just marvel at the displays of strength and endurance,
the Braemar Highland Gathering is an experience you won't forget in a hurry.

Below: The Royal Family at the annual Braemar Highland Gathering

MEMORY LANE

A S CHILDREN DUST OFF THEIR HISTORY BOOKS for the beginning of a new school year, Beamish Open Air Museum offers an alternative hands-on experience that will immerse them in the past. Spread over 120 hectares (300 acres) of County Durham countryside, this historical park features homes, shops and other buildings from the 19th and early 20th centuries, with costumed guides who'll tell you what life was like "way back when".

Behind the busy entrance hall you'll step into another world. Beamish focuses on two very different moments in history: 1825, when the lives of people in the northeast of England revolved around farming; and 1913, when the region was at its industrial peak. The first scene you come to is the 1913 Colliery Village, where you can take an underground tour of a real drift mine. At ground level, miners' cottages, with their vegetable gardens, show how the pitmen and their families lived, from the tin baths in front of the hearth to baking demonstrations. The three-room schoolhouse also provides a fascinating trip down memory lane.

Many buildings have been brought in from around the region and carefully reconstructed, but others, such as Pockerley Manor, have been here all along. The manor reveals the lifestyle of a yeoman farmer in the 1820s, and comprises a parlour, a kitchen pantry and servants' quarters. The 1913 Home Farm has also been restored; the farmer's wife bustles about in the kitchen and the farm buildings house an array of animals and machinery. Electric trams trundle along the cobbled street in the 1913 Town, passing the newspaper office and the Co-op, stocked with vintage tinned goods. The gruesome instruments in the dentist's surgery may help you resist the temptation of the old-fashioned sweets for sale in the Jubilee Confectionery.

Beamish is huge, but there is a delightful range of historic vehicles to transport you around the site. Take a ride on a horse-drawn dogcart, a restored omnibus or a steam-hauled carriage on the Pockerley Waggonway. Alternatively, the nearby woodlands and gentle fields are ideal for a peaceful walk, while casting a nostalgic eye on days gone by.

Main: Electric tram on the cobbled street of the 1913 Town
Below: Products on display in the Co-op of the 1913 Town

FURTHER DETAILS

BEAMISH OPEN AIR MUSEUM
Beamish, County Durham; open Jan–mid-Feb:
10am–4pm Tue–Thu and Sat–Sun; mid-Feb–mid-Mar:
10am–4pm daily; mid-Mar–Oct: 10am–5pm daily.
www.beamish.org.uk

WHAT ELSE TO SEE AND DO
Durham Cathedral
Dating from 1093, this cathedral, with its massive
carved stone pillars, rib-vaulted ceiling and rose window,
is one of Europe's great architectural masterpieces. You
can see the former monastery cloister and climb the
tower for splendid views.
www.durhamcathedral.co.uk

Durham City
Browse the crafts and foodstuffs in the charming
Indoor Market alongside the central Market Place.
Then hire a rowing boat beneath Elvet Bridge or take
a sightseeing cruise along the River Wear with the
Prince Bishop River Cruiser.
River Cruise: *www.princebishoprc.co.uk*
Durham Indoor Market: *www.durhammarkets.co.uk*

Crook Hall
This rare and atmospheric small medieval hall in
Durham dates from the 13th century. Hear tales of
resident ghosts and enjoy tea in the beautiful gardens.
www.crookhallgardens.co.uk

Auckland Castle
The medieval St Peter's Chapel is the highlight of
this former hunting lodge in Bishop Auckland,
County Durham.
www.aucklandcastle.org

Below (top to bottom): Re-enacting farming life on the 1913 Home
Farm; re-creation of an early-20th-century sweet shop at Beamish

THE ESSENTIALS

GETTING THERE AND AROUND
Windsor lies about 32 km (20 miles) west of London. The nearest airport is London Heathrow, 12 km (8 miles) away. Regular direct trains run to Windsor & Eton Riverside from London Waterloo. It's possible to visit the main sights on foot, but for trips to Legoland you'll need a car or to take a bus from the town centre.

WEATHER
Windsor enjoys a mild autumn climate with pleasant daytime temperatures of 8–14°C. Autumn rains are possible.

ACCOMMODATION
Splashing Out Harte & Garter, in Windsor, stands in a stunning location opposite Windsor Castle and is an elegantly refitted period building with very comfortable rooms.
www.harteandgarterhotel.com

On a Budget Travelodge Windsor Central offers friendly service and is just a five-minute walk from Windsor Castle.
www.travelodge.co.uk

EATING OUT
Splashing Out The Fat Duck in Bray (6 km/4 miles from Windsor) was voted Best Restaurant in the UK five years running (2008–12) by the Good Food Guide, and the cooking of its chef, Heston Blumenthal, continues to delight and amaze.
www.fatduck.co.uk

On a Budget Cornucopia Bistro on Windsor High Street is a reliable and unpretentious bistro with a great French menu.
www.cornucopia-bistro.co.uk

PRICE FOR A FAMILY OF FOUR
£180–260 a day for food, accommodation and entrance fees.

WEBSITE
www.windsor.gov.uk

Main: Autumn view of the Long Walk, leading to Windsor Castle
Above (top to bottom): St George's Chapel; Windsor Castle; Changing of the Guard of the Royal Household Division

A RIGHT ROYAL RESIDENCE

THE ROYAL ENCLAVE OF WINDSOR is one of England's superlative destinations. For family fun and entertainment, majestic views, great walks, river trips and extravagant pageantry, few places can compete. Windsor Castle sits high above the town, dominating the landscape, and its majesty provides a fascinating insight into the very heart of sovereign England. The earliest incarnation of the castle was built here by William the Conqueror in around 1070, and today's iconic building, finished in the 1820s, still serves as one of the Queen's main residences.

Beyond its distinctive exterior, the castle's most captivating sights are the glorious State Apartments (furnished with masterpieces by artists such as Canaletto, Gainsborough and Rubens), the quiet and hushed interior of St George's Chapel and the exquisite Queen Mary's Dolls' House. The latter, an exact replica of the castle rooms, offers a unique glimpse into the past. It was designed by Lutyens during the 1920s and includes copies of the very furniture,

FURTHER DETAILS

WINDSOR CASTLE
Windsor; open Mar–Oct: 9:45am–5:15pm daily;
Nov–Feb: 9:45am–4:15pm daily.
www.royalcollection.org.uk

Changing of the Guard
Usually 11am; Jun–Jul daily, Aug–Mar alternate days
only; check website for schedule.
www.royalcollection.org.uk

Windsor Great Park
Windsor; open from sunrise to sunset daily. Carriage
rides through the park leave from the High Street,
opposite the statue of Queen Victoria, at 12:30pm daily.
www.windsorgreatpark.co.uk

Boat Tours
Windsor Promenade. Dec–Oct: regular departures from
10am–5pm daily; Nov: 10am–4pm Sat–Sun only.
www.boat-trips.co.uk

Eton College
Eton, Windsor; open for guided visits only Mar–Nov;
times vary, see website for details.
www.etoncollege.com

Royal Windsor Wheel
This giant ferris wheel offers spectacular views over the
Windsor countryside; open 9am–5pm Mon–Sat.

Legoland Windsor
Winkfield Road, Windsor; open mid-Mar–Oct from
10am, closing times vary according to season.
www.legoland.co.uk

WHAT ELSE TO SEE AND DO
Hampton Court Palace
King Henry VIII's palace, 24 km (15 miles) southeast of
Windsor, is an astonishing monument to his extravagance.
The royal apartments, Great Hall, Privy Gardens, Chapel
Royal and famous maze are open to visitors daily, closing
times vary according to season.
www.hrp.org.uk/hamptoncourtpalace

Runnymede
In 1215 King John finally agreed to the terms of the
Magna Carta at Runnymede, setting his seal to the
document during negotiations that took place on these
very meadows. Lying 14 km (9 miles) southeast of
Windsor, the site is also famous today for its rare wildlife,
beautiful oxbow lake and many memorials, including
some designed by Sir Edwin Lutyens.
www.nationaltrust.org.uk

wallpaper, lights and paintings of the state rooms and servant's quarters at that
time. Autumn visitors to Windsor Castle are also given access to George VI's
private apartments, offering a glimpse of the monarch's semi-private life. The
castle has been a working palace for over 900 years, and its ancient traditions for
marking the sovereign's presence – such as the Changing of the Guard and the
raising of the Royal Standard – can still be seen today. To the south of the castle,
the royal Norman hunting chase, now known as Windsor Great Park, stretches
over 2,000 hectares (5,000 acres). Its magnificent Long Walk is an awe-inspiring
sight on a fine day.

The town itself also boasts a long history, and its old cobbled streets contain
intriguing buildings such as the Guildhall, designed by Sir Christopher Wren in
the 1680s. The River Thames is a glistening waterway here, with flocks of swans
and riverboats, and one of England's most illustrious public schools, the
15th-century Eton College, lies just across Windsor Bridge. But if you need to
give the children a 21st-century experience, take a ride on the giant Windsor
Wheel or head for the thrilling rides of nearby Legoland.

Below: Red deer stag and hinds in Windsor Great Park

THE ESSENTIALS

GETTING THERE AND AROUND
Blackpool is on the northwest coast of England, 85 km (53 miles) northwest of Manchester and 89 km (55 miles) north of Liverpool. It has its own small international airport, just to the south of the town. You can easily tour the town centre on foot, and can explore the Promenade by tram.

WEATHER
Blackpool has a temperate climate but autumn sees the wettest months of the year, and there can be cold sea breezes adding a chill factor. Average daytime temperatures range from 8 to 14ºC.

ACCOMMODATION
Splashing Out Number One, on St Luke's Road, in an enviably quiet area on the South Shore, is one of Blackpool's finest boutique B&Bs. *www.numberoneblackpool.com*

On a Budget The Berwyn Hotel, on the North Shore, is a traditional Blackpool hotel with its own large, attractive gardens. *www.berwynhotel.co.uk*

EATING OUT
Splashing Out Kwizeen, on King Street, offers original and interesting cooking, including a "Lancashire market" menu prepared from locally sourced produce. *www.kwizeenrestaurant.co.uk*

On a Budget Harry Ramsden's, on the Promenade, is a seaside institution that serves some of the best fish and chips you'll find anywhere in the country. *www.harryramsdens.co.uk*

PRICE FOR A FAMILY OF FOUR
Around £200 a day for accommodation, food and entrance fees.

WEBSITE
www.visitblackpool.com

NORTHERN LIGHTS

As THE DAYS DRAW IN, AN ELECTRIC RAINBOW of over a million light bulbs shines over Blackpool – "the Las Vegas of Lancashire". The Blackpool Illuminations – lasting 66 days and running a length of 10 km (just over 6 miles) along the town's famous Promenade – have been called "the greatest free light show on earth". You can become part of this awe-inspiring display by hopping aboard one of the illuminated trams that run up and down the seafront – it's the best way to enjoy this eye-popping extravaganza of colour.

The Illuminations began in 1879, after Blackpool became the first town in the world to install electric street lighting. In its first year, 100,000 people came from across Britain to see the "artificial sunshine". Within a few years, entire Lancashire villages would close down and decamp here for a week to enjoy their annual holiday. Today, the light show draws over 3.5 million visitors every year, who throng here to enjoy the bold and cheerful attractions of this quintessentially British seaside resort, from the big "Switch-On" in late August or early September to its conclusion in early November.

It's dazzling to be in town for the Big Switch On, when BBC Radio 2 broadcasts live from Blackpool's brightest occasion. A free concert, featuring live performances by pop bands and comedians, helps build excitement before the grand moment when the Illuminations are turned on by a celebrity guest. The Illuminations, like the city itself, have changed with the times – they now feature a startling array of light displays, including neon, lasers, fibre optics, three-dimensional scenes and moving figures. New technologies that cut energy consumption, from LED bulbs to wind turbines, are powering the lights in the new millennium.

Blackpool claimed another first in 1885, when trams were introduced along a stretch of the Promenade, becoming part of the first fully functioning electric tramway in the world. The network now extends for over 17 km (11 miles), and during the Illuminations the trams themselves are decked out in glorious colours and boast impressive designs.

Once you've had your fill of the town's dazzling lights, stroll along the North Pier with a portion of fish and chips, explore Blackpool Pleasure Beach or admire the sharks in the Sea Life aquarium. And what better way to end the day than a show at the iconic Blackpool Tower?

Main: Blackpool Tower at night during the Illuminations
Below: Rollercoasters at Blackpool Pleasure Beach

FURTHER DETAILS

BLACKPOOL

Blackpool Illuminations
The Promenade, Blackpool; late Aug/early Sep–Nov.
www.blackpool-illuminations.net

Blackpool Pleasure Beach
South Promenade, Blackpool. With a wealth of
shows, rides, indoor entertainment and outdoor
attractions, such as the Pepsi Max Big One – the tallest
rollercoaster in Europe – Blackpool Pleasure Beach
promises fantastic entertainment for all the family; open
Feb–Nov, with seasonal and daily variations.
www.blackpoolpleasurebeach.com

Sea Life Blackpool
The Promenade, Blackpool. This aquarium is home
to Europe's biggest collection of tropical sharks. You
can walk through an underwater tunnel and see more
than 1,000 sea creatures, including giant crabs and
Moray eels; 10am–4pm daily.
www.sealife.co.uk

Blackpool Tower
The Promenade, Blackpool. Blackpool's famous tower
is as much an icon of the town as the Eiffel Tower –
the inspiration for its design – is of Paris. There are
spectacular views of the town from the top, and the
tower also includes an aquarium, a circus, a 3-D cinema
and a ballroom. The tower is open 10am–6:30pm
daily; opening times of the attractions within it vary.
www.theblackpooltower.com

Below (top to bottom): The Blackpool Tower Ballroom;
Blackpool Tower from the North Pier

THE ESSENTIALS

GETTING THERE AND AROUND
The Chilterns are a range of hills in the south of England, between Oxford and London. Heathrow airport is about 47 km (29 miles) southwest of Stokenchurch. The best way to get to kite-viewing locations is by car. Some, such as Stokenchurch and Chinmoor, can be visited by bus from High Wycombe, where the nearest railway station – on the London Marylebone to Birmingham Snow Hill route – can be found.

WEATHER
In autumn the weather in the south of England is pleasant, with average daytime temperatures of between 7 and 14°C, but with a good chance of rain.

ACCOMMODATION
Splashing Out The Fox Country Inn, in Ibstone, is 300 years old and set in beautiful countryside.
www.foxcountryinn.co.uk

On a Budget Kenton House, in Marlow, is a cosy B&B and only 10 minutes' walk from the charming town center.
www.marlow-bedandbreakfast.co.uk

EATING OUT
Splashing Out The Hand and Flowers, in Marlow, serves award-winning food cooked by chef and owner Tom Kerridge, in warm and welcoming surroundings.
www.thehandandflowers.co.uk

On a Budget The Grouse and Ale, in High Wycombe, is a cheerful and homely pub serving good bar food as well as à la carte cuisine.
www.grouseandale.com

PRICE FOR TWO PEOPLE
Around £160 a day for accommodation and food.

WEBSITE
www.chilternsaonb.org

Main: Red kite in its characteristic swooping dive
Right (top to bottom): Kite with wings fully extended; at rest, but still watchful

LORDS OF THE AIR

JUST A SHORT JOURNEY NORTHWEST OF THE CAPITAL, the rolling, chalky Chiltern Hills provide a welcome refuge not just for London's stressed commuters but for a rich variety of wildlife. Chalk grasslands attract naturalists in search of orchids and other wild flowers, while the region's famous beech forests, the floors of which are carpeted with bluebells in the spring, turn into dazzling blurs of yellow and russet in the autumn. Since the 1980s, a majestic former resident – the red kite – has taken back its rightful place over the bucolic hills of the Chilterns. With a huge wingspan of up to 1.8 m (6 ft), warm russet, black and white plumage and a deeply forked tail, the red kite is unmistakable when seen soaring and spiralling as it catches thermals and performs its aerial acrobatics.

The red kite is one of Britain's great conservation success stories. These magnificent birds had been hunted to near national extinction in the mistaken belief that they fed on lambs and gamebirds (whereas they in fact subsist mainly on carrion) and by the 1960s there were just 30 left in the whole of Britain, all resident in mid-Wales. A reintroduction programme

FURTHER DETAILS

THE CHILTERNS
Watlington Hill
Near Watlington, Oxfordshire.
www.nationaltrust.org.uk

Cowleaze Wood
Near Stokenchurch, Oxfordshire.
www.forestry.gov.uk

The Ridgeway National Trail
This ancient 139-km- (87-mile-) long trail, possibly
Britain's oldest road, has been in use since Neolithic
times by herdsmen, soldiers and travellers. Its
picturesque route passes directly through the Chilterns,
and offers great views for walkers and access for horse
riders and cyclists along parts of its length.
www.nationaltrail.co.uk/ridgeway

WHAT ELSE TO SEE AND DO
The Hellfire Caves
Created by Sir Francis Dashwood, the founder of the
notorious 18th-century Hellfire Club of aristocratic
hedonists, the Hellfire Caves were both a meeting-place
and the site of much immoral behaviour. Today the
caves provide an atmospheric day out; you can explore
the passages and chambers running 1 km (half-a-
mile) under West Wycombe, and learn about the site's
shady history.
www.hellfirecaves.co.uk

The Roald Dahl Museum and Story Centre
This museum celebrates the life and work of Roald
Dahl, the author of *Charlie and the Chocolate Factory*,
James and the Giant Peach and *The BFG*, who lived in
the Chilterns in the town of Great Missenden. It contains
a biographical gallery as well as an interactive "story
centre", where you are encouraged to get creative.
www.roalddahl.com

Watlington
Reputedly Britain's smallest town, Watlington, near
High Wycombe, is steeped in the history of the region
and is packed with buildings dating from the 15th to
the 17th centuries. It's also within 1 km (half a mile)
of the Ridgeway Trail.
www.watlington.org

Below: Early morning mist over the Chiltern Hills

was launched in the 1980s, when 90 birds were brought over from Spain; the
first successful breeding took place in 1992, and numbers have since grown to
about 1,600 breeding pairs. Today, kites can be seen almost anywhere in the
Chilterns in autumn, casting their giant shadows even over large towns such as
High Wycombe. But for the best views, a good place to start is at Watlington
Hill, about 2 km (1 mile) southeast of the tiny historical town of Watlington, or
nearby Cowleaze Wood, about 5 km (3 miles) from Stokenchurch.

The Chilterns are a designated Area of Outstanding Natural Beauty (AONB),
so it's easy to combine a morning's kite-watching with a trip to one of the
region's pretty brick-and-flint villages or a ramble along the ancient Ridgeway
Trail. The long line of hills that makes up the Chilterns is perfect for an
afternoon ramble that may take you past sparkling chalk streams, through
wooded valleys and down quiet lanes.

A CRACKING GOOD TIME

OYSTERS AND GUINNESS form the staple diet of guests at the Galway Oyster Festival, which takes place in this charming Irish city at the end of September – the official start of the oyster season. Running since 1954, the festival was the brainchild of Brian Collins, proprietor of Galway's Great Southern Hotel, called Hotel Meyrick today. He wanted to increase the number of autumn guests to his establishment, and saw the oyster season as the perfect excuse to do so.

Today, the emphasis of the four-day-long Oyster Festival is on fun, food and, of course, filling up with Guinness – the national drink. After months of summer festivals and *fleadhs* (music festivals), there is always more than enough *craic* (fun) to go round at the last festival of the season, with the highlight being the "cracking" Guinness World Oyster Opening Championships. The festival's line-up, which includes a Mardi Gras party complete with jazz bands, continues to draw crowds from overseas every year. All the events are guaranteed sell-outs, and the entertainment is frequently described as some of the best in the world.

The oysters themselves are, of course, the focus of the festivities. They are carefully selected from beds beneath Galway Bay, where the native oyster still resides in the wild. After suffering at the hands of eager men frantically trying to beat the world record at the Oyster Opening

THE ESSENTIALS

GETTING THERE AND AROUND
Galway is situated on the west coast of Ireland, 215 km (135 miles) from Dublin. Galway Airport is 6 km (4 miles) from the city centre and is accessible by internal flights from Dublin. The city is well serviced by train and bus links. There are taxis and buses in the city and the centre is small enough to cover easily on foot. Hire a car if you want to travel further afield.

WEATHER
Autumn in Galway is generally mild and often sunny, with average daytime temperatures ranging from 7 to 12ºC, but rain is not unusual.

ACCOMMODATION
Splashing Out The award-winning Twelve boutique hotel, in Barna, near Galway, often has special deals during the festival.
www.thetwelvehotel.ie

On a Budget Sea Breeze Lodge, in Salthill near Galway, is an inexpensive but cosy guesthouse overlooking the beautiful Galway Bay.
www.seabreezelodge.org

EATING OUT
Splashing Out The casually elegant Malt House Restaurant in Galway serves a menu which changes seasonally and is based on regionally sourced produce.
www.thekingshead.ie

On a Budget McDonaghs, on Quay Street in Galway, is a combined seafood restaurant and fish-and-chip takeway that has a fantastic reputation in the city.
www.mcdonaghs.net

PRICE FOR TWO
£200–240 a day for accommodation, food and festival tickets.

FURTHER INFORMATION
www.galwaytourism.ie

Main: Hundreds of revellers enjoying the *craic* in the main marquee at the annual Galway Oyster Festival
Above: Festival staples – oysters and Guinness
Below: Competitors "shuck" piles of oysters at the World Oyster Opening Championship in Galway Town
Far right (top to bottom): Claddagh Quay in Galway Town; Twelve Ben mountain range in Connemara

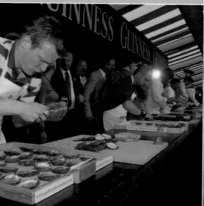

Championships on the Saturday afternoon, the oysters are served in all their glory in the festival marquee at the Claddagh, one of the oldest areas of the city. The marquee is erected on Nimmo's Pier, beside Galway Bay, and the festival's glamour is evident in the amount of *haute couture* you'll see making its way to the marquee via the Spanish Arch in Galway's Old Town.

Galway is conveniently located in the heart of the west of Ireland, and most of the 12,000 or so annual visitors to the festival make the most of their journey and venture beyond the folds of the marquee to search for a real sense of Irish life. The Aran Islands, Connemara, and The Burren are all on Galway's doorstep and await your discovery. Take the ferry over to Aran, an archipelago of three tiny islands where the primary language is Gaelic and life has a slower pace. A walk along the dramatic rocky coast will certainly awaken your Guinness-dulled senses as you stroll past fields that have been tamed over the years by the locals constantly working the craggy land. Or explore the eerie landscape of The Burren and the beauty of Connemara, and finish up in a cosy bar to start the *craic* all over again.

FURTHER DETAILS

GALWAY

Galway Oyster Festival
Various venues around Galway; four days in late Sep.
www.galwayoysterfestival.com

Aran Islands
Europe's westernmost point, these austere islands offer stunning coastal views and large prehistoric stone forts. You can reach them by taking a short flight from Connemara Airport or a ferry from Rossaveal.
www.aranislands.com

Connemara National Park
The unspoilt beauty of the Twelve Ben Mountains is home to a wealth of flora and fauna; open Mar–May and Sep–Oct: 10am–5.30pm daily; Jun–Aug: 9:30am–6.30pm daily.
www.connemaranationalpark.ie

The Burren
This desolate area of County Clare is a unique region in which Mediterranean and alpine plants can thrive.
www.burrennationalpark.ie

WHAT ELSE TO SEE AND DO

Our Lady Assumed into Heaven and St Nicholas
This magnificent cathedral in Galway was built in limestone and Connemara marble in 1965.
www.galwaycathedral.ie

Galway Market
This eclectic market is located outside the Collegiate Church of St Nicholas, the largest functioning medieval parish church in Ireland.
www.galwaymarket.ie

THE ESSENTIALS

GETTING THERE AND AROUND
Portmeirion is situated on the coast of North Wales on the estuary of the River Dwyryd. By public transport, travel to Porthmadog by train or bus, then take a train to Minffordd, which lies 2 km (1 mile) away from Portmeirion. You can walk from there or catch a bus. The village is 370 km (230 miles) from London.

WEATHER
Autumn in North Wales is often wet and windy, although spells of cool, dry, sunny weather are not uncommon. Daytime temperatures average 3–11°C on the coast and 0–5°C in the mountains.

ACCOMMODATION
Splashing Out Castell Deudraeth, in Portmeirion, is a castellated Victorian mansion that has been converted into a boutique hotel.
www.portmeirion-village.com

On a Budget The Travelodge in Porthmadog is only 3 km (2 miles) from Portmeirion. It is clean and comfortable, but has no food facilities – residents use local restaurants and cafés for meals.
www.travelodge.co.uk

EATING OUT
Splashing Out The Hotel Portmeirion Dining Room was designed by Clough Williams-Ellis in 1931 and redesigned in 2005 by Sir Jasper Conran. The menu features highlights of Welsh cuisine.
www.portmeirion-village.com

On a Budget Caffi Glas is an Italian-style restaurant in Portmeirion, offering pasta, pizzas, salads and snacks.
www.portmeirion-village.com

PRICE FOR TWO PEOPLE
Around £310 a day for food, accommodation, travel and entrance fees.

WEBSITE
www.visitwales.com
www.portmeirion-village.com

Previous page: Autumn in the acer glade at Westonbirt Arboretum, Gloucestershire

Main: Village of Portmeirion and the Dwyryd estuary **Right (top to bottom):** Black sheep sign above the wool shop; examples of Portmeirion's idiosyncratic style; Patrick McGoohan (left) in the TV series *The Prisoner*, set in Portmeirion

THE VILLAGE

THE IDIOSYNCRATIC VILLAGE OF PORTMEIRION is an extraordinary collection of Italianate buildings and sub-tropical gardens set high above the tranquil blue waters of the Dwyryd Estuary and against a background of the majestic mountains of Snowdonia. The village was built between 1925 and 1975 by an eccentric local architect, Sir Clough Williams-Ellis, who had vowed as a child to erect an ensemble of buildings that would represent his ideas on architecture, "and indeed be me". It is this sense of individual creativity that hits you very forcefully when you first see the surreal village he created and owned. How many architects would have thought to place together a collection of pastel-shaded, terracotta-roofed bungalows, colonnades, porticoes and Corinthian columns and set them among palm trees and fountains in North Wales? This is a rare sight indeed.

Williams-Ellis used "endangered" buildings from all over Britain, which were brought to Portmeirion and rebuilt, so that the steep slopes above the estuary now sport every architectural theme from Neo-Classical to Jacobean, and Gothic to Oriental, with Italianate

FURTHER DETAILS

PORTMEIRION VILLAGE
Portmeirion Village, Minffordd, Penrhyndeudraeth,
Gwynedd; open 9:30am–7:30pm daily.
www.portmeirion-village.com

WHAT ELSE TO SEE AND DO
Plas Brondanw
The family home of Sir Clough Williams-Ellis is not open
to the public, but you can visit the extraordinary gardens
and its charming cafe, which are divided into "rooms"
surrounded by hedges.
www.plasbrondanw.com

Ffestiniog Railway
The vintage steam trains of the world's oldest railway
company, established in 1832, run regular services from
Porthmadog to Blaenau Ffestiniog, climbing over 200 m
(700 ft) through the glorious Snowdonia landscapes
(see pp66–7). Alight at Minffordd for Portmeirion.
www.ffestrail.co.uk

Llechwedd Slate Caverns
There are 40 km (25 miles) of tunnels and 16
working levels at this massive slate mine near Blaenau
Ffestiniog, which can be visited on an organized visit
with spectacular Deep Mine Tour on the very steep
underground railway. There's also a reconstructed
Victorian mining village at ground level.
www.llechwedd-slate-caverns.co.uk

Below (top to bottom): Beach at Portmeirion; steam train
travelling down the Ffestiniog railway

style dominating. There's an architectural surprise around every corner as you
wend your way from the entrance down to the still, grey water of the Dwyryd
Estuary – one moment a Jacobean town hall stands proudly in front of you, the
next you find yourself walking through a Mediterranean piazza admiring a
sculpture of Buddha, or Siamese figures atop Ionic columns. It all sounds a bit
of a mish-mash of styles, but somehow it works, like a living museum of
world architecture.

    Wandering around Portmeirion is a chance to step away from real life for a few
hours, and if you visit in the autumn you'll avoid the often overcrowded cafés,
shops, gardens and woodland walks of summer. Consider an overnight stay at one
of the hotels or cottages here; the village is "closed" to the public in the evening,
so you'll get a more intimate feel for the place then. And really revel in the
other-worldly feel of Portmeirion, why not arrive by steam train on the Ffestiniog
Railway (see pp40–41)? It's as near as you're likely to get to stepping back in time.

MISTY MOUNTAINS

THE LOVELY MOUNTAINS OF MOURNE really do "sweep down to the sea", as the famous song proclaims. As you drive along the coast road south from the Irish resort of Newcastle, their rocky, wooded cliffs tower steeply above. When viewed from a distance inland, however, the grassy slopes appear deceptively gentle. It's only when you get up close that you can make out the rugged granite peaks and the steep flanks and moraines (glacial debris) leading up to them.

Tucked away in the southeast corner of Northern Ireland, between Carlingford Lough and the Irish Sea, the Mourne Mountains are designated as an Area of Outstanding Natural Beauty, and are excellent hiking country. They cluster together in a compact area stretching 24 km (15 miles) inland from the coast and measuring just over 11 km (7 miles) wide. The highest peak, Slieve Donard, rises 850 m (2789 ft) above sea level. A relatively easy trail leads from the coast at Bloody Bridge up to the summit, where there are incredible views across the mountains.

The best way to see beyond the mountains' perimeter is on foot, as only a few narrow roads penetrate the interior. Autumn is the best time to take to the trails, when the grasses and heathers erupt in golden and purple hues, and the skies and slopes play host to an amazing

Main: Walker looking over the Silent Valley from the summit of Slieve Bearnagh

THE ESSENTIALS

GETTING THERE AND AROUND
The Mountains of Mourne are on the east coast of Northern Ireland, between Newcastle and Newry. The nearest airports are Belfast City Airport and Belfast International Airport, 48 km (30 miles) and 84 km (52 miles) north of Newcastle respectively. Once there, an Ulsterbus "Mourne Rambler" service provides good access to the mountains.

WEATHER
The weather varies enormously in and around the mountains. In autumn, expect anything from sunny days to gales and pouring rain, with average daytime temperatures of 7–10°C.

ACCOMMODATION
Splashing Out The Slieve Donard Resort and Spa, in Newcastle, has earned a reputation as one of the most luxurious hotels in Northern Ireland.
www.hastingshotels.com

On a Budget The Briers, in Newcastle, is a beautiful 18th-century country house at the foot of the Mountains of Mourne, set in its own gardens.
www.thebriers.co.uk

EATING OUT
Splashing Out The Oak Restaurant, in the Slieve Donard Resort, has traditional decor and some of the best food for miles.
Tel: 028 4372 1066

On a Budget Cafe Mauds offers light bites and a range of ice creams with lovely views of the waterfront.
www.visitmournemountains.co.uk

PRICE FOR TWO PEOPLE
From around £150 a day for food and accommodation.

WEBSITES
www.mournelive.com
www.armaghanddown.com

variety of birdlife, from peregrine falcons and owls to skylarks, song thrushes, lapwings and red grouse. The author C S Lewis was so struck by these mountains' magical atmosphere that he declared that they made him feel that at any moment a giant might raise his head over the next ridge. The Mountains of Mourne were the inspiration for Lewis's mythical kingdom of Narnia, and whether you go on one of the challenging hikes to the high summits, or for a gentler walk in forest parks on the lower slopes, you can't help but be struck by the area's mysterious beauty.

Head inland from Annalong or Kilkeel, following signs to the Silent Valley, and you'll reach the starting point for the circular Viewpoint Walk, about 5 km (3 miles) long. This takes you around a reservoir and affords magnificent views of the surrounding peaks. Here you'll also see the remarkable Mourne Wall, a drystone wall that was built to define land boundaries in the early 1900s. It runs for 35 km (22 miles) and connects over 15 mountains – passing near or over the summits of all but one – making for a challenging but extraordinary walk.

FURTHER DETAILS

THE MOUNTAINS OF MOURNE
The Silent Valley Mountain Park, situated in the high Mournes, has an information centre and restaurant with impressive views over the mountain range. The visitor centre is open Jul–Aug: 11am–6:30pm daily; Jun and Sep: 11am–6:30pm Sat–Sun only.
www.mourne-mountains.com/mournes

WHAT ELSE TO SEE AND DO
Newcastle Beaches
The popular seaside resort of Newcastle, at the foot of Slieve Donard, has an 8-km (5-mile) expanse of beach and a busy promenade. Nearby is beautiful Tyrella Beach, a conservation area of mature dunes and scenic walks.
www.discovernorthernireland.com

Tollymore Forest Park
Giant Gothic gateways mark the entrance to Northern Ireland's oldest forest park, in the foothills of the Mourne Mountains, 3 km (2 miles) from Newcastle on the B180.
www.discovernorthernireland.com

Castlewellan Forest Park
Lying on the outskirts of Castlewellan, near Newcastle, this park forms the grounds of a baronial castle. Its highlights are a magnificent arboretum, dating from 1740, and superb views of the Mourne Mountains across the castle's lake.
www.discovernorthernireland.com

Downpatrick
North of the mountains, Downpatrick has several religious sites associated with St Patrick, including Down Cathedral, whose churchyard is reputed to be the burial place of Ireland's three patron saints: Patrick, Brigid and Colmcille.
www.discovernorthernireland.com

Below (top to bottom): Male red grouse, Mourne Wall

THE ESSENTIALS

GETTING THERE AND AROUND
Fountains Abbey and Studley Royal are in North Yorkshire, 47 km (29 miles) northwest of York. The nearest airport is Leeds/Bradford International Airport, 38 km (24 miles) to the south. The nearest town is Ripon, 6 km (4 miles) to the northeast; buses run from here to the abbey's visitor centre.

WEATHER
Autumn in North Yorkshire is generally mild but can be chilly. Although the weather is usually fair, it's wise to prepare for rain at all times. The average daytime temperature ranges from 4 to 11ºC.

ACCOMMODATION
Splashing Out The Old Deanery, in Ripon, is a charming 17th-century hotel and restaurant with immaculate rooms opposite Ripon Cathedral.
www.theolddeanery.co.uk

On a Budget The Old Coach House, in North Stainley, offers faultless rooms at a snug lakeside retreat a few kilometres from Fountains Abbey.
www.oldcoachhouse.info

EATING OUT
Splashing Out The Old Deanery, in Ripon, is a perfect place for atmospheric dining, with a grade-A menu and a splendid setting.
www.theolddeanery.co.uk

On a Budget Lockwoods, in Ripon, offers great food prepared using local produce, and has a relaxed vibe.
www.lockwoodsrestaurant.co.uk

PRICE FOR TWO PEOPLE
£160–210 a day for accommodation, food and entrance fees.

WEBSITE
www.yorkshire.com

BREATHTAKING RUINS

ENGLAND'S MOST SUBLIME ARCHITECTURAL RUIN, Fountains Abbey is also the largest and grandest of Britain's monastic sites. The roofless and skeletal abbey church with its staggeringly long nave – culminating in an arched window opening at each end – is the abbey's defining image, particularly at its eastern extremity where the Chapel of the Nine Altars stands. The nave is overlooked by the 50-m- (160-ft-) high Perpendicular Tower, a sturdy and dramatic edifice dating from the early 16th century. The remarkable arched Cellarium to the south, in which goods were stored and lay brothers ate their meals, is testament to the ambitious nature of Fountains Abbey – it is 90 m (300 ft) long and was built over the Skell River.

Dating from 1132, and located within a North Yorkshire landscape wreathed in history, Fountains Abbey was founded by Benedictine monks – who later adopted the more frugal monastic rule of the Cistercian order – in an area described at the time as "more fit for wild beasts than men to inhabit". The monastery's 400-year working life was brought to an end during the Dissolution of the Monasteries in Henry VIII's reign, and it was sold to Sir Richard Gresham, a London merchant. The abbey's lead, glass and stone were plundered: the building material for the neighbouring Jacobean mansion Fountains Hall was sourced from the site. In 1767 Fountains Abbey was purchased by William Aislabie, who incorporated it into the grand landscaping plans for Studley Royal, giving the ruins a new lease of life.

Fountains Abbey, set in over 320 hectares (800 acres) of prime North Yorkshire countryside, is an idyllic setting for lazy picnics and captivating walks. After you've spent the day exploring the monastery and its extraordinary countryside setting, in the midst of the autumnal blaze of reds and yellows, the complex begins to conjure up further magic at twilight. Saturdays in autumn bring the highlight of Fountains' year, when you can experience the floodlit monastic ruins echoing to the sound of nocturnal choir music and Gregorian chants – a perfect end to a truly atmospheric trip.

Main: Ruined nave of the abbey
Below: Fountain Abbey's impressive, vaulted Cellarium

FURTHER DETAILS

FOUNTAINS ABBEY
Fountains Abbey, near Ripon, North Yorkshire; open daily, check website for specific opening times.
www.nationaltrust.org.uk

Fountains Hall
A 16th-century mansion set in Studley Royal; opening times as for Fountains Abbey.

Fountains by Floodlight
In autumn the abbey is floodlit in the evening, while recorded Gregorian chant fills the air. A choir sings sacred and classical music from 8–9pm. Sep–Oct: dusk–10pm Sat only; last admission 9pm.

Studley Royal
Georgian water gardens, ornamental lakes and numerous follies; opening times as for Fountains Abbey. The Deer Park is open daily year-round during daylight hours. There are organized Deer Walks to watch the red, fallow and sika deer in rutting season (Aug–Nov).

WHAT ELSE TO SEE AND DO
Ripon
The North Yorkshire market town of Ripon is well worth exploring, especially for the small Ripon Cathedral and the nearby Market Place where the watchman sounds his horn every night at 9pm. For relaxation, take a walk along the peaceful and attractive Ripon Canal.
Ripon www.discoverripon.org
Ripon Cathedral www.riponcathedral.org.uk

Newby Hall
Lying southeast of Ripon, Newby Hall is an attractive 17th-century house set within 10 hectares (25 acres) of exquisite gardens. The interior of the house, designed by Scottish architect Robert Adam, is particularly stunning, and is beautifully accented by a lavish collection of paintings, porcelain and furniture.
www.newbyhall.com

Below: The Studley Royal Water Garden

THE ESSENTIALS

GETTING THERE AND AROUND
Lewes is in southeast England, 93 km
(58 miles) from London. Trains run
between Lewes and London Victoria
every 30 minutes from Monday to
Saturday, and every hour on Sunday
(journey time 70 minutes). There are
buses from Brighton to Lewes (journey
time 30 minutes) every 15 minutes from
Monday to Saturday, and every hour on
Sundays. The town is easily explorable
on foot.

WEATHER
In November the weather in Lewes
is relatively pleasant, but always be
prepared for rain and chilly winds, with
daytime temperatures from 4 to 10°C.

ACCOMMODATION
Splashing Out The Shelleys, on Lewes
High Street in the heart of town, is a
4-star 17th-century manor-house hotel
with buckets of character.
www.the-shelleys.co.uk

On a Budget Berkeley House, on Albion
Street, is a late-Georgian 4-star town
house B&B with considerable charm.
www.berkeleyhouselewes.com

EATING OUT
Splashing Out Pelham House Restaurant, on St Andrews Lane, is a 16th-
century house with a gorgeous menu
and fine views of the Downs.
www.pelhamhouse.com

On a Budget John Harvey Tavern, on
Cliffe High Street, is a traditional cosy
pub with a great range of beers and
pub food.
www.johnharveytavern.co.uk

PRICE FOR TWO PEOPLE
Around £160–210 a day for food,
accommodation and entrance fees.

WEBSITES
www.lewesonline.com
www.lewes.co.uk

Main: Costumed revellers at the bonfire night procession in Lewes

ALL FIRED UP

Sitting on the river Ouse and rising and falling with the gentle undulations of the magnificent South Downs, the East Sussex county town of Lewes is a fetching vignette of narrow lanes, time-warped wood-framed buildings and all the tidy elegance of a historic English market town. Lewes is charming all year round, but its cultural calendar literally explodes every 5 November, when it hosts Britain's largest and most famous bonfire night.

Lewes's remarkable anti-Catholic bonfire traditions, managed by local bonfire societies, honour the deaths of 17 Lewes Protestants martyred in the mid-16th century, as well as celebrating the anniversary of Guy Fawkes's demise in 1605. The festivities are highly tribal and religiously partisan, with smuggler costumes, riotous music, flying sparks, clouds of smoke and a tangibly martial flavour. The "Bonfire Boys" (and girls) of the seven societies blacken their faces, don striped smuggler's jerseys and raise flaming torches and crosses to parade through the streets as one, before dividing into their separate societies and returning to their respective "firesites" (home districts) to kindle bonfires and light fireworks. Effigies of Guy Fawkes and Pope Paul V (made head of the Catholic Church in 1605), along with more

FURTHER DETAILS

LEWES

Lewes Bonfire Night
Bonfire Night takes place on 5 November, unless this is a Sunday, in which case the celebrations are staged the night before; the first procession begins at around 5pm with the last one ending roughly at midnight. If you are planning to stay in Lewes on bonfire night, book your hotel room and restaurant table early. It can be wet and muddy at the bonfire sites, so wrap up and take waterproofs and suitable footwear. It's best to arrive in Lewes by train, as the streets are closed for the processions and it's very difficult to park in town.
www.lewesbonfirecouncil.org.uk

Lewes Castle
Open Mar–Oct: 10am–5:30pm Tue–Sat, 11am–5:30pm Sun–Mon and public Holidays; Nov–Feb: 10am–3.45pm Tue–Sat, 11am–3.45pm Sun–Mon and public Holidays (closed Mon in Jan).
www.sussexpast.co.uk/lewescastle

Anne of Cleves House
Open Mar–Oct: 10am–5pm Tue–Thu, 11am–5pm Sun, Mon and Bank Holidays; Nov–Feb: 10am–4pm Sat, 11am–5pm Sun.
www.sussexpast.co.uk/anneofcleves

WHAT ELSE TO SEE AND DO

Bluebell Railway
Taking its name from the bluebells that grow alongside the line in spring, this steam-engine railway runs on an old rail line between Sheffield Park, just north of Lewes, and East Grinstead. Trains run regularly in summer and autumn until October, and then for special events only over the winter months. Check the website for details.
www.bluebell-railway.co.uk

Brighton
A short bus or train trip takes you to the pebbly beaches, seaside charms and Georgian buildings of Brighton (*see pp38–9*). Visit the Royal Pavilion, amble to the tip of Brighton's famous Palace Pier and don't overlook wandering the Lanes, where a medley of small antique, knick-knack and jewellery shops share space with restaurants and bars.
www.visitbrighton.com

Glynde Place
A vast Elizabethan manor house 6 km (4 miles) from Lewes, with incredible views across the South Downs to the Weald. Treasures include art, craft and furniture pieces collected by the family over three centuries. The large gardens offer captivating walks.
www.glynde.co.uk

Below: Picturesque Keere Street in Lewes

current "villains", are sent up in flames. Some bonfire societies still propel burning barrels of tar into the river, which is a truly dramatic sight. The town heaves with visitors; if you can't make the 5 November celebrations, look out for others in the preceding and following weeks, both in Lewes and at the nearby villages of Battle, Newick and Mayfield.

Much of the appeal of Lewes draws from its historic street layout and its timber-framed buildings and "twittens", the Sussex name for the narrow lanes seen in these parts. The town also serves as a useful starting point for walks in the South Downs, which can be seen in all their rolling glory from Lewes Castle, a fortification erected in 1087 on a man-made hill, the town's highest point. Other highlights include the historic architecture and medieval charm of Keere Street – a steep and cobbled incline once famously navigated by the Prince Regent in his carriage – and Anne of Cleves House, a wood-framed Tudor building. The pretty Elizabethan gardens of Southover Grange provide a beautiful spot for a picnic.

THE ESSENTIALS

GETTING THERE AND AROUND
Stoke-on-Trent is 260 km (160 miles)
northwest of London. Birmingham,
Manchester and East Midlands airports
are all within 100 km (60 miles) of the
city. Trains from London Euston to
Stoke-on-Trent take approximately 90
minutes. Local buses run regularly from
the station to the main attractions; otherwise there are well-signed road links.

WEATHER
Autumn often brings spells of fine
weather to the area, but be prepared
for some wind and rain, with average
daytime temperatures ranging from
6 to 13°C.

ACCOMMODATION
Splashing Out A short drive from Stoke-
on-Trent, the 16-century Weston Hall is
a secluded luxury retreat set in beautiful
Staffordshire countryside.
www.weston-hall.co.uk

On a Budget New Hayes Farm B&B,
6 km (4 miles) from Stoke, is a Victorian
farmhouse on a working farm that
serves award-winning breakfasts.

EATING OUT
Splashing Out Located in a 14th-century
manor house in Acton Trussell, The
Moat House's award-winning restaurant
focuses on British game and seafood.
www.moathouse.co.uk

On a Budget The Dining Hall, at
the Wedgwood Visitor Centre, is an
open-plan restaurant open to non-visitors
that serves delicious home-cooked food
using local produce.
www.worldofwedgwood.com

PRICE FOR TWO PEOPLE
From around £160 a day for food,
entrance fees and accommodation.

WEBSITE
www.visitstoke.co.uk

POTTERING ABOUT

THE SPRAWLING CONURBATION OF STOKE-ON-TRENT – made up of six
smaller towns in England's industrial heartland – is inextricably linked
with the story of an entire industry. Ceramics have been made in the Potteries – the
towns of Burslem, Fenton, Hanley, Longton, Stoke and Tunstall – for centuries, and
a visit to Stoke-on-Trent provides a chance to learn about the region's long and
distinguished history of pottery-making. You can also browse the numerous factory
shops and stock up on classy tableware, and autumn is the ideal time to find that
perfect Christmas gift of fine bone china, before the busy festive season begins.

Stoke's pottery trade started in the 17th century, when farmer-potters used
the area's red and brown clays to make earthenware "butterpots". From the
mid-18th century the potters wanted white clay, similar to china from the Far
East, so they began to bring this up from Devon and Cornwall. Early innovators
included Josiah Wedgwood, who developed the highly-collectible "creamware",
and Joseph Spode, who invented bone china, the toughest form of porcelain.

The Potteries boomed during the Industrial Revolution of the 18th and 19th
centuries. The region, once covered with smoke from hundreds of brick bottle
kilns – so named for their bottle-like shape – supplied ceramic goods across the
British Empire. Stoke-on-Trent is unusual among British industrial cities in that
its key industry is still going strong: it has hundreds of pottery firms and
remains a world centre for ceramic design and production.

To get a real feel for the grimy old days, visit the Gladstone Pottery Museum at
Longton. This typical 19th-century bone-china pottery was saved from demolition
in the 1970s, and it is the last surviving complete Victorian pottery in the country.
It has plenty to offer: have a go at hands-on pot-throwing, and explore a huge
collection of ceramic artifacts, including a display of antique toilets. The
Middleport Pottery, home to the traditionally crafted and renowned Burleigh
ceramics, gives an insight into its Victorian past and its modern-day factory floor.
Sandwiched between two of the city's canals is the Etruria Industrial Museum,
home to a mill once used to crush bone and flint for the china industry.

Founded by Josiah Wedgwood in 1759, Wedgwood is the best-known china
pottery company in the city, and its visitor centre and museum at nearby Barlaston
are worth a visit. You can try throwing a pot, and there's a wonderful array of
priceless Wedgwood antiques on show, as well as contemporary jasper ware for sale.

Main: Red-brick interior of a bottle kiln at Gladstone Pottery Museum **Below (left to right):** Gladstone
Pottery Museum; the sign outside the Wedgwood Visitor Centre and Museum

FURTHER DETAILS

STOKE-ON-TRENT

Gladstone Pottery Museum
Uttoxeter Road, Longton, Stoke-on-Trent; open Apr–
Sep: 10am–5pm daily; Oct–Mar: 10am–4pm daily.
www.stokemuseums.org.uk

Middleport Pottery
Port Street, Burslem, Stoke-on-Trent; open 10am–
4pm daily.
www.ceramicauk.com

Etruria Industrial Museum
Lower Bedford Street, Etruria, Stoke-on-Trent;
opening hours vary – see website for details.
www.etruriamuseum.org.uk

Wedgwood Visitor Centre and Museum
Barlaston, Stoke-on-Trent; open 10am–5pm Mon–Fri,
10am–4pm Sat–Sun; closed 24 Dec–1 Jan.
www.worldofwedgwood.com

WHAT ELSE TO SEE AND DO

Emma Bridgewater
This contemporary working pottery, factory shop and
decorating studio in Hanley allows you to paint your
own pieces, and offers guided tours that give you the
opportunity to see a working pottery in action.
www.emmabridgewater.co.uk

The Potteries Museum and Art Gallery
This extensive, purpose-built free museum in Hanley
is home to the world's finest collection of Staffordshire
ceramics. There are also displays of pottery from across
the world, along with exhibits on local and natural
history and fine work by local artists.
www.stokemuseums.org.uk

Trentham Estate
First noted in the Domesday Book in 1086, this historic
estate offers stunning parkland, an Italian Garden, a
lake, a giant observation wheel and lots of
family activities.
www.trenthamleisure.co.uk

Below (top to bottom): The Potteries Museum and Art
Gallery; magnificent Italian Garden at the Trentham Estate

THE ESSENTIALS

GETTING THERE AND AROUND
Loch Lomond is 32 km (20 miles) – less than an hour's drive – from Glasgow, where the closest international airport is located. The Trossachs is easily reached from Stirling, 26 km (16 miles) away via Callander, or from Aberfoyle (32 km/20 miles away). You will need a car to explore the many beautiful drives within the national park. There are also scenic boat trips on Loch Katrine and Loch Lomond.

WEATHER
The weather can change rapidly here, especially in the mountains, so prepare for rain even on fine days. Average daytime temperatures range from 6 to12ºC.

ACCOMMODATION
Splashing Out The Roman Camp Hotel, in Callander, is a country-house hotel set in extensive grounds by the River Teith and has an acclaimed restaurant.
www.romancamphotel.co.uk

On a Budget The Balloch House offers stylish, comfortable accommodation in a historic lodge near Balloch Castle Country Park and right on the foot of Loch Lomond.
Tel: 01389 752579

EATING OUT
Splashing Out The Restaurant at the Roman Camp Hotel is simply named but serves up stunning flavours.
www.romancamphotel.co.uk

On a Budget The Byre Inn, in Brig o' Turk, uses locally sourced ingredients to make adventurous dishes with a Scottish twist.
www.byreinn.co.uk

PRICE FOR TWO PEOPLE
£170 a day for food and accommodation.

WEBSITES
www.visitscottishheartlands.com
www.trossachs.co.uk

Main: Low autumn cloud over Loch Lomond **Right (top to bottom):** Mountain biker exploring a trail by Loch Lomond; road winding through countryside in the Trossachs; steam boat on Loch Katrine

TAKE THE HIGH ROAD

WITH ITS BONNIE, BONNIE BANKS immortalized in the classic Scottish ballad, Loch Lomond is one of Scotland's most famous lochs. Less well-known, but equally beautiful, is the Trossachs region that surrounds it. Together they make up Scotland's first national park, which was established in 2002. Covering an area of around 1,865 sq km (720 sq miles), the park is like a miniature version of Scotland itself, encompassing its quintessential landscapes, from mountains, lochs and glens to forests and rolling lowlands.

At 37 km (23 miles) long, Loch Lomond is the largest expanse of fresh water in Great Britain. Known as the Queen of Scottish Lochs, its narrow, northern neck is bordered by steep mountains, while its southern half spreads out into a wide watery blue cloak, encrusted with dozens of jewel-like islands known as "inches". These privately owned islands, some of which appear only when the water levels are very low, have, over the years, provided havens for everyone from whisky-runners to saintly hermits, and you can see them up close from the pleasure boats that cruise the loch from several ports.

FURTHER DETAILS

LOCH LOMOND AND THE TROSSACHS
There is something for all tastes in the Loch Lomond and Trossachs National Park: hill-walking, cycling, boating, golf and, for the more adventurous, canoeing, kayaking, windsurfing and mountain biking.
www.lochlomond-trossachs.org

Loch Lomond Shores
This shopping, dining and activity complex is located at Balloch on the southern end of Loch Lomond. The Gateway Centre here is a visitor centre for Loch Lomond and Trossachs National Park. There are audio-visual shows, woodland walks, bike- and canoe-hire, cruises and more.
www.lochlomondshores.com

Trossachs Discovery Centre
The visitor centre on Aberfoyle's Main Street provides an overview of the history and geography of the region.
Tel: 01877 382 352

Lake of Menteith
The romantic ruins of Inchmahome, a 13th-century Augustinian priory, lie on an island in this scenic lake. They are accessible by ferry from the Port of Menteith.
www.historic-scotland.gov.uk

WHAT ELSE TO SEE AND DO
Stirling Castle
There are fantastic views from the ramparts of this impressive castle in Stirling, dating from 1496. It features striking Renaissance architecture and some period rooms.
www.historic-scotland.gov.uk

> The Trossachs… is like a miniature version of Scotland itself, encompassing its quintessential landscapes, from mountains, lochs and glens to forests and rolling lowlands.

Below: Port of Menteith Church reflected in the Lake of Monteith

Stretching north and east of Loch Lomond, the Trossachs has been a popular holiday spot since the late 18th century. Its lowlands contain one of the few Scottish "lakes", the Lake of Menteith, and the foothills around Aberfoyle mark the beginning of the Highlands. From here, a road winds up through Queen Elizabeth Forest Park and over Duke's Pass to Loch Katrine; it's a drive of exceptional beauty when the woodlands display their full autumn glory. Alternatively, a minor road west from Aberfoyle leads you into the wild glens along the shores of Loch Lomond, once the territory of the MacGregor clan. Some of the national park's most dramatic scenery lies in the Breadalbane region to the north. The scenic road from Killin to Tyndrum is spectacular, taking you past Ben More, the park's highest peak at 1,174m (3,852 ft). More mountains surround Argyll Forest Park, west of Loch Lomond. From Arrochar, drive up Glen Croe for stunning views, before descending through the atmospheric forest of Hell's Glen to Lochgoilhead.

THE ESSENTIALS

GETTING THERE AND AROUND
The Great North Run takes place in the northeast of England: it starts in Newcastle upon Tyne and finishes in South Shields. Newcastle International Airport is 11 km (7 miles) northwest of Newcastle. The Tyne and Wear Metro links the airport with the city centre and South Shields. Buses connect the quayside with the city centre.

WEATHER
In September the weather in Newcastle is normally cool and relatively dry, with average daytime temperatures ranging from 9 to 16ºC.

ACCOMMODATION
Splashing Out Malmaison Newcastle, on the quayside, has stunning views of the waterfront and is a short distance from the Millennium Bridge.
www.malmaison.com/locations/newcastle

On a Budget Jurys Inn Newcastle, on Scotswood Road, is a functional modern hotel about 10 minutes' walk from Newcastle city centre.
www.jurysinns.com/hotels/newcastle

EATING OUT
Splashing Out Café 21, in Newcastle's Trinity Gardens, is a smart restaurant in the heart of the quayside that offers contemporary European food and classic bistro dishes in stylish surroundings.
www.21newcastle.co.uk

On a Budget Panis Café, on High Bridge, Newcastle, is a genuine Italian establishment serving Sardinian and other regional dishes.
www.paniscafe.co.uk

PRICE FOR TWO
£160–210 a day, including food and accommodation.

WEBSITE
www.visitnortheastengland.com

ROAD RUNNERS

Since its inception in 1981, the Great North Run has become one of the biggest days in the British sporting calendar. With 50,000 runners cheered on by 30,000 spectators lining the route, the half-marathon – now the largest in the world – celebrates both the determination of the athletes taking part and the rejuvenated cityscapes of Newcastle, Gateshead and South Shields that provide the Run's backdrop. Elite runners tackling the 21-km (13-mile) route are joined by thousands of amateurs, many relying on sheer guts – rather than athleticism – to complete the route and raise millions of pounds for charity.

The tension builds as the competitors assemble at the starting point at Newcastle's Town Moor before the hooters sound to release the hordes of runners, their bobbing heads forming a rippling stream. The route takes the runners under the iconic arch of the Tyne Bridge, and those who have timed their run perfectly will cross from Newcastle to Gateshead just as the Red Arrows thunder overhead, leaving behind coloured smoke trails. But inspiration soon turns to perspiration as the runners spread out, pass Gateshead International Stadium, and head east towards the sea and South Shields. A sharp downhill section leads to the coast, where bands and supporters gather to provide the encouragement needed to move aching limbs. Eventually, the runners catch sight of the finish gantry, where the electronic clocks record times and stewards ensure chaos is avoided as the runners, in various stages of exhaustion and exuberance, cross the line and head towards their belongings and loved ones.

Once the hurly-burly of the run is over, competitors and spectators have time to explore the diverse urban heart of Tyneside, where world-class arts venues such as the Sage Gateshead, with its astonishing curved-glass structure, and the Baltic Centre for Contemporary Art, housed in a converted flour mill, vie for attention with Newcastle's famed nightlife. The city's tough face, which can be seen in the buildings that stand as memorials to the region's industrial past, has been softened by new architectural marvels, including the astonishing tilting Millennium Bridge over the Tyne, and public art along the quayside. Tyneside is a modern success story – a region that has successfully reinvented itself, some would say against the odds – and the Great North Run is the perfect symbol of its continued vitality.

Main: Red Arrows passing over runners on the Tyne Bridge
Below (left to right): Baltic Centre for Contemporary Art; Millennium Bridge over the Tyne

FURTHER DETAILS

THE GREAT NORTH RUN
The run takes place in either Sep or Oct annually.
www.greatrun.org

The Sage Gateshead
St Mary's Square, Gateshead Quays, Gateshead;
open 9am–11pm daily, subject to performance times.
www.thesagegateshead.org

The Baltic Centre for Contemporary Art
Gateshead Quays, South Shore Road; open 10am–6pm
Wed–Mon, 10:30am–6pm Tue.
www.balticmill.com

The Millennium Bridge
The Millennium Bridge links Newcastle to Gateshead,
and tilts daily at noon.
www.newcastlegateshead.com

WHAT ELSE TO SEE AND DO

Newcastle Castle Keep
Constructed in the 12th century to defend Newcastle
from Scottish invasions, the castle keep is a must-see.

St James' Park Tour
Football fans will enjoy taking a tour of St James' Park
stadium, home of Newcastle United.
www.nufc.co.uk

Bamburgh Castle
Standing guard over miles of uncrowded
Northumberland beaches, Bamburgh Castle is a
dramatic starting point for any historical tour of
the region.
www.bamburghcastle.com

The Alnwick Garden
These fabulous gardens in Alnwick were created by
the Duchess of Northumberland.
www.alnwickgarden.com

Durham The beautiful medieval city of Durham
features the UNESCO World Heritage Site of
Durham Cathedral.
www.thisisdurham.com

> Tyneside is a modern success
> story – a region that has
> successfully reinvented itself,
> some would say against the odds
> – and the Great North Run is a
> symbol of its continued vitality.

THE ESSENTIALS

GETTING THERE AND AROUND
Manchester is in the northwest of England. Manchester Airport is 16 km (10 miles) to the south of the city, and trains run from here to the city centre (Manchester Piccadilly station). Trains run from London approximately every 20 minutes and half-hourly from Liverpool. Most of central Manchester can be explored on foot, but there's also an extensive bus network.

WEATHER
Manchester enjoys a mild climate, with average autumn daytime temperatures ranging from 5 to 15ºC. The city gets less rain than many parts of the UK, but it's best to be prepared.

ACCOMMODATION
Splashing Out Velvet, on Canal Street, is a stunning hotel with lavishly equipped rooms and an exceptional restaurant with superb service.
www.velvetmanchester.com

On a Budget Ivy Mount Guesthouse, in Eccles, 6 km (4 miles) from the city centre, is a 3-star B&B with smart rooms and handy transport links to the city centre.
www.ivymountguesthouse.co.uk

EATING OUT
Splashing Out Gaucho Grill, on St Mary's Street, is a spacious Argentinian restaurant offering mouth-watering steaks and exceptional service.
www.gauchorestaurants.co.uk

On a Budget Set in Manchester's Little Italy district, next to the Northern Quarter, Ruby's Neapolitan Pizza uses traditional ingredients and authentic recipes.
www.facebook.com/RudysPizzaMcr

PRICE FOR TWO PEOPLE
From £190 a day for food, accommodation and entrance fees.

WEBSITE
www.visitmanchester.com

Previous page: A flock of fallow deer in Studley Royal Park, standing next to Ripon's renowned St Mary's Church

Main: Modern arched Merchants Bridge over the Bridgewater Canal **Right (top to bottom):** Statue outside Old Trafford Football Stadium; Central Library; one of the paintings on display in Manchester Art Gallery

INDUSTRIAL REVELATION

ONCE A MANUFACTURING GIANT processing more than 65 per cent of the world's cotton, Manchester still enjoys international fame. The city that grew up at the forefront of the Industrial Revolution is home to Manchester United, the wealthiest and most popular football club in the world. Fans from Mexico to China make pilgrimages just to visit Old Trafford in the southwest of the city, for guided tours of the hallowed stadium. The city has also given rise to some ground-breaking popular music – Oasis, the Stone Roses, the Happy Mondays, the Smiths and Take That are all on the roll-call of local bands.

Manchester's eclectic and stylish restaurant culture is also a great reason to visit. Although this cosmopolitan university city can be explored at any time of year, 250,000 people visit in autumn to sample the gastronomic delights on offer at the Manchester Food and Drink Festival. All of the city's restaurants, bars, cafés, pubs and delis put on special tastings and talks, the festival pavilion hosts "mini" festivals, of wine, whisky and real ale, and St Anne's Square is abuzz with chef demonstrations and busy market stalls selling delicious local food. In between bouts of eating and drinking, turn your attention to the rest of what Manchester

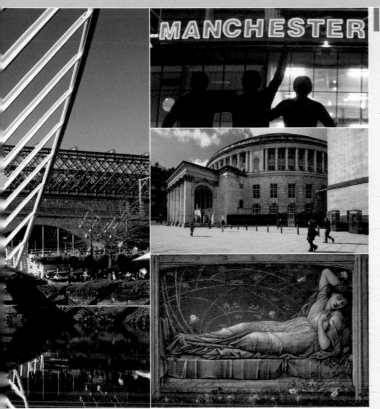

FURTHER DETAILS

MANCHESTER

Manchester United Museum and Stadium Tour
Old Trafford; **Museum:** open 9:30am–5pm Mon–Sat,
10am–6pm Sun (closed on match days); **Stadium
tours:** every 10 minutes from 9:40am–4:30pm
(except on match days).
www.manutd.com

Manchester Food and Drink Festival
Held in September or October at venues across the city.
www.foodanddrinkfestival.com

Manchester Art Gallery
Mosley Street; open 10am–5pm daily (to 9pm Thu).
www.manchesterartgallery.org

Albert Memorial
Albert Square.

Manchester Town Hall
Lloyd Street; open 9am–5pm Mon–Fri.
www.visitmanchester.com

Central Library
St Peter's Square; open 9am–8pm Mon–Thu,
9am–5pm Fri–Sat.

Free Trade Hall
St Peter's Square.

Manchester Cathedral
Victoria Street; open 8:30am–5:30pm Mon & Fri,
8:30am–6:30pm Tue–Thu, Sat & Sun.
www.manchestercathedral.org

Museum of Science and Industry
Liverpool St; open 10am–5pm daily.
www.msimanchester.org.uk

The Lowry Arts Centre
Pier 8, Salford Quays; open 11am–5pm Sun– Fri,
10am–5pm Sat.
www.thelowry.com

WHAT ELSE TO SEE AND DO

Chester
Enclosed within ancient walls, the historic city of Chester
has a clutch of interesting sights. From the half-timbered
Tudor and Victorian buildings that line The Rows to the
cathedral and castle, Roman relics and nearby Chester
Zoo, this small city offers something for everyone.
www.visitchester.com

has to offer. The impressive form of Manchester Art Gallery contains an
abundant and varied catalogue of art, including a strong selection of Pre-
Raphaelite oil paintings. The architecture, too, is worthy of attention. The most
magnificent structures owe much to the Mancunians' allegiance to Queen
Victoria: they demolished 100 buildings to erect Britain's first Albert Memorial
in 1865, and then built Albert Square around it, before adding the imposing
Neo-Gothic Town Hall and other Victorian gems. Neighbouring St Peter's
Square boasts its own architectural delights, including the Neo-Classical circular
Central Library and the palazzo-style Free Trade Hall. And Manchester
Cathedral, near the River Irwell, is home to an extraordinary Saxon carving, the
8th-century Angel Stone.

Don't overlook the canals and Victorian viaduct scenes of Castlefield, where
fragments of a Roman fort survive. On a rainy day, you can have a lot of fun
exploring the Museum of Science and Industry, or discovering more about
Manchester's industrial past through the works of its most famous painter,
L S Lowry (1887–1976), at The Lowry Arts Centre in Salford Quays. And if you're
still full of energy at the end of a satisfying day of exploration, Manchester's
famous nightlife and bar scene offer limitless entertainment.

Below: Lowry footbridge over the Manchester Ship Canal

THE ESSENTIALS

GETTING THERE AND AROUND
The New Forest is in Hampshire, in the south of England. The nearest airport is at Bournemouth, 27 km (17 miles) from Brockenhurst. Regular trains run to Brockenhurst from London Waterloo. Local buses run from both Brockenhurst and Lyndhurst to points within the forest; the New Forest Tour Bus runs from June to September between the forest's principal towns.

WEATHER
The New Forest enjoys a pleasant and mild climate in autumn, but prepare for changeable weather. Average daytime temperatures range from 7 to 14°C.

ACCOMMODATION
Splashing Out Rhinefield House Hotel, in Brockenhurst, is a secluded and grand 4-star country-house hotel in the heart of the New Forest.
www.handpickedhotels.co.uk

On a Budget Whitemoor House Hotel, in Lyndhurst, is a well-liked B&B with a handy central location.
www.whitemoorhouse.co.uk

EATING OUT
Splashing Out Lanes of Lymington, in Lymington, is a former schoolhouse converted into a stylish restaurant with a classy contemporary menu.
www.lanesoflymington.com

On a Budget La Pergola, in Lyndhurst, is an authentic family-run Italian restaurant in an attractive setting opposite open forest. Good value, popular puddings and a fun atmosphere.
www.la-pergola.co.uk

PRICE FOR TWO PEOPLE
£130–160 a day for accommodation, food and local transport.

WEBSITE
www.newforestnpa.gov.uk

A ROYAL FOREST

ORIGINALLY A HUGE SWATHE of uninterrupted woodland, the New Forest – recorded as "Nova Foresta" in the Domesday Book – is a scenic sanctuary for stressed urbanites and wildlife enthusiasts. Ranging over an area of 375 sq km (145 sq miles), this national park is today far less a forest than a vast, diverse patchwork of heathland, grassland, wetland and woodland, embracing a rich ecological diversity and a wonderful range of wildlife.

Deer have always populated the area, which was the principal reason why William the Conqueror designated it a "forest" – the medieval term for a royal hunting reserve – in the 11th century. Today, five species roam the forest; you'll need patience and a degree of luck to get close-up views of them, as they are extremely shy creatures. The largest and most impressive species is the red deer: the heftiest land mammal in the British Isles, the male is an imposing sight during the rutting (mating) season, which runs from mid-September to the end of October. Displaying their dense coats, muscular build and huge, magnificent antlers, the stags square off against each other in their challenge. The contest is usually decided through a mixture of performance and posturing, but if there is a battle, it can be ferocious.

The forest is also home to sika deer, originally from Japan, and the shy, rare muntjac deer from China. You may also catch a glimpse of the small roe deer, whose rutting season finishes in late summer. Fallow deer are among the most common animals in the forest, and you should see plenty of their white-spotted bodies flashing among the trees of this ancient royal park. Failing all else, you're virtually guaranteed to see them gathered beneath the viewing platform at the Bolderwood Deer Sanctuary in the forest, where they are fed regularly. But by far the most conspicuous animals in the forest are domesticated cattle and pigs, and, of course, the semi-wild New Forest ponies. As you watch them wandering lazily around villages and even poking their noses into shops, you'd be forgiven for thinking that all the local wildlife is friendly, but watch out for adders, which go slithering back to their hibernation sites in autumn.

Main: Red deer with bracken in its antlers **Below (left to right):** Red deer stags tussle during a "rut", New Forest ponies grazing on the forest floor

FURTHER DETAILS

NEW FOREST

New Forest Visitor Centre
Main car park, Lyndhurst; open 10am–5pm daily. There are also Visitor Information points scattered throughout the New Forest.
www.thenewforest.co.uk

The two main tourist towns in the New Forest are Lyndhurst and Brockenhurst.
Lyndhurst: www.newforest-online.co.uk/lyndhurst.asp
Brockenhurst: www.brockenhurst-newforest.org.uk

New Forest Tour Bus
The New Forest Tour offers one-day bus tickets that can be bought online, allowing you to hop on and off at will. Bicycles are allowed on board; runs mid-Jun–mid-Sep.
www.thenewforesttour.info

Bolderwood Deer Sanctuary
Deer are fed daily from April to September at this deer park, situated near the main Bolderwood car park. Several signposted, graded walks start here too, passing through ancient woodland.
www.new-forest-national-park.com/bolderwood-deer-sanctuary.html

WHAT ELSE TO SEE AND DO

Beaulieu
Lying within the New Forest, Beaulieu — pronounced "Bewley" — is a famous collection of sights, including the Palace House, home to the Montagu family since the 16th century; Beaulieu Abbey; the National Motor Museum; the World of Top Gear and stunning gardens.
www.beaulieu.co.uk

Below: Rambling through the New Forest National Park

WINDOWS ON THE PAST

THE SHANNON REGION OF WESTERN IRELAND is peppered with nearly 1,000 castles. While most stand in various stages of ruin and can only be glimpsed from a distance, Bunratty Castle is marvellously intact, and, together with its surrounding folk park, lets you experience history up close. Built on the site of a 10th-century Viking camp near the Shannon estuary, this imposing fortress dates back to 1425. It was sensitively restored in 1954 to its full medieval glory, inside and out, and now allows you to travel majestically back in time.

The castle is home to the extraordinary Bunratty Collection – some 450 pieces of medieval furniture, art and artifacts. But this is no staid museum. While parents admire the vaulted ceilings, tapestries and other highlights such as the rare 17th-century harpsichord in the South Solar Room, young imaginations will be fired by the castle's exciting features, such as "murder holes", gaps above passageways that were used to drop missiles or boiling liquids onto invaders passing beneath. Actors in medieval costume bring the past to life with entertaining tours, and there are great views from the ramparts.

In the evening, you can attend a medieval feast in the castle's splendid banqueting hall, with its minstrels' gallery. On the menu are dishes such as roast beef, which you eat with your fingers and wash down with mugfuls of mead. Then you can sit back and enjoy medieval and traditional Irish music. Autumn also offers seasonal pleasures such as September's Traditional Harvest Day and spooky Halloween events.

In the grounds around the castle, Bunratty Folk Park features more than 30 buildings that re-create local life in the 19th century, ranging from a fisherman's cottage to a Georgian gentleman's residence. Blacksmiths, thatchers, potters, weavers and other characters in period clothing demonstrate their workaday skills. You can buy flour freshly ground at the watermill or try a slice of hot griddle bread baked by the farmer's wife. Along the village street you'll find the schoolhouse, printworks, hardware shop and grocery. The pretty Walled Garden has been restored to a Regency style, and once again supplies fruit, vegetables and flowers to the castle.

THE ESSENTIALS

GETTING THERE AND AROUND
Bunratty Castle is in the town of Bunratty, which is about 13 km (8 miles) east of Shannon Airport and 12 km (7½ miles) west of Limerick, in County Clare on the west coast of Ireland. There are buses between Limerick and the airport at Shannon, which go directly past the castle, but it is most easily visited by car.

WEATHER
The weather in Bunratty in the autumn is usually mild, with average daytime temperatures of 9–14°C. Expect changeable conditions, however.

ACCOMMODATION
Splashing Out The Bunratty Castle Hotel is a luxury spa resort, offering a diverse range of rooms and facilities, a short stroll away from Bunratty Castle.
www.bunrattycastlehotel.com

On a Budget Bunratty Villa, in Bunratty, offers comfortable and affordable rooms set in elegant grounds, within walking distance of the castle.
www.bunrattyvilla.com

EATING OUT
Splashing Out The Bunratty Castle Hotel's Round Room is an upmarket restaurant serving excellent meals and fine wine.
www.bunrattycastlehotel.com

On a Budget The Original Durty Nelly's Pub has two reasonably priced restaurants, and there are cheaper bar meals available too.
www.durtynellys.ie

PRICE FOR A FAMILY OF FOUR
Around €360 a day for accommodation, food and entrance fees.

WEBSITE
www.shannonheritage.com

Main: South Solar Room at Bunratty Castle
Below: Re-creations of 19th-century housing in the Folk Park in Bunratty

FURTHER DETAILS

BUNRATTY CASTLE AND FOLK PARK

Bunratty, Shannon, County Clare; open 9am–5pm daily.
www.shannonheritage.com

WHAT ELSE TO SEE AND DO

Limerick
Sprawled at the head of the Shannon estuary,
Ireland's fourth-largest city has several attractions in
its medieval core. Visit King John's Castle, a Norman
fortress boasting historical and interactive exhibits, and
12th century St Mary's Cathedral with its old tombs and
carved oak misericords (carvings under seats). Don't
miss the outstanding Hunt Museum which houses
an eclectic collection ranging from Celtic treasures to
medieval artifacts and fine art.
King John's Castle: *www.shannonheritage.com*
St Mary's Cathedral: *www.cathedral.limerick.anglican.org*
Hunt Museum: *www.huntmuseum.com*

The Burren
For a scenic drive, head north into County Clare, where
you'll find the vast limestone plateau of the Burren –
one of the most unusual landscapes in Ireland. It's
dotted with tiny, rare plants as well as prehistoric
dolmens and medieval ruins. It stretches all the way
to the sea, to one of Ireland's prime beauty spots, the
Cliffs of Moher.
www.cliffsofmoher.ie

Craggaunowen
Authentically reconstructed buildings at the
archaeological open-air museum of Craggaunowen,
16 km (10 miles) north of Bunratty, demonstrate the
lifestyle of the ancient Celts. The exhibits include a ring
fort, a *crannog* (island settlement) and a medieval
castle. There are also rare-breed farm animals and the
leather-hulled Brendan Boat, used to re-enact the 6th-
century journey of St Brendan.
www.shannonheritage.com/craggaunowen

Below: Bunratty Castle illuminated at night and Durty Nelly's Pub

THE ESSENTIALS

GETTING THERE AND AROUND
Cornwall is in the southwest of the UK, about 5 hours' drive or train journey from London. The three main routes by car into the county are the A39 north coast road (which passes many good surf beaches), the A30 across Dartmoor and the A38 over the River Tamar. There are regular flights from London and other UK cities to Newquay's small airport.

WEATHER
Autumn daytime temperatures vary from 9 to 18°C, falling off considerably in late autumn when it may get close to freezing at night. Water temperatures vary from around 18°C early in the season to around 13°C later on.

ACCOMMODATION
Splashing Out Watergate Bay Hotel, in Watergate Bay, is literally right beside the surf and alongside the "Extreme Academy" for high-adrenaline sports. *www.watergatebay.co.uk*

On a Budget Reef Island, in Newquay, is a good option if you want to combine surfing and nightlife. *www.reefislandsurflodge.com*

EATING OUT
Splashing Out The Beach Restaurant, above Sennen Beach, overlooks the most consistent surf in Cornwall. *www.sennenbeach.com*

On a Budget Godrevy Café is based in an attractive wooden chalet overlooking Gwithian Towans, near St Ives. *www.godrevycafe.co.uk*

PRICE FOR TWO PEOPLE
From £160 a day for accommodation, food and transport.

WEBSITES
www.visitcornwall.com
www.magicseaweed.com

Main: Surfing enthusiasts taking to the water off Newquay **Right (top to bottom):** Riding the dramatic Atlantic surf off Fistral Beach, Newquay; blokarting on the beach near St Ives

SURF'S UP!

Beaches empty of summer visitors, swells rolling in from the North Atlantic and the warmest waters of the year make autumn the best time to hit the surf in North Cornwall. With more than 80 surfing locations off magical bays and coves, and plenty of surf schools, this rugged coast is the perfect place to feed your surfing addiction or try out exciting new activities, such as windsurfing, kite surfing, wave-skiing and blokarting.

Newquay is the obvious starting point: not only does it have several great surf beaches, but it is the centre of the county's après-surf action. Watergate Bay, just up the coast, promises glassy waves and a quieter setting; and if you want spectacularly blue seas, white sands and the chance of surfing with dolphins, check out Sennen, near Land's End. Alternatively, just strap your surfboard on to the roof of your car, throw your wetsuit in the back and go exploring as the autumn sun warms the sand and reflects rainbows off the back of the breaking waves.

The sea is never far away in Cornwall, and its call is irresistible: try a fishing safari aboard one of the boats departing from Newquay and catch some mackerel for supper, or take a

FURTHER DETAILS

NORTH CORNWALL

Surfing and Water Sports
North Cornwall has many surf schools, including the
Fistral Beach Surf School, Newquay. Speedsail UK,
based near St Ives, offers lessons in blokarting; the
Extreme Academy on Watergate Bay offers tuition and
rentals for many water- and beach-based sports.
Fistral Beach Surf School: *www.fistralbeach.co.uk*
Speedsail UK: *www.speedsailuk.com*
Extreme Academy: *www.watergatebay.co.uk*

Eden Project
Bodelva, Cornwall; opening times vary according to
season; see website for further details.
www.edenproject.com

The Lost Gardens of Heligan
Pentewan, Cornwall; open 10am daily; closing times
vary according to season.
www.heligan.com

Tate St Ives
Porthmeor Beach, St Ives, Cornwall; open Mar–Oct:
10am–5:20pm daily; Nov–Feb: 10am–4:20pm daily.
www.tate.org.uk/stives

Barbara Hepworth Museum and Sculpture Garden
Barnoon Hill, St Ives, Cornwall; open Mar–Oct: 10am–
5:20pm daily; Nov–Feb: 10am–4:20pm Tue–Sun.
www.tate.org.uk/visit/tate-st-ives

Below (top to bottom): Tideflats at Newquay Harbour; the
Eden Project site

wildlife-watching boat from Padstow harbour to spot peregrine falcons, seals and
dolphins. On wind-lashed days, when the sea's too wild for surfing and beach
rambles, there's still plenty to see and do; stroll around one of North Cornwall's
impossibly pretty fishing villages, squeezing down narrow lanes between
whitewashed cottages to find tiny pubs once frequented by smugglers. Or head
south to the Eden Project, where you can visit the giant geodesic domes housing
exotic plants from around the world. Nearby, the restored Lost Gardens of
Heligan at Pentewan are often less crowded than the Eden Project and just as
rewarding, with superb kitchen gardens, a wildlife hide and a boardwalk through
giant rhubarb and banana plantations. Culture vultures will enjoy the arty
enclave of St Ives, where the light has attracted many artists over the years. Here
is the Cornish outpost of the Tate Gallery, a museum and garden housing the
works of sculptor Barbara Hepworth, and other galleries where you can browse
and buy original artworks.

THE ESSENTIALS

GETTING THERE AND AROUND
Hereford is in the west of England, 2 hours 40 minutes from London by train. Trains and long-distance buses also link Hereford with Worcester (42 km/26 miles away), and Birmingham (108 km/67 miles away), home of the nearest international airport. Once in Herefordshire, cycling allows freedom, versatility and scenic enjoyment.

WEATHER
Herefordshire enjoys a mild and pleasant climate, with average autumn daytime temperatures of 9–17°C. Always be prepared for fickle weather, however, especially if cycling or walking.

ACCOMMODATION
Splashing Out The Feathers Hotel, in Ledbury, is located within a historic "black and white" coaching inn situated in the heart of town.
www.feathers-ledbury.co.uk

On a Budget Lowe Farm Bed and Breakfast, in Pembridge, is a working farm with a welcoming, homely atmosphere – a perfect escape in the heart of rural England.
www.bedandbreakfastlowefarm.co.uk

EATING OUT
Splashing Out Set on an organic cider-making farm, The Cider Barn prides itself in using local, seasonal produce, and its dining room has a welcoming atmosphere.
www.the-cider-barn.co.uk

On a Budget Cafe@All Saints is housed in the 13th-century All Saints Church in Hereford. The great setting is coupled with home-cooked breakfasts and lunches using regional ingredients.
www.cafeatallsaints.co.uk

PRICE FOR TWO PEOPLE
From £130 a day for accommodation and food.

WEBSITE
www.ciderroute.co.uk

Main: Apple orchards in Newton, near Leominster **Right (top to bottom):** Demijohns of cider; cider press in action; "black and white" timber-framed cottages at Pembridge

CIDER COUNTRY

ITS FERTILE LAND LARGELY DEVOTED TO AGRICULTURE, Herefordshire – nudging up against the Welsh border – is famed for its Hereford beef cattle and, of course, its glorious fruit, especially apples. The county is home to an extraordinary number of orchards and cider makers, making its pastoral villages ripe for scrumptious exploration. In autumn the cider apple harvest brings out the full richness, colour and flavour of the Herefordshire countryside.

Today's Herefordshire is delightfully dappled with cider orchards, spreading over 39 sq km (15 sq miles), and the county boasts the world's largest cider mill (Bulmers). A portion of the annual 286 million litres (63 million gallons) of Herefordshire cider enriches the local cuisine with apple aromas. A host of cider festivals – from the Cider-Making Festival and The Big Apple Festival in Hereford to the Ross-on-Wye Cider Festival – add extra sparkle to a tour of the county, with much consumption of the cloudy drink, festive music and a fair degree of merriment. At the Flavours of Hereford Food Festival in late October, apple pressing and tasting is just one part of a broader celebration of the outstanding local produce. Cycling through the rolling Herefordshire countryside is an ideal way to experience the rustic charms

FURTHER DETAILS

HEREFORDSHIRE

Hereford Tourist Office
Town Hall, St Owen St.
www.visitherefordshire.co.uk

Hereford Cider Museum
Pomona Place, Hereford; open Apr–Oct: 10am–5pm
Mon–Sat (and over the Cider-Making Festival
weekend); Nov–Mar: 11am–3pm Mon–Sat.
www.cidermuseum.co.uk

Hereford Cider-making Festival
Demonstrations of traditional cider-making, usually held
in late October at the Hereford Cider Museum.
www.cidermuseum.co.uk

The Big Apple Festival
This harvest festival celebrates apples and pears in
all their incarnations, as raw fruit, juices, alcoholic
drinks and even teas. It takes place across several
Herefordshire villages in early October each year.
www.bigapple.org.uk

Ross-on-Wye Cider Festival
The festival is held in September at Ross-on-Wye Cider
and Perry Company, Broome Farm, Peterstow.
www.rosscider.com

Cycling Routes
Leaflets detailing cycle routes are available from the
Ledbury Tourist Information Centre and other tourist
information centres.

Hereford Cathedral
College Cloisters, Cathedral Close, Hereford;
open 9:15am–5:30pm daily.
www.herefordcathedral.org

Mappa Mundi and Chained Library
The Chained Library is the cathedral's collection of
manuscripts, many dated earlier than 1500. The
Chained Library and Mappa Mundi are now housed
in the New Library at Hereford Cathedral; open
10am–4pm Tue–Thu; 10am–1pm first Sat of the
month; other times by appt.

Church of St Mary and St David
Kilpeck, near Hereford.

of this county – and you get to work off any weight you've accumulated from
cider-drinking by getting from A to B. Hop on a pair of wheels and embark upon
the 32-km (20-mile) Ledbury cycle route, which runs along tranquil lanes,
through pretty villages and past historic pubs. You can load up with fruit from
farms along the way. Or try the 30-km (19-mile) Pembridge cycle route, which
also winds its way past orchards and whisks you past Dunkertons Cider Mill,
an organic cider-making farm.

Be sure not to overlook Herefordshire's other charms. On the western flank of
the Malvern Hills, Ledbury is an attractive enclave of half-timbered Tudor and
Stuart architecture, a highlight on the Herefordshire "Black and White" villages trail.
Perched on the River Wye, the city of Hereford is where the eclectically styled
Hereford Cathedral can be found, dating from 1079, and the adjacent New Library
contains the Mappa Mundi, a 14th-century map of the world that ranks among the
country's finest historical documents. The nearby village of Kilpeck has a well-
preserved Norman church – the Church of St Mary and St David – that contains a
variety of exquisite religious carvings. Finally, take a walk around Ross-on-Wye,
a small town perfectly poised for scenic sojourns along the Wye River Valley.

Below: Herefordshire countryside on a frosty morning

THE ESSENTIALS

GETTING THERE AND AROUND
The River Tay runs for 193 km (120 miles) through central Scotland, reaching the sea outside the town of Perth. The nearest international airports are at Edinburgh and Glasgow, 66 km (41 miles) and 110 km (68 miles) from Perth. There are train connections from Glasgow and Edinburgh to Perth, then on to Dunkeld and Pitlochry. Car hire is available at the airports, and in Perth, Pitlochry and larger towns.

WEATHER
Early autumn weather on the Tay is often sunny, but mist, drizzle and heavy rain are always possible, with average autumn daytime temperatures of 6–11°C.

ACCOMMODATION
Splashing Out Hilton Dunkeld House, in Dunkeld, is a luxury hotel and leisure club that offers a range of rooms and activities on a landscaped estate by the river.
www.hiltondunkeld.com

On a Budget The Kenmore Hotel, in Kenmore, claims to be the oldest inn in Scotland, in a great location overlooking the river as it flows out of Loch Tay. Its restaurant serves good Scottish fare.
www.kenmorehotel.com

EATING OUT
Splashing Out Deans, in Perth, is a fine modern restaurant with an emphasis on tasty local produce prepared with culinary flair.
www.letseatperth.co.uk

On a Budget The Courtyard at Mains of Taymouth, in Kenmore, has a good, mid-priced restaurant and deli-style café.
www.taymouth.co.uk/restaurant

PRICE FOR TWO PEOPLE
£160 a day for accommodation, activities, food and entrance fees.

WEBSITE
www.visitscotland.com/see-do/active/fishing

A QUEST FOR SILVER

LIKE SILVER BLADES SLICING through the water, salmon carve a path from the North Sea to the headwaters of the Tay on an annual autumn journey to their spawning grounds. It's a prospect to thrill the heart of any angler – for many, the chance to dip a line into Scotland's longest river is the fulfilment of a lifetime's ambition.

There are a variety of methods you can use here to catch salmon: trolling on the loch, which involves dragging a baited line through the water from a boat; fly-fishing from land beside the Tay's upper reaches; and bait-fishing from boats or the river's banks. Each stretch of the Tay – from the mirror-calm waters of the loch to tree-lined stretches concealing deep underwater potholes, home to massive fish – calls for different angling skills and techniques, challenging even the most experienced of anglers. And the fish themselves are no easy catch; they are strong enough to swim upstream, leaping out of the rushing waters of rapids and waterfalls in their determination to return home. South of Perth, the River Earn – a tributary of the Tay that joins it at the wide Firth of Tay – is a great location to cast for hard-fighting sea trout, and also offers more opportunities for salmon fishing.

If you eventually sate your appetite for angling, pay a visit to Aberfeldy, where the Tay passes under the elegant Wade Bridge, designed by the Scottish architect William Adam in 1733. The little town has become a hub for adventure sports guaranteed to get the adrenaline flowing, from kayaking and slalom canoeing to white-water rafting on rapids. Sailing dinghies, motor cruisers and fishing boats can also be hired at nearby Kenmore, where the river exits Loch Tay between thickly wooded banks. On land, the region offers mountain-bike trails for novices and experienced riders, off-road quad biking and 4WD wildlife safaris.

There are plenty of golf courses to choose from. Perthshire has 40 courses, in glorious parkland, heathland and Highlands settings. Some back right on to the Tay. Anglers will be absorbed by their quest for silver in Scotland's famous river, but for their friends and families, its banks and tranquil lochs also provide a fantastic experience.

Main: River Tay near Dunkeld at sunset
Below (left to right): Salmon fishing at Kenmore; off-road quad biking; Kenmore and Loch Tay

FURTHER DETAILS

RIVER TAY

Tay Salmon Fisheries Company
Stockgreen Lodge, Lairwell, Kinfauns, Perth. You can fish for salmon in the river at Cargill and on the estuary near Perth, and for trout at the Willowgate fishery, home to rainbow, blue and brown trout. The Tay District Salmon Fisheries Board urges anglers to return all female fish and all males weighing over 7 kg (15 lb) to the water; open for salmon fishing 15 Jan–15 Oct: dawn until dusk Mon–Sat; open for trout fishing all year round, 8am–dusk daily.
www.taysalmon.co.uk

FishPal
This award-winning company offers guided fishing trips to many of Scotland's rivers, including the Tay. FishPal's local guides have specialist knowledge of the Tay and its inhabitants.
www.fishpal.com

WHAT ELSE TO SEE AND DO

Golf
The most popular golf course in the region is Dunkeld & Birnam Golf Club, a 100-year-old heathland course.
www.dunkeldandbirnamgolfclub.co.uk

Pitlochry Salmon Ladder
Thousands of salmon battle their way up the 34 artificial pools of the world's first "salmon ladder" each year on the River Tummel, a tributary of the Tay at Pitlochry.

Canoeing
The Scottish Canoe Association has a slalom site at the Grandtully rapids on the River Tay, and also maintains its own camp site near Grandtully village.
www.canoescotland.org

Quad Biking and Mountain Biking
Activity Scotland offers quad- and mountain biking, climbing, abseiling, gorge-walking and more.
www.activityscotland.com

Wildlife Safaris
Highland Safaris in Aberfeldy offer walking and 4WD safaris around the mountains and forests of Perthshire.
www.highlandsafaris.net

> For many anglers, the chance to dip a line into Scotland's longest river is the fulfilment of a lifetime's ambition

More Great Ideas for **Autumn**

| |

William the Conqueror's Battle Abbey in East Sussex

Red knot calidris flock over Snettisham in October

Inveraray, on the shores of Loch Fyne

BATTLE ABBEY SOUTHEAST ENGLAND

William the Conqueror, Duke of Normandy, built Battle Abbey on the site of the Battle of Hastings to commemorate his victory against the Saxon King Harold in 1066. The altar in the abbey church is said to mark the very spot where King Harold fell. Evocative audio tours pitch visitors into the bloody melee of the battlefield and "interviews" with monks, soldiers and other witnesses bring the day-long conflict to life. In the autumn, a battle re-enactment takes place on the site.
www.english-heritage.org/battleabbey

CROFT CASTLE
WEST MIDLANDS
With wonderful views over the Welsh Marches, this castellated late-17th-century house has a remarkable Georgian interior and is set in glorious parkland, which has miles of walking trails.
www.nationaltrust.org.uk

KILCHURN CASTLE
CENTRAL SCOTLAND
Abandoned after being struck by lightening in the 18th century, Kilchurn Castle sits on Loch Awe. It's a magnificent sight in autumn, when the hills behind it turn a flaming red.

DEVIL'S BRIDGE CENTRAL WALES

Near Aberystwyth are three bridges that span both the River Mynach and 900 years. Unusually, these bridges are built on top of each other: the lowest bridge dates from the 12th century, the middle one from the 18th century and, on top of that, an iron bridge built in 1901 that carries the Vale of Rheidol narrow-gauge railway. There are walks from the bridge to the 90-m (300-ft) Mynach Falls, the Devil's Punchbowl crater and steps known as "Jacob's Ladder".
www.tourism.ceredigion.gov.uk

TRAQUAIR HOUSE
SOUTHERN SCOTLAND
Visited by 27 kings and queens over its 900-year history, Scotland's oldest inhabited house exudes atmosphere. After a tour, sample Traquair House ales.
www.traquair.co.uk

WESTONBIRT ARBORETUM
SOUTHWEST ENGLAND
Heart-warming autumnal colour from a collection of more than 18,000 trees and shrubs, in 240 hectares (600 acres) of glorious parkland.
www.forestry.gov.uk

SNETTISHAM EASTERN ENGLAND

In the autumn, thousands of thrushes and finches migrate over this RSPB reserve on the Wash in Norfolk, described as an "avian motorway service station". Waders, noisy wigeon and Brent geese converge at Snettisham, while pink-footed geese roost on the Wash and fly inland at dawn to feed on sugar beet remnants. Look out for the breathtaking spectacle of giant flocks of knot – a species of wading bird – taking off in their hundreds as the tide covers their roost.
www.rspb.org.uk

INVEREWE GARDENS HIGHLANDS AND ISLANDS

Inverewe Gardens lie on the same latitude as Canada's Hudson Bay, yet warm currents from the Gulf Stream ensure that the site is mild all year round, enabling temperate plants to grow. The 20-hectare (50-acre) woodland gardens, on a craggy hillside, were created in 1862, and contain 2,500 species of plant. Its walled sections contain many unusual and exotic plants, and elsewhere otters, pine martens, seals and red deer can be found, along with marvellous views.
www.nts.org.uk

BOG OF ALLEN
EASTERN IRELAND
A massive peat bog covering 960 sq km (370 sq miles) in the Irish Midlands, the Bog of Allen is rich in history, ecology and walking routes, and there is also a nature centre to visit.
www.ipcc.ie

KIELDER FOREST
NORTHEAST ENGLAND
Among the many events that take place in England's largest forest is the autumnal forest foray. Some interesting wildlife can also be found here, such as red squirrels and bats.
www.forestry.gov.uk

INVERARAY CENTRAL SCOTLAND

Lying on the wooded shores of Loch Fyne, Inveraray is one of Scotland's most attractive towns in autumn, when the richly coloured trees create a vivid backdrop to its fine castle. Home of the Dukes of Argyll, the castle was redesigned and the town rebuilt by the second Duke in the 1740s. Heavily influenced by French architecture, yet unmistakably Scottish, Inveraray Castle houses magnificent interiors and a fascinating old jail that puts on ghost-hunting events.
www.inveraray-argyll.com

SELBORNE SOUTHEAST ENGLAND

This pretty village is famous for being the home of Gilbert White, the 18th-century naturalist who wrote the much-loved *The Natural History and Antiquities of Selborne.* His house hosts regular workshops and exhibitions, and is set against the backdrop of a beautiful beech wood, through which White built a steep zig-zag path. You can also visit the Oates Museum, which charts Lawrence Oates' part in Scott's expedition to the South Pole in 1910–1913.
www.hampshirescountryside.co.uk

DUNMORE EAST
SOUTHERN IRELAND
Pretty cottages and a bustling harbour characterize this charming fishing village, which hosts the Dunmore East Autumn Leaves Golf Classic competition in September.
www.waterford-dunmore.com

KENMARE SOUTHERN IRELAND

An up-market town boasting charming streets, gourmet restaurants, friendly pubs and a huge sweep of sandy bay. Kenmare is a great place to stay, especially out of season, when the roads are less crowded. Take the 170-km (105-mile) circular tourist trail, known as the "Ring of Kerry", which has breathtaking views of Macgillycuddy's Reeks mountain range, a glaciated valley and fantastic beaches. For a brush with history, search out the stone circle known as "The Shrubberies".
www.ringofkerrytourism.com

See also pp144–5, 164–5.

See also pp124–5, 134–5, 150–51, 158–9.

See also pp132–3, 140–1, 148–9, 156–7.

One of the statues of *Another Place*, on Crosby Beach

Tintagel Castle in Cornwall

Gothic fan enjoying the Goth Weekend in Whitby

ANOTHER PLACE NORTHWEST ENGLAND

The artist Antony Gormley put Crosby on the map when his installation, *Another Place*, was moved to the beach there. One hundred cast-iron, life-size statues, made from casts of the artist's own body, are set along 3 km (2 miles) of beach and 1 km (½ mile) out to sea. Previously exhibited abroad, the figures are now permanently placed at Crosby. A brisk beach walk offers a close encounter with the figures, which are best viewed at low tide.
www.visitsouthport.com

HOT-AIR BALLOON FESTIVAL NORTH WALES

Visit Llangollen in late summer and you'll see mass hot-air balloon launches and a night event, when the balloons are illuminated like giant light bulbs in the night sky.

GOTH WEEKEND IN WHITBY NORTHEAST ENGLAND

Whitby has literary associations with Dracula – in the novel, it is where the vampire arrives in England – and so it is the perfect spot for a celebration of all things Gothic. The event is held during the week of Halloween, with the main events on 31 October, and attracts people of all ages. Most of the events take place at the 1,000-capacity Whitby Pavilion, and include a strange bazaar, music and comedy acts, a charity football match and many fringe events.
whitbygothweekend.co.uk

SELF-GUIDED CYCLING TOURS
NORTHERN IRELAND

Cycling tours are offered around Ulster and Connaught until the end of October, in sparsely populated areas with frequently clear roads.
www.emeraldtrail.com

TINTAGEL CASTLE SOUTHWEST ENGLAND

Steep steps lead walkers to the romantic ruins of Tintagel Castle, set in a spectacular wave-lashed location on the cliffs of north Cornwall. Visitors have never let facts get in the way and they flock to this magical site keen to believe that it was, as legend has it, the birthplace of King Arthur. Splendid views can be enjoyed from the headland. Scramble down the rocks to Merlin's Cave, which lies just below Tintagel and leads on to a sandy cove.
www.english-hertiage.org.uk

OYSTER AND WELSH PRODUCE FESTIVAL
NORTH WALES

A celebration of Anglesey's high-quality food and drink, this is a weekend for tantalizing the taste buds at the Trearddur Bay Hotel in October. Thousands come to this friendly fair, where celebrity chefs give demonstrations and food and drink producers ply their wares. There are also crafts, a "sausage competition" and live music. Delicious foodstuffs include oyster fritters, crab cakes and laver bread.
www.angleseyoysterfestival.com

RAFT-BUILDING
CENTRAL WALES

Raft-building at Glasbury guarantees fun and a thorough soaking. Barrels, ropes and planks are used to make rafts that are strong enough to race on the River Wye.
www.blackmountain.co.uk

SEVINGTON LAKES
SOUTHWEST ENGLAND

These spring-fed lakes have pitches for coarse fishing and offer day-long sessions and night fishing by arrangement. Fish stocks include carp, rudd, perch, tench and roach.
www.go-fish.co.uk

HALLOWEEN AT WOOKEY HOLE
SOUTHWEST ENGLAND

For 50,000 years, the caves at Wookey Hole, set deep in the Mendip Hills, have been home to humans or animals. Evidence of this comes from archaeological artifacts, including flint tools and the bones of ice-age animals such as mammoths. Today the cavernous chambers are a major tourist attraction with a resident real-life "witch" and a circus, and at Halloween there are special spooky events.
www.wookey.co.uk

BARNSTAPLE OLD FAIR SOUTHWEST ENGLAND

Barnstaple's world famous fair is thought to date from 930. Throughout the centuries its traditions have been honoured, starting with toasts of spiced ale and a gloved hand being displayed from a window of the Guildhall to signify the hand of friendship to all-comers. The fair continues with a grand procession and the reading of the proclamation. It's only then that the thousands who attend the four-day event can really let their hair down and enjoy the fairground rides.
www.barnstapletowncouncil.co.uk/barnstaple-fair.asp

NORDIC WALKING SOUTHERN SCOTLAND

Nordic walking, also called "ski walking", involves the use of poles to increase the use of the upper body, turning walking into a full-body workout. Originating in Finland in the 1930s, it was designed to help competitive cross-country skiers keep fit in the off-season, but it became a popular recreational activity during the 1980s, and is now a mainstream activity in Scotland's many hiking regions. The gentle landscapes of Dumfries and Galloway are perfect beginner country.
www.cndoscotland.com

STONE SKIMMING AT EASDALE ISLAND
CENTRAL SCOTLAND

Easdale is a 5-minute ferry ride from the adjacent island, Seil, off the west coast of Argyll. A car-free island without roads, it was once an important slate-mining community, as evidenced by the abandoned, water-filled quarries. Easdale is famous today as the location of the one-day World Stone Skimming Championships, which take place on a quarry here in September. Just turn up to register and take part.
www.stoneskimming.com/easdale

INVERNESS
CENTRAL SCOTLAND

Fireworks illuminate the skies above Inverness on Guy Fawkes Night. There's also a torch-light procession, huge bonfire and funfair, all located in Bught Park.
www.inverness-scotland.com

WASDALE HEAD SHOW
NORTHWEST ENGLAND

This October country show features country delights such as fell races, wrestling, vintage cars and dog trials in a beautiful Lake District setting.
www.wasdaleheadshow.com

See also pp126–7, 142–3, 152–3, 162–3, 166–7.

See also pp128–9, 130–1, 160–1.

See also pp136–7, 146–7.

WINTER

Snow-covered
farmland in
Wiltshire,
England

WINTER IN GREAT BRITAIN AND IRELAND

WHEN DOES WINTER TRULY BEGIN? Some believe that it's marked by the end of British Summer Time in October, when the clocks are set back by an hour (ensuring that Britain and Ireland remain perpetually an hour out of step with countries in mainland Europe). But this would deny autumn its rightful place and ignore the seasonal change that occurs in the weather come December, when the days are at their shortest. Purists argue that the season's true beginning is the winter solstice, on 22 December, the shortest day of the year and the date of a pagan festival traditionally celebrated at Stonehenge. It's certainly true that over most of Britain and Ireland, real winter conditions of snow and ice rarely take hold until after Christmas or even the New Year. A "white Christmas" – even in northern Scotland – is an increasingly rare event. There has been widespread snow on Christmas Day only once since 1990, and bookmakers will happily take your money if you wish to bet that one snowflake will fall on the Meteorological Office on Christmas Day. But it wasn't always so. During the 17th and 18th centuries, the stretch of the River Thames that runs through London sometimes froze over completely, and "frost fairs" – complete with makeshift taverns, food stalls, river skating and other entertainment – took place on the ice. Most famously, the river froze solid for two whole months in the winter of 1683–84, and even King Charles II and his courtiers joined in the cavorting.

Christmas markets offer unusual gifts and delicacies from all over the world.

Some of Britain's winter traditions are truly ancient. We still deck homes, churches and public places with boughs of mistletoe and holly, one of the last relics of pagan tradition from the pre-Christian, Celtic winter solstice festival of 25 December, which became the Christian festival of Christmas. Many other aspects of the "traditional" British Christmas are much more recent embellishments. The Christmas tree, with its lights and decorations, is a German tradition, unheard of in Britain until it was popularized by Queen Victoria's German consort, Prince Albert. The Christmas turkey is another innovation: until well into the 20th century, the traditional Christmas roast was a goose or ham.

Christmas markets are a tradition that temporarily disappeared under Oliver Cromwell's puritanical reign. They resurfaced in Victorian times and today many cities, notably Dublin, Edinburgh, London and Birmingham, host colourful seasonal markets offering unusual gifts and delicacies from all over the world. The switching on of Christmas illuminations by local dignitaries is every town's official signal that the festive season has truly

Below (left to right): Christmas at Winchester Cathedral; Hogmanay fireworks, Edinburgh

begun. Great excitement accompanies the illumination of the mighty fir tree in London's Trafalgar Square, which is donated each year by the people of Norway in remembrance of British support during World War II. But despite the older pagan and newer commercial traditions, Christmas Eve and Christmas itself remain the greatest of Christian festivals, celebrated with carol singing and candlelit midnight services at the great cathedrals, such as Canterbury, York and Winchester, and in the tiniest of village churches. At home, Christmas Day is a private riot of unpacking stockings, ripping open presents and eating too much.

Marchers parade with great balls of fire that are hurled into the harbour at midnight.

If Christmas Day is the biggest family occasion of the year, New Year's Eve is the public party. Traditionally celebrated most gloriously in Scotland, Hogmanay has grown from an informal, one-night affair into a four-day festival that draws hundreds of thousands of visitors to Edinburgh to see out the old year. In Stonehaven, on the east coast of Scotland, marchers parade with great balls of fire that are hurled into the harbour at the stroke of midnight, while in smaller Scottish towns Hogmanay is a community party at which everyone is welcome – especially, according to tradition, a "tall, dark and handsome stranger". In London, revellers congregate along the Thames to hear the chimes of Big Ben and St Martin's in the Fields herald the New Year, while in Wales, Cardiff's Calennig (New Year) celebrations include a funfair and fire show in the Civic Centre.

Once the partying is over, winter begins to tighten its grip. In the far north, with only 6 hours of daylight in midwinter, dark skies may be lit by the flickering glow of the "dancers" – the poetic, old-fashioned name for the Northern Lights, or aurora borealis. With luck, skiers can enjoy deep snow on the Scottish runs of Aviemore and Glen Shee, and – on rare occasions – even Londoners can go tobogganning on the slopes of city parks, such as Primrose Hill and Hampstead Heath. Ironically, our heaviest snowfall often comes just after St Valentine's Day (14 February), the day that is held to signal the coming of spring, when songbirds choose their mates and couples become dewy-eyed and romantic. Everyone's hearts are thawing; winter is nearly over.

Below (left to right): Dawn on winter solstice at Stonehenge; aurora borealis rays over trees in Arran; skiers on the slopes of Glencoe

The Festive Season

Above: Artwork showing a traditional Christmas scene

Winter in Britain and Ireland ushers in a season of festivities ancient and modern. Some, such as the winter solstice fire festivals, have roots that extend deep into our history, pre-dating the advent of Christianity. In the West Country, "wassailing", a pagan luck-bringing ritual, can still be witnessed on Twelfth Night, and in Ireland, troupes of "mummers" continue a medieval tradition, taking chaotic performances to the winter streets. Other seasonal highlights are celebrated with the lighting of candles – these include Hanukkah, the Jewish Festival of Lights and Advent Sunday, the fourth Sunday before Christmas, which marks the beginning of the festive season.

But it is Christmas, with all its traditions and trappings, that truly dominates this time of year. While Christmas Day is, by and large, a family affair, the festive season builds for weeks before with the customary Christmas treats of carol concerts and nativity plays, pantomimes and office parties. In most parts of Britain and Ireland, New Year's Eve is the crescendo of the party season, and is marked with a night of revelry. This is followed, by some, with the decidedly more Puritan New Year's Day swim – an icy dip in the sea. In several cities, it is the colourful celebration of Chinese New Year at the end of January or in mid-February that brings the festive season to a close.

CHINESE NEW YEAR, LONDON

NORWEGIAN CHRISTMAS TREE IN TRAFALGAR SQUARE, LONDON

BRIGHTON WINTER SOLSTICE

Edinburgh's Hogmanay, Southern Scotland This is the biggest New Year's Eve celebration in the UK, with music, dancing and fireworks as the clock strikes midnight. *www.edinburghshogmanay.com*

Burns Night Celebrated in Scotland and further afield as close to the great poet's birthday (25 January) as possible, the event kicks off with pipe music, the Selkirk Grace and the address to the haggis.

Mumming, Northern Ireland Troupes of costumed players, or "mummers", perform ancient, rhyming, yuletide folk dramas in village halls or on house-to-house visits.

Twelve Days of Christmas Market, Eastern Ireland In the run-up to Christmas, St George's Dock on Dublin's waterfront is lined with carnival rides and stalls selling stocking-fillers, hot drinks and tasty snacks. *www.dublindocklands.ie/12daysofchristmas*

"Scroggling the Holly", Northeast England Children in Victorian costume, brass bands and morris dancers welcome Father Christmas in Haworth, Yorkshire, over a weekend in mid-November.

King's College Cambridge, Eastern England A solemn Christmas Eve service, A Festival in Nine Lessons and Carols features readings from undergraduates and commissioned carols *(see pp210–11)*.

Advent Carol Service and Procession at St Paul's Cathedral, London St Paul's Cathedral choir ushers in the festive season every year on Advent Sunday, with an atmospheric candlelit procession as well as traditional and contemporary carols.

Chinese New Year, London Vivid red lanterns, lion dancers and fireworks are highlights of Chinese New Year in London's Chinatown. *www.londonchinatown.org*

Norwegian Christmas Tree Ceremony, London The lights on this enormous tree in Trafalgar Square, an annual gift from the people of Norway to Londoners, are turned on in a ceremony close to Advent Sunday.

Harrods Winter Sale, London Bargain-hunters flock to this world-famous Knightsbridge store for its post-Christmas shopping frenzy, opened by celebrities in a glitzy ceremony. *www.harrods.com*

Sung Eucharist at Canterbury Cathedral, Southeast England The Eucharist sung by the cathedral choir is the moving climax of a Christmas Day morning of worship at England's greatest cathedral.

Brighton Winter Solstice Fire Festival, Southeast England An evening parade on 21 December through the city streets with home-made lanterns ends on the beach with a spectacular firework display.

Whimple Wassailing, Southwest England Locals parade through this Devon village on "Old Twelve Night" (17 January) in an age-old ritual thought to bring about a good apple harvest. *www.whimple.org*

New Year's Day Swim All over Britain and Ireland, from Achill on Ireland's west coast to Brighton in Sussex, hardy bathers plunge into chilly seas in a New Year's Day ritual, reputed to be the best cure for a hangover.

Hanukkah Jewish families all over Britain light the menorah for eight days and feast on *latkes* (potato pancakes) and doughnuts; the festival starts on the 25th day of Kislev in the Hebrew calendar, which falls any time from late November to late December.

Pantomime Season Plump men in drag, girls dressed as boys and broad innuendos are the hallmarks of the great British panto. Performances take place nationwide.

PANTOMIME

YORK MINSTER

TWELVE DAYS OF CHRISTMAS MARKET, DUBLIN

THE ESSENTIALS

GETTING THERE AND AROUND
The Giant's Causeway is just over 3 km (2 miles) north of the town of Bushmills, and about 80 km (50 miles) north of Belfast International Airport. When visiting in winter you will need a car or to use taxis to visit the Causeway.

WEATHER
In Northern Ireland in winter you can expect average daytime temperatures of 1–7°C, with the biting sea breeze adding an extra chill factor. You should also be prepared for some rainfall.

ACCOMMODATION
Splashing Out The Bushmills Inn, in the village of Bushmills, is a one-time coaching inn with oak beams, oil lamps and other characterful touches.
www.bushmillsinn.com

On a Budget The Causeway Hotel has spacious rooms right by the Causeway and has been here since 1836.
www.thecausewayhotel.com

EATING OUT
Splashing Out The Bushmills Inn also boasts an award-winning restaurant that uses local produce (including plenty of seafood) and offers Bushmills whiskey.
www.bushmillsinn.com

On a Budget The Harbour Bistro, on the waterfront in Portrush, has plenty of well-priced options including home-made burgers, salads and pasta dishes.
www.ramorerestaurant.com

PRICE FOR A FAMILY OF FOUR
£190–210 a day for accommodation, food and parking at the Causeway.

WEBSITE
www.nationaltrust.org.uk/giants-causeway

Main: Giant's Causeway, dramatically situated on the coast of County Antrim
Right (top to bottom): Interlocking geometric shapes of the basalt columns; Organ rock formation

WALKING WITH GIANTS

THERE ARE FEW PRETTIER OR MORE DRAMATIC DRIVES in the British Isles than the narrow road that hugs the Antrim coast between the mountains and the sea. It leads to Northern Ireland's most visited attraction, the phenomenal Giant's Causeway. Here an army of narrow basalt columns – around 40,000 of them – gathers en masse at the shoreline and marches haphazardly out to sea. As the sea and winter mists swirl around their disappearing forms, it's almost possible to imagine the giants of Irish legend – allegedly the builders of the Causeway – hurling insults at each other across the waves.

In fact, the Causeway is the work of geology, not giants. Around 60 million years ago, the explosion of an undersea volcano spewed molten lava into a depression along the shore. As it cooled, the shrinking and cracking produced tens of thousands of hexagonal columns of varying heights. The columns form stepping stones into the sea, and if you could follow them beneath the waves they would stretch along an underwater fissure, emerging in Scotland at the Isle of Staffa. In 1986 this geological marvel was named a UNESCO World Heritage Site.

FURTHER DETAILS

GIANT'S CAUSEWAY VISITOR CENTRE
Bushmills, County Antrim, Northern Ireland;
open Oct–Mar: 10am–5pm daily; Apr–Sep:
10am–7pm daily.
www.nationaltrust.org.uk

WHAT ELSE TO SEE AND DO
Old Bushmills Distillery
Located in Bushmills, this is the oldest legal distillery in
the world, dating its official production of whiskey back
to 1608, though alcohol was produced here for several
centuries before that. Children aged from 8 to 17 are
welcome on the tours, although younger children are
excluded for safety reasons.
www.bushmills.com

Dunluce Castle
Built in the 15th and 16th centuries, Dunluce is the
most impressive monument along the North Antrim
coast, a few miles west of Bushmills. It sits on a basalt
outcrop, the same stone that created the Giant's
Causeway, and is connected to the mainland by a
bridge. Don't miss the cave below the castle either,
though take care if scrambling down with children.
www.discovernorthernireland.com

Portrush
This seaside town on the North Antrim coast is famed
for its sandy beaches, and has many hotels, bars
and restaurants. The town is also home to the Royal
Portrush Golf Club – the only club in Ireland to have
hosted the British Open Championship.
www.portrush.org.uk

Below (top to bottom): Bushmills distillery and reservoir;
13th-century ruins of Dunluce Castle, perched on an outcrop
of the rocky Antrim coast

Down on the shoreline, the columns seem smaller than you might expect – the
tallest are around 12 m (39 ft) high – but it's the sheer mass of them that is so
impressive. As you stand atop them in the winter wind, watching the relentless
pounding of the waves, you can appreciate the ferocity of the storms that eroded
them over the centuries. The lack of crowds in this quieter season makes their
lonely beauty more intense.

The Causeway is backed by dramatic cliffs rising 100 m (328 ft). A variety of
sea birds make their home here. From the visitor centre you can walk along a
cliff-top path leading to other unusual rock formations, such as the Giant's
Chimney. The Shepherd's Steps will take you back down to the Causeway via 162
stone steps, making a circuit of about 3 km (2 miles). Alternatively, continue on
past the Organ, its long columns hugging the cliff face like cathedral organ pipes,
to the Port Reostan viewpoint. Here you can look back across a spectacular vista
of the Giant's Causeway, one of the most remarkable coastlines in the world.

A MEGALITHIC MARVEL

IT IS BRITAIN'S MOST IMPORTANT and well-known ancient monument – and its most mysterious. Rising out of Salisbury Plain, the megalithic circle of Stonehenge is an awesome and magical sight. Yet no one knows for sure who built it, and why. For centuries people have tried to unlock its secrets, theorizing that it was used as a religious temple, a royal palace, a Neolithic place of healing or a giant astronomical calendar – it is perfectly aligned with the points of sunrise and sunset on the winter and summer solstices.

Constructed in stages from around 3000 to 1500 BC, Stonehenge consists of colossal stones set in concentric circles, some linked by horizontal lintels, and all set within a larger earthwork of ditches and banks. The huge sandstones that form part of the original outer circle are local stones that stand over 6 m (21 ft) tall. But the smaller bluestones that formed the inner circle were transported here from Preseli in Wales, 240 km (150 miles) away.

Over the centuries, many myths and belief systems, from Arthurian tales to druidic traditions, have drawn inspiration from this enigmatic site. In 2008, after six years of excavations, archaeologists put forward the exciting theory that Stonehenge was a monument to the dead. Evidence from cremation burials at the site and further dating of stone fragments revealed that the bluestones were the first to be erected, in 3000 BC, and that hundreds of people were buried here over the next 500 years. What's more, Stonehenge stands in a wider landscape of even older burial mounds, processional avenues and timber circles, indicating that rituals of life and death were celebrated here much earlier.

Today, more than one million people visit this UNESCO World Heritage Site each year. The circle itself is cordoned off – you can walk all around Stonehenge but not within it unless you join an organized tour or arrange a private visit through English Heritage.

It is also opened for a few hours at dawn on the solstices and equinoxes that mark the seasons. It is well worth making the effort to be there for dawn on the winter solstice (21 or 22 December). There are few sights more extraordinary than watching the sun rise above the frosted ground and over the mighty stones.

THE ESSENTIALS

GETTING THERE AND AROUND
Stonehenge is on Salisbury Plain in Wiltshire, in southern England, about 11 km (7 miles) north of Salisbury itself. Salisbury is about 110 km (70 miles) southwest of London's Heathrow Airport. The Stonehenge Tour Bus departs from Salisbury, and it's even possible to walk the 3 km (2 miles) from Amesbury, though access is a lot easier with your own car. The site is located where the A303 and the A344 converge, just west of Amesbury.

WEATHER
Winter weather on Salisbury Plain can be bitter when cold winds are blowing, but there can also be crisp days when the stones look at their best. Average daytime temperatures range from 1 to 6°C.

ACCOMMODATION
Splashing Out Howard's House Country Hotel, in Teffont Evias, is 16 km (10 miles) from Stonehenge, and has luxurious accommodation and an exceptional restaurant.
www.howardshousehotel.co.uk

On a Budget The Victoria Lodge Guest House, in Salisbury, offers simple but fine accommodation.
www.victoria-guest-house.co.uk

EATING OUT
Splashing Out The Ship Inn, in Burcombe, is a splendid gastropub dating from the 17th century.
www.theshipburcombe.co.uk

On a Budget Charter 1227, in Salisbury, offers good, wholesome British grub at inexpensive prices.
www.charter1227.co.uk

PRICE FOR TWO PEOPLE
Around £185 a day for food, accommodation and entrance fees.

WEBSITE
www.english-heritage.org.uk/visit/places/stonehenge

Main: Aerial view of Stonehenge in winter
Below: Interior of the megalithic circle

FURTHER DETAILS

STONEHENGE
Open daily except 24 and 25 Dec. Opening hours vary and access may be reduced in bad weather. For all opening times, access times on the summer and winter solstices and spring and autumn equinoxes and details of small-group private visits, contact English Heritage.
www.english-heritage.org.uk

WHAT ELSE TO SEE AND DO
Avebury
Only 40 km (25 miles) north of Stonehenge, one of the largest prehistoric earthworks in Europe lies near the village of Avebury. Slightly older than Stonehenge, its magnificent stone circle has been re-erected and you can walk freely among the stones.
www.nationaltrust.org.uk

Silbury Hill
This green hill, 8 km (5 miles) west of Marlborough in Wiltshire, is the largest man-made prehistoric mound in Europe. You can only view the hill from a distance – there is no access – but you can follow a footpath to the nearby West Kennet Long Barrow, a prehistoric chamber tomb.
www.english-heritage.org.uk

Salisbury Cathedral
The finest 13th-century Gothic cathedral in Britain, Salisbury Cathedral is topped by a 123-m (404-ft) spire, the tallest in the country. Among its many highlights are Britain's largest cathedral cloisters and the chapter house, which contains an original copy of *Magna Carta*, one of only four still in existence.
www.salisburycathedral.org.uk

Old Sarum
On the edge of Salisbury, the remains of this Iron Age fort and Norman settlement include prehistoric earthworks and the scant ruins of a Norman castle, royal palace and cathedral.
www.english-heritage.org.uk

Below (top to bottom): Neolithic monument of Silbury Hill; standing stones outside Avebury at dusk

THE ESSENTIALS

GETTING THERE AND AROUND
The Shetland Islands are about 160 km (100 miles) from the north coast of Scotland. There are flights from Edinburgh, Glasgow, Inverness and Aberdeen to Sumburgh Airport, 40 km (25 miles) from Lerwick. Bus services, taxis and car hire are available at the airport. There are ferries to Lerwick from Aberdeen and Kirkwall. Flights (*www.directflight.co.uk*) connect the island of Mainland with outlying islands including Fair Isle, Foula and Papa Stour. Car ferries operate from Lerwick and connect Mainland with outlying islands.

WEATHER
Winter daytime temperatures in Shetland are between 3 and 5°C, and strong winds and sleet or rain are likely in winter. Shetland has less than 6 hours of light a day in January.

ACCOMMODATION
Splashing Out Brentham House, in Lerwick, is a small but cosy and stylish town-house hotel.
www.brenthamhouse.com

On a Budget Glen Orchy House in Lerwick is a comfortable guesthouse, close to the town centre, with modern facilities.
www.guesthouselerwick.com

EATING OUT
Splashing Out Hay's Dock Café Restaurant, in Lerwick, is an attractive modern waterside restaurant.
www.haysdock.co.uk

On a Budget Fjarå Cafe Bar, also in Lerwick, offers delicious food, great coffee and stunning views.
Tel: 01595 697388

PRICE FOR TWO PEOPLE
Around £120 a day for accommodation and food.

WEBSITE
www.shetland.org

Main: Northern Lights illuminating the sky over the Shetland Islands
Right (top to bottom): Gannet colony on a cliff edge; Scalloway harbour on the island of Mainland

FIRE AND LIGHT

SHETLANDERS CALL THEM THE "MERRY DANCERS" – wavering curtains of pale-green and white light that shimmer over the northern horizon on up to 100 nights a year, like a scene from a science fiction film. During the long days of a Shetland summer, when the sky never gets truly dark, the Northern Lights – or aurora borealis – are unremarkable, but during the long winter nights they can be truly spectacular, and on these distant islands there is little urban light pollution to interfere with one of the most magical phenomena in the night sky.

Shetland is a land apart: not just one island, but an archipelago of more than 100 far-flung, low-lying and surprisingly verdant isles and skerries (rocky reefs) where sheep graze, otters prowl for crabs in the rockpools, gannets soar over the clifftops and seals bask at low tide.

Far from Scotland's shores, Shetland is home to the proud descendants of Viking seafarers, and some Shetlanders have argued that, should Scotland ever achieve independence, the islands might be better off opting to become part of Norway. The capital, Lerwick, is closer to the Norwegian city of Bergen than to Edinburgh. Shetland's Viking heritage can be heard in the dialect spoken by islanders, and seen in historic buildings dating back to the 9th century and the first Norse settlers.

Perhaps the most potent symbol of the islands' Scandinavian ancestry is an annual event that takes place on the last Tuesday in January. On this night, the streets of Lerwick are lit by the flames of torches brandished by bearded islanders, known as *guizers*, in the fearsome garb of their Viking forebears. This is Up Helly Aa, perhaps the largest fire festival in Europe, and the climax of a year of planning and preparation that involves almost everyone in Lerwick.

At the head of a procession of almost 1,000 torch-bearers, the leader, known as Guizer Jarl, stands at the prow of his Viking longship – the galley. The ship is dragged through Lerwick, and finally meets a fiery end as hundreds of torches are hurled into its wooden hull to create a mighty bonfire. Only after the ship is well ablaze do the festivities really start. Revellers are welcomed into homes and halls throughout Lerwick, and a night of fiddle music, dancing and drinking gathers pace, with the last stragglers struggling home just in time for breakfast. For obvious reasons, the following day is traditionally a holiday in Lerwick, but there are further, slightly more subdued festivities, known as the "Guizers' Hop", that night. Come to Shetland for the eerie majesty of the Northern Lights, but stay for the wonderful festivities.

MONASTIC TRANQUILITY

I N A LAND SPRINKLED WITH MYSTERIOUS ROUND TOWERS and elaborate Celtic high crosses, Glendalough stands out as Ireland's finest early Christian monastic site. This "valley of the two lakes" has a timeless beauty, its sturdy stone ruins nestled at the base of two loughs that wind below forested folds in the Wicklow Mountains.

It's easy to love Glendalough in summer, when sunlight turns the loughs a sparkling blue, inviting pleasant strolls along their leafy shores. But in winter, when the crowds are gone and snow dusts the surrounding peaks, the dark towers of slate and granite rise starkly out of the valley into the crisp air and you can feel the mystical, magical pull of this tranquil place that attracted St Kevin so many centuries ago.

Kevin established a monastery here in 570 and its ruins, though of a later date (8th–12th centuries), are evocative and well preserved. From a distance you can spot the monastery complex's slender round tower, perfectly intact and rising 30 m (98 ft) from the ground. This style of tower, which served not only as a belfry but also as treasury and watchtower, is rare outside Ireland. With

Main: Frosty morning at Glendalough, with the round tower of the monastery visible beyond

THE ESSENTIALS

GETTING THERE AND AROUND
Glendalough is in the east of Ireland, 80 km (50 miles) south of Dublin. It is situated in Wicklow Mountains National Park, about 5 km (3 miles) west of the village of Laragh. It's about an hour's drive south from Dublin, but St Kevin's Bus Service (*www.glendaloughbus. com*) runs daily to Glendalough from Dublin via Bray.

WEATHER
In winter, the average daytime temperature at Glendalough is 3–8°C, with sub-freezing temperatures early in the morning. Be prepared for rain and light snow.

ACCOMMODATION
Splashing Out Lynham's Hotel, in the nearby village of Laragh, offers modern rooms with beautiful river views and has a bar and restaurant. *www.lynhamsoflaragh.ie*

On a Budget The tranquil Riversdale House near Glendalough has cosy rooms plus a self-catering cottage in a pretty riverside location. *www.glendalough.eu.com*

EATING OUT
Splashing Out The Wicklow Heather, in Laragh, serves traditional Irish and continental cuisine using organic produce. *www.wicklowheather.ie*

On a Budget Jake's Bar, in Lynham's Hotel, Laragh, serves good pub meals and family fare. *www.lynhamsoflaragh.ie*

PRICE FOR TWO PEOPLE
From around €160 a day for food, accommodation and admission to the Visitor Centre.

WEBSITE
www.glendalough.ie

its entrance about 4 m (13 ft) above the ground and accessible only by ladder, the tower was also a place of safety from invaders. The main entrance to the monastery complex is a double arched stone gateway. The largest building in the group is the 9th-century cathedral, now roofless but nonetheless impressive. In the surrounding cemetery, still used by local villagers, stands St Kevin's Cross, with Celtic decoration; carvings on the nearby Priests' House suggest that it once held Kevin's shrine. St Kevin's Church, an oratory or private chapel, is sometimes called St Kevin's Kitchen because of its chimney-like tower. Across a footbridge, a path along the Lower Lough leads to more sites on the Upper Lough: tiny Reefert Church, the ruined beehive hut called St Kevin's Cell and, higher up in the cliffs, a hermit's cave known as St Kevin's Bed.

Though Glendalough was raided by Vikings, Normans and the English, it remained a place of pilgrimage until the mid-19th century. Before exploring the ruins, first take a moment to stop at the Visitor Centre to discover why the historical site of Glendalough was as important as it is beautiful.

FURTHER DETAILS

GLENDALOUGH

Glendalough Visitor Centre
Glendalough, Bray, County Wicklow; open mid-Oct–mid-Mar: 9.30am–5pm daily; mid-Mar–mid-Oct: 9:30am–6pm daily.
www.heritageireland.ie

WHAT ELSE TO SEE AND DO

Wicklow Mountains National Park
Glendalough lies within this beautiful landscape of mountains, bogs, waterfalls and woodlands. Open year-round, the park is a popular area for walking, with nine way-marked trails around the Glendalough valley, including the long-distance Wicklow Way. Winter weather needn't prevent a hike on the shorter trails as long as you are prepared for conditions with suitable clothing and footwear; indeed, the surrounding mountains are stunning when capped with snow. The Glendalough Visitor Centre (above) serves as an information point for the park in winter. Walking trails are described on the park website.
www.wicklowmountainsnationalpark.ie

Avoca Handweavers
Ireland is famous for its fine woven goods, and winter is the perfect time to buy a cosy jumper or wrap up in a soft scarf. Avoca Handweavers are known for their creative take on traditional designs. They are based in Avoca village at Ireland's oldest working mill, which dates from 1723. On weekdays, you can watch the weavers at work on a guided tour. It's a beautiful drive from Glendalough via Rathdrum through the Vale of Avoca to get there.
www.avoca.ie

Wicklow Town
On the coast east of Glendalough, Wicklow's county town overlooks a broad bay. Stroll along its harbour and pebble beach, backed by the Broad Lough wildfowl lagoon and the ruins of the Black Castle. In the town, visit Wicklow's Historic Gaol.
Wicklow County: www.visitwicklow.ie
Wicklow's Historic Gaol: www.wicklowshistoricalgaol.com

Below (top to bottom): Oratory, or "St Kevin's Kitchen"; graveyard at Glendalough

THE ESSENTIALS

GETTING THERE AND AROUND
The Isle of Man lies in the Irish Sea, between England, Scotland and Northern Ireland. There are flights from all major British and Irish cities to Ronaldsway Airport, 16 km (10 miles) from the island's capital, Douglas. Ferries connect Douglas with Liverpool and Dublin. Buses link all towns on the island, operating from four main depots at Douglas, Peel, Ramsey and Port Erin. Several car-rental companies operate from Ronaldsway Airport.

WEATHER
The winter months are the wettest of the year, and strong winds are possible, with daytime temperatures of 0–10°C.

ACCOMMODATION
Splashing Out The Claremont, located on the promenade at Douglas, is the highest-rated hotel on the Isle. Rooms are opulent with modern features.
www.claremonthoteldouglas.com

On a Budget Hydro Hotel, in Douglas, has a grandiose exterior that conceals comfortable rooms with modern facilities.
www.hydrohotel.co.im

EATING OUT
Splashing Out A short walk from Douglas town centre, The Little Fish Café offers all day dining with a focus on freshly caught local seafood.
www.littlefishcafe.com

On a Budget Welbeck Hotel Restaurant, also in Douglas, serves traditional island fare such as Manx lamb and local beef.
www.welbeckhotel.com

PRICE FOR A FAMILY OF FOUR
Around £270 a day for accommodation, food and tours.

WEBSITES
www.visitisleofman.com
www.isleofman.com

Main: Mountain bikers exploring the Isle of Man's coastline at sunset

AN ISLAND APART

I F YOU LIKE SWEEPING VISTAS AND FRESH SEA BREEZES, then the Isle of Man is definitely the place to visit. Lying in the Irish Sea, midway between Ireland and Britain, this rocky island has a history and culture all of its own. Winter sees Man at its best, when the coasts and countryside are delightfully uncrowded and its many species of wildlife roam undisturbed.

Small though it is, the Isle of Man boasts an impressive variety of landscapes. The rugged sea-pounded cliffs are backed by sandy heathland at the Ayres National Nature Reserve, which is the perfect place for a bracing stroll. Rolling hills, moors and wooded glens, where waterfalls tumble into narrow streams, give way to fertile farmland. Set dramatically amid these diverse landscapes are ancient stone monuments left by the island's past inhabitants, from the first Stone-Age settlers to later Celts and Vikings. More than 200 elaborately carved early Christian crosses, adorned with complex Celtic patterns, are also scattered around the island.

Man attracts a variety of birdlife too, with Brent geese and Bewick's and whistler swans among the migrant species exchanging the harsh Arctic winter for Man's more clement

FURTHER DETAILS

ISLE OF MAN

Manx National Heritage
The Heritage Agency protects and maintains a portfolio of areas of natural beauty and special interest on the island. Most locations are freely accessible all year round.
www.manxnationalheritage.im

Ayres National Nature Reserve
Near Bride. The reserve's bird species include gannets, oystercatchers and ringed plovers. You can sometimes spot whales, basking sharks and grey seals off the coast from here; open all year round daily.
www.iomguide.com

Curraghs Wildlife Park
Ballaugh. More than 100 bird and animal species from around the world live in the natural wetland environment of this wildlife park and breeding centre; open summer: Mon–Fri 10am–6pm; winter: Fri–Sun 10am–4pm.
www.gov.im/wildlife

Cycle Hire
Sulby. Cycle Hire on the Isle of Man offers flexible and affordable cycle rental.
www.cyclehire.im

Riding Stables
Little London, Cronk-y-Voddy. The Ballahimmin Riding Centre offers off-road riding in beautiful countryside, with a wide selection of ponies and horses available; open all year round, reservations necessary.
www.ballahimmin.com

Boat Hire
Various companies offer boat charters and tours. See the Coast section of the Tourist Board website.
www.gov.im/tourism

Wildlife Tours
Douglas Sea Terminal. Isle of Man Wildlife Tours offers guided trips to the best spots for wildlife-watching; tours start at 10am Sat–Sun, lasting around 5 hours.
www.iomtours.co.uk

Below (top to bottom): Cliff formations; flock of Brent geese

climate. Ballaugh Curraghs, a region of peat wetlands, willow and bog myrtle scrub, is one of the best year-round wildlife sites. In winter it hosts the largest hen harrier roost in Europe and, if you're lucky, you might even spot one of its population of over 100 wild wallabies – the descendants of a pair that escaped from the nearby Curraghs Wildlife Park in the 1960s.

All you really need to explore the island is a good pair of walking boots, but if you prefer to travel on two wheels or four legs, there are several bike-hire companies and riding stables around the island – and there are plenty of trails that you can explore. And for stunning views of the rugged coastline and the tiny neighbouring island of the Calf of Man, along with opportunities to spot seals and a huge array of bird life, boat trips operate all year round from the Isle of Man's fishing harbours. Tour companies also offer guided driving and walking trips along the coast and inland, maximizing your chances of a great day spent watching wildlife.

THE ESSENTIALS

GETTING THERE AND AROUND
The Peak District National Park, the location of most of the caves, is in the northwest of England. The nearest airport is Manchester International Airport, 26 km (16 miles) northwest of Buxton. A car is the best way to explore the area, although there are also good bus connections.

WEATHER
Much of the Peak District National Park experiences higher than average rainfall in winter, and the weather can be changeable. Average daytime temperatures range from 3 to 5°C.

ACCOMMODATION
Splashing Out The Old Hall Hotel, in central Buxton, has been welcoming guests since the 16th century or earlier.
www.oldhallhotelbuxton.co.uk

On a Budget Swiss House in Castleton offers superior bed-and-breakfast accommodation in the heart of the Peak District.
www.swiss-house.co.uk

EATING OUT
Splashing Out The Columbine, in Buxton, combines sophisticated modern cuisine with the intimate feel of dining in a private home.
www.buxtononline.net/columbine

On a Budget Ye Olde Cheshire Cheese Inn, in Castleton, dates back to the 1600s and serves simple but tasty pub food in historic surroundings.
www.cheshirecheeseinn.co.uk

PRICE FOR TWO PEOPLE
Around £210 a day for accommodation, food and entrance fees.

WEBSITES
www.visitpeakdistrict.com
www.visitbuxton.co.uk

ROCK BOTTOM

THE UNSPOILED LANDSCAPE OF THE PEAK DISTRICT is green and rolling in some places and stark and rugged in others. In the depths of winter only the intrepid venture onto the windswept higher hills, but there is another terrain of stunning scenery open all year round: the underground world of Derbyshire's cave networks. Over millions of years, water trickling through the limestone hills and peaks has carved out a fantasy land of stalactites, stalagmites and crystal rock formations – a netherworld that is both beautiful and bizarre. Bad winter weather is good news for cave visitors, as melting snows or rainfall increase the volume of underground waterfalls and rivers, making this hidden realm all the more magnificent.

Two cave sites that have special appeal are near the towns of Buxton and Castleton. The Romans turned Buxton into an attractive spa town, as it remains today. Yet even the works of these mighty builders were dwarfed by the two-million-year-old cave network at Poole's Cavern on the edge of the town. Roman remains have been found here, but it was the Victorians who christened its most evocative rock formation the "Frozen Waterfall". Other strange formations in the cavern include Derbyshire's largest stalactite, the "Flitch of Bacon"– so named because of its resemblance to a side of pork.

There are impressive underground waterfalls in the cave networks around Castleton, 16 km (10 miles) northeast of Buxton. Blue John Cavern takes its name from the colourful mineral that is unique to the area's caves – fluorite, a mineral composed of calcium fluoride. The name Blue John is an anglicization of the French words *bleu et jaune*, or "blue and yellow". Due to its scarcity, the amount that can be mined is heavily restricted, but you can buy it when you visit the caves, and it is still mined in nearby Treak Cliff Cavern, where winter brings the added attraction of carol services held in the caves. You can also enjoy carol concerts in nearby Peak Cavern, which has the largest natural cave entrance in the British Isles and was once home to a whole village. Speedwell Cavern is the only show cave that you can explore by boat – and when you traverse its underground lake in the eerie half lit darkness, you can see why it has been called the "Bottomless Pit". In winter, the subterranean world of Derbyshire's caves is every inch as awe-inspiring as the peaks above.

Main: Potholing in Peak Cavern
Below (left to right): Navigating through Speedwell Cavern; Poole's Cavern on the edge of Buxton

FURTHER DETAILS

THE CAVES OF CASTLETON AND BUXTON

Poole's Cavern
Green Lane, Buxton. This cavern has been a local attraction for centuries, and Mary Queen of Scots is believed to have visited in it 1582; open Mar–Oct: 9:30am–5pm daily; Nov–Feb: 9:30am–4pm Sat–Sun.
www.poolescavern.co.uk

Blue John Cavern
Castleton. One of the many features of the Blue John Cavern is Lord Mulgrave's Dining Room, so called because the eponymous lord is said to have entertained miners to a meal here once; open from 9:30am daily, seasonal closing times vary.
www.bluejohn-cavern.co.uk

Treak Cliff Cavern
Cross Street, Castleton. Naturally occurring examples of Blue John stone can still be seen here; open 10am–5pm daily; carol services held on weekends throughout December at 11:30am and 2.00pm (until the weekend before Christmas).
www.bluejohnstone.com

Peak Cavern
Peak Cavern House, Peak Cavern Road, Castleton. The cave village here was inhabited until as recently as 1915, and its remains can still be seen; open Apr–Oct: 10am–5pm daily; Nov–Mar; 10am–5pm Sat–Sun; carol concerts are held in the caves in December on the three weekends before Christmas.
www.peakcavern.co.uk

Speedwell Cavern
Winnats Pass, Castleton. The deepest of the cave networks in the area, Speedwell Cavern is located some 183 m (600 ft) below ground; open 10am–5pm daily (later at peak times); guided boat tours take place daily.
www.speedwellcavern.co.uk

Below (top to bottom): The Crescent in Buxton; caver in a stream passage in Peak Cavern

THE ESSENTIALS

GETTING THERE AND AROUND
Glasgow is in the south of Scotland. Glasgow Airport is 13 km (8 miles) from the city centre, connected by a frequent shuttle bus service. Glasgow Central rail station has services to London Euston and elsewhere. Many attractions lie within walking distance of each other; the quickest way around the city is by Subway, Glasgow's underground metro system.

WEATHER
Be prepared for rain, wintry showers and cold daytime temperatures, averaging 2–5°C but often dropping below freezing.

ACCOMMODATION
Splashing Out Hotel du Vin, in Devonshire Gardens, is a fine boutique hotel in the fashionable West End district. Its bistro serves modern European dishes.
www.hotelduvin.com

On a Budget The Victorian House, on Renfrew Street, is a conveniently central guesthouse with 60 rooms, from singles to family suites.
www.thevictorian.co.uk

EATING OUT
Splashing Out The Ubiquitous Chip, on Ashton Lane, offers modern Scottish cuisine. Varied dining areas include a courtyard, brasserie and public bar.
www.ubiquitouschip.co.uk

On a Budget Babbity Bowster, on Blackfriars Street, offers a good blend of Scottish and international dishes, on its restaurant and bar menus.
www.babbitybowster.com

PRICE FOR TWO PEOPLE
Around £160 a day for food, accommodation, local transport and Winterfest activities.

WEBSITE
www.peoplemakeglasgow.com

Previous page: Members of the Jarl viking squad taking part in the annual Up Helly Aa Festival in the Shetland islands

Main: Ice skaters enjoy Glasgow on Ice in George Square **Right (top to bottom):** Glasgow's elegant, Neo-Classical Gallery of Modern Art; winter fireworks lighting up the sky above City Chambers

WINTER WONDERLAND

OFFERING A PULSATING PROGRAMME OF EVENTS, the Glasgow Loves Christmas festival easily justifies a visit to Scotland's biggest city, even at this chilly time of year. This umbrella organization brings together all of Glasgow's winter festivities from mid-November to mid-January. Its hub is George Square, a great civic set-piece in a city with an astonishing heritage of innovative Victorian architecture. Here you can don full winter garb and join the throng on what becomes the largest open-air ice-skating rink in Britain. There's also a festive market here in the lead-up to Christmas, with all kinds of tempting seasonal produce on offer.

Glasgow is one of Britain's top shopping cities, and the Christmas lights and decorations spectacularly transform the main drags of Sauchiehall, Argyle and Buchanan Streets, as well as some huge indoor shopping malls, such as the Buchanan Galleries. The window displays can be eye-catching, especially at the House of Fraser department store on Buchanan Street. It's panto season too, of course, and a clutch of theatres present their own takes on traditional seasonal offerings such as *Cinderella* or *Aladdin* – with an inimitable twist of Glaswegian humour.

FURTHER DETAILS

GLASGOW

Glasgow on Ice
George Square; late Nov–early Jan, 10am–10pm.
www.glasgowloveschristmas.com

Festive Market
George Square; open late-Nov–Dec: 10am–7pm
Mon–Fri, 9am–6pm Sat, 11am–5pm Sun and St
Andrew's Day.
www.glasgowloveschristmas.com

Theatre Royal
Hope Street; performances throughout the year.
www.atgtickets.com/venues/theatre-royal-glasgow

Glasgow Royal Concert Hall
Sauchiehall Street; musical performances all year.
www.glasgowconcerthalls.com

Hogmanay
George Square; 31 Dec. Tickets available from Nov.
www.hogmanay.net

Celtic Connections
Various venues, Jan.
www.celticconnections.com

Glasgow Film Festival
Various venues, Feb.
www.glasgowfilm.org/festival

WHAT ELSE TO SEE AND DO

City Chambers
These grandiose buildings were built in the 1880s,
when Glasgow was the "second city of empire".

Glasgow Museums
There are thirteen City of Glasgow museums to visit; the
most popular is Kelvingrove Art Gallery and Museum.
www.glasgowmuseums.com

Glasgow Botanic Gardens
Renowned gardens, glasshouses and arboretum.
www.glasgowbotanicgardens.com

Below (top to bottom): Kibble Palace glasshouses at
Glasgow's Botanic Gardens; Kelvingrove Museum.

If you're looking for high culture, the Scottish Ballet always performs a family favourite, such as *Swan Lake* or the *Nutcracker*, at the Theatre Royal, and the Royal Scottish National Orchestra puts on several Christmas concerts, including one special evening at the Royal Concert Hall, when live music is provided for a showing of the much-loved children's film, *The Snowman*.

Glasgow Loves Christmas continues into the New Year. On New Year's Eve, over 25,000 people pack into George Square to celebrate Hogmanay, with a massive music party featuring chart-topping bands and traditional pipers. It's ticket-only, but if you miss out, don't worry – there are street performances, concerts and ceilidhs throughout the city. January events continue with the huge Celtic Connections festival, featuring all types of Celtic music and musicians from around the world. In February, the Glasgow Film Festival provides opportunities to go to the UK premieres of films of all genres, from blockbusters to thoughtful shorts and documentaries.

THE ESSENTIALS

GETTING THERE AND AROUND
Dartmoor National Park is in the county of Devon, in the southwest of England. The nearest airport is Exeter International Airport. A car is recommended in winter, when the park's buses do not run. There are free guided walks provided by the Dartmoor National Park Authority.

WEATHER
The weather on Dartmoor is notoriously fickle, so it is always important to be prepared for extreme weather, including sudden storms, rain and snow, as well as thick mist and fog that can make navigation difficult. Average winter daytime temperatures range from 2 to 5°C.

ACCOMMODATION
Splashing Out The Horn of Plenty, in Gulworthy, Tavistock, offers the perfect location for a trip to Dartmoor, with gorgeous Tamar Valley views.
www.thehornofplenty.co.uk

On a Budget The Rosemont, in Yelverton, offers comfortable rooms and an excellent location in the southwest of the national park.
www.therosemont.co.uk

EATING OUT
Splashing Out 22 Mill St, in Chagford, is a modern restaurant offering tasty European fare.
www.22millst.com

On a Budget The Rugglestone Inn, in Widecombe-in-the-Moor, is a traditional pub serving real ales and good pub grub.
www.rugglestoneinn.co.uk

PRICE FOR TWO PEOPLE
From £160 a day for accommodation, food and entrance fees.

WEBSITES
www.dartmoor.gov.uk
www.visitdartmoor.co.uk

Main: Sunset over Saddle Tor on Dartmoor **Right (top to bottom):** Clapper bridge over the River Dart; Widgery Cross on Brat Tor near Lydford; prehistoric Merrivale Rows in Dartmoor National Park

GRANITE HILLTOPS

A SWATHE OF LANDSCAPE WITH AUSTERE NATURAL GRANDEUR, Dartmoor National Park occupies a vast chunk of England's southwest. The "grim charm" of this unspoilt, sweeping granite moorland, as Sir Arthur Conan Doyle poetically described it, is the antithesis of Britain's claustrophobic urban sprawls. The Ministry of Defence has laid claim to a large northwestern segment of the national park, and there's a scattering of peaceful villages and a web of roads, but otherwise this is sensationally boundless and empty rambling territory.

The bleak appeal of Dartmoor's barren moorland and tors (granite hilltops) is compelling at any time of the year, but for many visitors it reaches its full stature in winter. The waterfalls of Dartmoor, such as the tumbling Whitelady Waterfall at Lydford Gorge, are in full spate in the wet winter months. The air at this time of year is crisp and clear, ideal for raw and refreshing hikes and long, penetrating views, especially from highpoints such as rocky Bellever Tor (443 m/1453 ft), while winter dawns and sunsets create some fantastic panoramas. Rambling across the winter moorland – from Widgery Cross, a granite cross that sits high on Brat Tor, to the cascading waters of Doe Tor Brook and Falls – can be spectacular.

FURTHER DETAILS

DARTMOOR NATIONAL PARK

The Dartmoor National Park Authority publishes a handy guide to events and guided walks on Dartmoor over autumn and winter. It is essential to take a good map of Dartmoor and a compass with you when trekking. Don't underestimate the terrain, especially in winter: snow may make the landscape attractive, but it can also make it slippery underfoot. Always take water with you.
www.dartmoor.gov.uk

Some of the highest tors in Dartmoor, such as Yes Tor (619 m/2031 ft) and High Willhays (621 m/2037 ft), are located within an army firing range and are inaccessible if red flags are flying (signifying the range is in use). For further information on Dartmoor's firing ranges, consult
www.dartmoor-ranges.co.uk

National Park Information Centre
Princetown; open 10am–5pm daily.
www.dartmoor.gov.uk

Whitelady Waterfall
Lydford Gorge; opening times vary during the wet winter months; visit the website for more information.
www.nationaltrust.org.uk

Castle Drogo
Drewsteignton; opening times are variable over the winter; visit the website for further details.
www.nationaltrust.org.uk

WHAT ELSE TO SEE AND DO
Plymouth
The maritime town of Plymouth offers a number of significant historical sights. You can seek out the Mayflower Steps, marking the point where the Pilgrim Fathers set sail for the New World in 1620; explore Plymouth Hoe; join boat trips along Plymouth Sound; or peruse the Barbican area, the town's main concentration of old buildings, including Elizabethan House.
Plymouth: www.visitplymouth.co.uk
Elizabethan House: www.plymouth.gov.uk

Buckland Abbey
Established in Yelverton in the 13th century by Cistercian monks, Buckland Abbey is the one-time residence of Sir Francis Drake, who allegedly still haunts the property. It is also the home of "Drake's Drum", which, according to legend, beats when England is in danger.
www.nationaltrust.org.uk

Museum of Dartmoor Life
The three floors of exhibits in this Okehampton museum give a fascinating insight into Dartmoor's social history.
www.museumofdartmoorlife.org.uk

The Belstone Ring in north Dartmoor is a superb 4-hour circular walk that includes a climb to the summit of Cosdon Hill, where there are excellent views of Dartmoor, and encompasses Little Hound Tor, Oke Tor and Belstone Tor. You can also join organized overnight winter tours of Dartmoor, which provide opportunities to camp out in the wilderness. White-water kayaking and canoeing is also a popular pastime, especially along the River Dart.

It's not just the awesome natural drama of Dartmoor that seduces travellers: the national park is also riddled with archaeological and prehistoric sites, with a host of stone circles, cairns and burial chambers. Some of the area's prehistoric relics, such as the Bronze-Age settlement at Grimspound and the lines of standing stones known as the Merrivale Rows, are clearly defined, but others are more inconspicuous until a light dusting of snow brings their features into relief. Winter also sees a considerable number of farmers' markets on Dartmoor, such as the excellent Tavistock Farmers' Market. Furthermore, there is a host of historic houses and castles in the region, supplying architectural grandeur to the natural landscape. Castle Drogo, in the northeast of Dartmoor, is a particularly special building; designed by Sir Edwin Lutyens and completed as recently as 1930, it was the last castle to be built in England.

Below: Kayaking on the River Dart

THE ESSENTIALS

GETTING THERE AND AROUND
The Fens is a low-lying area of eastern England that stretches roughly from the north of Cambridge to Spalding and Boston in Lincolnshire, and from Rutland to western Norfolk. Several airports surround the Fens, notably London Stansted, Norwich and East Midlands, which is 40 km (25 miles) north of Leicester. Driving is the best way to get around, but you can also explore the Fens on foot.

WEATHER
The Fens can be damp and chilly in winter, with little shelter from cold winds, but heavy snow is uncommon. Average daytime temperatures range from 1 to 7ºC.

ACCOMMODATION
Splashing Out Congham Hall, in Grimston, is a luxury country house hotel with beautiful gardens and an acclaimed restaurant.
www.conghamhallhotel.co.uk

On a Budget The Old Rectory, in King's Lynn, is a friendly B&B in a fine Norfolk Georgian building.
www.theoldrectory-kingslynn.com

EATING OUT
Splashing Out The Anchor Inn at Sutton Gault, near Sutton, was one of the country's first gastropubs, and its fish dishes are renowned.
www.anchor-inn-restaurant.co.uk

On a Budget The Ship Inn, in Surfleet, has superb Fenland views and serves well-cooked steak, fish and chicken dishes.
www.shipinnsurfleet.com

PRICE FOR TWO PEOPLE
Around £160 a day for food and accommodation.

WEBSITE
www.visitcambridgeshire.org

BIG SKY COUNTRY

GREAT BRITAIN HAS MOUNTAINS AND MOORLAND, hills and dales, but of all its varied landscapes, one of the strangest is the Fens. In this low-lying region of eastern England the sky seems to go on forever over the vast, flat, endless expanse. In winter it has a desolate beauty, when the wind whistles in from the east and the flooded plains and marshes become home to thousands of water birds.

In their natural state, the Fens were broad marshlands, formed when rivers running from Middle England to the sea dropped sediment when they hit the flat plain. It was a murky landscape of shifting channels, sand bars, sedge banks and mires, with tufts of solid ground rising above standing pools thick with vegetation. But it was far from wasteland. Medieval fen-dwellers harvested reeds for thatching and cut peat for fuel. They had a plentiful diet of fish and wildfowl, and eels were so abundant here they were used as currency. This rich habitat was renewed by periodic flooding in winter.

Over the years, the low lying land of the Fens was drained to create agricultural land. Attempts at drainage began in Roman times, but in the 17th century a Dutch engineer, Cornelius Vermuyden, was hired to undertake widespread drainage over thousands of acres. This caused the land to sink below sea level as the peat topsoil dried out, resulting in more flooding. Steam-driven pumps finally brought it under control in the 1820s, and the land became useable; today it produces over a third of all of Britain's vegetables and flowers. When travelling around the Fens, you might well hear someone refer to a local person as a "Fen Tiger". This is a term of respect for a man or woman who was born and bred here, and who knows the Fenland skills that were once used to make a living.

The Fens are a haven for birds and wildlife, particularly breeding barn owls. Wicken Fen is Britain's oldest nature reserve, established in 1899, and preserves one of the last few pockets of undrained fenland. The Ouse Washes form the largest area of washland, or flood plain, in the country. When this area of pasture floods each winter, it attracts thousands of birds – from ducks and swans to waders, such as lapwings and golden plovers, and peregrines, merlins and other hunters – making winter the ideal time for nature-lovers to visit. The Great Fen Project, which aims to restore parts of the Fens to their natural state, will attract even more species back to this unique and atmospheric environment.

Main: Pink-footed geese soaring over the fens **Below (left to right):** Mute swans and pochard ducks, some of the diverse wildlife that, in winter, flocks to the Ouse Washes in Cambridgeshire; walkers on the Fens in Norfolk

FURTHER DETAILS

FENLAND NATURE RESERVES

Wicken Fen
The nature reserve is 14 km (9 miles) south of Ely, Cambridgeshire; reserve open daylight hours; visitor centre open 10am–5pm daily.
www.nationaltrust.org.uk/wicken-fen-nature-reserve

Ouse Washes
The RSPB visitor centre is 5 km (3 miles) from Manea village, near Chatteris, Cambridgeshire; visitor centre open 9am–5pm daily; birdwatching hides are open at all times.
www.rspb.org.uk/reserves/guide/o/ousewashes

WHAT ELSE TO SEE AND DO

Ely Cathedral
The monastery founded here by St Ethelreda in the 7th century was one of the great religious houses of East Anglia, and this abbey church, which dates from the 1180s, is among the most impressive cathedrals in Britain. Highlights include the Octagon Tower and the fan-vaulted Lady Chapel.
www.elycathedral.org

Straw Bear Festival
Each year in mid-January, the market town of Whittlesea, near Peterborough, holds the Straw Bear Festival, an ancient Fenland tradition in which the person chosen to be the "bear" is paraded through town in a costume made from the best harvest straw, accompanied by music, traditional street dancing and much merrymaking.
www.strawbear.org.uk

Wisbech and Fenland Museum
This museum contains a variety of rare and unusual artifacts that shine a light on the natural and cultural heritage of the town of Wisbech and the greater region.
www.wisbechmuseum.org.uk

Below: Ely Cathedral's nave and the Octagon Tower

THE ESSENTIALS

GETTING THERE AND AROUND
York is in the northeast of England. The nearest airport is Leeds Bradford Airport, about 40 km (25 miles) southwest of York. Excellent rail connections link the city with other destinations throughout England and into Scotland. York itself is fairly compact and so is easily explored on foot.

WEATHER
Sheltered in the Vale of York, the city's winter climate is temperate compared to the rest of Yorkshire, but rain or snow is still a possibility. Average winter daytime temperatures range from 4 to 6°C.

ACCOMMODATION
Splashing Out Middlethorpe Hall and Spa, on Bishopthorpe Road, is a luxury hotel surrounded by acres of parkland. *www.middlethorpe.com*

On a Budget The Bar Convent, on Blossom Street, is the oldest working convent in England, with characterful and very comfortable bedrooms. *www.bar-convent.org.uk*

EATING OUT
Splashing Out The Park Restaurant, on Peter's Grove, offers innovative tasting menus made from seasonal and local produce. *www.theparkrestaurant.co.uk*

On a Budget The Black Swan Pub, on Peasholme Green, is the oldest pub in York, built in 1417, and offers decent pub grub in an atmospheric setting. *www.blackswanyork.com*

PRICE FOR TWO PEOPLE
Around £190–230 a day for food, accommodation and entrance fees.

WEBSITE
www.visityork.org

Main: Intricate vaulted Chapter House ceiling of York Minster
Right (top to bottom): Participants at JORVIK Viking Festival; East end of York Minster in winter

VISITING THE VIKINGS

E ACH FEBRUARY, THE CITY OF YORK is overrun with Vikings, just as it was in days of old. This time, however, they're not here to conquer but to celebrate the city's heritage in the annual JORVIK Viking Festival. It's as if you've stumbled upon a gigantic fancy dress party, with scores of bearded, helmeted characters marauding through the narrow medieval streets. Over the five days of the festival, history is brought to life: you can hear Norse ballads and saga-telling, watch trials of strength and agility or full-scale battle re-enactments, and enjoy Viking crafts and food. A highlight is the longship races on the River Ouse.

While a visit to the festival is a great winter getaway, you can also see Vikings year-round at the JORVIK Viking Centre. This wonderful attraction arose from a city-centre archaeological dig that helped uncover how these Scandinavian trader-warriors lived when they ruled York – which the Vikings called *Jorvik* – from 866 until 954. Travel back in time on an underground journey through accurate recreations of the buildings, street life, sounds and even smells of the city in its Viking heyday. The tableaux of people going about their daily life are all the more fascinating when you discover that their faces are based on computer

FURTHER DETAILS

YORK

JORVIK Viking Centre and Festival
Coppergate; open winter: Apr–Oct: 10am–5pm; Nov–Mar: 10am–4pm. The JORVIK Festival takes place annually in the third week of February.
www.jorvik-viking-centre.co.uk

National Railway Museum
Leeman Road; open 10am–5pm daily.
www.nrm.org.uk

York Minster
Ogleforth; open 9am–5pm Mon–Sat, 12:45–5pm Sun.
www.yorkminster.org

WHAT ELSE TO SEE AND DO

Castle Museum
Founded by Dr John L Kirk, who collected items from his rural patients in lieu of fees, this museum is a treasure trove of everyday items and memorabilia from Georgian times to the mid-20th century. Exhibits include period costume, furniture, toys, crafts, tools, period rooms and even a recreation of a Victorian cobbled street.
www.yorkcastlemuseum.org.uk

York Art Gallery
A highlight of this fine art gallery on Exhibition Square is its extensive collection of British studio pottery. It also features paintings by 20th-century British artists, including L S Lowry's view of Clifford's Tower, as well as works by early Italian, Dutch and other European painters.
www.yorkartgallery.org.uk

Yorkshire Museum
Set in the grounds of the former St Mary's Abbey on Museum Street, this is one of the country's best archaeological museums. It contains an impressive collection of Roman remains from everyday life to the grave, as well as Viking and Anglo-Saxon artifacts and the ruins of the city's Benedictine abbey.
www.yorkshiremuseum.org.uk

Below (top to bottom): York's city wall; National Railway Museum

regenerations of actual skulls discovered at the site, and the artifacts are in the exact positions in which they were found.

When you have had your fill of Vikings, journey to the more recent past at the National Railway Museum – the largest of its kind in the world, with over 100 locomotives. Exhibits range from Thomas the Tank Engine to sumptuous royal carriages, the sleek Japanese bullet train – the only one outside Japan – and *Mallard*, the world's fastest steam locomotive.

The city's most famous landmark is York Minster, one of Britain's finest cathedrals and its largest Gothic building, with magnificent stained-glass windows. Perhaps the most atmospheric feature of York, however, is the medieval wall that still encircles the city, measuring 4 km (2½ miles) in circumference, with four original gates intact. Today, you can walk along a footpath atop this wall – the best place from which to admire one of the most beautiful cities of the north.

THE ESSENTIALS

GETTING THERE AND AROUND
Pembrokeshire forms the southwestern tip of Wales. It is accessed by car via the M4 and A40 and is approximately 4½ hours' drive from London. The nearest airport to the Pembrokeshire coast is Cardiff, about 145 km (90 miles) to the east; car hire is available at the airport. To explore Pembrokeshire's coastline, a car is essential, as the best storm sites are not well serviced by public transport.

WEATHER
Welsh winters tend to be wet and windy. Average temperatures in the daytime are 3–11°C, although they can drop below zero. Snow is very infrequent on the coast.

ACCOMMODATION
Splashing Out St Brides Spa Hotel, in Saundersfoot, has a clifftop location with superb views and a spa with an infinity pool heated to body temperature.
www.stbridesspahotel.com

On a Budget TYF Eco Lodge, in St Davids, is based in an old windmill on the outskirts of the country's smallest city.
www.tyf.com

EATING OUT
Splashing Out The Llys Meddyg Restaurant, in Newport, serves modern British dishes using plenty of locally sourced seafood, in a charming old-world setting.
www.llysmeddyg.com

On a Budget Cwtch, in St David's, is an intimate and informal venue for sampling high-quality Pembrokeshire produce including locally sourced crab, seabass, pork, steaks and cheeses.
www.cwtchrestaurant.co.uk

PRICE FOR TWO PEOPLE
From around £160 a day for accommodation and food.

WEBSITE
www.visitwales.com

Main: Breathtaking breakers crashing on the wild and windy Pembrokeshire coast

STORM-WATCHING

A MIGHTY STORM IS HOWLING IN FROM THE ATLANTIC against the Pembrokeshire coast, flinging streams of sea spray and salty rain at shoreline cottage windows, sending dune sand whistling through the air, bending trees and bushes until they creak and groan and smashing thundering steel-blue swells against towering, rain-lashed sea cliffs.

Pembrokeshire, jutting boldly out into the Atlantic, is hit by some of the most intense storms to batter the British Isles, and winter provides the best time for a breathtaking walk along the coast, into the teeth of a gale. This makes for an exhilarating expedition through what is possibly the only real wilderness environment left in Britain.

Few experiences are as raw and exciting as leaning into the screaming wind on a storm-swept beach to watch huge waves boom and break way offshore, or crash against cliffs and crags and hurl sea spray tens of metres into the air to cascade back to sea level like a

FURTHER DETAILS

PEMBROKESHIRE COAST NATIONAL PARK
Park Authority: *www.pembrokeshirecoast.org.uk*

National Park Visitor Centre
St Davids, Pembrokeshire; open Nov–Feb: 10am–4pm
daily; Mar–Oct: 9:30am–5pm daily.
www.pembrokeshirecoast.org.uk

Bear in mind that coastal storms can be dangerous as
well as spectacular:
- Be wary of storm surges, and rogue waves on beaches
  and low cliffs, which could sweep you out to sea
- Look out for loose and crumbling cliff faces after
  a storm
- Daylight hours are short in winter so, if you go for a
  long walk, bear this in mind
- Always let someone know your intended walking
  route and when you expect to be back
- Ensure you wear good waterproof clothing and
  footwear
- In an emergency dial 999 and ask for the Coastguard.
www.metoffice.gov.uk

WHAT ELSE TO SEE AND DO
Surfing in Mathry
Surf lessons are available at Preseli Venture near Mathry,
from £49 per half-day including all equipment.
www.preseliventure.com

St Davids
Britain's smallest city provides respite from the winter
storms. You'll find sanctuary in the 11th-century St
Davids Cathedral or the city's numerous pubs.
City: *www.stdavids.co.uk*
St Davids Cathedral: *www.stdavidscathedral.org.uk*

Below (top to bottom): Surfer riding the waves in
Pembrokeshire; waves pound the dramatic rocky coastline

waterfall from the heavens. Winter is the prime time to see this phenomenon on a regular basis. Most of the low-pressure systems that bring these storms to British shores pass by pretty quickly, so the chances are that if Saturday is windy and wet, Sunday will be breezy and sunny. Exposed coastlines such as Strumble Head and St Davids Head in North Pembrokeshire, and the vast white limestone cliffs of the Castlemartin region of South Pembrokeshire, offer unforgettable views of Mother Nature at her most raw and elemental, with the added bonus of welcoming B&Bs and warm, cosy pubs to scurry back to when you've had enough of being buffeted and blasted by wind, waves and sand.

The Pembrokeshire Coast National Park is Britain's only coastal national park, conserving over 620 sq km (240 sq miles) of this beautiful landscape. The park maintains the spectacular Pembrokeshire Coast Path – 299 km (186 miles) of trail you can follow around the peninsula, from St Dogmaels on Cardigan Bay to Amroth on the south coast. If you need a weekend winter break, nothing will blow away the cobwebs like a walk along this coastline.

NAVAL HEROES

PORTSMOUTH IS ENGLAND'S ONLY TRULY ISLAND CITY, as most of it lies on Portsea Island, where the Solent joins the English Channel. Nicknamed "Pompey", Portsmouth is a historic naval base of vast importance, and is home to the world's oldest dry dock. The city's powerful bond with the sea dates back to Roman times, but Portsmouth's great naval value made it a prime target for Luftwaffe bombing in World War II. The subsequent destruction led to some severe architectural reshaping, but the old town of Portsmouth maintains a historic charm, while a new, more innovative architectural impetus has given rise to the tall, graceful Spinnaker Tower – designed to resemble a spinnaker sail catching the wind.

It is Portsmouth's proud associations with the Royal Navy and British maritime history that truly define the city. Its Historic Dockyard is the resting place of three notable ships from very different periods: *HMS Victory*, *HMS Warrior* and the ill-fated *Mary Rose*. Nelson's ship, *HMS Victory*, sits today in dry dock, a world away from the roar and smoke of the Battle of Trafalgar. The imposing *HMS Warrior* entered service in 1861; it was Britain's first armour-plated

It is Portsmouth's proud associations with the Royal Navy and British maritime history that truly define the city.

battleship and the fastest vessel of its day, propelled by both steam engine and sails. You can admire a collection of fascinating objects retrieved from the wreck of the Tudor warship *Mary Rose* in a purpose-built museum. The dockyard also houses the Royal Naval Museum, which paints a detailed portrait of Portsmouth's role in British naval history, and Action Stations, a hands-on array of interactive games. A good way to get the city in full aerial perspective is to ascend the full 170 m (558 ft) of the elegant Spinnaker Tower.

Portsmouth can be visited in any season, but in late November and early December the atmosphere in the Historic Dockyard is at its most lively, when the Victorian Festival of Christmas brings the flavours of old Portsmouth to the fore. Join in the bustling festivities, when a host of street performers unite with Victorian characters, circus acts, policemen in period costume keeping order, traditional funfair attractions, marching bands, rides, shows and a galaxy of stalls to recreate the vibrant traditions of this historic city.

Main: Stern of *HMS Victory*
Far left (top to bottom): Gun deck on *HMS Victory*; prow of *HMS Victory*
Above: Ship figurehead of Admiral Horatio Nelson, alongside *HMS Victory*
Below: Spinnaker Tower at Gunwharf Quays

FURTHER DETAILS

PORTSMOUTH HISTORIC DOCKYARD
In addition to tickets for individual attractions, an annual pass for the Historic Dockyard is available, which allows unlimited entry to *HMS Warrior*, the Royal Naval Museum and Action Stations – the Royal Navy's interactive visitor attraction– but can be used once only for *HMS Victory*, the *Mary Rose* and harbour tours.
www.historicdockyard.co.uk

HMS Victory, HMS Warrior, Mary Rose
Portsmouth Historic Dockyard; open Apr–Oct: 10am–5:30pm daily; Nov–Mar: 10am–5pm daily.
HMS Victory: www.hms-victory.com
HMS Warrior: www.hmswarrior.org
Mary Rose: www.historicdockyard.co.uk

National Museum of the Royal Navy
Tickets to the museum can be bought separately or are included in the Historic Dockyard annual pass; open Apr–Oct: 10am–5pm daily; Nov–Mar: 10am–4:15pm daily.
www.nmrn.org.uk

Spinnaker Tower
Portsmouth Harbour; open 10am–5:30pm daily.
www.spinnakertower.co.uk

Victorian Festival of Christmas
Tickets include entry to *HMS Victory*, *HMS Warrior* and the *Mary Rose*; open 10am–6pm (last admission 4:30pm) daily.
www.christmasfestival.co.uk

WHAT ELSE TO SEE AND DO
Southsea
The seaside resort of Southsea, to the south of Old Portsmouth, has a largely gravel beach. The D-Day Museum offers fascinating insights into Portsmouth's role in the Normandy landings of 1944. Longer than the Bayeux Tapestry, the Overlord Embroidery at the museum relates the story of the invasion force.
Southsea: www.southsea.co.uk
D-Day Museum: www.ddaymuseum.co.uk

Portchester Castle
Originally dating from the 3rd century, Portchester Castle is unique as the last surviving Roman fort in northern Europe with walls still standing to their full height. Stationed at the head of Portsmouth Harbour, the castle served as a jail for French prisoners during the Napoleonic Wars.
www.english-heritage.org.uk

Below: *HMS Warrior* seen from the top of the Spinnaker Tower

Main: Brecon Beacons from Pen y Fan
Right (top to bottom): Hikers exploring the winter wilderness; waterfall in the Beacons

THE ESSENTIALS

GETTING THERE AND AROUND
The Brecon Beacons are in southeast Wales. The nearest international airport is Cardiff, 87 km (53 miles) south of Brecon. The nearest railway station is at Abergavenny, served by London trains via Newport. Buses run from Abergavenny to Brecon, which has bus and taxi services. Driving within the National Park can be slow, but it's a great area for walking, cycling and horse-riding.

WEATHER
The Beacons experience bright, cold weather in winter, as well as periods of wind and rain. Average winter daytime temperatures are 2–5°C.

ACCOMMODATION
Splashing Out Peterstone Court Country House and Spa, in Llanhamlach, offers luxurious spa and restaurant facilities with a mountainous backdrop.
www.peterstone-court.com

On a Budget The Bear, in Crickhowell, is an old-fashioned town coaching inn with antique furnishings and log fires.
www.bearhotel.co.uk

EATING OUT
Dining in the Beacons is limited to inns and pubs, so prices are quite consistent.

Nantyffin Cider Mill Inn, in Crickhowell, is a 16th-century inn serving high-quality British pub food in a bistro-style setting.
www.cidermill.co.uk

The Felin Fach Griffin Inn, near Brecon, has the motto of "simple things done well", which is reflected in its fantastic menu.
www.eatdrinksleep.ltd.uk

PRICE FOR TWO PEOPLE
Around £160 a day for accommodation and food.

WEBSITE
www.visitmidwales.co.uk

PANORAMIC VIEWS

WITH THE HIGHEST PEAKS IN WALES outside of Snowdonia, the Brecon Beacons National Park makes a superb winter escape. Hewn from sandstone, the snow-dusted Beacons rise skyward to the twin high-points of Pen y Fan and Cribyn. They immediately invite you to climb, but these summits can be treacherous in winter, so stop off first to speak to the experts at the National Park Visitor Centre in Libanus, who know when it's safest to set off.

Limber up with a walk on Mynydd Illtud Common, a protected area of grassland and wetland with stunning mountain vistas. Then pick a day with clear blue skies, wrap up warm to counter the inevitable biting wind and set off for one of the adjacent summits. The journey is astounding. The grassy ridges give way to dizzying drops from sheer cliff-like edges, and on a fine day a far-ranging panorama surrounds you, encompassing points over 160 km (100 miles) apart. To the north are the uplands of mid-Wales and pristine Snowdonia; to the east are the rolling Malverns and Cotswolds; the Bristol Channel and the

FURTHER DETAILS

THE BRECON BEACONS

Brecon Beacons National Park Visitor Centre
Libanus, Brecon; open Mar–Oct: 9:30am–5pm daily;
Nov–Feb: 9:30am-4pm daily.
www.breconbeacons.org

Mynydd Illtud Common
Between Libanus and Brecon, Brecon Beacons
National Park.
www.breconbeacons.org

Sgwd yr Eira
Near Penderyn, Brecon Beacons National Park.
www.breconbeacons.org

The Big Pit: National Coal Museum
Blaenavon, Torfaen; open 9:30am–5pm daily;
50-minute underground tours run between 10am
and 3.30pm.
www.museumwales.nc.uk/en/bigpit

Blaenavon Ironworks
North Street, Blaenavon; open Apr–Oct: 10am–5pm
daily; Nov–Mar: 10am–4pm Tue–Thu.
www.cadw.wales.gov.uk

WHAT ELSE TO SEE AND DO

Abergavenny Museum
Located in a ruined Norman castle and its grounds, in
Abergavenny's Castle Street, this local history museum
is home to a recreated old Welsh kitchen and a
grocer's shop. The museum's displays tell the story of
this centuries-old market town from prehistoric times
through to the present day.
www.abergavennymuseum.co.uk

Brecknock Museum & Art Gallery
Housed in the former Assize Court, in Captain's Walk
in Brecon, this museum and gallery houses displays
on local history and has changing exhibitions featuring
contemporary artists from all over Wales.
www.powys.gov.uk

Llangorse Multi-Activity Centre
The largest riding and indoor climbing centre in Wales
is at Gilfach Farm, Llangorse, near Brecon. It also
offers sky-wire rides, gorge-walking and pony trekking
(minimum trek time 1 hour).
www.activityuk.com

Taff Trail
A largely traffic-free cycling route, the Taff Trail runs
88 km (55 miles) between Brecon and Cardiff, through
the centre of the Brecon Beacons National Park.
www.tafftrail.org.uk

Below: Stone bridge over the River Usk at Crickhowell

heights of Exmoor in north Devon lie to the south, while the sea hides beyond the Black Mountains to the west.

South of the peaks is Brecon Beacons Waterfall Country, where the rivers Nedd, Hepste and Mellte carved their way through the land to form deep gorges during successive ice ages. The gorges are now cloaked with forests, but the rivers still run their course, tumbling over a series of tumultuous waterfalls. They are at their most dramatic after prolonged rain, so winter is an ideal time to experience them. Perhaps the most breathtaking of all the falls is Sgwd yr Eira, where an ancient route leads you along a rocky ledge and right beneath the curtain of the waterfall.

Once you've had your fill of the landscape, you might like to visit the compact, stone-built towns of Abergavenny, Brecon and Crickhowell, with their welcoming cosy inns and traditional shops that still serve the local farming communities. At the northeastern tip of the Beacons is the quaint book town of Hay-on-Wye (*see pp14–15*), while towards Cardiff are the famous Welsh "Valleys"– once scarred by mining and ironworking, but now a lush green landscape once again.

THE ESSENTIALS

GETTING THERE AND AROUND
The Burns Heritage Trail is in Ayrshire, on the southwest coast of Scotland. Alloway is 10 km (6 miles) south of Glasgow's Prestwick Airport and 67 km (42 miles) south of Glasgow's main international airport. The Burns sites are best visited by car, as public transport is relatively limited.

WEATHER
The mild sea air makes this corner of Scotland fairly pleasant in winter, and snow is not as common as elsewhere. Temperatures can be 2°C higher than in eastern Scotland, averaging 4–9°C during the daytime in winter.

ACCOMMODATION
Splashing Out Glenapp Castle, in Ballantrae, 48 km (30 miles) south of Alloway, is a luxurious 5-star retreat in a magnificent restored baronial castle. *www.glenappcastle.com*

On a Budget Greenan Lodge, in Doonfoot, is a small and friendly guesthouse a few minutes' drive from Burns Cottage in Alloway. *www.greenanlodge.com*

EATING OUT
Splashing Out The Cairndale Hotel's Reivers Restaurant in the centre of Dumfries offers classic Scottish and English dining in elegant surroundings. *www.cairndalehotel.co.uk*

On a Budget The Masonic Arms, in Gatehouse of Fleet, is a cosy pub with an open fire and a wide-ranging menu. *www.masonicarms.co.uk*

PRICE FOR TWO PEOPLE
Around £190–200 a day for food, car hire, accommodation and entrance fees.

WEBSITES
www.visitdumfriesandgalloway.co.uk
www.visitscotland.com

THE PLOUGHMAN POET

SCOTLAND'S BEST-LOVED NATIVE SON is not a warrior or a king but a poet – Robert Burns. People the world over ring in the New Year with his lyrics to "Auld Lang Syne", while Scots everywhere traditionally celebrate his birthday on 25 January with boisterous Burns Suppers, featuring recitations of his works and consumption of his favourite fare: whisky and haggis.

The Bard of Ayrshire was born in 1759 in a humble cottage built by his father's own hands in Alloway, near Ayr. The village became something of a place of pilgrimage after Burns's death, and much of it is now sequestered within the Burns National Heritage Park. His birthplace, Burns Cottage, has been restored to its original condition, and you can wander from here past places that formed the settings for his most famous poems, such as the eerie 16th-century kirk (church) and "Brig O'Doon", the medieval bridge that spans the beautiful river Doon. Climb to the Burns Monument at the edge of the village for far-reaching views over his beloved Ayrshire, before retreating to the cottage to read the great man's words again in his own hand – its museum contains the world's largest collection of his manuscripts and personal belongings.

Following in Burns's footsteps will take you through some of southwest Scotland's most beautiful scenery. Heading south through Galloway Forest Park, you'll travel through the ancient woodlands, lochs and moorland surrounding the Galloway Hills, a haven for wildlife, from red deer to red kites. In 1788, Burns took a lease on Ellisland Farm, just outside Dumfries, and its idyllic river setting inspired his best nature poetry. You can visit the artists' colony of Kirkcudbright and the old mill town Gatehouse of Fleet, where the cotton mill owned by Alexander Birtwhistle – immortalized by Burns as "Roaring Birtwhistle" – still stands.

Burns moved to the county town of Dumfries in 1791, and died here five years later, aged just 37. There is a memorial statue of him on Dumfries High Street, and you can explore the simple house where he spent his final years, or – perhaps most fitting of all – visit the Globe Inn, his favourite pub, and raise a glass to the great poet, Rabbie Burns.

Main: Loch Doon, Dumfries and Galloway
Below (left to right): Birthplace of Robert Burns, Alloway; statue of Burns in Dumfries

FURTHER DETAILS

THE BURNS HERITAGE TRAIL
Robert Burns Birthplace Museum
Alloway, Ayr; open 10am–5:30pm daily
(to 5:30pm Apr–Sep).
www.burnsmuseum.org.uk

Galloway Forest Park
Near Newton Stewart and New Galloway, Dumfries
and Galloway; open daily.
www.gallowayforestpark.com

Ellisland Farm
10 km (6 miles) north of Dumfries on the A76; open
Oct–Mar: 10am–1pm and 2–5pm Tue–Sat; Apr–Sep:
10am–5pm Mon–Sat, 2–5pm Sun.
www.ellislandfarm.co.uk

Burns House
Mill Road, Dumfries; open Oct–Mar: 10am–1pm
and 2–5pm Tue–Sat; Apr–Sep: 10am–5pm
Mon–Sat, 2–5pm Sun.
www.dumfriesmuseum.demon.co.uk

The Globe Inn
High Street, Dumfries; open 10am–11pm Mon–Wed,
10am–midnight Thu, 10am–1am Fri–Sat, 11:30am–
12am Sun.
www.globeinndumfries.co.uk

WHAT ELSE TO SEE AND DO
Sweetheart Abbey
The brooding ruins of the last great abbey built in
Scotland lie just outside Dumfries. Sweetheart Abbey
was named in honour of the undying love of its
founder, Lady Dervorgilla, for her husband John Balliol,
King of Scotland from 1292 to 1296. She is buried
in front of the High Altar with a casket containing his
embalmed heart.
www.historic-scotland.gov.uk

Caerlaverock Castle
A stunning castle with a moat, twin-towered gatehouse
and imposing battlements. This medieval stronghold
has a turbulent history, owing to its proximity to
England, which brought it into border conflicts. Visitors
can enjoy a siege warfare exhibition and a nature trail.
www.historic-scotland.gov.uk

Below (top to bottom): Burns Monument from the Brig O'Doon
in Alloway; walkers at the summit of Craiglee in the Galloway Hills

THE ESSENTIALS

GETTING THERE AND AROUND
Aviemore is in north-central Scotland.
The nearest airport is at Inverness,
58 km (36 miles) to the north. Aviemore
is also on the main rail route to the
Highlands; trains here from Edinburgh
take 2 hours. Most of the Cairngorms
National Park is only accessible on
foot, but a number of Aviemore-based
companies offer quad-bike tours, 4WD
trips and pony trekking on the fringes
of the park.

WEATHER
You will encounter freezing temperatures
and must be prepared for sleet, rain and
potential blizzard conditions, with low
to zero visibility from November until
March. Average daytime temperatures
range from -15 to 6°C, but depend
greatly on altitude and wind chill.

ACCOMMODATION
Splashing Out Macdonald Aviemore
Resort, in Aviemore, is made up of three
separate up-market hotels that share
extensive leisure facilities.
www.macdonaldhotels.co.uk/aviemore

On a Budget Aviemore Youth Hostel,
in the centre of Aviemore, offers
dormitory bunks and en suite and
family rooms.
www.syha.org.uk

EATING OUT
Splashing Out Aspects, in the
Macdonald Aviemore Resort, offers
elegant fine-dining using the best
Scottish produce.
www.macdonaldhotels.co.uk/aviemore

On a Budget The Old Bridge Inn, also
in Aviemore, offers hot soup and an
open fire in a quaint old building.
www.oldbridgeinn.co.uk

PRICE FOR TWO PEOPLE
From £190 a day for accommodation,
food and leisure activities.

WEBSITE
www.visitaviemore.com

Main: Ice-climbing in the Cairngorms
Right (top to bottom): Ski range at Glenshee Ski Centre in Cairnwell; sunset over the Cairngorm mountains

CAIRNGORMS CHALLENGE

Visiting the Cairngorms in winter is like entering a dazzling white universe. This is the largest wilderness area in Britain – a region of hills, moors and steep-sided glens that is home to birds and beasts found nowhere else in the country. Yet the gateways to this lonely and otherwordly kingdom are just a few hours' travel away from any of Scotland's major cities.

At the heart of the Cairngorms, 600 m (1,970 ft) above sea level, lies a unique Arctic world where wildlife such as ptarmigan grouse, mountain hares and stoats don their pure-white winter coats for concealment against the snow-covered landscapes. This can be an unforgiving environment, which, in the depths of winter, calls for an array of mountain survival skills in those who brave it. But if you dare, the Cairngorms National Park offers a heart-lifting experience unique to this part of the British Isles. Nothing beats the sight of a mighty golden eagle circling high in a brilliant, frosty blue sky, or the simple excitement of being the first to break a trail across a pristine expanse of newly fallen snow. If you obey the easily learned rules of survival, have the right kit and a modicum of common sense, an expedition in the hills can be a stroll in the park. At centres like Glenmore Lodge, Scotland's national outdoor training centre, expert mountain-climbers have passed on their hard-won

FURTHER DETAILS

WINTER SPORTS IN THE CAIRNGORMS

Cairngorms National Park Authority
www.cairngorms.co.uk

Mountaineering Council of Scotland
The Old Granary, West Mill, Perth; open 9am–5pm
Mon–Fri.
www.mcofs.org.uk

Scotland's National Outdoor Activities Centre
Glenmore Lodge, Glenmore.
www.glenmorelodge.org.uk

British Association of Snowsports Instructors
The Square, Grantown-on-Spey; open 9am–5pm
Mon–Fri.
www.basi.org.uk

Aviemore Sled Dog Rally
Aviemore; held annually in the last week of January.
www.siberianhuskyclub.com/aviemore

WHAT ELSE TO SEE AND DO

G2 Outdoor Centre
Winter survival skills training, snowboarding, skiing
and other winter sports are offered at this training
centre in Aviemore.
www.g2outdoor.co.uk

Glenshee Ski Centre
Based in Cairnwell, 35 km (22 miles) southeast
of Aviemore, the largest ski area in Britain offers
36 runs with an amazing diversity of natural terrain
for all standards of skiers and snowboarders.
www.ski-glenshee.co.uk

Rothiemurchus Estate
This private estate in Inverdruie, near Aviemore, offers a
huge number of outdoor activities, including hill-walking,
riding, quad-biking, canoeing and wildlife-watching, for
both families and corporate parties. It is possible to stay
on the estate's camp site and caravan park.
www.rothiemurchus.net

Highland Wildlife Park
At this park, in Kincraig near Kingussie, 20 km
(12 miles) south of Aviemore, open air enclosures
house threatened Highland wildlife, such as otters and
wildcats. Also found here are wolves and Arctic foxes
– species that were once native to the Highlands until
they were sadly hunted into near-extinction – and rather
more unlikely guests such as camels and Amur tigers.
www.highlandwildlifepark.org

Below: Golden eagle landing in snow

expertise for more than 60 years, and today you can enrol on a course in one of many mountain sports, such as skiing and rock- and ice-climbing. While taking a course at Glenmore can be a demanding and gruelling learning experience, it can also be great fun, leaving you with an empowering sense of achievement and skills that will last a lifetime.

With an array of places to stay, eat, drink and be merry, the purpose-built holiday village of Aviemore, on the northwest fringes of the national park, is a perfect base, offering a variety of outdoor activities. In January, it hosts the Aviemore Sled Dog Rally, the largest rally of its kind in Britain, with more than 250 squads and more than 1,000 sled dogs competing. Unlike in Alaska or Canada, where the dogs pull real sleds, heavy snow cannot always be guaranteed in Scotland, even at the height of winter – so the dog teams instead haul two-wheeled "sled-carts" over trails where the mud can often be deeper than the snow.

Whether you want to test your limits by learning the toughest of survival skills and taking on the fiercest mountain conditions, or would rather spend your time in the less demanding environs of Aviemore, a winter trip to the Cairngorms will certainly be an adventure.

THE ESSENTIALS

GETTING THERE AND AROUND
Birmingham is in the West Midlands of England, 190 km (120 miles) northwest of London and 153 km (95 miles) south of Manchester. Birmingham International Airport is 22 km (14 miles) east of the city. There are high-speed trains from London Euston, slower services from London Marylebone and hourly coaches from London Victoria. It's possible to walk between the main sites in Birmingham's city centre.

WEATHER
Freezing temperatures are not common in Birmingham until after Christmas, but be prepared for wind, rain and colder periods, with average daytime temperatures ranging from 3 to 5°C.

ACCOMMODATION
Splashing Out Hotel du Vin, on Church Street, is a stylish hotel and bistro located in the Jewellery Quarter, converted from a Victorian hospital.
www.hotelduvin.com/birmingham

On a Budget Premier Inn Birmingham, on Broad Street, is a handily located and cheap city-centre hotel.
www.premierinn.com

EATING OUT
Splashing Out Purnell's, on Cornwall Street, is a fantastic Michelin-starred restaurant serving contemporary cuisine.
www.purnellsrestaurant.com

On a Budget Kushi Balti Restaurant, on Moseley Road in the heart of the "Balti Belt", serves healthier recipes alongside more traditional South Asian dishes.
www.kushibalti.wordpress.com

PRICE FOR TWO PEOPLE
Around £190–210 a day for food, accommodation and entrance fees.

WEBSITE
www.visitbirmingham.com

CHRISTMAS CHEER

BIRMINGHAM'S STYLISHLY REGENERATED city centre comes as a very pleasant surprise to those who don't know it. At its heart lies Victoria Square, an exciting public space watched over by the elegant 19th-century domed Council House, and filled with fountains, weirs and notable sculptures. Antony Gormley's *Iron Man* attracts visitors, but the locals' favourite is the friendlier *River Goddess* – also known as "the floozie in the Jacuzzi" – by Dhruva Mistry.

From mid-November to 23 December the square plays host to the Frankfurt Christmas Market, which is the largest authentic German seasonal market outside Germany or Austria. This busy festive fair symbolizes Birmingham's partnership with its twin city and many vendors travel from Germany especially for the occasion. Crowds throng the area well into the evening, soaking up the atmosphere and sampling German delicacies, such as *glühwein* (mulled wine), grilled sausages, pretzels and beer, accompanied by music and a traditional fairground carousel.

Birmingham's city centre offers a host of other attractions, and is surprisingly compact and easy to explore. Close to Victoria Square, the Birmingham City Museum and Art Gallery

Main: German Frankfurt Christmas Market in Victoria Square
Above: *River Goddess* fountain in Victoria Square
Below: Festive gingerbread for sale on a stall at the Christmas Market

includes the finest collection of Pre-Raphaelite paintings in the world. Music is also central to city life here, and it's well worth visiting the Symphony Hall, home of the renowned Birmingham Symphony Orchestra. Their state-of-the art concert hall features a stunning auditorium and a 6,000-pipe organ, and is open for events and tours virtually every day.

The city is also home to the Jewellery Quarter, which dates back some 250 years and is still responsible for much of the nation's jewellery production. Admire its historic architecture, before heading to the Museum of the Jewellery Quarter. For more history, visit the Birmingham Back to Backs, a carefully resorted 19th-century courtyard of working people's homes.

For children, the National Sea Life Centre has spectacular displays of exotic marine species. Then there are Birmingham's canals – famously outdoing Venice's in extent. A stroll along the canal paths, past converted former warehouses, takes you to Gas Street Basin, now home to a buzzing concentration of bars and cafés too good to resist at the end of the day.

FURTHER DETAILS

BIRMINGHAM

Frankfurt Christmas Market
Victoria Square, Birmingham; open mid-Nov–23 Dec, 10am–9pm daily.
www.birmingham.gov.uk/frankfurtmarket

Birmingham Museum and Art Gallery
Chamberlain Square, Birmingham; open 10am–5pm Mon–Thu; 10:30am–5pm Fri; 10am–5pm Sat & Sun.
www.bmag.org.uk

Birmingham Symphony Hall
Broad Street, Birmingham; open at varying times for public tours and a full concert programme.
www.thsh.co.uk

National Sea Life Centre
The Waters Edge, Brindley Place, Birmingham; open 10am–4pm Mon–Fri, 10am–5pm Sat & Sun.
www.sealifeeurope.com

Museum of the Jewellery Quarter
The Smith and Pepper Building, Vyse Street, Hockley Birmingham; open 10:30am–4pm Tue–Sat, closed Sun and Mon except Bank Holidays.
www.birminghammuseums.org.uk/jewellery

Birmingham Back to Backs
Inge Street and Hurst Street, Birmingham; open 10am–5pm Tue–Sun (from 1pm Tue–Thu during school-term time), guided tours only (booking advised); closed Jan.
www.nationaltrust.org.uk

WHAT ELSE TO SEE AND DO

The Bull Ring
Birmingham's commercial centre since the Middle Ages, the Bull Ring is now the most-visited shopping complex outside London, and is easily recognizable due to the iconic aluminium-disc clad Selfridges building. Its latest incarnation was opened in 2003, on the site of the unloved 1960s development.
www.bullring.co.uk

Below (top to bottom): St Martin's Church and Selfridges department store; Symphony Hall auditorium

THE ESSENTIALS

GETTING THERE AND AROUND
Cambridge is in the east of England, 96 km (60 miles) north of London. The nearest international airport is London Stansted, 48 km (30 miles) south of the city and connected to it by bus and train. Once in the city, walking is the easiest way to see the main colleges and museums, as the centre is compact and pedestrianized.

WEATHER
Cambridge is in a very flat area of England and winter winds can be bitingly cold, though it only snows occasionally and not usually for long. Average winter daytime temperatures range from 2 to 8°C.

ACCOMMODATION
Splashing Out The Doubletree by Hilton, in Granta Place, is an upscale luxury hotel on the banks of the River Cam, just a stroll from the city centre. *http://doubletree.hilton.co.uk*

On a Budget Worth House, on Chesterton Road, a short walk north of the city centre, is a 4-star guesthouse with reasonably priced rooms. *www.worth-house.co.uk*

EATING OUT
Splashing Out Restaurant 22, also on Chesterton Road, is an old city favourite, serving consistently good cuisine with a *prix-fixe* menu. *www.restaurant22.co.uk*

On a Budget The Anchor, on Silver Street in the city centre, is a historic and lively riverside pub serving great food. Tel: 01223 353554

PRICE FOR TWO PEOPLE
Around £160 a day for food, accommodation and entrance fees.

WEBSITE
www.visitcambridge.org

Main: King's College and its magnificent chapel

CAROLS IN THE COLLEGE

T HE UNIVERSITY CITY OF CAMBRIDGE is one of the most beautiful in England. Its lofty spires and clock towers, ornately carved Tudor and Neo-Gothic façades, and colleges with neat courtyards and quadrangles contrast with its low, half-timbered and whitewashed city buildings that house charming shops, pubs and restaurants. In summer its narrow streets are packed with tourists and there's a steady flotilla of flat-bottomed punts poling along the River Cam. But winter is really the most romantic time to visit this historic city.

This is the season for the finest views of the university along the Backs – the long swathes of lawns and gardens alongside the river behind the colleges. When the trees drop their leaves, the impressive architecture really stands out. Walk from the Backs across graceful arched bridges to explore the colleges and admire their architectural and historical highlights at close hand – Trinity College, which boasts the Tudor-era Great Court and a library designed by the great architect Sir Christopher Wren; Magdalene College, whose library contains Samuel

FURTHER DETAILS

CAMBRIDGE

College Tours
Guided tours of the colleges can be booked through the Visitor Information Centre, Wheeler Street, Cambridge; open 10am–5:30pm Mon–Fri, 10am–5pm Sat; also May–Sep: 11am–3pm Sun and Bank Holidays.

Trinity College
Trinity Street, Cambridge.
www.trin.cam.ac.uk

Magdalene College
Magdalene Street, Cambridge.
www.magd.cam.ac.uk

St John's College
St John's Street, Cambridge.
www.joh.cam.ac.uk

King's College Chapel
King's Parade, Cambridge.
www.kings.cam.ac.uk

Art and Craft Market
All Saints Garden, Trinity Street, Cambridge; open Jan–Nov: 9am–5pm Sat; Dec: 9am–5pm Wed–Sat (weather permitting).
www.cambridge-art-craft.co.uk

Cambridge Market
Market Hill, Cambridge. This daily market sells a mixture of goods Mon–Sat, and becomes a farmers' market on Sun.

Sidney Sussex College
Sidney Street, Cambridge.
www.sid.cam.ac.uk

WHAT ELSE TO SEE AND DO

Great St Mary's
This Gothic building (the "university church") in Market Square has grand views from its 15th-century tower.
www.gsm.cam.ac.uk

Fitzwilliam Museum
The city's top museum, in Trumpington Street, contains a vast collection of European paintings, sculptures, drawings and prints, as well as Egyptian and Greek antiquities, illuminated manuscripts and Asian art and ceramics.
www.fitzmuseum.cam.ac.uk

Below: Art and Craft Market in All Saints Garden

Pepys's famous diary; and St John's College with its picturesque Bridge of Sighs. The star attraction is undoubtedly King's College Chapel – a late-Gothic masterpiece with magnificent fan-vaulting and exquisite stained-glass windows. A special carol service, "A Festival in Nine Lessons and Carols", is performed here by the King's College choir on Christmas Eve. Wrap up warm and join the queue before 9am if you hope to get a seat for the 3pm service; it's worth the long wait to hear traditional carols sung in such glorious surroundings.

Cambridge is also a delightful place to do your Christmas shopping. Visit the Art and Craft Market in All Saints Garden, where you can purchase quality gifts directly from the artists. Then browse the outdoor market, on Market Hill, which features everything from fashion to gourmet foodstuffs. A ramble down Cambridge's cobbled passages will lead you to quirky boutiques, cosy cafés and great second-hand bookshops. Or take a break from shopping by visiting one of the city's many museums or simply unwinding in one of its quaint old pubs.

More Great Ideas for **Winter**

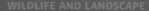

HISTORY AND HERITAGE

Rock of Cashel in Tipperary

WILDLIFE AND LANDSCAPE

Slavonian grebe at Dungeness

CITIES, TOWNS AND VILLAGES

Cornish fishing village of Mousehole

ROCK OF CASHEL SOUTHERN IRELAND
A winter visit to this ancient ecclesiastical stronghold in Tipperary is wonderfully atmospheric. It was once the seat of the ancient Kings of Munster, although most of the surviving buildings date from the 12th and 13th centuries. It flourished for centuries until Oliver Cromwell laid seige in 1647 and killed thousands, and it was eventually abandoned in the 18th-century. Cormac's Chapel is the best preserved of the ruins, but St Patrick's Cathedral is the Rock's heart.
www.cashel.ie

CORFE CASTLE SOUTHWEST ENGLAND
The magnificent windswept ruins of 1,000-year-old Corfe Castle offer breathtaking views across the Isle of Purbeck. Silhouetted against a bare winter sky, the castle dominates Corfe village as it has done for centuries. It is most famous as the home of Lady Bankes, who bravely defended the castle from a siege during the Civil War. In late winter, the castle's renowned ravens can be seen roosting. Legend says that when the birds leave, the castle suffers ill fortune.
www.corfe-castle.co.uk

WEST STOW VILLAGE
EASTERN ENGLAND
Set on an archaeological site in a large country park, West Stow is a reconstruction of an Anglo-Saxon village. Living history events in winter bring the village to life.
www.weststow.org

LLANDUDNO PIER NORTH WALES
This Y-shaped Victorian masterpiece is the longest pier in Wales. It was originally built in 1858, at a fraction of its present size, but storms damaged the structure the following year. A longer pier, measuring 376 m (1,234 ft), opened in 1877. Much of the original structure, including the promenade deck, the elaborate ironwork and the pavilion, still remains, and is classed as a Grade-II listed building. Visit for a reminder of the glory days of the seaside.
www.llandudnopier.com

DUNGENESS SOUTHEAST ENGLAND
Bleak, weird and strangely beautiful, Dungeness is the largest shingle expanse in Europe. The eerie landscape is interrupted by a shack "village", two nuclear power stations, two lighthouses, a miniature railway and fishing boats. The RSPB nature reserve here is a magnet for migrating birds, such as grebe, smew and bittern. Geese, swans and wigeons also visit in winter, as do several types of owls. Winter walks here will well and truly blow the cobwebs away.
www.rspb.org.uk

CHEVIOT HILLS
NORTHEAST ENGLAND
An isolated and romantic region of rounded hills and valleys, the Cheviot Hills are great walking country, with hundreds of ancient tracks and the chance to see timid otters.
www.cheviotwalks.co.uk

CAITHNESS HIGHLANDS AND ISLANDS
A landscape of massive cliffs, tiny islands, bleak moorland and sandy beaches, Caithness is as far north as you can get on mainland Britain. Rich in sea birds and rare plants, it feels like a world apart. In the winter months, there's an extra attraction – the Northern Lights, an extraordinary phenomenon that occurs when solar flares collide with Earth's magnetic field, producing a seemingly supernatural light show. One of the best places to view them is at Dunnett Head.
www.scotland-inverness.co.uk/caithness.htm

STOURHEAD GARDENS SOUTHWEST ENGLAND
Visiting Stourhead is like stepping into an 18th-century painting. Frosted ground, snowdrops, early rhododendrons and a tranquil lake make the gardens here a magical destination for winter visitors. It was laid out in the 1740s by Henry Hoare, who inherited the house and gardens. The fantastical landscape is beautifully choreographed to make the most of the splendid views across the lake to classical Italianate temples, grottoes, statues and bridges.
www.nationaltrust.org.uk/stourhead

MOUSEHOLE SOUTHWEST ENGLAND
Mousehole (pronounced "Mowzel") is an unspoilt coastal village looking out towards St Michael's Mount and Mounts Bay. It was the home of Dolly Pentreath, the last native Cornish-language speaker, who died 200 years ago. On 23 December, the village celebrates "Tom Bawcock's Eve" with songs and a huge "Stargazey" fish pie, commemorating a local fisherman whose fishing prowess once saved the village from starvation. The Christmas harbour lights are spectacular.
www.cornishlight.co.uk

ROBIN HOOD'S BAY NORTHEAST ENGLAND
This pretty village consists of a jumble of cottages clinging to a cliff. A maze of narrow cobbled alleyways and secret passages summons up images of smugglers, and on the sandy and rocky beach below, fossil hunters search for ammonite treasures. The North Sea Trail guides walkers along the beautiful coastline. In December, there's a Victorian Weekend with carol singing, street entertainment, and 19th-century-style food and drink.
www.robin-hoods-bay.co.uk

ENNIS
SOUTHERN IRELAND
The charming county town of Clare has a reputation as "the boutique capital of Ireland", and its narrow streets provide delightful shopping – just the place for winter retail therapy.
www.visitennis.ie

PORTHDINLLAEN
NORTH WALES
This tiny, idyllic village, which sits beside a golden beach, has magnificent walks that promise beautiful views, providing you with the perfect backdrop for a romantic Valentine's day.
www.walesdirectory.co.uk

CHESTER
NORTHWEST ENGLAND
Dating from Roman times, Chester is best seen by walking around the ancient city walls. The city's two-storey shopping streets, the Rows, lie inside the walls.
www.visitchester.com

See also pp178–9, 182–3, 200–201, 204–5, 210–11.

See also pp180–81, 186–7, 194–5, 202–3.

See also pp196–7, 208–9.

OUTDOOR ACTIVITIES   FAMILY GETAWAYS   FESTIVALS AND EVENTS

Mountain biking in the Dyfi Forest

Chinese dragon performance at Chinese New Year

Christmas illuminations at Kew Gardens

MOUNTAIN BIKING CENTRAL WALES

Machynlleth, on the southern side of Snowdonia, is the old capital of Wales, where Prince Owain Glyndwr held the first Welsh parliament. Today, it is a mountain-biking centre, where enthusiasts can tackle a 15-km (9-mile) circuit of trails in the nearby Dyfi Forest. Gravity-defying manoeuvres are required to tackle long descents and the "eye of the needle" jump, where cyclists have to land between two trees. "Design-your-own" routes are also available.
www.mbwales.com/machynlleth

CHINESE NEW YEAR SOUTHEAST ENGLAND

More than 50,000 people turn out to enjoy London's Chinese New Year, which falls between 21 January and 21 February. It starts with a grand parade that travels from Trafalgar Square along the Strand to Leicester Square. This is superb family entertainment, with dragon and lion dances, martial arts displays, opera and Chinese fireworks and firecrackers. At dusk revellers flock to the food stalls in a decorated Chinatown, for more dancing and celebration.
www.londonchinatown.org

ROYAL WELSH WINTER FAIR
CENTRAL WALES

Livestock, poultry and horses vie for attention with art and crafts at this popular fair at the South Glamorgan Hall in late November to early December.
www.rwas.co.uk

COTSWOLD WILDLIFE PARK
SOUTH EAST ENGLAND

Over-18s can become a keeper for a day at this wildlife park, where creatures including penguins, meerkats and big cats need feeding and cleaning.
www.cotswoldwildlifepark.co.uk

TIME OF GIFTS
SOUTHWEST ENGLAND

The Eden Project's "Time of Gifts" Christmas event is a winter wonderland. Ice-skating discos, music, decorated trees, markets and choirs are just some of the attractions.
www.edenproject.com

SIX NATIONS RUGBY
SOUTH WALES

Catch some of the Six Nations rugby matches in Cardiff's Millennium Stadium in February; the competing teams are England, Scotland, Ireland, Wales, France and Italy.
www.rbs6nations.com

OBAN WINTER FESTIVAL HIGHLANDS AND ISLANDS, SCOTLAND

Held in the picturesque Scottish town of Oban, this 10 day event in late November features an array of activities. There are street parades, international and local performing acts, pipers, lantern parades and plenty of other family-friendly events. The festival also coincides with St Andrew's Day, and provides the perfect spot to celebrate all things Scottish, with whisky tasting and a Haggisfest included in the programme.
www.obanwinterfestival.com

CURLING CENTRAL SCOTLAND

British interest in the sport of curling soared after the British team won a gold medal in the 2002 Winter Olympics, and courses on how to play this ancient game are now held at a number of venues in Scotland. An outside curling pond at the world's oldest curling centre in Kilsyth is often used on colder days, but it's more likely that beginner lessons and courses are held inside at the Dewar's Centre in Perth, which is also used by members of the Great British Olympic Curling teams.
www.liveactive.co.uk/sport/curling

CASTLE HOWARD NORTHEAST ENGLAND

Throughout most of December, Castle Howard, in North Yorkshire, opens from its winter break to show off in full Christmas regalia. The Great Hall and Long Gallery are decorated with garlands, roaring fires and giant Christmas trees dressed with thousands of baubles, and are filled with candlelight. Musical performances take place daily and Father Christmas welcomes visitors to his grotto, while in the stable courtyard, local and Christmas markets are held on set days.
www.castlehoward.co.uk

CHRISTMAS AT KEW LONDON

These magnificent gardens get a seasonal makeover in late November to December with dazzling illuminations covering the buildings, trails, trees and plants. The mile-long trail leads visitors past dancing lit-up fountains, a choir of holly bushes, a scented fire garden and decorated Christmas trees aplenty. There are festive refreshments available on the way, and even a miniature fairground with vintage rides, a christmas market and Santa's grotto. Guaranteed to bring Christmas cheer.
www.kew.org

STORM-WATCHING SOUTHWEST ENGLAND

A relatively new tourist phenomenon, winter storm-watching is quickly catching on, especially along Cornwall's north coast. Watching the crashing waves, which have amassed momentum over 5,000 km (3,000 miles) of open ocean, from cliffs above the wild sea, or at a safe distance on a beach, is always exciting and awe-inspiring. You can also watch experienced surfers catch the tail end of the storms on Newquay's beaches, such as Porthtowan (see also pp198–9).
www.newquayguide.co.uk

SANTA EXPRESS WEST MIDLANDS

The Severn Valley Railway runs Christmas specials for youngsters in December. The vintage engines pull their packed carriages for a distance of 26 km (16 miles) through the wintry countryside, from Kidderminster in Worcestershire to Bridgnorth in Shropshire. The route, punctuated by several sleepy country stations, follows the picturesque River Severn. Father Christmas himself tours the carriages, greeting families and handing out presents to children.
www.svr.co.uk

UP HELLY AA
HIGHLANDS AND ISLANDS

The ingredients for this festival go back 12 centuries. Crowds flock to watch the burning of a Viking galley made by the men of Lerwick, then celebrate by dancing until dawn.
www.uphellyaa.org

PANCAKE RACE
SOUTHEAST ENGLAND

Competitors in this famous 500-year-old Shrove Tuesday pancake race must be local housewives, and dressed accordingly in skirts, aprons and headgear.
www.olneytowncouncil.co.uk

See also pp192–3, 198–9, 206–7.   *See also pp176–7, 184–5.*   *See also pp190–91.*

SHETLAND
ISLANDS

ORKNEY
ISLANDS

Stornoway

Wick

Inverness

*HIGHLANDS
AND ISLANDS*

Aberdeen

Fort William

*CENTRAL
SCOTLAND*

Dundee

Glasgow

Edinburgh

*SOUTHERN
SCOTLAND*

Derry

*NORTHERN
IRELAND*

Dumfries

Newcastle
upon Tyne

Sunderland

Belfast

Bangor

Sligo

Armagh

*NORTHWEST
ENGLAND*

Middlesbrough

*NORTHEAST
ENGLAND*

*WESTERN
IRELAND*

Drogheda

Blackpool

York

Leeds

Hull

Galway

Athlone

Dublin

Blackburn

Liverpool

Manchester

Sheffield

Llandudno

*EASTERN
IRELAND*

Caernarfon

*NORTH
WALES*

Stoke-
on-Trent

EAST MIDLANDS

Nottingham

Limerick

Kilkenny

Carlow

Derby

Norwich

Peterborough

*SOUTHERN
IRELAND*

Waterford

Llandrindod
Wells

*WEST
MIDLANDS*

Birmingham

Coventry

Cambridge

Cork

*CENTRAL
WALES*

Milton Keynes

*EASTERN
ENGLAND*

Ipswich

Luton

*SOUTH
WALES*

Swindon

London

LONDON

Swansea

Cardiff

Bristol

Maidstone

*SOUTHWEST
ENGLAND*

Southampton

*SOUTHEAST
ENGLAND*

Brighton

Exeter

Bournemouth

Portsmouth

Plymouth

REGIONAL DIRECTORY

THIS DIRECTORY OFFERS FURTHER SUGGESTIONS for travel within Great Britain and Ireland in a concise and easy-to-use way. The five nations are divided into 18 regions *(see facing page)*, and for each region entries are listed for eight types of activity: Local Food, Farmers' Markets, Pubs and Bars, Places to Stay, Festivals and Events, Museums and Galleries, Things to Do With Kids, and Spas and Health Resorts. Entries are located on detailed regional maps and include essential practical information. Note that we have not always given specific opening times for pubs that are open throughout the day; these pubs, "open daily", are generally open from around 11am to 11pm, with slightly shorter hours on Sundays to comply with licensing bylaws.

Above: Tower Bridge in London

HIGHLANDS AND ISLANDS, SCOTLAND

LOCAL FOOD

The Bay Owl ⑤
Fresh crab, lobster and shellfish, all landed at nearby Dunbeath Harbour, are menu regulars, with snacks and takeaways.
Dunbeath, Morven, Highland; tel: 01593 731356; open noon–2:30pm and 5–8pm Tue–Sun. www.thebayowl.net

The River House Restaurant ⑮
Fine riverside restaurant with stunning views, serving local and seasonal cuisine.
1 Greig Street, Inverness; tel: 01463 222033; open 12:30–2:30pm Fri & Sat, 5:30pm–late Tue–Sat. www.riverhouseinverness.co.uk

Dizzy's Restaurant and Bar ㉔
Scottish and European fine dining at a classy restaurant in Aberdeen's West End.
70 Carden Place, Aberdeen; tel: 01224 625577; 10am–11pm Mon–Wed, 10am–midnight Thu & Fri, 11am–midnight Sat. www.dizzys.co.uk

Crannog at the Waterfront ㊲
Superb seafood on the menu here, including locally caught lobster and crab.
Town Pier, Fort William, Highland; tel: 01397 705589; open noon–2:30pm and 6–9pm daily. www.crannog.net/restaurant

Kinloch Lodge ㊻
The restaurant of a country hotel run by island aristocracy, serves delicious pies.
Sleat, Isle of Skye, Highland; tel: 01471 833333; open 8:30–9:30am, noon–2:30pm and 6:30–9:30pm daily. www.kinloch-lodge.co.uk

Plockton Shores Restaurant ㊸
A small, friendly restaurant that uses locally sourced produce.
30 Harbour Street, Plockton, Ross-shire; tel: 01599 544 263 www.plocktonshoresrestaurant.com

The Digby Chick ㉛
Specializes in fresh fish and shellfish.
5 Bank Street, Stornoway, Lewis, Outer Hebrides; tel: 01851 700026; open noon–2pm and 5:30–9pm Mon–Sat. www.digbychick.co.uk

Hoxa Tearooms and Gallery ④
A family run tearoom offering delicious cakes, snacks, freshly prepared lunches and incredible sea views.
St Margaret's Hope, South Ronaldsay, Orkney; tel: 01856 831366; open 10am–5pm daily. www.hoxatearooms.co.uk

Boath House ⑲
Acclaimed restaurant in a small country-house hotel, serving locally sourced seafood, game and lamb.
Auldearn, Nairn, Highland; tel: 01667 454896; open 8:30–9:45am, 12:30–1:15pm and 7pm–late daily. www.boath-house.com

The Bakehouse ⑳
Restaurant at the Findhorn Community eco-centre, serving home-grown organic produce and local meats and fish.
Findhorn, nr Forres, Morayshire; tel: 01309 691826; open 10am–4pm daily. www.findhorn.org

The Creel Inn ㉖
Clifftop gastropub with stunning sea views from Scotland's beautiful northeast coastline, offering a seafood menu that includes locally caught lobster.
Catterline, nr Stonehaven, Aberdeenshire; tel: 01569 750254; open noon–3pm and 6–11pm Mon–Thu, noon–3pm and 5pm–midnight Fri–Sat, noon–11pm Sun. www.thecreelinn.co.uk

Eleven Restaurant ㉛
The restaurant of the Caladh Inn Hotel; a choice of carvery buffet, à la carte grill and seafood menu.
Caladh Inn Hotel, James Street, Stornoway, Lewis, Outer Hebrides; tel: 01851 702740; open noon–2pm and 5–9pm Mon–Sat, noon–4pm and 5–8pm Sun. www.caladhinn.co.uk

Caberfeidh Restaurant ㊾
Seafood, steak, grills and pies make up a solid menu in this bar-restaurant, which also has a good choice of real ales.
Lochinver, Highland; tel: 01571 844321; opening hours vary seasonally, check website for details. www.thecaberfeidh.co.uk

FARMERS' MARKETS

Dingwall Farmers' Market ⑧
Meats and poultry, baked goods, fresh fruit and vegetables, as well as pottery.
High Street, Dingwall, Highland; tel: 01349 867941; second Sat of every month, 9am–2:30pm. www.dingwallcc.org.uk

Inverness Farmers' Market ⑮
Largest farmers' market in the Highlands.
Eastgate Precinct, High Street, Inverness; tel: 01309 651206; Feb–Jun and Oct–Nov: first Sat of every month; Jul–Sep and Dec: first and third Sat of every month, 8:30am–3pm. www.invernessfarmersmarket.co.uk

Lochaber Farm Shop ㊱
Local arts and crafts, cheeses, seafood, pickles, preserves, pies and cakes.
Lochaber Rural Complex, Torlundy, Highland; tel: 01397 708686; 10am–4pm Wed–Sat, 12–4pm Sun.

PUBS AND BARS

The Cawdor Tavern ⑱
Traditional country pub serving meals made from fresh local produce in the bar and à la carte restaurant.
Cawdor, nr Nairn, Morayshire, tel. 01667 404777; open daily. www.cawdortavern.co.uk

The Ship Inn ㉗
Authentic alehouse, the social hub of a thriving community of lobster-fishers.
The Square, Johnshaven, Aberdeenshire; tel: 01561 362257; open daily.

The Clachaig Inn ㉟
Cheerful, busy pub and B&B in the legendary "Glen of Weeping".
Glencoe, Highland; tel: 01855 811252; open daily. www.clachaig.com

Badachro Inn ㊹
Remote seaside pub in spectacular scenery, with a good menu, wine list and choice of ales and whiskies.
Badachro, nr Gairloch, Highland; tel: 01445 741255; open daily (from 4:30pm weekdays Jan–Mar). www.badachroinn.com

King's House Hotel Bar ㉞
Strategically perched between the wilds of Rannoch Moor and the slopes of Glencoe; popular with walkers and climbers.
Glencoe, Highland; tel: 01855 851259; open daily. www.kingshousehotel.co.uk

The Lock Inn ⑫
Waterside pub on the bank of the Caledonian Canal, not far from the southwest end of Loch Ness.
Fort Augustus, Highland; tel: 01320 366302; open daily.

Castlebay Bar ㊺
It's worth journeying to tiny Barra to spend an evening in this traditional island tavern.
Castlebay, Barra, Outer Hebrides; tel: 01871 810223; open daily. www.castlebayhotel.com

The Old Forge ㊶
Claims to be "the remotest pub in main-land Britain", with real ales and decent food.
Inverie, Knoydart, Highland; tel: 01687 462267; open daily. www.theoldforge.co.uk

Seumas Bar ㊼
At the foot of the Black Cuillin ridge, this cosy hotel pub has its own microbrewery, the Cuillin Brewery, next door.
Loch Sligachan, Isle of Skye, Highland; tel: 01478 650204; open daily. www.sligachan.co.uk

The Seaforth ㊽
Pub and brasserie offering more than 100 malt whiskies as well as solid pub grub.
Quay Street (corner of Shore Street), Ullapool, Highland; tel: 01854 612122; open daily. www.theseaforth.com

The Old Inn ㊺
Classic old-style Highland pub with traditional music in summer.
Old Bridge, Gairloch, Highland; tel: 01445 712006; open daily. www.theoldinn.net

Kylesku Hotel Bar ㊿
A cosy bar in a remote, small hotel, set in some of the best walking territory in Britain.
Kylesku, by Lairg, Highland; tel: 01971 502231; open daily. www.kyleskuhotel.co.uk

Marine Hotel ㉕
Award-winning tavern with rooms by the harbourside. It serves Scottish real ales, tasty European imports and good Highland cuisine in the restaurant upstairs.
Shorehead, nr Stonehaven, Aberdeenshire; tel: 01569 762155; open daily. www.marinehotelstonehaven.co.uk

PLACES TO STAY

Aberdeen Youth Hostel ㉔
Located within an historic building, this hostel is close to the city centre, and offers affordable private en suite and family rooms, as well as dormitory bunks.
8 Queen's Road, Aberdeen; tel: 01224 646988. www.syha.org.uk

Aberdeen Douglas Hotel ㉔
Comfortable, affordable hotel in the city centre with all the usual 3-star amenities.
43–45 Market Street, Aberdeen; tel: 01224 582255. www.aberdeendouglas.com

Rocpool Reserve ⑮
Stylish boutique hotel in the Highlands, with a bar and restaurant and 11 rooms.
14 Culduthel Road, Inverness; tel: 01463 240089. www.rocpool.com

Royal Hotel (51)
Well-priced hotel in a central location with a bar serving alcohol on Sundays, which is rare in the town of Stornaway.
Stornoway, Lewis, Outer Hebrides; tel: 01851 702109. www.royalstornoway.co.uk

Ayre Hotel ①
Highly rated family-run Orkney hotel on the Kirkwall quayside; affordable as well as comfortable.
Kirkwall, Orkney; tel: 01856 873001. www.ayrehotel.co.uk

Eilean Iarmain ㊻
Cosy and relaxing island hostelry with breathtaking surroundings and spectacular views across the Knoydart Hills.
Sleat, Isle of Skye, Highland; tel: 01471 833332. www.eilean-iarmain.co.uk

Plockton Hotel ㊸
Pretty hotel and excellent village pub, with good-value rooms in the cottage annexe.
41 Harbour Street, Plockton, Highland; tel: 01599 544274. www.plocktonhotel.co.uk

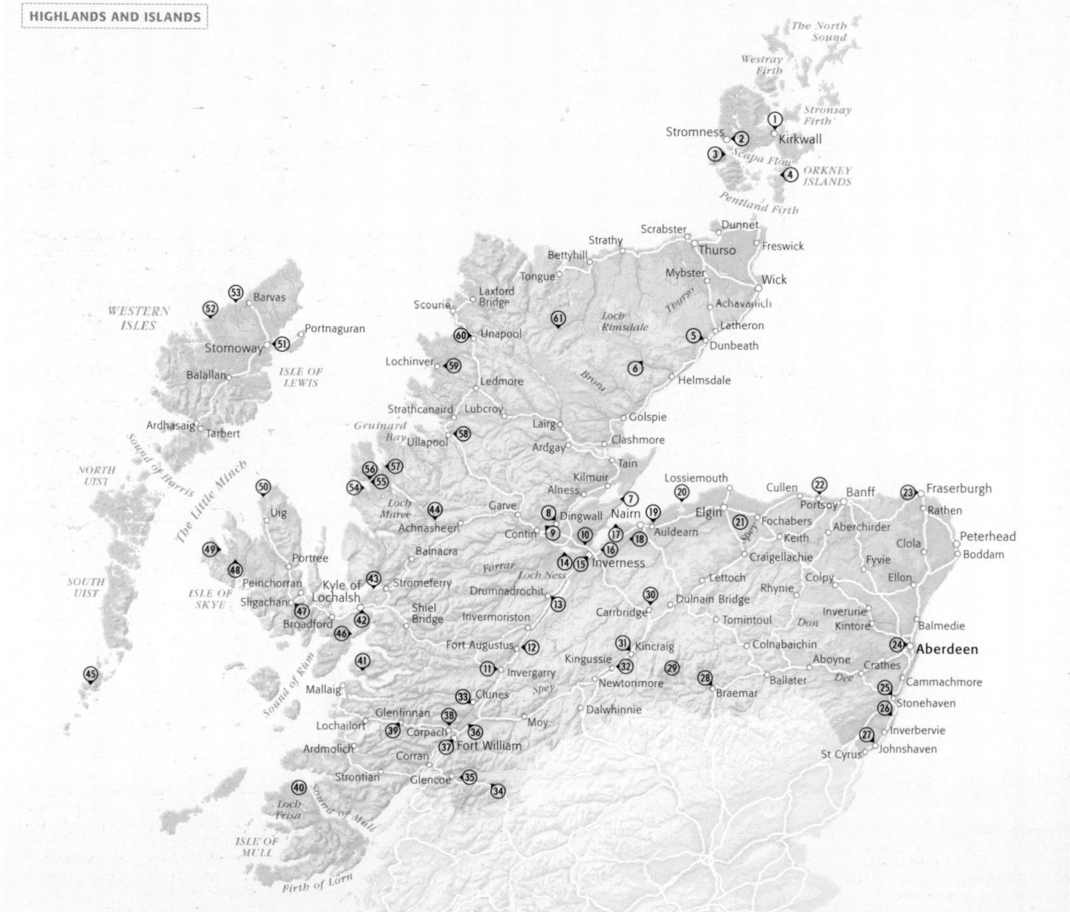

Woodwick House ③
It's worth staying in this affordable country-house hotel for the views out to sea, but the food is tasty too.
Evie, Orkney; tel: 01856 751330. www.woodwickhouse.co.uk

Saddle Mountain Hostel ⑪
A small, friendly, privately-owned hostel situated in the stunning Great Glen.
Mandally Road, Invergarry, Highland; tel: 01809 501412. www.saddlemountainhostel.co.uk

Bunchrew House ⑭
Mansion house overlooking the waters of the Beauly Firth. Popular for weddings.
Bunchrew, Inverness; tel: 01463 234917. www.bunchrew-inverness.co.uk

Culloden House ⑯
Ancestral home of the lairds of Culloden; now an opulent country-house hotel with a heated pool, huge Georgian rooms and luxury suites.
Culloden, Inverness; tel: 01463 790461. www.cullodenhouse.co.uk

The Station Hotel ㉒
Comfortable, small, family-run hotel in a tranquil fishing village on the south shore of the Moray Firth.
Portsoy, Highland; tel: 01261 842237. www.stationhotelportsoy.co.uk

Linnhe Lochside Holidays ㊳
Luxury self-catering chalets, set beside Loch Eil and surrounded by woodland.
Corpach, nr Fort William, Highland; tel: 01397 772376. www.linnhe-lochside-holidays.co.uk

The Three Chimneys ㊾
Delightful, reasonably priced hotel in a handy location on Skye.
Colbost, Isle of Skye, Highland; tel: 01470 511258. www.threechimneys.co.uk

Beaton's Croft House ㊿
A unique place to stay: from the outside, a traditional thatched cottage, but within you will find all modern amenities.
Bornesketaig, nr Uig, Isle of Skye, Highland; tel: 01314 580305. www.ntsholidays.com

The Torridon & Torridon Inn ㊹
Two hotels in one amid some spectacular Highland scenery. The Inn is cheaper, the nearby Torridon more luxurious.
Kinlochewe, Torridon, Highland; tel: 01445 700300. www.lochtorridonhotel.com

Pool House Hotel ㊾
Country-house hotel with seven gorgeous suites, ornamental gardens, a super restaurant and a lovely location.
Poolewe, Highland; tel: 01445 781272. www.pool-house.co.uk

Covesea Lighthouse ⑳
A single-storey house in the Covesea Skerries lighthouse complex, situated in the courtyard below the lighthouse tower.
Nr Lossiemouth, Moray, Highland; tel: 01314 580305. www.ntsholidays.com

Altnaharra Hotel ㉛
One of the classic Scottish fishing hotels, with some of the most famous trout waters in the Highlands nearby.
Altnaharra, Highland; tel: 01549 411222. www.altnaharra.com

FESTIVALS AND EVENTS

St Magnus Festival ①
Orkney's 12th-century cathedral is the hub of this five-day midsummer festival of classical music and the arts, which often features symphony orchestras.
Kirkwall, Orkney; tel: 01856 871445; mid–late Jun. www.stmagnusfestival.com

Shetland Folk Festival ㊶
A 4-day folk music event showcasing local, British and international acts.
Various venues across the isles; tel: 01595 694757; End of Apr–early May. www.shetlandfolkfestival.com

Tulloch Inverness Highland Games ⑮
Highland dancers, pipe bands, clan gatherings and strong-man events, such as tossing the caber, attract crowds to this popular day of games in the Highlands.
Bught Park, Inverness; tel: 01463 785006; Jul. www.invernesshighlandgames.com

Aberdeen Winter Festival ㉔
A stunning fireworks display kicks off eight weeks of events including a reindeer parade and St Andrew's day celebrations. The festival culminates in Aberdeen's famous Hogmanay Street Party on New Year's Eve.
Various venues, Aberdeen; early Nov–Dec 31. www.aberdeenchristmas.co.uk

Aberdeen Jazz Festival ㉔
A 5-day festival which attracts top performers from all over the world.
Various venues, Aberdeen; tel: 0045 111 0302; Mar. www.aberdeenjazzfestival.com

DanceLive ㉔
Scotland's only festival presenting contemporary dance, this two-week spectacular continues to dazzle ten years after it first started.
Various venues, Aberdeen; tel: 01224 611486; mid Oct. www.dancelivefestival.co.uk

Stonehaven Fire Festival ㉕
Breathtaking event where marchers parade through the streets, swinging giant balls of blazing tar before hurling them into the harbour on the stroke of midnight.
Stonehaven, Aberdeenshire; tel: 01569 764647; New Year's Eve (31 Dec). www.stonehavenfireballs.co.uk

Johnshaven Fish Festival ㉗
A pipe-band parade, live music, street stalls, fresh seafood and a dramatic cross-harbour raft race are highlights of this two-day village festival.
Johnshaven, Aberdeenshire; tel: 01561 361969; first or second weekend in Aug. www.johnshaven.com

Above: Up Helly Aa festival in Lerwick, Shetland

Royal Braemar Gathering ㉘
The most renowned Highland gathering attracts many visitors, including members of the British Royal family (*see pp126–7*).
Braemar Royal Highland Society, Braemar, Aberdeenshire; tel: 01339 741098; first Sat in Sep. www.braemargathering.org

Up Helly Aa ㊷
Torch-lit street procession by costumed "Vikings" culminates in a huge boat-burning bonfire and a night of drinking and dancing (*see pp180–81*).
Lerwick, Shetland; tel: 01595 693434; last Tue in Jan. www.uphellyaa.org

MUSEUMS AND GALLERIES

Inverness Museum and Art Gallery ⑮
A fine array of clan tartans, silver, jewellery, claymores, dirks and pistols, and traditional Highland dress.
Castle Wynd, Inverness; tel: 01463 237114; open 9am–5pm Mon–Sat. www.highlifehighland.com

Aberdeen Maritime Museum ㉔
Museum telling the story of Aberdeen's seaport, from the early days of the whaling industry to its decline in the 1980s.
Shiprow, Aberdeen; tel: 01224 337700; open 10am–5pm Tue–Sat, noon–3pm Sun. www.aberdeenships.com

Aberdeen Art Gallery ㉔
Varied collection of arts and crafts that includes an important portrait exhibition and extensive archaeological displays.
Schoolhill, Aberdeen; tel: 01224 523700; open 10am–5pm Mon–Sat, 2–5pm Sun. www.aagm.co.uk

Museum of Scottish Lighthouses ㉓
Many steps lead to the balcony of this historic lighthouse on the Moray Firth; it houses an extensive collection of glass lenses and lighting technology.
Kinnaird Head, Fraserburgh, Aberdeenshire; tel: 01546 511022; open 9am–5pm daily. www.lighthousemuseum.org.uk

Highland Folk Museum ㉜
The Kingussie section of this open-air museum comprises farming equipment, traditional costumes, musical instruments and more, while the Newtonmore annex contains a whole working farm township.
Newtonmore and Kingussie, Highland; tel: 01540 673551; open Apr–Aug: 10:30am–5:30pm daily; Sep: 11am–4:30pm daily; Oct: 11am–4:30pm Mon–Fri. www.highlandfolk.com

West Highland Museum ㊲
The best museum for anyone interested in the history of the Highland clans and the Jacobite cause.
Cameron Square, Fort William, Highland; tel: 01397 702169; open 10am–4pm Mon–Sat (to 5pm Apr–Oct); closed Jan & Feb. www.westhighlandmuseum.org.uk

Ullapool Museum and Visitor Centre ㊳
Museum highlighting the glory years of the local herring fishing industry and Ullapool's part in the great Highland emigrations of the 19th century.
West Argyle Street, Ullapool, Highland; tel: 01854 612987; open Apr–Oct: 10am–5pm Mon–Sat. www.ullapoolmuseum.co.uk

Above: Pair of rare Amur tigers at the Highland Wildlife Park

Cromarty Courthouse Museum ⑦
Life-like animatronic figures recreate the history of this village community.
Church Street, Cromarty, Highland; tel: 01381 600148; open Apr–Sep: 10am–5pm daily.
www.cromarty-courthouse.org.uk

The Highlanders' Museum ⑰
Fortress built in 1769 to repel the French and the Highland clans. It now houses a collection of military paraphernalia.
Fort George, nr Inverness, Highland; tel: 01313 108701; open Apr–Sep: 9:30am–5:30pm daily; Oct–Mar: 10am–4pm daily.
www.thehighlandersmuseum.com

Clan Cameron Museum ㉝
Museum painting a picture of Clan Cameron's support for the Jacobites and the history of the Cameron Highlanders.
Achnacarry, Spean Bridge, nr Fort William, Highland; tel: 01397 712480; open 1:30–5pm Apr–Sep (Jul and Aug:11am–4:30pm) daily.
www.clancameronmuseum.co.uk

Glenfinnan Station Museum ㊴
The story of the famous West Highland Line, Britain's most spectacular railway.
Station Cottage, Glenfinnan, Highland; tel: 01397 722295; open May–Oct: 9am–5pm daily.
www.glenfinnanstationmuseum.co.uk

Skye Museum of Island Life ㊽
Cottage-based museum that offers an entertaining recreation of the lives of 19th-century crofter families.
Kilmuir, Isle of Skye, Highland; tel: 01470 522206; open Easter–Oct: 9:30am–5pm Mon–Sat. www.skyemuseum.co.uk

The Pier Art Centre ②
Work by contemporary artists, including Barbara Hepworth and Naum Gaba.
Stromness, Orkney; tel: 01856 850209; open 10:30am–5pm Tue–Sat.
www.pierartscentre.com

Gairloch Heritage Museum ㊶
Re-creation of village life in Gairloch, with the schoolhouse, village shop and dairy.
Achtercairn, Gairloch, Highland; tel: 01445 712787; open Apr–Oct: 10am–5pm Mon–Fri; 11am–3pm Sat.
www.gairlochheritagemuseum.org

The Black House Village & Museum ㊿
Remarkable recreated hamlet, comprising the thatched cottages the islanders lived in well into the 20th century.
Gearrannan, Lewis, Outer Hebrides; tel: 01851 643416; open Apr–Sep: 9:30am–5:30pm Mon–Sat.

THINGS TO DO WITH KIDS

Loch Ness Centre and Exhibition ⑬
Fun-filled activity centre that reveals the stories behind the Loch Ness "monster".
Drumnadrochit, Loch Ness, Highland; tel: 01456 450573; open Nov–Mar: 10am–3:30pm; Easter–Jun: 9:30am–5pm; Jul & Aug: 9am–6pm; Sep & Oct: 9:30am–5pm. www.lochness.com

Highland Wildlife Park ㉛
Wolves, bison, lynx and other creatures that once roamed the Highlands can be seen in this excellent open-air zoo.
Kincraig, nr Kingussie, Highland; tel: 01540 651270; open Apr–Jun and Sep–Oct: 10am–5pm daily; Jul–Aug: 10am–6pm daily; Nov–Mar: 10am–4pm daily. www.highlandwildlifepark.org

Highland Museum of Childhood ⑨
Amusing collection of toys, games and dolls from bygone times in a quaint old railway station building.
The Old Station, Strathpeffer, Highland; tel: 01997 421031; open Apr–Oct: 10am–5pm Mon–Sat, 12–4pm Sun.
www.highlandmuseumofchildhood.org.uk

North Kessock Dolphin and Seal Centre ⑩
Seals and dolphins can sometimes be seen from the shore here, and there are daily dolphin-spotting cruises too.
North Kessock, nr Inverness, Highland; tel: 01463 731866; open Jun–Sep: 9:30am–4:30pm daily. www.wdcs.org.uk

Baile-an-Or ⑥
Pan for flecks of pure gold in the pristine Kildonan Burn, scene of a 19th century gold rush. Access is free.
Suisgill Estate, Helmsdale, Highland; tel: 01431 821372; open 10am–5:30pm Mon–Sat. www.helmsdale.org

Orkney Marine Life Aquarium ④
Enjoy a close-up encounter with the fascinating marine life found in the waters around Orkney and the Scottish coast.
Pool Farmhouse, Grimness, South Ronaldsay, Orkney; tel: 01856 831700; open Apr–Oct: 10am–6pm daily.
www.orkneymarinelife.co.uk

Seaprobe Atlantis ㊷
Trips in semi-submersible boats reveal the marine life teeming in the inshore waters of Scotland's west coast.
Kyle of Lochalsh, Highland; tel: 0800 980 4846; open Easter–Oct: at least five departures daily.
www.seaprobeatlantis.com

Landmark Forest Adventure Park ㉚
This forest adventure park has lots of rides and activities, such as rock climbing and sky diving, offering hours of fun for adults and children of all ages.
Carrbridge, Highland; tel: 0800 731 3446; open mid-Jul–mid-Aug: 10am–7pm daily; Sep–mid-Jul: 10am–5pm daily.
www.landmarkpark.co.uk

Treasures of the Earth ㊲
Claims to be Europe's finest private collection of crystals, gemstones and fossils, housed in caves and caverns.
Corpach, Fort William, Highland; tel: 01397 772283; open Apr–Oct: 10am–5pm, Jul & Aug: 9:30am–6pm, Nov: 10am–4pm.
www.treasuresoftheearth.co.uk

The Blackhouse at Arnol ㊼
This primitive home (lived in until the 1960s) will fascinate children and provide a healthy reminder that the "simple life" was far from idyllic.
Arnol, nr Stornoway, Lewis, Outer Hebrides; tel: 01851 710395; open Apr–Sep: 9:30am–5:30pm Mon–Sat; Oct–Mar: 10am–4pm Mon–Sat.
www.historic-scotland.gov.uk

SPAS AND HEALTH RESORTS

Best Western Inverness Palace Hotel and Spa ⑮
This comfortable hotel has an excellent leisure club with pool and offers a range of health and beauty treatments, as well as free car parking and WiFi internet access.
8 Ness Walk, Inverness; tel: 01463 223243. www.bw-invernesspalace.co.uk

Fantasia Health and Beauty Clinic ⑯
A hotel-based spa with highly qualified therapists, offering luxury packages including specialized laser treatments and aromatherapy massages.
Kingsmills Hotel Inverness, Culcabock Road, Inverness; tel: 01463 243244.
www.fantasiabeauty.com

Golf View Hotel and Spa ⑲
A tranquil spa located in a country-house hotel. The pool area overlooks the stunning Moray Firth.
63 Seabank Road, Nairn, Highland; tel: 01667 452301.
www.crerarhotels.com/golf-view-hotel-spa

The Marcliffe Hotel & Spa ㉔
Five-star luxury hotel and spa with 42 rooms and two restaurants, widely regarded as one of the best places to stay in Aberdeen.
North Deeside Road, Pitfodels, Aberdeen; tel: 01224 861000. www.marcliffe.com

OTHER SIGHTS IN THE BOOK

CENTRAL SCOTLAND

LOCAL FOOD

Jute Café Bar ①
Light lunches and a three-course evening menu are offered at this café. Dishes include steak and chocolate torte.
152 Nethergate, Dundee; tel: 01382 909 246; open 10am–midnight Sun–Thu and 10am–1am Fri–Sat. www.jutecafebar.co.uk

Dean's@Let's Eat ②
Vibrant Scottish menu based on local lamb, beef, salmon, scallops and more.
77–79 Kinnoull Street, Perth; tel: 01738 643377; open noon–3pm and 6–9pm Tue–Sat (to 9:30pm Sat), noon–5pm Sun. www.letseatperth.co.uk

Ostler's Close ⑧
The stunning dishes here range from fresh-picked wild chanterelles to game and seafood from the Fife fishing harbours.
25 Bonnygate, Cupar, Fife; tel: 01334 655574; open 6:30–11pm Tue–Sat. www.ostlersclose.co.uk

The Peat Inn ⑨
This legendary restaurant, not far from St Andrews, is simply superb.
Nr St Andrews, Fife; tel: 01334 840206; open 12:30–2pm and 6:30–9pm Tue–Sat. www.thepeatinn.co.uk

Anstruther Fish Bar ⑬
Rated by many as the best fish-and-chip shop in Scotland, this restaurant has stunning views over the Firth of Forth.
42–44 Shore Street, Anstruther, Fife; tel: 01333 310518; open 11:30am–9:30pm daily. www.anstrutherfishbar.co.uk

Sangster's ⑭
Michelin-starred restaurant where the menu is imaginative and the emphasis is on intense flavours.
51 High Street, Elie, Fife; tel: 01333 331001; open 12:30–1:30pm Sun, 7–8.30pm Tue–Sat. www.sangsters.co.uk

An Lochan Tormaukin ㉑
Wild (not farmed) venison, hand-dived scallops and home-made oatcakes to accompany some local cheeses are just some of the delights here.
Tormaukin Hotel, Glendevon, Perthshire; tel: 01259 781252; open noon–2pm and 6–9pm daily. www.tormaukinhotel.co.uk

Loch Fyne Oysters ㉟
The original, legendary seafood restaurant (which has spawned a chain of franchises), serving superb local oysters, kippers, smoked salmon and other fine seafood.
Clachan, Cairndow, Argyll and Bute; tel: 01499 600236; open 9am–6pm Mon–Sat, 10am–5pm Sun. www.lochfyne.com

Ee-Usk ㊲
Line-caught Atlantic halibut is among the specialities at this stylish seaside bistro.
North Pier, Oban, Argyll and Bute; tel: 01631 565666; open winter: noon–2:30pm and 5:45–9pm daily; summer: noon–3pm and 5:45–9:30pm daily. www.eeusk.com

Yann's at Glenearn House ④
Superb offerings, such as roast rump of lamb with four-bean casserole, blend French expertise with the best produce from Perthshire's hills and fields.
Perth Road, Crieff, Perth and Kinross; tel: 01764 650111; open 6–9pm Wed–Sat, noon–2pm and 6–9pm Sun. www.yannsatglenearnhouse.com

The Inn at Lathones ⑪
Game (such as hare and partridge), seafood (scallops, crab and lobster) and other rich delights feature on the menu at this 17th-century coaching inn, which also offers comfortable bedrooms and live music.
Largoward, nr St Andrews, Fife; tel: 01334 840494; open daily for breakfast, lunch and dinner. www.innatlathone.co.uk

Loch Leven's Larder ⑱
Home-grown vegetables and locally sourced cheeses, bacon and other produce appear on the menu in the café-restaurant of this working farm.
Channel Farm, Milnathort, Perth and Kinross; tel: 01592 841000; open 9:30am–5pm daily. www.lochlevenslarder.com

The Lion and Unicorn ㉕
Unpretentious restaurant serving excellent steaks (accompanied by real ale from the bar), conveniently located for those exploring the landscapes of the Trossachs.
Main St, Thornhill, Stirling; tel: 01786 850204; open noon–11pm Sun–Thu, noon–1am Fri–Sat. www.lion-unicorn.co.uk

Room With a View ⑯
The weekly menu here is dominated by fresh seafood from local harbours and produce sourced from nearby Fife farms. The river view is indeed spectacular.
Forth View Hotel, Aberdour, Fife; tel: 01383 860402; open noon–2pm and 6–9:30pm Wed–Sat, noon–2pm Sun. www.roomwithaviewrestaurant.co.uk

The Wee Restaurant ⑰
This tiny restaurant (it seats just 40) takes local culinary traditions and gives them a modern twist, and at a very affordable price.
17 Main Street, North Queensferry, Fife; tel: 01383 616263; open noon–2pm and 6:30–9pm Tue–Sun. www.theweerestaurant.co.uk

The Real Food Café ㉘
Café on a scenic road serving perfect crispy fish and chips, home-baked cakes, pies and hearty breakfasts; ideal for those on a day's walk.
Tyndrum, Perth and Kinross; tel: 01838 400235; open 7:30am–7:30pm Mon–Thu, 7:30am–8pm Fri–Sun. www.therealfoodcafe.com

FARMERS' MARKETS

Perth Farmers' Market ⑦
Established in 1999, the oldest farmers' market in Scotland is held in Perth's traditional market street.
King Edward Street, Perth; tel: 01738 582159; first Sat of every month (except Jan), 9am–2pm. www.perthfarmersmarket.co.uk

Cupar Farmers' Market ⑧
You'll meet friendly local producers at this bustling market in the heart of Fife's farming region.
Crossgate, Cupar, Fife; tel: 07773 280105; third Sat of every month, 9am–1pm. www.fifefarmersmarket.co.uk

Kirkcaldy Farmers' Market ⑮
Fine local cheeses and meats on sale in the reinvented industrial town of Kirkcaldy.
Town Square, Kirkcaldy, Fife; tel: 07773 280105; last Sat of every month (except Dec), 9am–1pm. www.fifefarmersmarket.co.uk

Stirling Farmers' Market ㉒
Large and popular farmers' market in the town's pedestrian area, boasting a superb variety of Scottish producers.
Port Street, Stirling; second Sat of every month (except Jan), 10am–4pm. www.stirlingfarmersmarket.co.uk

PUBS AND BARS

Taybridge Bar ①
A little-known gem of a bar, with a 1920s interior by the architect William Gauldie.
129 Perth Road, Dundee; tel: 01382 643973; open 11am–midnight daily.

The Grange Inn ⑩
Cosy pub not far from St Andrews, serving hearty meals. Booking is advised, particularly for lunch or dinner at weekends.
Nr St Andrews, Fife; tel: 01334 472670; open noon–2pm and 6–9pm Tue–Sat, noon–2pm Sun.

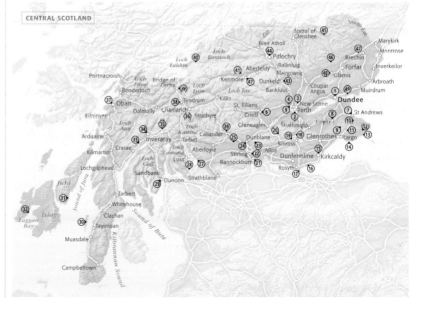

Above: Music fans at the T in the Park festival in Scotland

The Pitcairngreen Inn ④
Lively countryside pub, just outside Perth, offering real ales, mid-week acoustic music sessions and good pub food.
Almondbank, Perth; tel: 01738 583022; open daily. www.pitcairngreeninn.co.uk

The Bank Anstruther ⑬
Set in a charming fishing village, this pub has wonderful views over the harbour, and serves a wide variety of good ales and hearty pub meals.
23–25 High Street, Anstruther, Fife; tel: 01333 310189; open daily. www.thebank-anstruther.co.uk

The Ship Inn ⑭
This pub, which has its own cricket team, boasts a great location overlooking the sea in one of Scotland's more picturesque east-coast villages.
Elie, Fife; tel: 01333 330246; open daily. www.shipinn.scot

The Portcullis ㉒
A few steps from Stirling Castle, the Portcullis serves pies, steaks and other traditionally filling dishes, as well as a huge choice of real ales.
Castle Wynd, Stirling; tel: 01786 472290; open daily. www.theportcullishotel.com

The Lade Inn ㉖
In the heart of "Rob Roy Country", the Lade Inn brews its own humorously named beers ("Ladeback", for example), serves great food and has its own shop stocked with Scottish brews and malts.
Kilmahog, nr Callander, Stirling; tel: 01877 330152; open daily. www.theladeinn.com

Skipinnish Ceilidh House ㊲
Fiddle music, Highland dancing, live bands and a good range of ales and whiskies are offered at the region's top folk-music venue.
34–38 George Street, Oban, Argyll and Bute; tel: 01631 569599; open 6pm–1am Mon–Sat (to 3am Sat). www.skipinnishceilidhhouse.com

The Moulin Inn ㊹
A couple of miles from the town centre, this pub brews its own ales and has occasional live music on Sundays.
Pitlochry, Perth and Kinross; tel: 01796 472196; open daily. www.moulinhotel.co.uk

The Oak Tree Inn ㉗
This pub, in a quaint lochside village, is the ideal place for a heartening pint or dram before commencing an assault on the West Highland Way or a hike up nearby Conic Hill.
Balmaha, Loch Lomond, Stirling; tel: 01360 870357; open daily. www.oaktreeinn.co.uk

Bridge of Orchy Hotel ㊴
This welcoming small hotel bar offers outstanding views and good food.
Bridge of Orchy, nr Tyndrum, Stirling; tel: 01838 400208; open daily. www.bridgeoforchy.co.uk

The Taybank ㊸
There are few better places for a pint on a sunny summer day in Perthshire than the tables outside this aptly named pub, well known for live music.
Tay Terrace, Dunkeld, Perth and Kinross; tel: 01350 727340; open daily. www.thetaybank.co.uk

Fisherman's Tavern ㊾
Superb traditional pub with a good selection of ales on tap, and cosy bedrooms upstairs too.
10–16 Fort Street, Broughty Ferry, Dundee; tel: 01382 775941; open daily. www.fishermanstavern-broughtyferry.co.uk

PLACES TO STAY

Salutation Hotel ②
Opened in 1699, this claims to be the oldest hotel in Scotland; famously, Bonnie Prince Charlie slept here.
34 South Street, Perth; tel: 01738 630066. www.strathmorehotels.com

St Andrews Youth Hostel ⑦
Cheap single or double en suite rooms within modern self-catering apartments.
David Russell Apartments, Buchanan Gardens, St Andrews, Fife; tel: 01334 467100. http://bnb.st-andrews.ac.uk/resbus/bnb

Cook's of Stirling ㉒
Stylish restaurant with rooms within walking distance of Stirling town centre.
78 Upper Craigs, Stirling; tel: 01786 430890. www.cooksofstirling.co.uk

Stirling Youth Hostel ㉒
Hotel-style en suite rooms as well as dorm bunks are available in this town-centre hostel within a converted historic church.
St John Street, Stirling; tel: 01786 473442. www.syha.org.uk

Huntingtower Hotel ⑤
Very stylish rooms and good food, well located for an overnight stop en route between the Highlands and Lowlands.
Crieff Road, Perth and Kinross; tel: 01738 583771. www.huntingtowerhotel.co.uk

The Sheriffmuir Inn ㉓
Two comfortable bedrooms attached to an excellent restaurant make this strategically located establishment an excellent overnight stop on a tour of Scotland.
Sheriffmuir, nr Dunblane, Stirling; tel: 01786 823285. www.sheriffmuirinn.co.uk

Cromlix House ㉔
Serene country-house hotel set in a vast, wooded estate with its own fishing loch. Superb food and great atmosphere.
Cromlix Estate, nr Dunblane, Stirling; tel: 01786 822125. www.cromlix.com

The Gigha Hotel ㉚
Choose from cosy rooms or self-catering cottages. The restaurant and bar serve excellent locally caught seafood.
Isle of Gigha, Argyll and Bute; tel: 01583 505254. www.gigha.org.uk

Port Charlotte Hotel ㉜
Unquestionably the finest place to stay and eat on the marvellous island of Islay. Great range of whiskies at the bar and fresh local produce in the restaurant.
Port Charlotte, Isle of Islay, Argyll and Bute; tel: 01496 850360. www.portcharlottehotel.co.uk

Moor of Rannoch Hotel ㊵
Inexpensive hotel with a fine restaurant, the perfect jumping-off point for the Rannoch Moor section of the West Highland Way (see pp46–7).
Rannoch Station, Perth and Kinross; tel: 01882 633238. www.moorofrannoch.co.uk

Fortingall Hotel ㊶
Attractive 17th-century inn with a highly regarded restaurant, not far from picturesque Loch Tay.
Fortingall, Aberfeldy, Perth and Kinross; tel: 01887 830367. www.fortingall.com

Kenmore Hotel ㊷
Very pleasant country-house hotel in a picturesque village, overlooking the River Tay and Loch Tay.
The Square, Kenmore, Perth and Kinross; tel: 01877 830205. www.kenmorehotel.com

Glen Clova Hotel ㊺
Comfortable hotel with bunkhouse and en suite rooms, a cosy bar and good food, at the head of a picturesque glen.
Clova, Glen Clova, Angus; tel: 01575 550350. www.clova.com

Jura Hotel ㉛
This small, no-frills affordable hotel is by far the best base for exploring the island's landscapes and sampling its malt whisky. The views are spectacular.
Craighouse, Isle of Jura, Argyll and Bute; tel: 01496 820243. www.jurahotel.co.uk

FESTIVALS AND EVENTS

Scottish Game Fair ③
This annual three-day event celebrates all that's best in the world of game, tweed, tackle, shotguns and gun dogs.
Scone Palace, Scone, Perth and Kinross; tel: 01738 554826; first weekend of Jul. www.scottishfair.com

T in the Park ⑲
Scotland's answer to Glastonbury is a line-up of the best contemporary bands over three days, without the typical traditions of other Scottish events.
Strathallan Castle, Perth and Kinross; second weekend of Jul. www.tinthepark.com

Cowal Highland Gathering ㉙
One of the largest Highland games in the world, this three-day event features pipers, caber-tossers, dancing and local food.
Dunoon, Argyll and Bute; tel: 01369 703206; last weekend of Aug. www.cowalgathering.com

MUSEUMS AND GALLERIES

Dundee Contemporary Arts ①
Highly regarded modern arts centre with an ever-changing calendar of cutting-edge exhibitions, a cinema, a printmakers' workshop and an excellent café-restaurant.
152 Nethergate, Dundee; tel: 01382 909900; open (galleries): 11am–6pm daily (until 8pm Thu). www.dca.org.uk

The McManus ①
Enter this Victorian Gothic building and discover the fascinating story of Dundee's industrial heritage, with exhibitions of archaeology and Victorian art.
Albert Square, Meadowside Dundee; tel: 01382 307200; open 10am–5 Mon–Sat, 12:30–4:30pm Sun. www.mcmanus.co.uk

Fergusson Gallery ②
Wonderful array of works by one Scotland's most important 19th– century artists, J D Fergusson.
Marshall Place, Perth; tel: 01738 open 10am–5pm Tue–Sat (May, also noon–4:30pm Sun). www.scottishmuseums.crg.uk

The Black Watch Museum ②
Poignant museum following the of one of Scotland's oldest regim from its foundation up to its pres incarnation as 2nd Battalion, Regiment of Scotland.
Balhousie Castle, Hay Street, tel: 01738 638152; open 9:30am–4:30pm daily; 10am–4pm daily. www.theblackwatch.co.uk

Fenton Barns ⑥
Farm shop café specializing in fresh
ingredients and local produce. Enjoy light
meals, tarts and scones.
Nr Drem, East Lothian; tel: 01620 850294;
open 10am–4:30pm daily.
www.fentonbarnsfarmshop.com

The Garvald Inn ⑨
Cosy pub-restaurant that serves up an
array of rich and tasty dishes.
Main Street, Garvald, nr Haddington, East
Lothian; tel: 01620 830311; open
noon–11pm Tue–Thu, noon–midnight
Fri–Sat, 12:30–6:30pm Sun.

The Black Bull ⑪
Former coaching inn serving delicious beef
sourced from nearby St Boswells Market.
Market Place, Lauder, Borders; tel: 01578
722208; open daily
www.blackbull-lauder.com

The Oyster Bar ㉒
Probably the best fish and seafood on
the southwest coast, freshly caught and
brilliantly prepared.
Harbour Road, Troon, South Ayrshire;
tel: 01292 319339; open noon–2:30pm
and 6:30–9:30pm Tue–Sat, noon–
2:30pm Sun.

Creelers Seafood Restaurant ㉓
Serving delicious locally sourced seafood
treated in its artisan smokehouse.
Home Farm, Brodick, Arran, North
Ayrshire; tel: 01770 302810; open
12:30–2:30pm and 6–9pm Tue–Sat.
www.creelers.co.uk

Braidwoods ㉔
Michelin-starred restaurant that prepares
the finest local produce, such as Wester
Ross scallops, with cosmopolitan flair.
Saltcoats Road, Dalry, North Ayrshire;
tel: 01294 833544; open 7–9pm Tue;
noon–1:30pm and 7–9pm Wed–Sat.
www.braidwoods.co.uk

Glenskirlie House ㉗
Seasonal Scottish ingredients dominate
a modern-British menu in this restaurant
at a boutique hotel.
Nr Banknock, Stirling; tel: 01324 840201;
open noon–2pm daily, 6–9pm Mon–Fri,
6–9.30pm Sat, 5–8pm Sun).
www.glenskirliehouse.com

FARMERS' MARKETS

Edinburgh Farmers' Market ①
Seafood, organic bread, honey, cheeses,
meats and fruit wines are on sale here,
with Edinburgh Castle as the backdrop.
Castle Terrace, Edinburgh; tel: 01312
208580, every Sat, 9am–2pm.
www.edinburghfarmersmarket.com

Kelso Farmers' Market ⑬
Around 18 local producers, with the
emphasis on sheep-related products, from
organic lamb to sheepskin, wool and tweed.
Kelso, Borders; tel: 01573 410797; last Sat
of every month, 9:30am–1:30pm.
www.scottishfarmersmarkets.co.uk

Haddington Farmers' Market ④
Fine local cheeses, organic vegetables and
North Sea line-caught fish.
Corn Exchange, Court Street, Haddington,
East Lothian; tel: 01368 863593; last Sat
of every month, 9am–1pm.
www.haddingtonfarmersmarket.co.uk

Falkirk Farmers' Market ㉘
Vibrant market with much to offer,
including cakes, cuts of meat, smoked
foods and vegetables.
High Street, Falkirk; tel: 01560 484861;
first Fri of every month, 11am–4pm.
www.scottishfarmersmarkets.co.uk

PUBS

The Magnum ①
Spacious, gracious and verging on grand,
the Magnum is great for a pint in the
summer sun or a dram on a winter's night.
1 Albany Street, Edinburgh; tel: 01315
574366; open daily.

The Doric Tavern ①
Formerly a legendary rugby supporters'
pub, the Doric pulls a mean pint as well
as serving fine solid Scots cooking.
15–16 Market Street, Edinburgh; tel: 01312
251084; open daily. www.the-doric.com

Café Royal ①
Victorian pub, adorned with remarkable
tiled portraits of great inventors, with
excellent ales and a fine atmosphere.
17 West Register Street, Edinburgh;
tel: 01315 561884; open daily.
www.caferoyaledinburgh.co.uk

Oxford Bar ①
Fine traditional Edinburgh pub, favoured by
the fictional Scottish Detective Inspector
Rebus and his creator, author Ian Rankin.
8 Young Street, Edinburgh; tel: 01315
39/119; open daily.
www.oxfordbar.co.uk

The Sheep Heid ①
Dating back to 1360, this is a great place
for a pint after walking up Arthur's Seat. It's
also home to the world's oldest functional
skittle alley.
43–45 The Causeway, Duddingston
Village, Edinburgh; tel: 01316 617974;
open 11am–11pm Mon–Thu; 11am–
midnight Fri–Sat, 12:30–11pm Sun.
www.sheepheid.co.uk

Joseph Pearce's ①
Bright, airy and child-friendly bar with
comfy sofas, WiFi access, a good choice
of wines and beers.
23 Elm Row, Leith Walk, Edinburgh;
tel: 01315 564140; open 11am–midnight
Sun–Thu, 11am–1am Fri–Sat.
www.bodabar.com

Kay's ①
Tucked away on a quiet corner on the
edge of the New Town, Kay's is a gem
of a pub with a great selection of ales.
39 Jamaica Street, Edinburgh; tel: 01312
251858; open 11am–midnight Mon–Thu
(until 1am Fri & Sat), 12:30–11pm Sun.

Above: The Balmoral hotel in Edinburgh

Poosie Nansie's ㉑
Immortalized in Robert Burns's *Tam O
Shanter*, this Ayrshire pub is a classic. Little
has changed here since Burns's day.
21 Loudoun Street, Mauchline, East
Ayrshire; open daily.

The Horse Shoe ㉖
This grand Victorian pub in the city centre
serves a variety of Scottish whiskies and
has a horse theme running throughout.
17–21 Drury Street, Glasgow; tel: 01412
486368; open daily.
www.horseshoebar.co.uk

The Scotia Bar ㉖
A favourite with local writers, poets and
musicians, this pub hosts live music
most evenings.
112 Stockwell Street, Glasgow; tel: 01415
528681; open 11am–midnight
Mon–Sat, 12:30pm–midnight Sun.
www.scotiabar.net

Babbity Bowsters ㉖
Great pub in Glasgow's trendy Merchant City,
with a French-Scottish restaurant upstairs,
plus real ales, malt whiskies and live music.
There are a few outside tables.
16–18 Blackfriars Street, Glasgow;
tel: 01415 525055; open daily.
www.babbitybowster.com

The Four Marys ㉙
Renowned real-ale pub close to the
evocative ruin of Linlithgow Palace.
65–67 High Street, Linlithgow, West
Lothian; tel: 01506 842171; open daily.
www.fourmarys-linlithgow.co.uk

PLACES TO STAY

The Balmoral ①
The *grande dame* of Edinburgh hotels,
the Balmoral has a superb spa, as well as
a Michelin-starred restaurant, champagne
bar and a central location in the city's main
shopping area.
1 Princes Street, Edinburgh; tel: 01315
562414. www.thebalmoralhotel.com

The Scotsman ①
A three-level gym and health centre
and Scotland's largest stainless-steel
swimming pool embellish this luxury
hotel in the city centre.
20 North Bridge, Edinburgh, tel. 01315
565565. www.thescotsmanhotel.com

The Grassmarket Hotel ①
Cheap and cheerful budget hotel with
its own pub, Biddy Mulligan's, on the
ever-popular Grassmarket.
94–96 Grassmarket, Edinburgh, tel. 01312
202299. www.grassmarkethotel.co.uk

The Lodge at Carfraemill ⑩
This roadside inn offers cosy rooms and
good solid cooking. An excellent overnight
stop while touring.
Carfraemill, nr Lauder, Borders; tel: 01578
750750. www.carfraemill.co.uk

Hotel du Vin ㉖
This pioneering boutique hotel, comprising
a block of five Georgian town houses,
boasts a classy bar and bistro.
1 Devonshire Gardens, Glasgow;
tel: 01413 700305.
www.hotelduvin.com/glasgow

Malmaison ㉖
Stylish, comfortable boutique hotel
with well-appointed rooms and a good
brasserie-style restaurant.
278 West George Street, Glasgow;
tel: 01413 780384.
www.malmaison-glasgow.com

Abode Glasgow ㉖
Trendy town house hotel with individually
styled bedrooms and suites.
129 Bath Street, Glasgow; tel: 01412
216789. www.abodehotels.co.uk

CitizenM ㉖
Located in the heart of Glasgow, this
super-stylish hotel comes equipped with
free WiFi and comfy beds.
60 Renfrew Street, Glasgow; www.
citizenm.com

Above: Boat lift at the Falkirk Wheel

The Victorian House ㉖
Centrally located hotel that's comfortable and very good value for money.
212 Renfrew Street, Glasgow; tel: 01413 320129. www.thevictorian.co.uk

Ednam House ⑬
Unpretentiously cosy hotel in the centre of a pretty Borders market town, offering fine views of the River Tweed from its classy restaurant.
Bridge Street, Kelso, Borders; tel: 01573 224168. www.ednamhouse.com

Dakota Forth Bridge ㉛
Distinctive futuristic black glass monolith just off the motorway near the famous bridge, with king-size beds, cocktails and an award-winning seafood restaurant.
A90 Forth Bridge Approach, South Queensferry, Midlothian; tel: 01313 193690. www.dakotaforthbridge.co.uk

The Black Bull ⑪
This inn offers eight en suite rooms – including two family rooms – above a noted gastropub.
Market Place, Lauder, Borders; tel: 01578 722208. www.blackbull-lauder.com

Roxburghe Hotel ⑫
Aristocratic owners the Duke and Duchess of Roxburghe ensure that this country-house hotel lives up to its reputation for grandeur and fine dining.
Heiton by Kelso, Borders; tel: 01573 450331.www.roxburghe.net

Cringletie House ⑮
Comfortable rooms in an imposing 19th-century mock-baronial mansion.
Edinburgh Road, Peebles, Borders; tel: 01721 725750. www.cringletie.com

Stobo Castle ⑰
Splendid baronial-style hotel, with service and facilities to match its grand exterior.
Stobo, Borders; tel: 01721 725300. www.stobocastle.co.uk

Glasgow International Jazz Festival ㉖
Jazz musicians from across the world gather in Glasgow to perform in concert halls, theatres, bars and restaurants.
Various venues, Glasgow; late Jun. www.jazzfest.co.uk

Glasgow Film Festival ㉖
A major fixture attracting leading British and international actors, writers and directors over ten days.
Various venues, Glasgow; tel: 01413 326535; mid–late Feb. www.glasgowfilm.org

Celtic Connections ㉖
Musicians and performers from all over the "Celtic Fringe" converge on Glasgow for this three-week celebration of contemporary and traditional music.
Various venues, Glasgow; tel: 01413 538000; late Jan–early Feb. www. celticconnections.com

Edinburgh International Book Festival ㉖
Authors from across the globe descend on Edinburgh to discuss literature. Inspiring, informative and entertaining.
Charlotte Square Gardens, Edinburgh; tel: 08453 735888; mid- to late Aug. www.edbookfest.co.uk

Royal Highland Show ㉚
Celebration of all that is best from Scotland's farms and countryside, with a week of food and best-of-breed contests for rare breeds and traditional livestock.
Ingliston, nr Edinburgh; tel: 01313 356207; last week of Jun. www.royalhighlandshow.org

National Museum of Scotland ①
Magnificent collection in a superb modern building displays the story of Scotland.
Chambers Street, Edinburgh; tel: 03001 236789; open 10am–5pm daily. www.nms.ac.uk

Scottish National Gallery of Modern Art ①
One of the world's finest collections of contemporary, Dadaist and Surrealist art.
75 Belford Road, Edinburgh; tel: 01316 246200; open 10am–5pm daily. www.nationalgalleries.org

National Museum of Flight ⑤
Astounding collection of civil and military aircraft, including Concorde, at a historic airfield near Edinburgh.
East Fortune Airfield, East Lothian; tel: 03001 236789; open mid-Mar–Oct 10am–5pm daily; Nov–mid-Mar: 10am–4pm Sat & Sun (open 10am-4pm daily during Feb half term). www.nms.ac.uk

New Abbey Corn Mill ⑱
Watch as this restored water-powered mill produces the nation's favourite food: oatmeal.
New Abbey, Dumfries and Galloway; tel: 01387 850260; open late Mar–Sept: 9:30am–5:30pm daily; Oct–Mar: 10am–4pm Mon–Wed and Sat & Sun. www.historic-scotland.gov.uk

Kelvingrove Art Gallery and Museum ㉖
The largest civic museum and art gallery in Britain boasts an impressive and eclectic collection.
Argyle Street, Glasgow; tel: 01412 769500; open 10am–5pm Mon–Thu and Sat, 11am–5pm Fri and Sun. www.glasgowmuseums.com

Scottish Storytelling Centre ①
Scottish stories old and new, told and reinterpreted for young and old.
43–45 High Street, Edinburgh; tel: 01315 569579; open Sep–Jun: 10am–6pm Mon–Sat; Jul–Aug: 10am–6pm daily. www.scottishstorytellingcentre.co.uk

Museum of Childhood ①
A collection of toys and games, guaranteed to delight children of all ages, and even the accompanying adults.
42 High Street, Edinburgh; tel: 01315 294142; open 10am–5pm Mon–Sat, noon–5pm Sun. www.edinburghmuseums.org.uk

Our Dynamic Earth ①
Journey through the hidden world of geology within this imaginative, interactive visitor attraction beneath Edinburgh's own extinct volcano.
Holyrood Road, Edinburgh; tel: 01315 507800; open late Mar–Oct: 10am–5:30pm daily (Jul–Aug: 10am-6pm daily); Nov–Mar: 10am–5:30pm Wed–Sun. www.dynamicearth.co.uk

Scottish Museum of Football ㉖
At Scotland's national stadium, this museum celebrates the country's footballing greats. A must for soccer-crazy youngsters.
Hampden Park, Glasgow; tel: 01416 166139; open 10am–5pm Mon–Sat, 11am–5pm Sun. www.scottishfootballmuseum.org.uk

Falkirk Wheel ㉘
This unique high-tech lift links the Forth & Clyde and Union canals by hoisting boats 35m into the air. An attraction which brings Scotland's 19th-century canal network back to life.
Lime Road, Tamfourhill, Falkirk; tel: 01324 61988; open 10am–5:30pm daily (check website for specific seasonal opening times). www.thefalkirkwheel.co.uk

Dalhousie Castle ②
Seat of the chieftans of Clan Ramsay, this country-house hotel and spa lies between Edinburgh and the Borders. Enjoy a unique dining experience in the castle's barrel-vaulted dungeon restaurant.
Bonnyrigg, Midlothian; tel: 01875 820153. www.dalhousiecastle.co.uk

Peebles Hotel Hydro ⑯
Right in the heart of the Tweed Valley, this historic spa hotel, built in 1907, offers top-quality treatments.
Innerleithan Road, Peebles, Borders; tel: 01764 651846. www.peebleshydro.co.uk

Mar Hall ㉕
A superbly luxurious baronial house, with a spa offering a number of relaxing treatments, set in its own wooded grounds overlooking the Clyde and conveniently close to Glasgow Airport.
Mar Hall Drive, Bishopton, nr Glasgow; www.marhall.com

Edinburgh Festival ① *(see pp114–15).*
Common Ridings ⑭ *(see pp78–9).*
Burns Heritage Trail ⑲ *(see pp204–5).*
Glasgow Winterfest ㉖ *(see pp190–91).*

NORTHERN IRELAND

LOCAL FOOD

Deane's Deli and Bistro ①
Superior snacks at Michelin star-winning chef Michael Deane's excellent deli, café and wine bar.
44 Bedford Street, Belfast; tel: 02890 248800; open noon–3pm and 5:30–10pm Mon–Sat. www.michaeldeane.co.uk

Kitsch Belfast ①
Enjoy delicious food made from locally-sourced produce at this eclectic eatery.
61-63 Dublin Road, Belfast; tel: 02890 333353; open 12–10pm Mon–Sat, 8am–6pm, 5–10pm Sun. www.wearekitch.com

Café Conor ①
Irish breakfasts, home-baked scones and a full menu in a place that's always busy.
11A Stranmillis Road, Belfast; tel: 02890 663266; open 9am–11pm daily. www.cafeconor.com

CarGoes Café and Deli ①
One of the best-known cafés and delis in Belfast; winner of a Best Breakfast Award.
613 Lisburn Road, Belfast; tel: 02890 665451; open 9am–4:30pm Mon–Fri, 9am–5pm Sat, 10am–3pm Sun. www.cargoescafe.co.uk

Swantons Gourmet Foods ①
One of Belfast's best delis; the home-made desserts are an irresistible treat.
639 Lisburn Road, Belfast; tel: 02890 683388; open 9am–5pm Mon–Sat.

Long's Fish Restaurant ①
The oldest – and many say the greatest – fish-and-chip shop in Belfast. A classic!
39 Athol Street, Belfast; tel: 02890 321848; open 11:30am–6:30pm Mon–Sat. www.johnlongs.com

Bay Tree Coffee House ②
Great café, considered to have the best cinnamon scones in the UK.
118 High Street, Holywood, County Down; tel: 02890 421419; open 8am–9:30pm Mon, Wed–Fri; 8am–5pm Tue; 9:30am–9:30pm Sat. www.baytreeholywood.com

The Boathouse Restaurant ④
Enjoy exquisite fine dining at this award-winning restaurant while taking in stunning views of the marina.
1a Seacliff Road, Bangor, County Down; tel: 02891 469253; open 12:30–2:30pm, 5:30–9:30pm Wed–Sat, 1–8pm Sun. www.theboathouseni.co.uk

Yellow Door Deli, Bakery and Café ⑲
Home-made chutneys, jams and ice cream at this wonderful award-winning bakery.
74 Woodhouse Street, Portadown, County Armagh; tel: 02838 353528; open 9am–5pm Mon–Sat.

Donnelly's Bakery and Coffee House ㉞
Beautiful Irish breads, such as wheaten and potato, baked in-house.
Ann Street, Ballycastle, County Antrim; tel: 02820 763236; open 7am–6pm Mon–Sat. www.donnellysbakery.co.uk

Picnic ⑦
Home-made fare and good local food in this quaint-looking deli-café across from Killyleagh Castle.
47 High Street, Killyleagh, County Down; tel: 02844 828525; open 7am–5pm Mon–Fri, 10am–4pm Sat & Sun.

Mourne Seafood Bar ⑬
You know you'll get the best fresh shellfish and seafood here, as the owner also runs an oyster farm on Carlingford Lough.
10 Main Street, Dundrum, County Down; tel: 02843 751377; open noon–late Mon -Sat, noon–8:30pm Sun. www.mourneseafood.com

Seasalt Delicatessen and Bistro ⑮
Irish cheeses and foodstuffs from around the world make the perfect picnic.
Central Promenade, Newcastle, County Down; tel: 02843 725027; open 9am–6pm Sun–Thu, 9am–9pm Fri–Sat.

The Loft Coffee Bar ㉑
A stylish coffee bar offering a wide range of sandwiches, cakes, milkshakes and home-made Italian ice cream.
The Linen Green, Moygashel, County Tyrone; tel: 02887 729929; open 9am–5pm Mon–Sat. www.theloftcoffeebar.com

FARMERS' MARKETS

Belfast City Food & Garden Market ①
Every Saturday, this lively Belfast market offers a wide range of local and international produce.
St George's Street, Belfast; tel: 02890 435704; every Sat, 9am–3pm.

Lisburn Farmers' Market ⑩
Some of the best regional produce, plus entertaining street performers.
15 Lisburn Square, Lisburn; tel: 02892 509250; first Sat of every month, 10am–4pm.

Portadown Market ⑱
The number and quality of local growers and makers selling here has won this market a "Best Farmers' Market" award.
Craigavon, nr Portadown, County Armagh; Fri and Sat 7am–4pm.

Templepatrick Farmers' Market ㊱
Locally grown and produced foods, including fruit and vegetables, meats, artisan breads and cheeses.
Coleman's Garden Centre, Ballyclare Road, Templepatrick, County Antrim; tel: 02894 432513; fourth Sun of every month, 11am–6pm.

Tyrone Farmers' Market ㉒
Only around 15 stalls, but a great mix of meats, fruit and vegetables (some organic), baked goods, jams and local crafts.
Tesco's car park, Dungannon, County Tyrone; tel: 02889 521943; first Sat of every month, 8:30am–12:30pm.

PUBS AND BARS

The Crown Bar ①
Historic watering hole, dating back to 1849, with Arabian-themed saloons.
46 Great Victoria Street, Belfast; tel: 02890 243187; open daily. www.crownbar.com

The Spaniard ①
Fashionable pub offering a large variety of food and drink, great music, good craic and quirky decor.
3 Skipper Street, Belfast; tel: 02890 232448; open daily.

McHugh's Bar and Restaurant ①
Housed in the oldest building in Belfast, McHugh's centuries of atmosphere behind it. It puts on live music nights in its basement bar.
29–31 Queen's Square, Belfast; tel: 02890 509999; open noon–3pm and 5–11pm Mon–Fri, noon–1:30am Sat, noon–10pm Sun. www.mchughsbar.com

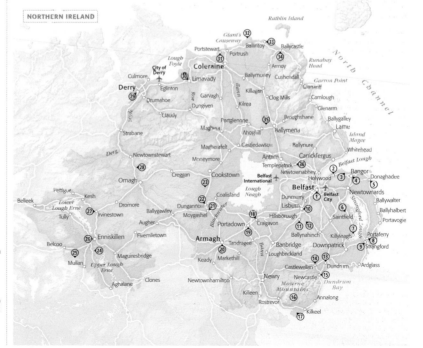

NORTHERN IRELAND

The Old Inn ③
Founded in about 1600, this inn has a large, traditional bar with an open fire, and a great award-winning restaurant.
11–15 Main Street, Crawfordsburn, County Down; tel: 02891 853255; open daily.
www.theoldinn.com

Grace Neill's ⑤
Ireland's oldest pub has a lounge bar held up by old ship timbers, and two snugs decorated with the booty of long-dead smugglers. The food is great too.
33 High Street, Donaghadee, County Down; tel: 02891 884595; open daily.
www.graceneills.com

The Pheasant ⑫
With its atmospheric old Highland Bar and a Neo-Gothic restaurant, this tavern has character galore.
410 Upper Ballynahinch Road, Annahilt, County Down; tel: 02892 638056; open daily. www.ploughgroup.com/pheasant

Blakes of the Hollow ㉖
This Victorian classic is the most famous pub in town and rated as one of Ireland's best.
6 Church Street, Enniskillen, County Fermanagh; tel: 02866 322143; open daily, noon–late. www.blakesofthehollow.com

Malmaison ①
A boutique hotel in stylishly converted warehouses in the centre of Belfast.
34–38 Victoria Street, Belfast; tel: 02890 220200. www.malmaison.com

Anna's House ⑥
Peaceful retreat describing itself as a luxury B&B, overlooking a pretty lake and serving its own organically grown food.
Tullynagee, 35 Lisbarnett Road, Comber, County Down; tel: 02897 541566.
www.annashouse.com

Barholm Portaferry ⑧
A tastefully-restored Victorian house occupying an outstanding location on Portaferry's shorefront. A mixture of single, double and family rooms are available.
11 The Strand, Portaferry, County Down; tel: 02842 729967.
www.barholmportaferry.co.uk

The Cuan ⑨
The heart of Strangford life – a restaurant, pub and fish-and-chip shop with superb, affordable accommodation.
Strangford Village, County Down; tel: 02844 881222. www.thecuan.com

Carriage House ⑬
Charming, family-run B&B that serves a great traditional breakfast in a sun room overlooking a walled garden.
71 Main Street, Dundrum, County Down; tel: 02843 751635.
www.carriagehousedundrum.com

The King's Inn ⑭
The King's Inn is a tidy, traditional family run bar-restaurant with seven simple but cosy en suite bedrooms.
28 Lower Square, Castlewellan, County Down; tel: 02043 788247.
www.kingsinn.weebly.com

Lurganconary Organic Farms ⑰
Award-winning, 5-star, self-catering cottages stunningly set in 40 hectares (100 acres) by the Mountains of Mourne.
25 & 27 Lurganconary Road, Kilkeel, County Down; tel: 02830 254595.
www.lurganconaryfarms.com

Tullylagan Country House Hotel ㉓
Rural Ireland with modern facilities; a manor hotel in 12 hectares (30 acres) of grounds, with two award-winning restaurants.
40b Tullylagan Road, Cookstown, County Tyrone; tel: 02886 765100.
www.tullylaganhotel.com

Westville Hotel ㉖
Chic boutique hotel in the centre of Enniskillen, with a stylish restaurant and open kitchen.
14–20 Tempo Road, Enniskillen, County Fermanagh; tel: 02866 320333.
www.westvillehotel.co.uk

Arch House Bed and Breakfast ㉗
A well-established B&B in a scenic spot overlooking Belmore, Benlaughlin and Cuilcagh mountains.
65 Marble Arch Road, Florencecourt, Enniskillen, County Fermanagh; tel: 02866 348452. www.archhouse.com

Beech Hill Country House Hotel ㉙
Four-star country retreat with acclaimed Ardmore Restaurant, which serves signature dishes such as Finnebrogue venison wellington.
32 Ardmore Road, Derry; tel: 02871 349279. www.beech-hill.com

Belfast International Arts Festival ①
Ireland's biggest arts festival brings world-class musicians, dancers, dramatists and comedians to the city for two weeks.
Various venues; Belfast; tel: 02890 982707; last three weeks of Oct.
www.belfastfestival.com

Festival of Fools ①
Wonderfully bizarre three-day mix of international comedy and street-theatre.
Various venues; Belfast; tel: 02890 236007; first May Bank Holiday weekend.
www.foolsfestival.com

St Patrick's Day ①
Although more associated with Dublin *(see pp42–3)*, the celebrations in Belfast are also a day of parades, music and fun.
Belfast city centre; 17 Mar.

Cathedral Quarter Arts Festival ①
Week-long festival of the arts, including theatre, dance, comedy, music, literature, visual arts and events for children.
Cathedral Quarter, Belfast; tel: 02890 232403; end Apr–May. www.cqaf.com

Open House Festival ①
Everything from traditional Irish ballads to bluegrass at this five-day folk-music event.
Cathedral Quarter, Belfast; tel: 02890 246609; Sep. www.openhousefestival.com

The Feile Festival ①
This ten-day festival grew up in response to the Troubles, and is now one of Europe's biggest community festivals.
Various venues; Belfast; tel: 02890 313440; Jul–Aug. www.feilebelfast.com

Hillsborough Oyster Festival ⑪
Four-day-long World Oyster Eating Championships, plus a masquerade ball.
Hillsborough, County Down; tel: 02892 689717; Sep.
www.hillsboroughoysterfestival.com

Apple Blossom Festival ⑳
Four-day festival in Northern Ireland's orchard capital, home of the Bramley apple.
Armagh, County Armagh; tel: 02837 521800; May.

Banks of the Foyle Halloween Carnival ㉙
Music and parades are part of this vibrant week-long festival by the river.
Various venues, Derry; tel: 02871 376545; last week of Oct.
www.derrycity.gov.uk/halloween

International North West 200 ㉛
Ireland's biggest one-day outdoor sporting event attracts 150,000 motorcycle fans.
Portstewart, County Derry; May.
www.northwest200.org

Ould Lammas Fair ㉞
One of the oldest surviving fairs in Ireland; two days of music and entertainment.
Ballycastle, County Antrim; last Mon and Tue of Aug.

Below: St Patrick's Day celebrations in Belfast

MUSEUMS AND GALLERIES

The Ulster Museum ①
One of the best local collections of
archaeology, art and historical artifacts,
housed in a Renaissance-style setting.
Also has visiting exhibitions.
*Stranmillis Road, Belfast; tel: 02890
428428; open 10am–6pm Mon–Sat,
11am–6pm Sun.
www.ulstermuseum.org.uk*

The MAC ①
The Metropolitan Arts Centre offers an
eclectic mix of music, theatre, dance and
art, bringing the very best of local and
international talent to Belfast.
*10 Exchange Street West, Belfast; tel:
02890 235053; open 10am–7pm daily.
www.themaclive.com*

Ulster Folk and Transport Museum ②
Voted Museum of the Year in 2007, this
museum is home to the largest transport
collection in Ireland and a reconstructed
village from the early 1900s.
*Cultra, Holywood, County Down;
tel: 02890 428728; open 10am–5pm
Tue–Sun. www.uftm.org.uk*

Armagh County Museum ⑳
Eclectic collection of local artifacts, art,
natural-history and local-history displays.
*The Mall East, Armagh, County Armagh;
tel: 0283/ 523070; open 10am– 5pm
Mon- Fri, 10am–1pm and 2–5pm Sat.
www.nimni.com/acm*

Royal Irish Fusiliers Museum ⑳
Archives, uniforms, weapons and other
exhibits tell the story of this brave and
historic regiment that served in many
conflicts, including the Napoleonic Wars.
*Sovereigns House, The Mall, Armagh,
County Armagh; tel: 0283/ 522911;
open 10am–12:30pm and 1:30–4pm
Mon–Fri (& first Sat of month May–Sep).*

The Navan Centre and Fort ⑳
Excellent centre offering modern
multimedia and interactive insights into
the ancient fort of the Kings of Ulster.
*Killylea Road, Armagh, County Armagh;
tel: 02837 510180; open Jan–Mar and
Oct–Dec: 10am–4pm daily; Apr–Sep:
10am–6:30pm daily.
www.armagh.co.uk/navan-centre-fort*

Enniskillen Castle and
Museums ㉖
An impressive 600-year-old castle
incorporating two museums.
*Castle Barracks, Enniskillen, County
Fermanagh; tel: 02866 325000; opening
times vary throughout the year; check
website for details.
www.enniskillencastle.co.uk*

Ulster American Folk Park ㉘
This fascinating museum brilliantly tells
the incredible story of Irish migration
to America.
*Castletown, Omagh, County Tyrone;
tel: 02882 243292; open 10am–4pm
daily. www.nmni.com*

Sheelin Antique Irish Lace Museum ㉔
The finest collection of antique lace
in the country, with a tempting shop.
*Bellanaleck, Enniskillen, County
Fermanagh; tel: 02866 348052;
open 10am–6pm Mon–Sat.
www.irishlacemuseum.com*

Tower Museum ㉙
Award-winning museum exploring Derry's
turbulent history, complete with treasures
recovered from Spanish Armada wrecks.
*Union Hall Place, Derry; tel: 02871
372411; open 10am–5:30pm daily.
www.derrycity.gov.uk/museums/
tower-museum*

Harbour Museum ㉙
Listed building with a collection that
includes a replica of St Columba's boat.
*Harbour Square, Derry; tel: 02871
377331; open 10am–1pm and 2–4:30pm
Mon–Fri. www.culturenorthernireland.org/
features/heritage/harbour-museum*

The Nerve Centre ㉙
Northern Ireland's leading creative media
arts centre. Features a wide-ranging
programme of events and exhibitions.
*7-8 Magazine Street, Derry; tel: 02871
260562; open 10am–5pm.
www.nervecentre.org*

THINGS TO DO WITH KIDS

Belfast Zoo ①
A wonderful collection of over 1,200
exotic animals, from agoutis to zebras.
*Antrim Road, Belfast; tel: 02890 776277;
open Apr–Sep: 10am–7pm daily; Oct–Mar:
10am–4pm daily. www.belfastzoo.co.uk*

Belfast Castle Estate ①
The castle and its grounds are within Cave
Hill Country Park, so you've got plenty of
space to explore. There is also an
award-winning adventure playground
*Antrim Road, Belfast; tel: 02890 776925;
open 9am–10pm Tue–Sat, 9am–5:30pm
Sun & Mon. www.belfastcastle.co.uk*

Titanic Belfast ①
This interactive exhibition has a live
undersea exploration centre.
*Queen's Island, Belfast; tel: 02890
766386; open 10am–5pm Oct–Mar,
Apr–May and Sep 9am–6pm, June–
August, 9am–7pm. www.titanicbelfast.com.*

W5 ①
Science museum with lots of interactive
fun and educational things to do.
*W5@Odyssey, Queen's Quay, Belfast;
tel: 02890 467700; open 10am–5pm
Mon–Fri, 10am–6pm Sat, noon–6pm Sun.
www.w5online.co.uk*

Titanic Boat Tours ①
Take a boat-trip around Belfast's shipyards,
where the ill-fated *Titanic* was constructed.
*Lagan Boat Company, 48 St John's Close,
2 Laganbank Road, Belfast; tel: 02890
240124; trips Mar–Oct daily; Nov–Dec
weekends only. www.laganboatcompany.
com*

Above: Palm House in Belfast Botanic Gardens

St Patrick's Trian Visitor Complex ⑳
Exhibitions include the scenes of a Viking
raid, the funeral of an Irish High King and
the Land of Lilliput, where a 6 m (20 ft)
giant describes *Gulliver's Travels*.
*40 English Street, Armagh, County
Armagh; tel: 02837 521801; open Jul–
Aug: 10am–5:30pm Mon–Sat, 2–6pm
Sun; Sep–Jun: 10am–5pm Mon–Sat,
2–5pm Sun.*

Armagh Astropark ⑳
An amazing scale model of the universe
is set in the grounds of the excellent
Armagh Observatory.
*College Hill, Armagh, County Armagh;
tel: 02837 522928; park open dawn–dusk
daily. www.arm.ac.uk*

Armagh Planetarium ⑳
Exhibitions, rocket-building activities and
demonstrations, together with special
events such as talks and films about
space and astronauts.
*College Hill, Armagh, County Armagh;
tel: 02837 523689; open 10am–5pm
daily. www.armaghplanet.com*

Marble Arch Caves ㉓
Take a boat trip then walk through
an awe-inspiring cave network, with
underground rivers and waterfalls.
*Marlbank, Florencecourt, County
Fermanagh; tel: 02866 348855;
open mid Mar–mid Oct daily.
www.marblearchcavesgeopark.com*

Castle Archdale Country Park ㉗
Deer herds, a butterfly garden, bike hire
and pony trekking are just a few of the
activities to keep children amused here.
*Irvinestown, County Fermanagh; tel:
02868 621588; open 9am–dusk daily.*

Carrick-a-Rede Rope Bridge ㉝
The simple pleasures are sometimes the
best, and kids love taking the rope bridge
to a little island here.
*119a Whitepark Road, Ballintoy,
County Antrim; tel: 02820 769839; Sep–
Oct & mid–Feb–May: open 9:30am–6pm
daily; Jun–Aug: open 10am–
7pm daily; Nov–mid-Feb 9:30am–
3:30pm daily. www.nationaltrust.org.uk/
carrick-a-rede*

SPAS AND HEALTH RESORTS

Culloden Estate & Spa ②
This 5-star estate, built in the Holywood
Hills for the Bishops of Down, has
breathtaking country views as well as
modern spa facilities.
*Bangor Road, Holywood, County Down; tel:
02890 421066. www.hastingshotels.com*

The Slieve Donard Resort & Spa ⑮
One of Europe's finest spas in a 4-star
resort overlooking the County Down coast.
*Downs Road, Newcastle, County Down;
tel: 02843 721066.
www.hastingshotels.com*

Killyhevlin Lakeside Hotel &
Chalets ㉖
A health club and Elemis Spa in a hotel
that has been voted as one of the top
places to stay in Northern Ireland by
Ulster TV viewers.
*Killyhevlin, Enniskillen, County Fermanagh;
tel: 02866 323481. www.killyhevlin.com*

Lough Erne Golf Resort ㉖
Northern Ireland's newest resort,
offering a Thai spa and two championship
golf courses. It's refreshingly eco- and
child-friendly too.
*Belleek Road, Enniskillen, County
Fermanagh; tel: 02866 323230.
www.lougherneglfresort.com*

Roe Park Resort ㉚
The north coast's most deluxe resort,
with a £1-million Roe Spa and its own
golf course.
*Limavady, County Derry; tel: 02877
722222. www.roeparkresort.com*

Galgorm Resort and Spa ㉟
With 66 hectares (163 acres) of lush
parkland, the Galgorm is a rural retreat
within 30 minutes' drive of Belfast.
*136 Fenaghy Road, Galgorm, County
Antrim; tel: 02825 881001.
www.galgorm.com*

OTHER SIGHTS IN THE BOOK

Mountains of Mourne ⑯ (see pp142–3).
Derry ㉚ (see pp30–31). **Giant's Causeway**
㉜ (see pp176–7).

WESTERN IRELAND

LOCAL FOOD

The Green Man ①
A wonderful deli that stocks food and drink from around the world, but is especially renowned for its local produce, including farmhouse cheeses, honey and bacon.
Main Street, Dunfanaghy, County Donegal; tel: 074 910 0800; open 9:30am–6pm Mon–Sat, 10am–2pm Sun.

Aroma Coffee ⑱
This unpretentious little café features home-baked items, good local ingredients and gives a nod to the chef's Mexican roots.
The Craft Village, Donegal, County Donegal; tel: 074 972 3222; open 9:30am–5:30pm Mon–Sat.

The Blueberry Tea Room ⑩
From sandwiches to home-baked pastries and cakes, this is the kind of perfect tea room every town should have.
Castle Street, Donegal, County Donegal; tel: 074 972 2933; open 9am–7pm Mon–Sat.

Moran's Oyster Cottage ㉙
A 300-year-old thatched cottage houses an award-winning restaurant, renowned for its delicious local oyster dishes.
The Weir, Kilcolgan, County Galway; tel: 091 796113; open noon–10pm daily. www.moransoystercottage.com

Anton's ㉛
A simple family-run café that has a loyal local following due to its good-value, home-cooked food.
12 Father Griffin Road, Galway, County Galway; tel: 091 582067; open 9am–6pm Mon–Fri. www.antonscafe.com

Goya's ㉛
One of Galway's best delis and bakeries, which has a café too. The indulgent chocolate cakes are not to be missed.
2–3 Kirwan's Lane, Galway, County Galway; tel: 091 567010; open 9am–6pm Mon–Sat. www.goyas.ie

Cullen's at the Cottage ㉞
Café in the grounds of the Ashford Castle Hotel, serving less formal food from the hotel's superb kitchen.
Ashford Castle, Cong, County Mayo; tel: 094 954 5332; 11:30am–9:30pm daily. www.ashford.ie

Hungry Monk Café ㉞
A friendly eaterie offering both home-baked snacks and wholesome meals.
Abbey Street, Cong, County Mayo; tel: 094 954 5842; open Mar–Oct: 10am–5:30pm Mon–Sat, 11am–5pm Sun; Nov–Dec: 10am–5:30pm Sat, 11am–5pm Sun.

McCormacks at the Andrew Stone Gallery ㊵
Fantastic Irish cooking; all the food is local and the home-made desserts are excellent.
Bridge Street, Westport, County Mayo; tel: 098 25619; open 10:15am–4:45pm Mon–Tue and Thu–Sat.

Lyons Café ⑮
The café may be one of the oldest in town, but its modern menu has some of the best organic snacks and meals around.
Lyons Department Store, Quay Street, Sligo, County Sligo; tel: 071 914 2969; open 9am–noon and 12:30–2pm daily. www.lyonscafe.com

Brigit's Garden Café ㉜
The gardens here are some of the best in the Galway area, and in season their produce is used in the café's menu.
Brigit's Garden, Pollagh, Roscahill, County Galway; tel: 091 550905; open May–Sep: 10:30am–5pm daily; Apr: 10:30am–5pm Sun; Oct–Mar: by arrangement. www.brigitsgarden.ie

Market Kitchen ㊻
A popular restaurant situated in an historic building above Brennan's Lane Bar, with a gluten-free take on local dishes.
Clare Street, Ballina, County Mayo; tel: 096 74971; open 3pm–late daily. www.marketkitchen.ie

Ballybofey Farmers' Market ⑨
Busy weekly market offering the best local produce of eastern Donegal.
GAA Grounds, Ballybofey, County Donegal; tel: 086 817 8854; every Fri, noon–4pm.

Donegal Farmers' Market ⑩
A typical array of produce, with live music!
The Diamond, Donegal, County Donegal; tel: 087 973 0539; third Sat of every month, 10am–2pm.

Athenry Farmers' Market ㉚
The riches gathered from the fields of Athenry are well represented at this weekly organic farmers' market.
Market Cross, Athenry, County Galway; tel: 087 627 2017; every Fri, 9:30am–4pm.

Galway Farmers' Market ㉛
Hundreds of stalls selling fresh produce, homemade jams and chutneys, cheeses and locally made crafts.
St Nicholas's Church, Galway; 8am–6pm Sat, Sun, Bank Holidays and Fridays in Jul and Aug. www.galwaymarket.com

Boyle Farmers' Market ㉑
An award-winning market that sells a huge range of food, plus very good crafts.
King House, Boyle, County Roscommon; tel: 071 966 3033; every Sat, 10am–2pm. www.unabhan.ie/boyle-farmers-market

Roscommon Farmers' Market ㉕
Fresh breads, fish and organic meats are among the produce on sale every week.
Market Square, Roscommon, County Roscommon; tel: 0861298317; every Fri, 10am–2pm.

Ballinasloe Farmers' Market ㉖
One of the best markets in the area, with dozens of excellent stalls.
Croffy Yard, Ballinasloe, County Galway; tel: 087 256 3167; every Fri, 8.30am–1pm.

Kinvara Farmers' Market ㉘
A great cross-section of food, from shellfish to award-winning cheeses.
Johnston's Hall, Main Street, Kinvara, County Galway; tel: 086 949 5769; every Fri, 10am–2pm.

WESTERN IRELAND

Manorhamilton Farmers' Market ⑭
At this enterprising cross-border market you can buy artisan cheeses, soda bread and other home-baked goodies, plus local honey, yogurts, olive oil and craft items.
Bee Park Resource Centre, New Line, Manorhamilton, County Leitrim; tel: 071 985 6935; every Fri, 10am–2pm.

Sligo Farmers' Market ⑯
Here you'll find freshly caught fish, organic local meats, cheeses, fruit and vegetables, delicious home-baked bread and, in summer, a selection of crafts stalls too.
IT College Car Park, Ballinode, County Sligo; tel: 071 914 7007; every Sat, 10am–2pm.

PUBS AND BARS

McGrory's of Culdaff ③
Whether you're after a bar, live music, a guesthouse or a highly rated restaurant, this is an essential port of call in Culdaff.
Culdaff, County Donegal; tel: 074 937 9104; open daily. www.mcgrorys.ie

Nancy's Bar ⑦
Brilliant family-owned Irish bar that attracts some of the best local session musicians, and serves good pub food in summer too.
Front Street, Ardara, County Donegal; tel: 074 954 1187; open daily.

The Bridge Bar ⑬
Whether you want good food, a few drinks, music or the chance to hang out with surfers, the Bridge Bar is the place to be.
West End, Bundoran, County Donegal; tel: 071 984 2050; open daily. www.maddensbridgebar.com

The Beach Bar ⑱
A 17th-century pub, which is also now a B&B and live-music venue, with an excellent reputation for its food.
Aughris Head, Templeboy, County Sligo; tel: 071 917 6465; open Apr–Oct: 1pm–late daily; Nov–Mar: 1pm–late Sat & Sun. www.thebeachbarsligo.com

The Oarsman ㉒
Regarded as one of the best pubs in western Ireland, gaining plaudits for its fine food, with dishes such as Kettyle lamb.
Bridge Street, Carrick-on-Shannon, County Leitrim; tel: 071 962 1733; open daily. www.theoarsman.com

Keogh's ㉘
This fine family-run pub has a bar and separate dining area serving traditional food, such as local salmon or black pudding.
The Square, Kinvara, County Galway; tel: 091 637145; open daily. www.kinvara.com/keoghs

Cronin's Sheebeen ㊵
Who could resist a drink in a thatched pub with a name like this? Good food too, from Thai fishcakes to loin of venison.
Rosbeg, Westport, County Mayo; tel: 098 26528; open mid-Mar–Oct: noon–midnight daily; Nov–mid-Mar 4:30pm–12:30am Mon–Thu, noon–midnight Fri–Sun.

Matt Molloy's ㊵
This music bar is owned by Matt Molloy of the folk band The Chieftains, and features live artists every night of the week.
Bridge Street, Westport, County Mayo; tel: 098 27663; open daily, hours flexible. www.mattmolloy.com

The Quays ㉛
Located in the vibrant 'Latin Quarter', The Quays is one of Galway's most famous pubs with some of the interior imported from a medieval French church. Renowned as a thriving live music venue.
11 Quay Street, Galway, County Galway; tel: 091 568347; open 10.30am–2am. www.louisfitzgerald.com/quaysgalway

J J Gannons ㉝
A pub offering luxury accommodation and gastropub food, serving champagne as well as Guinness.
Ballinrobe, County Mayo; tel: 094 954 1008; open daily. www.jjgannons.com

John J Burke ㉟
A family-run pub and restaurant, with wonderful home-cooked food and lovely views from the restaurant balcony.
Mount Gable House, Clonbur, County Galway; tel: 094 954 6175; open daily. www.burkes-clonbur.com

Crockets on the Quay ㊻
An old-fashioned bar, overlooking the River Moy, serving superb traditional dishes.
The Quay Village, Ballina, County Mayo; tel: 096 75930; open daily. www.crocketsonthequay.ie

PLACES TO STAY

Woodhill House ⑦
A characterful 17th-century coastal manor house offering occasional music events and an excellent restaurant which uses local produce in French-style cuisine.
Ardara, County Donegal; tel: 074 954 1112. www.woodhillhouse.com

Donegal Organic Farm ⑧
Biodynamic farm set in idyllic Donegal countryside, offering accommodation in the farmhouse and in separate flats.
Doorian, Glenties, County Donegal; tel: 074 955 1177.

Ard Na Breatha ⑩
A country house on a working farm only a short walk from Donegal, Ard Na Breatha won a prestigious EU award for eco-tourism.
Drumrooske Middle, Donegal, County Donegal; tel: 074 972 2288. www.ardnabreatha.com

Donegal Manor ⑩
Donegal Manor combines 4-star luxury with the friendliness of a family B&B, so it's no surprise this hotel has won all kinds of awards.
Letterkenny Road, Donegal, County Donegal; tel: 074 972 5222. www.donegalmanor.com

Above: Performers at the Galway Arts Festival

Rathmullen House ④
Beautiful Georgian house with gardens that drop down to the beach. The food, surrounding scenery and leisure facilities are top-class.
Rathmullan, County Donegal; tel: 074 915 8200. www.rathmullenhouse.com

Highlands Hotel ⑥
Housed in a 19th-century fishing and shooting lodge, this gracious family-run hotel and restaurant has plush rooms and opulent decor and furnishings.
Main Street, Glenties, County Donegal; tel: 074 955 1111. www.highlandshotel.ie

Ard Nahoo ⑰
An eco-retreat and health farm in stunning Yeats country, with accommodation in three Scandinavian-inspired eco-cabins.
Mullagh, Dromahair, County Leitrim; tel: 071 913 4939. www.ardnahoo.com

Keenan's ㉔
A boutique hotel, bar and restaurant, dating back to 1838, that combines luxury with a healthy respect for Irish tradition.
Tarmonbarry, County Roscommon; tel: 043 26098. www.keenans.ie

Caheroyan House and Farm ㉚
Eighteenth-century manor house and organic farm offering accommodation, nature walks and the chance for children to feed newborn farm animals.
Athenry, County Galway; tel: 091 844858. www.caheroyanhouseathenry.com

The Twelve ㉛
Award-winning luxury boutique hotel and spa. Its location, in a village close to the centre of Galway, adds to its chic appeal.
Barna Village, Galway, County Galway; tel: 091 597000. www.thetwelvehotel.ie

Ben View House ㊲
Stylish yet inexpensive family-run B&B in an 1848 town house with original features.
Bridge Street, Clifden, County Galway; tel: 095 21256. www.benviewhouse.com

Wyatt Hotel ㊵
Successfully blends a traditional setting with modern stylish comfort; the brasserie is award-winning.
The Octagon, Westport, County Mayo; tel: 098 25027. www.wyatthotel.com

Enniscoe ㊺
A country house with fantastic views of the breathtaking Mayo countryside, offering B&B and self-catering accommodation.
Castlehill, Ballina, County Mayo; tel: 096 31112. www.enniscoe.com

FESTIVALS AND EVENTS

Mary from Dungloe Festival ⑤
A huge eight-day festival with international music acts celebrating the famous Irish folk song, Mary from Dungloe.
Dungloe, County Donegal; Jul–Aug; tel: 087 449 1144. www.maryfromdungloe.com

Yeats Festival ⑮
Two-week period of events in Sligo and across the county celebrating one of Ireland's leading literary figures, W B Yeats.
County Sligo; tel: 071 914 2693; Jul. www.yeatssociety.com

Ballinasloe October Fair and Horse Festival ㉖
The biggest horse fair in Ireland takes place over two weeks, offering music, parades, horse auctions and other entertainment.
Ballinasloe, County Galway; Oct; tel: 090 964 4793. www.ballinasloeoctoberfair.com

Cruinniu na mBád ㉘
The three-day "Gathering of the Boats" in Galway Bay features the traditional sailing boats of the west coast.
Kinvara, County Galway; tel: 086 251 0922; Aug. www.cruinniunambad.com

Fleadh na gCuach ㉘
The "Cuckoo Festival" is a long weekend of traditional Irish music and the arts held every year on the early May Bank Holiday weekend.
Kinvara, County Galway; tel: 091 637131; May. www.kinvara.com/cuckoo/

Galway Arts Festival ㉛
For two weeks Galway welcomes theatre, spectacle, street art, music and comedy in a huge, exciting celebration.
Galway, County Galway; tel: 091 509700; Jul. www.giaf.ie

Galway Film Fleadh ㉛
Ireland's leading film festival brings stars, glamour and thought-provoking films to Galway for six days each July.
Various venues, Galway; tel: 091 562200; Jul. www.galwayfilmfleadh.com

Galway International Oyster Festival ㉛
One of Ireland's most famous food festivals has been running since 1954 (see pp136–7).
Galway, County Galway; tel: 091 394637; Sep. www.galwayoysterfestival.com

Ballyshannon Folk and Traditional Music Festival ⑫
A three-day festival that has been bringing some of Ireland's top music acts to this estuary town for over 30 years.
Ballyshannon, County Donegal; tel: 086 252 7400; Aug Irish Bank Holiday weekend (late Jul/early Aug). www.ballyshannonfolkfestival.com

Connemara Pony Show ㉔
A one-day gathering for those who want to admire the semi-wild Connemara ponies in all their splendour.
Clifden, County Galway; tel: 095 21863; Aug. www.cpbs.ie

Croagh Patrick Pilgrimage ㊴
More than 15,000 pilgrims climb Mayo's third-highest peak, the name of which means "Patrick's Stack" in English, to honour Ireland's patron saint, St Patrick.
Croagh Patrick, County Mayo; tel: 098 64114; last Sun in Jul. www.croagh-patrick.com

Westport International Sea Angling Festival ㊵
The longest-running and biggest sea angling festival in Ireland runs for four days.
Clew Bay, Westport, County Mayo; tel: 098 27297; Jun. www.westportseaanglingfestival.eu

Castlebar Blues Festival ㊶
For one weekend every year, Castlebar hosts the longest-running blues festival in Ireland, with concerts, a blues trail and a CD and record fair
Castlebar, County Mayo; tel: 094 902 3111; May–Jun.

Ballina Salmon Festival ㊻
Held in the "salmon capital of the world", this huge ten-day festival also celebrates local arts, culture and communities.
Ballina, County Mayo; tel: 096 79814; Jul. www.ballinasalmonfestival.ie

MUSEUMS AND GALLERIES

Galway City Museum ㉛
A range of good exhibitions telling the intriguing story of the city of Galway.
Spanish Parade, Galway, County Galway; tel: 091 532460; open 10am–5pm Tues–Sat; Easter–Sep only: 12pm–5pm Sun. www.galwaycitymuseum.ie

Nora Barnacle House Museum ㉛
The former home of Nora Barnacle, who married James Joyce, now restored to the way it was when she lived there as a child.
Bowling Green, Galway, County Galway; tel: 091 564743; open summer only, call to join a tour.

Claddagh Ring Museum ㉛
Tiny museum in the Claddagh Gold shop with a collection of traditional Irish lovers' rings, including some of the oldest made.
1 Quay Street, Galway, County Galway; tel: 091 566365; open 10am–5:30pm Mon–Sat, noon–4pm Sun. www.claddaghring.ie

Above: Bogwood tree at the Céide Fields Visitor Centre

Sligo County Museum ⑮
Strong on local history, but the main interest here is the W B Yeats Memorial Room, which contains items relating to the poet's life and works, including his 1923 Nobel Prize for Literature medal.
Stephen Street, Sligo, County Sligo; tel: 071 911 1679; open Oct–Apr: 9.30am–12.30pm Tues–Sat; May–Sept: 9.30am–12.30pm and 2–4:30pm Tue–Sat. www.sligoarts.ie/venuesprofile/sligomuseum

Knock Museum ㊸
Learn the story of the apparition of the Virgin Mary in Knock, experienced by two women near the village church in 1879.
Knock, County Mayo; tel: 094 938 8100; open 10am–6pm daily. www.knockshrine.ie/museum

Kiltimagh Museum ㊹
Excellent local museum in a former railway station, exploring the history of the town and its inhabitants.
Kiltimagh, County Mayo; tel: 094 938 1132; open Jun–Sep: 2–6pm daily. www.museumsofmayo.com

Enniscoe Museum ㊺
This museum and family history centre displays household and farm artifacts, and you can also explore the grounds and Victorian walled garden.
Mayo North Heritage Centre, Castlehill, Ballina, County Mayo; tel: 096 31809; open Apr–Oct: 9am–6pm Mon–Fri, 2–6pm Sat–Sun; Nov–Mar: family history section only, 9am–4pm Mon–Fri. www.museumsofmayo.com

Céide Fields Visitor Centre ㊼
This startling pyramid-shaped visitor centre has won an architectural award; inside it tells the story of the unusual surrounding landscape and blanket bogs.
Ballycastle, County Mayo; tel: 096 43325; open mid-Mar–May and Oct–Nov: 10am–5pm daily; Jun–Sep: 10am–6pm daily; Dec–mid-Mar: bookings only. www.museumsofmayo.com

THINGS TO DO WITH KIDS

Deane's Farm Equestrian Centre ⑪
Deane's 40-hectare (100-acre) farm on the Donegal coast offers pony rides, horse-trekking trips and riding lessons.
Darney, Bruckless, County Donegal; tel: 074 973 7160; open 10am–6pm Wed–Sun.

Eagles Flying ⑲
Ireland's largest centre for birds of prey and owls is a must-see, with daily hour-long flying demonstrations and a Pet Zoo.
Ballymote, County Sligo; tel: 071 918 9310; open Mar–Nov: 10:30am–12:30pm and 2:30–4:30pm daily. www.eaglesflying.com

Slieve Aughty Centre ㉗
Riding holidays are available in summer, as well as working stays at the stables and lake and forest trail riding.
Kylebrack West, Loughrea, County Galway; tel: 090 974 5246. www.slieveaughtycentre.com

Ireland's School of Falconry ㉞
Falconry school in the grounds of Ashford Castle offering classes in hawk-flying within the gardens and woodlands.
Ashford Castle, Cong, County Mayo; tel: 094 954 6820; by appointment only. www.falconry.ie

An Trá Mhóir ㊱
A 3-mile (5-km) popular surfing beach, "The Great Beach" is the perfect place to be when the sun is shining.
Creggoduff, Bunowen, Ballyconneely, County Galway.

Killary Adventure Company ㊳
Exciting adventure sports such as bungee-jumping, kayaking, and abseiling; daily activites and residential stays.
Leenane, County Galway; tel: 095 43411. www.killaryadventure.com

Westport House ㊿
An 18th-century country house, with a pirate-themed adventure park and outdoor activity centre.
Westport, County Mayo; tel: 098 27766; open Mar–May: 10am–4pm; Jun 10am–4pm Mon–Fri, Sat–Sun 10am–6pm; Jul–Aug: 10am–6pm daily; Sep–Nov: 10am–4pm daily; Dec: wkends. www.westporthouse.ie

Mayo Horsedrawn Caravan Holidays ㊷
Hire a traditional Irish horse-drawn caravan and explore the area at a leisurely pace, staying overnight at pre-arranged farm sites.
Belcarra, Castlebar, County Mayo; tel: 094 903 2777. www.horsedrawncaravan.com

SPAS AND HEALTH RESORTS

Kee's Hotel and Leisure Club ⑧
This family-run hotel has its own leisure club with fitness room, pool, steam room, sauna and in-house beauticians.
Stranorlar, Ballybofey, County Donegal; tel: 074 913 1018. www.keeshotel.com

Jackson's Hotel and Leisure Centre ⑨
On the banks of the River Finn, Jackson's is an award-winning hotel with a sauna, Jacuzzi, swimming pool and gym, offering yoga classes, massages and treatments.
Ballybofey, County Donegal; tel: 074 913 1021. www.jacksonshotel.ie

Villa Rose Hotel and V-Spa ⑨
Boutique hotel with an award-winning contemporary spa offering a thermal suite and a wide range of therapies, massages and other spa treatments.
Main Street, Ballybofey, County Donegal; tel: 074 913 2266. www.villarose.net

Ballyliffin Lodge and Spa ②
A 4-star hotel with spectacular views of Malin Head. Its Rock Crystal Spa has nine treatment rooms, a pool, gym, 12-seater Jacuzzi and a dry flotation chamber.
Shore Road, Ballyliffin, County Donegal; tel: 074 937 8200. www.ballyliffinlodge.com

Kilronan Castle Estate and Spa ⑳
This majestic, modernized castle retreat on the shores of Lough Meelagh offers the ultimate in luxurious pampering and individualized treatments.
Ballyfarnon, County Roscommon; tel: 071 961 8000. www.kilronancastle.ie

Lough Rynn Castle ㉓
This castle hotel by Lough Rynn boasts spa and leisure facilities, as well as a golf course designed by Nick Faldo.
Mohill, County Leitrim; tel: 071 963 2700. www.loughrynn.ie

Abbey Hotel ㉕
An 18th-century manor house set in large, pretty gardens, this 4-star luxury hotel has a big indoor pool, treatment room, gym, sauna, Jacuzzi and steam room.
Galway Road, Roscommon, County Roscommon; tel: 090 662 6021. www.abbeyhotel.ie

Raheen Woods Hotel ㉚
A luxurious contemporary haven, with a "Tranquility" spa offering yoga and gym classes, massage and spa therapies and a steam room, sauna, pool and Jacuzzi.
Athenry, County Galway; tel: 091 875888. www.raheenwoodshotel.ie

The Twin Trees Hotel ㊻
This family hotel's Eagles Leisure Club offers a swimming pool, steam room, Jacuzzi and exercise classes.
Ballina, County Mayo; tel: 096 21033. www.twintreeshotel.ie

Mount Falcon Country House Hotel and Spa ㊻
Mount Falcon is hidden in 40 hectares (100 acres) of woodland, with a gym, pool, steam room, sauna and spa.
Ballina, County Mayo; tel: 096 74472. www.mountfalcon.com

OTHER SIGHTS IN THE BOOK

Galway Oyster Festival ㉛ *(see pp136–7).*

EASTERN IRELAND

LOCAL FOOD

Chapter One ①
Michelin-starred restaurant at the Dublin Writers Museum, known for its imaginative contemporary use of Irish ingredients.
Basement of the Writers Museum, 18 Parnell Square, Dublin; tel: 01 873 2266; open 12:30–2pm and 6–11pm Tue–Fri, 6–11pm Sat. www.chapteronerestaurant.com

Chapterhouse Café ①
The café of the Dublin Writers Museum, offering less expensive, but exceptionally fine, food from the same kitchen as its parent restaurant, Chapter One (*above*).
18 Parnell Square, Dublin; tel: 01 872 2077; open 10am–5pm Mon–Sat, 11am–5pm Sun. www.writersmuseum.com

Blazing Salads ①
Amazing deli that makes everything on the premises except for bread, which is baked in an organic bakery. Several soups and dishes, such as vegetarian stews and shepherd's pie, are made daily.
42 Drury Street, Dublin; tel: 01 671 9552; open 10am–4pm Mon–Fri, 9am–5pm Sat. www.blazingsalads.com

Queen of Tarts ①
One of two branches, this café specializes in tarts, home-baked breads, muffins, scones, cakes and pastries.
4 Cork Hill, Dame Street, Dublin; tel: 01 670 7499/633 4681; open 8am–7pm Mon–Fri, 9am–7pm Sat–Sun. www.queenoftarts.ie

The Gourmet Store ㉒
Deli selling delicious local cheeses, meats and home-made sandwiches, paninis, wraps and bagels. The hot bacon, sausage and white-pudding sandwich is a speciality.
56 High Street, Kilkenny, County Kilkenny; tel: 056 777 1727; open 8am–6pm daily. www.thegourmetstorekilkenny.com

Bradbury's Bakery ㉘
In business since 1938, this deli makes everything from fresh bread to wedding cakes and even the local school dinners – try one of the diet or spelt breads.
Leinster Street, Athy, County Kildare; tel: 059 863 1845; open daily 8am–6pm. www.bradburys.ie

Spago Italian Bistro ㉚
The stylish restaurant of the Heritage Hotel specialises in stone-cooked Irish steaks
Portlaoise, County Laois; tel: 057 867 8588; open 6pm–9:30pm Sun–Thu, until 10pm Fri and Sat. www.theheritagehotel.com

Ramparts Coffee Shop ㊸
Ireland is known for its wonderful baking and this is a great place to sample home-made breads, scones, sandwiches, bagels and more substantial meals too, close to the entrance to Trim Castle.
Castle Street, Trim, County Meath; tel: 046 943 7227; open 9:30am–5:30pm Mon–Sat.

Blackrock Market ②
Fine arts, crafts and furniture on sale alongside a range of fresh food produce.
19A Main Street, Blackrock, Dublin; tel: 01 283 3522; every Sat and Sun, 11am–5.30pm. www.blackrockmarket.com

Monkstown Village Market ③
Friendly market featuring a wide range of fresh Irish produce.
Parish Church, Monkstown, County Dublin; tel: 087 234 9419; every Sat, 10am–4pm.

Poppies ⑤
From a cup of tea or a take away salad to delicious traditional dishes, such as homity pie, Poppies prides itself on its country cooking. Unmissable if you're in the area.
The Square, Enniskerry, County Wicklow; tel: 01 282 8869; open 8am–6pm daily. www.poppies.ie

Avoca (Fern House Café) ⑥
One of the best-known names in Ireland for crafts and foods, Avoca serves up some of the tastiest dishes around, including a Wicklow Blue cheese salad.
Kilmacanogue, County Wicklow; tel: 01 274 6990; open 9.30am–4.30pm Mon–Sat, dinner 6–9.30pm Thurs–Sat, 9.30am–5pm Sun. www.avoca.ie

Leitrim Lounge ⑩
Award-winning riverside pub with live music, a beer garden and a solid traditional menu.
Leitrim Place, Wicklow Town, County Wicklow; tel: 0404 67443; open daily.

Avenue Café ㊱
Stylish café-restaurant in a university town serving cheap and cheerful options, such as Irish-beef burgers, and local dishes, such as Bantry Bay mussels.
Main St, Maynooth, County Kildare; tel: 01 628 5003; open from noon (last orders 9:30pm) Mon–Sat, 1–10pm Sun (last orders 7:30pm). www.avenuecafe.ie

Malahide Market ㊴
Very popular market offering arts, crafts and fashion indoors, with fresh fish and local farm produce outside.
St Sylvester's GAA Hall, 2 Church Road, Malahide, Dublin; tel: 086 056 2896; every Sat, 1.30pm–6pm.

FARMERS' MARKETS

Dublin Docklands Farmers' Market ①
Fashion and design items as well as fresh breads and home-made desserts at this popular market in Ireland's capital.
Excise Walk, International Financial Services Centre, Dublin; every Wed, noon–2:30pm. www.dublindocklands.ie

Harcourt Street Farmers' Market ①
The old railway station arches have been transformed into a thriving food venue in the centre of the city
Park Place, Station Buildings, Upper Hatch Street, Dublin; every Thurs, 10am–4pm. www.irishfarmersmarkets.ie

Kilkenny Farmers' Market ㉒
One of the best in the area with producers of honey, meats, breads, cakes and jams.
Mayor's Walk, Kilkenny, County Kilkenny; tel: 056 779 4513; every Thu, 9am–2.30pm.

Portlaoise Farmers' Market ㉚
Only a handful of local stalls, but they offer a good range of top-quality local produce.
Market Square, Portlaoise, County Laois; tel: 057 866 4205; every Fri, 10am–3pm.

Ballymun Farmers' Market ㊳
Organic produce, home-made bread, cakes and jams, as well as arts and crafts.
Ballymun Shopping Centre, Ballymun, Dublin; tel: 087 698 1093; every Thu 9am–3.30pm. www.ballymunmarket.ie

Wexford Market ⑯
Excellent local market selling a range of local produce, such as bacon, sausages, organic chicken and lamb, fish, yogurt, honey, butter and bread.
Super Valu car park , Key West, Wexford, County Wexford; tel: 087 794 8830; every Fri, 9am–2pm.

Howth Market ㊵
A vast array of organic produce, locally baked goods, jewelry, clothing and antiques. A permanent selection of shops are also open daily in addition to the weekend market.
3A Harbour Road, Howth, nr Dublin; tel: 01 839 4141; every Sat, Sun and Bank Holiday, 9am–6pm. www.howthmarket.e

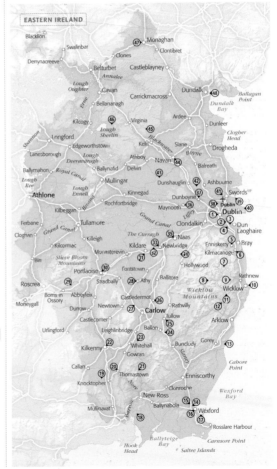

EASTERN IRELAND

PUBS AND BARS

Davy Byrnes ①
Legendary Dublin pub, famous for its appearance in James Joyce's *Ulysses*, and the place to be on 16 June for Bloomsday (see *Festivals and Events*).
21 Duke Street, Dublin; tel: 01 677 5217; open daily. www.davybyrnes.com

McDaids ①
Famous pub popular in the 1950s with Brendan Behan and other Dublin literary figures, though it dates from 1779.
3 Harry Street, Dublin; tel: 01 679 4395; open daily.

The Coach House ⑦
Award-winning pub with great food, in an ideal location for tourists.
Main Street, Roundwood, County Wicklow; tel: 01 281 8157; open daily. www.thecoachhouse.ie

The Lobster Pot ⑬
Country pub specializing in the freshest of seafood – the Wexford cockles and mussels are very popular.
Ballyfane, Carne, County Wexford; tel: 053 913 1110; closed Mon (except Bank Holidays when closed Tue) and also Jan and first week Feb. www.lobsterpotwexford.com

The Yard ⑭
Acclaimed modern restaurant and coffee shop, located right in the heart of Wexford town, serving imaginative fusion cooking in a relaxed atmosphere.
3 Lower Georges Street, Wexford, County Wexford; tel: 053 914 4083; open daily. www.theyard.ie

Kyteler's Inn ㉒
The oldest inn in Kilkenny serves traditional food, such as Irish stews, Irish lamb and boiled bacon and cabbage, and puts on a variety of entertainment.
St Kieran's Street, Kilkenny, County Kilkenny; tel: 056 772 1064; open daily. www.kytelersinn.com

Ballymore Inn ㉞
Renowned for its good country food, ranging from simple bar fare to fancier steaks and fish dishes.
Ballymore, Eustace, County Kildare; tel: 045 864585; open 12:30–9pm daily. www.ballymoreinn.com

Thomas Fletcher ㉟
One of the best-loved pubs in the area, Thomas Fletcher dates back to the 1800s and remains unspoilt by modern times.
Commercial House, Main Street, Naas, County Kildare; tel: 045 897328; open 4pm–late Sun–Fri, noon–late Sat.

Andy's Bar and Restaurant ㊼
Family pub in the centre of town; a great place if you just want a drink, but it would be a shame not to sample the superb food.
12 Market Street, Monaghan, County Monaghan; tel: 047 82277; open from 4pm Tue–Fri, noon Sat, 3:30pm Sun.

Above: "James Joyce" and "Molly Bloom", Bloomsday

Marble City Bar ㉒
This historic bar now has stylish modern touches, but it is the quality of the food that draws people here.
66 High Street, Kilkenny, County Kilkenny; tel: 056 776 1143; open daily until 10pm.

The Hanged Man's ㉝
Gastropub noted for creative Irish cuisine, especially the local fish and seafood, though its steak is also rightly renowned.
Milltown, Newbridge, County Kildare; tel: 045 431515; open 5–11pm Mon–Sat, noon–10pm Sun. www.hangedmans.ie

Fitzpatrick's Bar and Restaurant ㊽
With several bars, a beer garden, a bistro and a restaurant, there's something for every budget at this very popular pub.
Rockmarshall, Jenkinstown, Dundalk, County Louth; tel: 042 937 6193; open Apr–Oct: daily; Nov–Mar: Tue–Sat. www.fitzpatricks-restaurant.com

PLACES TO STAY

Brooks Hotel ①
One of the best boutique hotels in Dublin, with a fashionable restaurant and bar.
Drury Street, Dublin; tel: 01 670 4000. www.brookshotel.ie

Quay House ⑱
In the heart of a delightful fishing village, Quay House and its helpful owners offer simple but comfortable accommodation.
Kilmore Quay, County Wexford; tel: 053 912 9988. www.quayhouse.net

Ballindrum Farm ㉘
Only an hour's drive from Dublin but in the middle of rolling Kildare countryside, this farm has won awards for its hospitality.
Athy, County Kildare; tel: 059 862 6294. www.ballindrumfarm.com

Highfield House B&B ㊸
Lovely 18th-century house in a great location overlooking Trim Castle and the River Boyne, with beautiful private gardens.
Castle Street, Trim, County Meath; tel: 046 943 6386. www.highfieldguesthouse.com

Killiane Castle ⑰
Working farm and B&B, built in the ruins of a 13th-century Norman castle, and set in beautiful Wexford countryside.
Drinagh, County Wexford; tel: 053 915 8885. www.killianecastle.com

Croan Cottages ⑲
Four-star self-catering cottages hidden in the grounds of the 18th-century Croan House, a small farm next to a forest.
Dunmaggan, County Kilkenny; tel: 056 776 6868. www.croancottages.com

Ballyduff House ⑳
Built in 1760, this is an active farm as well as a B&B and is set in beautiful parkland, overlooking the River Nore.
Thomastown, County Kilkenny; tel: 056 775 8488. www.ballyduffhouse.com

Lorum Old Rectory ㉓
Luxury manor house built in 1863 in the Barrow Valley, at the foot of the Blackstairs Mountains. Exceptional home cooking includes home-grown organic produce.
Kilgreaney, Bagenalstown, County Carlow; tel: 059 977 5282. www.lorum.com

Ballin Temple ㉔
Set deep in the Carlow countryside, this private house has cottages to rent and acres of woodland to explore.
Ardattin, County Carlow; tel: 059 915 5037/086 817 9238. www.ballintemple.com

Kilkea Lodge Farm ㉖
This small, child-friendly family farm has just a handful of rooms and sometimes runs music and painting courses.
Castledermot, County Kildare; tel: 059 914 5112. www.kilkealodgefarm.com

Coolanowle Cottages ㉗
Peaceful holidays are on offer in these cottages on a working organic farm an hour's drive from Dublin, with simple B&B or self-catering options also available.
Ballickmoyler, Carlow, County Laois; tel: 059 862 5176. www.coolanowle.com

Lakeview Organic Farm ㊸
Self-catering accommodation with fishing rights on adjacent Mullagh Lake. You can buy produce from the owners' organic farm.
Mullagh, County Cavan; tel: 086 8633 922. www.lakeview.com

Ross House ㊻
A working farm and equestrian centre right on the shores of Lough Sheelin, described as the perfect rural Irish retreat.
Mountnugent, County Cavan; tel: 0498 540218. www.ross-house.com

FESTIVALS AND EVENTS

The Audi Dublin International Film Festival ①
This 10-day event brings movie premieres and leading Irish film-makers and actors to Ireland's capital.
Various venues, Dublin; tel: 01 662 4260; Feb–Mar. www.diff.ie

Dublin Theatre Festival ①
Irish writers have produced remarkable drama, and for almost three weeks each year the city's theatres put on a wide range of plays celebrating their work.
Various venues, Dublin; tel: 01 677 8439; Sep–Oct. www.dublintheatrefestival.com

Bloomsday ①
Dublin brings alive the day on which James Joyce's *Ulysses* was set in 1904, with events all over the city, especially in bars.
Various venues, Dublin; 16 June. www.bloomsdayfestival.ie

Taste of Dublin ①
Spread over four days and held in pretty Iveagh Gardens, this festival celebrates the best of Dublin's food and drink.
Iveagh Gardens, Dublin; tel: 01 497 2020; Jun. www.tasteofdublin.ie

The Wicklow 200 ⑪
Ireland's biggest bicycle race is a huge fixture in the calendar, and attracts over 1,000 cyclists hoping to cover 200 km (125 miles) over the course of a day.
Rathdrum (main checkpoint), County Wicklow; tel: 059 648 1350; Jun. www.wicklow200.ie

Wexford Opera Festival ⑯
One of the world's biggest festivals of opera, running since 1951, the 12-day event stages a huge array of performances in a variety of operatic styles.
Wexford Opera House, Wexford, County Wexford; tel: 053 912 2400; late Oct. www.wexfordopera.com

Town of Books Festival ㉑
Readers and writers unite in this little town for a weekend in late August, with readings, workshops and music events.
Various venues, Graiguenamanagh, County Kilkenny; Aug. www.graiguenamanaghtownofbooks.com

The Cat Laughs ㉒
An international selection from the world's top stand-up comedians livens up Kilkenny over a long weekend.
Various venues, Kilkenny, County Kilkenny; May–Jun. www.thecatlaughs.com

Kilkenny Arts Festival ㉒
Art and music are celebrated over 10 days in Kilkenny, including street theatre and special events for children.
Kilkenny, County Kilkenny; tel: 056 776 3663; Aug. www.kilkennyarts.ie

Irish Derby Festival ㉜
This three-day festival is a spectacle of fashion, music and world-class horse racing.
Curragh Racecourse, County Kildare; late Jun. www.curragh.ie

Irish Grand National ㊷
This two-day race meeting rivals only the Irish Derby in the horse-racing calendar.
Fairyhouse Racecourse, Ratoath, County Meath; tel: 01 825 6167; Mar/Apr. www.fairyhouse.ie

MUSEUMS AND GALLERIES

National Museum of Ireland ①
This fascinating museum is home to a huge collection of Irish historical artifacts, art and natural-history displays.
Kildare Street, Dublin; tel: 01 677 7444; open 10am–5pm Tue–Sat, 2–5pm Sun. www.museum.ie

National Gallery of Ireland ①
Displays on W B Yeats and other Irish writers and artists, as well as a wide European collection – unmissable.
Merrion Square West and Clare Street, Dublin; tel: 01 661 5133; open 9:30am–5:30pm Mon–Wed, Fri, Sat; 9:30am–8:30pm Thu; noon–5.30pm Sun. www.nationalgallery.ie

Chester Beattie Library ①
A fine museum, with a breathtaking collection of rare books and manuscripts.
Dublin Castle, Dublin; tel: 01 407 0750; open May–Sep: 10am–5pm Mon–Fri, 11am–5pm Sat, 1–5pm Sun; Oct–Apr: 10am–5pm Tue–Fri, 11am–5pm Sat, 1–5pm Sun. www.cbl.ie

Irish Museum of Modern Art ①
A delightful and thought-provoking gallery housed in the restored former hospital.
Royal Hospital, Kilmainham, Dublin; tel: 01 612 9900; open 10am–5:30pm Tue and Thu–Sat, 10:30am–5:30pm Wed, noon–5:30pm Sun. www.imma.ie

Dublin Writers Museum ①
Excellent displays comprising manuscripts by many fine Irish writers.
18 Parnell Square, Dublin; tel: 01 872 2077; open Sep–May: 10am–5pm Mon–Sat, 11am–5pm Sun, Jun–Aug: 10am–5pm Mon–Sat, 11am–6pm Sun. www.writersmuseum.com

Dublin City Gallery The Hugh Lane ①
Lovely gallery featuring modern European art and the studio of Francis Bacon.
Charlemont House, Parnell Square North, Dublin; tel: 01 222 5550; open 10am–6pm Tue–Thu, 10am–5pm Fri–Sat, 11am–5pm Sun. www.hughlane.ie

The Guinness Storehouse ①
Imaginative displays and interactive exhibits designed to appeal to all ages tell the story of the national tipple (adults get a free one at the end).
St James's Gate, Dublin; tel: 01 408 4800; open Sep–Jun: 9:30am–5pm daily; Jul–Aug: 9:30am–7pm daily. www.guinness-storehouse.com

The Irish National Stud ㉛
The best place to see racing thoroughbreds at rest. Also on site are the National Horse Museum, Saint Fiachra's Garden and extensive Japanese Gardens.
Tully, County Kildare; tel: 045 521251; open Feb–Dec: 9am–6pm. www.irishnationalstud.ie

THINGS TO DO WITH KIDS

Dublin Zoo ①
From African hunting dogs and Arctic foxes to tigers, wolves and zebras, Dublin Zoo has a large collection of animals in simulated natural environments.
Phoenix Park, Dublin; tel: 01 474 8900; open Mar–Sep: 9:30am–6pm daily; Oct: 9:30am–5:30pm daily; Nov–Dec: 9:30am–4pm daily; Jan: 9:30am–4:30pm daily; Feb: 9:30am–5pm daily. www.dublinzoo.ie

Dublinia and the Viking World ①
This heritage centre brings early and medieval Dublin to life with detailed models and audio-visual displays.
St Michael's Hill, Christchurch, Dublin; tel: 01 679 4611; open Mar–Sep: 10am–6.30pm daily; Oct–Feb: 10am–5.30pm daily. www.dublinia.ie

Viking Splash Tours ①
Guided tours around Dublin by land and water in amphibious World War II vehicles, taking in Viking and more recent historical sites. Tours finish with a splashy drive around the Grand Canal Docklands.
St Stephen's Green North, Dublin; tel: 01 707 6000; tours operate all year, departing every 30 min in summer. www.vikingsplash.ie

Airfield Estate ④
Working farm with beautiful gardens, a café and heritage experience.
Overend Way, Dundrum, Dublin; tel: 01 969 6666; open Sep–May: 9.30am–5pm daily; Jun: 9.30am–5pm Mon–Fri, 9.30am–7pm Sat and Sun; Jul and Aug: 9.30am–7pm daily. www.airfield.ie

Wexford Wildfowl Reserve ⑭
Bird reserve famous for the thousands of geese it attracts in the winter.
North Slob, County Wexford; tel: 076 100 2660; open 10am–5pm daily.

Irish National Heritage Park ⑮
Educational open-air museum covering 9,000 years of Irish history (see pp104–5).
Ferrycarrig, County Wexford; tel: 053 912 0733; open May–Aug: 9:30am–6:30pm daily; Sep–Apr: 9:30am–5:30pm daily. www.inhp.com

Kilkenny Castle ㉒
Set in huge grounds, this is one of the most fascinating castles in Ireland.
The Parade, Kilkenny, County Kilkenny; tel: 056 770 4100; open Feb–Feb: 9:30am–4:30pm daily; Mar: 9:30am–5pm daily; Apr–May and Sep: 9:30am–5:30pm daily; Jun–Aug: 9am–5:30pm daily. www.kilkennycastle.ie

Kilvahan Horse-Drawn Caravans ㉙
Rent a traditional horse-drawn caravan for a week and sample life in the slow lane.
Coolrain, County Laois; tel: 057 873 5178. www.horsedrawncaravans.com

Malahide Castle ㊴
A haunted castle and model railway in huge grounds, just north of Dublin
Malahide, County Dublin; tel: 01 816 9538; open 10am–5pm daily. www.malahidecastleandgardens.ie

SPAS AND HEALTH RESORTS

The Dawson ①
Hip combination of boutique hotel and spa right in the centre of Dublin.
35 Dawson Street, Dublin; tel: 01 612 7900. www.thedawson.ie

Ballycullen Lodge and Yoga Retreat ⑨
Reflexology, acupuncture, massage, reiki and homeopathy; other healthy options include forest walks and organic food.
Birch Hill, Ballycullen, Ashford, County Wicklow; tel: 0404 40000. www.ballycullenlodge.com

Brook Lodge and Wells Spa ⑫
The wells in the name of this hotel provide the spa water used in the flotation rooms, Finnish baths and pools.
Macreddin Village, County Wicklow; tel: 0402 36444. www.brooklodge.com

Kilmokea Country Manor and Gardens ⑰
The small spa in this 18th-century rectory includes an indoor pool, sauna and gym, and offers aromatherapy treatment.
Great Island, Campile, County Wexford; tel: 051 388109. www.kilmokea.com

Mount Juliet Golf and Spa Hotel ㉖
ESPA spa and health club with a swimming pool, sauna, steam room and gymnasium.
Thomastown, County Kilkenny; tel: 056 777 3000. www.mountjuliet.ie

Mount Wolseley Hotel Spa and Golf Resort ㉕
Set in green rolling hills, this has a championship golf course and tennis courts, as well as a Sanctuary Spa.
Tullow, County Carlow; tel: 059 918 0100. www.mountwolseley.ie

Osprey Hotel and Spa ㉝
Features a sauna, steam room, salt grotto and full- and half-day spa packages.
Devoy Quarter, Naas, County Kildare; tel: 045 881111. www.ospreyhotel.ie

Dunboyne Castle Hotel and Spa ㊲
Historic Dunboyne Castle has extensive mature gardens and is the perfect location for a spa, handy for Dublin Airport.
Dunboyne, County Meath; tel: 01 801 3500. www.dunboynecastlehotel.com

Castleknock Hotel and Country Club ㊶
The Tonic Health and Day Spa here offers yoga and Pilates classes, an indoor pool, sauna, steam room and Jacuzzi.
Porterstown Road, Castleknock, Dublin; tel: 01 640 6300. www.castleknockhotel.com

Bellinter House ㊹
Georgian house, home to the Bellinter Bathhouse, which specializes in seaweed baths and other spa indulgences.
Navan, County Meath; tel: 046 903 0900. www.bellinterhouse.com

OTHER SIGHTS IN THE BOOK

Left: Malahide Castle

SOUTHERN IRELAND

LOCAL FOOD

The Sage Café ①
Serving everything from sandwiches to delicious Dingle crab risotto, and with a deli counter doing takeaways too, the Sage Café is understandably always busy.
67–68 Catherine Street, Limerick, County Limerick; tel: 061 409458; open 9am–6pm Mon–Sat. www.thesagecafe.com

The Pantry ②
From big breakfasts to lunch and afternoon teas, the Pantry café and deli serves a great range of home-made food.
12 Quentin's Way, Nenagh, County Tipperary; tel: 067 31237; open 8:30am–6pm Mon–Sat. www.thepantrycafe.ie

Café Lucia ⑦
For breakfast, lunch or an early dinner, this is one place you'll find locals visiting for good home-cooked food at good prices.
2 Arundel Lane, Waterford; tel: 051 852553; open Mon–Sat 9am–5pm (until 7pm Fri).

Quealy's Café Bar ⑫
As the name says, Quealy's is part-café and part-bar, and has a lively atmosphere; make a pit stop here for inexpensive but exceptionally good local food, such as a seafood platter or smoked haddock pie.
82 O'Connell Street, Dungarvan, County Waterford; tel: 058 24555; open noon–9pm daily.

Farm Gate Café and Restaurant ⑲
You won't find fresher produce or better local eating than at this café-restaurant in Cork's famous English Market.
English Market, Cork; tel: 021 427 8134; open 8.30am–4.30pm Mon–Fri (until 5pm Sat). www.farmgate.ie

Crawford Gallery Café ⑲
The café at Crawford's Art Gallery is run by the granddaughter of the acclaimed Irish chef Myrtle Allen, and the menu focuses on local dishes and local produce.
Emmet Place, Cork; tel: 021 427 4415; open 8:30am–4pm Mon–Sat.

Denise's Delicious Gluten-Free Bakery ⑲
Artisan bakery selling gluten-free goods, made naturally with local ingredients; also available online and throughout Ireland.
Unit 17/18 Euro Business Park, Little Island, Cork; tel: 021 435 5536; open 9am–5pm Mon–Fri. www.delicious.ie

Fishy Fishy Café ㉑
Friendly quayside restaurant serving beautifully fresh local fish and seafood, run by the same people who own a fine fish-and-chip shop nearby.
Crowley's Quay, Kinsale, County Cork; tel: 021 470 0415; opening times subject to change during the season, reservations advisable. www.fishyfishy.ie

Cathleen's Country Kitchen ㉟
Good local produce, inexpensive home-cooked food, with delicious local dishes such as bacon and cabbage.
17 New Street, Killarney, County Kerry; tel: 064 663 3778; open 9am–6pm Mon–Sat.

Murphy's Ice Cream ㊳
With its fine dairy produce it's not surprising Ireland produces some good ice cream, and here at Murphy's it's all made in Dingle with milk from Kerry cows.
Strand Street, Dingle, County Kerry; tel: 066 915 2644; open 11am–6pm daily (until 10pm in summer). www.murphysicecream.ie

Annie May's ㉔
All-day restaurant-bar serving breakfast, lunch and dinner using local produce, with lots of Irish favourites on the menu.
11 Bridge Street, Skibbereen, County Cork; tel: 028 22930; open 8:30am–9pm daily. www.anniemays.ie

Glebe Gardens and Café ㉕
Seasonal produce from the gardens is used in wonderful dishes, such as the elderflower pannacotta.
Glebe Gardens, Baltimore, County Cork; tel: 028 20579; open Easter–Sep: 10am–10pm Wed–Sat, 10am–6pm Sun. www.glebegardens.com

FARMERS' MARKETS

Milk Market Limerick ①
One of the best markets in southern Ireland with fresh, local produce including seafood, breads, cheeses, sausages and jams;
Mungret Street, Limerick; Fri 10am–3pm, Sat 8am–3pm, Sun 11am–3pm. www.milkmarketlimerick.ie

Cahir Farmers' Market ④
An exceptionally good market highlighting the rich variety of local produce, including organic wines, juices, breads, meats, fish and, of course, fruit and vegetables.
Craft Granary Car Park, Church Street, Cahir, County Tipperary; every Sat, 9am–1pm. www.cahirfarmersmarket.ie

Dunhill Farmers' Market ⑨
Small, select monthly market with a chance to buy local speciality cheeses, eggs, vegetables, meats and breads baked fresh on site.
Parish Hall, Dunhill, County Waterford; tel: 051 396 234; last Sun of every month, 11:30am–2pm.

Carrick-on-Suir Farmers' Market ⑥
There are only a few stalls here, but the produce is excellent and there's a chance to chat with the producers.
Heritage Centre, Main Street, Carrick-on-Suir, County Tipperary; every Fri, 10am–2pm.

Dungarvan Farmers' Market ⑫
Here you can find farmhouse cheeses, traditional and not-so-traditional breads and cakes, organic meats, fruit and vegetables, and tempting puddings.
Grattan Square, Dungarvan, County Waterford; tel: 086 328 4594; every Thu, 9:30am–2pm. www.dungarvanmarket.wordpress.com

Midleton Farmers' Market ⑭
A small but select market with only a handful of stalls, but offering top produce, including seafood, shellfish, organic pork, vegetables and local cheeses.
Hospital Road, Midleton, County Cork; tel: 021 463 1323; every Sat, 9.30am–1pm. www.midletonfarmersmarket.com

Clonakilty Farmers' Market ㉓
Held twice a week, this market has a small selection of stalls selling local meat and fish, bread, cakes, honey and cheese.
Recorder's Alley, Clonakilty, County Cork; tel: 086 826 3429; every Fri and Sat, 9am–3pm. www.clonakiltymarket.com

Skibbereen Farmers' Market ㉔
The smell of fresh bread and pastries fills the air here at this thriving market, where cheeses, honeys, organic vegetables and arts and crafts are also on sale.
The Fairfield, Skibbereen, County Cork; tel: 087 285 1897; every Sat, 9:30am–1:30pm. www.skibbereenmarket.com

Schull Country Market ㉖
From burgers to herbal teas, sushi to pizzas, the range sold here, in this lovely harbour village on the southwest coast, is enormous.
Pier car park, Schull, County Cork; tel: 028 27824; every Sun, 11am–3pm. www.schullmarket.com

Listowel Farmers' Market ㊶
Cheeses and chutneys, breads and patisserie, seafood, vegetables, pies and herbs – all sold at this busy little market.
The Square, Listowel, County Kerry; tel: 087 613 5799 every Fri, 9am–2pm.

PUBS AND BARS

Henry Downes ⑦
Quirky, very Irish pub – in business since 1759 – that bottles its own whiskey and, bizarrely, has its own squash court – if you can find it (second right after the Bridge Hotel).
8–10 Thomas Street, Waterford; tel: 051 874 118; open from 5pm daily.

Left: Picturesque harbour village of Schull

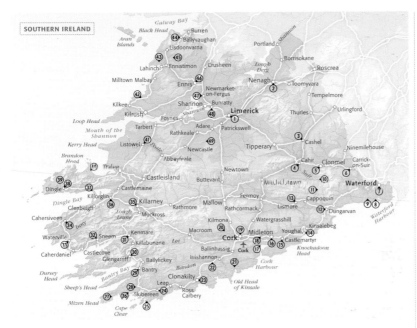

SOUTHERN IRELAND

Map references in circles correspond to the numbered entries below and in the Places to Stay panel.

Aulber House ③
Grand modern guesthouse with a sumptuous period feel, just a few minutes' walk from the centre of Cashel.
Golden Road, Cashel, County Tipperary; tel: 062 63713.
www.aulberhouse.com

Kilmaneen Farmhouse ⑤
On land farmed by the same family for six generations, this 200-year-old farmhouse has self-catering and B&B accommodation.
Newcastle, Clonmel, County Tipperary; tel: 052 613623.
www.kilmaneen.com

Glenorney ⑧
Beautiful house overlooking Tramore Bay on the Waterford coast, with comfortable rooms; the Irish breakfasts using local produce are outstandingly good.
Newtown, Tramore, County Waterford; tel: 051 381056.
www.glenorney.com

Glasha Farmhouse B&B ⑩
Welcoming B&B set in the lovely Nire Valley, offering packed lunches for walkers and a tasty home cooked evening meal.
Via Clonmel, Ballymacarbry, County Waterford; tel: 052 6136108.
www.glashafarmhouse.com

Sliabh gCua Farmhouse ⑪
A real rural retreat with breathtaking views and remarkable food, and with four championship golf courses nearby.
Ballynamult, Nr Dungarvan, County Waterford; tel: 058 47120.
www.waterfordfarms.com/sliabhgcua/

Dún Ard ⑫
Spectacular location with views of the Comeragh Mountains and Dungarvan Bay. The perfect base to explore the area's cosy pubs and fine restaurants.
Na Ceithre Gaotha, Dungarvan, County Waterford; tel: 058 46782.
www.dunard.ie

Hagal Farm ㉙
A farm stay like no other, with holistic treatments and massages in a 150-year-old farmhouse set in 2 hectares (5 acres).
Coomleigh West, Bantry, County Cork; tel: 027 66838. www.hagalfarm.com

Kingfisher Lodge ㊱
One of the best B&Bs in Killarney; generous breakfasts, a lovely garden, and just a few minutes' stroll to the town centre.
Lewis Road, Killarney, County Kerry; tel: 064 663 7131.
www.kingfisherkillarney.com

Drumcreehy Guesthouse ㊸
With views over Galway Bay, friendly hosts, open fires, and complimentary tea, coffee and cakes, this is a dream of a guesthouse in which to stay while exploring the Burren.
Ballyvaughan, County Clare; tel: 065 707 7377.
www.drumcreehyhouse.com

The Fairways Bar ②
Country pub with a cosy snug bar, with cushion-strewn banquettes and, in winter, an open fire. There is a large bar-dining area with an upmarket menu and a fancier gourmet restaurant, the Orchard, attached.
Kilruane, Nenagh, County Tipperary; tel: 067 41444; open daily.
www.thefairwaysbar.ie

Dalton's ㉑
This Kinsale mainstay has been popular for years, and combines exceptionally good pub lunches with a typical Irish bar atmosphere in the evenings.
3 Market Street, Kinsale, County Cork; tel: 021 477 7957; open daily.
www.ireland-guide.com

The Poachers Inn ㉒
Local seafood is the draw here at what looks like an ordinary, cosy little pub – but which also happens to have a marvellous menu created by a top chef.
Clonakilty Road, Bandon, County Cork; tel: 023 884 1159; open daily; restaurant 12–9pm Wed–Sat, 12.30–3:30pm Sun.

An Súgán ㉓
There's no missing this busy, brightly coloured and cheerful pub, and the food and drink is some of the best in town, from smoked salmon to the local Clonakilty black pudding.
41 Wolfe Tone Street, Clonakilty, County Cork; tel: 023 883 3719.
www.ansugan.com

Mary Ann's Bar and Restaurant ㉔
A 19th-century pub in a 15th-century building, but the menu, including crab, salmon and the catch of the day, is as fresh and modern as they come.
Castletownshend, Skibbereen, County Cork; tel: 028 36146; open daily.
www.westcorkweek.com/maryanns

Levis's Bar ㉘
This 150-year-old bar-cum-grocery store, now run by just one of the two Levis sisters, is exactly the kind of Irish pub that visitors hope to find – a warm welcome and a wonderful, traditional interior full of people having a good time.
Corner House, Main Street, Ballydehob, County Cork; tel: 028 37118; open daily.

The Horseshoe ㉛
It's almost impossible to resist this place, with an outside adorned with colourful flowers; the unpretentious interior belies an award-winning menu and wine list.
3 Main Street, Kenmare, County Kerry; tel: 064 664 1553; open daily.
www.horseshoebarkenmare.com

The Smugglers Inn ㉝
This inn was once a farmhouse and has almost 200 years of history, plus stunning views and a highly rated seafood restaurant, with fresh lobsters a speciality. *Cliff Road, Waterville, County Kerry; tel: 066 947 4330; open daily.*
www.thesmugglersinn.com

O'Neill's ㉞
In the same family for 150 years, this simple but very hospitable pub is at the tip of the Iveragh peninsula; the summer seafood bar has made this place a legendary spot.
Renard Point, Cahirciveen, County Kerry; tel: 066 947 2165; open daily; food served Apr–Oct only.

Morrissey's Seafood Bar and Restaurant ㊷
With a lovely setting by the River Cree, the waterside terrace of this family-run bar is the perfect spot to enjoy everything from a refreshing pint to fish and chips.
Doonbeg, County Clare; tel: 065 9055304; open daily.
www.morrisseysdoonbeg.com

Vaughans Anchor Inn ㊸
Near the stunning Cliffs of Moher, this multi-award-winning pub serves superb seafood but remains a family establishment with a shop attached.
Main Street, Liscannor, County Clare; tel: 065 708 1548; open daily.
www.vaughans.ie

Vaughans Pub ㊹
One of the best music venues in southern Ireland, in a homely bar with an open fire and hearty food; Céilidh dance every Sunday evening.
Main Street, Kilfenora, County Clare; tel: 065 708 8004; open daily.
www.vaughanspub.ie

Fortview House ㉗
Working farm, in a glorious location near Mizen Head, offering both self-catering and B&B accommodation; the breakfasts are outstandingly good.
Gurtyowen, Toormore, Goleen, County Cork; tel: 028 35324.
www.fortviewhousegoleen.com

The Shores Country House B&B ㊵
Modern house furnished in traditional style; some rooms have views of Brandon Bay on the Dingle Peninsula. It offers much-acclaimed breakfasts and dinners.
Cappatigue, Castlegregory, County Kerry; tel: 066 713 9196.
www.shorescountryhouse.com

Newpark House ㊻
Farmhouse on a grand country-house scale surrounded by beech and oak trees; some rooms have canopied beds.
Roslevan, Ennis, County Clare; tel: 065 682 1233.
www.newparkhouse.com

FESTIVALS AND EVENTS

Spraoi ⑦
Waterford's annual Spraoi Festival takes over the city for three days and includes street parades with bands and buskers from all over the world.
Various venues, Waterford; tel: 051 841808; late Jul.www.spraoi.com

Waterford Imagine Arts Festival ⑦
This ten-day annual festival includes music, dance, literature, theatre, film, visual arts and special events for children.
Various venues, Waterford; tel: 076 110 2856; late Oct or early Nov.
www.imagineartsfestival.com

Cork Film Festival ⑲
Spread over eight days, Ireland's biggest and oldest film festival has premieres of documentaries and short films, and attracts famous actors and directors.
Various venues, Cork; tel: 021 427171; Nov. www.corkfilmfest.org

Cork Folk Festival ⑲
The four-day Cork Folk Festival has been going since 1980, with numerous stage performances, masterclasses and impromptu sessions in the pubs too.
Various venues, Cork; early Oct. www.corkfolkfestival.com

Cork Jazz Festival ⑲
Four days of the world's top musicians turn Cork into a jazz-lover's dream, with some drama productions thrown in.
Various venues, Cork; tel: 021 427 8979; late Oct.
www.guinnessjazzfestival.com

Killorglin Puck Fair ㊱
Ireland's oldest fair is held, without fail, for three days on the same dates every year: see parades, music, street theatre and the crowning of a goat as King Puck.
Killorglin, County Kerry; tel: 066 976 2366; 10–12 Aug. www.puckfair.ie

Above: Lismore Heritage Centre

Cobh Peoples Regatta ⑰
Historically one of the biggest sailing regattas in Europe, this three-day event is still going strong in Cobh Harbour.
Cobh, County Cork; tel: 021 481 1347; Aug. www.cobhpeoplesregatta.com

Baltimore Fiddle Fair ㉕
Baltimore comes to life for four days with concerts and countless fiddle sessions.
Baltimore, County Cork; tel: 086 375 3380; early May. www.fiddlefair.com

Baltimore Seafood Festival ㉕
Cork is renowned for its seafood and this three-day festival is the chance to join in and celebrate it, with rowing races, net-mending competitions and more.
Baltimore, County Cork; tel: 028 20125; late May. www.baltimoreseafoodfest.com

Killarney Summerfest ㉟
This eclectic festival lasts for over two weeks, and has arts and outdoor events as well as activities for children.
Scotts Garden, Killarney, County Kerry; tel: 064 667 1560; Jul. www.killarneysummerfest.com

Dingle Regatta ㊳
A day of boat races in the harbour and carousing in the evening, all celebrating the skills of local sailors and boatmen.
Dingle Harbour, Dingle, County Kerry; tel: 066 915 1907; Aug.

Dingle Races ㊳
For a weekend in August, a Dingle field is transformed into a racecourse, with over 20 races and tens of thousands of people from all over Ireland and beyond.
Ballintaggart, Dingle, County Kerry; tel: 087 927 2556; Aug. www.dingleraces.ie

MUSEUMS AND GALLERIES

Cork Butter Museum ⑲
This unique and entertaining museum tells the fascinating story of one of Ireland's most famous products.
The Tony O'Reilly Centre, O'Connell Square, Cork; tel: 021 4300 600; open Mar–Oct: 10am–5pm daily (till 6pm Jul–Aug); Nov–Feb 11am–3pm Sat and Sun only. www.corkbutter.museum

The Hunt Museum ①
Picasso, Renoir and Henry Moore are just some of the famous names in this extensive private art collection.
Rutland Street, Limerick; tel: 061 312833; open 10am–5pm Mon–Sat, 2–5pm Sun. www.huntmuseum.com

Nenagh Heritage Centre and Museum ②
Housed in what was the Governor's House and the gatehouse for the town jail, this museum includes a re-created school room, dairy, kitchen, condemned cells and the execution area.
The Governor's House, Kirkham Street, Nenagh, County Tipperary; tel: 067 33850; open 10am–4pm Tues–Fri. www.nenagh.ie/places-of-interest/details/nenagh-heritage-centre

Brú Ború Cultural Centre ③
Found at the foot of the Rock of Cashel, this is a wonderful multimedia exploration of Irish culture and, in particular, its music, with evening shows.
Cashel, County Tipperary; tel: 062 61122; open 9am–5pm Mon–Fri; mid-Jun–late August: also Tues–Sat until 11pm . www. bruboru.ie

Tipperary County Museum ⑤
This museum, which tells the story of the county of Tipperary, has won several awards for its imaginative displays, and houses visiting exhibitions too.
Mick Delahunty Square, Clonmel, County Tipperary; tel: 052 613 4551; open 10am–4.45pm Tue–Sat. www.tipperarycoco.ie/museum

Carrick-on-Suir Heritage Centre ⑥
This former church now combines an interesting heritage museum with the town's Tourist Information Centre, making it any visitor's first port of call.
Main Street, Carrick-on-Suir, County Tipperary; tel: 051 640200; open 10am–1pm and 2pm–4pm Tues–Fri. www.carrickonsuirheritagecentre.ie

Waterford Treasures at the Granary Museum ⑦
Waterford's main museum contains exceptionally good and imaginative displays that tell the city's story using many impressive multimedia techniques.
Merchants Quay, Waterford; tel: 076 110 2501; open 9.15am–6pm Mon–Fri (until 5pm Sep–May), 9:30am–6pm Sat (10am–5pm Sep–May), 11am–6pm Sun (until 5pm Sep–May). www.waterfordtreasures.com

Waterford County Museum ⑫
Run by enthusiastic volunteers, this interesting museum houses fascinating artifacts, including coins and militaria. There's also maritime history, a shop and genealogical information.
St Augustine Street, Dungarvan, County Waterford; tel: 058 45960; open 10am–5pm Mon–Fri. www.waterfordcountymuseum.ie

Lismore Heritage Centre ⑬
There was a monastery in Lismore as long ago as AD 636, and this excellent centre tells the town's story through to the present day with entertaining audio-visual displays.
Main Street, Lismore, County Waterford; tel: 058 54975; open 9am–5.30pm Mon–Fri; Apr–Nov: also open 10am–5pm Sat, noon–5pm Sun. www.discoverlismore.com

Fox's Lane Folk Museum ⑭
One of those fascinating little museums that displays all sorts of everyday items from the past – from sewing machines to glove stretchers – showing how previous generations lived.
North Cross Lane, Youghal, County Cork; tel: 024 91145; open Jul–Sep: 10am–1pm and 2–6pm Tue–Sat; other times by appointment.

Crawford Municipal Art Gallery ⑲
Here you can view an extensive permanent collection of art by important 19th- and 20th-century Irish and international artists, as well as frequent visiting exhibitions.
Emmet Place, Cork; tel: 021 480 5042; open 10am–5pm Mon–Sat (till 8pm Thu). www.crawfordartgallery.ie

Cork Public Museum ⑲
Everything from ancient archaeology to modern sport in the city is presented in this first-class and sizeable museum.
Fitzgerald Park, Cork; tel: 021 427 0679; open 11am–1pm and 2:15–5pm Mon–Fri, 11am–1pm and 2:15–4pm Sat; Apr–Sep: also open 3–5pm Sun. www.corkcity.ie/services/corporateandexternalaffairs/museum/

Kinsale Regional Museum ㉑
This comprehensive collection covers everything to do with Kinsale, including the story of the Kinsale Giant, the Battle of Kinsale, and the sinking of the Cunard liner Lusitania off the coast here in 1915.
Market Square, Kinsale, County Cork; tel: 021 477 7930; open 10am–1pm and 2–5pm Mon–Sat, 2–5pm Sun. http://homepage.eircom. net/~kinsalemuseum/index.html

THINGS TO DO WITH KIDS

Fota Wildlife Park ⑱
The park is designed to allow the animals to roam as freely as possible; the cheetahs' feeding time is not to be missed.
Carrigtwohill, County Cork; tel: 021 481 2678; open 10am–4.30pm Mon–Sat, 10.30am–4.30pm Sun. www.fotawildlife.ie

Cork City Gaol Heritage Centre ⑲
One of the city's major visitor attractions, this atmospheric centre really brings home what prison conditions were like for the inmates.
Convent Avenue, Sunday's Well, Cork; tel: 021 430 5022; Apr–Sep: open 9.30am–5pm daily; Oct–Mar: 10am–4pm daily. www.corkcitygaol.com

Mitchelstown Cave ④
One of the finest show caves in Europe; guided tours lead visitors through just a fraction of the enormous underground network to see some of the most unusual shapes and structures.
Burncourt, Cahir, County Tipperary; tel: 052 746 7246; open Feb: 10am–4pm daily; Mar–Oct: 10am–5pm daily; Nov: 10am–4pm daily; Dec–Jan: weekends only.

Cahir Castle ④
Dating from 1142, Cahir Castle is one of the biggest and best-preserved castles in Ireland, thanks to 19th-century restoration work. There are plenty of nooks, crannies and rooms for children to explore.
Cahir, County Tipperary, tel: 052 744 1011, open mid-Oct–Feb: 9.30am–6.30pm daily; Mar–mid-Jun: 9:30am–5:30pm daily; mid-Jun–Aug: 9am–6.30pm daily; Sep–mid-Oct 9.30am–5.30pm daily.

West Cork Model Railway Village ㉓
There are road-train rides to be had around Clonakilty town, as well as the delightful and detailed scale model of the West Cork Railway as it would have looked in the 1940s.
The Station, Inchydoney Road, Clonakilty, County Cork; tel: 023 883 3224; open 11am–5pm daily. www.modelvillage.ie

Schull Planetarium ㉖
The Republic of Ireland's only planetarium is situated in the little Cork town of Schull. It is run through the Community College and offers a variety of shows throughout the summer months.
Community College, Schull, County Cork; tel: 028 28315; open Jun–Sep: show times vary.
www.westcorkweb.ie/planetarium/index.html

Celtic and Prehistoric Museum ㊳
Mammoth fossils, dinosaur eggs and skeletons: there's a lot to entertain both children and adults at this museum, which tells the intriguing story of ancient Dingle and its environs.
Dingle, Peninsula, County Kerry; tel: 087 915 9191; open Mar–Nov: 10am–5:30pm daily.
www.celticmuseum.com

Dingle Oceanworld Aquarium ㊳
Plenty of hands-on experiences for children in this top-class aquarium, which explores maritime life both locally and internationally. At the Touch Tank, friendly rays swim up to be petted.
The Wood, Dingle, County Kerry; tel: 066 915 2111; open 10am–5pm daily. www.dingle-oceanworld.ie

Fungi the Dolphin ㊳
Take the children to the harbour in Dingle and look out for its most famous resident, Fungi the bottlenose dolphin, or admire his bronze sculpture. Hire a boat from the pier to see Fungi up close *(see pp86–7).*
The Harbour, Dingle, County Kerry.

International Sailing Centre ⑰
Older children have the chance to learn sailing skills or surfing in this sheltered harbour; youngsters can join in supervised sessions of canoeing and water fun.
East Hill, Cobh, County Cork; tel: 021 481 1237; courses available to book all year round. www.sailcork.com

Blarney Castle ⑳
Famous for its Stone of Eloquence, kissed by millions, but also a magical place for exploring ruins and curious rock formations, including the Wishing Steps and the Witch's Kitchen.
Blarney, County Cork; tel: 021 438 5252; open Nov–Feb: 9am–5pm daily; Mar–Apr: 9am–6pm daily; May: 9am–6.30pm Mon–Sat, 9am–6pm Sun; Jun–Aug: 9am–7pm Mon–Sat, 9am–6pm Sun; Sept: 9am–6.30pm Mon–Jul, 9am–6pm Sun; Oct: 9am–6pm daily.
www.blarneycastle.ie

Glengarriff Nature Reserve ㉚
Take the children out to this lovely wooded nature reserve to look for otters, stoats, bats, owls and more.
Glengarriff, County Cork; tel: 027 63636; open access daily.
www.glengarriffnaturereserve.ie

Inch Strand Beach ㊲
The most famous and beautiful beach in Ireland is a movie star in its own right – it famously featured in the 1970 film *Ryan's Daughter* – and has huge stretches of beautiful sand to explore.
Inch, south of Dingle, County Kerry.

SPAS AND HEALTH RESORTS

Radisson Blu Hotel and Spa Limerick ①
In a handy location, this hotel's spa has its own steam room, tropical rain shower and outdoor hot tub.
Ennis Road, Limerick; tel: 061 456200.
www.radissonblu.ie/hotel-limerick

Coolbawn Quay Lakeshore Spa ②
On the shores of Lough Derg, this spa is modelled on an Irish village, and has luxurious "cottages". Its facilities include a natural spring-water pool, a eucalyptus steam room and a sauna.
Coolbawn, Lough Derg, County Tipperary; tel: 067 28158. www.coolbawnquay.com

Hayfield Manor Hotel ⑲
A 5-star hotel right in the centre of Cork, with mature gardens, nine spa-treatment rooms, an acclaimed restaurant, and many "Hotel of the Year" awards to its name.
Perrott Avenue, College Road, Cork; tel: 021 484 5900.
www.hayfieldmanor.ie

Dingle Skellig Hotel and Spa ㊳
This 4-star hotel is situated on the most westerly tip of Europe, in an area that *National Geographic* magazine described as the most beautiful on Earth.
Dingle, County Kerry; tel: 066 915 0200.
www.dingleskellig.com

Castlemartyr ⑮
The luxury 5-star Castlemartyr is set in 50 hectares (220 acres) of woodland and has a stunning modern spa, a championship golf course, archery, heritage trails and many other activities right in the grounds.
Castlemartyr, County Cork; tel: 021 421 9000. www.castlemartyrresort.ie

Carlton Kinsale Hotel and Spa ㉑
This 4-star resort lies in 36 hectares (90 acres) of woodland and has extensive views over Oysterhaven Bay; its spa has ten treatment rooms, plus a swimming pool, sauna and gym.
Rathmore Road, Kinsale, County Cork; tel: 021 470 6000.
www.carltonkinsalehotel.com

Inchydoney Island Lodge and Spa ㉓
With its views over the ocean and two sweeping beaches, this is certainly one of the most idyllic retreats to be found in the country. Treatments include seawater therapy.
Clonakilty, County Cork; tel: 023 883 3143.
www.inchydoneyisland.com

Park Hotel Kenmare ㉛
This 5-star spa hotel retreat is a short walk from the centre of Kenmare, and includes a lap-pool and sauna, as well as tennis, t'ai chi courses, aquaerobics and even a 12-seater cinema.
Kenmare, County Kerry; tel: 064 664 1200. www.parkkenmare.com

Parknasilla Resort ㉜
Luxury spa resort with its own 12-hole golf course and outdoor activities for all the family.
Sneem, County Kerry; tel: 064 667 5600. www.parknasillresort.ie

Dromoland Castle Hotel ㊼
This medieval fortress can trace its history back 1,000 years, but today it is a 5-star, fabulously furnished luxury resort hotel with a spa set within the castle grounds.
Newmarket-on-Fergus, County Clare; tel: 061 368144. www.dromoland.ie

Bunratty Castle Hotel ㊽
This luxury hotel has its own spa, and there's also a leisure club, pool, sauna and steam room.
Bunratty, County Clare; tel: 061 478700. www.bunrattycastlehotel.com

The Mustard Seed at Echo Lodge ㊼
Beautiful, homely country house with stylish ambience in abundance. Comfortable rooms with old-world charm will ensure you won't want to check out.
Ballingarry, County Limerick; tel: 069 68508. www.mustardseed.ie

OTHER SIGHTS IN THE BOOK

Cork ⑲ *(see pp52–3).* **Dingle Peninsula** ㊴ *(see pp86–7).* **Bunratty Castle** ㊼ *(see pp160–1).*

Below: Cahir Castle in County Tipperary

NORTH WALES

LOCAL FOOD

The Seahorse Restaurant ①
A choice of local meat, fresh fish and seafood is served in this Grade-II-listed building with a daily changing menu.
7 Church Walks, Llandudno, Gwynedd; tel: 01492 875315; open from 4:30pm daily. www.the-seahorse.co.uk

West Shore Beach Café ①
This delightful café, with stunning views of Conwy bay, serves tasty homemade dishes using local recipes.
West Shore Promenade, Dale Road, Llandudno, Gwynedd; tel: 01492 872958; open Feb–Mar and Nov–early Dec: 10am–4:30pm Wed–Sun; Apr–Oct: 10am–5pm daily. www.westshorebeachcafe.com

Edwards of Conwy ④
Traditional, award-winning master butcher renowned for its Welsh lamb and beef.
18 High Street, Conwy; tel: 01492 592443; open 7am–5:30pm Mon–Sat. www.edwardsofconwy.co.uk

The Sun Trevor ㉓
Scenic, family-friendly inn close to the Llangollen Canal, offering substantial meals.
Sun Bank, Llangollen, Denbighshire; tel: 01978 860651; bar menu: noon–5pm daily; evening menu: noon–8:30pm daily. www.suntrevor.co.uk

Penhelig Arms ㉗
Stylish restaurant serving fresh local seafood in an 18th-century seafront inn.
27–29 Terrace Road, Aberdovey, Gwynedd; tel: 01654 767215; open noon–10:30pm Mon–Thu, noon–11pm Fri–Sat, noon–2:30pm Sun. www.penheligarms.com

SugarPlum Tearoom ⑮
Choose from a wide selection of freshly made sandwiches here, as well as quiches and cakes, or indulge in afternoon tea.
The Old Station, Rhewl, Ruthin, Denbighshire; tel: 01824 702852; open 9:30am–4:30pm Mon–Sat, 10am–4pm Sun. www.sugarplumtearoom.co.uk

On the Hill ⑮
A seasonally changing menu, featuring delicious dishes made with locally sourced produce, is offered at this bistro.
1 Upper Clwyd St, Ruthin, Denbighshire; tel: 01824 707736; open noon–2pm and 6:30–9pm Tue–Sat, 5–9pm Sun. www.onthehillrestaurant.co.uk

Yr Hen Fecws ㉛
Try imaginative local specialities with an international twist at this popular restaurant with seven guest rooms.
16 Lombard Street, Porthmadog, Gwynedd; tel: 01766 514625; open 8am–4pm Mon–Sat. www.henfecws.com

Iechyd Da Delicatessen ㊷
Buy local cheeses, smoked fish, honey, chocolates and a range of international delicacies here.
Station Road, Betws-y-Coed, Conwy; tel: 01690 710994; open 9:30am–5.30pm daily. www.delinorthwales.co.uk

Wal Restaurant ㊿
Enjoy succulent Welsh black cow steaks sourced from Llanfair Hall (4 miles away), plus Italian dishes and all-day-breakfasts.
Palace Street, Caernarfon, Gwynedd; tel: 01286 674383; open 9am–3pm Sun–Tue, 9am–9pm Wed–Sat. www.walrestaurant.co.uk

Lle Hari Restaurant ㊸
Try local lamb, venison, pork and fish at this smart and popular hotel restaurant.
The Meadowsweet Hotel, Station Road, Llanrwst, Conwy; tel: 01492 642111; open 5pm–9pm Tue–Sat, 6pm–8pm Sun–Mon. www.eating-northwales.co.uk

Blas ar Fwyd ㊸
Deli with a huge range of cheeses, chutneys, preserves, cakes and more, with a restaurant opposite.
Heol yr Orsaf, Llanrwst, Conwy; tel: 01492 640215; deli open 9am–5:30pm Mon–Sat; restaurant open 10:30am–8pm Mon–Fri, 10:30am–9pm Sat, 10:30am–4:30pm Sun. www.blasarfwyd.com

Hooton's Homegrown (51)
Pick your own strawberries, raspberries and vegetables in season at two sites with views of Mount Snowdon.
Gwydryn Hîr, Brynsiencyn, Anglesey; tel: 01248 430322; open from mid-Jun. www.hootonshomegrown.co.uk

The Lobster Pot (57)
Long-established seafood restaurant serving fresh local crab, lobster, oysters and scallops, as well as meat dishes.
Church Bay, Anglesey; tel: 01407 730241; open noon–1:30pm and 6pm–late Tue–Sat, noon–2pm Sun. www.thelobsterpotrestaurant.co.uk

Pier House Bistro (64)
Feast on local mussels here, while admiring the stunning views of the Menai Strait and the Snowdonia Mountain Range.
Seafront, Beaumaris, Anglesey; tel: 01248 811055; open 9am–9pm daily. www.pierhousebistro.com

Kyffin Café Deli (53)
Sample flavourful dishes from around the world at Bangor's only vegetarian café and tuck into home-made cakes.
129 High Street, Bangor, Gwynedd; tel: 01248 355161; open 9:30am–5:30pm Mon–Sat. www.courtyardcuisine.com

The Old Boathouse Café & Restaurant (62)
Enjoy sea views and a menu featuring salads, grills, fish, lamb and lobster.
Red Wharf Bay, Anglesey; tel: 01248 852731; open 10am–9pm daily (from 9am in summer). www.boathouserestaurantanglesey.co.uk

FARMERS' MARKETS

Mold Farmers' Market ⑬
Buy locally produced organic meats and veg, as well as handmade crafts.
St Mary's Church Hall, King Street, Mold, Flintshire; tel: 01745 561999; first and third Sat of every month, 9am–1pm. www.celynfarmersmarket.co.uk

Wrexham Farmers' Market ⑳
Local producers sell everything from meats and eggs to cakes and honey.
Queen's Square, Wrexham; tel: 01978 292540; third Fri of every month, 9:30am–1pm. www.fmiw.co.uk

Glyndwr Farmers' Market ㉔
Fruit, veg, preserves, cheeses and more are sold at this market on a working farm.
Rhug Estate, Corwen, Denbighshire; tel: 07813 020933; May–Oct: first Sun of every month, 10am–4pm. www.fmiw.co.uk

Dolgellau Farmers' Market ㉖
Plenty of local food and drink is on offer at this busy monthly market in the Snowdonia National Park.
Eldon Square, Dolgellau, Gwynedd; tel: 01341 450211; Mar–Dec: third Sun of every month, 10am–2pm. www.fmiw.co.uk

Anglesey Farmers' Market (65)
Local fruit, veg and much more at this popular monthly market.
David Hughes School, Pentraeth Road, Menai Bridge, Anglesey; tel: 01248 725700; third Sat of every month, 9am–1pm. www. angleseyfarmersmarket.co.uk

PUBS AND BARS

George & Dragon ④
Historic pub full of character near Conwy Castle, with beer garden, restaurant and guest rooms.
21 Castle Street, Conwy; tel: 01492 592305; open daily. www.georgeanddragonconwy.co.uk

We Three Loggerheads ⑭
Facing the picturesque Loggerheads Country Park outside Mold, this inn serves a range of cask ales and home-cooked meals.
Ruthin Road, Loggerheads, Gwernymynydd, Denbighshire; tel: 01352 810337; open daily. www.we-three-loggerheads.co.uk

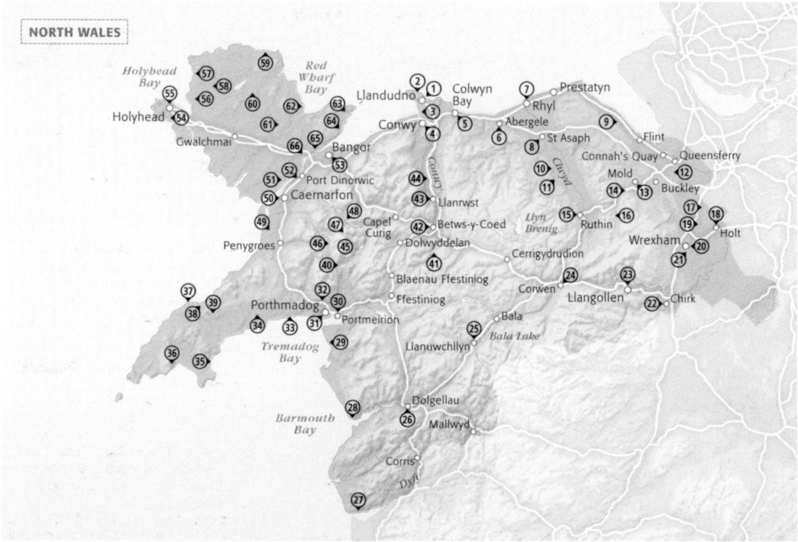

Glan Yr Afon Inn ⑨
Picturesque village pub with microbrewery
ales, restaurant and guest rooms.
*Dolphin, Milwr, Hollywell, Flintshire;
tel: 01352 710052; open daily.
www.glanyrafoninn.co.uk*

**Guildhall Tavern Hotel &
Restaurant** ⑩
A former 16th-century coaching inn with
plenty of character and offering traditional
pub food and Sunday lunches.
*Hall Square, Denbigh, Denbighshire;
tel: 01745 816533; open daily.
www.guildhalltavernhotel.co.uk.*

Pant-Yr-Ochain ⑲
Sample a wide range of real ales at this
pub built into an historic manor house.
*Old Wrexham Road, Gresford, Wrexham;
tel: 01978 853525; open daily
www.brunningandprice.co.uk/pantyrochain*

Ty Coch Inn ㊲
Quaint red-brick village inn on the Lleyn
Peninsular that serves real ales and food
in friendly surroundings.
*Porthdinllaen, Gwynedd, tel: 01758
720498; open 11am–11pm Mon–Sat,
11am–4pm Sun. www.tycoch.co.uk*

Cwellyn Arms ㊻
A popular pub in the heart of Snowdonia,
with a range of dormitory, B&B and
camp-site accommodation.
*Rhyd Ddu, Gwynedd; tel: 01766 890321;
open daily. www.snowdoninn.co.uk*

The Black Boy Inn ㊾
The oldest pub in town, this is a cosy
stop for local ales.
*Northgate Street, Caernarfon, Gwynedd;
tel: 01286 673604; open daily.
www.black-boy-inn.com*

The Ship Inn ㊼
Historic, award-winning pub on the shore,
serving regional real ales and 48 whiskies.
*Red Wharf Bay, Anglesey; tel: 01248
852568; open daily.
www.shipinnredwharfbay.co.uk*

Ye Olde Bull's Head Inn ㊽
Historic 15th-century inn with oak-beamed
ceilings, log fire, restaurant, brasserie and
elegant guest rooms.
*Castle Street, Beaumaris, Anglesey;
tel: 01248 810329; open daily.
www.bullsheadinn.co.uk*

Four Crosses Inn ㊾
Family-friendly pub with an extensive
menu and views of the Menai Strait.
*Pentraeth Road, Menai Bridge, Anglesey;
tel: 01248 712230; open daily.
www.robinsonsbrewery.com*

PLACES TO STAY

Bodysgallen Hall & Spa ①
Historic mansion with a fine restaurant,
15 spacious rooms and 16 cottage suites
in the extensive grounds.
*Llandudno, Conwy; tel: 01492 584466.
www.bodysgallen.com*

Above: Gladstone's Library in Hawarden

The Quay Hotel & Spa ③
Luxurious waterfront hotel that boasts
smart rooms and suites, a gym and an
excellent restaurant.
*Deganwy Quay, Deganwy, Conwy; tel:
01492 564100. www.quayhotel.com*

The Kinmel Arms Hotel ⑥
Choose from four individually designed
suites, with balconies or patios.
*The Village, St George, Abergele,
Conwy; tel: 01745 832207.
www.thekinmelarms.co.uk*

Pier Hotel Rhyl ⑦
Seafront adult-only hotel with a choice
of cosy rooms, plus bar and restaurant.
*23 East Parade, Rhyl, Denbighshire;
tel: 01745 350280.
www.pierhotelrhyl.co.uk*

The Talardy Hotel ⑧
Attractive, child-friendly boutique hotel
with 11 imaginatively themed rooms, two
restaurants, a wine bar and a pub.
*The Roe, St Asaph, Denbighshire; tel: 01745
799314. www.talardyhotelstasaph.co.uk*

Gladstone's Library ⑫
Grand Victorian residential library, with
26 peaceful en suite rooms, a restaurant
and 250,000 books to browse.
*Church Lane, Hawarden, Flintshire; tel:
01244 532350. www.gladstoneslibrary.org*

Beaufort Park Hotel ⑬
Large modern hotel and conference centre
with comfortable rooms and suites,
restaurant and coffee house.
*Mold, Flintshire; tel: 01352 758646.
www.beaufortparkhotel.co.uk*

Rossett Hall Hotel ⑰
Attractive Georgian house with tasteful
en suite rooms and an upmarket restaurant.
*Chester Road, Rossett, Wrexham;
tel: 01244 571000.
www.rossetthallhotel.co.uk*

The Hand Hotel ㉒
Welcoming 17th-century coaching inn with
en suite rooms, a restaurant and bar.
*Church Street, Chirk, Wrexham; tel: 01691
773472. www.thehandhotelchirk.co.uk*

Cartref Guest House ㉗
Peaceful Edwardian house not far from the
beach, with five neat rooms and a garden.
*Aberdovey, Gwynedd; tel: 01654 767273.
www.cartref-aberdovey.co.uk*

Ty'r Graig Castle ㉘
Grand, cliff-top Victorian mansion offering
11 period-style rooms with views of
Cardigan Bay.
*Llanaber Road, Barmouth, Gwynedd; tel:
01341 280470. www.tyrgraigcastle.co.uk*

Snowdon Lodge ㉜
Busy, friendly hostel for groups, with a
range of dormitory accommodation and
private rooms, plus a cosy lounge.
*Lawrence House, Church Street, Tremadog,
Porthmadog, Gwynedd; tel: 01766
515354. www.snowdonlodge.co.uk*

Venetia ㉟
Trendy boutique hotel with five chic,
individually designed rooms and a classy
seafood restaurant.
*Lon Sarn Bach, Abersoch, Gwynedd; tel:
01758 713354. www.venetiawales.com*

Caeau Capel Hotel ㊳
Homely, old-fashioned country-house
hotel in large gardens near the coast,
with 16 restful rooms.
*Rhodfa'r Mor, Nefyn, Gwynedd;
tel: 01758 720240.
www.caeaucapelhotel.com*

The Old Rectory ㊴
Homely B&B rooms in a Georgian house
and a separate self-catering cottage and
lodge in the heart of the Llyn Peninsula.
*Boduan, nr Pwllheli, Gwynedd; tel:
01758 721519. www.theoldrectory.net*

Swallow Falls Complex ㊷
Beautifully located Edwardian hotel with
smart modern rooms, high-quality hostel
dorms and a camp site.
*Holyhead Road, Betws-y-Coed, Conwy;
tel: 01690 710796.
www.swallowfallshotel.co.uk*

Plas Maenan Country House ㊹
Tastefully furnished rooms and large suites
are available in this welcoming mansion
with mountain views.
*Conwy Valley, nr Llanrwst, Conwy;
tel: 01492 660232.
www.plas-maenan-hotel.co.uk*

Ben's Bunkhouse ㊽
Simple dorm rooms, with kitchen and
lounge, at the foot of Mount Snowdon.
*Nant Peris, Llanberis, Gwynedd; tel: 07989
500657. www.bensbunkhouse.co.uk*

Eryl Môr Hotel ㊾
Country house hotel overlooking the
Menai Strait with neat en suite rooms
and a restaurant.
*2 Upper Garth Road, Bangor,
Gwynedd; tel: 01248 354042.
www.erylmorhotel.co.uk*

The Trearddur Bay Hotel ㊾
Family-run hotel on a blue-flag beach,
with spacious rooms, a pool and restaurant.
*Trearddur Bay, Anglesey; tel: 01407
860301. www.trearddurbayhotel.co.uk*

Penrhyn Farm ㊼
Choose between five luxury self-catering
cottages at this seaside farm.
*Llanfwrog, Anglesey; tel: 01407 730134.
www.penrhynfarm.com*

Drws-y-Coed Farm Guest House ㊿
Working cattle and sheep farm offering
spacious en suite rooms in a peaceful
rural setting.
*Llanerch-y-Medd, Anglesey; tel: 01248
470473. www.drwsycoedguesthouse.co.uk*

The Liverpool Arms Hotel (64)
Attractively renovated Georgian inn, with 10 stylish rooms, some with four-poster beds, and a traditional tavern.
Castle Street, Beaumaris, Anglesey; tel: 01248 810362. www.liverpoolarms.co.uk

Auckland Arms Hotel (65)
Cosy B&B accommodation in a family-run hotel with a bar and pleasant garden.
Water Street, Menai Bridge, Anglesey; tel: 01248 712545.

Plas Cadnant (65)
Self-catering in five beautifully restored cottages set in private parkland.
Cadnant Road, Menai Bridge, Anglesey; tel: 01248 717007. www.plascadnantgardens.co.uk

FESTIVALS AND EVENTS

Conwy River Festival (4)
Major yachting festival with nine days of competitions, live music, RAF displays and a children's procession.
Conwy Quay, Conwy; tel: 01492 596253; Aug. www.conwyriverfestival.org

Conwy Seed Fair (4)
Founded by Edward I, this day-long, twice-annual fair has stalls selling plants, seeds and honey.
High Street and Lancaster Square, Conwy; tel: 01492 650851; Mar and Sep. www.conwybeekeepers.org.uk

Gwledd Conwy Feast (4)
Popular two-day food festival featuring produce stalls, cookery demonstrations and entertainment.
Quayside, Conwy; tel: 01492 338083; Oct. www.conwyfeast.co.uk

Focus Wales Festival (20)
Three-day festival, showcasing the best new emerging talents in Welsh music, including over 200 bands.
Various venues, Wrexham; tel: 01978 345230; May. www.focuswales.com

Llangollen Food Festival (23)
Two-day international culinary festival, with numerous producers exhibiting their cheeses, meats, wine and chocolate.
The Llangollen Pavilion, Llangollen, Denbighshire; tel: 01978 860111; Oct: 10am–5pm (both days). www.llangollenfoodfestival.com

Barmouth Walking Festival (28)
Ten-day exploration of beautiful local scenery; guided walks along the coast or inland.
Barmouth, Gwynedd; tel: 01341 242646; Sep. www.barmouthwalkingfestival.co.uk

Trefriw Walking Festival (44)
Explore the spectacular mountains and lakes of Snowdonia on a three-day series of guided walks, plus a programme of other events hosted in Trefriw.
Trefriw, nr Llanrwst, Conwy; tel: 07901 628367; May. www.trefriwwalkingfestival.co.uk

Abersoch Jazz Weekend (35)
Annual three-day festival with performers from across the UK and overseas.
Various venues, Abersoch, Gwynedd; tel: 01758 712929; Sep. www.abersochlife.com

Bangor Music Festival (53)
Annual six-day showcase for both contemporary and experimental music, with concerts and workshops.
Bangor University, College Road, Bangor, Gwynedd; tel: 01248 382181; Mar. www.bangormusicfestival.org.uk

Anglesey Oyster & Welsh Produce Festival (54)
Local producers exhibit their food and drink, with cookery demonstrations, talks and music over two days.
Trearddur Bay Hotel, Lon Isallt, Trearddur Bay, Anglesey; tel: 01248 725700; Oct. www.angleseyoysterfestival.com

Copperfest (59)
Three-day, free music festival, featuring Welsh and international pop artists.
Various venues, Amlwch, Anglesey; tel: 01407 831599; Aug. www.copperfest.co.uk

MUSEUMS AND GALLERIES

Conwy Castle (4)
One of the great medieval Welsh castles, with eight towers and a dramatic setting.
Conwy; tel: 01492 592358; open Mar–Oct: 9:30am–5pm daily (Jul–Aug: to 6pm); Nov–Feb: 10am–4pm Mon–Sat, 11am–4pm Sun. www.cadw.gov.wales

Plas Mawr (4)
The UK's best-preserved Elizabethan town house, with elaborate carvings, plaster ceilings and furnishings.
High Street, Conwy; tel: 01492 580167; open Apr–Sep: 9:30am–5pm daily; Oct: 9:30am–4pm daily. www.cadw.gov.wales

Above: Caernarfon Castle, a UNESCO World Heritage Site

Great Orme Mines (2)
Take a guided tour through this fascinating Bronze Age copper mine and museum.
Great Orme, Llandudno, Conwy; tel: 01492 870447; open mid-Mar–Oct: 10am–4pm daily. www.greatormemines.info

Chirk Castle (22)
Explore the sumptuous rooms, galleries and gardens of this 14th-century castle.
Chirk, Wrexham; tel: 01691 777701; open Apr–Sep: noon–5pm daily; Mar, Oct and 3 weeks in Dec: noon–4pm daily. www.nationaltrust.org.uk

Harlech Castle (29)
Picturesque 13th-century castle with exhibitions on its tumultuous history.
Harlech, Gwynedd; tel: 01766 780552; open Mar–Oct: 9:30am–5pm daily (Jul–Aug: to 6pm); Nov–Feb: 10am–4pm Mon–Sat, 11am–4pm Sun. www.cadw.gov.wales

Sygun Copper Mine (40)
Explore the old mines then visit the museum, kids' play area and lakeside paths.
Beddgelert, Gwynedd; tel: 01766 890595; open Mar–Oct: 9:30am–5pm daily. www.syguncoppermine.co.uk

Tŷ Mawr Wybrnant (41)
A Tudor farmhouse, birthplace of Bishop Morgan, translator of the first Welsh Bible.
Penmachno, Betws-y-Coed, Conwy; tel: 01690 760213; open Apr–Sep: noon–5pm Thu–Sun; Oct–Nov: noon–4pm Thu–Sun. www.nationaltrust.org.uk

National Slate Museum (48)
See demonstrations and tour old workshops and quarrymen's houses (see p41).
Padarn Country Park, Llanberis, Gwynedd; tel: 0300 111 2333; open Easter–Oct: 10am–5pm daily; Nov–Easter: 10am–4pm Sun–Fri. www.museumwales.ac.uk

Erddig Hall (21)
Georgian stately home with original furnishings, extensive parkland, coach rides and servants' outbuildings.
Wrexham; tel: 01978 355314; open Feb–Mar and Nov–Dec: 11am–4pm daily; Apr–Oct: 10am–5pm daily. www.nationaltrust.org.uk

The Lloyd George Museum (33)
Displays on the life and times of the World War I Prime Minister, at his boyhood home.
Llanystumdwy, Criccieth, Gwynedd; tel: 01766 522071; open Easter–May: 10:30am–5pm Mon–Fri; Jun: 10:30am–5pm Mon–Sat; Jul–Sep: 10:30am–5pm daily; Oct: 11am–4pm Mon–Fri. www.gwynedd.llyw.cymru

Plas Yn Rhiw (36)
Charming Tudor manor house with landscaped gardens and woodland walks.
Rhiw, Pwllheli, Gwynedd; tel: 01758 780219; open late Mar–May: noon–5pm Thu–Mon; Jun–Jul: noon–5pm Wed–Mon; Aug: noon–5pm daily; Oct: noon–4pm Thu–Sun; school holidays: open daily (check website). www.nationaltrust.org.uk

Caernarfon Castle (50)
Wales's most impressive medieval castle is a UNESCO World Heritage Site, with exhibitions on its long history.
Castle Ditch, Caernarfon, Gwynedd; tel: 01286 677617; open Mar–Oct: 9:30am–5pm daily (Jul–Aug: to 6pm); Nov–Feb: 10am–4pm Mon–Sat, 11am–4pm Sun. www.cadw.gov.wales

Swtan Cottage (57)
Visit Anglesey's last-remaining thatched cottage, restored to its circa-1900 appearance, with displays on rural life.
Porth Swtan, Church Bay, Anglesey; tel: 01407 730186; open Easter–Sep: noon–4pm Fri–Sun. www.swtan.co.uk

Holyhead Maritime Museum ⑤⑤
Wales's oldest lifeboat station houses
displays on Holyhead's seafaring history
and model ships.
*Newry Beach, Beach Road, Holyhead,
Anglesey; tel: 01407 769745; open
Apr–Oct: 10am–4pm Tue–Sun.
www.holyheadmaritimemuseum.co.uk*

Llynnon Mill ⑤⑧
Visit Wales's only working windmill,
with a reconstructed bakery and
Iron Age roundhouses.
*Llanddeusant, Holyhead, Anglesey;
tel: 01407 730407; open Easter–Sep:
11am–5pm Tue–Sat, 1–5pm Sun.
www.visitanglesey.co.uk*

Oriel Ynys Mon ⑥①
Exhibitions from local artists, including
the Sir Kyffin Williams collection.
*Rhosmeirch, Llangefni, Anglesey; tel:
01248 724444; open 10:30am–5pm
daily. www.kyffinwilliams.info*

Plas Newydd ⑥⑥
Beautiful country home of the Marquess
of Anglesey, with a collection of fine art.
*Llanfairpwll, Anglesey; tel: 01248 714795;
open mid Mar–early Nov: 11am–4:30pm
daily. www.nationaltrust.org.uk*

THINGS TO DO WITH KIDS

Great Orme Tramway ①
View the Great Orme headland from
Britain's only cable-hauled tramway.
*Victoria Station, Church Walks,
Llandudno, Conwy; tel: 01492 577877;
open Apr–Sep: 10am–6pm daily;
late Mar and Oct: 10am–5pm daily.
www.greatormetramway.co.uk*

Bodafon Farm Park ①
Feed the animals, meet the owls and have
fun at the adventure playground on this
working farm with a delightful café.
*Bodafon Road, The Promenade,
Llandudno, Conwy; tel: 01492 549060;
open Mar–Sep: 10am–8:30pm Mon–Fri,
10am–6pm Sat–Sun; Oct–Feb: 10am–
5pm daily. www.bodafonfarmpark.com*

Welsh Mountain Zoo ⑤
A beautifully sited zoo with tigers, snow
leopards, chimps, sea lions and more.
*Colwyn Bay, Conwy; tel: 01492 532938;
open Apr–Oct: 9:30am–6pm daily;
Nov–Mar: 9:30am–5pm daily.
www.welshmountainzoo.org*

Harlequin Puppet Theatre ⑤
Enchanting and entertaining puppet
shows for the whole family.
*Cayley Promenade, Rhos-on-Sea, Colwyn
Bay, Conwy; tel: 01492 548166; open
during school holidays; shows at 3pm.
www.puppets.uk.com*

Rhyl SeaQuarium ⑦
Get close to sharks, rays, conger eels, sea
lions and more at this seafront aquarium.
*East Parade, Rhyl, Denbighshire; tel:
01745 344660; open 10am–5pm daily.
www.seaquarium.co.uk*

Horse-Drawn Canal Boat Trips ㉓
Take a trip along the Llangollen Canal in
a horse-drawn canal boat *(see pp101).*
*Llangollen Wharf, Wharf Hill, Llangollen,
Denbighshire; tel: 01978 860702; trips
run Easter–Oct from 11am.
www.horsedrawnboats.co.uk*

Bala Lake Railway ㉕
A 15-km (9-mile) steam-train journey takes
in the stunning scenery of Lake Bala.
*The Station, Llanuwchllyn, Gwynedd;
tel: 01678 540666; open Easter–Oct:
see website for departure times.
www.bala-lake-railway.co.uk*

Ffestiniog Railway ㉛
This vintage steam train takes the scenic
route from Porthmadog to Blaenau
Ffestiniog *(see pp40–1).*
*Harbour Station, Porthmadog, Gwynedd;
tel: 01766 516000; trains run all year;
see website for timetables.
www.ffestiniograilway.co.uk*

Glasfryn Activity Park ㉞
Go-karting, quad-biking, archery, bowling
and fishing are on offer at this busy activity
centre, with toddlers' play area.
*Y Ffôr, Pwllheli, Gwynedd; tel: 01766
810000; open from 9:30am daily
www.glasfryn.co.uk*

The Fun Centre ㊱
Younger children love the slides, ball pools,
maze and mini-cars at this play centre.
*Christchurch, Bangor Street, Caernarfon,
Gwynedd; tel: 01286 671911; open
daily (hours vary, phone for details);
from 10am during school holidays.
www.thefuncentre.co.uk*

Anglesey Sea Zoo ㊿
See everything from sea horses to
sharks at Wales's largest aquarium.
*Brynsiencyn, Llanfairpwll, Anglesey;
tel: 01248 430411; open mid-Feb–
mid-Oct: 10am–6pm daily.
www.angleseyseazoo.co.uk*

Foel Farm Park ⑤①
Take a tractor tour of the farm, feed the
animals and see chocolate-makers at work.
*Brynsiencyn, Anglesey; tel: 01248 430646;
open mid-Feb–Mar: 10:30am–5pm Sat–
Sun (daily during Feb half-term); Apr–Nov:
10:30am–5:30pm daily www.foelfarm.co.uk*

Greenwood Forest Park ⑤②
Ride the world's only eco-friendly roller
coaster, or try the mini-tractors, boardwalk
maze or forest theatre.
*Y Felinheli, Gwynedd; tel: 01248 670070;
open Feb half term and mid Mar–Oct:
10am–5:30pm daily.
www.greenwoodforestpark.co.uk*

Pili Palas Nature World ⑥⑤
A fascinating artificial jungle, home to
butterflies, exotic birds and reptiles.
*Penmynydd Road, Menai Bridge,
Anglesey; tel: 01248 712474; open
10am–5:30pm daily. www.pilipalas.co.uk*

SPAS AND HEALTH RESORTS

The Wild Pheasant Hotel & Spa ㉓
Charming Victorian country house
with spacious rooms and suites, and
a separate modern spa centre.
*Berwyn Road, Llangollen,
Denbighshire; tel: 01978 860629.
www.wildpheasanthotel.co.uk*

Llanrhaeadr Springs ⑪
Luxurious spa using "healing water" from
St Dyfnog's well. The spa offers beauty
treatments and gym, yoga and pilates
classes in relaxing surroundings.
*The Coach House, Stable Yard,
Llanrhaeadr, Denbighshire; tel: 01745
775751. www.springs-spa.co.uk*

The Secret Spa ⑱
Beauty treatments, holistic therapies,
massages and reflexology sessions
to give you the "feel-good factor".
*Lilac Cottage, The Cross, Holt,
Wrexham; tel: 01829 271693.
www.thesecretspa.co.uk*

**Tre-Ysgawen Country House
Hotel & Spa** ⑥①
Pool, sauna, beauty treatments, gym
and yoga in the converted stables of
a Victorian mansion.
*Capel Coch, Llangefni, Anglesey,
tel: 01248 750750.
www.treysgawen-hall.co.uk*

Anglesey Healing Centre ⑥③
Small, private retreat offering *reiki,*
reflexology and aromatherapy
treatments and workshops.
*Llangoed, Beaumaris, Anglesey; tel: 01248
490814. www.angleseyhealingcentre.co.uk*

OTHER SIGHTS IN THE BOOK

Below: Great Orme Tramway in Llandudno

CENTRAL WALES

LOCAL FOOD

Pilgrims Tea Rooms and Restaurant ⑱
Award-winning tearoom serving traditional home cooking using local ingredients.
Cathedral Close, Brecon, Powys; tel: 01874 610610; open 10am–5pm daily (until 4pm in winter). www.breconcathedral.org.uk

Mrs Brown's ㉖
Enjoy delicious home-made Welsh cakes alongside excellent coffee at this delightful café. Quiches, pies, baguettes, wraps, jacket potatoes and salads are just some of the choices available for lunch.
1 New Road, Llandeilo, Carmarthenshire; tel: 07920 865642; open 8am–3pm Mon–Fri

The Treehouse (61)
Popular organic food shop and café, with lots of fresh local produce on the menu.
14 Baker Street, Aberystwyth, Ceredigion; tel: 01970 615791; open 9am–5pm Mon–Sat. www.treehousewales.co.uk

Ultracomida Delicatessen (61)
A vast range of Welsh, French and Spanish cheeses, cured meats, olives and more.
31 Pier Street, Aberystwyth, Ceredigion; tel: 01970 630686; open 10am–6pm Mon–Sat, noon–5pm Sun. www.ultracomida.co.uk

The Blue Ball Restaurant ㊲
Relaxed, trendy restaurant offering a menu of local seafood and international dishes.
Upper Frog Street, Tenby, Pembrokeshire; tel: 01834 843038; open 6–9pm Tue–Sat, 12:30–2:30pm Sun. www.theblueballrestaurant.co.uk

Martha's Vineyard Restaurant ㊸
Overlooking the Cleddau Estuary, Martha's offers a varied menu of fresh local seafood.
Cleddau House, Milford Marina, Milford Haven, Pembrokeshire; tel: 01646 697083; open noon–11pm Sun–Thu, noon–midnight Fri–Sat. www.marthasvineyardrestaurant.co.uk

The Harbour Inn ㊽
Local seafood and traditional pub meals, with picturesque views over the harbour.
Main Street, Solva, Pembrokeshire; tel: 01437 720013; restaurant open noon–2:30pm and 6–8:30pm Sun–Thu, noon–3pm and 6–9pm Fri–Sat. www.harbourinnsolva.com

Cardigan Brasserie (53)
Friendly brasserie offering delicious meals prepared with fresh local produce.
Cross House, 3 High Street, Cardigan, Ceredigion; tel: 01239 758088; open 11am–3pm and 5:30–late Mon–Sat. www.cardiganbrasserie.co.uk

Llanelli Market ㉛
Find Welsh delicacies such as cockles, laverbread and the haggis-like Felinfoel faggots at this friendly covered market with over 50 family-run stalls.
Market Precinct, Llanelli, Carmarthenshire; tel: 01554 773984; open 8:30am–5pm Mon–Sat. www.carmarthenshiremarkets.co.uk

Llwynhelyg Farm Shop (54)
Local vegetables and cheeses, meats and jams are sold at this award-winning shop.
Sarnau, Llandysul, Ceredigion; tel: 01239 811079; open 9am–6pm Mon–Sat, 9:30am–1:30pm Sun. www.llwynhelygfarmshop.co.uk

The Hungry Trout (55)
Seafood restaurant offering a creative menu of fresh local fish and shellfish.
2 South John Street, New Quay, Ceredigion; tel: 01545 560680; open 9am–3pm and 6–9pm daily. www.thehungrytrout.co.uk

New Quay Honey Farm (55)
See working bees and sample Welsh mead at this honey-themed tearoom.
Cross Inn, New Quay, Ceredigion; tel: 01545 560822; open Easter–Oct 10am–5pm Tue–Sat. www.thehoneyfarm.co.uk

La Cuccina (60)
Home-made cakes, pastries and organic breads are served at this pleasant café.
35 Alban Square, Aberaeron, Ceredigion; tel: 01545 571012; open 9am–3:30pm Mon, 9am–4:30pm Tue–Sat.

FARMERS' MARKETS

Welshpool Farmers' Market ①
Buy local fruit, veg, cheeses and more at this monthly market.
Coed-y-dinas, Welshpool, Powys; tel: 01938 555545; first Sat Mar–Dec, 9am–2pm. www.coedydinas.co.uk

Knighton Community Market ⑥
Farmers and small producers from across the region offer fruit, vegetables and more.
Community Centre, Bowling Green Lane, Knighton, Powys; second and fourth Sat of every month, 9:30am–12:30pm. www.knightoncommunitycentre.com

Brecon Farmers' Market ⑱
A tempting array of home-baked cakes, farmhouse cheeses, fresh fruit and veg.
Market Hall, Brecon, Powys; tel: 01874 612275; second Sat of every month, 9:30am–2pm. www.breconfarmersmarkets.co.uk

Carmarthen Farmers' Market ㉝
All manner of local produce is on sale at this bi-weekly food and drink market.
Carmarthen town centre; first and third Fri of every month, 9am–1pm. www.tmiw.co.uk

Fishguard Farmers' Market (51)
Local fruit, vegetables, fish, poultry, honey, cheeses, butter, cakes and more.
Town Hall, Fishguard, Pembrokeshire; tel: 01348 840689; every Sat, 9am–1pm. www.pembrokeshire.gov.uk

Lampeter Farmers' Market (57)
Local food and drink direct from the producers at this popular market.
Market Street, Lampeter, Ceredigion; tel: 01570 423200; every other Fri, 9am–2pm. www.fmiw.co.uk

PUBS

The Dragon Hotel ④
Try potent local real ales in the cosy bar of this 17th-century coaching inn and hotel.
Market Square, Montgomery, Powys; tel: 01686 668359; open daily. www.dragonhotel.com

Kilvert's Inn ⑫
Busy family-run inn in the foothills of the Brecon Beacons, serving several local ales. There are also regular live music nights.
The Bullring, Hay-on-Wye, Powys; tel: 01497 821042; open daily. www.kilverts.co.uk

The Crown Inn ㊲
Traditional family-run pub, with regular live music and special events.
Lower Frog Street, Tenby, Pembrokeshire; tel: 01834 842796; open daily. www.sabrain.com

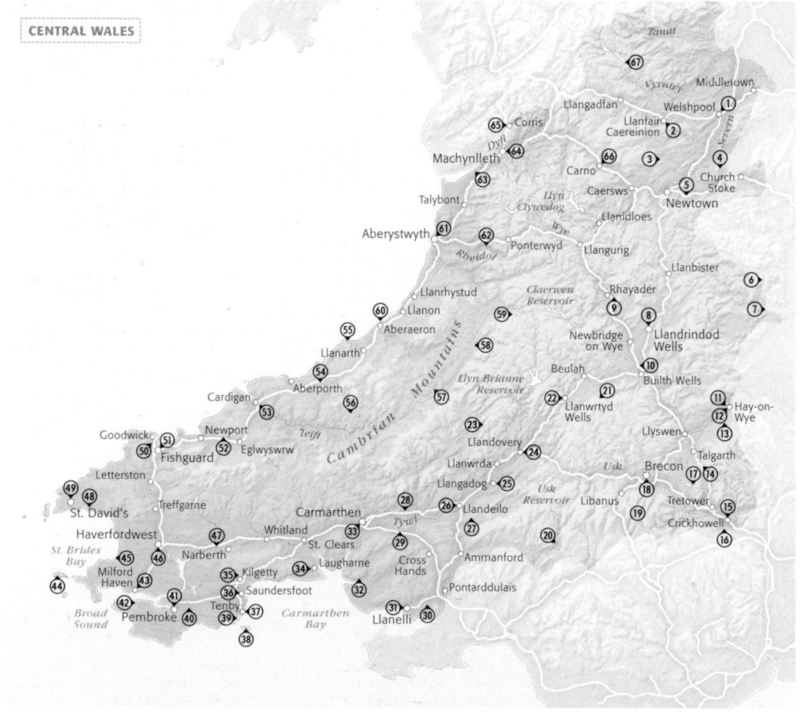

Above: Gwesty Cymru hotel in Aberystwyth

The Bear ⑮
Medieval pub recommended by the Campaign for Real Ale serving a range of local real ales in historic surroundings.
High Street, Crickhowell, Powys; tel: 01873 810408; open daily.
www.bearhotel.co.uk

The Red Lion Hotel ㉕
Historic village pub with an excellent restaurant and B&B rooms.
Church Street, Llangadog, Carmarthenshire: tel: 01550 777228; open 11am–11pm Tue–Sun.
www.theredlionllangadog.com

White Hart Thatched Inn and Brewery ㉙
Picturesque 14th-century thatched village pub, with a range of ales brewed on site, a beer garden and a restaurant.
Llanddarog, Carmarthenshire; tel: 01267 275395; open noon–3:30pm and 6–11pm Mon, Tue, Thu–Sat, noon–3:30pm and 7–10:30pm Sun.
www.thebestpubinwales.co.uk

The Aleppo Merchant Inn ㉖
Historic rural pub with a large beer garden, restaurant serving traditional pub food, and a few guest rooms.
Carno, Caersws, Powys; tel: 01686 420210; open daily. www.thealeppo.co.uk

The Castle ㊹
Friendly Victorian pub and restaurant in a stunning coastal location, with two rooms.
1 Grove Place, Little Haven, Pembrokeshire; tel: 01437 781445; open 11am–11pm daily (to midnight Fri–Sat).

The Grove Hotel ㊾
Sample regional real ales and Welsh spirits at this attractively restored old inn set in idyllic grounds just outside the little cathedral city of St Davids.
High Street, St Davids, Pembrokeshire; tel: 01437 720341; open daily.
www.grovestdavids.co.uk

Watermans Arms ㊶
Located on the Mill Pond, this pub serves excellent pub fare and has lovely views of the castle.
2 The Green, Pembroke, Pembrokeshire; tel: 01646 682718; open daily.
www.watermansarmspembroke.co.uk

Penwig ㊾
Friendly, family-run pub overlooking Cardigan Bay, serving home-cooked meals in a bright, modern bar-restaurant.
South John Street, New Quay, Ceredigion; tel: 01545 560910; open daily.
www.penwig.co.uk

Yr Hen Orsaf ㊶
Occupying the town's old 1920s railway station, this family-friendly chain pub serves food throughout the day.
Alexandra Road, Aberystwyth, Ceredigion; tel: 01970 636080; open daily.
www.jdwetherspoon.com

Inn on the Pier ㊶
Party on the pier at the only all-night-long pub in Ceredigion, a lively nightspot with great sea views.
The Royal Pier, Marine Terrace, Aberystwyth, Ceredigion; tel: 01970 636102; 11:30am–1am Sun–Thu, 11:30am–5am Fri–Sat. www.royalpier.co.uk

Royal Oak ①
Renovated Grade II-listed coaching inn with 25 tasteful rooms and a restaurant in a pleasant small market town.
The Cross, Welshpool, Powys; tel: 01938 552217. www.royaloakwelshpool.co.uk

The Forest Country House ⑤
Five en suite rooms are offered in this peaceful family-run Victorian country house, with tennis court and garden.
Gilfach Lane, Kerry, Newtown, Powys; tel: 01686 621821.
www.bedandbreakfastnewtown.co.uk

The Metropole ⑧
Long-established family-run hotel in the town centre, with smart rooms and excellent facilities.
Temple Street, Llandrindod Wells, Powys; tel: 01597 823700.
www.metropole.co.uk

Baskerville Hall Hotel ⑪
Imposing Gothic country mansion, with ornate rooms, indoor pool, camp site and dorms.
Clyro Court, Hay-on-Wye, Powys; tel: 01497 820033.
www.baskervillehall.co.uk

The Old Post Office Bed & Breakfast ⑬
Converted post office in an excellent location for the Hay Festival.
Llanigon, nr Hay-on-Wye, Powys; tel: 01497 820008. www.oldpost-office.co.uk

The Dragons Back ⑭
Four comfortable rooms in the inn, plus dorm accommodation and a camp site.
Pengenffordd, nr Talgarth, Powys; tel: 01874 711353.
www.thedragonsback.co.uk

The Old Rectory Country Hotel ⑯
Attractive 16th-century countryside mansion with stylish en suite rooms, restaurant and nine-hole golf course.
Llangattock, Crickhowell, Powys; tel: 01873 810373.
www.rectoryhotel.co.uk

The Beacons Guest House ⑱
Georgian town house with lots of period charm and neat modernized rooms.
16 Bridge Street, Brecon, Powys; tel: 01874 623339. www.thebreconbeacons.co.uk

Warpool Court Hotel ㊾
Attractive Victorian hotel with a popular restaurant. It has 22 en suite modern bedrooms, many with sea views.
St Davids, Pembrokeshire; tel: 01437 720300. www.warpoolcourthotel.com

The Black Lion Hotel ㊾
This hotel has a restaurant, bar and garden, as well as nine spacious rooms overlooking scenic Cardigan Bay.
Glan Mor Terrace, New Quay, Ceredigion; tel: 01545 561144.
www.blacklionnewquay.co.uk

The New White Lion ㉔
Elegant Grade II-listed building with six stylish bedrooms, a restaurant and regular music and poetry nights.
43 Stone Street, Llandovery, Carmarthenshire; tel: 01550 720685.
www.newwhitelion.com

Middle Mill Guest House ㉜
Rustic guesthouse with neatly furnished rooms, set in large grounds with a private river for fishing.
Middle Mill, Carmarthen Road, Kidwelly, Carmarthenshire; tel: 01554 891728.
www.middlemill.talktalk.net

The Boat House Bed & Breakfast ㉞
Most of the spacious, elegant rooms at this B&B have views of the estuary and Laugharne castle.
1 Gosport Street, Laugharne, Carmarthenshire; tel: 01994 427263.
www.bed-breakfast-holiday.co.uk

St Brides Spa Hotel ㊱
Light, airy rooms, many with sea views, in this classy hotel equipped with a restaurant and spa.
St Brides Hill, Saundersfoot, Pembrokeshire; tel: 01834 812304.
www.stbridesspahotel.com

Penally Abbey ㊴
With views of Caldey Island and beautiful rooms, this is a peaceful coastal hotel with an excellent restaurant.
Penally, nr Tenby, Pembrokeshire; tel: 01834 843033.
www.penally-abbey.com

Nantgwynfaen Organic Farm ㊱
Three restful rooms are offered on this working organic farm, with on-site farm shop.
Penrhiwllan Road, Croeslan, Llandysul, Ceredigion; tel: 01239 851914.
www.organicfarmwales.co.uk

Coed Parc Farm ㊲
Homely B&B accommodation is available at this friendly working farm that overlooks a lovely wooded valley.
Lampeter, Ceredigion; tel: 01570 422402.
www.coedparcfarmbedandbreakfast.co.uk

Y Talbot ㊸
Make yourself at home in one of the stylish rooms at this Grade-II-listed inn.
Tregaron, Ceredigion; tel: 01974 298208.
www.ytalbot.com

Gwesty Cymru ㊱
Trendy modern hotel on the seafront, with eight stylish rooms and terrace restaurant.
19 Marine Terrace, Aberystwyth, Ceredigion; tel: 01970 612252.
www.gwestycymru.com

Ynyshir Hall ㊹
This grand country-house hotel, set in lush landscaped gardens, was once owned by Queen Victoria.
Eglwysfach, Machynlleth, Powys; tel: 01654 781209.
www.ynyshirhall.co.uk

FESTIVALS AND EVENTS

Gregynog Festival ③
Held in various beautiful historic locations in North Powys, this 11-day classical music festival features performances by the world's leading musicians.
Various venues, Powys; tel: 01686 207100; Jun. www.gregynogfestival.org

Presteigne Festival ⑦
A six-day celebration of classical music, including some by contemporary composers, in a countryside location.
Various venues, Presteigne, Powys; tel: 01544 267800; Aug. www.presteignefestival.com

Llandrindod Wells Victorian Festival ⑧
For a week, costumed locals and visitors re-create the spa town's Victorian heyday, with street entertainment and fireworks.
Various venues, Llandrindod Wells, Powys; tel: 01597 823441; Aug. www.llandrindod-wells.com/victorian.html

Royal Welsh Show ⑩
One of the UK's biggest agricultural and country shows, with livestock competitions and entertainment over four days.
Royal Welsh Showground, Llanelwedd, Builth Wells, Powys; tel: 01982 553683; Jul. www.rwas.co.uk

Brecon Jazz Festival ⑱
Wales's premier jazz festival, with big-name acts from across the world performing over a weekend around town.
Various venues, Brecon, Powys; tel: 0870 9901299; Aug. www.breconjazzfestival.org

World Bog Snorkelling Championships ㉒
Bizarre swimming competition held in bog trenches, attracting numerous international participants over two days.
Waen Rhydd Bog, Llanwrtyd Wells, Powys; tel: 01591 610666; Aug. www.green-events.co.uk

Man Versus Horse Marathon ㉒
Annual 35-km (22-mile) countryside race between runners and horse-riders, only twice won by a human.
Llanwrtyd Wells, Powys; tel: 01591 610666; Jun. www.green-events.co.uk

Tenby Arts Festival ㊲
A week of amateur dramatics, classical and jazz music, dancing, talks and poetry readings.
Various venues, Tenby, Pembrokeshire; tel: 01834 845523; Sep. www.tenbyartsfest.co.uk

Pembrokeshire Fish Week ㊸
This week-long celebration of fish and the seaside opens in Milford Haven harbour and continues across Pembrokeshire, with barbecues, cooking demonstrations, fishing competitions and music.
Various locations, Pembrokeshire; tel: 01437 776169; late Jun/early Jul. www.pembrokeshirefishweek.co.uk

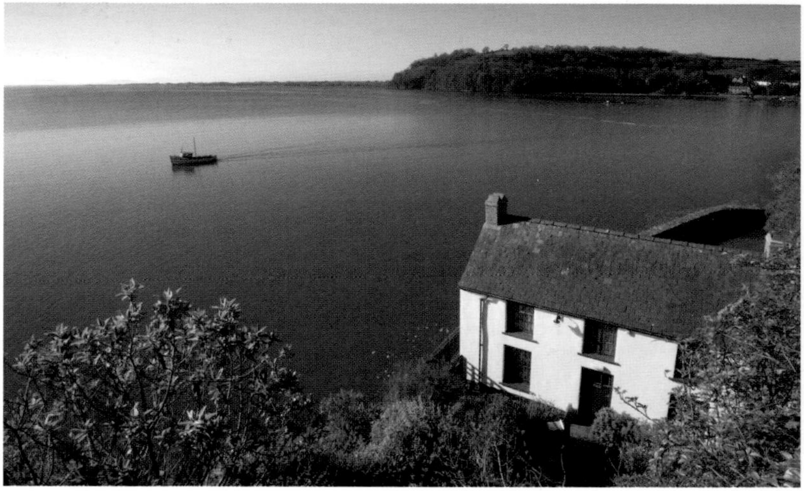

Above: Dylan Thomas Boathouse at Laugharne

Really Wild Festival ㊾
A weekend event showcasing Welsh produce, plus fun activities such as foraging walks.
Pwllcaerog Farm, nr St Davids, Pembrokeshire; tel: 01348 837405; May. www.reallywildfestival.co.uk

Fishguard International Music Festival (51)
Prestigious eight-day music festival featuring classical concerts, operatic performances, string quartets and soloists.
Various venues, Fishguard and St Davids, Pembrokeshire; tel: 01348 873237; Jul. www.fishguardmusicfestival.co.uk

MUSEUMS AND GALLERIES

Powis Castle and Garden ①
Dramatic medieval castle housing a fine collection of paintings, plus Italian gardens.
Welshpool, Powys; tel: 01938 551944; open Mar, Oct–Dec: 11am–4pm daily; Apr–Aug: 11am–5pm daily. www.nationaltrust.org.uk

Powysland Museum ①
Exhibitions covering Montgomeryshire's prehistoric, Roman and Viking past.
Canal Wharf, Welshpool, Powys; tel: 01938 554656; open Jun–Aug: 10:30am–1pm and 2–5pm Mon–Fri, 10:30am–3pm Sat; Sep–May: 11am–1pm and 2–5pm Mon, Tue, Thu–Fri, 11am–2pm Sat. www.powys.gov.uk

The Old Bell Museum ④
Displays on local archaeology and social history can be found at this museum, run entirely by volunteers, in an evocative 16th-century former inn.
Arthur Street, Montgomery, Powys; tel: 01686 668313; open Apr–Sep: 1:30–5pm Wed–Fri and Sun, 10:30am–5pm Sat. www.oldbellmuseum.org.uk

The Judge's Lodging ⑦
Award-winning museum in this plush Victorian judge's residence, with re-created interiors, including the Judge's apartments and servants' quarters. Sit in the Judge's chair in the courtroom and visit the damp cells.
Broad Street, Presteigne, Powys; tel: 01544 260650; open Mar–Oct: 10am–5pm Tue–Sun; Nov: 10am–4pm Wed–Sun; Dec: 10am–4pm Sat–Sun. www.judgeslodging.org.uk

Radnorshire Museum ⑧
Displays on the local history of this small spa town, as well as Neolithic and Roman artifacts, can be seen here.
Temple Street, Llandrindod Wells, Powys; tel: 01597 824513; open Apr–Sep: 10am–4pm Tue–Sat; Oct–Mar: 10am–4pm Tue–Fri, 10am–1pm Sat. www.powys.gov.uk

Kidwelly Castle ㉜
Well-preserved and outstanding example of a 12th-century Norman castle, with exhibitions on its long and fascinating military history.
Castle Road, Kidwelly, Carmarthenshire; tel: 01554 890104; open Mar–Jun and Sep–Oct: 9:30am–5pm daily; Jul–Aug: 9:30am–6pm daily; Nov–Feb: 10am–4pm Mon–Sat. www.cadw.gov.wales

The Dylan Thomas Boathouse at Laugharne ㉞
An exhibition on the famous Welsh poet's life, including his writing shed, at the house where he wrote *Under Milk Wood.*
Dylan's Walk, Laugharne, Carmarthenshire; tel: 01994 427420; open May–Oct: 10am–5pm daily; Nov–Apr: 10:30am–3pm daily. www.dylanthomasboathouse.com

Dolaucothi Gold Mines ㉓
Underground tours of this unique Roman gold mine and exhibition.
Pumsaint, Llanwrda, Carmarthenshire; tel: 01558 650177; open mid-Mar–Jun and Sep–Oct: 11am–5pm daily; Jul–Aug: 10am–6pm daily. www.nationaltrust.org.uk

Carreg Cennen Castle ㉗
One of Wales's best medieval castles *(see pp110–11)*, with magnificent views over the Carmarthenshire countryside.
Tir Y Castell Farm, Trapp, Llandeilo, Carmarthenshire; tel: 01558 822291; open 9:30am–6:30pm daily (last adm Apr–Oct: 5:30pm; Nov–Mar: 4pm). www.carregcennencastle.com

Milford Haven Museum ㊸
This fascinating maritime and heritage museum explores the impact the whaling, fishing and oil industries had on the town.
The Old Customs House, The Docks, Milford Haven, Pembrokeshire; tel: 01646 694496; open 10:30am–4pm Mon–Sun. www.milfordhavenmuseum.co.uk

Haverfordwest Town Museum ㊻
Varied displays on local history including paintings, vintage costumes and archaeological artifacts.
Castle House, Haverfordwest, Pembrokeshire; tel: 01437 763087; open Apr–Oct: 10am–4pm Mon–Sat (Aug: to 5pm). www.haverfordwest-town-museum.org.uk

Ceredigion Museum (61)
In a restored Edwardian theatre, the Ceredigion Museum houses exhibitions on local culture and industry.
Coliseum, Terrace Road, Aberystwyth, Ceredigion; tel: 01970 633088; open 10:30am–4pm Tue–Sat, noon–4pm Sun. www.ceredigion.gov.uk

Castell Henllys Iron Age Hill Fort (52)
Reconstructed Iron Age roundhouses, prehistoric livestock breeds, costumed villagers, craft workshops and story-telling.
Meline, nr Crymych, Pembrokeshire; tel: 01239 891319; open Apr–Oct: 10am–5pm daily; Nov–Mar: 11am–3pm daily. www.pembrokeshirecoast.org.uk

Strata Florida Abbey (59)
View the picturesque ruins of this 12th-century Cistercian abbey, with an on-site museum.
Ystrad Meurig, Ceredigion; tel: 01974 831261; open Apr–Oct: 10am–5pm daily; Nov–Mar: 10am–4pm daily. www.cadw.wales.gov.uk

MOMA Machynlleth (64)
The four galleries of this Museum of Modern Art feature 20th-century and contemporary Welsh paintings and sculpture.
The Tabernacle, Heol Penrallt, Machynlleth, Powys; tel: 01654 703355; open 10am–4pm Mon–Sat. www.moma.machynlleth.org.uk

THINGS TO DO WITH KIDS

Welshpool and Llanfair Light Railway (2)
Hop aboard a vintage narrow-gauge steam train for a trip across beautiful countryside.
The Station, Llanfair Caereinion, Welshpool, Powys; tel. 01938 810441; open mid-Mar–Oct: see website for full timetable. www.wllr.org.uk

Red Kite Feeding Centre – Gigrin Farm (9)
A rare chance to see wild red kites up close on this family-run farm, which has its own feeding station for the birds of prey
Gigrin Farm, South Street, Rhayader, Powys; tel: 01597 810243; open 12:30 5pm daily (feeding time 3pm summer, 2pm winter). www.gigrin.co.uk

National Showcaves Centre for Wales (20)
Tours around a spectacular series of caves, plus a dinosaur park and shire horse centre for younger children.
Abercrave, Swansea; tel: 01639 730284; open mid-Mar–Oct: 10am–3pm daily. www.showcaves.co.uk

Llanelli Wetland Centre (30)
Nature reserve with bird-watching hides, lakes, lagoons, discovery centre, canoe safari and bike trail.
Llwynhendy, Llanelli, Carmarthenshire; tel: 01554 741087; open 9:30am–5pm daily. www.wwt.org.uk

Folly Farm (33)
As well as an adventure playground and Europe's largest undercover vintage funfair, there are animals galore in this country park, farm and zoo.
Begelly, Kilgetty, Pembrokeshire; tel: 01834 812731; open mid-Feb–Jun and Sep–Oct: 10am–5pm daily; Jul–Aug: 10am–5:30pm daily; Nov–mid-Feb: 10am–4pm Sat–Sun.. www.folly-farm.co.uk

Skomer Island (44)
Take a day trip to this nature reserve and discover dolphins, seals, puffins and Manx shearwaters.
Pembrokeshire; tel: 01646 636800; day trips depart from Martin's Haven Apr–Sep: 10am–noon Tue–Sun. www.welshwildlife.org

Oakwood Theme Park (47)
Fun for kids of all ages, with a huge selection of funfair rides and roller coasters, plus calmer boat rides for parents.
Canaston Bridge, Narberth, Pembrokeshire; tel: 01834 891373; open Apr–Oct: from 10am (see website for details). www.oakwoodthemepark.co.uk

The Magic of Life Butterfly House (62)
Walk among hundreds of exotic, colourful butterflies – some of which are the largest in the world – and see giant caterpillars, unusual insects and an array of rare and endangered plants at this butterfly house.
CwmRheidol, Aberystwyth, Ceredigion; tel: 01970 880928; open late Mar–Oct: 10am–5pm daily. www.magicoflife.org

Corris Railway and Museum (65)
Ride this 19th-century steam railway through the picturesque Dulas Valley and visit the railway museum.
Station Yard, Corris, Machynlleth, Powys; tel: 01654 761303; open weekends May–Sep: trains hourly from 11am. See website for full timetable. www.corris.co.uk

Below: Puffin feeding on Skomer Island

Llangorse Multi Activity Centre (17)
Wales's largest indoor climbing centre, plus horse-riding and outdoor obstacle courses.
The Gilfach, Llangorse, Powys; tel: 0333 600 2020; open 9am–10pm Mon–Sat, 9am–5pm Sun. www.activityuk.com

Caldey Island (38)
Picturesque island owned by Cistercian monks, with an abbey, churches, a museum and a long sandy beach.
Pembrokeshire, tel: 01834 844453; boats sail from Tenby, May–Aug from 10am Mon–Sat; Sep from 10:30am Mon–Sat; Apr and Oct from 10:30am Mon–Fri www.caldey-island.co.uk

SPAS AND HEALTH RESORTS

Lake Country House and Spa (21)
A range of spa treatments and a lakeside hot tub are offered at this hotel, which is in the perfect location for a truly relaxing break.
Llangammarch Wells, Powys; tel: 01591 620202. www.lakecountryhouse.co.uk

Four Seasons Health and Leisure (28)
A heated indoor pool, Jacuzzi, steam room and gym in a tranquil rural location.
Cwmtwrch Farm, Nantgaredig, Carmarthenshire; tel: 01267 290238. www.fourseasonswales.co.uk

Three Rivers Hotel & Spa (33)
State-of-the-art spa with swimming pool, Jacuzzi, sauna, steam rooms and gym.
Ferryside, Carmarthen; tel: 01267 267270. www.threerivershotel.co.uk

Monks Health Club & Spa (31)
Spa and gym at a luxurious country club with pool, sauna and numerous treatments.
Machynys Peninsula Golf Club & Premier Spa, Nicklaus Avenue, Machynys, Llanelli, Carmarthenshire; tel: 01554 744888. machynys.com/healthclub-and-spa.html

Lamphey Court Hotel & Spa (40)
Peaceful Georgian mansion offering modern luxury, including heated pool, sauna, gym, tennis courts and various therapies and treatments.
Lamphey, nr Tenby, Pembrokeshire; tel: 01646 672273. www.lampheycourt.co.uk

The Ivybridge Spa (50)
Day and overnight packages are available and numerous massages, facials and body treatments are offered.
Drim Mill, Goodwick, Pembrokeshire, tel: 01348 875347 www.ivybridgespa.co.uk

Lake Vyrnwy Hotel & Spa (67)
A luxury 4-star hotel and spa resort with fitness centre, spa pool, sauna, gym and fine views over the beautiful Lake Vyrnwy nature reserve.
Llanwddyn, Powys; tel: 01691 870692. www.lakevyrnwy.com

OTHER SIGHTS IN THE BOOK

Hay Festival (12) (see pp14–15). **The Brecon Beacons** (19) (see pp202–3). **Pembrokeshire Coast** (42) (see pp198–9).

SOUTH WALES

LOCAL FOOD

The Secret Garden Café ⑩
A warm welcome awaits at this popular café known for its brunches, burgers, steak grills and excellent coffee.
25 Charles Street, Newport; tel: 01633 223559; open 10am–5pm Tue–Sat.

Junction 28 ⑪
Welsh lamb, venison, steaks, fish and a range of local cheeses are on the menu at this artfully converted railway station outside Newport.
Station Approach, Bassaleg, Newport; tel: 01633 891891; open noon–2pm and 5:30pm–9:30pm Mon–Sat; 11:30–8pm Sun. www.junction28.com

Berry Hill Fruit Farm ⑪
Pick your own pears, plums, berries, beans, rhubarbs and peas in season at this farm.
Coedkernew, Newport; tel: 01633 680938; open 9am–5pm Mon & Tue and Thu–Sat, 9am–1pm Sun. www.berryhillfruitfarm.co.uk

The Farmer's Daughter Restaurant ⑪
Try traditional home-cooked fare or exotic dishes such as zebra or kangaroo at this farm-based restaurant.
Croescarneinion Farm, Bassaleg, Newport; tel: 01633 892800; open 5:30pm–late Thu & Fri, 6:30pm–late Sat, from noon Sun. www.thefarmersdaughter.co.uk

Prince's Cafe ⑰
Historic establishment offering home-made cakes and pies to take away, and traditional meals upstairs.
74 Taff Street, Pontypridd, Rhondda Cynon Taf; tel: 01443 402376; open 9am–5pm Mon–Sat.

Zerodegrees ⑳
A modern restaurant and microbrewery, serving British and European cuisine.
27 Westgate Street, Cardiff; tel: 029 2022 9494; open noon–midnight Mon–Sat, noon–11pm Sun. www.zerodegrees.co.uk

Wally's Delicatessen ⑳
Cardiff institution selling a huge variety of cheeses, meats, sweet treats and food from around the world.
38–46 Royal Arcade, Cardiff; tel: 029 2022 9265; open 8:30am–5:30pm Mon–Fri, 8:30am–6pm Sat, 11am–4pm Sun.www.wallysdeli.co.uk

Cardiff Market ⑳
There are regional cheeses, meats, fish, fruit and vegetables and much more on offer at this bustling market.
Entrances on Trinity Street and St Mary Street, Cardiff; tel: 029 2087 1214; open 8am–5:30pm Mon–Sat. www.cardiffcouncilproperty.com

Thé Pot ⑳
Excellent French style bistro serving dishes, such as boeuf bourguigon and Welsh rack of lamb, all made with fresh local produce.
138 Crwys Road, Cardiff; tel: 029 2025 1246; open 9am–4pm Tue, 9am–4pm and 6–10pm Wed–Sat, 9am–3pm Sun. www.thepotcafe.co.uk

Gelynis Farm ㉔
Come here to sample the superb award-winning ice cream, as well as a wide selection of home-made cakes.
Morganstown, Cardiff; tel. 029 2084 4440; open Apr–Oct: 10:30am–4:30pm Sat–Sun. www.gelynisfarm.co.uk

Oscars of Cowbridge ㉙
A friendly, stylish restaurant that gives classic Welsh dishes a contemporary twist.
65 High Street, Cowbridge, Vale of Glamorgan; tel: 01446 771984; open 11am–11pm Mon–Sat. www.oscarsofcowbridge.com

Zia Nina ㉝
Authentic southern Italian dishes, including plenty of pasta and pizzas, are served at this smart family-run restaurant.
28 Dunraven Place, Bridgend; tel: 01656 660045; open noon–2pm and 6–10pm Tue–Sat. www.zianinarestaurant.com

Cobbles Kitchen and Deli ㉜
Located in a beautiful Grade II-listed building, this eatery serves tasty breakfasts, light lunches and numerous home-made treats. The Deli stocks an array of local produce.
Ty Maen Farm Buildings, Ogmore-by-Sea, Bridgend; tel: 01656 661954; open 9:30am–4pm daily. www.cobbleskitchen.co.uk

The Loft Lounge ㉝
Popular café-bar with chic decor and a varied menu that features toasties, sandwiches and coffee by day, and grills, tapas, beer and cocktails by night.
Unit 8, Gentle Way, Broadlands District Center, Bridgend; tel: 01656 857232; open from 9am daily. www.loftloungebar.com

Sidoli Bros ㉞
The place to go for traditional fish and chips and a variety of seafood dishes.
13–14 Well Street, Porthcawl, Bridgend; tel: 01656 783766; open 11:30am–11pm Mon–Fri, 11am–11pm Sat & Sun.

Swansea Market ㊳
Try the famous local cockles, laverbread (seaweed) and Welsh cakes in Wales's largest indoor market.
Oxford Street, Swansea; tel: 01792 654296; open 8am–5:30pm Mon–Fri, 7:30am–5:30pm Sat, 10am–4:30pm Sun. www.swanseaindoormarket.co.uk

The Chattery ㊳
Relaxed, friendly restaurant, with local produce on the menu and occasional music nights.
59 Uplands Crescent, Uplands, Swansea; tel: 01792 473276; open 10am–5pm Mon–Fri, 10am–5pm and 7–10pm Fri & Sat; open later for live music nights. http://homepage.ntlworld.com/thechattery

Nicholaston Farm ㊵
Pick your own strawberries, raspberries and gooseberries at this working farm and camp site, with farm shop and café.
Penmaen, Gower, Swansea; tel: 01792 371209; shop open 8am–6pm daily, PYO open mid-Jun–Jul/Aug. www.nicholastonfarm.co.uk

The Walnut Tree Restaurant ㊿
High-quality regional and international cuisine is on the menu at this highly regarded countryside restaurant.
Llanddewi Skirrid, Abergavenny, Monmouthshire; tel: 01873 852797; open noon–2pm and 7–10pm Tue–Sat. www.thewalnuttreeinn.com

FARMERS' MARKETS

Caerphilly Farmers' Market ⑮
A variety of local food, drink and crafts, including jewellery and pottery are on sale at this market.
The Twyn, Caerphilly; tel: 07805 563809; second Sun of every month, 10am–2pm. www.caerphillyfarmersmarket.co.uk

Riverside Farmers' Market ⑳
This weekly market has a huge selection of local fruit, vegetables, meat, cheeses, fish and seafood, as well as home-made chocolates, baked goods, preserves and much more.
17 Fitzhamon Embankment, Cardiff; tel: 029 2019 0036; every Sun 10am–2pm. www.riversidemarket.org.uk

Cowbridge Farmers' Market ㉙
Locally produced cheeses, bread, fruit and vegetables can be bought at this twice-monthly market.
Arthur Johns Car Park, North Road, Cowbridge, Vale of Glamorgan; tel: 01446 771033; first and third Sat of every month, 9:30am–12:30pm. www.valefarmersmarket.com

Abergavenny Farmers' Market ㊾
A good range of food and drink produced in the area, along with occasional cooking and crafts demonstrations.
Market Hall, Cross Street, Abergavenny, Monmouthshire; tel: 01873 735811; fourth Thu of every month, 9am–2:30pm. www.abergavennyfarmersmarket.co.uk

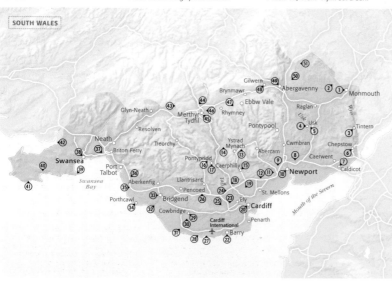
SOUTH WALES

PUBS

The Punch House ①
Historic, Grade II-listed inn with resident
ghost. Live music on Fridays and popular
Sunday roasts.
*Agincourt Square, Monmouth;
tel: 01600 713855; open daily.
www.punchhousemonmouth.com*

The Queen's Head ①
This welcoming Tudor pub plays host
to regular live jazz sessions and also
offers accommodation and meals.
*1 St James' Street, Monmouth;
tel: 01600 712767; open daily.
www.queensheadmonmouth.co.uk*

The Church Inn ⑲
Quaint and sociable medieval pub in
a picturesque setting, with quiz nights
and live music.
*Ty-Glas Road, Llanishen, Cardiff;
tel: 029 2076 3601; open daily.
www.churchinnllanishen.co.uk*

The Goat Major ⑳
This traditional pub, with dark wood
panelling and black leather sofas, serves
a good choice of regional real ales.
*High Street, Cardiff; tel: 029 2033 7161;
open daily. www.sabrain.com*

The Maltsters Arms ⑳
Dating back to around 1310, this is
believed to be Cardiff's oldest pub.
*42–44 Cardiff Road, Llandaff, Cardiff;
tel: 029 2033 3096; open daily.
www.maltsterscardiff.com*

The Woodville ⑳
Lively Victorian pub in the heart of Cardiff's
student neighbourhood. Popular with a
younger crowd.
*1–5 Woodville Road, Cathays, Cardiff;
tel: 029 2039 7889; open daily.
www.thewoodvillecardiff.co.uk*

Terra Nova ⑳
Large, modern pub on the bay with an
outdoor terrace and a good menu.
*Mermaid Quay, Stuart Street, Cardiff Bay,
Cardiff; tel: 029 2045 0947; open daily
(until 2am Fri & Sat).
www.terranovacardiff.com*

The Plymouth Arms ㉓
Atmospheric former Victorian hunting
lodge, complete with oak beams,
fireplaces and a large garden.
*Crofft Y Genau Road, St Fagans,
Cardiff; tel: 029 2056 9173; open daily.
www.vintageinn.co.uk*

The Sportsmans Rest ㉕
Rustic, countryside pub with a menu
featuring plenty of hearty food.
*Peterston-Super-Ely, Vale of Glamorgan;
tel: 01446 760675; open daily*

Duke of Wellington ㉙
Award-winning medieval pub with open
fires, a beer garden and traditional pub grub.
*High Street, Cowbridge, Vale of Glamorgan,
tel: 01446 773592; open daily.
www.dukeofwellingtoncowbridge.com*

The Westbourne ㊳
In the Uplands area, this independent
pub is popular with students and features
a heated beer terrace.
*1 Bryn y Mor Road, Swansea;
tel: 01792 476637; open daily.
www.westbourneswansea.com*

The Pumphouse ㊳
Modern pub in an attractive quayside
building with an outside terrace and a
wide range of ales.
*Pumphouse Quay, Maritime Quarter,
Swansea; tel: 01792 651080; open daily.
www.sabrain.com*

Salt at the George ㊴
Modern, airy and family-friendly seaside
pub with an outdoor terrace and good
wine selection.
*Mumbles Road, Mumbles, Swansea;
tel: 01792 368129; open daily
www.georgeswansea.com*

Red Lion Inn ㊸
A favourite with the locals, this pub has
good food and a wide range of real ales.
*Church Road, Penderyn, Rhondda Cyon
Taf; tel: 01685 811914; open daily.
www.redlionpenderyn.com*

PLACES TO STAY

Ciderhouse Cottage ②
Self-catering accommodation in a restored
barn with all mod cons, on a peaceful
Monmouthshire farm.
*Penylan Farm, Hendre, Monmouthshire;
tel: 01600 716435. www.penylanfarm.co.uk*

Llancayo Windmill ④
For a holiday home with a difference,
try this rural, handsomely restored
five-storey windmill deep within
beautiful Monmouthshire countryside.
*Morspan Holdings Ltd, Beech Hill Farm,
Usk, Monmouthshire; tel: 01291 672539.
www.llancayowindmill.com*

Olway Inn ⑤
Fishing trips can be arranged at this
quaint 17th century countryside inn,
which also has a restaurant.
*Chepstow Road, Gwernesney, Usk,
Monmouthshire; tel: 01291 672047.
www.olwayinn.co.uk*

Crescent Guest House ⑩
Good-quality hotel close to the city
centre, with tasteful en suite rooms.
*11 Caerau Crescent,, Newport; tel: 01633
776677. www.crescentguesthouse.com*

Heritage Park Hotel ⑯
A comfortable modern hotel with
restaurant and spa, opposite the
Heritage Park Museum.
*Coed Cae Road, Trehafod, Pontypridd,
Rhondda Cynon Taf; tel: 01443 687057.
www.heritageparkhotel.co.uk*

The Big Sleep Hotel ⑳
In a converted office block, this is a
modish, simply furnished central hotel.
*Bute Terrace, Cardiff; tel: 029 2063 6363.
www.thebigsleephotel.com*

Above: Terra Nova, in Cardiff's trendy bay area

NosDa Hostel ⑳
Smart backpacker hostel in Cardiff city
centre, with en suite rooms and a gym.
*53–59 Despenser Street, Riverside, Cardiff;
tel: 029 2037 8866. www.nosda.co.uk*

Jolyons at The Bay ⑳
Elegant six-room boutique hotel in the
Cardiff Bay area with king-size beds and
whirlpool baths.
*Bute Crescent, Cardiff; tel: 029 2048
8775. www.jolyons.co.uk*

Aberthaw House Hotel ㉒
Comfortable guesthouse near the
town centre, with neat en suite rooms.
*28 Porthkerry Road, Barry, Vale of
Glamorgan; tel: 01446 737314
www.aberthawhousehotel.org.uk*

Llanerch Vineyard ㉖
Self-catering and B&B accommodation in
farm buildings on Wales's largest vineyard.
*Hensol, Vale of Glamorgan; tel: 01443
225716. www.llanerch-vineyard.co.uk*

Fontygary Leisure Park ㉗
Popular seafront caravan and camping
park with entertainment and leisure
centre, gym and restaurants.
*Rhoose, Barry, Vale of Glamorgan; tel:
01446 710386. www.fontygaryparks.co.uk*

Limpert Bay Guest House ㉘
Delightful guest house located on the
beach with fabulous sea views.
*The Leys, Gileston, Barry, Vale of
Glamorgan; tel: 01446 751073.
www.limpertbay.co.uk*

Sheepleys ㉚
Charming and friendly B&B with
tastefully decorated en-suite rooms.
*Llandow, nr Cowbridge, Vale of
Glamorgan; tel: 01446 776228
www.sheepleys.co.uk*

Newcourt Bed and Breakfast ㉛
Self-contained accommodation with
an open fire in the lounge, plus a well-
stocked fridge in the kitchen containing
an array of choices for breakfast.
*Cowbridge Road, Llantwit Major,
Vale of Glamorgan; tel: 01446 794368*

Foam Edge Guest House ㉞
Welcoming town house on the seafront
with comfortable, well-appointed rooms.
*9 West Drive, Porthcawl, Bridgend; tel: 01656
782866. www.welcometoporthcawl.co.uk*

Seabank Hotel ㉞
Grand 19th-century hotel near the beach;
most rooms enjoy spectacular sea views.
*Esplanade, Porthcawl, Bridgend; tel: 01656
782261. www.leisureplex.co.uk*

Trecco Bay Holiday Park ㉞
Family-friendly caravan park on a blue-flag
beach, with a pool and golf course.
*Porthcawl, Bridgend; tel: 0344 335 3450.
www.parkdeanholidays.com*

Protea Guest House ㉞
Smart Edwardian town house near the
seafront, with tastefully furnished rooms.
*25 Esplanade Avenue, Porthcawl,
Bridgend; tel: 01656 786526.
www.proteaguesthouse.com*

Above: Chepstow Castle in Gwent

The Dragon Hotel ㊳
Swansea's swankiest hotel, with 106 stylish rooms, two restaurants, a health club and pool.
The Kingsway, Swansea; tel: 01792 657100. www.dragon-hotel.co.uk

Port Eynon Youth Hostel ㊶
Fresh modern dorms and rooms in a restored lifeboat station, just off the beach.
Old Lifeboat House, Port Eynon, Gower, Swansea; tel: 0845 371 9135. www.yha.org.uk

Llwyn Onn Guest House ㊹
Pleasant rural guesthouse in the Brecon Beacons with simple airy rooms.
Llywyn Onn, Cwmtaf, Merthyr Tydfil; tel: 01685 384384. www.llwynonn.co.uk

Queen Bee & B ㊺
The well-appointed, luxurious rooms at this B&B are inspired by Laura Ashley and Julian McDonald.
Atalanta House, Fothergill Street, Merthyr Tydfil; tel: 07535 309235. www.queenbeeandb.co.uk

Beaufort Arms ㊽
A historic inn situated at the foot of the Black Mountains with four comfortable rooms.
Main Road, Gilwern, nr Abergavenny, Monmouthshire; tel: 01873 832235. www.beaufortarms.co.uk

The Old Rectory (51)
Three elegant rooms in a 17th-century former rectory, set in a charming hamlet.
Llangattock Lingoed, nr Abergavenny Monmouthshire; tel: 01873 821326. www.oldrectorystayinwales.co.uk

FESTIVALS AND EVENTS

Monmouth Festival ①
A nine-day free music festival, featuring established and upcoming acts from a variety of musical genres.
Various venues, Monmouth; Jul. www.monmouthfestival.co.uk

Coral Welsh Grand National ⑥
Join in the festivities at Wales's most prestigious horse-racing meeting on the day after Boxing Day.
Chepstow Racecourse, Chepstow, Monmouthshire; tel: 01291 622260; Dec. www.chepstow-racecourse.co.uk

The Big Cheese® ⑱
Caerphilly's rich heritage and culture is celebrated with three days of street theatre, music, re-enactments, funfair rides and fireworks.
Owain Glyndwr Playing Fields, Twyn Square, Caerphilly; tel: 029 2088 0011; Jul. www.caerphilly.gov.uk/bigcheese

Porthcawl Elvis Festival ㉞
Europe's biggest gathering of Elvis Presley tribute artists, with three days of shows and singing competitions.
Various venues, Porthcawl, Bridgend; Sep. www.elvies.co.uk

Cardiff Festival ⑳
City-wide festivities on weekends in the summer, including open-air theatre performances, concerts, comedy, acrobats and a carnival.
Various venues, Cardiff; tel: 029 2087 2087; Jun–Sep. www.cardiff-events.com

Welsh Proms ⑳
Annual musical festival in the heart of Cardiff, featuring eight days of performances, including classical, folk and world music, and the Children's Proms.
St David's Hall, The Hayes, Cardiff; tel: 029 2087 8444; Jul. www.welshproms.com

Swansea International Festival of Music and The Arts ㊳
Long-running musical festival featuring classical music, opera, jazz, gospel and musical comedy over three weeks.
Various venues, Swansea; tel: 01792 411570; Sep–Oct. www.swanseafestival.org

Abergavenny Food Festival ㊾
Major two-day culinary festival, with food stalls, cookery demonstrations and entertainment *(see p123)*.
Various venues, Abergavenny, Monmouthshire; tel: 01873 851643; Sep. www.abergavennyfoodfestival.com

MUSEUMS AND GALLERIES

Nelson Museum & Local History Centre ①
One of the world's best collections of Admiral Nelson memorabilia, including personal letters and his sword. The Local Hitory Centre displays items from the Monmouth Borough archive and includes an exhibition about the Rolls family.
New Market Hall, Priory Street, Monmouth; tel: 01600 710630; open Mar–Oct: 11am–1pm and 2–5pm Mon–Sat, 2–5pm Sun; Nov–Feb: 11am–1pm and 2pm–4pm Mon–Sat, 2–4pm Sun. www.monmouthshire.gov.uk

Usk Rural Life Museum ④
Displays recall rural life in Monmouthshire, with a reconstructed farm kitchen and agricultural equipment.
The Malt Barn, New Market Street, Usk, Monmouthshire; tel: 01291 673777; open Mar–Oct: 10:30am–5pm Tue–Sun. www.uskmuseum.org

Chepstow Castle ⑥
Dating from 1067, this is one of Britain's earliest stone castles. It commands spectacular views over the River Wye.
Chepstow, Monmouthshire; tel: 01291 624065; open Mar–Oct: 9:30am–5pm daily (Jul–Aug: to 6pm); Nov–Feb: 10am–4pm Mon–Sat, 11am–4pm Sun. www.cadw.wales.gov.uk

Caldicot Castle ⑦
Take an audio tour around this stunning Norman castle and its extensive parkland.
Church Road, Caldicot, Monmouthshire; tel: 01291 420241; open Easter–Oct: 11am–4pm Tue–Sun (to 5pm in school holidays). www.visitmonmouthshire.com

National Roman Legion Museum ⑧
See Britain's best-preserved Roman amphitheatre, legionary barracks, countless artifacts and a re-created Roman garden.
High Street, Caerleon, Monmouthshire; tel: 0300 111 2333; open 10am–5pm Mon–Sat, 2–5pm Sun. www.museumwales.ac.uk/roman

Fourteen Locks Canal Centre ⑨
Discover the history of the Brecon and Monmouthshire Canal, and go for a boat trip on the waterway.
Cwm Lane, Rogerstone, Newport; tel: 01633 892167, open 10am–4:30pm daily. www.fourteenlocks.mbact.org.uk

Tredegar House ⑩
Explore this grand 17th-century mansion with costumed guides. Regular themed events are also held.
Newport; tel: 01633 815880; open mid-Feb–end Mar: 11am–4pm; end Mar–Sep: 11am–5pm daily. www.nationaltrust.org.uk

Llancaiach Fawr Manor ⑭
Costumed guides take you back in time at this 16th-century manor house.
Gelligaer Road, Nelson, Treharris, Caerphilly; tel: 01443 412248; open 10am–5pm Tue–Sun. www.your.caerphilly.gov.uk/llancaiachfawr

Rhondda Heritage Park ⑯
A reconstructed mining village street and tours of the old buildings at the pit's head.
Lewis Merthyr Colliery, Coed Cae Road, Trehafod, Rhondda Cynon Taf; tel: 01443 682036; open 10:30am–4:30pm Tue–Sat. www.tourism.rctcbc.gov.uk/en

Castell Coch ⑱
Victorian "fairy-tale" castle in medieval style, with lush Neo-Gothic interiors.
Tongwynlais, Cardiff; tel: 029 2081 0101; open Feb: 10am–4pm Mon–Sat, 11am–4pm Sun; Mar–Oct: 9:30am–5pm daily (Jul–Aug: to 6pm). www.cadw.wales.gov.uk

Butetown History & Arts Centre ⑳
Discover the history of Cardiff's docklands
at this unique community centre.
4 Dock Chambers, Bute Street, Cardiff;
tel: 029 2025 6757; open 11am–5pm
Tue–Fri, 11am–4:30pm Sat–Sun.
www.bhac.org

National Museum Cardiff ⑳
Fascinating displays on natural history,
archaeology, social history and art.
Cathays Park, Cardiff; tel: 0300 111 2333;
open 10am–5pm Tue–Sun.
www.museumwales.ac.uk/cardiff

Bay Art ⑳
Stylish gallery, situated in Cardiff's bay
area, regularly hosts major exhibitions
of works by contemporary Welsh and
international artists.
54B/C Bute Street, Cardiff Bay; tel. 029
2065 0016; open noon–5pm Tue–Sat.
www.bayart.org.uk

Cosmeston Medieval Village ㉑
Faithfully reconstructed 14th-century
village, complete with costumed
villagers and rare farm animals.
Cosmeston, Lavernock Road,
Penarth, Vale of Glamorgan;
tel: 029 2070 1678;
open Apr–Sep: 10am–5pm daily;
Oct–Mar: 10am–4pm daily.
www.valeofglamorgan.gov.uk

St Fagans Museum of Welsh Life ㉓
Visit restored historic buildings brought
here from across Wales, and watch
traditional craftspeople at work.
St Fagans, Cardiff; tel: 0300 111
2333; open 10am–5pm daily.
www.museumwales.ac.uk/stfagans

National Waterfront Museum ㊳
Explore Wales's industrial and maritime
heritage through fascinating displays.
Oystermouth Road, Maritime Quarter,
Swansea; tel: 0300 111 2333;
open 10am–5pm daily.
www.museumwales.ac.uk/swansea

Dylan Thomas Centre ㊳
Displays on the life and works of the poet,
plus a café and bookshop.
Somerset Place, Swansea; tel: 01792
463980; open 10am–4:30pm daily.
www.dylanthomas.com

Ynysfach Engine House ㊺
Once part of the 19th-century Cyfarthfa
Ironworks, this building houses displays
on local industrial heritage.
Ynysfach Road, Merthyr Tydfil; tel: 01685
727371; open 10am–4pm Mon–Fri.
www.cyfarthfa.com

**Cyfarthfa Castle Museum & Art
Gallery** ㊺
A Regency-era mansion house, home
to displays on local industrial history.
Cyfarthfa Park, Brecon Road, Merthyr
Tydfil; tel: 01685 723112; open Apr–Sep:
10am–5:30pm daily; Oct–Mar: 10am–
4pm Tue–Fri, noon–4pm Sat–Sun.
www.cyfarthfa.com

Bedwellty House and Park ㊼
Restored Regency mansion and gardens
with displays on local history.
Morgan Street, Tredegar, Blaenau Gwent;
tel: 01495 353370; open 11am–5pm daily.
www.bedwelltyhouseandpark.co.uk

THINGS TO DO WITH KIDS

Old Station, Tintern ③
Explore the series of trails around this
restored Victorian country railway station with
a signal box, train carriages and a play area.
Tintern, Chepstow, Monmouthshire; tel:
01291 689566; open Apr–Sep: 10:30am–
5:30pm daily; Oct: 10:30am–4pm daily.
www.visitmonmouthshire.com/
oldstationtintern

Cefn Mably Farm Park ⑫
Younger kids will love the pony rides,
indoor and outdoor play areas and petting
the animals at this farm.
Began Road, Cefn Mably, nr Castleton,
Cardiff; tel: 01633 680312; open 10am–
5pm daily. www.cefnmablyfarmpark.com

Techniquest ⑳
Here kids can get hands-on with a variety
of interactive science experiments.
Stuart Street, Cardiff Bay, Cardiff;
tel: 029 2047 5475; open 9:30am–
4:30pm Tue–Fri, 10am–5pm Sat–Sun
www.techniquest.org

Doctor Who Experience ⑳
Costumes and props from the BBC TV
series here – watch out for the Daleks!
Discovery Quay, Porth Teigr, Cardiff Bay,
Cardiff; tel: 0208 433 3162; open 10am–
5pm daily (days can vary, see website for
details). www.doctorwhoexhibition.com

Below: Interactive exhibits at Techniquest in Cardiff

Barry Island Pleasure Park ㉒
Wales's premier amusement park will
provide plenty of thrills and spills for
all the family.
Friars Road, Barry Island, Vale of
Glamorgan; tel: 01446 722100;
open noon–6pm daily.
www.barryislandpleasurepark.co.uk

Welsh Hawking Centre ㉒
Get close to over 200 birds of prey and
watch displays of falconry in attractive
parkland at this centre.
Weycock Road, Barry, Vale of Glamorgan;
tel: 01446 734687; open 10:30am–5pm
Wed–Mon. www.welsh-hawking.co.uk

Ogmore Farm Riding Centre ㉜
Saddle up a horse for a guided trek
along wide beaches, sand dunes and
open countryside.
Ogmore Farm, Ogmore Road,
Bridgend; tel: 01656 880856.
www.rideonthebeach.co.uk

Ocean Quest ㉞
A water-sports centre that offers kayaking,
surfing and power-boating tuition.
49 New Road, Porthcawl, Bridgend;
tel: 01656 783310; see website for course
details. www.ocean-quest.co.uk

Margam Country Park ㊱
Explore the magnificent Gothic mansion,
orangery, narrow-gauge railway, adventure
playground, deer park and bike trails in
glorious country parkland.
Margam, Port Talbot; tel: 01639 881635;
open Apr–early Sep: 10am–5pm daily;
mid-Sep–Oct and end Jan–Mar:
10am–4:30pm; Nov–mid-Jan: 1–4:30pm
Mon–Tue). www.margamcountrypark.co.uk

Kenfig National Nature Reserve ㉟
The coastal dunes and wetlands here
are ideal for bird-watching or just enjoying
countryside walks.
Ton Kenfig, nr Porthcawl, Bridgend; tel:
01656 743386; open daily (visitor centre
open 2–4:30pm Mon–Fri, 10am–4:30pm
Sat–Sun).

Brecon Mountain Railway ㊻
Take a steam-train ride through the
stunning landscape of the Brecon Beacons
and visit the workshop where repairs are
made to the locomotives and carriages.
Off Heads of the Valleys trunk road, Pant
Station, Merthyr Tydfil; tel: 01685 722988;
open mid-Feb–Oct: trains depart from
10:30am (see website for full timetable).
www.breconmountainrailway.co.uk

Parc Bryn Bach ㊼
Several instructor-led activities on offer,
including mountain-biking, kayaking and
archery, with on site accommodation.
Merthyr Road, Tredegar, Blaenau Gwent;
tel: 01495 355920; phone for details
(visitor centre open from 8:30am daily).
www.parcbrynbach.co.uk

SPAS AND HEALTH RESORTS

The Celtic Manor Resort ⑩
Luxurious resort with two spas offering
various facial and body treatments.
Coldra Woods, Newport; tel: 01633
413000. www.celtic-manor.com

Bryn Meadows Spa ⑬
Luxurious boutique spa with pool,
sauna, Jacuzzi and sun terrace.
Maes-y-Cwmmer, nr Ystrad Mynach,
Caerphilly; tel: 01495 225590.
www.brynmeadows.co.uk

Laguna Health & Spa ⑳
A wide variety of beauty treatments
and massages in the heart of Cardiff.
Park Plaza Hotel, Greyfriars Road,
Cardiff; tel: 029 2011 1110.
www.lagunahealthandspa.com

The St Davids Hotel & Spa ⑳
A top-class spa and restaurant in a modern
5-star hotel overlooking Cardiff Bay.
Havannah Street, Cardiff Bay, Cardiff;
tel: 029 2045 4045.
www.thestdavidshotel.com

The Towers Hotel & Spa ㊲
A sauna, swimming pool and various
beauty treatments are available here.
Jersey Marine, Swansea Bay,
Swansea; tel: 01792 814155.
www.thetowersswanseabay.com

Nant Ddu Lodge ⑪
Relax and be pampered at this country
hotel in the Brecon Beacons.
Cwmtaf, Merthyr Tydfil; tel: 01685 379111.
www.nant-ddu-lodge.co.uk

OTHER SIGHTS IN THE BOOK

NORTHWEST ENGLAND

LOCAL FOOD

Earth Café ⑯
Buddhist-inspired, alcohol-free vegetarian café that has its (healthy) heart in the right place.
16–20 Turner Street, Northern Quarter, Manchester; tel: 0161 834 1996; open 10am–4pm Mon–Fri, 10am–5pm Sat. www.earthcafe.co.uk

Nawaab ⑯
Palatial Indian restaurant with an extensive and mouthwatering menu of dishes.
1008 Stockport Road, Levenshulme, Manchester; tel: 0161 224 6969; open 5:30–11pm Mon–Thu, 5–11pm Fri and Sat, 1–11pm Sun. www.nawaab.co.uk

Manchester Real Food Market ⑯
Full of seasonal fare and local produce, from cakes to cheeses and real ale.
Piccadilly Gardens, Manchester; tel: 0161 234 7357; second and fourth Fri and Sat of every month, 10am–5:30pm.

The Quarter ㉓
Splendid pizzas, pasta, salads and home-made cakes at this relaxing bistro.
7 Falkner Street, Liverpool; tel: 0151 707 1965; open 8am–11pm Mon–Fri, 9am–11pm Sat and Sun. www.thequarteruk.com

Below: "The Beats" pose at Liverpool's Cavern Club

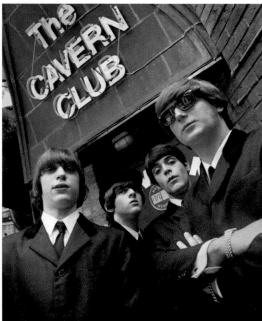

Village Bakery ③
This increasingly well-known bakery uses local ingredients and renewable energy to make artisan, organic produce. There's also a lovely café attached.
Lazonby, Penrith, Cumbria; tel: 01768 898437; open 9am–5pm Mon–Sat, 9:30am–5pm Sun during summer months (opening times vary outside this). www.village-bakery.com

Joseph Benjamin ⑳
Award-winning restaurant, bar and deli that swears by locally-sourced, seasonal ingredients and has a relaxed atmosphere.
134–140 Northgate Street, Chester; tel: 01244 344295; open Tue, Wed & Sun for lunch, Thu–Sat for dinner. www.josephbenjamin.co.uk

Chez Jules Restaurant ⑳
Located within a lovely half-timbered building, this busy French eatery is one of Chester's most popular.
71 Northgate Street, Chester; tel: 01244 400014; open noon–10:30pm Mon–Sat, noon–9:30pm Sun. www.chezjules.com

Seniors ㉘
Every day, apart from Sunday, is "fryday" at this chippie, which has a loyal following. Note that it closes early.
106 Normoss Road, Blackpool, Lancashire; tel: 01253 393529; open 11:30am–2pm and 4:30–8pm Mon–Sat. www.seniorsfishandchips.co.uk

William Peat Butchers ⑨
Award-winning Cumbrian butchers famed for its top-quality pork.
2 Finkle Street, Sedbergh, Cumbria; tel: 015396 20431; open 7am–5pm Mon–Fri, 7am–4pm Sat. www.castlebankbutchers.co.uk

Brough's ㉕
Celebrated butchers with award-winning sausages and local meats on offer.
583b Liverpool Road, Ainsdale, Southport, Merseyside; tel: 01704 578025; open 8am–5:30pm Mon–Thu & Sat, 8am–6:30pm Fri.

FARMERS' MARKETS

Penrith Farmers' Market ⑤
A must for anyone on the trail of fresh produce, local specialities and crafts.
Market Square, Penrith, Cumbria; tel: 01768 817817; third Tue of month, Mar–Dec, 9:30am–2:30pm.

Colne Farmers' Market ⑩
Small market with an appetizing spread of vegetables, meats and other organic fare.
Market Street, Colne, Lancashire; tel: 01282 661240; third Sat of every month, 9am–2pm.

Lancaster Charter Farmers' & Producers' Market ㉙
Bustling outdoor market with a cornucopia of fresh and tasty local produce.
Market Square, Lancaster; tel: 01524 414251; 9am–4:30pm Wed & Sat.

Orton Farmers' Market ㉝
Mind-boggling range of local Cumbrian food and produce in the deliciously picturesque village of Orton.
Orton, Cumbria; second Sat of every month, 9am–2pm. www.ortonfarmers.co.uk

PUBS AND BARS

Peveril of the Peak ⑯
Traditional and distinctive-looking early-19th-century pub with a green-tiled exterior and a healthy range of real ales.
127 Great Bridgewater Street, Manchester; tel: 0161 236 6364; open noon–11pm Mon–Wed, noon–11:30pm Thu, noon–midnight Fri & Sat, noon–10:30pm Sun.

The Metropolitan ⑯
Gorgeous red-brick railway tavern full of period charm; bar and restaurant menus.
2 Lapwing Lane, West Didsbury, Manchester; tel: 0161 438 2332; open daily. www.the-metropolitan.co.uk

Cavern Club ㉓
Eternally associated with the Fab Four, the Cavern Club is an iconic spot for a drink and for catching live bands.
10 Mathew Street, Liverpool; tel: 0151 236 1965; open from 10am daily; closes midnight Mon–Wed, late Thu–Sun (with evening admission charges for live performances). Families welcome before 7pm. www.cavernclub.org

The Greyhound Hotel ⑧
Hotel and pub with 17th-century roots and much-championed dining and drinking.
Main Street, Shap, Cumbria; tel: 01931 716474. www.greyhoundshap.co.uk

The Three Fishes ⑬
Lovely outpost of fine cuisine and real ale in the Ribble Valley.
Mitton Road, Mitton, nr Whalley, Lancashire; tel: 01254 826888; open daily. www.thethreefishes.com

Alma de Cuba ㉓
An altar-equipped church conversion that is dedicated to fine food and drink.
St Peter's Church, Seel Street, Liverpool; tel: 0843 504 4690; open daily. www.alma-de-cuba.com

The Water Witch ㉙
Perched on the side of the Lancaster Canal, these converted stables provide an excellent place to slake a thirst.
Canal Tow Path, Aldcliffe Lane, Lancaster; tel: 01524 63828; open daily. www.thewaterwitch.co.uk

The Drunken Duck Inn ㊷
This magnificently named inn is a classic watering hole, set in massive grounds in the heart of the Lake District.
Barngates, Ambleside, Cumbria; tel: 01539 436347; open daily. http://drunkenduckinn.co.uk

The Bitter End ㊿
Traditional Lake District pub with on-site brewery. Serves mussels in white wine and other delicious dishes.
15 Kirkgate, Cockermouth, Cumbria; tel: 01900 828993; open 4–11pm Mon–Fri, 11am–11pm Sat & Sun. www.bitterend.co.uk

PLACES TO STAY

Warwick Lodge Guesthouse ①
Very clean and comfortable: large rooms, superb breakfasts and friendly proprietors.
112 Warwick Road, Carlisle; tel: 01228 523796. www.warwicklodgecarlisle.co.uk

Hard Day's Night ㉓
Highly fashionable Beatles-dedicated accommodation in a lovely historic building in the heart of Liverpool.
Central Buildings, North John Street, Liverpool; tel: 0151 668 0475. www.harddaysnighthotel.com

Malmaison Liverpool ㉓
Carbon-grey and black industrial decor at this hotel, with stylish rooms, smooth dining and entertainment facilities.
William Jessop Way, Princes Dock, Liverpool; tel: 0151 363 3640. www.malmaison-liverpool.com

The Nadler ㉓
Great value contemporary conversion of an old warehouse. No add-ons, no restaurant/bar but mini-kitchens in rooms.
29 Seel Street, Liverpool; tel: 0151 705 2626. www.thenadler.com/liverpool

The Rampsbeck Country Manor Hotel ⑥
In an absolutely stunning lakeside position by Ullswater, and set in attractive grounds, this magnificent country-house hotel makes for a memorable stay.
Watermillock, Ullswater, Cumbria; tel: 01768 486442. www.rampsbeck.co.uk

Appleby Manor Country House Hotel ⑦
Delightfully located 19th-century house in the Eden Valley, with considerate staff and excellent dining.
Roman Road, Appleby in Westmorland, Cumbria; tel: 01768 351571. www.applebymanor.co.uk

The Welbeck ⑲
Just off the Central Promenade in Douglas, this hotel offers comfy, clean rooms, sea views and attentive service.
Mona Drive, Douglas, Isle of Man; tel: 01624 675663. www.welbeckhotel.com

Edgar House ⑳
This period Georgian house is peacefully situated atop the ancient city walls.
22 City Walls, Chester; tel: 01244 347007. www.edgarhouse.co.uk

The Chester Grosvenor ⑳
The height of luxury in Chester, this gorgeous-looking historic hotel has everything you might need, including an invigorating spa.
Eastgate, Chester; tel: 01244 324024. www.chestergrosvenor.com

Higher Huxley Hall ⑳
Fine-looking manor house dating back to the 13th century, with huge grounds.
Red Lane, Huxley, Chester; tel: 01829 781100. www.huxleyhall.co.uk

Ash Farm ㉑
This handsome 18th-century farmhouse, set in gorgeous Cheshire countryside, is a perfect romantic getaway.
Park Lane, Little Bollington, Altrincham, Cheshire; tel: 0161 929 9290. www.ashfarm.co.uk

The Big Blue ㉘
Guests are full of praise for the modern, roomy accommodation and family-oriented facilities at this hotel right next to the Pleasure Beach.
Ocean Boulevard, Pleasure Beach, Blackpool, Lancashire; tel: 0871 222 4000. www.bigbluehotel.com

Manor House Hotel ㊿
Expect a warm welcome and excellent food at this traditional hotel.
Crown Street, Cockermouth, Cumbria; tel: 01900 828663. www.manorcockermouth.co.uk

New House Farm ㊿
Hidden away within 6 hectares (15 acres) of scenic Lakeland, this 17th-century house has the added allure of a garden hot tub.
Lorton, Cockermouth, Cumbria; tel: 07841 159818. http://newhouse-farm.com

Number 43 ㉚
Lovingly designed and cared-for Victorian boutique B&B overlooking the Kent estuary, with more than a measure of style and modern flair.
The Promenade, Arnside, Cumbria; tel: 01524 762761. www.no43.org.uk

The Pennington ㊵
Very relaxing seafront hotel in Ravenglass with modern, comfortable rooms and excellent dining.
Main Street, Ravenglass, Cumbria; tel: 01229 717222. www.penningtonhotel.co.uk

The Archway ㉟
Truly charming B&B with Victorian charm; grade-A breakfasts and packed lunches.
13 College Road, Windermere, Cumbria; tel: 01539 445613. www.the-archway.com

The Old Dungeon Ghyll Hotel ㊸
Hotel in a 300-year-old building with a perfect location in the Langdale Valley.
Great Langdale, Ambleside, Cumbria; tel: 01539 437272. www.odg.co.uk

Beck Allans Bed & Breakfast ㊺
Lovely Lake Disctrict B&B with delightful views over the River Rothay.
College Street, Grasmere, Cumbria; tel: 01539 435079. www.beckallans.com

The Cottage in the Wood Country House Hotel & Restaurant ㊽
With welcoming owners, a great restaurant, a cosy feel and a secluded mountain forest location overlooking Skiddaw, this is a great place for a relaxing break.
Magic Hill, Whinlatter Forest, Braithwaite, nr Keswick, Cumbria; tel: 01768 778409. www.thecottageinthewood.co.uk

Cumberland County Show ①
One-day celebration of food and farming with games, rides and performances.
Carlisle Racecourse, Durdar Road, Carlisle, Cumbria; tel: 01228 812601; Jun. www.cumberlandshow.co.uk

Potfest ⑤
Two separate three-day gatherings for creative potters from all over Europe to show off their creations.
Penrith, Cumbria; Potfest in the Park at Hutton-in-the-Forest; Jul; Potfest in the Pens at Skirsgill Auction Mar; Aug. www.potfest.co.uk

The Great British R&B Festival ⑩
Three-day gathering of seasoned blues musicians, from Steve Cropper to The Yardbirds, Chicken Shack and beyond.
Colne, Lancashire; Aug. www.bluesfestival.co.uk

Manchester International Festival ⑯
Biennial festival celebrating new and original performance art, visual arts and music events over two weeks.
Various venues, Manchester; tel: 0161 817 4500; every other Jul. www.mif.co.uk

Liverpool Irish Festival ㉓
Music, art, theatre, literature, Gaelic football and dance at this two-week celebration of traditional and contemporary Irish culture.
Various venues, Liverpool; Oct. www.liverpoolirishfestival.com

Grasmere Rushbearing Festival ㊺
Traditional bearing of rushes to St Oswald's Church by local children; the festival dates back hundreds of years when rushes were strewn on the floor of local churches.
Grasmere, Cumbria; Sat closest to St Oswald's Day (5 Aug). www.grasmereandrydal.org.uk

NORTHWEST ENGLAND

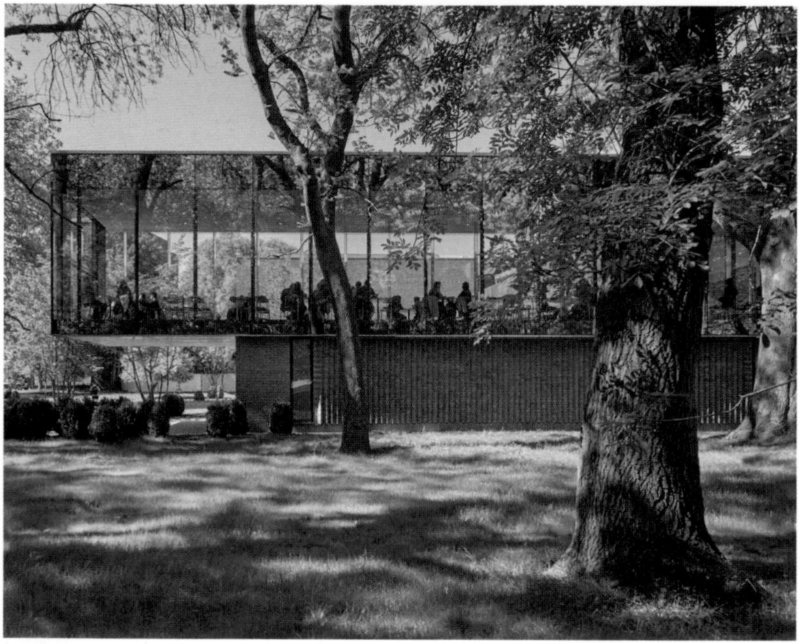

Left: Whitworth Art Gallery

Grasmere Lakeland Sports and Show ㊺
Largest meeting for traditional Lakeland sports, such as fell-running, hound trails and bouts between the inimitably dressed Cumberland wrestlers. Military bands provide the music.
Grasmere, Cumbria; Aug Bank Holiday Sun. http://grasmeresportsandshow.co.uk

Appleby Horse Fair ⑦
Attracting thousands of travellers and a constellation of caravans and wagons, this week-long festival is an annual highlight.
Appleby in Westmorland, Cumbria; first Thu in Jun (unless first Thu is 1 Jun, when it is held on 8 Jun). www.applebyfair.org

Coniston Country Fair ㊲
Events at this taditional show include falconry, hang-gliding and egg throwing.
Coniston Water, Cumbria; Jul. www.conistoncountryfair.co.uk

Lakeland Country Fair ㊳
One-day celebration of traditional country crafts and skills, with sheepdog shows, fell races and children's activities.
Torver, nr Coniston, Cumbria; Aug. www.lakelandcountryfair.co.uk

Great North Swim ㉟
Be one of the 20,000 or so who flock to see swimmers take part in this challenging one-mile open water charity event.
Windermere, Cumbria; Jun. www.greatswim.org

Balloons and Tunes ⑭
Hot-air balloons of all descriptions fill the skies in this weekend-long extravaganza.
Witton Country Park, Preston Old Road, Blackburn, Lancashire; Jul. www.visitblackburn.co.uk.

Accrington Food & Drink Festival ⑮
A celebration of Lancashire gastronomy, including cooking demonstrations, stalls, music and dance.
Market Hall, Blackburn Road, Accrington, Lancashire; tel: 01282 426846; Jun. www.accringtonfoodfestival.co.uk

Ambleside Christmas Lights Festival ㊹
Heart-warming procession with paper lanterns through the winter streets of Ambleside one evening in November, with fireworks and other seasonal events.
Ambleside, Cumbria; mid-Nov. www.amblesidechristmaslights.co.uk

Keswick Beer Festival ㊼
The north's largest beer festival is a two-day exercise in real-ale indulgence.
Keswick Rugby Club, Davidson Park, Keswick, Cumbria; Jun. www.keswickbeerfestival.co.uk

Solway Festival (52)
Annual summer Cumbrian music festival with a strong programme of bands over the August Bank Holiday weekend.
Silloth, West Cumbria; late Aug. www.solfest.org.uk

Pendle Walking Festival ⑪
Guided walks, pub walks and the Pendle Way Challenge – a five-day hike.
Pendle, Lancashire; Aug–Sep. www.visitpendle.com/countryside/walking-festival

Ulverston Walking Festival ㉝
For all who appreciate the scenic Lakeland outdoors – on foot – with walks led by experienced volunteers.
Ulverston, Cumbria; Apr–May. www.ulverstonwalkfest.co.uk

Keswick Mountain Festival ㊼
Try ghyll scrambling, moonlight canoeing or a 70km cycle at this popular festival.
Crow Park, Keswick, Cumbria; mid-May. www.keswickmountainfestival.co.uk

MUSEUMS AND GALLERIES

Whitworth Art Gallery ⑯
Superb collection including rare Turner and Pre-Raphaelite watercolours.
Oxford Road, Manchester; tel: 0161 275 7450; open 10am–5pm Mon–Wed and Fri–Sun, 10am–9pm Thu. www.whitworth.manchester.ac.uk

The Imperial War Museum North ⑯
Modern museum with an extensive collection of military artifacts.
The Quays, Trafford Wharf Road, Manchester; tel: 0161 836 4000; open 10am–5pm daily. http://north.iwm.org.uk

Tullie House Museum and Art Gallery ①
Fascinating glimpses into the history, natural history, arts and culture of Carlisle.
Castle Street, Carlisle; tel: 01228 618718; open Nov–Mar: 10am–4pm Mon–Sat, noon–4pm Sun; Apr–Oct: 10am–5pm Mon–Sat, 11am–5pm Sun. www.tulliehouse.co.uk

The Manx Museum ⑲
Bursting with historical treasures unique to the island, this museum uses film, galleries and interactive displays to explore Manx culture and heritage.
Kingswood Grove, Douglas, Isle of Man; tel: 01624 648000; open 10am–5pm Mon–Sat. www.manxnationalheritage.im

Grosvenor Museum ⑳
Superb collection of Chester-related artifacts and displays including a first-rate range of Roman exhibits.
27 Grosvenor Street, Chester; tel: 01244 972197; open 10:30am–5pm Mon–Sat, 1–4pm Sun. www.grosvenormuseum.co.uk

Walker Art Gallery ㉓
Sumptuous collection of paintings from Pre-Raphaelite masters to Impressionist visionaries, as well as Turner and Hockney.
William Brown Street, Liverpool; tel: 0151 478 4199; open 10am–5pm daily. www.liverpoolmuseums.org.uk

Magical Mystery Tour ㉓
Essential Beatles bus tours where the streets become museum exhibits, organized by the Cavern Club, where the band first played *(see Pubs and Bars).*
Cavern City Tours, Liverpool; tel: 0151 703 9100. www.cavernclub.org

Laurel and Hardy Museum ㉝
Stan Laurel was born in Ulverston and this absorbing museum is dedicated to the sheer comic genius of the famous duo.
Roxy Cinema, Brogden Street, Ulverston, Cumbria; tel: 01229 582292; open 10am–5pm daily (closed Mon & Wed Nov-Easter). www.laurel-and-hardy-museum.co.uk

Ruskin Museum ㊲
Art and artifacts associated with John Ruskin, plus a selection of items relating to Donald Campbell and his record-breaking speedboat, *Bluebird*, which tragically crashed on Coniston Water in 1967.
Coniston, Cumbria; tel: 01539 441164; open mid-Mar–mid-Nov: 10am–5:30pm daily; mid-Nov–mid Mar: 10:30am–3:30pm Tue–Sun. www.ruskinmuseum.com

Keswick Museum and Art Gallery ㊼
Victorian-era museum crammed with oddities, from a mummified cat to musical stones, a mantrap and Napoleon's teacup. This is one of the world's strangest museums.
Station Road, Keswick, Cumbria; tel: 01768 773263; open 10am–4pm daily. www.keswickmuseum.org.uk

Lady Lever Art Gallery ㉒
A fantastic collection of Victorian art, including an internationally renowned selection of Pre-Raphaelite paintings.
Port Sunlight Village, Wirral, Merseyside; tel: 0151 478 4136; open 10am–5pm daily. www.liverpoolmuseums.org.uk

The National Football Museum ㉗
Now housed in the spectacular Urbis Building, this unfettered celebration of the "beautiful game" is a must for all football fans, young and old.
*Urbis Building, Cathedral Gardens, Manchester; tel: 0161 605 8200; open 10am–5pm daily.
www.nationalfootballmuseum.com*

Dock Museum ㉛
Built over a former dry dock, with an emphasis on the shipbuilding and maritime history of Barrow-in-Furness.
North Road, Barrow-in-Furness, Cumbria; tel: 01229 876400; open 11am–4pm Wed–Sun. www.dockmuseum.org.uk

Blackwell, The Arts and Crafts House ㉞
House near Lake Windermere associated with the Arts and Crafts movement and designed by M H Baillie Scott.
Bowness-on-Windermere, Cumbria; tel: 01539 446139; open Mar–Oct: 10:30am–5pm daily; Nov–Feb: 10:30am–4pm daily. www.blackwell.org.uk

Hill Top Farm ㊱
Beatrix Potter's 17th-century Lake District bolt hole is perfectly picturesque. Full of her favourite things, the cottage has a lovely garden to explore.
*Nr Sawrey, Ambleside, Cumbria; tel: 01539 436269; open Jun–Aug: Mon–Thu daily.
www.nationaltrust.org.uk/hill-top*

THINGS TO DO WITH KIDS

South Tynedale Railway ⑦
Scenic steam-train trips run along Northern England's highest narrow-gauge railway – 3.2 km (2 miles) of line stretch from Alston to Kirkhaugh.
The Railway Station, Alston, Cumbria; tel: 01434 338214 (talking timetable 01434 382828); operating hours vary: see website or contact for details. www.south-tynedale-railway.org.uk

World Museum Liverpool ㉓
Fascinating fun for wide-eyed kids, from the Ancient Egypt Gallery to the fish-filled aquarium, plus bundles of ongoing events.
*William Brown Street, Liverpool; tel: 0151 478 4393; open 10am–5pm daily.
www.liverpoolmuseums.org.uk*

Sandcastle Waterpark ㉘
With slides, chutes, pools and a wave machine, little ones will have plenty to keep them entertained.
*South Beach, Blackpool, Lancashire; tel: 01253 343602; open throughout the year (check website for availability).
www.sandcastle-waterpark.co.uk*

Dewa Roman Experience ⑳
Family-run attraction featuring recreations of Roman street scenes and relics from Roman Empire-era Chester.
*Pierpoint Lane, off Bridge Street, Chester; tel: 01244 343407; open Feb–Nov: 9am–5pm Mon–Sat, 10am–5pm Sun; Dec–Jan: 10am–4pm daily.
www.dewaromanexperience.co.uk*

The World of Beatrix Potter Attraction ㉞
Potter's magical world brought colourfully to life, with a much-loved tea room.
*Crag Brow, Bowness-on-Windermere, Cumbria; tel: 0844 504 1233; open 10am–5:30pm daily (last entry 4:30pm).
www.hop-skip-jump.com*

Ravenglass and Eskdale Railway ㊴
Hop aboard one of the steam trains running between Ravenglass and Dalegarth for a scenic journey.
*Ravenglass, Cumbria; tel: 01229 717171; trains run at least six times per day Feb–Oct (check website for availability outside these months).
www.ravenglass-railway.co.uk*

The Puzzling Place ㊼
Stuffed with puzzles, gadgets and curiosities to keep the kids entertained.
*Museum Square, Keswick, Cumbria; tel: 01768 775102; open mid-Mar–Oct: 11am–5:30pm daily; Nov–mid-Mar: 11am–5pm Tue–Sun (weekends only Jan).
www.puzzlingplace.co.uk*

Crafty Monkeys ④
Kids will love getting creative – and as messy as possible – at this interactive pottery studio. Do decopatch, make a pot, or paint a piggy bank.
Corney Square, Penrith, Cumbria; tel: 01768 398975; check website for opening times. www.craftymonkeys.org

Go Ape ㉖
Hidden in beautiful woodland, this action-packed obstacle course gives you a bird's eye view. Traverse the tree tops, jump off swings and fly down zip lines.
*Rivington Lane, Horwich, Bolton, Lancashire; tel. 0845 519 7072; open Feb–Nov (check site for availability).
https://goape.co.uk*

South Lakes Safari Zoo ㉜
From its white rhinos to red kangaroos and Colombian spider monkeys, this beautifully designed zoo is a joy.
*Melton Terrace, Lindal, Ulverston, Cumbria; tel: 01229 466086; open 10am–4:30pm daily.
www.southlakessafarizoo.com*

SPAS AND HEALTH RESORTS

Holbeck Ghyll Country House Hotel ㉟
With gorgeous Lake Windermere views and a Michelin-starred restaurant, this excellent hotel boasts a fantastic health spa, designed for full-on pampering.
Holbeck Lane, Windermere, Cumbria; tel: 01539 432375. www.holbeckghyll.com

Formby Hall Golf Resort and Spa ㉔
All-round winner on the Golf Coast with soothing spa and great fitness packages.
*Southport Old Road, Formby, Southport, Merseyside; tel: 01704 875699.
www.formbyhallgolfresort.co.uk*

Low Wood Hotel ㊶
This Lake Windermere shoreside hotel has a lovely location, great for family getaways.
*Ambleside Road, nr Windermere, Cumbria; tel: 01539 433338.
www.englishlakes.co.uk*

Lodore Falls Hotel ㊻
Highly relaxing getaway with health treatments that include waterfall therapy.
*The Lodore Falls Hotel, Borrowdale, Keswick, Cumbria; tel: 0800 840 1246.
www.lakedistricthotels.net/lodorefalls*

Armathwaite Hall Hotel ㊾
Stately luxury near Bassenthwaite Lake, spectacular scenery and a marvellous spa.
*Bassenthwaite Lake, Keswick, Cumbria; tel: 01768 776551.
http://armathwaite-hall.com*

OTHER SIGHTS IN THE BOOK

Pendle Hill ⑫ *(see pp26–7).* **Manchester** ⑯ *(see pp156–7).* **Cheshire Ring** ⑰ *(see pp112–13).* **Isle of Man** ⑱ *(see pp184–5).* **Liverpool** ㉓ *(see pp20–21).* **Blackpool** ㉘ *(see pp132–3).* **Lake District** ㊸ *(see pp50–51).*
Below: Ravenglass and Eskdale Railway

THE GREEN

NORTHEAST ENGLAND

LOCAL FOOD

The Factory Kitchen ①
An art gallery and café serving imaginative British cooking with local ingredients.
The Biscuit Factory, 16 Stoddart Street, Newcastle; tel: 0191 261 1103; open 10am–4pm Mon–Fri, 10am–5pm Sat, 11am–4pm Sun. www.thebiscuitfactory.com

Bistro Hotel du Vin ①
Simple dishes, expertly prepared, with a menu that changes seasonally and is based on local seafood, meats and veg.
Allan House, City Road, Newcastle; tel: 0191 389 8628; open daily for breakfast, lunch and dinner. www.hotelduvin.com

Helmsley Market ⑦
This weekly market is worth a visit just for a stroll around the picturesque square, but you can also browse for fresh local food.
Helmsley, North Yorkshire; tel: 01653 600666; every Fri. www.northyorkmoors.org.uk

Walmgate Ale House and Bistro ⑪
Fresh-picked watercress, freshly caught mackerel, York ham and rare-breed lamb, beef and pork are on the menu here.
25 Walmgate, York; tel: 01904 629222; open noon–10:30pm Mon–Fri, 9:30am–10:30pm Sat, 9:30am–9:30pm Sun. www.walmgateale.co.uk

Lanterna ⑬
This Italian restaurant is a Scarborough highlight, serving tasty local seafood.
33 Queen Street, Scarborough, North Yorkshire; tel: 01723 363616; open Apr–mid-Oct: 7–9:30pm Mon–Sat; mid-Oct-Mar: 7–9:30pm Tue–Sat. www.lanterna-ristorante.co.uk

The Star Inn at Harome ⑧
This old-fashioned inn, with its thatched roof, is now a gastropub, acclaimed for its superb way with fresh local produce.
Harome, nr Helmsley, North Yorkshire; tel: 01439 770397; open 6:15–9:30pm Mon, 11:30am–2pm and 6:15–9:30pm Tue–Sat, noon–6pm Sun. www.thestaratharome.co.uk

The Pipe and Glass Inn ⑮
This 15th-century inn serves local Burdass lamb, beef and sausages, game in season and freshly caught local seafood.
West End, South Dalton, Beverley, East Yorkshire; tel: 01430 810246; open noon–2pm and 6–9:30pm Tue–Sat, noon–4pm Sun. www.pipeandglass.co.uk

The Old Vicarage ⑰
Tessa Bramley's innovative menu is embellished by ingredients from the restaurant's own kitchen garden.
Ridgeway, nr Sheffield; tel: 0114 247 5814; open for lunch and dinner Tue–Fri, dinner only Sat. www.theoldvicarage.co.uk

Brasserie Blanc ㉝
Famed chef Raymond Blanc's city-centre brasserie in Leeds offers his modern approach to classic French cooking.
Sovereign Street, Leeds; tel: 0113 220 6060; open 7:30am-10pm Mon–Fri, 9am–10:30pm Sat, 9am–9pm Sun. www.brasserieblanc.com

Kirkgate Market ㉝
Kirkgate is Europe's largest indoor market, with 400 stalls in the market building and, on most days, 200 more outside.
Vicar Lane, Leeds; tel: 0113 378 1950; 8am–5:30pm Mon–Sat. www.leedsmarkets.co.uk

Below: Interior of the Kirkgate Market in Leeds

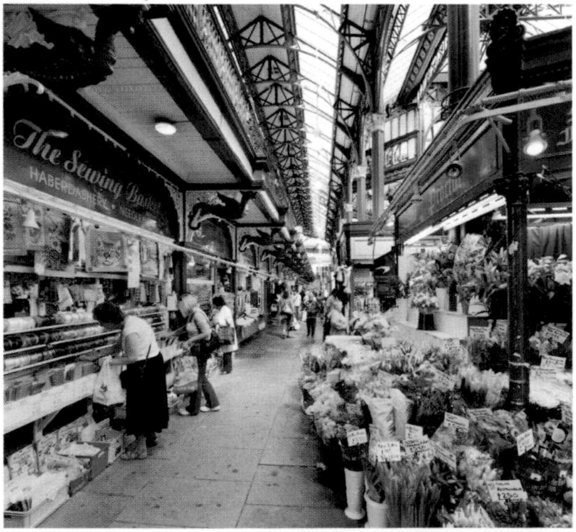

The Three Acres ㉓
Superb pub-restaurant serving classic dishes; seafood is a speciality.
Roydhouse, Shelley, nr Huddersfield; tel: 01484 602606; open daily. www.3acres.com

Box Tree Restaurant ㊴
Chef Simon Gueller's sumptuous menu puts the emphasis on local produce.
35–37 Church Street, Ilkley, West Yorkshire; tel: 01943 608484; open 7–9:30pm Wed and Thu, noon–2pm and 7–9:30pm Fri and Sat, noon–3pm Sun. www.theboxtree.co.uk

Knaresborough Market ㊶
Caters for the everyday needs of locals, not just visiting gourmets; stalls are piled with locally sourced fruit and vegetables.
Knaresborough, North Yorkshire; every Wed, 8:30am–4pm. www.knaresborough.co.uk

General Tarleton ㊸
The signature dish in this luxury hotel and restaurant is the chef's "little moneybags" (seafood parcels in lobster sauce), but the menu changes daily.
Ferrensby, Knaresborough, North Yorkshire; tel: 01423 340284; open noon–2pm and 6–9pm daily (to 8:30pm Sun). www.generaltarleton.co.uk

The Blue Lion (59)
Romantic, candlelit restaurant priding itself on the wide variety of local Yorkshire ingredients used. Good vegetarian options.
East Witton, nr Leyburn, North Yorkshire; tel: 01969 624273; open noon–2:15pm and 6:30–9:15pm Mon–Sat, noon–9:15pm Sun. www.thebluelion.co.uk

Fernaville's Rest (63)
Fine pub and restaurant in a picturesque village, with real ales and dishes based on seasonal produce from local farms.
Whorlton, County Durham; tel: 01833 627341; open daily. www.fernavilles.com

FARMERS' MARKETS

Hartlepool Farmers' Market ⑤
Hand-reared meats, game and poultry, and home-made chutneys, cheeses and jams.
Historic Quay, Hartlepool, County Durham; second Sat of every month, 8:30am–2:30pm. www.northerndalesfarmersmarkets.com

Grassington Farmers' Market (62)
Great for locally baked cakes, tea loaves and curd tarts, cheeses and unusual preserves, such as blueberry and lavender jam.
Grassington, Upper Wharfedale, North Yorkshire; third Sun of every month, 9:30am–1:30pm. www.gonorthyorkshire.co.uk

Hexham Farmers' Market (69)
Look out for Northumberland hill lamb at this award-winning market. Market Place, *Hexham, Northumberland; tel: 01434 230605; second and fourth Sat of every month, 9am–1:30pm. www.hexhamfarmersmarket.co.uk*

Northallerton Farmers' Market ㊽
Everything from cheeses and organic dairy products to pork, lamb and even buffalo.
High Street, Northallerton, North Yorkshire; fourth Wed of every month, 8:30am–2:30pm. www.northerndalesfarmersmarkets.com

PUBS

The Bacchus ①
Busy and popular city-centre pub with a big choice of local microbrewery beers, cask ales and a long wine list.
42–48 High Bridge, Newcastle; tel: 0191 261 1008; open all day Mon–Sat, noon–11pm Sun. www.sjf.co.uk

The Victoria ④
The plain exterior of this family-run pub conceals a cosy interior with an open fire.
86 Hallgarth Street, Durham; tel: 0191 386 5269; open daily. www.victoriainn-durhamcity.co.uk

The Golden Fleece ⑪
More than 400 years old, this pub in the historic heart of York is said to be haunted.
Pavement Lane, York; tel: 01904 625171; open daily. www.thegoldenfleeceyork.co.uk

The Kelham Island Tavern ⑱
Yorkshire "Pub of the Year" in 2015, with a large selection of hand-drawn ales.
62 Russell Street, Sheffield; tel: 0114 272 2482; open noon–midnight daily. www.kelhamtavern.co.uk

Whitelocks ㉝
Classic Leeds pub serving authentic ales on this site for almost 300 years.
Turk's Head Yard, Briggate, Leeds; tel: 0113 245 3950; open daily. www.whitelocksleeds.com

The Cross Keys ㉝
Fine real-ale pub in the centre of Leeds, with beers by Rooster's Brewery at Knaresborough and a selection of stouts.
107 Water Lane, Leeds; tel: 0113 243 3711; open daily. www.the-crosskeys.com

The Bingley Arms ㊵
With its "priest's hole", original Dutch oven and snug bars, this country pub is one of the oldest in Britain.
Church Lane, Bardsley, nr Leeds; tel: 01937 572462; open daily. www.bingleyarms.co.uk

The Old Fleece ㊽
Charles Dickens enjoyed a drink in this venerable pub in the centre of a busy North Yorkshire market town.
89 High Street, Northallerton, North Yorkshire; tel: 01609 773345; open daily.

The Lister Arms ㊿
Classic Yorkshire country inn with bags of atmosphere, good home cooking and cosy rooms, as well as local ales.
Malham, nr Skipton, North Yorkshire; tel: 01729 830330; open daily. www.listerarms.co.uk

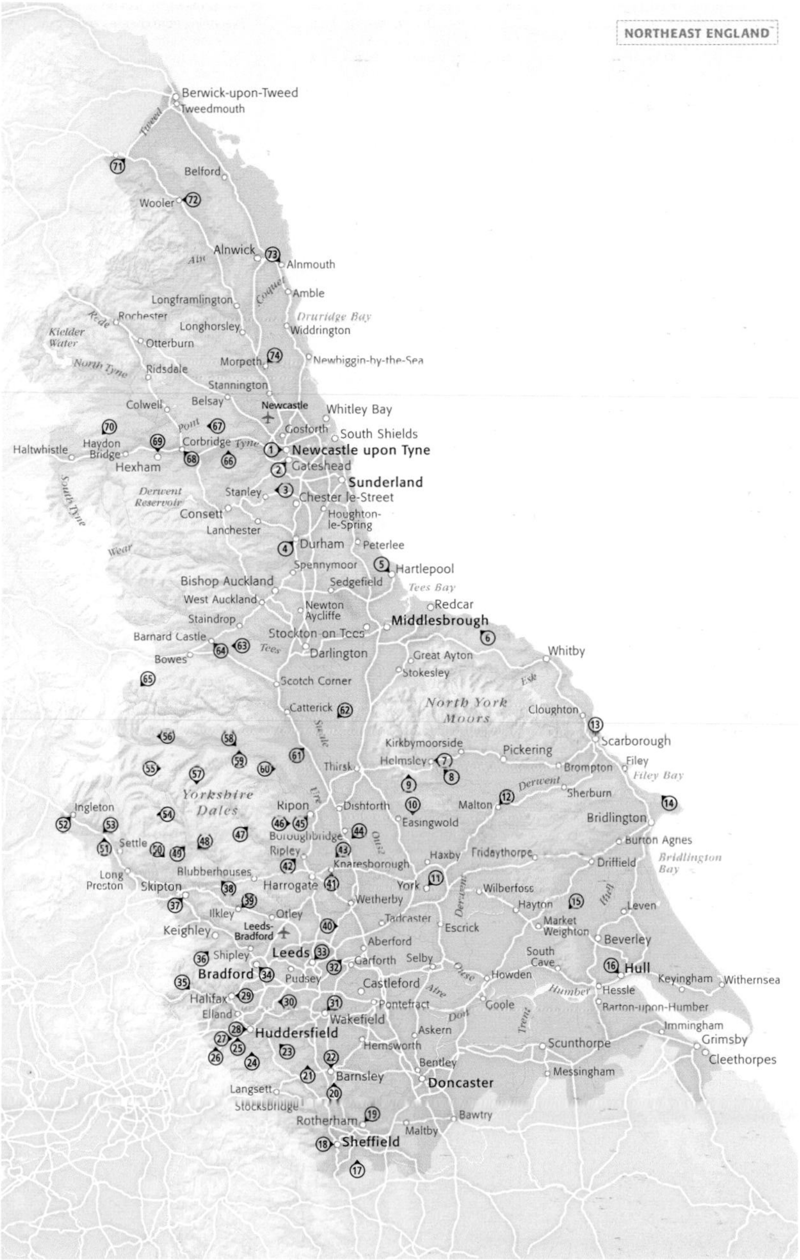

The Durham Ox ⑩
Award-winning pub and restaurant with three centuries of history.
Crayke, North Yorkshire; tel: 01347 821506; open daily.
www.thedurhamox.com

The Farmer's Arms ㉔
This pub has won awards for its choice of ales and wines and its excellent menus.
2-4 Liphill Bank Road, Holmfirth, West Yorkshire; tel: 01484 683713; open daily.

The Rat and Ratchet ㉘
Town-centre pub acclaimed for its array of real ales and ciders.
40 Chapel Hill, Huddersfield, North Yorkshire; tel: 01484 542400; open 3pm–late Mon–Thu, noon–late Fri–Sun.
www.ossett-brewery.co.uk

The Woolly Sheep Inn ㊲
This pub is favoured by locals for its excellent range of real ales, including those from regional brewery Timothy Taylor.
38 Sheep Street, Skipton, North Yorkshire; tel: 01756 700966; open daily.
www.woollysheepinn.co.uk

Ye Olde Punch Bowl ㊹
Good pub food and a selection of real ales from this inn's microbrewery.
Marton cum Gratton, North Yorkshire; tel: 01423 322519; open daily.
www.thepunchbowlmartoncumgrafton.com

The One Eyed Rat ㊺
Local fruit wines, mulled wine in winter, and a fine range of English real ales.
51 Allhallowgate, Ripon, North Yorkshire; tel: 01765 607704; open 5–11pm Mon–Thu, noon–11pm Fri and Sat, noon–10:30pm Sun. www.oneeyedrat.com

The Old Hall Inn ㊾
Dignified, traditional Yorkshire country inn on the edge of Grassington National Park.
Threshfield, North Yorkshire; tel: 01756 752441; open daily.
www.oldhallinnandcottages.co.uk

Falcon Inn (54)
The Falcon Inn is the very epitome of a rustic Yorkshire Dales tavern, with a well-deserved reputation for its excellent home cooking.
Arncliffe, nr Skipton, North Yorkshire; tel: 01756 770205; open daily.
www.thefalconinn.com

The White Lion (55)
Claiming to be the highest pub in Wharfedale, this is an excellent place for a pint after tackling nearby Buckden Pike.
Cray, North Yorkshire; tel: 01756 760262; open daily (but closed Jan).
www.bestpubinthedales.co.uk

The Green Dragon Inn (61)
Cosy, classic country pub with a good range of traditional ales and a more than adequate menu, just off the A1 motorway.
Exelby, Bedale, North Yorkshire; tel: 01677 422233; open daily.

The Tan Hill Inn ⑥⑤
Way up in the Yorkshire Dales, this inn claims to be the highest pub in Britain, and offers rooms and self-catering cottages. *Tan Hill, Reeth, Swaledale, North Yorkshire; tel: 01833 628246; open daily.* www.tanhillinn.co.uk

The Boathouse ⑥⑥
With at least eight guest beers at any given time, the Boathouse is also the "brewery tap" for the local Wylam microbrewery. *Station Road, Wylam, Northumberland; tel: 01661 853431; open daily.* www.theboathousewylam.com

Dipton Mill ⑥⑨
Delightful pub in an old mill building with ales from the local Hexhamshire Brewery. *Hexham, Northumberland; tel: 01434 606577; open noon–2:30pm and 6–11pm Mon–Sat, noon– 3pm Sun.* www.diptonmill.co.uk

The Red Lion Inn ⑦③
Good food and drink at this friendly 18th-century coaching inn in the prettiest village on the Northumberland coast. *22 Northumberland Street, Alnmouth, Northumberland; tel: 01665 830584; open daily.* www.redlionalnmouth.com

PLACES TO STAY

Jesmond Dene House ①
A grand and spacious Arts and Crafts mansion with 40 comfortable rooms. *Jesmond Dene Road, Newcastle; tel: 0191 212 3000.* www.jesmonddenehouse.co.uk

Hotel du Vin ①
Boutique hotel offering monsoon showers and plasma screen TVs in the rooms, and a bistro with alfresco dining. *Allan House, City Road, Newcastle; tel: 0191 389 8628.* www.hotelduvin.com

The Pheasant Hotel ⑧
Lovely country-house hotel on a charming village green, perfectly located for exploring the North Yorkshire countryside. *Harome, nr Helmsley, North Yorkshire; tel: 01439 771241.* www.thepheasanthotel.com

Byland Abbey Inn ⑨
A uniquely romantic inn with a fine-dining restaurant opposite the evocative Cistercian ruins of Byland Abbey. *Byland, North Yorkshire; tel: 01347 868204.* www.bylandabbeyinn.com

The Calls ㉝
This hotel by the River Aire, within walking distance of Leeds city centre, is everything a boutique town-house hotel should be. *42 The Calls, Leeds; tel: 0113 244 0099.* www.42thecalls.co.uk

Yorebridge House ㉟⑥
A traditional stone building with classy facilities and an outstanding restaurant. *Bainbridge, Wensleydale, North Yorkshire; tel: 01969 652060.* www.yorebridgehouse.com

Above: Sheep-racing at the Masham Sheep Fair

Ashfield House ㉔②
Cosy haven on the main street of a pretty village, yards from a cobbled market square. *Grassington, nr Skipton, North Yorkshire; tel: 01756 752584.* www.ashfieldhouse.co.uk

Boar's Head ㊷②
Opposite Ripley Castle, this olde-worlde inn's aristocratic owner has furnished the bedrooms luxuriously. *Ripley, nr Harrogate, North Yorkshire; tel: 01423 771888.* www.boarsheadripley.co.uk

Yorke Arms ㊼
Michelin-starred restaurant with rooms, two of which are in the charming Ghyll Cottage, a short walk away. *Ramsgill-in-Nidderdale, Pateley Bridge, nr Harrogate, North Yorkshire; tel: 01423 755243.* www.yorke-arms.co.uk

The Traddock ㉟③
Elegant small guesthouse with just 10 rooms, all en suite, set in the beautiful Dales countryside. *Austwick, nr Settle, North Yorkshire; tel: 01524 251224.* www.thetraddock.co.uk

Swinton Park ⑥⓪
Outstanding, grand castle hotel, set in 80 hectares (200 acres) of grounds, with luxurious bedrooms. See falconry displays at the hotel's own Birds of Prey Centre. *Masham, North Yorkshire; tel: 01765 680900.* www.swintonpark.com

Burgoyne Hotel ⑥⑤
A late-Georgian house set in an idyllic village. Bedrooms have four-posters and drawing rooms have open log fires. *The Green, Reeth, Swaledale, North Yorkshire; tel: 01748 884292.* www.theburgoyne.co.uk

The Angel Inn ㊽
Stylish coaching inn (the oldest in historic Corbridge) with a fine restaurant, a good bar and bright, well-appointed bedrooms. *Corbridge, Northumberland; tel: 01434 632119.* www.theangelofcorbridge.com

The Collingwood Arms ⑦①
Historic coaching inn on the banks of the River Tweed, popular with anglers. *Cornhill on Tweed, Northumberland; tel: 01890 882424.* www.collingwoodarms.com

Eshott Hall ⑦④
Set in 200 hectares (500 acres), this fine 17th-century mansion is now a country-house hotel. A kitchen garden provides organic produce for the restaurant. *Morpeth, Northumberland; tel: 01670 787454.* www.eshott.com

FESTIVALS AND EVENTS

JORVIK Viking Festival ⑪
Re-enactments, river events, music and arts and crafts (see pp196–7). *Coppergate Walk, York; tel: 01904 615505; mid-Feb.* www.jorvik-viking-centre.co.uk

York Festival of Food and Drink ⑪
Sample local food and drink from street stalls, gourmet restaurants and gastropubs, during this 10-day festival. *Various venues, York; tel: 01904 635149; Sep–Oct.* www.yorkfoodfestival.com

Huddersfield Carnival ㉘
A boisterous, Afro-Caribbean-inspired weekend of "freedom and friendship". *Huddersfield, West Yorkshire; mid-Jul.* www.huddersfieldcarnival.com

Leeds CAMRA Beer, Cider and Perry Festival ㉝
Real ale, beers and ciders from all over Britain and the world, live music and an array of local food, held by the Campaign for Real Ale (CAMRA) over three days in spring. *Various venues, Leeds; Mar.* www.leedsbeerfestival.co.uk

Bradford International Film Festival ㉞
This major 10-day event in Yorkshire's official "City of Film" is now established as a leading international fixture. *Various venues, Bradford; mid-Mar.* www.bradfordfilmfestival.org.uk

Ilkley Literature Festival ㊴
This top literary event attracts leading authors and poets, as well as new talent. *Various venues, Ilkley, West Yorkshire; tel: 01943 816714; Sep–Oct.* www.ilkleyliteraturefestival.org.uk

Masham Sheep Fair ⑥⓪
Local farmers compete for coveted prizes over two days. There is even a sheep race. *Masham, North Yorkshire; last weekend in Sep.* www.mashamsheepfair.com

Masham Steam Engine and Fair Organ Rally ⑥⓪
Two days of steam-traction engines and wagons, fair organs, and opportunities to sample local food and drink. *Masham, North Yorkshire; tel: 01765 689569; third weekend in Jul.* www.visitmasham.com

Slaithwaite Moonraking Festival ㉗
A week of storytelling, music and dancing culminates with a lantern parade and a firework display. *Slaithwaite, West Yorkshire; mid-Feb.* www.slaithwaitemoonraking.org

Wakefield Festival of Food, Drink & Rhubarb ㉛
Celebrates the very best local food and produce, including the local speciality. *Wakefield, West Yorkshire; tel: 0345 601 8353; third weekend in Feb.* www.experiencewakefield.co.uk

Bradford Festival ㉞
Multicultural celebration with theatre, dance, live music, and great street food. *Various venues, Bradford city centre; second weekend in Jun.* www.bradfordfestival.org.uk

Hebden Bridge Arts Festival ㉟
An enjoyable fortnight of comedy, performance, music and literary events. *Hebden Bridge, West Yorkshire; late June–early Jul.* www.hebdenbridgeartsfestival.co.uk

Haworth Victorian Christmas Weekend ㊱
Six weekends of Christmas events, traditions, shopping and festive fun in a picturesque Yorkshire village. *Haworth, West Yorkshire; early Dec.* www.christmas.yorkshire.com

Dales Festival of Food and Drink ㊺⑧
Three days of "food, farming and fun": plenty of opportunities to sample local ales, cheeses, sausages, organic meats and more. *Leyburn, Wensleydale, North Yorkshire; mid-June.* www.dalesfestivaloffood.org

Glendale Show ⑦②
Northumberland's major annual agricultural show: a day of sheepdog trials, equestrian events, food and drink, and competitions for livestock breeders and producers. *Wooler, Northumberland; tel: 01668 283868; last Mon in Aug.* www.glendaleshow.com

MUSEUMS AND GALLERIES

Great North Museum ①
Exciting and eclectic displays range from a large-scale interactive model of Hadrian's Wall to a *Tyrannosaurus rex* skeleton and a collection of Egyptian mummies. *Barras Bridge, Newcastle; tel: 0191 208 6765; open 10am–5pm Mon–Fri, 10am–4pm Sat, 11am–4pm Sun.* www.twmuseums.org.uk

Discovery Museum ①
This interactive museum celebrates Newcastle's shipbuilding and engineering heritage, and highlights inventions that changed the world. *Blandford Square, Newcastle; tel: 0191 232 6789; open 10am–4pm Mon–Fri, 11am–4pm Sat and Sun.* www.twmuseums.org.uk

Baltic Centre for Contemporary Art ②
Dynamic centre for contemporary arts in a landmark converted industrial building.
Gateshead Quays, Gateshead, Tyne and Wear; tel: 0191 478 1810; open daily. www.balticmill.com

National Railway Museum ⑪
Three giant halls crammed with railway history, including the world's fastest steam locomotive, "Mallard", and the legendary "Flying Scotsman".
Leeman Road, York; tel: 0844 815 3319; open 10am–5pm daily. www.nrm.org.uk

Eden Camp Modern History Theme Museum ⑫
Award-winning museum dedicated to Britain's role in the major conflicts of the 20th century.
Malton, North Yorkshire; tel: 01653 697777; open 10am–5pm daily (closed 23 Dec–11 Jan). www.edencamp.co.uk

Millennium Gallery ⑱
This marvel of glass and white concrete houses cutting-edge contemporary art.
Arundel Gate, Sheffield; tel: 0114 278 2600; open 10am–5pm Mon–Sat, 11am–4pm Sun. www.museums-sheffield.org.uk

Thwaite Mills Watermill ㉝
Explore Leeds' industrial heritage at one of the country's last remaining water-powered millls.
Thwaite Lane, Stourton, Leeds; tel: 0113 378 2983; open 10am–5pm Tue–Fri, 1–5pm Sat and Sun. www.leeds.gov.uk/museumsandgalleries

Royal Armouries ㉝
Awe-inspiring collection of weaponry, from axes, swords and daggers to muskets, modern pistols and machine guns. Outdoor events in summer include medieval jousting.
Armouries Drive, Leeds; tel: 0113 220 1999; open 10am–5pm daily. www.royalarmouries.org

National Media Museum ㉞
Behind-the-scenes tours, two world-class cinemas, an IMAX giant-screen experience and an exhibition dedicated to the history of TV are among the attractions here.
Bradford; tel: 0844 856 3797; open 10am–6pm Tue–Sun (cinemas till late). www.nationalmediamuseum.org.uk

Brontë Parsonage Museum ㊱
Set amid desolate moorland, Haworth Parsonage was the lifelong home of Charlotte, Emily and Anne Brontë.
Church Street, Haworth, West Yorkshire; tel: 01535 642323; open daily (but closed Jan). www.bronte.org.uk

The Bowes Museum (64)
A truly magnificent French-château-style building housing stunning collections of fine and decorative arts, but with family-friendly features too.
Barnard Castle, County Durham; tel: 01833 690606; open 10am–5pm daily. www.thebowesmuseum.org.uk

Cleveland Ironstone Mining Museum ⑥
Explore Britain's first ironstone mine with a tour into deep underground galleries.
Deepdale, Skinningrose, North Yorkshire; tel: 01287 642877; open Mar–Nov: 10am–3:30pm Mon–Fri, 1–3:30pm Sat (call to check opening times Dec–Feb). www.ironstonemuseum.co.uk

Worsbrough Mill Museum ⑳
This museum comprises a working water mill dating from the 17th century and a powered mill from the 19th century.
Worsbrough Bridge, Barnsley, South Yorkshire; tel: 01226 774527; open 10am–4pm Sat and Sun (10am–4pm daily during school holidays). www.worsbrough-mill.com

Cannon Hall Museum, Park and Gardens ㉑
Georgian mansion housing outstanding antiques and two regimental museums.
Bark House Lane, Barnsley, South Yorkshire; tel: 01226 790270; open Apr–Oct: 10am–4pm Tue–Fri, 11am–4pm Sat and Sun; Nov–late Mar: noon–4pm Sat and Sun (closed late Dec–mid-Feb). www.cannon-hall.com

Cooper Gallery ㉒
Fine collection of oil and watercolour paintings, drawings and prints.
Church Street, Barnsley, South Yorkshire; tel: 01226 242905; open 10am–4pm Mon–Fri, 10am–3pm Sat. www.cooper-gallery.com

THINGS TO DO WITH KIDS

The Deep ⑯
Spectacular aquarium with 3,500 fish – including 40 sharks – viewed from an underwater tunnel and a glass lift ride.
Tower Street, Hull; tel: 01482 381000; open 10am–6pm daily. www.thedeep.co.uk

Eureka! The National Children's Museum ㉙
More than 400 interactive exhibits, with lots of special events and activities at weekends and during school holidays.
Discovery Road, Halifax, West Yorkshire; tel: 01422 330069; open 10am–4pm Mon–Fri, 10am–5pm Sat and Sun. www.eureka.org.uk

Ripley Castle ㊷
This 700-year-old castle has beautiful walled gardens, lakes and a deer park.
Ripley, nr Harrogate, North Yorkshire; tel: 01423 770152; open daily, kids tours 1pm Sat and Sun. www.ripleycastle.co.uk

Housesteads Roman Fort (70)
Explore the dramatic ramparts of Hadrian's Wall *(see pp36–7)* from one of the most accessible of its frontier fortresses.
Haydon Bridge, Northumberland; tel: 01434 344363; open Apr–Oct: 10am–6pm daily; Nov–Mar: 10am–4pm daily. www.english-heritage.co.uk

Magna Science Adventure Centre ⑲
Launch rockets, fire water cannons, board an airship and enjoy Europe's largest science and technology playground.
Sheffield Road, Rotherham, South Yorkshire; tel: 01709 720002; open 10am–5pm Sat and Sun. www.visitmagna.co.uk

Standedge Tunnel ㉖
Take a glass-roofed-barge cruise through the longest and deepest tunnel in Britain.
Waters Road, Marsden, Huddersfield, West Yorkshire; tel: 01484 844298; tours run daily Apr–Nov. www.standedge.co.uk

Ponderosa Rural Therapeutic Centre ㉚
See exotic, rare-breed domestic animals in the lakes and gardens here.
Smithies Lane, Heckmondwike, West Yorkshire; tel: 01924 235276; open mid-Apr–mid-Nov: 10am–5pm daily; mid-Nov–mid-April: 10am–4pm Sat and Sun. www.ponderosa-park.co.uk

Yorkshire Dales Falconry Centre (51)
Eagles, falcons, owls and hawks can be seen in three separate daily flying displays.
Crows Nest Road, nr Settle, North Yorkshire; tel: 01729 822832; open noon–3:30pm daily. www.falconryandwildlife.com

White Scar Cave (52)
The longest show-cave in Britain, spectacularly located on the Yorkshire Dales.
Ingleton, North Yorkshire; tel: 01524 241244; open Feb–Oct: 10am–4pm daily; Nov–Jan: 10am–4pm Sat & Sun. www.whitescarcave.co.uk

SPAS AND HEALTH RESORTS

Titanic Hotel & Spa ㉕
The UK's first "eco-spa", with an emphasis on organic products.
Low Westwood Lane, Linthwaite, Huddersfield, West Yorkshire; tel: 01484 843544. www.titanicspa.com

Thorpe Park Hotel & Spa ㉜
A touch of the Mediterranean in Yorkshire with its glass atrium, stylish bedrooms and seven spa treatment rooms.
1150 Century Way, Thorpe Park, Leeds; tel: 0113 264 1000. www.thorpeparkhotel.com

The Devonshire Arms ㊳
Aristocratic 18th-century exterior conceals 21st-century comforts, including a health, beauty and fitness club with a pool, whirlpool, steam room and sauna.
Bolton Abbey, Skipton, North Yorkshire; tel: 01756 710441. www.thedevonshirearms.co.uk

Matfen Hall (67)
Spacious country-house hotel and spa with a fine restaurant and its own 27-hole and 9-hole golf courses.
Matfen, Northumberland; tel: 01661 886400. www.matfenhall.com

OTHER SIGHTS IN THE BOOK

Great North Run ① *(see pp152–3).* **Beamish** ③ *(see pp128–9).* **York** ⑪ *(see pp196–7).* **Bempton Cliffs** ⑭ *(see pp32–3).* **Fountains Abbey** ㊻ *(see pp144–5).* **Yorkshire Dales** (57) *(see pp94–5).* **Hadrian's Wall** (70) *(see pp36–7).*

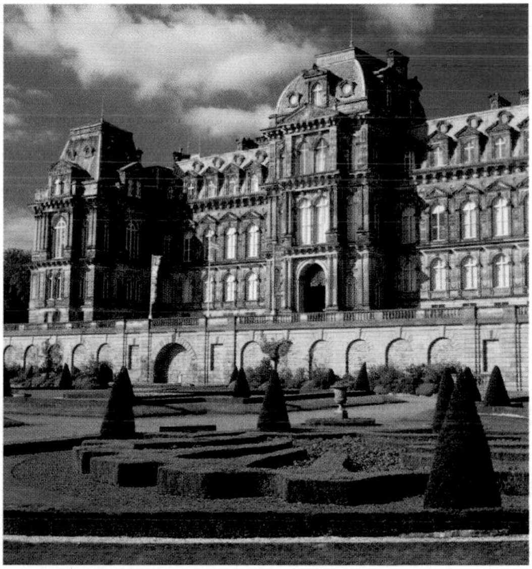

Right: Bowes Museum at Barnard Castle

WEST MIDLANDS

LOCAL FOOD

Siam Corner Ma Ma Thai ④
First-rate menu with vegetarian dishes and outstanding service.
17 Bird Street, Lichfield, Staffordshire; tel: 01543 411911; open 5–10:30pm daily, noon–2:30pm Tues–Sun. www.siamcornermamamathai.co.uk

Café Opus at IKON ⑨
A stylish and modern café on the ground floor and outdoor terrace of the contemporary art gallery, IKON.
1 Oozells Square, Brindleyplace, Birmingham; tel: 01212 483226; open Tue–Sun: 10am–5pm. www.cafeopus.co.uk

Rupali Tandoori Restaurant ⑪
Much-admired Indian restaurant with a full-flavoured, authentic menu.
337 Tile Hill Lane, Coventry; tel: 02476 422500; open 5–11pm daily. www.rupali.co.uk

My Dhabba ⑪
A wide variety of Indian street food served by friendly staff at this popular restaurant.
1–3 Lower Holyhead Road, Coventry; tel: 02476 559900; open 5pm–11pm daily. www.mydhabba.co.uk

Mr Underhills ㉗
A Michelin-starred, seven-course set dinner menu in a beautiful riverside location.
Dinham Weir, Ludlow, Shropshire; tel: 01584 874431; orders taken 7:15–8:15pm Wed–Sun. www.mr-underhills.co.uk

Harp Lane Deli ㉗
A fabulous range of cheeses, meats, pickles and juice await visitors along with great coffee, hot deli sandwiches and freshly-made salads.
4 Church Street, Ludlow, Shropshire; tel: 01584 877355; open 9am–5pm Mon–Sun. www.harplane.com

The Clive Bar and Restaurant ㉗
A former farmhouse that serves delicious dishes made from locally sourced produce.
Bromfield, Ludlow, Shropshire; tel: 01584 856565; open 11am–11pm Mon–Sat, noon–10:30pm Sun. www.theclive.co.uk

Café Catalan ⑬
Serves tapas at lunchtime and in the afternoon and Catalan dishes at night.
6 Jury Street, Warwick; tel: 01926 498930; open noon–3pm and 6–9:30pm Mon–Sat. www.cafecatalan.com

BurgerWorks ⑱
Much-loved Italian eatery with great pizzas, a pleasant ambience and polite staff.
12 Friar Street, Worcester; tel: 01905 27770; open 12:30–2:30pm and 5–9:30pm Tue–Thu, 12:30–2:30pm and 5–10pm Fri, noon–11pm Sat, noon–5pm Sun.

Abbey Road Coffee ⑳
The perfect place for a light bite, serving a range of delicious homemade soups, sandwiches, paninis, cakes and artisan coffee.
11 Abbey Road, Malvern, Worcestershire; tel: 01684 899901. www.thegreatmalverndeli.co.uk

La Dolce Vita ㉞
An intimate, family-run restaurant offering a true taste of Italy in the heart of Shrewsbury.
35 Hills Lane, Shrewsbury; tel: 01743 249126; open 12–2pm Thu–Sat, 6:30–10pm Wed–Sun. www.ladolcevitashrewsbury.co.uk

FARMERS' MARKETS

Warwick Farmers' Market ⑬
A selection of fresh and organic produce, all from local farmers.
Market Square, Warwick; tel: 01926 800750; fifth Sat of the month (if applicable), 9am–2pm. www.warwickdistrictmarkets.co.uk

Stratford-upon-Avon Farmers' Market ⑰
Warwickshire's largest farmers' market, with a plethora of meats, cheeses, beverages, breads and cakes.
Rother Street, Stratford-upon-Avon, Warwickshire; first and third Sat of the month, 9am–3pm. www.stratforduponavonmarkets.co.uk

Ross-on-Wye Farmers' Market ㉓
A wholesome spread of tasty local produce sourced from local farmers.
High Street, below the Market House, Ross-on-Wye, Herefordshire; tel: 01568 797427; first Fri of the month, 9am–1pm. www.hfmg.org

Hereford Farmers' Market ㉕
Excellent opportunity to get your hands on bundles of the very freshest local produce.
High Town, nr Buttermarket, Hereford; first Sat of every month, 9am–2pm.

PUBS AND BARS

The Manor Arms ⑤
Claims to be one of England's oldest pubs (12th century), in a scenic position by the Rushall Canal.
Park Road, Walsall, West Midlands; tel: 01922 642333; open daily.

The Jam House ⑨
Easy-going and popular over-21s venue playing live jazz and rhythm-and-blues music, aimed at a smart-casual audience.
St Pauls Square, Jewellery Quarter, Birmingham; tel: 01212 003030; open 6pm–late Tue–Sat. www.thejamhouse.com

The Lord Clifden ⑨
With an impressive collection of urban artwork –including pieces by Banksy – this pub serves wide range of real ales.
34 Great Hampton Street, Hockley, Birmingham; tel: 01215 237515; open 10am–midnight Sun–Thu, 10am–late Fri–Sat. www.thelordclifden.com

The Town Wall Tavern ⑪
Historic pub oozing with character, charm and traditional pub cosiness. Serves a selection of real cask ales.
Bond Street, Coventry; tel: 02476 220963; open daily. www.townwalltavern.co.uk

The Old Swan ⑧
Excellent Black Country pub – nicknamed Ma Pardoe's after a long-serving landlady – with home-brewed beer, including "Old Swan" itself.
87 Halesowen Road, Netherton, Dudley, West Midlands; tel: 01384 253075; open daily.

The Prince of Wales ㉒
Fantastic ciders including draught pear, plus real ales and a lovely location.
Church Lane, Ledbury, Herefordshire; tel: 01531 577001; open daily. www.powledbury.com

The Mill Race ㉔
First-rate food plus excellent ale and cider; its own farm supplies many of the ingredients.
Walford, nr Ross-on-Wye, Herefordshire; tel: 01989 562891; open 11am–3pm and 6–10pm Mon–Fri, 10am–11pm Sat, 11:30am–9pm Sun. www.millrace.info

The Harp Hotel ㉛
A lovely village pub offering an ever-changing selection of cask beers, real ciders, continental lagers and wine.
40 High Street, Albrighton, nr Wolverhampton; tel: 01902 374381; open daily. www.hopback.co.uk

The Inn at Grinshill ㉟
Steeped in historic character, with some tempting accommodation and an extensive menu from the kitchen.
The High Street, Grinshill, nr Shrewsbury, Shropshire; tel: 01939 220410; open 11am–3pm and 6–11pm Mon–Sat, noon–4pm Sun. www.theinnatgrinshill.co.uk

PLACES TO STAY

Prince Rupert Hotel ㉞
Historic charm and medieval elegance, with a range of rooms including the 12th-century "Mansion House" suites.
Butcher Row, Shrewsbury, Shropshire; tel: 01743 499955. www.princeruperthotel.co.uk

Albright Hussey Manor ㉞
Magnificently restored Tudor house in superb Shropshire countryside with wonderful food and service.
Shrewsbury, Shropshire; tel: 01939 290523. www.albrighthussey.co.uk

Netherstowe House ④
Tremendous Georgian boutique hotel with bags of charm, modern furnishings and lovely, individually named rooms.
Lichfield, Staffordshire; tel: 01543 254270. www.netherstowehouse.com

Malmaison ⑨
Former Royal Mail sorting office given a luxurious and trendy renovation making it a real destination stay.
One Wharfside Street, Birmingham; tel: 0121 7943004. www.malmaison.com

Above: Warwick Folk Festival in the grounds of Warwick school

Hyatt Regency Birmingham ⑨
Comfortable rooms and excellent service
– the full range of top-notch Hyatt facilities
in a central location.
*Bridge Street, Birmingham; tel: 01216
431234. www.hyatt.com*

Church Hill Farm B&B ⑮
Charming farmhouse in a tranquil rural
location southeast of Warwick; with only
three rooms, booking is advised
*Lighthorne, Warwickshire; tel: 01926
651251. www.churchhillfarm.co.uk*

Stratford-upon-Avon Youth Hostel ⑯
A wide range of rooms are offered at this
Georgian mansion, set in extensive grounds
in Alveston, near to Stratford-upon-Avon.
*Hemmingford House, Alveston, Stratford-
upon-Avon, Warwickshire; tel: 0845 371
9661. www.yha.org.uk*

Riverside Caravan Park ⑰
Lovely perch on the banks of the River
Avon, with friendly staff, good facilities and
access to Stratford upon Avon by river taxi.
*Tiddington Road, Stratford-upon-Avon,
Warwickshire; tel: 01789 292312.*

Copper Beech House ⑳
Tons of Victorian charm, a gorgeous
garden and comfortable rooms in the
setting of the Malvern Hills.
*32 Avenue Road, Malvern, Worcestershire;
tel: 01684 565013.*
www.copperbeechhouse.co.uk

Barnacle Hall ⑩
Historic farmhouse B&B with plenty of
draws: charm, comfort, time-worn
textures and a friendly owner.
*Shilton Lane, Shilton, Coventry; tel: 02476
612629. www.barnaclehall.co.uk*

Coombe Abbey Hotel ⑫
Stately former abbey surrounded by
stunning Warwickshire parkland.
*Brinklow Road, Binley, Coventry;
tel: 02476 450450.*
www.coombeabbey.com

Colwall Park Hotel ㉑
Exemplary service, fantastic food and very
comfy rooms in a handsome hotel; the
perfect base for walks in the Malvern Hills.
*Colwall, Malvern, Worcestershire;
tel: 01684 540000. www.colwall.co.uk*

Woodend Farm House ㉒
Quiet accommodation in converted
18th-century timbered barn and its
outbuildings.
*Ledbury, Herefordshire; tel: 01432 890227.
www.bed-breakfast-herefordshire.co.uk*

The Feathers Hotel ㉒
Gorgeous black-and-white former coaching
inn, dating from Elizabethan times, with a
relaxing spa and fine dining. Located in
the heart of market town Ledbury
*High Street, Ledbury, Herefordshire;
tel: 01531 635266.*
www.feathers-ledbury.co.uk

Linden Guest House ㉓
Appealing and great value B&B with comfy
rooms and tasty breakfasts.
*14 Church Street, Ross-on-Wye,
Herefordshire; tel: 01989 565373.*
www.lindenguesthouse.com

Castle House ㉕
Elegant and grand Georgian townhouse
located within a two minute walk of
Hereford Cathedral.
*Castle Street, Hereford; tel: 01432 356321.
www.castlehse.co.uk*

Priory Hotel ㉖
Fabulous former rectory with plenty of
period character and comfort.
*Priory Lane, Stretton Sugwas,
Herefordshire; tel: 01432 760264.
www.hotelpriory.co.uk*

Fishmore Hall ㉗
High degree of comfort, service, cuisine
and countryside views from a boutique
hotel in a restored Georgian house.
*Fishmore Road, Ludlow, Shropshire;
tel: 01584 875148.
www.fishmorehall.co.uk*

The Library House Guest House ㉚
Welcoming and comfy B&B in a beautiful
Grade II-listed Georgian building just along
from the Iron Bridge.
*Severn Bank, Ironbridge, nr Telford,
Shropshire; tel: 01952 432299.*
www.libraryhouse.com

Wilderhope Manor ㉘
A Grade I listed Elizabethan manor turned
refined hostel; a perfect base for hikes in
the surrounding landscape.
*Longville in the Dale, Shropshire; tel: 0845
371 9149. www.yha.org.uk*

The Raven Hotel & Restaurant ㉙
Handsome 17th-century coaching inn with
large rooms and a popular restaurant.
*Barrow Street, Much Wenlock, Shropshire;
tel: 01952 727251. www.ravenhotel.com*

Abbots Bromley Horn Dance ③
Highly distinctive ancient folk dance where
the dancers carry reindeer antlers.
*Abbots Bromley, Staffordshire; Wakes
Monday, day after Wakes Sunday (first
Sunday after 4 Sep).*
www.abbotsbromley.com/horn_dance

Lichfield Festival ④
Excellent four-day international festival
of music, theatre, dance, poetry and more.
*Lichfield, Staffordshire; tel: 01543 306270;
early Jul. www.lichfieldfestival.org*

Warwick Folk Festival ⑬
Festive celebration of folk music, with
three days of dance, workshops and a
full schedule of folk-music performances.
*Warwick School, Warwick;
tel: 02476 678738; late Jul.
www.warwickfolkfestival.co.uk*

Black Country Boating Festival ⑧
Hundreds of vessels congregate along
the canal for a long weekend of fun.
*Bumble Hole Nature Reserve, Windmill
End, Netherton; tel: 0844 800 5076; Sep.
www.bcbf.com*

Birmingham Weekender ⑨
Birmingham's leading cultural festival,
bursting with talent and innovation across
the creative spectrum, takes place over
three days in September.
*Various venues, Birmingham; Sep.
www.birminghamweekender.com*

**Birmingham Jazz and Blues
Festival** ⑨
A diverse 10-day appreciation of jazz, in
which hundreds of musicians perform.
*Various venues, Birmingham city centre;
tel: 0121 454 7020; Jul.
www.birminghamjazzfestival.com*

Ludlow Food Festival ㉗
A three-day celebration of food and drink
comprising talks, exhibits and workshops.
*Various venues, Ludlow, Shropshire;
tel: 01584 873957; Sep.
www.foodfestival.co.uk*

Above: Water ride at the Alton Towers theme park

MUSEUMS AND GALLERIES

Selly Manor Museum ⑨
Charming Tudor half-timbered house
dating from the 16th century, with a
great collection of historic furniture.
*Maple Road, Bournville, Birmingham;
tel: 01214 720199; open 10am–5pm
Tue–Fri (also Apr–Sep: 2–5pm Sat–Sun
and Bank Holiday Mondays).
www.sellymanormuseum.org.uk*

Coventry Transport Museum ⑪
A veritable A–Z of British and Coventry-
built motor vehicles plus half-term holiday
activities for car-obsessed children.
*Millennium Place, Hales Street, Coventry;
tel: 02476 234270; open 10am–5pm
daily (last admission at 4:30pm).
www.transport-museum.com*

Museum of Royal Worcester ⑱
The world's largest collection of Worcester
porcelain, dating from the 18th century to
the present day.
*Severn Street, Worcester; tel: 01905
21247; open 10am–5pm Mon–Sat.
www.worcesterporcelainmuseum.org*

The Commandery ⑱
Attractive half-timbered museum that
chronicles the history of Worcester.
*Sidbury, Worcester; tel: 01905 361821;
open 10am–5pm Mon–Sat, 1:30–5pm
Sun. www.worcestershire.gov.uk/museums*

Malvern Museum ⑳
Explore the curative properties of Malvern
spring water and the Victorians' fascination
with its healing powers.
*The Priory Gatehouse, Abbey Road,
Malvern, Worcestershire; tel: 01684
576811; open Easter–30 Oct: 10:30am–
5pm daily (closed Wed in term time).
www.malvernmuseum.co.uk*

The Elgar Birthplace Museum ⑲
The life and music of Sir Edward Elgar is
celebrated in this historic cottage, which is
filled with mementoes and personal effects.
*Crown East Lane, Lower Broadheath,
Worcester; tel: 01905 333224;
open 11am–5pm Fri–Tue.
www.elgarfoundation.org*

The Old House Hereford ㉕
Delve into Hereford history at this
traditional timber-framed house which
offers a fascinating insight into daily life
in Jacobean times.
*High Town, Hereford; tel: 01432 260694;
open 11am–4pm Tue–Sat.*

Museum of the Gorge ㉚
Absorbing museum detailing the history
and industrial culture of the Ironbridge
Gorge World Heritage Site.
*Ironbridge, Shropshire; tel: 01952 433424;
open 10am–5pm daily.
www.ironbridge.org.uk*

Coalbrookdale Museum of Iron ㉚
History of iron-smelting with fine examples
of cast iron from the Coalbrookdale
company, located in the old iron foundry.
*Coalbrookdale, Ironbridge, Shropshire;
tel: 01952 433424; open 10am–5pm
daily. www.ironbridge.org.uk*

Coalport China Museum ㉚
Fantastic collection of richly glazed
Coalport ceramics, with a range of
workshops for young potters.
*Coalport, Ironbridge, Shropshire;
tel: 01952 433424; open 10am–5pm
daily. www.ironbridge.org.uk*

Wroxeter Roman City ㉝
Roman Britain's fourth-largest city –
known then as Viroconium – with an
on-site museum detailing its appearance.
*Wroxeter, Shropshire; tel: 01743 761330;
open Mar–Oct: 10am–5pm daily;
Nov–Mar: 10am–4pm Sat & Sun.
www.english-heritage.org.uk/wroxeter*

THINGS TO DO WITH KIDS

**Thinktank, Birmingham Science
Museum** ⑨
Interactive, hands-on educational displays
and scientific exhibits for young Einsteins
(and their parents), plus a state-of-the-art
digital planetarium and IMAX theatre.
*Millennium Point, Curzon Street,
Birmingham; tel: 0121 348 8000;
open 10am–5pm daily (last admission
at 4pm). www.thinktank.ac*

Ludlow Castle ㉗
Fantastic day out for the children at this
11th-century castle ruin, which also boasts
self-catering accommodation.
*Castle Square, Ludlow, Shropshire;
tel: 01584 874465; open Dec–Jan:
10am–4pm Sat–Sun; mid-Feb–Mar:
10am–4pm daily; Apr–Jul: 10am–5pm
daily; Aug: 10am–7pm daily; Sep:
10am–5pm daily; Oct–Nov:
10am–4pm daily.
www.ludlowcastle.com*

Alton Towers ②
Popular amusement park and resort with
thrilling rides, a water park and a spa for
all-in-one family entertainment.
*Alton, Staffordshire; tel: 0871 222 3330;
open late Mar–early Nov, times vary
through the year. www.altontowers.com*

Dudley Zoo and Castle ⑦
History, heritage and wildlife all combined
in an educational and fun experience.
*Dudley, West Midlands; tel: 01384 215313;
open Sep–Easter: 10am–3pm (grounds
close at 4pm); Easter–Sep: 10am–4pm
(grounds close at 5pm).
www.dudleyzoo.org.uk*

Green Frog Pottery ⑳
Pottery painting, glazing and firing for
young potters at a Malvern studio.
*107 Barnards Green Road, Malvern,
Worcestershire; tel: 01684 561778;
open 10am–5:30pm Tue–Sat.
www.greenfrogpottery.co.uk*

Blists Hill Victorian Town ㉚
Victorian-themed town, that is perennially
popular with school children.
*Madeley, Shropshire; tel: 01952 433424;
open Apr–Oct: 10am–5pm daily; Nov–
Mar: 10am–4pm daily. www.ironbridge.
org.uk*

Royal Airforce Museum Cosford ㉜
Huge museum with a wealth of warplanes
and ever-changing displays and exhibits.
*Shifnal, Shropshire; tel: 01902 376200;
open 10am–5pm daily.
www.rafmuseum.org.uk*

SPAS AND HEALTH RESORTS

Fairlawns Hotel Spa ⑤
Excellent spa packages are on offer here,
plus highly professional service and
beautiful grounds.
*Little Aston Road, Aldridge, nr Walsall,
West Midlands; tel: 01922 455122.
www.fairlawns.co.uk*

New Hall Hotel and Spa ⑥
Beautiful 800-year-old manor-house hotel
(with moat) set in exquisite grounds.
*Walmley Road, Sutton Coldfield, nr
Birmingham; tel: 0845 072 7577.
www.handpickedhotels.co.uk/newhall*

Amala Spa ⑨
A range of packages tailored to meet
individual health needs, including
massages and skin treatments.
*Hyatt Regency Birmingham, 2 Bridge
Street, Birmingham; tel: 0121 632 1690.
www.birmingham.regency.hyatt.com*

**Ardencote Manor Hotel, Country Club
and Spa** ⑭
Fully equipped with health facilities and a
golf course, this hotel is set in splendid and
peaceful surroundings.
*Lye Green Road, Claverdon, Warwickshire;
tel: 01926 843111. www.ardencote.com*

OTHER SIGHTS IN THE BOOK

Stoke-on-Trent ① *(see pp148–9).*
Birmingham ⑨ *(see pp208–9).*
Stratford-upon-Avon ⑰ *(see pp34–5).*
Herefordshire ㉕ *(see pp164–5).*

EAST MIDLANDS

LOCAL FOOD

The Old Bakery Restaurant ①
Homely restaurant in the historic Uphill area, serving tasty dishes with ingredients sourced from its own vegetable garden.
26–28 Burton Road, Lincoln; tel: 01522 576057; open noon–1:30pm Thu–Sun and 7–8:30pm Tue–Sat.
www.theold-bakery.co.uk

The Wheatsheaf Inn ⑧
This Boston restaurant is much celebrated for its wide range of fine food and real ales.
Hubberts Bridge, Boston, Lincolnshire; tel: 01205 290347; open 5–9pm Mon–Wed, noon–2pm and 5–9pm Thu–Sat, 12–2pm Sun. www.the-wheatsheaf inn-hubberts-bridge.co.uk

The Church Restaurant ⑮
Modern dishes served up in the ecclesiastical setting of a former church.
67–83 Bridge Street, Northampton; tel: 01604 603800; open noon–late Mon–Sat. www.thechurchrestaurant.com

Cini Restaurant and Bar ⑲
Well-presented contemporary and innovative Italian dishes, made with locally sourced produce, are on offer here. Sleep off your meals in modern bedrooms.
26 High Street, Enderby, Leicester; tel: 0116 286 3009; open noon–2pm and 5–10pm Mon–Thu, noon–2pm and 5:30–10pm Fri & Sat.
www.cinirestaurant.co.uk

Dickinson & Morris Ye Olde Pork Pie Shoppe ㉒
Purchase a mouth watering range of pork pies, sausages, cheeses and bacon from this 160 year-old establishment.
10 Nottingham Street, Melton Mowbray, Leicestershire; tel: 01664 482068; open Mar–Dec: 8am–5pm Mon–Sat; Jan–Feb: 8am–4pm Mon–Sat.
www.porkpie.co.uk

World Service ㉗
A stylish fine-dining restaurant that offers outstanding food in the beautiful setting of 17th-century Newdigate House.
Newdigate House, Castlegate, Nottingham; tel: 0115 847 5587; open noon–2pm and 7–10pm Mon–Sat, noon–3:30pm Sun.
www.worldservicerestaurant.com

Koinonia Restaurant ㉙
Tasty South Indian cuisine focusing on the distinctive flavours of Kerala cooking.
19 St Marks Lane, Newark, Nottinghamshire; tel: 01636 706230; open 11:30am–3pm and 6–11pm Mon–Fri, 11:30am–11:30pm Sat, 11:30am–7:30pm Sun. www.koinoniarestaurant.com

The Old Original Bakewell Pudding Shop ㊵
Tasty Bakewell puddings, jams, chutneys, marmalades and biscuits are sold here; there is also a restaurant on the first floor.
The Square, Bakewell, Derbyshire; tel: 01629 812193; open daily.
www.bakewellpuddingshop.co.uk

Piedaniel's ㊵
Enjoy beautifully presented food, cooked using local ingredients, at this stylish Bakewell restaurant.
Bath Street, Bakewell, Derbyshire; tel: 01629 812687; open noon–2pm and 7pm–late Mon–Sat.
www.piedaniels-restaurant.com

Rose Cottage Cafe ㊾
A snug and cosy cottage in Castleton serving great home-made food. There is also a lovely garden.
Cross Street, Castleton, Derbyshire; tel: 01433 620472; open 10am–5pm Sat–Thu.

Columbine Restaurant ㊿
Popular Buxton restaurant with ample servings and considerable culinary flair.
7 Hall Bank, Buxton, Derbyshire; tel: 01298 78752; open 7–10pm Mon, Wed–Sat.
www.columbinerestaurant.co.uk

FARMERS' MARKETS

Bakewell Farmers' Market ㊵
A focus on organic produce, selling everything from chocolate to sausages.
Bakewell, Derbyshire; tel: 01629 813777; last Sat of every month, 9am–2pm.

Buxton Farmers' Market ㊿
A huge variety of local produce in Buxton's fantastic Pavilion Gardens.
St John's Road, Buxton, Derbyshire; tel: 01298 23114; first Thu of every month, 9:30am–2:30pm.

PUBS

The Strugglers Inn ①
Cosy pub at the foot of the walls of Lincoln Castle, named after prisoners who would struggle on the way to the nearby gallows.
83 Westgate, Lincoln; tel: 01522 535023; open daily.

The Tobie Norris ⑪
A fabulous range of brews are available at this stylish pub, located in a building dating from 1280, and containing seven uniquely decorated rooms.
12 St Pauls Street, Stamford, Lincolnshire; tel: 01780 753800; open daily.
www.tobienorris.com

The King's Head ⑭
Scenic riverside location with the Nene Way long-distance footpath right outside.
Church Street, Wadenhoe, Northamptonshire; tel: 01832 720024; open daily.
www.wadenhoekingshead.co.uk

Ye Olde Trip to Jerusalem ㉗
"The oldest inn in Britain" and the assembly point for Crusading knights.
Brewhouse Yard, Nottingham; tel: 0115 947 3171; open daily.
www.triptojerusalem.com

EAST MIDLANDS

Above: Joining in the fun at the Robin Hood Festival

The Plough Inn ㉗
Traditional Nottingham brewery pub with a friendly atmosphere and a wide range of beer and cider.
17 St Peter's Street, Radford, Nottingham; tel: 07815073447; open daily.
www.nottinghambrewery.com

Chequers at Woolsthorpe ㉓
Snug Vale of Belvoir pub with a focus on relaxation and excellent food. Plush accommodation is also available.
Main Street, Woolsthorpe by Belvoir, Grantham, Lincolnshire; tel: 01476 870701; open daily.
www.chequersinn.net

The Boat Inn ⑯
In the same family since the 19th century, this stone-floored pub has stunning canal views and offers trips on the pub's narrow boat, Indian Chief.
Shutlanger Road, Stoke Bruerne, Northamptonshire; tel: 01604 862428; open daily. www.boatinn.co.uk

The Druid Inn ㊳
Located in a 17th-century building, this atmospheric pub is famed for its excellent restaurant.
Main Street, Birchover, Matlock, Derbyshire; tel: 01629 653836; open noon–11pm Tue–Sat, noon–10:30pm Sun. www.thedruidinn.co.uk

Eyre Arms ㊶
Dating back to the mid-18th century, the haunted Eyre Arms is a traditional pub with Grade II-listed status, a seasoned interior and quaint beer garden.
Hassop, Bakewell, Derbyshire; tel: 01629 640390; open 11am–3pm and 6:30–11pm daily (to 10:30pm Sun).
www.eyrearms.com

The Crispin ㊸
A welcoming traditional Peak District pub near Bakewell serving cask-conditioned ales from Cheshire brewer Robinson's.
Main Road, Great Longstone, Derbyshire; tel: 01629 640237; open noon–3pm and 6–11pm Mon–Fri, noon–11pm Sat & Sun. www.thecrispin.co.uk

The Barrel Inn ㊸
Pop in for a drink or spend the night at this charming Inn that claims to be the highest pub in Derbyshire.
Bretton, Eyam, Hope Valley, Derbyshire; tel: 01433 630856; open daily.
www.thebarrelinn.co.uk

The Old Nag's Head ㊼
This pub, which dates back to the 16th century, stands invitingly at the beginning of the Pennine Way.
Grindsbrook Booth, Edale, Hope Valley, Derbyshire; tel: 01433 670291; open daily.

PLACES TO STAY

Washingborough Hall Hotel ②
Magnificent Georgian country house with particularly good-value rooms and a gorgeous garden.
Church Hill, Washingborough, Lincolnshire; tel: 01522 790340.
www.washingboroughhall.com

Kildare Hotel ④
This popular and very well-kept Skegness B&B is a short stroll from the beach.
80 Sandbeck Avenue, Skegness, Lincolnshire; tel: 01754 762935.
www.kildare-hotel.co.uk

Plummers Place Guesthouse ⑨
With a lovely location in the Lincolnshire fens, this B&B is bursting with historic character and charm.
Shore Road, Freiston Shore, Boston, Lincolnshire; tel: 01205 761490.
www.plummersplace.com

The George of Stamford ⑪
Marvellous old hotel with particularly congenial service, excellent dining and a variety of comfy rooms.
71 St Martins, Stamford, Lincolnshire; tel: 01780 750750.
www.georgehotelofstamford.com

Lake Isle Hotel & Restaurant ⑫
Elegant 18th-century house with outstanding dining and 12 fine rooms.
16 High Street East, Uppingham, Rutland; tel: 01572 822951. www.lakeisle.co.uk

The Regency Hotel & Restaurant ⑲
Impressive-looking Victorian town house with modest prices, decent rooms and murder-mystery dinners.
360 London Road, Leicester; tel: 01162 709634. www.the-regency-hotel.com

Hotel Maiyango ⑲
Neat and effortlessly cool boutique hotel at the heart of Leicester, offering a superlative dining experience and a rooftop terrace bar.
13–21 St Nicholas Place, Leicester; tel: 0116 251 8898. www.maiyango.com

Bridge House B&B ㉘
Comfortable and very well-run Edwardian establishment with first-rate breakfasts.
4 London Road, New Balderton, Newark, Nottinghamshire; tel: 01636 674663.
www.arnoldsbandb.co.uk

Harts Hotel ㉗
Delightful modern-looking boutique hotel with first-rate service.
Standard Hill, Park Row, Nottingham; tel: 0115 988 1900. www.hartshotel.co.uk

Hartington Hall Hostel ㊱
Excellent-value former manor house and youth hostel with accommodating staff.
Hall Bank, Hartington, nr Buxton, Derbyshire; tel: 0845 371 9740.
www.yha.org.uk

Harthill Hall ㊲
A handsome group of historic buildings offering a range of rooms plus spa, indoor swimming pool and other facilities.
Alport, Bakewell, Derbyshire; tel: 01629 636190. www.harthillhall.co.uk

Bagshaw Hall ㊵
Imposing 350-year-old building with a Queen Anne interior, gorgeous grounds and great views.
Bagshaw Hill, Bakewell, Derbyshire; tel: 01629 810333.
www.bakewellholidayapartments.com

Riverside House ㊷
Serene and relaxing Peak District retreat on the banks of the River Wye.
Ashford-in-the-Water, Bakewell, Derbyshire; tel: 01629 812475.
www.riversidehousehotel.co.uk

Swiss House ㊾
Tastefully-decorated B&B lodgings in the Peak District, with helpful owners and great breakfasts.
How Lane, Castleton, Hope Valley, Derbyshire; tel: 01433 621098.
www.swiss-house.co.uk

Griff House Bed and Breakfast ㊿
A refurbished Victorian property ideally located for exploring the historic spa town of Buxton and the Peak District.
2 Compton Road, Buxton, Derbyshire; tel: 01298 23628.
www.griffhousebuxton.co.uk

FESTIVALS AND EVENTS

Lost Village Festival ③
Lost Village is a music festival "experience", set amongst secluded woodland and featuring world-class DJs, artists and bands.
In woodland, Lincoln; end of May.
www.lostvillagefestival.com

Northampton Balloon Festival ⑮
Hot-air balloons galore makes for a thrilling and memorable three-day spectacle.
Billing Aquadrome, Crow Lane, Great Billing, Northampton; tel: 01604 784948; mid-Aug.
www.northamptonballoonfestival.net

Hare Pie Scramble and Bottle Kicking ⑱
This tradition, which involves scrambling for pieces of hare pie and then kicking bottles of beer between two streams, is over 200 years old.
Hallaton, Leicestershire; Easter Mon.

Melton Mowbray Food Festival ㉑
A lavish spread of pies, cheeses and wines, with live cooking demonstrations and celebrations of all things gastronomic over a food-filled weekend.
The Cattle Market, Scalfold Rd, Melton Mowbray, Leicestershire; tel: 07894 229449; Oct.
www.meltonmowbrayfoodfestival.co.uk

CAMRA Summer Beer Festival ㉖
Five-day celebration of beer, organized by the Campaign for Real Ale, with live music.
Market Place, Derby; Jul.
www.derbycamra.org.uk

Robin Hood Festival ㉛
This week-long celebration of the life of Robin Hood and his Merry Men is perfect for little ones.
Sherwood Forest Visitor Centre, Edwinstowe, Nottinghamshire; tel: 08444 775678; Aug.
www.nottinghamshire.gov.uk/robinhoodfestival

International Byron Festival ㉝
Fans of Lord Byron flock to his family home at Newstead Abbey for a ten-day reflection on his life and poetic legacy.
Newstead Abbey, Nottingham; tel: 01159 639633; Jul.
www.newsteadabbeybyronsociety.org

Wirksworth Festival ㉞
Popular arts festival with a focus on everything from performance art to poetry, visual arts, film and sculpture – with workshops.
Wirksworth, Derbyshire; tel: 01629 824003; Sep.
www.wirksworthfestival.co.uk

Royal Shrovetide Football ㉟
Dating from the 12th century, this game of football takes place across the entire town.
Ashbourne, Derbyshire; Shrove Tue and Ash Wed. www.ashbourne-town.com/events/football.html

The Big Session ㊿
Hosted by Oysterband, the best English folk bands and artists gather in Buxton for two days and nights to welcome in May.
Buxton Opera House, Buxton, Derbyshire; tel: 01298 72190; end of Apr–early May.
www.buxtonoperahouse.org.uk/the-big-session

Buxton Festival ㊿
Major event that attracts opera-goers, musicians, poets and writers for two weeks of festivities.
Opera House and various venues, Buxton, Derbyshire; tel: 01298 72190; Jul.
www.buxtonfestival.co.uk

Buxton Festival Fringe ㊿
Offshoot of the Buxton Festival, with an emphasis on drama, comedy, poetry, film and music over two weeks.
Various venues, Buxton, Derbyshire; tel: 01298 79351; Jul.
www.buxtonfringe.org.uk

MUSEUMS AND GALLERIES

Battle of Britain Memorial Flight Visitors Centre ④
A nostalgic hangar tour displays World War II planes, including Spitfires and Hawker Hurricanes, up close.
RAF Coningsby, Dogdyke Road, Coningsby, Lincolnshire; tel: 01526 344041; open 10am–5pm Mon–Fri.
www.lincolnshire.gov.uk/bbmf

The Cottage Museum ⑤
This quaint museum outlines the history of the attractive village of Woodhall Spa.
Iddesleigh Road, Woodhall Spa, Lincolnshire; tel: 01526 352456; open Easter–Oct: 10:30am–4:30pm daily.
www.cottagemuseum.co.uk

Stamford Arts Centre ⑪
The gallery displays a varied programme of contemporary exhibitions from local and international artists including photography, painting, textile, drawing and sculpture.
27 St Mary's Street, Stamford Lincolnshire; tel: 01780 763203; open 9:30am–9pm Mon–Sat. www.stamfordartscentre.com

Northampton Museum & Art Gallery ⑮
Outstanding historic collection of footwear in a famous shoe museum and gallery.
4–6 Guildhall Road, Northampton; tel: 01604 838111; open 10am–5pm Tue–Sat, 2–5pm Sun.
www.northampton.gov.uk

Canal Museum, Stoke Bruerne ⑯
Fascinating waterways exhibition housed in a former corn mill alongside the canal.
Stoke Bruerne, Towcester, Northamptonshire; tel: 01604 862229; open Apr–Oct: 10am–5pm daily; Nov–Mar: 11am–3pm Wed–Fri, 11am–4pm Sat–Sun. www.canalrivertrust.org.uk

New Walk Museum & Art Gallery ⑲
Magnificent museum, with collections from the natural world to art and beyond.
53 New Walk, Leicester; tel: 0116 225 4900; open 10am–5pm Mon–Sat, 11am–5pm Sun. www.leicester.gov.uk

Derby Museum and Art Gallery ㉖
Intriguing museum housing a collection of paintings by local artist Joseph Wright.
The Strand, Derby; tel: 01332 641901; open 10am–5pm Tue–Sat, noon–4pm Sun. www.derby.gov.uk

Harley Gallery ㉚
Excellent venue showcasing work from contemporary craftspeople and artists.
Welbeck, Worksop, Nottinghamshire; tel: 01909 501700; open 10am–5pm Mon–Sat, 10am–4pm Sun.
www.harleygallery.co.uk

Chatsworth House ㊴
Spectacular 17th-century estate and gardens with a wealth of antiquities.
Bakewell, Derbyshire; tel: 01246 565300; open Mar–Oct: 10:30am–6pm daily.
www.chatsworth.org

Althorp House ⑰
Explore the magnificent stately home of Althorp House to discover one of Europe's finest private collections of furniture, pictures and ceramics.
Althorp, Northamptonshire; tel: 01604 770107; open Jul–Aug: noon–5pm and selected dates in Feb.
www.spencerofalthorp.com

Nottingham Castle ㉗
Seventeenth-century mansion, on the site of the original castle, stuffed with history and culture, including the Castle Museum.
Off Friar Lane, Maid Marian Way, Nottingham; tel: 01158 761400; open Mar–Sep: 10am–5pm Tue–Sun; Oct–Feb: 10am–4pm Tue–Sun.
www.nottinghamcastle.org.uk

Eyam Museum ㊹
Explore the ins and outs of this "plague village", which imposed isolation on itself to quarantine the bubonic plague in 1665.
Hawkhill Road, Eyam, Derbyshire; tel: 01433 631371; open Mar–Nov: 10am–4:30pm Tue–Sun.
www.eyam-museum.org.uk

THINGS TO DO WITH KIDS

Lincoln Castle ①
A fascinating 11th-century castle offering a host of summer events, from jousting to drama.
Castle Hill, Lincoln; tel: 01522 782040; open Oct–Mar: 10am–4pm daily; Apr–Sep: 10am–5pm daily.
www.lincolncastle.com

National Space Centre ⑲
The UK's largest planetarium and interactive space centre, dedicated to the story of the universe.
Exploration Drive, Leicester; tel: 0845 605 2001; open 10am–4pm Tue–Fri, 10am–5pm Sat–Sun;
www.spacecentre.co.uk

Heckington Windmill ⑦
Dating back to 1830, England's sole surviving eight-sailed windmill is a fantastic sight.
Hale Road, Heckington, Sleaford, Lincolnshire; tel: 01529 461919; open Apr–mid-Jul: noon–5pm Thu–Sun; mid-Jul–Sep: noon–5pm daily; Oct–Mar: noon–4pm Sat–Sun.
www.heckingtonwindmill.org.uk

Bosworth Battlefield Heritage Centre and Country Park ⑳
Medieval history gruesomely brought to life, plus nature walks for the squeamish.
Sutton Cheney, nr Market Bosworth, Nuneaton, Warwickshire; tel: 01455 290429; open Apr–Oct: 10am–5pm daily; Nov–Mar: 10am–4pm daily.
www.bosworthbattlefield.com

Ashby-de-la-Zouch Castle ㉔
Famous ruin, often hosting children's events, such as a medieval-style combat in August.
Ashby-de-la-Zouch, Leicestershire; tel: 01530 413343; open Apr–Jun and Sep–Oct: 10am–5pm Thu–Mon; Jul–Aug: 10am–5pm daily; Nov–Mar: 10am–4pm Sat–Sun. www.english-heritage.org.uk

Donington Park Grand Prix Exhibition ㉕
Give young petrol-heads something to roar about with the world's largest collection of Grand Prix racing cars.
Donington Park, Castle Donington, Derby; tel: 01332 810048; open 10am–5pm daily. www.donington-park.co.uk

Sherwood Forest Natural Nature Reserve ㉛
Great trekking opportunities in historic parkland that is forever associated with Robin Hood and his Merry Men.
Edwinstowe, Mansfield, Nottinghamshire; tel: 01623 823202; open Apr–Oct: 10am–5pm daily; Nov–Mar: 10am–4:30pm daily. www.nottinghamshire.gov.uk

World Conker Championship ⑬
A truly international battle of the conkers, with events for men and women plus junior competitions.
New Lodge Fields, nr Oundle, Northamptonshire; tel: 01832 272735; second Sun in Oct.
www.worldconkerchampionships.com

Go Ape ㉜
High-wire adventures, zip-lines and obstacle courses in the trees make up this popular woodland adventure park.
Sherwood Pines, Nottinghamshire; tel: 0333 331 7820; open Mar–Oct: daily; Nov: Sat–Sun. www.goape.co.uk

Chestnut Centre Otter, Owl and Wildlife Park ㊽
Inspiring wildlife park in the Peak District National Park, home to otters, polecats, red foxes, deer and more.
Chapel-en-le-Frith, High Peak, Derbyshire; tel: 01298 814099; open Mar–Sep: 10:30am–5:30pm daily; Oct–Feb: 10:30am–dusk daily.
www.chestnutcentre.co.uk

SPAS AND HEALTH RESORTS

Barnsdale Hall Hotel ⑩
Country house equipped with spa and leisure facilities in a fabulous location.
Stamford Road, Barnsdale, Oakham, Rutland; tel: 01572 757901.
www.barnsdalehotel.co.uk

Losehill House Hotel & Spa ㊻
Lovely Peak District hotel in a secluded location, with swimming pool and spa.
Edale Road, Hope, Derbyshire; tel: 01433 621219. www.losehillhouse.co.uk

OTHER SIGHTS IN THE BOOK

Derbyshire Peak District ㊹ *(see pp/6–7).*
Caves of Castleton and Buxton ㊾
(see pp186–7).

Below: National Space Centre in Leicester

EASTERN ENGLAND

LOCAL FOOD

Cotto ㉛
Fantastic European menu using a wide variety of local ingredients – a large proportion of which is sourced from Cambridge Market – with a heavy bias towards organic produce.
183 East Road, Cambridge; tel: 01223 302010; open 6:30pm–late Wed–Sat. www.cottocambridge.co.uk

Midsummer House ㉛
A Michelin-starred restaurant, housed in a quaint old building, that sources ingredients from local suppliers to create fantastic contemporary cuisine.
Midsummer Common, Cambridge; tel: 01223 369299; open 7–9:30pm Tue, noon–1:30pm and 7–9:30pm Wed–Sat. www.midsummerhouse.co.uk

The Last Wine Bar & Restaurant ①
Award-winning restaurant with a relaxed vibe; delicious English fare and fine wine.
70–76 St George's Street, Norwich; tel: 01603 626626; open noon–3:30pm and 5pm–12:30am Mon–Sat. www.lastwinebar.co.uk

The Deli and Restaurants, Jarrold ①
Take time out in one of several delicious eateries at this iconic department store.
1–11 London Street, Norwich; open 9am–5:30pm Mon–Fri (to 6pm Sat), 10:30am-4:30pm Sun. www.jarrold.co.uk

The Old Fire Engine House ㉝
Handsome restaurant and art gallery with a focus on traditional English dishes.
25 St Mary's Street, Ely, Cambridgeshire; tel: 01353 662582; open 12:15–2pm, 3:30–5:15pm and 7:15–9pm daily (closed Sun eve). www.theoldfireenginehouse.co.uk

The Lifeboat Inn ㊼
Delightful seafood restaurant, pub and charming hotel in a superb coastal setting.
Ship Lane, Thornham, Norfolk; tel: 01485 512236; restaurant open noon–2:30pm and 6–9pm Mon–Fri, all day Sat & Sun. www.lifeboatinnthornham.com

The Hoste Arms ㊿
Pretty former coaching inn offering locally sourced food and the catch of the day.
The Green, Burnham Market, Norfolk; tel: 01328 738777; open 7:30–9:30am, noon–9:15pm daily. www.thehoste.com

Wiveton Hall (55)
Gorgeous Jacobean house where you can pick your own fruit and eat in a lovely café.
Wiveton Hall, Holt, Norfolk; tel: 01263 740515; open Easter–Christmas, 10:30am–5pm daily. www.wivetonhall.co.uk

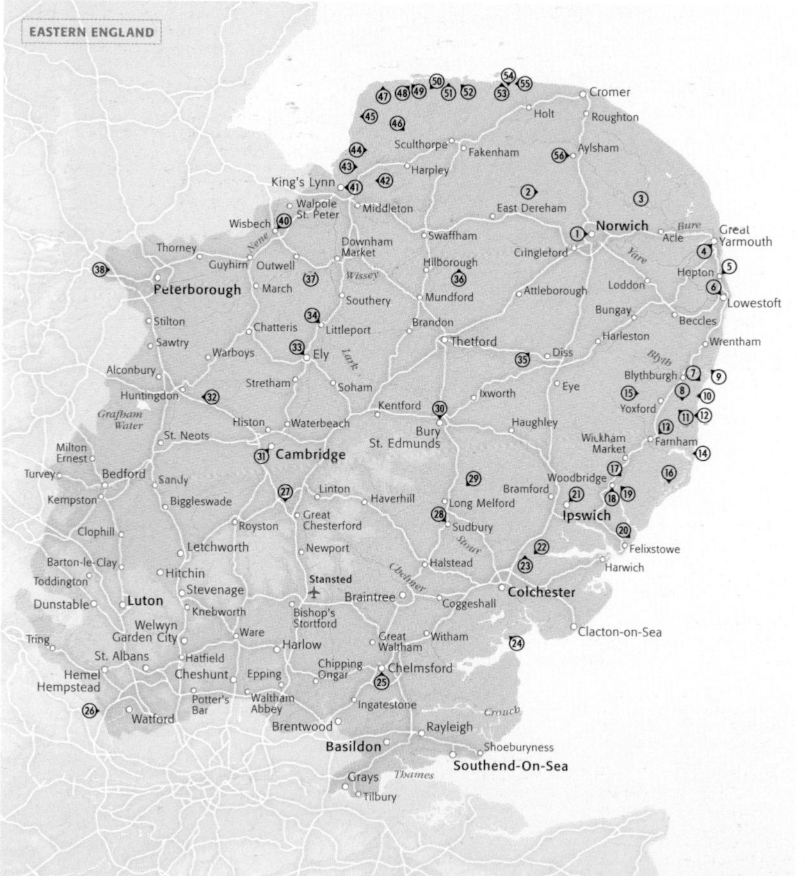

The Westleton Crown ⑧
Historic former coaching inn dating back to the 12th century, with log fires and an award-winning restaurant.
The Street, Westleton, Southwold, Suffolk; tel: 01728 648777; open 7:15–10am, noon–2:30pm and 7–9:30pm Mon–Fri, 7:30–10:30am, noon–2:30pm and 7–9:30pm Sat & Sun. www.westletoncrown.co.uk

Emmett's of Peasenhall ⑮
Delicious range of hams, organic wines, cheeses, chocolates, olives and chutney.
Peasenhall, Saxmundham, Suffolk; tel: 01728 660250; open 8:30am–5:30pm Mon–Fri, 8:30am–5pm Sat. www.emmettsham.co.uk

Reckford Farm Shop ⑪
A range of goodies, from home-made pies to fish and cheeses, locally sourced from responsible producers.
Reckford Farm, Westleton Road, Middleton, Saxmundham, Suffolk; tel: 01728 648253; open 9am–5pm daily. www.onesuffolk.co.uk

Railway Farm Market Garden & Farm Shop ⑬
Bursting with home-grown and locally sourced goodies, from vegetables to honey and free-range eggs.
Main Road, Benhall, Saxmundham, Suffolk; tel: 01728 605793; open 8am–5:30pm Mon–Sat, 9am–2pm Sun.

The Lighthouse Restaurant ⑭
Agreeable Aldeburgh restaurant with a very dependable English and European menu.
77 High Street, Aldeburgh, Suffolk; tel: 01728 453377; open noon–2pm and 6:30–10pm Mon–Fri, noon–2:30pm and 6:30–10pm Sat & Sun. www.lighthouserestaurant.co.uk

Butley Orford Oysterage ⑯
Superb seafood is on the menu here, with oysters from the restaurant's oyster bed.
Market Square, Orford, Suffolk; tel: 01394 450277; open noon–2:15pm daily; also Apr–Jul and Sep–Oct: 6:30–9pm Wed–Fri, 6–9pm Sat; Aug: 6:30–9pm daily (from 6pm Sat); Nov–Apr: 6:30–9pm Fri, 6–9pm Sat only. www.butleyorfordoysterage.co.uk

The Whistle Stop Café ⑱
Glorious food, light snacks and coffee served in the former Woodbridge railway station. There are also bedrooms available upstairs.
Woodbridge Station Guesthouse, Station Road, Woodbridge, Suffolk; tel: 01394 384831; open 9am–4pm Mon–Fri, 9am–5pm Sat & Sun. www.woodbridgestationguesthouse.co.uk

Salthouse Eaterie ㉑
Delicious British and Mediterranean food served up in a stunning waterside location.
Salthouse Harbour Hotel, Neptune Quay, Ipswich, Suffolk; tel: 01473 226789; open 7am–10pm daily. www.salthouseharbour.co.uk

The Company Shed (24)
Simple, no-frills seafood eatery; the oysters alone are worth the trip out here.
129 Coast Road, West Mersea, Colchester, Essex; tel: 01206 382700; open 9am–4pm Tue–Sat, 10am–4pm Sun.
www.thecompanyshed.co

FARMERS' MARKETS

Aldeburgh Farmers' Market (14)
Wholesome spread of locally produced edibles and drinks in a pleasant Suffolk coastal town.
Church Hall, Victoria Road, Aldeburgh, Suffolk; third Sat of every month, 9am–12:30pm.

Lavenham Farmers' Market (29)
Huge and wholesome range of local produce in this delightful village near Bury St Edmunds.
Lavenham Village Hall or Market Place, Church St, Lavenham, Suffolk; fourth Sat of every month, 10am–1pm.

Ely Farmers' Market (33)
Small, friendly market featuring excellent local produce, from traditional fruit and veg to farmed ostrich meat.
Off Market Square, Ely, Cambridgeshire, tel: 01353 665555; second and fourth Sat of every month, 8:30am–2pm.
www.visitely.eastcambs.gov.uk

Wayland Farmers' Market (24)
Diverse range of locally reared, grown and prepared produce at a small market town in the heart of Norfolk.
Watton High Street, Watton, Norfolk; tel: 01953 883915; first Sat of every month except Jan, 8:30am–12:30pm.
www.wayland.org.uk

Aylsham Farmers' Market (56)
A bounty of locally reared meats, locally grown vegetables and other produce.
Market Place, Aylsham, Norfolk; tel: 01263 733354; first and third Sat of every month, 9am–1pm.
www.aylsham-tc.gov.uk

PUBS

Adam and Eve (1)
An historic Norwich alehouse, thought to date from the 12th century, offering good food, great beer and a delightful garden.
Bishopsgate, Norwich; tel: 01603 667423; open daily.

The Rumbold Arms (4)
Great wine list, a host of real ales, an extensive menu and huge back garden (once a bowling green).
107 Southtown Road, Great Yarmouth, Norfolk, tel: 01493 653887; open daily.
www.therumboldarms.co.uk

The Ship Inn (10)
This nautically flavoured inn at the once-flourishing port of Dunwich is a joy.
St James Street, Dunwich, Saxmundham, Suffolk; tel: 01728 648219; open daily.
www.shipatdunwich.co.uk

Above: Historic windmill at Cley, now converted into holiday accommodation

The Anchor (7)
An emphasis on beach views, fresh local ingredients and organic produce matched by an ambitious range of beers.
Main Street, Walberswick, Suffolk; tel: 01502 722112; open 11am–4pm and 6–11pm Mon–Fri, all day Sat & Sun
www.anchoratwalberswick.com

Land of Liberty, Peace and Plenty (26)
A splendid range of real ales greets customers at this atmospheric pub in a 19th-century house with a great garden.
Long Lane, Heronsgate, Hertfordshire; tel: 01923 282226; open daily.
www.landoflibertypub.com

The Old Cannon (30)
Fantastic brew-pub in a converted brewery at the heart of Bury St Edmunds, with fine food and own-brewed beer.
86 Cannon Street, Bury St Edmunds, Suffolk; tel: 01284 768769; open lunch and evening Mon–Fri, all day Sat & Sun.
www.oldcannonbrewery.co.uk

The Eagle (31)
Former coaching inn associated with Francis Crick and James Watson, who celebrated their discovery of the DNA double-helix here.
8 Benet Street, Cambridge; tel: 01223 505020; open daily.

Free Press (31)
Great food and ale and a traditional vibe that's a pleasant contrast to modern pubs.
Prospect Row, Cambridge; tel: 01223 368337; open daily. www.freepresspub.com

The Sun Inn (23)
Sleepy former coaching inn, steeped in real-ale aromas, with a lovely garden.
High Street, Dedham, Essex; tel: 01206 323351; open daily.
www.thesuninndedham.com

The Cock (32)
Much-loved quaint pub with an admirable European menu, good-value set meals and bucketloads of character, right at the heart of the village.
47 High Street, Hemingford Grey, Huntingdon, Cambridgeshire; tel: 01480 463609; open 11:30am–3pm and 6–11pm Mon–Sat, noon–4pm and 6:30–10:30pm Sun.
www.cambscuisine.com

The Rose and Crown (45)
Stuffed with nooks, timber beams, uneven floors and 14th-century charm, this pub has its own bedrooms if you simply can't pull yourself away.
Old Church Road, Snettisham, Norfolk; tel: 01485 541382; open daily.
www.roseandcrownsnettisham.co.uk

The White Horse (48)
Stunningly situated on the North Norfolk coastline with fantastic sea views: eat, drink, stay overnight and enjoy the unique atmosphere. *Brancaster Staithe, Norfolk; tel: 01485 210262; open daily.*
www.whitehorsebrancaster.co.uk

PLACES TO STAY

Dedham Hall (23)
Fifteenth-century manor house deep in the heart of Constable Country *(see pp80–81)*, complete with a celebrated restaurant and luxury rooms.
Brook Street, Dedham, Essex; tel: 01206 323027.
www.dedhamhall.co.uk

Lavenham Priory (29)
Gorgeous, half-timbered, 13th-century B&B with a lovely, large garden, in the middle of a pretty village.
Water Street, Lavenham, Sudbury, Suffolk; tel: 01787 247404.
www.lavenhampriory.co.uk

Cathedral House (33)
Fine Georgian period B&B with charming owners, breakfast cooked to order and a fabulous location in the shadow of Ely Cathedral.
17 St Mary's Street, Ely, Cambridgeshire; tel: 01353 662124.
www.cathedralhouse.co.uk

The Gate House Bed & Breakfast (34)
Luxurious en suite rooms and excellent breakfasts at this friendly B&B.
2b Lynn Road, Littleport, Ely, Cambridgeshire; tel: 01353 863840.
www.thegatehousebandb.co.uk

Elme Hall Hotel (40)
Particularly spacious roofing in a large Georgian-style mansion offering both luxury and budget accommodation.
69 Elm High Road, Wisbech, Cambridgeshire; tel: 01945 475566.
www.elmehall.co.uk

The Old Rectory (41)
Former Georgian rectory swishly converted with comfy, good value en suite rooms and a courtyard, terrace and garden.
33 Goodwins Road, King's Lynn, Norfolk; tel: 01553 768544.
www.oldrectory-kingslynn.com

Deepdale (43)
Hostel accommodation and camp site at a fun and atmospheric spot on the north Norfolk coast. Yurts are also available.
Deepdale Farm, Burnham Deepdale, Norfolk; tel: 01485 210256.
www.deepdalefarm.co.uk

Vine House (50)
Elegant Georgian boutique hotel with a cosy study area, rooms that boast a flawless attention to detail and butler service in the evenings.
The Green, Burnham Market, Norfolk; tel: 01328 738777.
www.thehoste.com

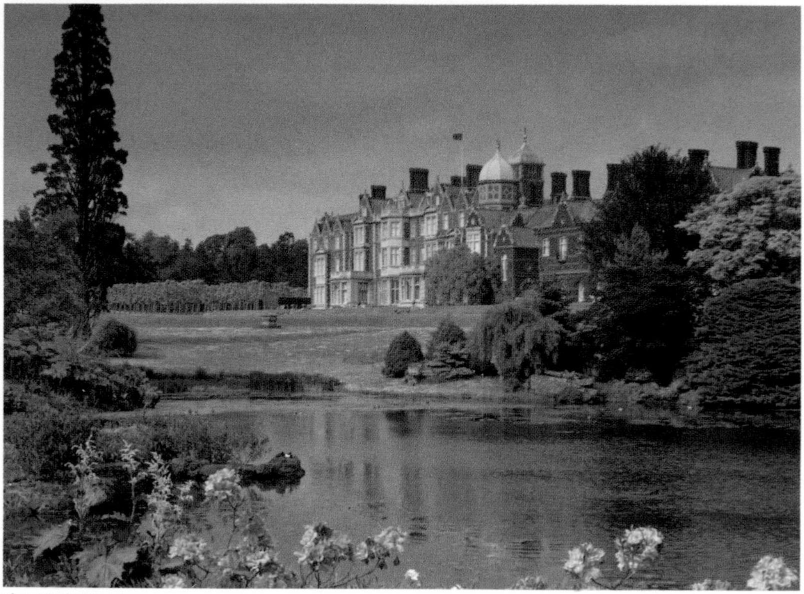

Above: Sandringham House

The Crown (52)
Excellent former coaching inn with rooms, on a Georgian square in a quintessential seaside town with long Norfolk views; the food is first-rate.
The Buttlands, Wells-next-the-Sea, Norfolk; tel: 01328 710209. www.crownhotelnorfolk.co.uk

Cley Windmill (54)
Bedrooms in a fabulous historic windmill and in converted stables and boathouses.
Cley-next-the-Sea, Holt, Norfolk; tel: 01263 740209. www.cleywindmill.co.uk

FESTIVALS AND EVENTS

Norfolk and Norwich Festival ①
Music, theatre, dance and the arts – including original commissions – celebrated with gusto over 16 days.
Various venues, Norwich and Norfolk; tel: 01603 877750; May. www.nnfestival.org.uk

Ely Folk Festival ㉝
Folk fans converge on the cathedral town of Ely for three days of music, dance, merrymaking and festive fun.
Ely Outdoor Centre, Ely, Cambridgeshire; tel: 07500 527334; Jul. www.elyfolk.co.uk

Aldeburgh Festival ⑭
A two-week event focusing on classical music by past and contemporary composers, in a charming Suffolk seaside town.
Various venues, Aldeburgh, Suffolk; tel: 01728 687100; Jun. www.aldeburgh.co.uk

Aldeburgh Poetry Festival ⑭
Three-day celebration of the written and spoken word complete with poetry workshops and open-mic events.
Various venues, Aldeburgh, Suffolk; tel: 01986 835950; Nov. www.aldeburghpoetryfestival.org

Latitude Festival ⑨
A four-day festival that pulls in big names from the worlds of music, literature, poetry, comedy and theatre.
Henham Park, Southwold, Suffolk; Jul. www.latitudefestival.com

Essex Poetry Festival ㉕
A month of poetry readings, workshops, open-mic events and poetry competitions.
The Cramphorn Theatre, Fairfield Road, Chelmsford, Essex; tel: 01245 606505; Sep–Oct. www.essex-poetry-festival.co.uk

King's Lynn Festival ㊶
A varied two-week programme of music, including classical, jazz and folk, with special celebrity guests.
Various venues, King's Lynn, Norfolk; tel: 01553 767557; Jul. www.kingslynnfestival.org.uk

Holkham Country Fair (51)
Two-day celebration of rural England held every other year (in odd-numbered years) in the dazzling grounds of this Palladian hall.
Holkham Hall, Wells-next-the-Sea, Norfolk; tel: 01328 821821; Jul. www.holkhamcountryfair.co.uk

MUSEUMS AND GALLERIES

Castle Museum and Art Gallery ①
Appealing museum housed in an 11th-century castle, with artworks from the Norwich School, displays on Norfolk's history and the largest collection of ceramic teapots in the world.
Castle Meadow, Norwich; tel: 01603 493625; open 10am–4:30pm Mon–Sat, 1–5pm Sun. www.museums.norfolk.gov.uk

Sainsbury Centre for the Visual Arts ①
Superb permanent collection of art, ranging from Yüan dynasty effigies to works by Francis Bacon and Henry Moore.
University of East Anglia, Norwich; tel: 01603 593199; open 10am–6pm Tue–Fri, 10am–5pm Sat & Sun. www.scva.org.uk

Dunwich Museum ⑩
Displays about the once-magnificent medieval town of Dunwich, now reduced to a tiny coastal village because of erosion.
St James Street, Dunwich, Suffolk; tel: 01728 648796; open Apr–Sep: 11:30am–4:30pm. www.dunwichmuseum.org.uk

Bawdsey Radar Museum ⑳
The world's first radar station is a must for all World War II and Battle of Britain fans.
Bawdsey Quay, Suffolk, tel: 07821 162879; open some Sundays in Apr–Aug, 12:30–4:30pm; see website for details. http://www.bawdseyradar.org.uk

Aldeburgh Museum ⑭
Delightful old timbered Tudor building exhibiting local artifacts and exploring legends such as the "Aldeburgh Witches".
Moot Hall, Aldeburgh, Suffolk; tel: 01728 454666; open Apr–May and Sep–Oct: 2:30–5pm daily; Jun–Aug: noon–5pm daily. www.aldeburghmuseum.org.uk

Sutton Hoo Exhibition Hall ⑲
Celebrated collection of artifacts from the excavated burial mounds of the Anglo-Saxon kings of East Anglia.
Tranmer House, Sutton Hoo, Woodbridge, Suffolk; tel: 01394 389700; opening times vary according to season, check website for details. www.nationaltrust.org.uk

Bridge Cottage ㉒
Thatched cottage by the River Stour, devoted to Constable *(see pp80–81)*. It featured in a couple of his paintings.
Flatford, Suffolk; tel: 01206 298260; open Jan–Feb: 11am–3:30pm Sat & Sun; Mar: 11am–5pm Wed–Sun; Apr–Oct: 10:30am–5:30pm daily; Nov–Dec: 11am–3:30pm Wed–Sun. www.nationaltrust.org.uk

Duxford Imperial War Museum ㉗
Tremendous fleet of aircraft, including crowd-pulling Spitfires and Concorde. A great day out for aviation buffs.
Duxford, Cambridgeshire; tel: 01223 835000; open mid-Mar–Oct: 10am–6pm daily; Nov–mid-Mar: 10am–4pm daily. www.iwm.org.uk

Gainsborough's House ㉘
Splendid collection of the works of Sudbury's most notable artistic resident, the portrait-painter Thomas Gainsborough, in his place of residence.
46 Gainsborough Street, Sudbury, Suffolk; tel: 01787 372598; open 10am–5pm Mon–Sat. www.gainsborough.org

The Edmund Gallery ㉚
The iconic cathedral's primary exhibition space, hosting a varied programme of exhibitions throughout the year.
Angel Hill, Bury St Edmunds, Suffolk; tel: 01284 748720; open 10am–4:30pm daily. www.stedscathedral.co.uk

Whipple Museum of the History of Science ㉛
A great variety of fascinating models, instruments and contraptions from the archives of scientific endeavour.
Free School Lane, Cambridge; tel: 01223 330906; open 12:30–4:30pm Mon–Fri. www.hps.cam.ac.uk/whipple

Sedgwick Museum of Earth Sciences ㉛
A compendium of fossils, minerals, dinosaurs and other geological exhibits from around the world.
University of Cambridge, Downing Street, Cambridge; tel: 01223 333456; open 10am–5pm Mon–Fri, 10am–4pm Sat. www.sedgwickmuseum.org

Babylon Gallery ㉝
Waterside art gallery located in a former warehouse, with a wide range of works.
Waterside, Ely, Cambridgeshire; tel: 01353 616993; open 10am–4pm Tue–Sun, 11am–5pm Sun.
www.babylonarts.org.uk

Stained Glass Museum ㉝
An interesting little museum based in the stunning Ely Cathedral, offering a colourful look at the history of stained-glass manufacture.
The South Triforium, Ely Cathedral, Ely, Cambridgeshire; tel: 01353 660347; open 10:30am–5pm Mon–Sat, noon–4:30pm Sun.
www.stainedglassmuseum.com

Ely Museum ㉝
Packed with local relics and housed in a 13th-century building, this intriguing museum was once the Bishop's Gaol.
The Old Gaol, Market Street, Ely, Cambridgeshire; tel: 01353 666655; open Mar–Nov: 10:30am–5pm Mon–Sat, 1–5pm Sun, Oct–Feb: 10:30am–4pm Mon–Sat, 1–4pm Sun. www.elymuseum.org.uk

Castle Rising ㊸
This Norman castle, not far from Sandringham, dates from 1140. It is surrounded by a defensive mound, and boasts seasonal events and guided tours.
King's Lynn, Norfolk; tel: 01553 631330; open Apr–Oct: 10am–6pm daily; Nov–Mar: 10am–4pm Wed–Sun.
www.castlerising.co.uk

Sandringham House and Museum ㊹
Simply magnificent stately home and gardens – the retreat for four generations of British royals – with a museum containing a huge collection of keepsakes.
Sandringham, Norfolk; tel: 01485 545400; open Apr–Oct: 11am–5pm daily.
www.sandringhamestate.co.uk

Norwich Dragon Festival ①
A celebration of the fire-breathing serpent, its place in myth and its links with Norwich.
Various venues, Norwich; tel: 01603 599576; Jan–Feb.

Pleasure Beach ④
Vast seaside amusement park with thrilling rides, activities and amusements.
South Beach Parade, Great Yarmouth, Norfolk; tel: 01493 844585; open May–Sep, see website for details.
www.pleasure-beach.co.uk

Duxford Airshows ㉗
Historic aircraft from the Duxford Imperial War Museum take to the skies on selected dates during the summer months.
Duxford Imperial War Museum, Duxford, Cambridgeshire; tel: 01223 035000; museum open daily, airshows in May, Jul & Sep. www.iwm.org.uk

Strawberry Fair ㉛
Family-oriented arts and crafts festival offering samba bands, circus acts, face-painting, locally made films and more.
Midsummer Common, Cambridge; first Sat in Jun. www.strawberry-fair.org.uk

Snettisham Park ㊺
Kids will love the deer safari and bottle-feeding lambs at this huge park farm.
Snettisham, King's Lynn, Norfolk; tel: 01485 542425; open 10am–5pm daily (lambing season Feb–May).
www.snettishampark.co.uk

Wells and Walsingham Steam Railway ㉜
Board a steam train from Wells to Walsingham and enjoy the glorious views.
Stiffkey Road, Wells-next-the-Sea, Norfolk; tel: 01328 711630; open Apr–Nov.
www.wellswalsinghamrailway.co.uk

Africa Alive! ⑥
Home to over 80 species of animals from around Africa – including rhinos, giraffes, lions, cheetahs and monkeys.
Whites Lane, Kessingland, Lowestoft, Suffolk; tel: 01502 740291; open 9:30am–5pm daily (to 4pm in winter).
www.africa-alive.co.uk

Southwold Pier ⑨
Bundles of amusements, including the fantastic "Under the Pier Show", plus fish and chips and gift shops.
Southwold, Suffolk; tel: 01502 7221055; open Nov–Mar: 10am–5pm daily; Apr–Oct: 10am–7pm daily.
www.southwoldpier.co.uk
www.underthepier.com

Bircham Windmill ㊻
Children and adults alike will fall in love with this wonderfully restored 19th-century windmill set in the pastoral fields of Norfolk.
Bircham Windmill, Great Bircham, Norfolk; tel: 01485 578393; open Apr–Sep, 10am–5pm daily.
www.birchamwindmill.co.uk

Blakeney Seal Trips ㉝
One hour boat trips to view seals and birds in their natural habitat on Blakeney Point on the north Norfolk coast.
Morston Quay, Morston, Norfolk; tel: 0800 0740 753; Apr–Oct: daily; see website for winter trips.
www.norfolksealtrips.co.uk

Dinosaur Adventure Park ②
Forty hectares (100 acres) of evocative woodland dedicated to all things Jurassic and Neanderthal. There are also displays about prehistoric life and a playground.
Weston Park, Lenwade, Norfolk; tel: 01603 876310, open Mar–mid-Jul and Sep–Oct: 10am–5pm daily; mid-Jul–Aug: 9:30am–6pm daily; Nov–Feb: 10am–4pm daily.
www.dinosauradventure.co.uk

Bressingham Steam Museum & Gardens ㉟
Museum of all things train-related, from gleaming engines built during the age of steam, to Thomas the Tank Engine rides for kids and train journeys for all ages.
Low Road, Bressingham, Norfolk; tel: 01379 686900; open Apr–Nov: from 10:30am daily. www.bressingham.co.uk

Sacrewell Farm & Country Centre ㊳
Children will love visiting this farm, which also offers camping, caravanning and party facilities from March to October.
Thornhaugh, Peterborough; tel: 01780 782254; open Mar–Sep: 9:30am–5pm daily; Oct–Feb: 10am–4pm daily.
www.sacrewell.org.uk

Sprowston Manor Hotel Spa ①
Seven treatment rooms boasting a vast range of beauty and holistic treatments, in beautiful woodland surroundings.
Sprowston, Norwich; tel: 01603 410871.
www.marriott.co.uk

Hopton Holiday Village ⑤
Sporty family getaway in a sandy beach setting, with swimming pools, sauna and sports courts.
Hopton-on-Sea, nr Great Yarmouth, Norfolk; tel: 0871 230 1922.
www.haven.com/parks/norfolk_essex/hopton

Potters Leisure Resort ⑤
Five-star holiday village with private beach and an impressive range of spa and sports facilities.
Coast Road, Hopton-on-Sea, nr Great Yarmouth, Norfolk; tel: 0870 112 9631.
www.pottersholidays.com

Best Western Ufford Park Golf, Hotel and Spa ⑰
Sweeping parkland, an 18-hole golf course and excellent health and spa facilities: relaxation is the watchword.
Yarmouth Road, Melton, Woodbridge, Suffolk; tel: 01394 383555.
www.uffordpark.co.uk

The Varsity Hotel and Spa ㉛
Located on the edge of the River Cam, this spa offers a wide range of luxury treatments.
Thompson's Lane, Cambridge; tel: 01223 306030.
www.thevarsityhotel.co.uk

Congham Hall Hotel ㊷
Idyllically situated, luxury Georgian manor finely attuned to the art of pampering and relaxation, with Sandringham nearby.
Congham Hall, Grimston, King's Lynn, Norfolk; tel: 01485 600250.
www.conghamhallhotel.co.uk

Norfolk Broads ③ (see pp72–3). **Suffolk Heritage Coast** ⑫ (see pp18–19). **Stour Valley** ㉒ (see pp80–81). **Cambridge** ㉛ (see pp210–11). **The Fens** ㉗ (see pp194–5).

Below: Seals on a sandbank at Blakeney Point in Norfolk

LONDON

LOCAL FOOD

Diwana Bhel Poori House ⑩
Inexpensive south-Indian vegetarian diner near Euston station, with a popular lunchtime buffet.
121-3 Drummond Street NW1; tel: 020 7387 5556; open noon–11:30pm Mon–Sat, noon–10:30pm Sun. www.diwanabph.com

Number Twelve Restaurant ⑪
Well-presented, good-value modern Italian cuisine; very handy for the British Museum.
12 Upper Woburn Place, Camden WC1; tel: 020 7693 5425; open noon–3pm and 5:30–10:30pm Tue–Fri, 5:30pm–10:30pm Sat. www.numbertwelverestaurant.co.uk

North Sea Fish Restaurant ⑫
Family-run fish-and-chip restaurant with cosy decor in Bloomsbury, serving a good range of fish in huge portions.
7/8 Leigh Street, Bloomsbury WC1; tel: 020 7387 5892; open noon–2:30pm and 5:30–11pm Mon–Sat. www.northseafishrestaurant.co.uk

Simpson's-in-the-Strand ㊺
Classic British dining in a Victorian setting; roast beef is carved at the table.
100 Strand, Westminster WC2; tel: 020 7836 9112; open 12:15–2:45pm and 5:45–10:45pm Mon–Sat, 12:15–3pm and 6–9pm Sun. www.simpsonsinthestrand.co.uk

Rules Restaurant ㊼
Allegedly London's oldest restaurant, established in 1798; traditional British food including beef from their own estate.
35 Maiden Lane, Covent Garden WC2; tel: 020 7836 5314; open noon–11:30pm Mon–Sat, noon–10:30pm Sun. www.rules.co.uk

Gay Hussar ⑯
A Soho institution with tremendous atmosphere, serving hearty and authentic Hungarian food.
2 Greek Street, Soho W1; tel: 020 7437 0973; open 12:15–2:30pm and 5:30–10:45pm Mon–Sat. www.gayhussar.co.uk

Veeraswamy (51)
Britain's oldest surviving Indian restaurant, with delicious food and opulent decor.
Mezzanine Floor, Victory House, 99 Regent Street, Westminster W1; tel: 020 7734 1401; open noon–2:15 pm and 5:30–10:30pm Mon–Fri, 12:30–2:30pm and 5:30–10:30pm Sat, 12:30–2:30pm and 6–10:30pm Sun. www.veeraswamy.com

Bentley's Oyster Bar & Grill (54)
Classy fish restaurant, grill and oyster bar off Piccadilly, opened in 1916.
11–15 Swallow Street, Westminster W1; tel: 020 7734 4756; oyster and champagne bar open 11:30am–11:30pm Mon–Sat, 11:30am–10:30pm Sun; restaurant open noon–3pm and 5:30–11pm Mon–Sat. www.bentleys.org

Manna ②
As organic, vegetarian, seasonal, local, ethical and detoxifying as possible, the food at Manna is from heaven.
Erskine Road, Primrose Hill NW3; tel: 020 722 8028; open noon–3pm and 6:30–10pm Tue–Sat, noon–8:30pm Sun. www.mannav.com

Brick Lane Beigel Bake ㉕
An East End institution: clubbers queue with locals for fresh bagels.
159 Brick Lane, Tower Hamlets E1; tel: 020 7729 0616; open 24 hours a day.

Borough Market ㉝
London's oldest food market; a huge range of stalls in a Dickensian setting.
Off Southwark Street, Southwark SE1; open 10am–5pm Mon–Thu, 10am–6pm Fri, 8am–5pm Sat. www.boroughmarket.org.uk

Oxo Tower Restaurant and Brasserie ㊱
Modern European food and spectacular Thames views from a London landmark.
Oxo Tower Wharf, Barge House Street, South Bank SE1; tel: 020 7803 3888; open noon–3pm and 6–11pm Mon–Sat, noon–3:30pm and 6:30–10pm Sun. www.harveynichols.com

Polpo ㊻
One of several London branches of this popular venetian tapas style restaurant.
6 Maiden Lane, Covent Garden WC2; tel: 020 7836 8448; open noon–11:30pm Mon–Sat, noon–10:30pm Sun. www.polpo.co.uk

Parlour Restaurant ㊿
Viennese cakes, hot chocolate and ice-cream treats for children of all ages.
First floor, Fortnum and Mason, 181 Piccadilly W1; tel: 020 7734 8040; open 10am–7pm Mon–Sat, 11:30am–5pm Sun. www.fortnumandmason.com

G. Kelly Pie & Mash (82)
Classic pies, mash and jellied eels in an East End street market, established in 1937.
526 Roman Road, Bow, E3; tel: 020 8980 3165; open 10am–4pm Tue–Thu, 10am–7pm Fri, 10am–5:30pm Sat, 11am–4pm Sun–Mon. www.gkelly.london

Billingsgate Market (83)
Get up early to see the largest selection of fresh fish in the UK. The market also offers great fish-preparation and cookery classes.
Trafalgar Way, Poplar E14; tel: 020 7987 1118; open 4–8am Tue–Sat. www.billingsgatefishmarket.org

Bibendum (89)
Classic French cuisine in a light and spacious restaurant housed in a converted Art Deco building.
Michelin House, 81 Fulham Road, Fulham SW3; tel: 020 7581 5817; open noon–2:30pm and 7–11pm Mon–Fri, 12:30–3pm and 7–11pm Sat, 12:30–3pm and 7–10:30pm Sun. www.bibendum.co.uk

FARMERS' MARKETS

Marylebone Farmers' Market ⑦
One of London's largest, surrounded by many individual shops and cafés.
Cramer Street, off Marylebone High Street, Westminster W1; every Sun, 10am–2pm. www.lfm.org.uk/markets

Pimlico Road Farmers' Market (66)
Held in a leafy square and serving prosperous Chelsea and Belgravia.
Orange Square, off Pimlico Road and Ebury Street, Westminster SW1; every Sat, 9am–1pm. www.lfm.org.uk/pimlico.asp

Notting Hill Gate Farmers' Market (76)
Plenty of organic produce at this market, very close to Notting Hill tube station.
Off Kensington Church Street, Kensington W8; every Sat, 9am–1pm. www.lfm.org.uk/nott.asp

Islington Farmers' Market (80)
Serving stylish Islington, and near its boutiques and antique shops.
William Tyndale School, Upper Street, Islington N1; every Sun, 10am–2pm. www.lfm.org.uk/isling.asp

Blackheath Farmers' Market (86)
Close to the up-market shops and airy parkland of Blackheath village.
Blackheath rail station car park, 2 Blackheath Village SE3; every Sun, 10am–2pm. www.lfm.org.uk/black.asp

Lavender Hill Farmers' Market (88)
An incredible variety of cheeses, meats, jams, cakes, breads and fresh produce.
Shaftesbury Park Primary School, Ashbury Road, Battersea SW11; every Sat, 10am–2pm. www.lfm.org.uk/markets/lavender-hill

Hammersmith Farmers' Market (91)
Wide range of fresh takeaway food as well as regional produce.
Off King Street, Hammersmith, W6; every Thu, 10am–3pm. www.weareccfm.com/locations/hammersmith/

PUBS

The George Inn ㉜
National Trust-owned former coaching terminus, with a striking 16th-century galleried courtyard.
Off Borough High Street, Southwark SE1; tel: 020 7407 2056; open daily. www.nationaltrust.org.uk/george-inn

The Market Porter ㉝
Busy Victorian pub, open very early on weekdays for Borough Market workers.
9 Stoney Street, London Bridge SE1; tel: 020 7407 2495; open 6–8:30am and 11am–11pm Mon–Fri, noon–11pm Sat, noon–10:30pm Sun. www.markettaverns.co.uk

The Holly Bush (92)
Little-changed Hampstead village local with old-fashioned rooms and alcoves.
22 Holly Mount, Hampstead NW3; tel: 020 7435 2892; open daily. www.hollybushhampstead.co.uk

The Spaniards Inn (92)
Good food and a large garden at this former toll house on Hampstead Heath.
Spaniards Road, Hampstead NW3; tel: 020 8731 8406; open daily. www.thespaniardshampstead.co.uk

The Cutty Sark Tavern (85)
Lovely old tavern offering a good range of food made from locally-sourced produce.
4–6 Ballast Quay, Greenwich SE10; tel: 020 8858 3146; open daily. www.cuttysarktavern.co.uk

The Dove (91)
William Turner painted from the riverside terrace of this 17th-century pub.
19 Upper Mall, Hammersmith W6; tel: 020 8748 9474; open daily. www.dovehammersmith.co.uk

Below: View over the Thames from the Oxo Tower Restaurant and Brasserie

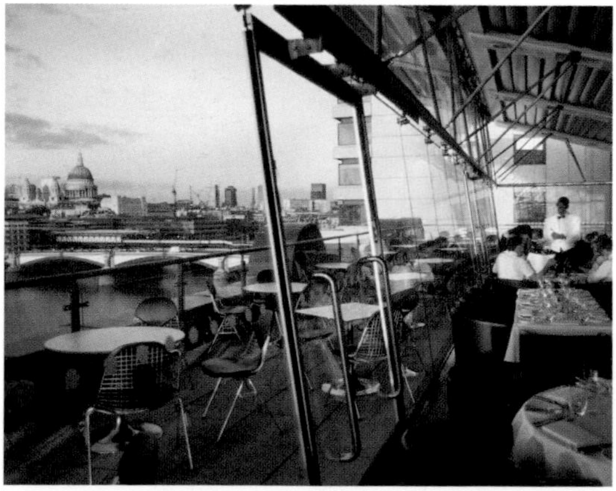

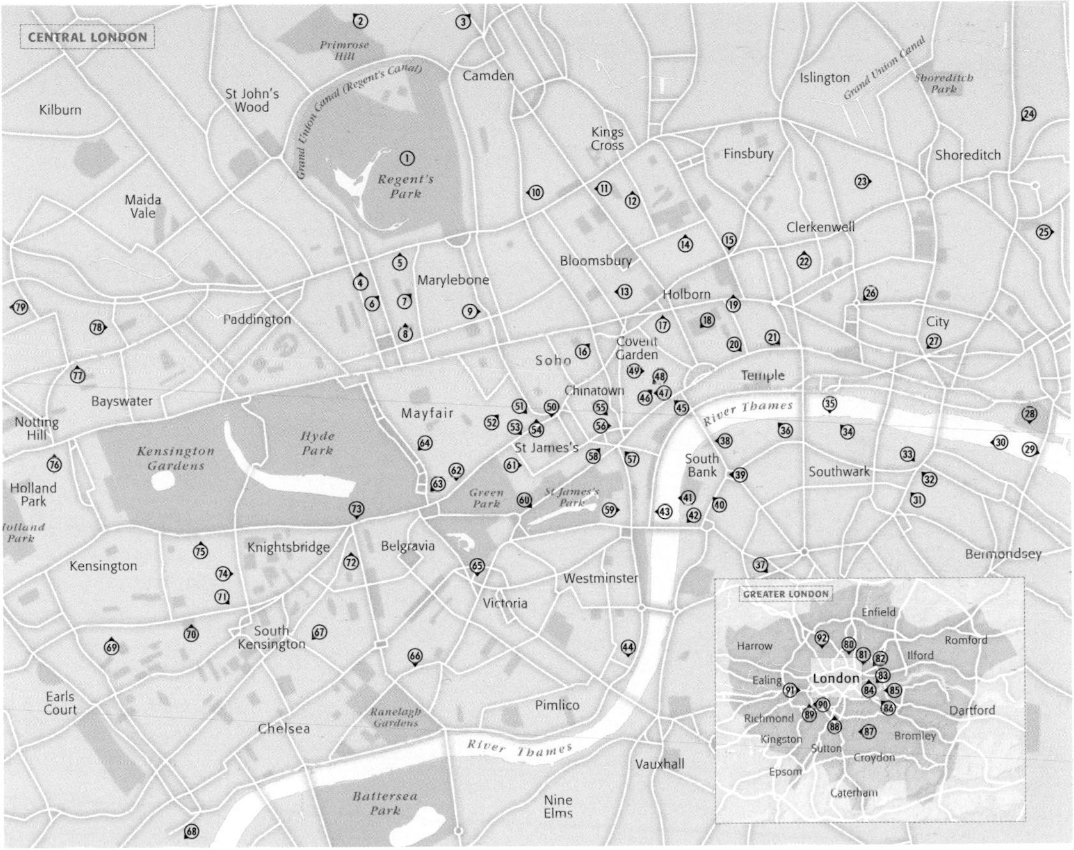

The Lamb ⑭
Full of Victorian character, with original etched glass screens and traditional tables.
94 Lamb's Conduit Street, Camden WC1; tel: 020 7405 0713; open noon–11pm Mon–Wed, noon–midnight Thu–Fri, 11am–midnight Sat, noon–10:30pm Sun. www.thelamblondon.com

Cittie of Yorke ⑲
Bustling City pub with a high-beamed roof and three bar areas, with cosy booths off the back bar.
22 High Holborn, Holborn WC1; tel: 020 7242 7670; open 12am–11pm Mon–Sat.

The Grapes (84)
Welcoming 18th-century inn in Docklands with a waterside balcony and a fish restaurant upstairs with river views.
76 Narrow Street, Tower Hamlets E14; tel: 020 7987 4396; open noon–11pm Mon–Sat, noon–11pm Sat, noon–10:30pm Sun. www.thegrapes.co.uk

The Princess Louise ⑰
Friendly, beautifully restored Victorian "gin palace" with mirrors and engraved glass.
208 High Holborn, Holborn WC1; tel: 020 7405 8816; open daily.

Old Bank of England ⑳
Grand conversion of a former bank, with chandeliers and a courtyard; good pies.
194 Fleet Street, City EC4; tel: 020 7430 2255; open 11am–11pm Mon–Fri, noon –6pm Sat. www.oldbankofengland.co.uk

The Olde Cheshire Cheese ㉑
Engaging warren of little-changed 17th-century rooms. Good-value beer.
145 Fleet Street, City, EC4; tel: 020 7353 6170; open daily.

The Jerusalem Tavern ㉒
Atmospheric eighteenth-century tavern with beers from Suffolk brewery St Peters.
55 Britton Street, Clerkenwell, EC1; tel: 020 7490 4281; open 11am–11pm Mon–Fri. www.stpetersbrewery.co.uk/london

The Greenwich Union (85)
Distinctive pub serving European-style beers produced by a small local brewery.
56 Royal Hill, Greenwich SE10; tel: 020 8692 6258; open noon–11pm Mon–Fri, 11am–11pm Sat, 11:30am–10:30pm Sun. www.greenwichunion.com

PLACES TO STAY

Ambassadors Bloomsbury Hotel ⑪
Contemporary rooms in Bloomsbury, well-positioned for the British Museum.
12 Upper Woburn Place, Camden, WC1; tel: 020 7693 5400. www.ambassadors.co.uk

Northumberland House (57)
Inexpensive but stylish student residences available over the summer holidays.
Edward VII Rooms, 8a Northumberland Avenue, Westminster WC2; tel: 020 7107 5603; open Jun–Sep only. www.lsevacations.co.uk/residences/northumberland.htm

22 York Street ④
Enjoy delicious breakfasts round a curved antique table in this elegant and friendly bed-and-breakfast.
22 York Street, Marylebone, W1; tel: 020 7224 2990. www.22yorkstreet.co.uk

The Langham ⑨
A refurbished grand Victorian hotel; have tea in the famous Palm Court.
1c Portland Place, Regent Street W1; tel: 020 7636 1000. www.langhamhotels.com

Athenaeum Hotel and Apartments (62)
Luxury accommodation in a distinctive hotel with exterior vertical "wall garden".
116 Piccadilly, Mayfair W1; tel: 020 7499 3464. www.athenaeumhotel.com

Miller's Residence (77)
Antiques and exotic memorabilia fill this romantic hideaway in Notting Hill.
111a Westbourne Grove, Kensington W2; tel: 020 7243 1024. www.millershotel.com

Above: Costumed street performer at the Notting Hill Carnival

St Christopher's Inn ③
Three well-located backpackers' hostels, one with its own traditional English pub, close to London Bridge.
121 Borough High Street, Southwark SE1; tel: 0207 407 2392.
www.st-christophers.co.uk

London Marriott Hotel County Hall ④
Fantastic central location right on the river by the London Eye and South Bank, in stately ex-London council headquarters.
Westminster Bridge Road, Southwark SE1; tel: 020 7928 5200.
www.marriott.co.uk

The Trafalgar Hotel ㊽
Handsome old building refitted as a smart contemporary hotel with a rooftop garden overlooking Trafalgar Square.
2 Spring Gardens, Trafalgar Square SW1, tel: 020 7870 2900.
www.thetrafalgar.com

The Goring Hotel ㊺
Traditional English elegance near Buckingham Palace; run by the same family since 1910.
15 Beeston Place, Westminster SW1; tel: 020 7396 9000. www.thegoring.com

Searcy's Roof Garden Bedrooms ㊼
Charming rooftop bed-and-breakfast rooms in a country-house styled building near Harrods and Hyde Park.
30 Pavilion Road, Knightsbridge SW1; tel: 020 7584 4921.
www.30pavilionroad.co.uk

St James Club and Hotel ㊽
Elegantly restored London town house in a secluded location; excellently placed for upmarket shopping.
7–8 Park Place, St James's SW1; 020 7316 1600. www.stjamesclubandhotel.co.uk

The Chelsea Harbour Hotel ㊽
London's only all-suite hotel, with spectacular marina views.
Chelsea Harbour SW10; tel: 0207 823 3000. www.millenniumhotels.co.uk

The Nadler Kensington ㊾
Stylish and good-value rooms, each with a small kitchenette with a sink, microwave and fridge.
25 Courtfield Gardens, Kensington SW5; tel: 020 7244 2255.
www.thenadler.com

FESTIVALS AND EVENTS

Pride in London ⑥
Colourful festival and parade celebrating the LGBT community.
Baker Street to Trafalgar Square W1; tel: 0844 884 2439; Sat, late Jun.
www.prideinlondon.org

Totally Thames ㉟
A month-long festival of river-related events. Includes river pageants and rallies by day, and carnivals, fireworks and dancing by night.
Thames-side, Westminster Bridge to Tower Bridge and beyond, Sep.
www.totallythames.org

Lord Mayor's Show ㉗
A 5-km- (3-mile-) long procession celebrating the city's newly elected mayor. The day ends with a firework display.
Between Bank and Aldwych; mid-Nov.
www.lordmayorsshow.london

London Film Festival ㊳
A two-week feast of new films from around the world.
BFI, South Bank SE1 and other venues; tel: 020 7928 3232; mid-Oct.
www.bfi.org.uk/lff

Royal Academy Summer Exhibition ㊾
The world's largest open-submission contemporary art show, running over eight weeks or more.
Royal Academy of Arts, Burlington House, Piccadilly W1; tel: 020 7300 8090; Jun–Aug. www.royalacademy.org.uk

Trooping the Colour ㊿
Pageantry between Buckingham Palace and Whitehall, marking the monarch's official birthday.
The Mall, W1; 10am–noon, second Sat in Jun (rehearsals on the two previous Sats).
www.householddivision.org.uk

The Boat Race ⑨⓪
Spectators crowd the river banks at the start point at Putney Bridge for the annual rowing contest between boats from Oxford and Cambridge universities.
Between Putney and Mortlake, west London; held annually on a Saturday in Mar or Apr. www.theboatrace.org

The Proms ㊌
Famous eight-week music festival featuring informal concerts, all with inexpensive standing ("prom") tickets available. "Last Night" tickets are hard to obtain, but this concert is relayed on giant outdoor screens to cheerful crowds in Hyde Park.
Royal Albert Hall, Kensington Gore SW7; tel: 0845 401 5040; nightly, mid-Jul–mid-Sep. www.bbc.co.uk/proms

Notting Hill Carnival ㊻
Europe's largest street festival; three days of Caribbean-inspired music and spectacle.
Notting Hill W11; Aug Bank Holiday weekend. www.nottinghillcarnival.biz

Frieze Art Fair ①
One of the world's leading contemporary art fairs, this four-day event brings together internationally renowned artists and galleries. Visitors can browse or buy.
Regents Park NW1; tel: 0203 372 6111; early Oct. www.friezelondon.com

MUSEUMS AND GALLERIES

Wallace Collection ⑧
Fine-art collection and exquisite interiors: feels like a small French palace.
Hertford House, Manchester Square W1; tel: 020 7563 9500; open 10am–5pm daily. www.wallacecollection.org

British Museum ⑬
The grandest and oldest museum of all, with treasures and artifacts from every corner of the globe.
Great Russell Street, Bloomsbury WC1; tel: 020 7323 8299; open 10am–5:30pm daily (to 8:30pm Fri).
www.britishmuseum.org

Sir John Soane's Museum ⑱
Architect's early-19th-century home crammed with an eccentric collection of antiquities and artworks, just as he left it.
13 Lincoln's Inn Fields, Camden WC2; tel: 020 7405 2107; open 10am–5pm Tue–Sat. www.soane.org

Geffrye Museum ㉔
Gem of a museum, reconstructing domestic interiors from different eras.
Kingsland Road E2; tel: 020 7739 9893; open 10am–5pm Tue–Sun.
www.geffrye-museum.org.uk

Victoria and Albert Museum ㊀
Vast, sumptuous collection of art, architecture, craftsmanship and design with an impressive roster of visiting exhibits.
Cromwell Road, Kensington SW7; tel: 020 7942 2000; open 10am–5:45pm Sat–Thu. www.vam.ac.uk

National Maritime Museum ㊄
Greenwich's flagship museum, setting out Britain's history as a maritime power. The grounds also house the Royal Observatory, with more displays, planetarium shows and sky-watching evenings.
Romney Road, Greenwich SE10; tel: 020 8858 4422; open 10am–5pm daily.
www.rmg.co.uk

Museum of London ㉖
Explore the city of London's development from prehistoric times to the modern day.
London Wall, City EC2; tel: 020 7001 9844; open 10am–6pm daily. www.museumoflondon.org.uk

Tate Modern ㉞
Modern art on show in a cavernous Thames-side former power station.
Bankside, Southwark SE1; tel: 020 7887 8888; open 10am–6pm Sun–Thu, 10am–10pm Fri–Sat. www.tate.org.uk

Imperial War Museum ㊲
Museum documenting the social effects of war and the technology involved.
Lambeth Road, Lambeth SE1; tel: 020 7416 5000; open 10am–6pm daily. www.iwm.org.uk

National Portrait Gallery ㊵
Famous figures through British history, as portrayed by artists and photographers.
Trafalgar Square WC2; tel: 020 7306 0055; open 10am–6pm Sat–Wed, 10am–9pm Thu–Fri. www.npg.org.uk

National Gallery ㊶
Magnificent European art collection, from medieval works to French Impressionism.
Trafalgar Square WC2; tel: 020 7747 2885; open 10am–6pm Sat–Thu, 10am–9pm Fri. www.nationalgallery.org.uk

Tate Britain ㊸
British artists from 1500 to the present, including Turner and the pre-Raphaelites.
Millbank, Westminster SW1; tel: 020 7887 8888; open 10am–6pm daily. www.tate.org.uk/britain

Museum of London Docklands ㊸
Engaging displays in an old waterside warehouse revealing London's fascinating history as a port.
No. 1 Warehouse, West India Quay E14; tel: 020 7001 9844; open 10am–6pm daily. www.museumoflondon.org.uk

THINGS TO DO WITH KIDS

London Zoo ①
Penguins, giraffes, big cats, reptiles and all manner of other wildlife living on the edge of Regent's Park.
Outer Circle, Regent's Park NW1; tel: 0344 225 1826; open Oct–Feb: 10am–4pm daily; Mar–Nov: 10am–5:30pm daily. www.zsl.org

London Transport Museum ㊽
From old London buses to Underground trains, posters, models and toys.
Covent Garden Piazza, Covent Garden WC2; tel: 020 7379 6344; open 10am–6pm Sat–Thu, 11am–6pm Fri. www.ltmuseum.co.uk

Museum of Childhood ㊶
Absorbing collection of children's toys, from the 17th century to the present day.
Cambridge Heath Road, Tower Hamlets E2; tel: 020 8983 5200; open 10am–5:45pm daily. www.vam.ac.uk/moc

Walker's Quay Canal Trips ③
Circular sightseeing canal trips with commentary from Camden Lock to Little Venice and back, passing London Zoo.
250 Camden High Street, Camden NW1; tel: 020 7485 4433; cruise timetables vary throughout the year, check website for details. www.walkersquay.com

Madame Tussauds ⑤
Famous names from history, politics, sport and entertainment recreated in an eerily lifelike form in this waxwork museum.
Marylebone Road, Westminster NW1; tel: 0871 894 3000; open 9:30am–5:30pm Mon–Fri, 9am–6pm Sat–Sun, school holidays and most Bank Holiday Mondays. www.madametussauds.com

Tower of London ㉘
Real dungeons, medieval weapons and tales of executions to thrill the bloodthirsty; also home to the Crown Jewels.
Tower Hill, Tower Hamlets EC3; tel: 020 3166 6000; open Mar–Oct: 9am–5:30pm Tue–Sat, 10am–5:30pm Sun–Mon; Nov–Feb: 9am–4:30pm Tue–Sat, 10am–4:30pm Sun–Mon. www.hrp.org.uk/toweroflondon

Tower Bridge ㉙
Walk high along this famous bridge, close to the Tower of London, which raises to allow river traffic to pass through.
Tower Bridge Road, Bermondsey SE1; tel: 020 7403 3761; open Apr–Sep: 10am–5:30pm daily; Oct–Mar: 9:30am–5pm daily. www.towerbridge.org.uk

HMS Belfast ㉚
A 1938 warship that had significant roles in both World War II and the Korean War, moored near Tower Bridge.
Morgan's Lane, Tooley Street, Southwark SE1; tel: 020 7940 6300; open Mar–Oct: 10am–6pm daily; Nov–Feb: 10am–5pm daily. www.hmsbelfast.iwm.org.uk

Below: Tate Modern

BFI IMAX ㊴
Astounding cinema with a screen nearly as tall as five double-decker buses.
1 Charlie Chaplin Walk, South Bank, Waterloo SE1; tel: 0330 333 7878; bookings 10:30am–7:30pm daily; programme times vary. www.bfi.org.uk

London Duck Tours ㊵
A tour with a big surprise: the amphibious vehicle takes a sightseeing route on land before driving straight into the Thames.
55 York Road, Lambeth SE1; tel: 020 7928 3132; tours 10am–dusk daily, according to demand. www.londonducktours.co.uk

London Eye ㊶
Riverside "big wheel" giving a bird's-eye view of the river and city.
Riverside Building, County Hall, Westminster Bridge Road SE1; tel: 0871 781 3000; open May–Sep: 10am–9pm daily, Oct–Apr: 10am–8:30pm daily. www.londoneye.com

Thames River Services ㊸
Take a river trip past London's old docks to visit Greenwich.
Westminster Pier, Embankment SW1; tel: 020 7930 4097; Apr–Oct: boats run half-hourly between 10am and 4pm; Nov–Mar: boats run every 40 minutes from 10:30am to 3.20pm. www.thamesriverservices.co.uk

Churchill War Rooms ㊾
Churchill's World War II headquarters beneath Whitehall.
Clive Steps, King Charles Street, Westminster SW1; tel: 020 7930 6961; open 9:30am–6pm daily. http://cwr.iwm.org.uk

Natural History Museum ㊲
An amazing range of natural-history exhibits set in beautiful Victorian halls, including a spectacular dinosaur gallery.
Cromwell Road, Kensington SW7; tel: 020 7942 5000; open 10am–5:50pm daily. www.nhm.ac.uk

Science Museum ㊴
The history and future of science explored in impressive exhibits and activities.
Exhibition Road, Kensington SW7; tel: 020 7942 4000; open 10am–6pm daily. www.sciencemuseum.org.uk

Crystal Palace Park ㊼
Victorian park with terrific views and life-size dinosaur figures around a lake.
Upper Norwood, Crystal Palace SE19; open 7:30am–dusk daily. www.crystalpalacepark.org.uk

SPAS AND HEALTH RESORTS

Spa London ㊶
Bethnal Green's former Turkish baths, now offering affordable steam and sauna rooms with concessions.
York Hall Leisure Centre, Old Ford Rd, Bethnal Green E2; tel: 020 8709 5845; open 11am–8pm Mon–Fri, 9am–7pm Sat–Sun. www.spa-london.org

The Rosebery Rooms ⑮
Intimate and good value; best for express treatments rather than lounging.
168 Clerkenwell Road Islington, EC1; tel: 0333 320 4001; open 10am–8pm Mon–Fri, 10am–5pm Sat. www.roseberyrooms.com

Bliss Spa ㊻
A stylish and modern spa featuring eight multi-purpose spa treatment rooms and several quick service stations for smaller treatments.
60 Sloane Ave, South Kensington SW3; tel: 020 7590 6146; open 9:30am–8pm Mon–Sat, 10am–7pm Sun. www.blissworld.co.uk

Ironmonger Row Baths ㉓
Victorian Turkish baths with a 30-m (100-ft) swimming pool; affordable and inclusive.
Ironmonger Row Islington, EC1; tel: 020 3642 5521; open 11am–9pm Mon, 10am–9pm Tue–Wed & Fri, 10am–5:30pm Thu, 9am–6pm Sat–Sun (most sessions are single-sex only; check before visiting). www.spa-london.org/ironmonger-row-baths

The Health Club at One Aldwych ㊾
A members-only spa offering a wide range of treatments and a chlorine-free swimming pool with mood lighting.
1 Aldwych, Covent Garden WC2; tel: 020 7300 1000; open 6:30am–10pm Mon–Fri, 8am–8pm Sat–Sun. www.onealdwych.com/health-club

Spa at Brown's ㉜
Three luxurious, soothingly decorated private treatment rooms.
Brown's Hotel, Albemarle St, Mayfair W1; tel: 020 7518 4009; open 10am–8pm daily. www.brownshotel.com

Spa Intercontinental ㊻
Five elliptical therapy rooms with striking decor and a "steam temple".
First floor, 1 Hamilton Place, Mayfair W1; tel: 020 7318 8691; open 9am–9pm Mon–Fri, 10am–7pm Sat–Sun. www.spaintercontinental.com

Dorchester Hotel Spa ㊹
Full-on 1930s glamour, cocktails and rose-tinted mirrors in a relaxed spa.
The Dorchester Hotel, Park Lane W1; tel: 020 7319 7109; open 7am–9pm Mon–Sat, 8am–9pm Sun. www.thedorchester.com/dorchester-spa

The Porchester Spa ㊻
Turkish baths with original features from 1929 and a sizeable swimming pool.
The Porchester Centre, Queensway W1; tel: 020 7792 3980; open 10am–10pm daily.

Mandarin Oriental Hyde Park Spa ㉓
A luxurious retreat spread over two floors, offering indulgent spa packages.
66 Knightsbridge SW1; tel: 020 7235 2000; 8am–10pm Mon–Fri, 8am–9pm Sat–Sun. www.mandarinoriental.com/london/luxury-spa

SOUTHEAST ENGLAND

LOCAL FOOD

Rumsey's Chocolaterie ④
Coffee shop inspired by the film *Chocolat* and serving hand-made local chocolates.
Rumsey's of Wendover, The Old Bank, 26 High Street, Wendover, Buckinghamshire; tel: 01296 625060; open 8:30am–6pm Mon–Sat, 10am–6pm Sun.
www.rumseys.co.uk

The Greene Oak ⑫
Gastropub where both the decor and the menu blend traditional British cuisine with French country style.
Oakley Green, Windsor, Berkshire; tel: 01753 864294; food served noon–2:30pm and 6:30–9:30pm Mon–Sat, noon–4pm Sun.
www.thegreeneoak.co.uk

Denbies Wine Estate ⑮
There are all-year wine-making displays, with "vineyard train" tours from spring to October, two restaurants and a shop.
London Road, Dorking, Surrey; tel: 01306 876616; open 9:30am–5pm Mon–Sat, 10am–5pm Sun (Apr–Oct: till 5:30pm daily).
www.denbies.co.uk

National Collection of Cider and Perry ㊹
A vast range of ciders to sample, and a shop, restaurant and 250-hectare (625-acre) working farm.
Middle Farm, Firle, Lewes, East Sussex; tel: 01323 811324; open 9:30am–5:30pm daily.
www.middlefarm.com

English's Seafood Restaurant and Oyster Bar ㊻
Celebrated old restaurant near Brighton's Lanes, featuring locally caught seafood.
29–31 East Street, Brighton, East Sussex; tel: 01273 328645; open noon–10pm Mon–Sat, 12:30–9:30pm Sun.
www.englishs.co.uk

Nutbourne Vineyards ㊽
Walk among lakes and vineyards, and sample wines in a historic windmill.
Gay Street, nr Pulborough, West Sussex; tel: 01798 815196; open May–Oct: 2–5pm Tue–Fri, 11am–5pm Sat.
www.nutbournevineyards.com

The Old Customs House ㊿
Spacious gastropub in a historic Georgian waterfront building, good for breakfasts and coffees as well as enjoyable traditional dishes and real ales.
Gunwharf Quays, Portsmouth; tel: 02392 832333; food served noon–8pm daily.
www.theoldcustomshouse.com

Brogdale Farm ㉓
Pay a visit to the National Fruit Collection and take in orchard tours, the apple-themed tearoom and farm shop.
Brogdale Road, Faversham, Kent; tel: 01795 530013; open 9am–5pm Mon–Sat, 9am–4pm Sun.
www.brogdalecollections.org

Macknade Fine Foods ㉓
Enterprising farm-shop complex and delicatessen blending Kentish heritage with Italian gastronomy.
Faversham Flagship Foodhall, Selling Road, Faversham, Kent; tel: 01795 534497; open 9am–6pm Mon–Sat, 10am–4pm Sun.
www.macknade.com

Whitstable Oyster Company ㉔
Oysters harvested offshore are served in the company's beachside fish restaurant.
The Royal Native Oyster Stores, Horsebridge, Whitstable, Kent; tel: 01227 276856; open noon–2:30pm Mon–Fri, 6:30–9pm Tue–Thu, 6:30–9:30pm Fri, noon–9:45pm Sat, noon–8:30pm Sun.
www.whitstableoystercompany.com

Wykeham Arms ㉒
Find classic pub dishes and smart sandwiches at this quirky old city inn; some seating is at Victorian school desks from nearby Winchester College.
75 Kingsgate Street, Winchester, Hampshire; tel: 01962 853834; food served noon–2:30pm and 7–9pm Mon–Sat, 12:30–2:30pm Sun.
www.wykehamarmswinchester.co.uk

Hog's Back Brewery ㉙
An independent brewery, housed in 18th-century barns; weekend and evening tours (booking required).
Manor Farm, The Street, Tongham, Surrey; tel: 01252 783000; open 9am–6pm Mon–Tue and Sat, 9am–8:30pm Wed–Fri, 10am–4:30pm Sun.
www.hogsback.co.uk

Kimbridge on the Test ㉑
Farm shop and restaurant on a fishing estate where you can sample or catch trout.
Kimbridge, Romsey, Hampshire; tel: 01794 340777; open 10am–4:30pm Mon–Sat, 11am–4pm Sun.
www.kimbridgeonthetest.com

Cobbs Farm Shop and Kitchen ㊶
Fruit farm with farm shop, butcher, baker, fishmonger and licensed restaurant.
Bath Road, Hungerford, Berkshire; tel: 01488 686770; open 9am–5pm Mon–Sat, 10am–4pm Sun.
www.cobbsfarmshop.co.uk

Millets Farm Centre ㊵
A farm shop, delicatessen, bakery and restaurants with pick-your-own in season.
Kingston Road, Frilford, Abingdon, Oxfordshire; tel: 01865 392200; open 9am–6pm daily (restaurant till 5pm).
www.milletsfarmcentre.com

Browns Bar & Brasserie Oxford ㊻
Colonial-style restaurant, popular for breakfast, afternoon tea or cocktails.
5–11 Woodstock Road, Oxford; tel: 01865 511995; open 9am–11pm Mon–Thu, 9am–11:30pm Sat, 9am–10:30pm Sun.
www.browns-restaurants.co.uk

Wild Thyme ㊼
Cornish monkfish tails and Tamworth pork in an old setting with window seats.
10 New Street, Chipping Norton, Oxfordshire; tel: 01608 645060; open noon–2pm Thu–Sat, 7–9pm Tue–Thu, 6:30–9:30pm Fri & Sat.
www.wildthymerestaurant.co.uk

FARMERS' MARKETS

Maidenhead Farmers' Market ⑪
Berkshire's longest-running farmers' market, with its own loyalty scheme.
Grove Road car park, Maidenhead, Berkshire; tel: 01628 670272; second Sun of every month, 10am–1pm.
www.maidenheadfarmersmarket.org.uk

Windsor Farmers' Market ⑫
A wide range of produce on offer, a short walk from the town centre.
St Leonard's Road, Windsor, Berkshire; tel: 01235 227266; first Sat of every month, 9am–1pm. www.tvfm.org.uk

Rochester Farmers' Market ㉑
Running since 2000, and selling produce from the "Garden of England".
Blue Boar lane car park, Rochester, Kent; tel: 01634 338155; third Sun of every month, 9am–1pm.
www.kfma.org.uk

Wye Farmers' Market ㉛
One of Kent's oldest farmers' markets, in an attractive village on the North Downs.
Village Green, Wye, nr Ashford, Kent; tel: 07804 652156; first and third Sat of every month, 9am–noon.
www.wyefarmersmarket.co.uk

Lewes Farmers' Market ㊽
One of Britain's first farmers' markets, operating since 1998.
Pedestrian precinct, Cliffe, Lewes, East Sussex; tel: 07555 902677; first and third Sat of every month, 9am–1pm.
www.commoncause.org.uk

SOUTHEAST ENGLAND

Heathfield Farmers' Market ④①
Market in a South Downs town in the heart of the Sussex Weald country.
Co-op car park, 110 High Street, Heathfield, East Sussex; tel: 01892 610314; third Sat of every month, 9am–12:30pm. www.heathfield.net

Ryde Farmers' Market ⑥⓪
Market recently set up to bring fresh, local produce to Isle of Wight customers and tourists alike.
Anglesea Street, Ryde, Isle of Wight, Hampshire; tel: 07800 727 903; every Sat, 8:30am–12:30pm. www.islandfarmersmarket.co.uk

Southsea Farmers' Market ⑥③
All featured produce is from Hampshire or within 16 km (10 miles) of its border.
Palmerston Road Precinct, Southsea, Hampshire; tel: 01420 588671; third Sun of every month, 10am–2pm. www.hampshirefarmersmarkets.co.uk

Andover Farmers' and Crafts Market ⑦④
A range of stalls selling local produce line the historic high street.
High Street, Andover, Hampshire; third Sun of Mar–Dec, 10am–2pm. www.testvalley.gov.uk

Hungerford Farmers' Market ⑧⓪
Fresh local produce to sample, as well as the chance to chat with the suppliers.
High Street, Hungerford, Berkshire; tel: 01235 227266; fourth Sun of every month, 10am–1:30pm. www.tvfm.org.uk

Newbury Farmers' Market ⑧①
Most produce here is grown or made within 48 km (30 miles) of west Berkshire.
Market Place, Newbury, Berkshire; tel: 01235 851911; first and third Sun of every month, 9am–1pm. www.tvfm.org.uk

Woodstock Farmers' Market ⑧⑧
Popular market conveniently located for Oxford and the Cotswolds.
By Town Hall, Woodstock, Oxfordshire; tel: 07779 400421; first and third Sat of every month, 8:30am–1pm. www.tvfm.org.uk

Chipping Norton Farmers' Market ⑧⑨
All produce here is sourced from within an 80-km (50-mile) radius.
Town centre, Chipping Norton, Oxfordshire; tel: 07779 400421; third Sat of every month, 8:30am–1:30pm. www.tvfm.org.uk

PUBS AND BARS

The Cricketers Arms ④④
Classic South Downs village pub, with flint walls and traditional beamed and panelled interiors.
Berwick Village, East Sussex; tel: 01323 870469; open 10am–10:30pm Mon–Fri, 11am–11pm Sat, noon–8pm Sun. www.cricketersberwick.co.uk

The Old Queens Head ⑦
Characterful 17th-century inn, carefully reinvented as a classy dining pub.
Hammersley Lane, Penn, High Wycombe, Buckinghamshire; tel: 01494 813371; open 11am–11pm Mon–Sat, noon–10:30pm Sun. www.oldqueensheadpenn.co.uk

The Harrow Inn ②⓪
A friendly country-dining pub with a broad menu and an attractive garden terrace.
Common Road, Ightham Common, Kent; tel: 01732 885917; open noon–3pm and 6–11pm Thu–Sat, noon–3pm Sun.

The Royal Oak ④⑦
Old-fashioned and welcoming pub, with beer from the cask and country food.
Wineham Lane, Wineham, West Sussex; tel: 01444 881252; open 11am–2.30pm and 6–11pm Mon–Sat, noon–5pm and 7–10:30pm Sun.

The Harrow ⑤④
This 17th-century Hampshire pub has changed very little over the centuries.
Harrow Lane, Steep, Hampshire; tel: 01730 262685; open noon–2:30pm and 6–11pm Mon–Fri, 11am–11pm Sat, noon–3pm and 7–10:30pm Sun (closed Sun evening late Sep–May). www.harrow-inn.co.uk

The Anchor Bleu ⑤⑦
Harbourside views from a cosy beamed old bar, which serves local fish dishes.
High Street, Bosham, West Sussex; tel: 01243 573956; open 11:30am–10pm Mon & Tue, 11:30am–11pm Wed & Thu, 11:30am–11:30pm Fri, 11am–11:30pm Sat, noon–10pm Sun.

The Three Horsehoes ⑦⑦
Cheerful local in the Surrey hills, owned by villagers; good walking country.
Dye House Road, Thursley, Surrey; tel: 01252 703268; open noon–3pm and 5:30–11pm daily. www.threehorseshoesthursley.com

The Bell Inn ⑧③
Unspoilt village pub with simple food, in the same family for 200 years.
Bell Lane, Aldworth, Reading, Berkshire; tel: 01635 578272; open 11am–3pm and 6–11pm Tue–Sat, noon–3pm and 7–11pm Sun.

The Swan Inn ⑧⑦
Riverside Cotswold dining pub with a menu of imaginative contemporary food.
Swinbrook, nr Burford, Oxfordshire; tel: 01993 823339; open 11am–11pm Mon–Thu, 11am–11:30pm Fri, 11:30am–11:30pm Sat, noon–10:30pm Sun. www.theswanswinbrook.co.uk

The Falkland Arms ⑨⓪
Traditional, thatched and ivy-hung pub and restaurant in an unspoilt estate village.
Great Tew, Chipping Norton, Oxfordshire; tel: 01608 683653; open 8am–11pm daily. www.falklandarms.co.uk

Above: Spectators at the Henley Royal Regatta

The Three Chimneys ③③
A traditional country pub with beers and local cider served from the cask, and a reputation for great modern British food.
Hareplain Road, Biddenden, Kent; tel: 01580 291472; open 11:30am–11pm Mon–Sat, noon–10:30pm Sun. www.thethreechimneys.co.uk

The Royal Oak ③⑤
Romney Marsh inn mixing original features with modern design. It offers a good variety of bar food.
High Street, Brookland, Kent; tel: 01797 334215; open noon–3pm Mon–Fri, 6–9pm Mon–Thu, 6–9:30pm Fri, noon–9:30pm Sat, noon–5pm Sun. www.theroyaloakbrookland.co.uk

PLACES TO STAY

The Five Arrows ⑦
A striking Victorian hotel, built by the Rothschild family for craftsmen working on Waddesdon Manor.
High Street, Waddesdon, Aylesbury, Buckinghamshire; tel: 01296 651727. www.thefivearrows.co.uk

Gravetye Manor ①⑥
Luxurious hotel in an Elizabethan manor house on its own wooded estate.
Nr East Grinstead, West Sussex; tel: 01342 810567. www.gravetyemanor.co.uk

Cathedral Gate Hotel ②⑤
A 15th-century building near Canterbury's cathedral; oak beams and sloping floors.
36 Burgate, Canterbury, Kent; tel: 01227 464381. www.cathgate.co.uk

The Royal Hotel ②⑧
Nautical-themed beachside guesthouse, run by the Kent brewer Shepherd Neame.
Beach Street, Deal, Kent; tel: 01304 375555. www.theroyalhotel.com

Seaview Hotel ⑤⑨
Stylish waterside accommodation with the warm atmosphere of a genuine pub.
High Street, Seaview, Isle of Wight, Hampshire; tel: 01983 612711. www.seaviewhotel.co.uk

Elvey Farm ③②
High-class accommodation and seasonal food on a medieval farm in rural Kent.
Elvey Lane, Pluckley, Kent; tel: 01233 840442. www.elveyfarm.co.uk

Jeakes House ③⑦
A 17th-century building with cosy and comfortable rooms that commemorate local literary figures, such as Conrad Aiken.
Mermaid Street, Rye, East Sussex; tel: 01797 222828. www.jeakeshouse.com

Sandy Balls Holiday Centre ⑥⑧
Peaceful, long-established centre with New Forest cabins and outdoor activities.
Godshill, Fordingbridge, New Forest, Hampshire; tel: 08446 931050. www.sandyballs.co.uk

The Peat Spade Inn ⑦③
A rural retreat with stylish rooms lying in the heart of the Test Valley, the fly-fishing capital of the world.
Village Street, Longstock, Stockbridge, Hampshire; tel: 01264 810612. www.peatspadeinn.co.uk

The Elephant ⑧③
Quirky hotel with an Indian/colonial theme throughout its individually styled rooms, and models of elephants everywhere.
Church Road, Pangbourne, Berkshire; tel: 0118 984 2244. www.elephanthotel.co.uk

The Kings Arms ⑧⑧
Sitting on the edge of the Cotswolds, this hotel is a stone's throw from Blenheim Palace, home of the Duke of Marlborough and birthplace of Winston Churchill.
19 Market Street, Woodstock, Oxfordshire; tel: 01993 813636. www.kings-hotel-woodstock.co.uk

FESTIVALS AND EVENTS

Henley Royal Regatta ①⓪
Dressing up for this five-day festival of rowing is part of the society calendar.
Henley-on-Thames, Oxfordshire; tel: 01491 572153; Jun–Jul. www.hrr.co.uk

South of England Show ①⑦
Massive three-day annual showcase for agriculture, equestrianism and countryside activities, with arena entertainments.
The South of England Centre, Ardingly, West Sussex; tel: 01444 892700; Jun. www.seas.co.uk

Winchester Hat Fair ⑦②
This long-running street festival provides four days of events and art installations.
Various venues, Winchester, Hampshire; tel: 01962 844600; Jul. www.hatfair.co.uk

Didcot Railway Centre Steamdays ⑧④
Old steam locomotives from the former Great Western Railway in action.
Didcot, Oxfordshire; tel: 01235 817200; Jul–Aug: weekends, also some school holidays. www.didcotrailwaycentre.org.uk

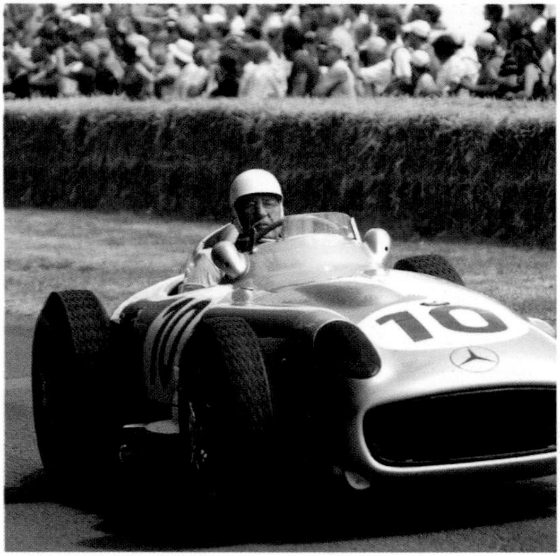

Above: Legendary racing driver Sir Stirling Moss at the Goodwood Festival of Speed

Kent County Show (22)
Kent's largest outdoor event, with country pursuits and forestry, food and farming exhibits over three days.
Kent Showground, Detling, Maidstone, Kent; tel: 01622 630975; Jul.
www.kentshowground.co.uk

Battle of Hastings Re-Enactment (39)
A two-day annual event with living-history demonstrations, culminating in a re-enactment of the famous battle of 1066 that changed English history.
Battle Abbey, Battle, East Sussex; tel: 01424 775705; Oct.
www.english-heritage.org.uk/1066

Airbourne (42)
Eastbourne's free international aerial fair is the world's largest seaside airshow, with four days of synchronized flying displays and historic aircraft to admire.
Seafront, Eastbourne, East Sussex; tel: 01323 415415; Aug.
www.eastbourneairshow.com

Goodwood Festival of Speed (53)
World-renowned celebration of motorsport and classic vehicles over three days on the famous Goodwood circuit.
Goodwood House, Goodwood, Chichester, West Sussex; tel: 01243 755000; Jul (booking required).
www.grrc.goodwood.co.uk

Festival of Chichester (56)
An eclectic summer festival that offers music, talks, comedy, exhibitions and outdoor events over 17 days.
Various venues, Chichester, West Sussex; tel: 01243 813595; Jun–Jul.
www.festivalofchichester.co.uk

Isle of Wight Walking Festival (61)
Over 300 walking trips for all tastes, from easy family rambles to ghost-hunting and dinosaur fossil walks.
Various venues, Isle of Wight, Hampshire; tel: 01983 823070; two weeks in May, plus a weekend in late Oct.
www.isleofwightwalkingfestival.co.uk

New Forest and Hampshire Country Show (66)
Three-day country show in the New Forest, with vintage farm machinery on display alongside livestock.
The Showground, New Park, Brockenhurst, Hampshire; tel: 01590 622400; Jul.
www.newforestshow.co.uk

Grange Park Opera (75)
Classy opera festival, where performances take place over two months in a theatre built in the grounds of a ruined mansion.
The Grange, nr New Alresford, Hampshire; tel: 01962 737373; Jun–Jul.
www.grangeparkopera.co.uk

Surrey County Show (78)
One-day agricultural show bringing the country into the centre of Guildford, including best-of-breed competitions and working dog trials.
Stoke Park, Guildford, Surrey; tel: 01483 890810; late May Bank Holiday Mon.
www.surreycountyshow.co.uk

Royal County of Berkshire Show (82)
Two-day county agricultural show that ends with a mass hot-air balloon ascent.
Newbury Showground, Priors Court Road, Hermitage, Thatcham, Berkshire; tel: 01635 247111; Sep.
www.berkshireshow.co.uk

MUSEUMS AND GALLERIES

Bletchley Park (1)
A fascinating exploration of how those who worked here cracked wartime Nazi codes in secret.
The Mansion, Bletchley Park, Milton Keynes, Buckinghamshire; tel: 01908 640404; open Mar–Oct: 9:30am–5pm daily; Nov–Feb: 9:30am–4pm daily.
www.bletchleypark.org.uk

Chiltern Open Air Museum (6)
Working Victorian farm featuring endangered old buildings that have been saved and re-erected here.
Newland Park, Gorelands Lane, Chalfont St Giles, Buckinghamshire; tel: 01494 871117; open Mar–Oct: 10am–5pm daily.
www.coam.org.uk

Brooklands Museum (14)
Vintage racing cars and planes displayed around this 1930s racing circuit.
Brooklands Road, Weybridge, Surrey; tel: 01932 857381; open Apr–Oct: 10am–5pm daily; Nov–Mar: 10am–4pm daily. www.brooklandsmuseum.com

Rochester Guildhall Museum (21)
Fine 17th-century building, with displays on local history and exhibits relating to Charles Dickens, who lived nearby.
High Street, Rochester, Kent; tel: 01634 332900; open 10am–5pm Tue–Sun.
www.medway.gov.uk/tourism

How We Lived Then: Museum of Shops (42)
A quirky personal collection that recreates old shops with thousands of nostalgic products and fixtures and fittings.
20 Cornfield Terrace, Eastbourne, East Sussex; tel: 01323 737143; open daily from 10am; closing times vary according to season. www.how-we-lived-then.co.uk

Towner Art Gallery (42)
A striking gallery of modern and contemporary art, including a large collection of Eric Ravilious's paintings.
Devonshire Park, College Road, Eastbourne, East Sussex; tel: 01323 434670; open 10am–5pm Tue–Sun.
www.townereastbourne.org.uk

Weald and Downland Open Air Museum (53)
Rescued and relocated old local buildings, with farm animals and craftspeople.
Singleton, Chichester, West Sussex; tel: 01243 811363; open Jan–Feb: 10:30am–4pm Wed, Sat & Sun; Feb–Mar and Nov–Dec: 10:30am–4pm daily; Apr–Oct: 10am–6pm daily.
www.wealddown.co.uk

Pallant House Gallery (56)
A Queen Anne town house home to a collection of 20th-century British art.
9 North Pallant, Chichester, West Sussex; tel: 01243 774557; open 10am–5pm Tue & Wed and Fri & Sat, 10am–8pm Thu, 11am–5pm Sun.
www.pallant.org.uk

Tunbridge Wells Museum (19)
Includes costumes, toys and the decorative wooden boxes known as Tunbridge Ware.
Civic Centre, Mount Pleasant, Royal Tunbridge Wells, Kent; tel: 01892 554171; open 9:30am–5pm Tue–Sat.
www.tunbridgewellsmuseum.org

Hastings Museum and Art Gallery (38)
Richly eclectic collection including displays on distinguished Hastings residents, such as John Logie Baird, inventor of television.
Johns Place, Bohemia Road, Hastings, East Sussex; tel: 01424 451052; open Apr–Oct: 10am–5pm Tue–Sat, noon–5pm Sun; Nov–Mar: 10am–4pm Tue–Sat, noon–4pm Sun.
www.hmag.org.uk

Shipwreck and Coastal Heritage Centre (38)
Seafront museum telling the story of local shipwrecks.
Rock-a-Nore Road, Hastings, East Sussex; tel: 01424 437452; open Apr–Oct: 10am–5pm daily; Nov–Mar: 11am–4pm Sat & Sun.
www.shipwreckmuseum.co.uk

Petworth House (51)
The National Trust's finest art collection, including works by Turner and Van Dyck.
Petworth, West Sussex; tel: 01798 342207; open Mar–Oct: 11am–5pm Sat–Wed. www.nationaltrust.org.uk

Tangmere Military Aviation Museum (55)
A great collection of aircraft memorabilia, located on a former RAF station.
Tangmere Road, Tangmere, West Sussex; tel: 01243 790090; open Mar–Oct: 10am–5pm daily; Feb and Nov: 10am–4:30pm daily.
www.tangmere-museum.org.uk

National Motor Museum (65)
Over 250 vehicles from every motoring era, plus motorcycles and a 1930s garage.
Beaulieu, Brockenhurst, Hampshire; tel: 01590 612345; open Jun–Sep: 10am–6pm daily; Oct–May: 10am–5pm daily. www.beaulieu.co.uk

Christ Church Picture Gallery (86)
An 18th-century collection of old masters in one of Oxford's grandest colleges.
Christ Church College, Oxford; tel: 01865 276172; open Oct–May: 10:30am–1pm Mon & Wed–Sat, 2–4:30pm Mon & Wed–Sun; Jun: 10:30am–5pm Mon & Wed–Sat, 2–5pm Sun; Jul–Sep: 10:30am–5pm Mon–Sat, 2pm–5pm Sun.
www.chch.ox.ac.uk

THINGS TO DO WITH KIDS

Roald Dahl Museum and Story Centre (5)
Fun-filled interactive galleries that commemorate the great storyteller and promote creative writing.
81–83 High Street, Great Missenden, Buckinghamshire; tel: 01494 892192; open 10am–5pm Tue–Fri, 11am–5pm Sat & Sun. www.roalddahl.com/museum

Bekonscot Model Village ⑧
Enchanting miniature landscape with six 1930s villages linked by a model railway.
Warwick Road, Beaconsfield, Buckinghamshire; tel: 01494 672919; open mid-Feb–Oct: 10am–5:30pm daily. www.bekonscot.com

Ashdown Forest Centre ⑱
Explore "Winnie the Pooh" country with a picnic and children's games in this enchanting forest.
Wych Cross, Forest Row, East Sussex; tel: 01342 823583; open Apr–Sep: 2–5pm Mon–Thu, 2–4:30pm Fri, 11am–5pm Sat & Sun; Oct–Mar: 11am–4pm Sat & Sun. www.ashdownforest.org

Diggerland ㉑
Over-5s can ride on – and even drive – real dumper trucks and giant diggers.
Roman Way, Medway Valley Leisure Park, Strood, Kent; tel: 0871 227 7007; open mid-Feb: 10am–4pm; Mar–Oct: 10am–5pm Sat & Sun and daily during school holidays (except Christmas). www.diggerland.com

Canterbury Heritage Museum ㉕
Family-focused museum with well-loved children's characters and activities including a medieval discovery gallery.
Stour Street, Canterbury, Kent; tel: 01227 475202; open 11am–5pm daily during school holidays. www.canterbury.co.uk/museums

Kent and East Sussex Railway ㉞
Take a vintage train ride on this rural light railway, and end up exploring medieval Bodiam Castle.
Tenterden Town Station, Station Road, Tenterden, Kent; tel: 01580 765155; timetables vary, see website for details. www.kesr.org.uk

Observatory Science Centre ㊵
Astronomy demonstrations and giant outdoor interactive exhibits at a world-famous observatory, home to six historical telescopes that the public can try out.
Herstmonceux, East Sussex; tel: 01323 832731; open Feb–Mar and Oct–Nov: 10am–5pm daily; Apr–Sep: 10am–6pm daily. www.the-observatory.org

Drusillas Park ㊸
Thoroughly child-friendly zoo and park where visitors can interact with a large variety of animals up close; there is also a huge adventure playground.
Alfriston, East Sussex; tel: 01323 874100; open Apr–Oct: 10am–5pm daily; Nov–Mar: 10am–4pm daily. www.drusillas.co.uk

Fort Nelson (64)
Napoleonic-era fort with underground tunnels to explore and huge cannons fired daily.
Portsdown Hill Road, Fareham, Hampshire; tel: 01329 233734; open Apr–Oct: 10am–5pm daily; Nov–Mar: 10:30am–4pm daily. www. royalarmouries.org/visit-us/fort-nelson

Camber Sands ㊱
A vast, safe, sandy seashore, backed by dunes, which is excellent for a family day out. You can cycle here from Rye.
Nr Rye, East Sussex.

Chichester Harbour Water Tours (58)
Cruise Chichester harbour in a former lifeboat, and see the yachts and wildfowl.
12 The Parade, East Wittering, West Sussex; tel: 01243 670504; times vary, see website for up to-date timetables. www.chichesterharbourwatertours.co.uk

Marwell Wildlife (70)
Rolling parkland where animals, including penguins and rhinos, roam in generously sized enclosures. Amazing experiences for children and evening safaris are also on offer. There is a hotel on site.
Thompsons Lane, Colden Common, Winchester, Hampshire; tel: 01962 777407; open from 10am daily, closed between 4 and 6pm depending on season. www.marwell.org.uk

Winchester Cathedral (72)
An imaginative children's programme includes free tours around the cathedral, workshops and summer-holiday activities.
The Close, Winchester, Hampshire; tel: 01962 857200; open 9:30am–5pm Mon–Sat, 12:30pm–3pm Sun; activity times vary. www.winchester-cathedral.org.uk

Port Lympne Wild Animal Park ㉚
Bringing the African safari experience to the Kent countryside; featuring gorillas, tigers, rhinos and giraffes among many others.
Lympne, nr Hythe, Kent; tel: 01303 264647; open Apr–Oct: 9:30am–3pm daily; Nov–Mar: 9:30am–2:30pm daily. www.aspinallfoundation.org

SPAS AND RESORTS

Hartwell House and Spa ③
Seventeenth-century country-house hotel, with an elegant spa building modelled on an orangery.
Oxford Road, Aylesbury, Buckinghamshire; tel: 01296 746500. www.hartwell-house.com

Donnington Valley Hotel (81)
A contemporary hotel with an affordable spa offering a range of treatments, plus access to an 18-hole private golf course.
Old Oxford Road, Donnington, Newbury, Berkshire; tel: 01635 551199. www.donningtonvalley.co.uk

Vineyard Hotel and Spa (81)
Pampering with Balinese massage and chocolate-, wine- and truffle-themed treatments, as well as gourmet food at a Michelin-starred restaurant.
The Vineyard at Stockcross, Stockcross, Newbury, Berkshire; tel: 01635 589415. www.the-vineyard.co.uk

Below: Relaxing in the sun at Camber Sands

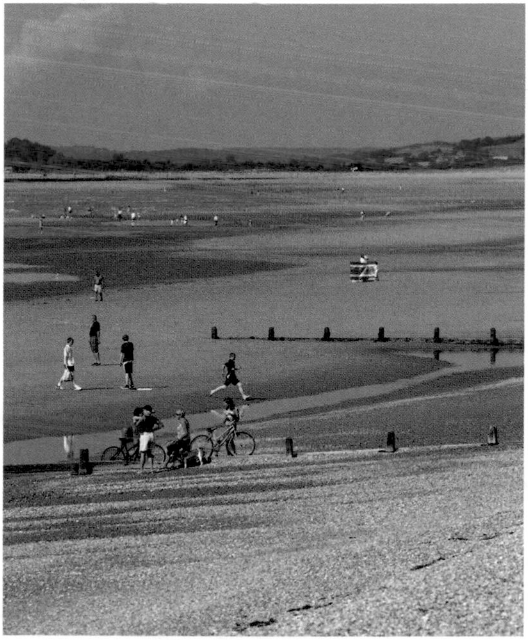

Pennyhill Park Hotel and The Spa ⑬
Super-spacious and relaxing luxury spa with eight indoor and outdoor pools.
London Road, Bagshot, Surrey; tel: 01276 486100. www.thespa.uk.com/exclusive_hotels/the_spa.aspx

Ashdown Park Hotel and Country Club ⑱
Victorian Gothic hotel in its own parkland, with an 18-hole golf course and a spa.
Wych Cross, Forest Row, East Sussex; tel: 01342 824988. www.ashdownpark.com

Tor Spa Retreat ㉖
Indian-inspired, down-to-earth spa emphasizing healthy vegetarian food and Ayurvedic treatments.
Ickham, Canterbury, Kent; tel: 01227 728500. www.torsparetreat.com

Bailiffscourt Spa ㊾
Spacious, airy spa in an oak-framed building with an outdoor pool.
Climping, West Sussex; tel: 01903 723511. www.hshotels.co.uk

The Spread Eagle Hotel & Spa (52)
Scandinavian-style spa in the grounds of a historic coaching inn. Good value.
Spread Eagle Hotel, South Street, Midhurst, West Sussex; tel: 01730 816911. www.hshotels.co.uk

SenSpa at Careys Manor (66)
Hotel near the New Forest with an extensive Thai-themed spa, ice room and large hydrotherapy pool.
Careys Manor Hotel, Brockenhurst, Hampshire; tel: 01590 624467. www.careysmanor.com/luxury–spa.html

New Park Manor Bath House Spa (66)
Old country manor with a purpose-built spa, outdoor hot tub and forest views.
Lyndhurst Road, Brockenhurst, Hampshire; tel: 01590 623467. www.newparkmanorhotel.co.uk

Chewton Glen (67)
Country house spa resort near the New Forest and the coast. Offers holistic programmes and indulgent treatments.
New Milton, Hampshire; tel: 01425 275341. www.chewtonglen.com/spa

Grayshott Spa (77)
Country-house spa that offers fitness programmes alongside a range of health and beauty treatments.
Headley Road, Grayshott, Hindhead, Surrey; tel: 01428 602020. www.grayshottspa.com

OTHER SIGHTS IN THE BOOK

The Chilterns ⑨ *(see pp134–5).* **Windsor** ⑫ *(see pp130–31).* **Broadstairs** ㉗ *(see pp74–5).* **Dover Castle** ㉙ *(see pp16–17).* **Lewes** ㊺ *(see pp146–7).* **Brighton** ㊻ *(see pp38–9).* **Arundel** ㊿ *(see pp96–7).* **Isle of Wight** (62) *(see pp68–9).* **Portsmouth** (63) *(see pp200–201).* **The New Forest** (69) *(see pp158–9).* **New Alresford** (76) *(see pp24–5).* **Oxford** (86) *(see pp56–7).*

SOUTHWEST ENGLAND

LOCAL FOOD

The Old Butcher's ①
Friendly, modern brasserie that serves modern cuisine using local ingredients. *Park Street, Stow-on-the-Wold, Cheltenham, Gloucestershire; tel: 01451 831700; open noon–2pm and 6:30–9:30pm Mon–Sat (until 10pm Sat), noon–2pm and 7–9pm Sun. www.theoldbutchers.com*

Stroud Market ⑥
Popular multi-award winning market with up to 60 regular and guest stalls. *Cornhill Market Place, Stroud, Gloucestershire; tel: 01453 758060; every Sat, 9am–2pm. www.fresh-n-local.co.uk*

Jesse's ⑦
This intimate bistro serves seasonal produce. Ask to sit in the courtyard. *The Stableyard, Black Jack Street, Cirencester, Gloucestershire; tel: 01285 641497; open noon–2:30pm daily, 7–9:30pm Tue–Sat. www.jessesbistro.co.uk*

Swindon Market ⑫
Highly regarded market offering high-quality seasonal and local produce. *Swindon Designer Outlet, Kemble Road, Swindon, Wiltshire; tel: 01453 758060; every Sun, 10am–4pm. www.fresh-n-local.co.uk*

Riverstation ⑭
A contemporary riverside restaurant with stylish but informal à la carte dining. The menu changes every day. *The Grove, Bristol; tel: 0117 914 4434; open noon–2:30pm and 6–10:30pm Mon–Sat (until 11pm Fri & Sat), noon–3pm Sun. www.riverstation.co.uk*

Wednesday Market ⑭
An award-winning market in Bristol, offering local honey, cheeses and fruit. *Corn Street and Wine Street, Bristol; tel: 0117 922 4016; every Wed, 9:30am–2:30pm. www.bristol.gov.uk*

Bath Market ⑮
An established market, priding itself on sustainability and fresh, seasonal produce. *Green Park Station, Green Park Road, Bath; tel: 01761 490624; every Sat, 9am–1:30pm. www.bathfarmersmarket.co.uk*

Sally Lunn's Historic Eating House ⑮
The oldest house in Bath and home to the original Bath Bun. These mammoth creations are part bun, part bread and part cake. Too famous to miss. *Sally Lunn's House, 4 North Parade Passage, Bath; tel: 01225 461634; open 10am–6pm Mon–Sat, 11am–6pm Sun. www.sallylunns.co.uk*

Britford Farm Shop ㉓
Award-winning shop in sight of Salisbury Cathedral selling first-rate local food. *Bridge Farm, Britford, Salisbury, Wiltshire; tel: 01722 413400; open 10:30am–4pm Mon–Fri, 11am–4:30pm Sat. www.britfordfarmshop.co.uk*

Pitney Farm Shop ㉞
Award-winning organic food, such as speciality sausages from local pigs. *Glebe Farm, Woodsbirdshill Lane, Pitney, Langport, Somerset; tel: 01458 253002; open 9am–5:30pm Mon, Tue and Thu–Sat. www.pitneyfarmshop.co.uk*

Museum Inn ㊳
Fabulous local foods, such as game from neighbouring estates; luxury rooms too. *Farnham, Dorset; tel: 01725 516261; open noon–3pm and 6–11pm Mon–Sat, noon–3pm and 7–10:30pm Sun. www.museuminn.co.uk*

Crab House Café ㊽
Beachside wooden shack serving varied and inventive seafood and farmed oysters. *Ferryman's Way, Portland Road, Wyke Regis, Dorset; tel: 01305 788867; open noon–2pm and 6–8:30pm Wed–Thu; noon–2:30pm and 6–9:30pm Fri & Sat; noon–3:30pm Sun. www.crabhousecafe.co.uk*

Bakery at Lacock ⑱
Highly tempting and picturesque bakery with a café and a garden. *8 Church Street, Lacock, Chippenham, Wiltshire; tel: 01249 730457; open 10am–5pm daily.*

Wells Market ㉚
An all-year-round market with weekly variations of stallholders and produce. *The Market Place, Wells, Somerset; tel: 01934 837285; every Wed, 9am–2:30pm. www.somersetfarmersmarket.co.uk*

Newton Abbot Market ㉓
This town-centre market has a reputation for quality and variety. *Courtenay Street, Newton Abbot, Devon; tel: 01626 25426; every Tue & Fri, 9am–3pm. www.teignbridge.gov.uk*

Truro Market ⑦⑦
County-town market with heaps of delicious local temptations. *The Piazza, Lemon Quay, Truro, Cornwall; tel: 01326 376244; every Tue & Fri, 9am–4pm. www.trurofarmers.co.uk*

Lizard Pasty Shop ㊼
Anne Mullen's famous pasties, freshly made. Don't visit late, as they often sell out. *Beacon Terrace, The Lizard, Helston, Cornwall; tel: 01326 290889; open 9am–3pm Mon–Sat, 9–2pm Sun in summer.*

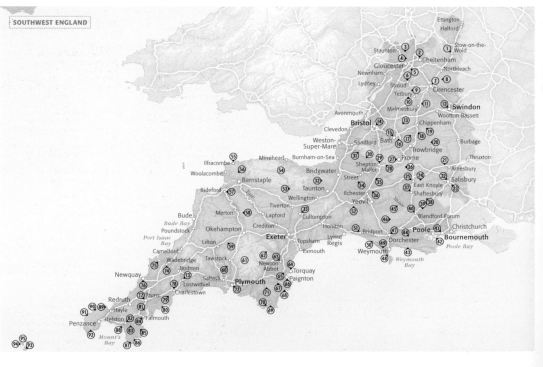

The Seahorse (68)
Riverside fish restaurant with squid, cuttlefish, sole and mussels on the menu.
5 South Embankment, Dartmouth, Devon; tel: 01803 835147; open noon–2:30pm and 6–9:30pm Tue–Sat. www.seahorserestaurant.co.uk

South Devon Chilli Farm (71)
Thousands of chilli varieties and extensive information about growing chillis.
Wigford Cross, Loddiswell, Devon; tel: 01548 550782; open 10:30am–4:30pm daily (closed Sat and Sun between Christmas and Easter). www.southdevonchillifarm.co.uk

Relish Food and Drink (74)
Popular deli and café with lovely staff who have a passion for organic food.
Foundry Court, Wadebridge, Cornwall; tel: 01208 814214; open 9am–4pm Mon–Sat. www.relishcornwall.co.uk

Lobbs Farm Shop (79)
Cornish cheeses, including nettle-wrapped Yarg and Heligan Slab, and other delights such as hog's pudding and saffron cake.
Heligan, St Ewe, St Austell, Cornwall; tel: 01726 844411; open Apr–Sep: 9:30am–5:30pm Mon–Sat, 10:30am–4:30pm Sun; Oct–Mar: 9:30am–5pm Mon–Sat, 10:30am–4.30pm Sun. www.lobbsfarmshop.com

Quayside Fish (88)
Selling from Newlyn's sustainable catches only. Fresh meat is also for sale.
The Harbourside, Porthleven, Cornwall; tel: 01326 562008; open 9am–4pm Tue–Fri, 9am–1pm Sat. www.quaysidefish.co.uk

Roskilly's Farm (85)
Delicious icecream, fudge and yogurts at a working dairy farm. Perfect for families.
Tregellas Barton Farm, St Keverne, Cornwall; tel: 01326 280479; open 11am–5pm Sat & Sun. www.roskillys.co.uk

Porthminster Beach Café (89)
Serves the freshest seafood direct from sea to plate in a stunning beach location.
Porthminster Beach, St Ives, Cornwall; tel: 01736 795352; open noon–4pm and 6–9:30pm daily. www.porthminstercafe.co.uk

FARMERS' MARKETS

Cirencester Farmers' Market ⑦
Independently run market, selling treats such as organic Old Spot sausages.
Market Place, Cirencester, Gloucestershire; tel: 01453 834777; second and fourth Sat of every month, 9am–1pm.

Axbridge Farmers' Market ㉛
Twenty-five stalls pop up every week in the picturesque 400-year-old market square.
Town Square, Axbridge, Somerset; tel: 01934 837285; first Sat of every month, 9am–1pm. www.somersetfarmersmarkets.co.uk

Stow-on-the-Wold Farmers' Market ①
Trout from nearby lakes and locally reared meats are on offer at this Cotswold market in a picture-postcard town.
Market Square, Stow-on-the-Wold, Gloucestershire; tel: 01453 758060; second Thu of every month, 9am–1pm. www.fresh-n-local.co.uk

Cheltenham Farmers' Market ②
At this award-winning market, 40 stalls sell produce including handmade Scotch eggs and charcuterie.
The Promenade, Cheltenham, Gloucestershire; tel: 01608 652662; second and fourth Fri of every month, 9am–2pm. www.cheltenham.gov.uk

Devizes Farmers' Market ⑳
Outdoor market with a great range of locally produced fresh and seasonal foods.
Market Place, Devizes, Wiltshire; tel: 07541 762497; first Sat of every month, 9am–1pm. www.wiltshirefarmersmarkets.co.uk

Frome Farmers' Market ㉗
One of Somerset's largest markets, with 30 stalls and nearby parking.
Market Yard, Frome, Somerset; tel: 01934 837285; second Sat of every month, 9am–1pm. www.somersetfarmersmarkets.co.uk

Blandford Farmers' Market ㊵
Heaps of local food including handmade fishcakes and Dorset Blue Vinney cheese.
Market Place, Blandford Forum, Dorset; tel: 01258 454510; every Thu and Sat, 8:30am–4:30pm. www.dorsetforyou.com

Poundbury Farmers' Market ㊼
Largest market in Dorset selling some of the county's best local produce. Poundbury was a Roman city and overlooks the Iron Age hill town of Maiden Castle.
Queen Mother Square, Poundbury, Dorchester, Dorset; tel: 01258 454510, first Sat of every month, 9am–1pm. www.dorsetforyou.com

Bridport Farmers' Market (51)
Award-winning market where celebrity chef Hugh Fearnley-Whittingstall often sells produce from River Cottage.
The Arts Centre, South Street, Bridport, Dorset; tel: 01297 678318; second Sat of every month, 9am–1pm. www.bridportandwestbay.co.uk

Ilfracombe Farmers' Market (55)
Wide range of produce including dairy, fish, meats and preserves. There are often performances from local music acts.
The Lantern Centre, Ilfracombe, Devon; tel: 01271 865824; first Sat of every month. www.visitilfracombe.co.uk

St Mary's Farmers' Market (93)
Selection of fresh local produce, including shellfish, preserves and dairy products.
Town Hall or on Holgates Green (depending on weather), St Mary's, Isles of Scilly; tel: 01720 424355; first Thu of every month, 10am–2pm.

Above: Floating pontoon at the Pandora Inn

Plymouth Farmers' Market (72)
City-centre market selling ostrich meat, strawberries, vegetables, cheeses and pies.
The Piazza, Plymouth, Devon; tel: 01752 306552; second and fourth Sat of every month, 8am–4pm.

Lostwithiel Farmers' Market (73)
All produce comes from within a 56-km (35-mile) radius of the town.
Community Centre, Lostwithiel, Cornwall; tel: 01840 250586; every other Fri, 10am–1:30pm. www.cornishassociations smallholdersandproducers.co.uk

Helston Farmers' Market (82)
Organic eggs, pasties and herbs are among the local produce on offer here.
Cattle Market Building, Boating Lake, Helston, Cornwall; tel: 01326 560606; first Sat of every month, 9:30am–1pm. www.helstonfarmersmarket.co.uk

PUBS

The Boat ③
Delightful riverside pub that has belonged to the same family for 350 years.
Ashleworth Quay, Gloucestershire; tel: 01452 700272; open daily (Nov–Apr: 6–11pm Mon & Wed). boatinn.wordpress.com

The Weighbridge Inn ⑨
Stylish pub serving "2-in-1" pies, half filling of your choice and half cauliflower cheese.
Longfords, Minchinhampton, Gloucestershire; tel: 01453 832520; open daily. www.weighbridgeinn.co.uk

The Gumstool Inn ⑩
Imaginative food in a traditional pub within the grounds of the Calcot Manor Hotel.
Calcot Manor Hotel, Tetbury, Gloucestershire; tel: 01666 890391; open daily. www.calcotmanor.co.uk

The George Inn ⑱
Busy, child-friendly pub with lots of cosy corners, situated in a National Trust village.
4 West Street, Lacock, Chippenham, Wiltshire; tel: 01249 730263; open daily. www.georgeinnlacock.co.uk

The Fox and Hounds ㉕
Pretty pub offering views of Blackmore Vale, an imaginative menu and good beers.
The Green, East Knoyle, Wiltshire; tel: 01747 830573; open daily. www.foxandhounds-eastknoyle.co.uk

The Half Moon Inn ㊲
Large edge-of-town pub, with helpful staff and more than decent food.
Salisbury Road, Shaftesbury, Dorset; tel: 01747 852456; open daily. www.halfmoonshaftesbury.co.uk

The Brace of Pheasants ㊻
Smart old thatched village pub with excellent food in lovely walking country.
Plush, Dorset; tel: 01300 348357; open noon–3pm and 7–11pm Tue–Sat, 7–10:30pm Sun. www.braceofpheasants.co.uk

The Lord Poulett (52)
Idyllic inn serving tasty food, and boasting lovely views and a *petanque* piste.
Hinton St George, Somerset; tel: 01460 73149; open noon–11pm daily. www.lordpoulettarms.com

The Culm Valley Inn ㉝
Olde-worlde appeal and good food in a charmingly scruffy pub that originally served as a railway house.
Culmstock, Cullompton, Devon; tel: 01884 799823; open noon–3pm and 5–11pm Mon–Thu, noon–11pm Fri & Sat, noon–3pm Sun. www.culmvalleyinn.co.uk

Woods (53)
Very Exmoor – stuffed animals, hunting prints and wood-burning stoves, as well as great food and drink.
4 Bank Square, Dulverton, nr Minehead, Somerset; tel: 01398 324007; open daily. www.woodsdulverton.co.uk

The Duke of York (58)
A great find – a proper pub, simply furnished, friendly and unspoilt, offering homely food.
Iddesleigh, Winkleigh, Devon; tel: 01837 810253; open daily. dukeofyorkdevon.co.uk

The Millbrook Inn (69)
Tiny, historic creekside pub in an idyllic village setting.
South Pool, Kingsbridge, Devon; tel: 01548 531581; open daily. www.millbrookinnsouthpool.co.uk

The Pandora Inn (81)
Gorgeous waterside setting and tables on a floating pontoon – one of Cornwall's most endearing inns.
Restronguet Creek, Mylor Bridge, Falmouth, Cornwall; tel: 01326 372678; open daily. www.pandorainn.com

Cadgwith Cove Inn (86)
An unfussy, old-fashioned inn with a great atmosphere and good, straightforward food on the menu.
Cadgwith, nr Helston, Cornwall; tel: 01326 290513; open daily. www.cadgwithcoveinn.com

PLACES TO STAY

The Bradley ②
This family-run Regency town house's rooms are furnished with antiques as well as modern comforts.
19 Royal Parade, Bayshill Road, Cheltenham, Gloucestershire; tel: 01242 519077. www.thebradleyhotel.co.uk

Bibury Court Hotel ⑧
Jacobean mansion with four-poster beds and an award-winning restaurant menu.
Bibury, Gloucestershire; tel: 01285 740337. www.biburycourt.com

The Catherine Wheel ⑬
Friendly B&B and inn in a splendid building located in a quiet village near Bath.
High Street, Marshfield, Chippenham, Wiltshire; tel: 01225 892220. www.thecatherinewheel.co.uk

The Pear Tree ⑰
Lovely rustic-chic farmhouse hotel offering inventive food sourced from local suppliers.
Top Lane, Whitley, Melksham, Wiltshire; tel: 01225 704966. www.peartreewhitley.co.uk

St Ann's House ㉒
Four-star Georgian house with Cathedral views and a large breakfast menu.
33–4 St Ann St, Salisbury, Wiltshire; tel: 01722 335657. www.stannshouse.co.uk

The Lamb at Hindon ㉔
Gorgeous inn providing country elegance, comfort and good food.
High Street, Hindon, Salisbury, Wiltshire; tel: 01747 820573. www.lambathindon.co.uk

The Pilgrims at Lovington ㉟
Lovely individual rooms at a popular dining pub just off the Roman Fosse Way.
Pilgrims Way, Lovington, Somerset; tel: 01963 240600. www.thepilgrimsatlovington.co.uk

The Bull Hotel (51)
This lavish 16th-century former coaching inn is bathed in modern glamour. There is also a popular pub on site.
34 East Street, Dorset; tel: 01308 422878. www.thebullhotel.co.uk

Plumber Manor ㊺
Dreamy hotel in the hands of the Prideaux-Brunes family for 400 years.
Sturminster Newton, Dorset; tel: 01258 472507. www.plumbermanor.com

Broomhill Art Hotel and Sculpture Park (56)
Quirky hotel with an art gallery and 300 sculptures in lovely wooded grounds.
Muddiford, Barnstaple, Devon; tel: 01271 850262. www.broomhillart.co.uk

Riverside House (67)
Riverbank B&B and self-catering accommodation with beautiful views.
Tuckenhay, Totnes, Devon; tel: 01803 732837. www.riverside-house.co.uk

Above: Great Dorset Steam Fair

Moonfleet Manor ㊾
Faded but still glorious, magical and child-friendly hotel behind the Fleet lagoon in a sleepy coastal backwater.
Fleet, Weymouth, Dorset; tel: 01305 786948. www.moonfleetmanorhotel.co.uk

Lewtrenchard Manor (59)
Numerous awards confirm this Jacobean manor's hotel and restaurant credentials.
Lewdown, nr Okehampton, Devon; tel: 01566 783222. www.lewtrenchard.co.uk

The Lugger Hotel (80)
The sea laps at the feet of this cute hotel, with small but sumptuous rooms, a spa and excellent cream teas.
Portloe, Truro, Cornwall; tel: 08431 787155. www.luggerhotel.co.uk

The Hen House (85)
B&B and self-catering retreat for green enthusiasts or for those craving peace.
Tregarne, Manaccan, Helston, Cornwall; tel: 01326 280236. www.thehenhouse-cornwall.co.uk

The Gurnard's Head (90)
Sophisticated inn in a coastal setting; comfortable bedrooms, fabulous food.
Treen, Zennor, St Ives, Cornwall; tel: 01736 796928. www.gurnardshead.co.uk

Flying Boat Club (94)
New-England-style self-catering at an island World War II "flying-boat" base.
Bryher, Scilly Isles; tel: 01720 422849. www.tresco.co.uk

FESTIVALS AND EVENTS

Salisbury International Arts Festival ㉒
Two weeks of music, dance, theatre, film, photography, literature and much more.
Salisbury, Wiltshire; tel: 01722 332241; late May–early Jun. www.salisburyfestival.co.uk

The Times and The Sunday Times Cheltenham Literature Festival ②
The world's oldest literature festival is held here over two weeks in autumn. The event usually attracts high-profile names.
Various venues, Cheltenham, Gloucestershire; tel: 01242 850270; Oct. www.cheltenhamfestivals.com/literature

Cheese Rolling ⑤
Open to all, this demented tussle sends vast Double Gloucesters down a steep hill.
Cooper's Hill, Brockworth, Gloucestershire; usually second May Bank Holiday Monday. www.cheese-rolling.co.uk

Cotswold Show ⑦
A weekend of arena performances, family entertainment and country pursuits.
Cirencester Park, Cirencester, Gloucestershire; tel: 01285 652007; early Jul. www.cotswoldshow.co.uk

WOMAD Festival ⑪
Scores of acts on stage at this three-day melting-pot of amazing world music.
Charleton Park, Malmesbury, Wiltshire; tel: 0845 146 1735; late Jul. www.womad.org/festivals

Bath International Music Festival ⑮
Seventeen days of music, from classical to contemporary *(see pp90–91)*.
Various venues in and around Bath; tel: 01225 462231; late May–early Jun. www.bathfestivals.org.uk

Great Dorset Steam Fair ㊴
Largest event of its kind in western Europe, displaying plenty of puff over five days in early autumn.
Tarrant Hinton, between Salisbury and Blandford, Dorset; tel: 01258 860361; early Sep. www.gdsf.co.uk

Stock Gaylard Oak Fair ㊺
A day celebrating the wonders of wood, with crafts, demonstrations and stalls.
Stock Gaylard Estate, Sturminster Newton, Dorset; tel: 01963 23511; Aug. www.stockgaylard.com

Widecombe Fair (62)
A day of Devon delights, such as sheep-shearing and tug-of-war, suitable for everyone, "Uncle Tom Cobley and all".
Widecombe-in-the-Moor, Newton Abbot, Devon; second Tue in Sep. www.widecombefair.com

Royal Cornwall Show (74)
The county's biggest annual agricultural event, held over three days.
Wadebridge Showground, Wadebridge, Cornwall; tel: 01208 812183; Jun. www.royalcornwallshow.org

Minack Theatre Performances (92)
Spectacular open-air theatre with views across Mounts Bay. There are both evening and matinée performances in summer.
Porthcurno, Penzance, Cornwall; tel: 01736 810181; open for day visitors 10am–3pm daily; theatre performances Apr–Sep, times vary. www.minack.com

Royal Bath and West Show ㉙
From Pimm's to tractors, a huge, traditional and varied four-day show.
Shepton Mallet, Somerset; tel: 01749 822200; June. www.bathandwest.com

The International Agatha Christie Festival (65)
A week-long celebration of the "Queen of Crime", timed to coincide with her birthday.
Torquay, Devon; mid-Sep. www.agathachristiefestival.com

'Obby 'Oss Day (75)
Boisterous Celtic celebration to welcome in May with singing and dancing.
Padstow, Cornwall; tel: 01841 533449; noon–late, 1 May.

World Pilot Gig Championships (93)
Four days of colourful and energetic races in traditional wooden boats.
St Mary's, Scilly Isles; tel: 01720 423569; May. www.worldgigs.co.uk

MUSEUMS AND GALLERIES

The Wilson ②
Displays of the 19th-century Arts and Crafts movement in all its glory.
Clarence Street, Cheltenham, Gloucestershire, tel: 01242 237431; open 9:30am–5:15pm daily. www.cheltenhammuseum.org.uk

Nature in Art ④
Unique museum and gallery dedicated to artistic inspiration from nature.
Wallsworth Hall, Sandhurst Lane, Sandhurst, Gloucestershire; tel: 01452 731422; open 10am–5pm Tue–Sun and Bank Holiday Mondays. www.natureinart.org.uk

American Museum ⑯
American history, culture and decorative arts in a beautiful Neo-Classical manor.
Claverton Manor, Claverton, Bath; tel: 01225 460503; open mid-Mar–Oct: noon–5pm Tue–Sun (Bank Holiday Mondays and Aug: noon–5pm daily). www.americanmuseum.org

Salisbury and South Wiltshire Museum ㉒
Gallery covering Stonehenge and the nearby Neolithic settlement of Old Sarum.
The King's House, 65 The Close, Salisbury, Wiltshire; tel: 01722 332151; open 10am–5pm Mon–Sat; Jun–Sep: also open noon–5pm Sun, 10am–5pm Bank Holiday Mondays. www.salisburymuseum.org.uk

Russell Cotes Art Gallery and Museum ㊶
Renaissance-style baronial house, crammed with treasures and notable art. Highlights include works by the Pre-Raphaelites and the Japanese collection.
Russell Cotes Road, East Cliff, Bournemouth, Dorset; tel: 01202 451858; open 10am–5pm Tue–Sun and Bank Holiday Mondays. www.russellcotes.com

Fleet Air Arm Museum (36)
Centre of naval aviation history, with Concorde and an aircraft carrier to explore.
HMS Heron, Royal Naval Air Station, Yeovilton, Yeovil, Somerset; tel: 01935 840565; open mid-Mar–Nov: 10am–5:30pm daily (last admission 4pm); 1 Dec–24 Mar: 10am–4:30pm Wed–Sun (last admission 3pm). www.fleetairarm.com

Tank Museum (44)
Rides in a tracked vehicle, trenches and an extensive collection of tanks.
Bovington, Dorset; tel: 01929 405141; open 10am–5pm daily. www.tankmuseum.org

Torquay Museum (64)
From Agatha Christie to insects; this museum is ranked among the finest in the southwest.
529 Babbacombe Road, Torquay, Devon; tel: 01803 293975; open 10am–4pm Mon–Sat (last entry 3pm); mid-Jul–Sep: also open 1:30–5pm Sun. www.torquaymuseum.org

Morwellham Heritage Centre (60)
A living-history industrial museum in the heart of the Cornwall and West Devon Mining Landscape World Heritage Site.
Morwellham Quay, nr Tavistock, Devon; tel: 01822 832766; open Nov–Feb: 10am–4pm daily; Mar–May & Sep–Oct: 10am–5pm daily; Jun–Aug: 10am–6pm daily. www.morwellham quay.co.uk

Charlestown Shipwreck and Heritage Centre (78)
Fascinating collection of shipwreck artifacts and maritime history, the largest of its kind in Europe. *Quay Road, Charlestown, St Austell, Cornwall; tel: 01726 69897; open Mar–Oct: 10am–5pm daily. www.shipwreckcharlestown.com*

Tate St Ives (89)
Internationally renowned exhibitions of contemporary art, plus talks, music, workshops and fabulous views.
Porthmeor Beach, St Ives, Cornwall; tel: 01736 796226; open Mar–Oct: 10am–5:20pm daily; Nov–Feb: 10am–4:20pm Tue–Sun. www.tate.org.uk/stives

Geevor Tin Mine (91)
Centuries of mining history brought to life in tours of underground tunnels, as well as collections of rocks, minerals and tools.
Pendeen, Penzance, Cornwall; tel: 01736 788662; open 9am–5pm Sun–Fri. www.geevor.com

THINGS TO DO WITH KIDS

Flambards (82)
One of Cornwall's most-visited attractions boasts a theme park with a variety of rides, events and attractions, as well as living-history exhibits and beautiful gardens.
Helston, Cornwall; tel: 01326 573404; open school summer holidays: 10am–5pm; times vary outside the school summer holidays – check before visiting. www.flambards.co.uk

Cornish Seal Sanctuary (83)
From one distressed, newly born seal rescued in 1958 to scores of seals, sea lions, penguins and otters, the sanctuary on the Helford Estuary is a haven for the injured and orphaned.
Gweek, near Helston, Cornwall; tel: 01326 221361. www.visitsealife.com

Bowood House Adventure Playground ⑲
An acclaimed playground that features a life-size pirate galleon and a large collection of slides and walkways.
Derry Hill, Calne, Wiltshire; tel: 01249 812102; house open 11am–5:30pm daily; playground open Apr–Nov: 11am–6pm daily. www.bowood.org

Longleat Safari Park ㉖
Drive-through attraction – made famous on the BBC's *Animal Park* – with lions, tigers, wolves, vultures and much more.
Nr Warminster, Wiltshire; tel: 01985 844400; opening times vary – check before visiting. www.longleat.co.uk

East Somerset Railway ㉘
Steam railway that offers special themed events, such as steam galas and Thomas the Tank Engine rides for kids.
Cranmore Railway Station, Cranmore, Shepton Mallet, Somerset; tel: 01749 880417; see website for train timetables. www.eastsomersetrailway.com

Oceanarium ㊶
The wonders of the deep are displayed here for all the family. Exhibits include an underwater tunnel, penguins, otters, sharks and piranhas.
Pier Approach, West Beach, Bournemouth, Dorset; tel: 01202 311993; opening times vary – check before visiting. www.oceanarium.co.uk

Below: Lioness at Longleat Safari Park

Cheddar Caves and Gorge ㉛
World-famous attraction with stunning sights and walks – enough to keep you busy for a whole day.
Cheddar, Somerset; tel: 01934 742343; open 10am–5pm daily. www.cheddargorge.co.uk

Abbotsbury Swannery ㊿
Unique swan colony with fluffy cygnets (hatching time mid-May–late June), mass-feeding and a willow maze.
New Barn Road, Abbotsbury, nr Weymouth, Dorset; tel: 01305 871858; open Mar–Nov: 10am–5pm daily (last entry 4pm). www.abbotsbury-tourism.co.uk

Big Sheep (57)
Pony rides, mini-tractors and lamb-feeding add to the fun at this all-weather attraction which focuses on traditional sheep-rearing.
Abbotsham, Bideford, Devon; tel: 01237 472366; open 10am–5pm Sat, Sun & school holidays. www.thebigsheep.co.uk

Paignton Zoo (66)
Celebrated zoo, home to thousands of amazing and exotic animals and plants; the crocodile swamp is a must-see.
Totnes Road, Paignton, Devon; tel: 01803 697500; from 10am daily, closing times vary – check before visiting. www.paigntonzoo.org.uk

SPAS AND HEALTH RESORTS

Relaxation Centre ⑭
City-centre spa offering holistic treatments, a meditation garden and a floatation room.
9 All Saints Road, Clifton, Bristol; tel: 0117 970 6616; open 10am–9pm Sun–Fri, 9am–10pm Sat. www.relaxationcentre.co.uk

Chase Hotel Spa ⑤
Four-star hotel-spa offering dozens of ways to relax and be pampered.
Shurdington Road, Brockworth, Gloucestershire; tel: 01452 519988. www.qhotels.co.uk

Bath House Spa at The Royal Crescent ⑮
Extensive spa with a pool, plunge tubs, sauna, gym and holistic therapies.
The Royal Crescent Hotel, 16 Royal Crescent, Bath; tel: 01225 823333. www.royalcrescent.co.uk

Combe Grove Manor ⑯
Hotel spa overlooking beautiful Claverton Down woodland just outside Bath.
Monkton Combe, nr Bath; tel: 01225 834644. combegrove.com

Bowood Hotel and Spa ⑲
Modern spa in brand-new country-chic hotel on the Bowood Estate.
Derry Hill, Calne, Wiltshire; tel: 01249 823883. www.bowood.org

Haven Hotel ㊷
Award-winning hotel and spa with uninterrupted views of Poole Harbour.
Sandbanks, Poole, Dorset; tel: 01202 707323. www.fjbhotels.co.uk

Cedar Falls Health Farm ㉜
Hotel spa and centre for natural beauty; perfect for a relaxing weekend.
Bishop's Lydeard, Taunton, Somerset; tel: 01823 433233. www.cedarfalls.co.uk

Imperial Hotel (64)
Five-star luxury: the latest gym technology, expert advice and professional treatments.
Park Hill Road, Torquay, Devon; tel: 01803 294301. www.thehotelcollection.co.uk

Lorrens Ladies' Health Hydro (64)
A women-only retreat offering slimming and sculpting treatments, day-long specials and relaxation packages.
Cary Park, Babbacombe, Torquay, Devon; tel: 01803 329994. www.lorrens-health-hydro.co.uk

Carlyon Bay Hotel Spa (79)
Sanctuary in a dramatic setting on the Cornwall coast, with modern facilities.
Sea Road, St Austell, Cornwall; tel: 01726 812304. www.carlyonbay.com

St Michael's Hotel and Spa (84)
Top coastal spa with sub-tropical gardens. Winner of the Best Spa in Cornwall for 2013 and 2014 at the Cornwall Today Awards.
Gyllyngrase Beach, Falmouth, Cornwall; tel: 01326 312707. www.stmichaelshotel.co.uk

OTHER SIGHTS IN THE BOOK

Bristol ⑭ *(see pp88–9).* **Bath** ⑮ *(see pp90–91).* **Stonehenge** ㉑ *(see pp178–9).* **Lulworth Ranges** ㊸ *(see pp102–3).* **Exmoor** (54) *(see pp106–7).* **Salcombe** (70) *(see pp84–5).* **Dartmoor** (61) *(see pp192–3).* **North Cornwall** (76) *(see pp162–3).* **Isles of Scilly** (95) *(see pp54–5).*

Acknowledgments

The publisher would like to thank the following for text contributions: Alf Alderson; Will Ham Bevan; Donna Dailey; Mo Farrell; Nigel Farrell; Rebecca Ford; Robin Gauldie; Jenny Geal; Mike Gerrard; Damian Harper; Tim and Anne Locke; Sinead McGovern; Paul Shawcross; Richard Watkins.
We would also like to thank the following for their assistance

with sourcing images: Jacki Winstanley (Beamish Museum), Joya Kuin (Cork International Choral Festival), Shelley Keeling (The Wedgwood Visitor Centre), Sue Easton (New Forest District Council), Mary Andrews (Guardian and Observer), Lynne McPhee (Culture and Sport Glasgow), Janet Major (Llangollen International Musical Eisteddfod) and Finn Beales

(Surestate Ltd). Thanks also to Tracy Smith for design assistance; Caroline Elliker, Fay Franklin and Vivienne Watton for editorial assistance; Clare Currie, Rebecca Ford, Deborah Stansfield and Jo and Trevor Wright for their help with compiling lists of ideas for the book; Sarah Tomley for proofreading; and Hilary Bird for indexing.

Picture Credits

The publisher would like to thank the following for their kind permission to reproduce their photographs:

KEY: a-above; b-below/bottom; c-centre; l-left; r-right; t-top:

4Corners Images Ltd: SIME/ Massimo Ripani 137br.
Alamy Images: aber 243tl; Albarmages 166; Kevin Allen 72–3; Per Andersen 254bl; David Angel 101br; John Angerson 59crb; Anna Stowe Landscapes UK 179br; Bailey-Cooper Photography 4 197c; Anthony Baker 187br; Roger Bamber 120br, 263br; Andrew Barker 79br; Howard Barlow 157c; Martin Beddall 117ca; BL Images Ltd 161br; David Boag 11bl; Martin Bond 147br; Mark Boulton 59da, 124br; Kevin Britland 277tc; Brotch Travel 191tc; Ed Brown 131br; camera lucida lifestyle 199cr; John Cameron 123c; David Chapman 131c; Adrian Chinery 97tc; Peter Chisholm 151tc; Carolyn Clarke 168cla; Colin Palmer Photography 185cr; colinpics 121bl; Gary Cook 230tc; Ashley Cooper 1; Roger Coulam 212c, 257br; CountryCollection/Homer Sykes 56c; Craig Joiner Photography 124bc; David Cunningham 130c; Alan Curtis 175ca; Colin Curwood 210–11; CW Images 100c, 116rта; Maciej Czajka 34bc; Ian Dagnall 148br; Andrew Darrington 120bl; David Cordner Main 3 33c; David Noble Photography 10bl, 50–1, 141ca; David Noton Photography 124–5, 130–1, 183br, 207c; Gareth Davies 58ca; Danita Delimont 160–1; Detail Parenting 262tl; John Devlin 37br; Digital-Fotofusion Gallery 213cra; Thomas Dobner 2007 193br; Dual Aspect Photography 67c; earthscapes/Tony Wright 197tr; Patrick Eden 28–9, 62br; Greg Balfour Evans 24–5, 58da, 74bl, 163br; Martyn Evans 201br; eye35.com 241br; David Fernie 78–9; Andrew Fox 208c; fstop2 55br; Victor George 187cr; Les Gibbon 58cb; Globuss Images 31cr; Chris Gomersall 134–5, 168ca; Goplaces 77br; Gavin Gough 63br; Stan Green 117cdb; Guy Edwardes Photography 106c; Brian Harris 81crb; Allan Hartley 132–3; Headline Photo Agency 260tr; Paul Heinrich 117cr; Jim Henderson 173bc; Mark Hicken 116cb; Holmes Garden Photos 16bc; Peter Horree 23bl, 87br; Michael Howell 80–1; James Hughes 125br; Darryl Hunt 33br; ICP 256tc; image france 97br; Images of Birmingham Premium 208–9; Oleksandr Ivanchenko 121br; John James 208bc; Jeff Morgan food and drink 122–3b; Jeff Morgan heritage 165; JFox images 183cr; Wendy Johnson 54c; Jon Arnold Images Ltd 17c; David Jones 165br; John Keates 148–9; Gail Mooney-

Kelly 268bc; Stuart Kelly 39c; David Kilpatrick 116crb; Mike Kipling 145br; Chris Knapton 178bc; Stan Kujawa 130ca; Lancashire Images 27c, 27cr; Lebrecht Music and Arts Photo Library 209br; Barry Levers 76–7; Chris Lewington 195br; Steve Lewis ARPS 41bc; Tony Lilley 74bc; Paul Lindsay 143br, 229tc; Simon Litten 159bl; Peter T Lovatt 41br; Vincent Lowe 205br; David Lyons 197br; Vincent MacNamara 105crb; Manor Photography 75br, 179cr; John Martin 35c; Francisco Martinez 57br; Alan Mather 128–9, 129cr; Gareth McCormack 92c, 142–3; John McKenna 151c; Rod McLean 204–5; Paul Melling 157ca; Renee Morris 195bl; Joanne Moyes 113c; nagelestock.com 47br, 172bl; The National Trust Photolibrary 51bl, 145bc; Alan Novelli 117da, 140–1; Graham Oliver 58bc, 197cr; James Osmond 138–9; Pagan Festivals/ Roger Cracknell 10 79c, 79ca; Andrew Page 34–3; Andrew Palmer 212db; Paul Felix Photography 203br; Ed Pavelin 193ca; pbpgalleries 278tc; PBstock 168crb; PCL 175br, 275bc; Peter Adams Photography Ltd 209cr; Photolibrary Wales 213cr; The Photolibrary Wales 13br, 67br, 100–1, 203c; Pictorial Press Ltd 141c; Powered by Light / Alan Spencer 168cra; Premier 110–11; Realimage 27tc; Robert Estall photo agency 81br; Robert Harding Picture Library Ltd 49br, 137cr, 195bc; David Robertson 114–15, 151br, 172br, 205bc; Seb Rogers 106bc, 184–5, 213cla; Mark Salter 67tc; South West Images Scotland 79tc; Scottish Viewpoint 173br, 205bl; Neil Setchfield 89ca, 247tr; Shenval 23br, 207tc; Steven Shepperdson 169cla; Adrian Sherratt 279bc; Robbie Shone 186–7; SHOUT 57c; Jon Sparks 27br; Michael Spence 41crb; Brian Stark 116cl; STARN 207br; Stephen Saks Photography 105tc; Steve Atkins Photography 159bc; StockImages 115bl; Derek Stone 135c; Striking Images 43crb; Jack Sullivan 59ca; Mark Sunderland 211br; thislife pictures 64tl; Peter Titmuss 24c; Topix 239tr; travelib europe 212br, 213clb; Travelshots.com 16c; Felipe Trueba 213ca; UK City Images 127tc; Colin Underhill 161tc; UrbanLandscapes 103bc; Adam van Bunnens 174–5b; Mike Weatherstone 122cl; Robin Weaver 249bc; Terry Whittaker 63bc; Rob Whitworth 177c; World Pictures 141cr.
ArenaPAL: Marilyn Kingwill 175cl.
The Art Archive: Eileen Tweedy 122tc; V&A/Theatre Museum London 174tc.
AWL Images: Alan Copson 98–9; Travel Pix Collection 82–3.
Axiom Photographic Agency: The Irish Image Collection 44–5.
Aztec West (Flickr): 89c.
Beamish Museum Limited: 128bc.

Cardiff Council/Cyngor Caerdydd: 122bl.
Corbis: Agliolo/Sanford 198–9; Arcaid/Benedict Luxmoore 224tl; Arcaid/Edifice/Philippa Lewis 38c; Arcaid/Florian Monheim 196–7; Arcaid/Joe Cornish 156–7; Atlantide Phototravel 20tc, 20–1, 49bc; Annie Griffiths Belt 15cr; Niall Benvie 172–3; Mark Bolton 164–5; Construction Photography 21br, 89tc; Corbis 185br; Cordaiy Photo Library Ltd/ Chris North 69b, 103cr; Marco Cristofori 22–3; Richard Cummins 105c, 182–3, 237br; Destinations 64d, 117bc; Ecoscene/Andrew Brown 202–3; Ecoscene/Rosemary Greenwood 113tc; Ric Ergenbright 177br; Robert Estall 81bl; Eurasia Press/Steven Vidler 91bl; Macduff Everton 177cr; Eye Ubiquitous/ Bryan Pickering 51ca; Eye Ubiquitous/ Paul Seheult 201c; Eye Ubiquitous/ Paul Thompson 38cr; Richard Glover 191cr; Paul Hardy 49bl; John Harper 12bl; Jason Hawkes 97c, 135br; Robert Holmes 163cr; Angelo Hornak 58crb; Image Source 67cr; The Irish Image Collection/Design Pics 30–1; Robbie Jack 34c; Catherine Karnow 223tr; Herbert Kehrer 51c; Richard Klune 157br; Bob Krist 59ca; Barry Lewis 199br; Loop Images/ Colin Read 201bc; Loop Images/ Roy Shakespeare 244tr; Loop Images/Steve Bardens 68–9; National Trust/Robert Estall 113br; Reuters/Luke MacGregor 146–7; Leo Mason 68c; George McCarthy 143cr; Colin McPherson 157tc; Gideon Mendel 14bc; Michael Nicholson 200–1; Charles O'Rear 58ca; Micha Pawlitzki 177tc; Photo Images/Lee Snider 53br; Reuters 117cra; Reuters/David Moir 220tl; Reuters/Jeff J Mitchell 217tr; Robert Harding World Imagery 77bc, 133br; Robert Harding World Imagery/Adam Burton 107bl; Robert Harding World Imagery/ Adam Woolfitt 169ca; Robert Harding World Imagery/Gavin Hellier 176–7; Robert Harding World Imagery/John Miller 96–7, 106–7; Robert Harding World Imagery/Matthew Davison 91bc; Robert Harding World Imagery/ Yadid Levy 20ca; Skyscan 178c, 37c, 178–9; Geray Sweeney 227tr, 232tc; Sygma/Sion Touhig 250bl; Homer Sykes 93c; Paul Thompson 141tc; Sandro Vannini 129bca, 154–5, 168bl, 221br; Patrick Ward 51tc, 253br; Nik Wheeler 35bc; Adam Woolfitt 91br, 116da, 173bl, 212cra.
Culture and Sport Glasgow: 190–1, 191c.
Dorling Kindersley: Joe Cornish 71br; Andrew Downes 136bc, 136–7; Kim Sayer 65tl.
Dreamstime.com: Atgimages 153bl; Stanko07 259t;
Rob Eavis: 187bl.
Glen Fairweather: 40–1.
fotolia: Airi Pung 70bc; Steve Smith

94–5; Studio Pookini 153br.
Mark Freeman: 47crb.
Roy Gentry: 24bc, 25c.
Getty Images: 20cb; Peter Adams 63bl, 212–13; AFP/Ben Stansall 270tl; AFP/Carl De Souza 188–9; AFP/Max Nash 274tl; Altrendo Nature 33tc; Richard Ashworth 92cr; Axiom Photographic Agency 95br; Axiom/ IIC 31br, 87bl, 160bc; Christina Bollen 109c; TAdie Bush 162–3; Matt Cardy 14–15, 69c, 91cb, 168cb; Neale Clark 35br; Chris Close 46–7; Gary Cralle 191br; Ian Cumming 37tc; Richard Cummins 87bc; DEA/Pubbli Aer Foto 181cr; Dorling Kindersley 271bc; Michael Dunning 48–9, 56–7t; Echo 122–3c; Guy Edwardes 15br, 86, 192–3; James Emmerson 36–7, 68bc; Geoff du Feu 73bc; Flickr/Scott Masterton 2–3; John & Eliza Forder 95bc; Ed Freeman 212cla; Christopher Furlong 115bc, 133crb, 169cra; Suzanne & Nick Geary 103br; Tim Graham 73bl, 127ca, 130tc; Jorg Greuel 215tr; Paul Harris 141br; Chris Jackson 126–7, 127br; Frank Krahmer 62–3; Brian Lawrence 167br; Life File/Andrew Ward 11br; Peter Macdiarmid 200c, 273tc; Paul McErlane 226bl; Michael McQueen 150–1; Jose Maria Mellado 151ca; Jeff J Mitchell 115br, 167bl, 181br, 218tl; E Nagele 266tr; National Geographic/Thad Samuels Abell Ii 107c; Elliott Neep 109cr; James Osmond 66–7; Oxford Scientific / Photolibrary 11bc; Panoramic Images 64–5b, 102, 116–17t; Andrew Parkinson 116ca; Photographer's Choice RF/Alice 168–9; Photographer's Choice/ Brian Lawrence 118–19; Photographer's Choice/Fraser Hall 174bl; Photographer's Choice/ Guy Edwardes 60–1; Photographer's Choice/Lyn Holly 64cr; Photographer's Choice/Michael Rosenfeld 123br; R H Productions 54–5, 55br; Roy Rainford 248tl; Riser/Terje Rakke 85c; Riser/Tom Stock 62bl; Robert Harding World Imagery/Neale Clark 65cr; Ellen Rooney 84c; Andy Rouse 10br, 55c, 59bl; Kevin Schafer 92–3; Slow Images 70–1, 240tr; Andrew Stuart 127c; Taxi/Ghislain & Marie David de Lossy 167bc; David Tipling 32–3; Travel Ink 200bc; David Trood 206–7; Bruno Vincent 56cr; Ian Walton 152–3; Dougal Waters 73br; Ronald Wittek 135tc; Sven Zacek 212cra.
Hereford Cider Museum Trust: 165ca.
iStockphoto.com: Ana Abejon 73tc; Anthony Brown 90; John Butterfield 109br; Ewan Chesser 33c; Crisma 120–1; Rachel Dewis 58–9; Thomas Dickson 265cr; fotoVoyager 203tc; Joe Gough 245br; Bjorn Hotting 163cc; David Joyner 73bl; Karen Kelly 70c, 105br; Roman Krochuk 180–1; lleerogers 120bc; Jonathan Maddock 112–13; Stephen Rees 54bc;

Iain Sarjeant 93br; slowfish 10–1; Matthew Stansfield 163tc; whitemay 265tc.
Lluniau Llwyfan: 100cb.
Lonely Planet Images: Oliver Strewe 136c.
The National Trust Photo Library ©NTPL: Joe Cornish 144–5; Stephen Robson 12–13b.
naturepl.com: William Osborn 170–1.
New Forest District Council: 159br.
Gary Newman: 88–9, 89br.
photographersdirect.com: www.Skyscanner.co.uk 16–17.
Photolibrary: AGE Fotostock 43br, 52bc; AGE fotostock/EA. Janes 8–9; Charles Bowman 39br; Britain on View 84bc, 84–5, 95bl, 132bc, 148bc, 267bl; Britain on View/ Daniel Bosworth 12–13c; Britain on View/Grant Pritchard 174c; Cotswolds Photo Library 4–5; Jorg Richard Cummins 236tc; F1 Online 181c; Kevin Galvin 234bl; Garden Picture Library/J S Sira 13c; Garden Picture Library/Martin Page 12d; Robert Harding 19br, 42–3, 74–5; Adrian Houston 100bc; Image State 109tc; imagebroker.net/Norbert Eisele–Hein 169d; imagebroker.net/ White Star/Monica Gumm 6–7; Imagestate/James Jagger 64bl; Irish Images 52–3; The Irish Image Collection 71cr, 104–5, 233bl; OSF/David Clapp 193tc; OSF/ Enrique Aguirre 158–9; OSF/ Splashdown 108–9; Photononstop 181tc; Robert Harding Travel/ James Emmerson 25br; Robert Harding Travel/Robert Cousins 85br; The Travel Library 38–9.
Photolibrary Wales: Peter Lane 169c; Dave Newbould 110bc; Ben Smith 111br.
Lee Pilkington: 26–7.
Gaol Rehault: 47bc.
Rex Shutterstock: View Pictures 252tl.
rspb–images.com: Richard Brooks 18–19; David Tipling 19bc, 19cr, 194–5.
Stoke-on-Trent City Council: 149crb.
Superstock: Manchester Art Gallery/ Sleeping Beauty by Edward Burne-Jones (detail) 157c.
Tan Wei Jin: 187bc.
The Trentham Estate: Joe Wainwright 149br.

Jacket images

Front and Spine: **AWL Images:** Adam Burton.
Back: **4Corners:** Colin Dixon r; **AWL Images:** Peter Adams cr; Alan Copson cl; **Getty Images:** Britain On View/Stephen Dorey l.

For further information see: www. dkimages.com